Statistics Pedagogy in the Age of AI:

Challenges, Strategies, and Global Case Studies

Roel Famat Ceballos
https://orcid.org/0000-0001-8267-6482
University of Southeastern Philippines, Phillipines

IGI Global
Scientific Publishing
Publishing Tomorrow's Research Today

Vice President of Editorial Melissa Wagner
Director of Acquisitions Mikaela Felty
Director of Book Development Jocelynn Hessler
Production Manager Mike Brehm
Cover Design Jose Rosado

Published in the United States of America by
IGI Global Scientific Publishing
701 East Chocolate Avenue
Hershey, PA, 17033, USA
Tel: 717-533-8845 | Fax: 717-533-7115
Website: https://www.igi-global.com E-mail: cust@igi-global.com

Library of Congress Cataloging-in-Publication Data

Names: Ceballos, Roel Famat, 1988- editor
Title: Statistics pedagogy in the age of AI : challenges, strategies, and global case studies / edited by Roel Famat Ceballos.
Other titles: Statistics pedagogy in the age of artificial intelligence
Description: Hershey, PA : IGI Global Scientific Publishing, [2026] | Includes bibliographical references and index. | Summary: "This book explores how statistics education is evolving in the age of artificial intelligence. It highlights innovative teaching practices, ethical considerations, and curriculum reforms, offering global perspectives and practical strategies to equip learners with critical statistical thinking for an AI-driven, data-centric world"-- Provided by publisher.
Identifiers: LCCN 2025041862 (print) | LCCN 2025041863 (ebook) | ISBN 9798337362595 hardcover | ISBN 9798337362601 paperback | ISBN 9798337362618 ebook
Subjects: LCSH: Statistics--Study and teaching | Artificial intelligence--Educational applications
Classification: LCC QA276.18 .S725 2026 (print) | LCC QA276.18 (ebook)
LC record available at https://lccn.loc.gov/2025041862
LC ebook record available at https://lccn.loc.gov/2025041863

British Cataloguing in Publication Data
A Cataloguing in Publication record for this book is available from the British Library.

This book is dedicated first and foremost to God, the Lord Jesus Christ, the source of wisdom, strength, and guidance throughout my academic and professional journey. To Him I offer my gratitude for the grace and purpose that continue to sustain my work and life.

I also dedicate this book to my students, past, present, and future, whose curiosity, perseverance, and commitment to learning continue to inspire my work as an educator. In an era shaped by artificial intelligence and rapid technological change, it is your critical thinking and sense of responsibility that give deeper meaning to the discipline of statistics.

I further dedicate this work to my family, whose love and support have been my greatest source of strength. To my wife, Melody, and our son, Liam Roel, thank you for your patience, understanding, and unwavering encouragement throughout this journey. To my mother, Alicia, and my father, Eduardo, I offer my deepest gratitude. Your sacrifices, hard work, and dedication in providing me with an education have shaped who I am today and made this achievement possible.

Table of Contents

Detailed Table of Contents

This chapter examines how artificial intelligence (AI), machine learning (ML), and remote sensing are reshaping the teaching and practice of environmental and risk statistics. It integrates core concepts of environmetrics, such as uncertainty quantification, spatial and temporal modeling, and hazard assessment, with modern AI methods including LSTM networks, ensemble learning, ConvLSTM, and hybrid statistical and machine learning approaches. The chapter highlights applications in air pollution analysis, climate and hydrological modeling, drought and flood forecasting, land cover change detection, and disease surveillance. Ethical considerations such as algorithmic bias, transparency, explainable AI, and environmental justice are emphasized as essential to responsible modeling. Philippine case studies, including PM2.5 and respiratory health, dengue and Mpox dynamics, flood and drought risk, and disaster preparedness indices, demonstrate real-world contexts for instruction.

Bayesian statistics, grounded in Bayes' theorem, has evolved into a central paradigm in modern data analysis. While its computational feasibility emerged after the 1950s, advances such as MCMC in the 1990s further accelerated its adoption across disciplines. Yet, teaching Bayesian reasoning remains challenging due to its conceptual complexity. This chapter introduces an interactive pedagogical model using RShiny visualizations and AI tools to teach Bayesian mean estimation. By enabling students to manipulate priors, explore posterior updates, and engage in AI-guided reflection, the approach fosters active, inquiry-based learning. It demonstrates how combining interactivity and AI support can make Bayesian reasoning more accessible, engaging, and conceptually meaningful.

Artificial intelligence is no longer confined to research labs or industry; it has entered the classroom as both partner and provocateur. This chapter explores the role of AI as a teaching assistant in statistics education, with a particular focus on intelligent tutoring systems that adapt to learners' needs. By blending algorithmic precision with human-centered pedagogy, these systems offer individualized feedback, foster student engagement, and reduce the burden of repetitive instruction. Yet, the integration of AI in statistics teaching raises pressing questions about trust, equity, and the preservation of critical thinking. Drawing on global case studies, the chapter examines both the promise and the pitfalls of AI-driven tutoring, proposing a vision in which human educators and AI systems collaborate to create richer, more inclusive learning environments. The argument advanced here is not that machines should replace teachers, but that they can extend their reach and sharpen their effectiveness in transformative ways.

The rapid integration of Artificial Intelligence (AI) technologies into educational environments has significantly transformed assessment practices, particularly in the field of statistical education. Traditional evaluation methods—often rigid, summative, and limited in scope—fail to capture the depth of conceptual understanding and reasoning required in statistics. This chapter explores how AI-powered tools such as natural language processing, intelligent tutoring systems, machine learning, and learning analytics can foster more personalized, responsive, and equitable assessment strategies. Grounded in theoretical frameworks including constructivism, cognitive load theory, and formative assessment principles, the chapter proposes a multi-layered framework for AI-based statistical evaluation. It further analyzes international case studies from South Korea, Finland, the United States, and Indonesia, revealing the contextual factors influencing successful AI adoption.

This chapter advances a conceptual-theoretical blueprint for statistics education in AI-adjacent learning ecologies, where predictive pipelines and generative synthesis can amplify computation yet erode epistemic agency. Centering variability, transnumeration, and validity-bounded inference, it reframes competence as disciplined judgment under uncertainty, not procedural throughput or platform fluency. AI is positioned as scaffold, simulator, and critic, while learners retain accountability for assumption articulation, calibration, robustness under distribution shift, and harm-aware thresholding. The chapter specifies a tiered curriculum architecture, orchestration routines, and integrity-by-design assessment, integrating equity-of-opportunity, privacy-by-design, and contestability as pedagogical constraints. Five internally coherent tables operationalize big ideas, competency progressions, tool-phase guardrails, analytic rubrics, and multi-source evidence ecologies, yielding an audit-ready, globally portable design for academics, policymakers, and learning technologists.

This chapter examines how artificial intelligence (AI) has transformed the teaching and learning processes in modern statistics through discussions of the intelligent tutoring systems and automated modeling algorithms that are redefining modern statistical education. Conventional methods of statistics may pose a challenge to learners especially in abstract conceptualization, interpretation, and application of models to real data. Using AI-managed tools, teachers will be able to deliver personalized learning experiences, feedback, and intelligent guidance that support a variety of learning styles. The intelligent tutoring systems provide customized routes to the probability, hypothesis testing and data analysis mastery, and the automated modeling platforms represent by AI simplify the tasks involved in model selection, validation and interpretation. The chapter also points to pedagogical advantages of these technologies, such as increased engagement, better conceptual understanding, and better accessibility by learners of various levels of proficiency.

Artificial Intelligence (AI) is revolutionizing education across disciplines, and its impact on statistics education is especially profound. As a field rooted in data interpretation, quantitative reasoning, and analytical thinking, statistics benefits uniquely from AI's capabilities in data processing, pattern recognition, and adaptive learning. The integration of AI in statistics education is not merely a trend but a transformative shift that redefines how students learn statistical concepts, how educators teach them, and how both groups interact with data. By leveraging AI tools, intelligent tutoring systems, predictive analytics, and interactive platforms, educators can create more personalized, engaging, and effective learning experiences. This comprehensive examination explores the multifaceted role of AI in statistics education, highlighting its benefits, applications, challenges, and future potential. Intelligent Tutoring Systems (ITS): AI-powered intelligent tutoring systems simulate human-like guidance by interpreting student input and offering instant feedback.

The integration of Artificial Intelligence (AI) and Data Science into education marks a transformative shift in the way teaching and learning are conceptualized, delivered, and assessed. These technologies are reshaping educational environments at every level, from primary classrooms to higher education and lifelong learning platforms. By harnessing the power of AI and data analytics, educators and institutions can personalize learning experiences, improve administrative efficiency, enhance student engagement, and make data-driven decisions that lead to improved academic outcomes. AI, through machine learning algorithms and natural language processing, enables the creation of intelligent tutoring systems, adaptive learning platforms, and automated grading tools that cater to the unique needs and learning paces of individual students. These tools can identify knowledge gaps, suggest tailored content, and even provide real-time feedback, thereby fostering a more inclusive and student-centered educational approach.

Artificial intelligence (AI) is rapidly transforming the landscape of data literacy and redefining how statistical concepts are learned, understood, and applied in educational settings. As data-driven technologies increasingly influence decision-making across fields, it has become essential for learners to understand statistical reasoning and develop the ability to critically interpret AI-generated analyses. This chapter explores how the teaching of confidence intervals (CIs) can serve as an effective platform for fostering both statistical and AI literacy. Building on decades of research showing that students develop a deeper grasp of inferential reasoning through interactive visualization and guided inquiry, this chapter proposes a pedagogical model that integrates dynamic simulation tools with AI-assisted questioning. The central goal of this instructional approach is twofold: first, to strengthen students' conceptual understanding of statistical inference, and second, to cultivate their capacity to interrogate and evaluate AI-generated explanations.

Earthquake detection provides a compelling context for rethinking statistics pedagogy through the integration of classical inference and artificial intelligence (AI). Traditional techniques such as STA/LTA and matched filtering illustrate key statistical principles like signal processing and interpretability but rely on assumptions (e.g., stationary noise) and handcrafted features that limit performance in complex environments. AI-driven models, including CNNs, EQTransformer, and CRED, improve sensitivity by learning hierarchical patterns, yet introduce challenges in interpretability, domain generalization, and uncertainty quantification. These issues are amplified in data-sparse settings like the Philippines. This chapter advocates an integrative pedagogical approach that combines statistical reasoning with AI, using strategies such as transfer learning and uncertainty-aware modeling to develop robust, explainable, and context-sensitive analytical skills.

Rapid integration of artificial intelligence into statistical education presents critical risks to the scientific values of reproducibility, transparency, and openness. This chapter examines how AI tools can generate polished yet unverifiable outputs, fostering an illusion of competence that undermines genuine statistical understanding. Grounded in the open science movement and the broader reproducibility crisis, the chapter advocates for embedding reproducible computational workflows using R, Python, Quarto, and Git into statistics curricula. It presents the Transparency, Reproducibility, Openness, and Provenance (TROPE) framework for aligning classroom practices with core scientific values. Strategies for teaching critical evaluation of AI-generated results, FAIR data principles, and ethical AI attribution are also discussed. The chapter argues that teaching students to document, verify, and openly share their analytical workflows is a foundational obligation for producing trustworthy researchers.

In an era defined by the rapid integration of artificial intelligence (AI), the discipline of statistics and its pedagogical approaches face a critical inflection point. This chapter explores this transformative landscape, examining the profound challenges and opportunities for statistics education. In response, this chapter presents a comprehensive set of pedagogical strategies designed to foster deep data literacy and computational thinking. These strategies include leveraging generative AI as a

Preface

INTRODUCTION

The teaching and learning of statistics now unfold in a world increasingly shaped by algorithmic decision-making. AI systems influence public health surveillance, environmental risk assessment, disaster preparedness, economic forecasting, and social policy. Machine learning models are routinely embedded in software platforms that students encounter in classrooms, workplaces, and everyday life. Consequently, statistical education faces a critical inflection point: educators must prepare learners not only to operate AI-driven tools but also to interrogate their assumptions, limitations, and societal implications.

Globally, educational systems are undergoing curriculum reforms aimed at strengthening data literacy, computational thinking, and interdisciplinary problem-solving. International frameworks increasingly recognize statistics and data science as core competencies for the 21st century. At the same time, concerns about algorithmic bias, opaque decision processes, and unequal technological access highlight the urgent need for ethical and critical statistics education. Students must learn how uncertainty propagates through models, how predictions affect vulnerable populations, and how data-driven systems can reinforce or mitigate inequities.

Within this context, statistics pedagogy cannot remain anchored in procedural calculation alone. When AI automates analytical workflows, the educational focus must shift toward reasoning, interpretation, communication, and ethical judgment. This volume is situated directly within this global moment of transformation. By integrating AI-enhanced instructional strategies with foundational statistical concepts, the book offers educators and policymakers a roadmap for navigating the opportunities and risks of AI-mediated learning.

OVERVIEW OF THE CHAPTERS

Statistics has long served as the intellectual foundation for understanding variability, uncertainty, and evidence-based decision-making across disciplines. Traditionally, statistics education has emphasized probabilistic reasoning, inferential logic, and the interpretation of data-driven conclusions. However, the rapid emergence of artificial intelligence (AI), machine learning (ML), and automated analytics has fundamentally altered how statistical reasoning is practiced, interpreted, and taught. In this new era, statistical computation is increasingly delegated to algorithms capable of generating models, predictions, and insights at unprecedented speed and scale. While these developments have expanded the reach of statistics, they have also raised profound pedagogical, epistemic, and ethical challenges.

Statistics Pedagogy in the Age of AI: Challenges, Strategies, and Global Case Studies responds to this transformation by examining how statistics education must evolve when automation reshapes analytical practice. The volume brings together theoretical perspectives, methodological innovations, and globally grounded case studies to explore how statistical thinking can be taught responsibly, meaningfully, and equitably in AI-mediated learning environments. Rather than positioning AI as a replacement for statistical reasoning, the book emphasizes the continued importance of conceptual understanding, inferential judgment, uncertainty awareness, and ethical accountability.

The subject matter spans multiple dimensions of statistics pedagogy. These include environmetrics and hazard analysis, Bayesian reasoning, intelligent tutoring systems, AI-assisted assessment, curriculum redesign, faculty development, and discipline-specific applications such as environmental monitoring and earthquake detection. Collectively, the chapters explore how AI can be used not merely to optimize instruction, but to deepen learners' engagement with uncertainty, causality, fairness, and real-world consequences.

Each chapter in this volume contributes a distinct yet interconnected perspective on statistics pedagogy in the age of AI.

Chapter 1 establishes the interdisciplinary foundation of the book by integrating environmetrics with modern AI methodologies. Through applications in air pollution, climate modeling, hydrology, disease surveillance, and disaster risk assessment, it demonstrates how probabilistic reasoning and ethical reflection can be embedded within AI-enhanced instruction. The inclusion of Philippine case studies grounds abstract concepts in socially relevant, real-world contexts, highlighting statistics education as a tool for environmental justice and public decision-making.

Chapter 2 covers Bayesian reasoning which represents a paradigm shift in statistical thinking, which remains pedagogically challenging. This chapter addresses these challenges through interactive visualization and AI-guided inquiry, enabling learners to explore prior beliefs, likelihoods, and posterior updates dynamically. The chapter underscores how interactivity and AI scaffolding can support conceptual understanding rather than replace cognitive engagement.

Chapter 3 focusing on intelligent tutoring systems, examines how AI can personalize learning pathways and provide timely feedback while preserving human-centered pedagogy. Global case studies illustrate both pedagogical potential and ethical concerns, positioning AI as a collaborator rather than a substitute for educators.

Understanding the assessment lies at the heart of pedagogical reform, Chapter 4 explores AI-assisted assessment models that move beyond static testing toward formative, adaptive evaluation of statistical reasoning. Drawing on international case studies, it demonstrates how AI can support equity and responsiveness when grounded in sound educational theory.

Chapter 5 is a theoretically grounded chapter advances a vision of statistics education centered on epistemic responsibility. By foregrounding causal reasoning, fairness metrics, and validity constraints, it reframes statistical competence as disciplined judgment under uncertainty. The chapter offers an audit-ready curriculum framework aligned with global accountability standards.

Chapter 6 examines how AI tools can reduce cognitive barriers while enhancing conceptual learning. Automated modeling platforms are discussed not as ends in themselves, but as opportunities to redirect student attention toward interpretation, assumptions, and model evaluation.

Sustainable pedagogical reform requires empowered educators. Chapter 7 emphasizes professional development strategies that equip faculty with both technical fluency and pedagogical confidence in AI-integrated environments. It highlights the institutional responsibilities accompanying AI adoption.

Curriculum reform is explored through the lens of inclusivity, interdisciplinarity, and future readiness. Chapter 8 outlines principles for aligning statistics curricula with AI and data science trends while preserving statistical foundations.

Chapter 9 introduces interactive tools in analyzing confidence intervals. Confidence intervals serve as a vehicle for strengthening inferential reasoning and AI literacy. Through simulation-based learning and AI-assisted questioning, this chapter demonstrates how students can be trained to critically evaluate automated analyses.

Chapter 10 bridges statistics education with seismology and disaster risk reduction. It illustrates how machine learning extends classical statistical methods while reinforcing the importance of probabilistic reasoning, uncertainty quantification, and model validation, particularly in resource-limited settings.

Chapter 11 examines the critical roles of reproducibility, transparency, and open science in AI-driven statistical education. It highlights the need for students to understand not only how models are built, but also how results can be replicated, validated, and openly communicated. The chapter discusses tools and practices such as open data, reproducible workflows, and transparent reporting standards, positioning these as essential competencies in an era of automated analytics.

Serving as the integrative conclusion, Chapter 12 synthesizes pedagogical insights across the volume. It offers a forward-looking framework for teaching statistics in AI-rich environments, emphasizing generative AI as a learning partner, simulation-based inference, and redesigned assessments.

CONCLUSION

Statistics Pedagogy in the Age of AI contributes to the field by articulating a coherent, globally informed vision of statistics education for an era defined by automation and uncertainty. Rather than yielding to technological determinism, the book asserts that AI heightens the need for statistical reasoning grounded in conceptual clarity, ethical awareness, and social responsibility.

The volume advances the field in four key ways. First, it reframes statistics education around epistemic stewardship, emphasizing judgment under uncertainty rather than procedural fluency alone. Second, it demonstrates how AI can be pedagogically integrated to support, rather than erode, deep learning. Third, it foregrounds ethical considerations such as fairness, transparency, and equity as central to statistical instruction. Finally, it provides globally relevant case studies that illustrate how context matters in pedagogy, policy, and practice.

In an age when algorithms increasingly shape decisions that affect lives, environments, and societies, statistics education must rise to the challenge. This book offers educators, researchers, and policymakers both conceptual guidance and practical strategies for doing so. Its ultimate contribution lies in reaffirming statistics not merely as a technical discipline, but as a cornerstone of informed, ethical, and democratic participation in an AI-driven world.

Acknowledgement

I wish to express my sincere gratitude to all those who contributed to the completion of this volume. This book is the result of a collective effort, and I am deeply indebted to the chapter authors for their scholarly insights, dedication, and commitment to advancing statistics education in the age of artificial intelligence. Their contributions reflect both intellectual rigor and a shared vision for a more responsive and future ready discipline.

I also extend my appreciation to the peer reviewers and academic colleagues who generously shared their time and expertise to provide constructive feedback. Their critical perspectives have significantly strengthened the quality and coherence of this book.

My heartfelt thanks go to my institution, the University of Southeastern Philippines, for fostering an environment that values research, innovation, and collaboration. The support provided, through resources, encouragement, and opportunities for engagement, has been instrumental in bringing this project to fruition.

I am equally grateful to my students, past, present, and future, whose curiosity, questions, and evolving needs continue to shape how statistics is taught and practiced. In an era shaped by artificial intelligence and rapid technological change, it is their critical thinking and sense of responsibility that give deeper meaning to the discipline of statistics. They remain at the heart of this endeavor.

Chapter 1
Environmetrics and Ethical Hazard Analysis in Teaching Environmental and Risk Statistics in the AI Era

Roel F. Ceballos
http://orcid.org/0000-0001-8267-6482
University of Southeastern Philippines, Philippines

Resa Mae R. Sangco
Northeastern Mindanao State University, Philippines

Alan Prahutama
Diponegoro University, Indonesia

ABSTRACT

This chapter examines how artificial intelligence (AI), machine learning (ML), and remote sensing are reshaping the teaching and practice of environmental and risk statistics. It integrates core concepts of environmetrics, such as uncertainty quantification, spatial and temporal modeling, and hazard assessment, with modern AI methods including LSTM networks, ensemble learning, ConvLSTM, and hybrid statistical and machine learning approaches. The chapter highlights applications in air pollution analysis, climate and hydrological modeling, drought and flood forecasting, land cover change detection, and disease surveillance. Ethical considerations such as algorithmic bias, transparency, explainable AI, and environmental justice are

DOI: 10.4018/979-8-3373-6259-5.ch001

emphasized as essential to responsible modeling. Philippine case studies, including PM2.5 and respiratory health, dengue and Mpox dynamics, flood and drought risk, and disaster preparedness indices, demonstrate real-world contexts for instruction.

1.0 INTRODUCTION

Environmental systems today are under increasing stress from climate change, rapid urbanization, population growth, and resource overexploitation. These pressures manifest in more frequent and severe extreme weather events—such as floods and droughts—as well as increased air and water pollution, ecosystem degradation, and the spread of vector-borne diseases (Gacu et al., 2025). These dynamics make understanding and managing uncertainty, risk, and long-term environmental change more critical than ever, positioning statistical literacy not merely as a technical skill, but as a fundamental capacity for interpreting, evaluating, and communicating quantitative evidence to support environmental decision-making under uncertainty (Lipič & Ovsenik, 2020).

In this chapter, statistical literacy is understood as encompassing probabilistic reasoning, awareness of uncertainty and variability, critical evaluation of model assumptions and limitations, and the ethical use of data-driven evidence in applied environmental contexts. These competencies are essential for students and practitioners engaged in environmental science, sustainability, public health, and disaster risk reduction, where statistical outputs directly inform policy, planning, and risk communication.

Concurrently, artificial intelligence (AI) and machine learning (ML) are reshaping how environmental data are collected, analyzed, and interpreted. Predictive models powered by ML—such as neural networks and ensemble methods—are increasingly used to forecast climate impacts with high spatial and temporal resolution, providing decision support for resource allocation, hazard warning systems, and environmental planning (Gacu et al., 2025). In parallel, remote sensing combined with ML facilitates the monitoring of environmental variables such as land cover change, vegetation health, and air pollution concentrations (Feng et al., 2025; Aljanabi et al., 2024). However, with the power of AI comes significant risk: models may suffer from bias, lack transparency, or be overfitted, particularly when trained on unrepresentative or noisy environmental data (McGovern et al., 2021).

These risks raise pedagogical challenges: teaching environmental statistics in the AI era requires more than technical competence. Educators must support students to critically evaluate the strengths and limitations of AI models, grasp interpretability issues, and understand when algorithmic approaches are appropriate versus when classical statistical methods are preferable. Recent scholarship highlights the need for hybrid pedagogical frameworks that integrate core statistical theory—such as uncertainty quantification and spatio-temporal modeling—with AI literacy, domain expertise, and ethical reasoning (McGovern et al., 2021; Gacu et al., 2025).

From an educational perspective, AI is already influencing postgraduate and undergraduate sustainability curricula. Studies show that AI can personalize learning experiences, model complex environmental systems, and reveal student behavior, but also raise concerns about equity, data privacy, algorithmic bias, and potential overreliance undermining critical thinking (Leal Filho et al., 2025). As AI becomes more embedded in environmental research, bibliometric analyses reveal rapid growth in AI applications, especially in ecological decision support, pollution monitoring, and disaster risk management (Springer, 2025).

Given this landscape, environmental statistics pedagogy must evolve. Effective instruction should integrate: (1) rigorous statistical foundations for uncertainty and risk; (2) AI-based and algorithmic tools for prediction and forecasting; and (3) ethical frameworks addressing fairness, transparency, and environmental justice. Framed pedagogically, this integration links methods, data, ethics, and instructional practice, enabling educators to prepare learners not only to analyze environmental data, but to make responsible, context-aware, and ethically grounded decisions in a complex, uncertain, and AI-augmented world.

2.0 CORE CONCEPTS: ENVIRONMETRICS, HAZARD RISK, AND UNCERTAINTY

In teaching environmental statistics in the age of AI, grounding learners in the right core conceptual frameworks is essential. This ensures they appreciate both the traditional statistical foundations and the complexities introduced by modern, data-rich, AI-driven contexts.

2.1 Environmetrics as a Statistical Discipline

Environmetrics refers to the application of statistical methods to environmental data. It aims to model, analyze, and make inferences about environmental systems, often characterized by spatial and temporal dependency, non-stationarity, and multiple interacting variables (Bonas, Datta, Wikle, et al., 2024). Recent work in environmetrics emphasizes hybrid modeling, which combines interpretable statistical models (e.g., linear models, Gaussian processes) with more flexible machine learning approaches, to better capture environmental complexity while retaining insight (Bonas et al., 2024).

For example, in the study of air pollution, spatio-temporal joint modeling has become more common: Wang, Ling, and Chen (2023) developed a Bayesian model for both moderate and extreme pollution levels in Spain, combining extreme-value theory and spatial dependence to better represent the behavior of pollutant concentrations across space and time. Their work illustrates how classical statistical theory (e.g., probabilistic models, Bayesian inference) remains deeply relevant, even when dealing with complex environmental data (Wang et al., 2023).

Another frontier is spatio-temporal stochastic volatility models, which aim to model not only the mean of environmental variables (e.g., pollutant concentrations) but also their time-varying risks or volatility. Otto, Doğan, and Taşpınar (2022) proposed a Bayesian spatio-temporal stochastic volatility model to assess environmental risk, allowing for explicit spatial and temporal spillovers and location-specific volatility. This kind of model helps quantify how the uncertainty (or variability) of environmental outcomes evolves over space and time.

Moreover, environmetrics must grapple with extremes—rare but high-impact events such as severe pollution episodes, floods, and heat waves. Traditional max-stable processes, often used in extreme value theory, may be insufficient. Recent reviews argue for new modeling approaches, as environmental data science is shifting away from max-stable models toward more flexible and scalable frameworks that can accommodate non-stationarity and more realistic dependence structures (Huser et al., 2025).

Altogether, these developments show that environmetrics as a discipline is evolving rapidly. For pedagogy, this means teaching must not only cover classical theory (regression, time-series, spatial statistics) but also advanced methods (Bayesian modeling, stochastic volatility, extremes) and how they connect with AI-driven approaches.

2.2 Hazard, Risk, and Probability

When discussing risk in environmental contexts, a useful working definition is that risk reflects the probability of an adverse event multiplied by its severity or consequence, acknowledging that risk is inherently probabilistic and uncertain. In risk education, four core components frequently emerge as central to understanding and decision-making: uncertainty, probability, severity, and consequences (Schenk, Drechsel-Grau, & Stefanek, 2024). These components highlight that risk is not a single measurable quantity, but a construct that integrates likelihood, impact, and incomplete knowledge.

In environmental risk assessment, risk is commonly decomposed into more specific and operational dimensions:

- Hazard: the inherent potential of a natural or anthropogenic process to cause harm (e.g., flooding, extreme heat, pollutant release);
- Exposure: the presence of populations, ecosystems, infrastructure, or assets in locations where hazards may occur;
- Vulnerability: the susceptibility of exposed elements to damage or loss, influenced by physical sensitivity, adaptive capacity, resilience, and socio-economic conditions.

Conceptually, these relationships are often summarized as (Schenk et al., 2024):

$$\text{Risk} = \text{Hazard} \times \text{Exposure} \times \text{Vulnerability}$$

While this expression is not a literal mathematical formula, it provides a powerful pedagogical framework for understanding how different drivers of risk interact. Importantly, each component is itself characterized by uncertainty and variability, which must be modeled and interpreted probabilistically.

From a statistical perspective, hazards are typically represented using probability distributions that describe the frequency and intensity of events (e.g., flood peak distributions, drought duration distributions, or pollutant concentration exceedances). Exposure is often modeled spatially, using population density, land-use, or infrastructure data, where uncertainty may arise from data resolution, temporal mismatch, or classification error. Vulnerability is commonly expressed through damage or impact functions, which relate hazard intensity to expected loss and often exhibit substantial uncertainty due to behavioral, structural, and socio-economic heterogeneity.

Effective teaching of risk therefore requires students to understand how uncertainty enters at each stage and how it propagates through the risk system. Small uncertainties in hazard frequency or vulnerability assumptions can lead to disproportionately large changes in estimated risk, particularly when nonlinear damage functions or extreme events are involved. This insight is foundational for later topics such as loss exceedance curves, expected annual damage, and probabilistic risk assessment.

Pedagogically, this decomposition allows instructors to design learning activities that isolate and recombine components of risk. For example, students can examine how improved flood defenses lower vulnerability without altering hazard probability, or how urban expansion increases exposure even if hazard frequency remains unchanged. Such exercises reinforce the distinction between risk reduction strategies that target physical processes versus those that address social or structural vulnerability.

Moreover, framing risk in probabilistic terms prepares students to engage critically with AI-based environmental models introduced later in the chapter. While AI may enhance hazard prediction or exposure mapping, it does not eliminate uncertainty; instead, it often redistributes it across system components. Integrating probability theory with hazard–exposure–vulnerability frameworks enables learners to assess whether AI-generated risk estimates are credible, interpretable, and appropriate for decision-making.

Overall, teaching hazard, risk, and probability as interdependent and uncertain constructs provides students with a conceptual bridge between foundational statistics and applied risk analysis. This foundation is essential for understanding subsequent topics such as probabilistic risk assessment, Monte Carlo simulation, and multi-criteria decision analysis, where uncertainty is no longer an abstract concept but a central driver of environmental decisions.

2.3 Uncertainty: Types and Quantification

Uncertainty is central to environmental statistics and risk analysis. There are multiple sources of uncertainty in environmental models, and recent literature highlights the importance of making students aware of them, how to quantify them, and how to communicate them.

1. Sources of Uncertainty
    - o *Variability*: natural heterogeneity in environmental systems (e.g., differences in pollutant dispersion across sites).
    - o *Parameter uncertainty*: lack of precise knowledge about model parameters.
    - o *Model uncertainty*: uncertainty about the correct functional form or model structure.
    - o *Measurement error*: noise in data collected from sensors or estimated exposures (Hayes, Regan, & Burgman, 2021).
2. Quantifying Uncertainty
    - o Recent work in uncertainty quantification emphasizes predictive uncertainty in machine learning, showing that traditional ML models need to be paired with methods that estimate their predictive distributions, not just point predictions (Tyralis & Papacharalampous, 2024).
    - o Bayesian approaches are particularly powerful, since they naturally provide posterior distributions over parameters and predictions, allowing full propagation of uncertainty (Bonas et al., 2024).

- o For climate variables, best practices recommend propagating uncertainty through aggregation or merging of data, and carefully presenting uncertainty to avoid misinterpretation (Andersson et al., 2023).

3. Communicating Uncertainty
   - o It is not enough to compute uncertainty; students must also learn how to interpret it and communicate it meaningfully. In risk education, learners must grapple with how uncertainty interplays with values, ethical tradeoffs, and decision-making (Schenk et al., 2024).
   - o The precautionary principle often guides decision-making when uncertainty is large but potential consequences are severe: this ethical orientation is fundamental in risk pedagogy (Schenk et al., 2024).

2.4 Interpretability vs. Flexibility: Hybrid Modeling

A persistent tension in modern environmetrics, and in statistical modeling more broadly, lies in the trade-off between interpretability and flexibility. Interpretable statistical models, such as linear regression, generalized additive models, and Gaussian processes, are valued because they make assumptions explicit, allow parameters to be directly linked to environmental processes, and facilitate uncertainty quantification. These qualities enable explanation, transparency, and trust, which are especially important in environmental decision-making contexts where statistical outputs often inform policy, risk communication, and resource allocation.

At the same time, machine-learning models such as neural networks, random forests, and ensemble methods offer a high degree of flexibility. Their ability to capture complex nonlinear relationships, interactions, and high-dimensional patterns has led to substantial gains in predictive accuracy across many environmental applications. However, this flexibility often comes at the cost of interpretability. Many ML models function as "black boxes," making it difficult to understand how predictions are generated, to assess whether learned relationships are physically plausible, or to evaluate the reliability of predictions when models are applied outside the domain of their training data.

Hybrid modeling provides a useful middle ground for addressing this tension, particularly in educational settings. By combining interpretable statistical components with machine-learning elements, hybrid models allow learners to engage simultaneously with explanation and prediction. Bonas et al. (2024) explicitly discuss this trade-off in the context of environmental time-series analysis, highlighting three critical considerations: interpretability of model components, adaptability in dynamic and non-stationary environments, and the risks associated with extrapolation into previously unobserved conditions. These concerns are particularly salient in environmental systems, which are increasingly shaped by climate change, land-use transformation, and evolving human–environment interactions.

From a pedagogical perspective, hybrid models make the structure of environmental systems more visible to students. For example, a model may use interpretable components to represent long-term trends or seasonal cycles, while a machine-learning component captures short-term anomalies or residual nonlinear behavior. Such configurations help students distinguish between theoretically motivated structure and data-driven pattern recognition. This distinction reinforces core statistical concepts such as bias–variance trade-offs, overfitting, and uncertainty propagation, while also demonstrating how AI-based tools can complement rather than replace statistical reasoning.

Teaching interpretability and flexibility in this integrated way encourages students to think critically about model design and validation. Learners are prompted to consider not only predictive performance, but also robustness, plausibility, and transparency—especially when models are used to inform high-stakes environmental decisions. Attention to validation across both interpolation and extrapolation settings further reinforces the idea that models trained on historical data may fail when environmental conditions shift, and that high accuracy within a training domain does not guarantee reliability under changing future scenarios.

By framing interpretability and flexibility as a continuum rather than a binary choice, this section supports a central pedagogical message of the chapter: effective environmental statistics education must prepare students to balance explanation, prediction, and ethical responsibility. Hybrid modeling offers a concrete and teachable approach for achieving this balance, enabling learners to engage with AI-enhanced methods while maintaining the foundational principles of statistical inference and critical evaluation.

3. AI-ENHANCED METHODS FOR TEACHING ENVIRONMENTAL STATISTICS

The integration of artificial intelligence (AI) into environmental statistics instruction has transformed how learners engage with data, models, and uncertainty. Modern AI tools allow students to work with rich spatiotemporal datasets, develop predictive models, and examine real-world environmental risks. These tools also support deeper learning by enabling students to compare traditional statistical methods with AI-driven approaches and critically evaluate the interpretability, accuracy, and ethical implications of different models (Oddo et al., 2025).

3.1 Machine Learning for Environmental Prediction

Machine learning (ML) has become a core component of modern environmental modeling and provides students with opportunities to build, evaluate, and critique predictive systems.

Land-Use and Land-Cover (LULC) Classification

Deep learning models such as LSTM and hybrid optimization–classification systems provide powerful tools for analyzing land-use changes. For example, hybrid PSO–LSTM models have demonstrated high accuracy in LULC classification and can be used in teaching to illustrate spatial prediction and temporal patterns in environmental change (Babu et al., 2020).

Flood Susceptibility Mapping

Ensemble ML models—such as random forests and gradient boosting—are widely used to model flood susceptibility, outperforming traditional logistic regression in many contexts. Reviews from 2024–2025 indicate that hybrid ML systems consistently improve the accuracy of flood forecasting models (Asif, Kuglitsch, Pelivan, & Albano, 2025).

Rainfall and Streamflow Forecasting

Deep learning approaches, particularly LSTMs, have been shown to outperform linear hydrological models for rainfall–runoff prediction. LSTM networks have been integrated into real-time flood forecasting systems, including Google's operational flood forecasting architecture, which demonstrates improved performance in river-stage prediction (Bogner et al., 2021).

Drought Severity Prediction

Gradient boosting and deep learning models can predict drought indices using hydrometeorological and remote-sensing features. Recent applications show that LSTM combined with vegetation and soil-moisture data can effectively forecast drought conditions under climate change scenarios (Afan et al., 2024).

Damage Mapping

Zhang et. al (2021) Using Landsat 8 imagery on Google Earth Engine with random forest and univariate image differencing, the study mapped forest damage caused by Typhoon Lekima in Zhejiang Province, China. It resulted in high accuracy, showing that 4598.87 km^2 (8.44%) of forest was affected and net canopy loss reached 2.57%. Damage severity and spatial patterns were strongly influenced by elevation, slope, precipitation, and forest type, and the methods and results support post-typhoon restoration planning and sustainable forest management.

Mapping Forest Cover Change

Nguyen et. al (2025) monitored forest cover changes in three Vietnamese provinces—Thanh Hoa, Kon Tum, and Dong Nai—using remote sensing and GIS with Random Forest classification in Google Earth Engine. Land cover was grouped into five classes, revealing substantial changes from 2010 to 2020: broadleaf forests expanded in Thanh Hoa but declined in Kon Tum, while both broadleaf and mixed forests increased in Dong Nai. Classification reliability was high (Kappa 0.81–0.89). Forest cover for 2030 was predicted by comparing CA-Markov and MOLUSCE, with MOLUSCE more accurate and showing strong impacts of agriculture, deforestation, and restoration on future forest dynamics.

In the classroom, these models allow learners to compare interpretability (e.g., linear regression) with predictive accuracy (e.g., LSTM or random forest), fostering critical thinking about model selection under uncertainty.

3.2 Remote Sensing and Satellite Data

Remote sensing datasets create accessible and authentic learning opportunities in environmental statistics. In the current era of machine learning (ML) and artificial intelligence (AI), the use of big data such as satellite data is growing rapidly. Researchers are increasingly using satellite data to analyze various aspects of the environment, such as land cover changes (Alam et al., 2020), water quality (Hassan and Woo, 2021), forest fires (Jaiswal et. al, 2002), and the impacts of climate change (Yang et al., 2013). The availability of open source, standardized data with broad spatial-temporal coverage is the main reason for the widespread use of satellite data. Furthermore, it is possible to integrate satellite data with field survey data (in situ) to obtain more comprehensive and accurate analysis results. This integration enables the development of more reliable ML models, as information from direct field measurements can be used for calibration, validation, and improving the accuracy of satellite image interpretation.

Here are possible applications for Environmental Statistics Education:

1. Air pollution and atmospheric analysis.

Students can work with open-access datasets such as MODIS or Sentinel to analyze aerosol optical depth, PM concentrations, or thermal anomalies.

2. Vegetation health and NDVI dynamics.

ConvLSTM architectures have proven effective in predicting NDVI patterns and can be used as a teaching tool to explain spatial-temporal modeling (Robin et al., 2022). Students engage with concepts like autocorrelation, multicollinearity among spectral bands, and spatiotemporal smoothing.

3. Urban heat islands and thermal monitoring.

Satellite-derived land surface temperature allows students to examine urban heat dynamics. Clustering and ML prediction models can be introduced to identify hotspots and simulate heat mitigation scenarios.

4. Radar precipitation and hydrological data.

Radar-derived precipitation estimates (e.g., IMERG) have been used in hybrid LSTM + process-based flood models (Natural Hazards, 2024). These datasets help students practice data cleaning, feature extraction, and integration of AI with classical hydrological models.

Da Silveria et. al (2021) combined WorldView-3 and Landsat-8 imagery with machine learning to map suitable habitats for *Millepora alcicornis* in marine protected areas of Northeast Brazil.

SVM classification produced 15 benthic classes with 79% accuracy, while MaxEnt modeling showed that distance from shore and depth limit coral settlement and growth.

Ecological variables were the most important predictors, highlighting the role of high biodiversity.

Comparing habitat suitability with human use indicated that tourism and fishing may inhibit coral development, reinforcing the need for no-take zones and other protective measures.

3.3 Early Warning Systems (EWS) and AI Dashboards

AI-enhanced early warning systems represent a high-impact area for instruction in environmental risk analysis.

Flood Forecasting and Real-Time Dashboards

Hybrid flood EWS that combine ML (such as LSTM) with physically based hydrodynamic models are now used operationally in coastal and estuarine systems, demonstrating strong predictive performance in real-time forecasting (Natural Hazards, 2024).

Automated Rainfall–Runoff and Hydrological Modeling

Students can explore automated hydrological systems that process rainfall data and forecast streamflow using ML. This reinforces concepts of uncertainty propagation and sensitivity analysis.

IoT Networks and Real-Time Environmental Monitoring

Sensor networks for rainfall, river level, soil moisture, and groundwater allow learners to simulate real-time prediction and decision-making systems. These systems also introduce important lessons about data latency, missing data, and sensor noise.

Disease and Environmental Health Surveillance

AI-driven EWS for vector-borne disease outbreaks (e.g., dengue, malaria) incorporate environmental predictors such as temperature, rainfall, and humidity. These can be used in teaching to illustrate multidisciplinary environmental risk modeling.

Students also learn key ethical considerations: false alarms, public trust, data privacy, and responsible communication of risk (Pandey et al., 2025).

3.4 AI-Assisted Environmental Models

Beyond prediction, AI is used to build comprehensive environmental models that reinforce statistical principles.

AI-Based Drought Forecasting

Recent research shows that integrated LSTM models using NDVI, soil moisture, and precipitation provide strong predictive skill in arid region drought forecasting (Afan et al., 2024).

Clustering for Watershed Classification

Unsupervised algorithms (k-means, hierarchical clustering) can classify watersheds based on geophysical and hydrological attributes. This reinforces topics such as distance metrics, scaling, and cluster validation.

Anomaly Detection for Pollution and Environmental Monitoring

Autoencoders, isolation forests, and one-class SVMs detect pollution spikes or anomalous temperature events. Teaching these models helps students understand variance, thresholds, outliers, and extreme value theory.

These applications allow students to apply fundamental statistical concepts—distribution, correlation, variability, uncertainty—to complex real-world systems enriched by AI insights.

4. TEACHING HAZARD AND DISASTER RISK ANALYSIS IN AN AI CONTEXT

The increasing frequency and severity of natural hazards—including floods, droughts, extreme heat, landslides, and vector-borne disease outbreaks—has intensified the need for educational approaches that prepare students to analyze, model, and manage risk. Integrating AI into hazard and disaster risk analysis enhances students' ability to understand uncertainty, interpret complex systems, and evaluate the consequences of multiple hazard scenarios (Rana & Routray, 2023). This section outlines how traditional frameworks in risk analysis can be strengthened through AI-driven tools.

4.1 Probabilistic Risk Assessment (PRA)

Probabilistic Risk Assessment (PRA) is fundamental in environmental and disaster risk education because it provides a structured framework for quantifying uncertainty and estimating the likelihood and consequences of adverse events. Rather than relying on deterministic "worst-case" scenarios, PRA emphasizes probabilistic reasoning and explicitly models the variability inherent in natural hazards, exposure patterns, and system response. As such, PRA is well suited for teaching students how uncertainty propagates through environmental systems and influences risk-informed decision-making.

In environmental applications, PRA typically involves the evaluation of several key components:

- hazard probability distributions, which describe the likelihood and intensity of events such as floods, earthquakes, droughts, or typhoons;
- exposure and vulnerability curves, which link hazard intensity to potential damage, losses, or impacts on populations and infrastructure;
- loss exceedance curves (LECs), which express the probability that losses will exceed a given threshold; and
- Expected Annual Damage (EAD), a summary metric representing the long-term average loss weighted by event probability.

These concepts remain central in operational domains such as flood risk management, seismic risk assessment, and cyclone-loss estimation, and are widely adopted in policy-oriented risk frameworks (UNDRR, 2022). From an educational perspective, PRA enables students to move beyond point estimates and engage directly with probability distributions, tail risks, and nonlinear loss behavior.

Artificial intelligence enhances PRA by expanding the ways in which hazard scenarios and exposure data can be generated and analyzed. AI-based models can produce large ensembles of plausible hazard realizations, extract complex patterns from historical records, and improve probabilistic forecasting under data-rich conditions. For example, machine-learning techniques—including deep neural networks embedded within Bayesian frameworks—have been used to generate synthetic hazard scenarios under non-stationary climate conditions, allowing risk models to reflect changing hazard dynamics rather than assuming stationarity (Majumder & Reich, 2023). In PRA education, such approaches allow students to explore how assumptions about climate non-stationarity influence estimated risk.

AI-enabled PRA also supports the integration of high-resolution exposure data, such as satellite-derived population density, building footprints, or land-use layers, which can substantially improve local-scale risk estimates. When combined with vulnerability functions, these datasets help students understand how spatial heterogeneity in exposure interacts with hazard intensity to drive loss outcomes. Importantly, this integration highlights that increases in model complexity must be accompanied by careful treatment of uncertainty, data quality, and representativeness—reinforcing core statistical principles rather than bypassing them.

Pedagogically, PRA combined with AI-generated scenarios provides powerful instructional opportunities. Educators can use scenario ensembles to demonstrate how small changes in hazard probability, exposure distribution, or vulnerability assumptions can lead to nonlinear changes in expected losses, particularly in the tails of loss distributions. These exercises help students appreciate why extreme events, though rare, often dominate long-term risk metrics such as EAD. Moreover, PRA-based teaching naturally connects to subsequent topics such as Monte Carlo simulation, sensitivity analysis, and multi-criteria decision analysis, making it a central integrative component in environmental risk statistics curricula.

4.2 Monte Carlo and Stochastic Simulation

Monte Carlo simulation remains a cornerstone of hazard modeling and environmental risk education because it provides a clear and intuitive way to demonstrate how uncertainty propagates through complex environmental systems. By simulating thousands of plausible future states, Monte Carlo methods allow students to visualize the range of potential outcomes associated with hazards such as floods, droughts, landslides, or storm surges, rather than focusing on single deterministic predictions. This approach reinforces core statistical concepts such as variability, probability distributions, tail risk, and the cumulative effects of uncertain inputs on overall impact.

Recent research highlights how artificial intelligence can further enhance Monte Carlo-based hazard modeling. AI-assisted simulation frameworks that incorporate surrogate models, neural networks, or active learning strategies enable faster and more computationally efficient generation of hazard scenarios while maintaining realistic representations of system behavior. These approaches have been shown to improve both predictive accuracy and the characterization of uncertainty, particularly in data-intensive or high-dimensional modeling contexts (Meresa et al., 2021; Pickering et al., 2022). From a teaching perspective, such tools allow learners to work with richer ensembles of simulated outcomes without prohibitive computational cost.

In instructional settings, students can engage with simulated rainfall ensembles, stochastic drought indices, generated storm-surge heights, or probabilistic ground-shaking fields and observe how uncertainty in inputs—such as precipitation intensity, soil moisture conditions, or tide levels—translates into variability in hazard intensity and resulting impacts. These exercises help learners understand that uncertainty is not confined to a single model component, but accumulates across the modeling chain, often leading to nonlinear responses in damage, losses, or risk metrics.

Stochastic simulation is especially valuable in climate-change education, where future conditions cannot be represented by a single forecast. By exploring multiple plausible futures under different Representative Concentration Pathway (RCP) or

Shared Socioeconomic Pathway (SSP) scenarios, students can examine how assumptions about emissions, socio-economic development, or climate sensitivity influence projected hazards and risks. This exposure encourages probabilistic thinking and helps learners appreciate the fundamental distinction between scenario-based exploration and prediction.

Hybrid approaches that combine AI with Monte Carlo simulation—often referred to as multi-fidelity or surrogate-assisted methods—have been shown to improve predictive fidelity in climate-related hazard modeling by reducing computational burden while preserving accuracy (Gruber et al., 2023). In a pedagogical context, these methods offer an opportunity to teach students how approximation, model hierarchy, and computational efficiency interact with uncertainty quantification. More importantly, they reinforce the idea that sophisticated tools do not eliminate uncertainty, but instead provide new ways of representing and managing it within decision-relevant frameworks.

4.3 Multi-Criteria Decision Analysis (MCDA)

Environmental management and disaster risk reduction frequently require decisions that involve balancing multiple, and often conflicting, criteria. Decision-makers must weigh hazard likelihood against social vulnerability, economic costs, environmental impacts, and ethical considerations, all under conditions of uncertainty. Within environmental statistics education, Multi-Criteria Decision Analysis (MCDA) provides a structured framework for helping students understand how complex decisions can be formally represented, evaluated, and justified when no single criterion is sufficient.

MCDA methods enable learners to decompose complex problems into manageable components and to make explicit the trade-offs inherent in environmental decision-making. Techniques such as the Analytic Hierarchy Process (AHP) and Delphi-based expert elicitation allow students to structure problems hierarchically, integrate diverse sources of knowledge, and translate qualitative judgments into quantitative weights. Extensions such as fuzzy decision-making methods, including fuzzy AHP and fuzzy TOPSIS, help students address ambiguity and imprecision in expert assessments, which are common in hazard and vulnerability evaluations. When combined with geographic information systems (AHP–GIS), MCDA further supports spatial risk assessment, allowing learners to visualize how multiple criteria interact across space.

The integration of artificial intelligence enhances MCDA by automating and refining several stages of the decision process. AI-enhanced MCDA frameworks can support automated weighting schemes, improve consistency checking in pairwise comparisons, and facilitate the integration of MCDA with predictive models and scenario-based risk assessments. This integration is particularly valuable in educational settings, where students can explore how changes in assumptions, weights, or data sources influence ranking and prioritization outcomes.

Empirical studies indicate that AI-assisted MCDA, particularly AI-enhanced AHP, can improve decision-making accuracy and reduce subjective bias in hazard prioritization and environmental planning contexts (Kiker et al., 2021). Pedagogically, this allows students to critically examine the balance between expert judgment and algorithmic support, reinforcing the idea that decision-support systems do not replace human responsibility but instead structure and inform it.

4.4 Spatiotemporal Modeling for Hazards

Many environmental hazards exhibit strong spatial and temporal dynamics, making spatiotemporal modeling a central component of environmental risk analysis. Teaching students how to analyze these patterns offers an opportunity to integrate geographic information systems (GIS), statistical modeling, and machine-learning approaches within a unified instructional framework. Through spatiotemporal modeling, learners can examine how hazards evolve across space and time and how spatial dependence, temporal autocorrelation, and non-stationarity influence risk estimates.

Within educational settings, spatiotemporal hazard modeling can be applied to a wide range of environmental and public-health challenges. Common learning contexts include the detection of dengue hotspots, analysis of spatiotemporal drought progression, mapping of flood-prone barangays, modeling pollution plume dispersion, assessing landslide susceptibility, and identifying heatwave anomalies. These applications allow students to work with real or realistic datasets while reinforcing key statistical concepts such as spatial autocorrelation, temporal dependence, and uncertainty propagation.

Artificial intelligence enhances spatiotemporal modeling by enabling automated spatial feature extraction from sources such as satellite imagery, learning complex nonlinear relationships, and efficiently handling large geospatial datasets. Recent studies demonstrate that deep learning architectures—including convolutional neural networks (CNNs), convolutional long short-term memory (ConvLSTM) models, and hybrid spatial–temporal frameworks—often outperform classical statistical models in detecting environmental hotspots and forecasting spatial risk (Robin et al., 2022). From a pedagogical perspective, these AI-based methods provide students with powerful tools to contrast predictive performance against interpretability and model transparency.

Empirical examples further illustrate these approaches. In dengue forecasting, machine-learning models such as LSTM, Bi-LSTM, CNN-LSTM, and related architectures have been shown to improve predictive accuracy by capturing complex temporal patterns in disease incidence (Jaya et al., 2025). Drought propagation has similarly been monitored using AI-extracted indicators such as NDVI and soil-moisture anomalies, allowing students to explore how vegetation and hydrometeorological signals interact over time (Afan et al., 2024). In flood susceptibility mapping, ensemble machine-learning methods such as random forests and gradient boosting have consistently demonstrated higher accuracy than traditional logistic regression, highlighting the advantages of nonlinear modeling in spatial risk assessment (Pathak & Muralidharan, 2023).

At the same time, classical spatial statistical models remain essential for instruction, particularly when interpretability and inference are central goals. Prahutama et al. (2021), for example, applied geographically weighted negative bivariate binomial regression to model dengue cases and mortality in East Nusa Tenggara Province, Indonesia, identifying key drivers such as population density, poverty levels, availability of health facilities, and sanitation coverage. Similarly, Ispriyanti et al. (2018) used the Spatial Durbin Model to analyze the spread of dengue fever in Central Java Province, comparing weighting techniques and highlighting spatial spillover effects. These examples allow students to compare theory-driven spatial regression approaches with data-driven machine-learning models, reinforcing the interpretability–flexibility trade-off discussed earlier in the chapter.

Teaching spatiotemporal hazard modeling within this integrated framework provides students with hands-on experience in environmental prediction, spatial risk mapping, and uncertainty quantification. More importantly, it equips learners to critically evaluate both statistical and AI-based approaches, understand their assumptions and limitations, and apply them responsibly in real-world environmental and public-health decision-making contexts.

5. ETHICS, EQUITY, AND RESPONSIBLE AI IN ENVIRONMENTAL DECISIONS

As AI-driven tools become increasingly embedded in environmental monitoring, disaster forecasting, and risk communication, the ethical dimensions of algorithmic decision-making have become central to statistics pedagogy. Teaching environmental statistics in the age of AI therefore requires more than technical competence in modeling or computation. It demands a critical understanding of how data, models, and algorithms interact with issues of bias, transparency, accountability, community participation, and justice. This section examines key ethical considerations that must be integrated into environmental statistics education to ensure that AI-enhanced analyses support equitable and responsible decision-making.

5.1 Algorithmic Bias and Environmental Justice

AI systems used for environmental prediction—such as flood susceptibility modeling, wildfire risk assessment, or pollution exposure estimation—are particularly vulnerable to algorithmic bias when training data are incomplete, spatially uneven, or socially unrepresentative (Holstein et al., 2019; Shankar et al., 2017). In many regions of the Global South, including parts of Southeast Asia, environmental datasets are dense in urban centers but sparse in coastal, indigenous, and rural communities. As a result, AI-based models may systematically underestimate flood or landslide risks in marginalized barangays, misclassify indigenous territories due to coarse spatial resolution, disproportionately prioritize areas with better monitoring infrastructure, or reinforce historical inequities in environmental resource allocation (Milojevic-Dupont & Creutzig, 2021).

From a pedagogical standpoint, these challenges underscore the importance of teaching students how algorithmic bias emerges from data collection practices, model design choices, and evaluation metrics. Students must learn to identify, measure, and mitigate bias through statistical diagnostics, spatial representativeness checks, and fairness-aware modeling approaches. Embedding environmental justice considerations into statistical training helps learners recognize that AI-driven environmental decisions are not value-neutral, and that technical outputs can have unequal real-world consequences across communities.

5.2 Transparency and Explainability

Because environmental models often inform high-stakes policies—such as evacuation orders, land-use zoning, infrastructure investment, and climate adaptation measures—decision-makers require statistical evidence that is trustworthy, interpretable, and transparent. Environmental statistics education must therefore emphasize the principles and practices of explainable AI (XAI) alongside conventional modeling techniques. Transparency practices include clear documentation of datasets and models, assessment of feature importance, explicit quantification and communication of uncertainty, and the use of interpretable modeling alternatives in parallel with more complex black-box systems.

Explainability is particularly important in environmental hazard contexts, where errors or misclassifications can affect thousands of lives. For example, an opaque landslide susceptibility model that cannot be scrutinized or explained may undermine public trust and complicate accountability (Roscher et al., 2020). XAI also aligns with broader calls for "environmentally responsible AI," which emphasize transparency, participation, and accountability in algorithmic systems deployed in public decision-making (Taddeo & Floridi, 2020).

Traditional statistical inference provides one pathway to explanation through parameter estimation and hypothesis testing, enabling explicit interpretation of relationships between variables. In contrast, many machine-learning approaches prioritize predictive accuracy, often without built-in mechanisms for explanation (Breiman, 2001). Recent advances in XAI seek to bridge this divide by introducing post-hoc interpretability tools that complement predictive models. Techniques such as SHAP (Shapley Additive Explanations) (Lundberg & Lee, 2017) and LIME (Local Interpretable Model-Agnostic Explanations) (Yang et al., 2023) allow students to interrogate model behavior, examine local and global feature contributions, and better understand the conditions under which AI models may fail or behave unpredictably. Teaching these tools alongside classical statistical interpretation reinforces the idea that explanation is a core component of responsible modeling, not an optional add-on.

5.3 Ethical Risk Communication

Ethical environmental decision-making also depends on the ability to communicate statistical uncertainty and risk in ways that are clear, actionable, and socially responsible. Misinterpretation of hazard forecasts may lead to alarmism, complacency, or erosion of trust, particularly when probabilistic information is poorly conveyed. Statistics education must therefore prepare students to communicate risk effectively to diverse audiences, including policymakers who require concise yet accurate summaries, community leaders who need context-sensitive explanations, journalists who may amplify or oversimplify probabilities, and disaster-risk managers responsible for operational readiness.

Ethical risk communication involves avoiding unnecessary technical jargon, clearly articulating uncertainty ranges, and explicitly acknowledging model assumptions and limitations (Fischhoff & Davis, 2014). In culturally and linguistically diverse settings such as the Philippines, it is especially important for students to engage with community-centered communication strategies that respect local knowledge, values, and perceptions of risk. Teaching these skills helps learners appreciate that effective risk communication is as critical to disaster preparedness as accurate modeling.

5.4 Indigenous and Local Knowledge (ILK)

Despite its importance, Indigenous and Local Knowledge (ILK) is rarely incorporated into traditional statistics curricula. Yet ILK plays a vital role in environmental prediction, ecosystem monitoring, and disaster resilience. Empirical research shows that ILK can enhance environmental analysis by providing long-term historical memory of hazards, offering locally grounded indicators of droughts, floods, or ecosystem change, supplying ground-truth for validating AI-generated predictions, and improving spatial accuracy through participatory GIS and community-based monitoring (Liu et al., 2018; Purwitaningsih et al., 2022).

Integrating ILK into environmental statistics education promotes pluralism in knowledge systems and challenges the assumption that algorithmic outputs are complete or neutral representations of reality. ILK complements statistical and AI-based methods by adding context-specific insights that are often invisible in purely data-driven models. Incorporating these perspectives helps students develop culturally relevant, ethically grounded approaches to environmental decision-making, reinforcing the broader goal of responsible and inclusive AI-enabled environmental analytics.

6. GLOBAL CASE STUDIES AND APPLICATIONS FROM THE PHILIPPINES

Environmental statistics pedagogy is greatly enriched by applied, place-based case studies that demonstrate how statistical theory, AI-based methods, and ethical considerations converge in real-world decision-making. The Philippines—one of the most hazard-prone countries globally—offers a particularly valuable context for such instruction. Its exposure to typhoons, floods, droughts, air pollution, and infectious disease outbreaks, combined with growing availability of environmental and public-health data, provides compelling opportunities for students to engage deeply with environmetrics, risk analysis, and AI-driven modeling. The following case studies illustrate how core statistical concepts can be taught through pressing environmental and societal challenges, while reinforcing responsible and context-aware use of AI.

Case Study 1: Air Pollution (PM2.5) and Respiratory Health

The analysis of $PM_{2.5}$ exposure and its association with child respiratory illness and mortality offers a strong example of how environmental statistics can elucidate public-health risk patterns (Ceballos et al., 2024). In the Philippines, chronic exceedances of $PM_{2.5}$ guidelines are driven by transportation emissions, biomass burning, and industrial activity (Cohen et al., 2017; Guttikunda et al., 2021). Using air-quality and health datasets, students can model exposure–response relationships through generalized additive models or distributed lag models, explore delayed effects of pollution exposure in time-series data, and distinguish anthropogenic from natural pollution sources using source-apportionment or classification techniques.

AI-based pollutant forecasting models, such as hybrid SARIMA–BiLSTM approaches, further allow learners to compare predictive performance and interpretability relative to classical regression or ARIMA models (Necula et al., 2025). These exercises introduce key epidemiological concepts, including exposure misclassification, uncertainty, and causal inference, while highlighting the trade-offs between predictive accuracy and model transparency.

Case Study 2: Flood Susceptibility Mapping

Floods are among the most frequent and damaging disasters in the Philippines, making flood susceptibility mapping a particularly relevant pedagogical application. Students can develop baseline statistical models using logistic regression, then extend analyses using AI-based spatial classifiers such as random forests or gradient boosting. Expert-driven approaches such as the Analytic Hierarchy Process (AHP) can also be introduced to incorporate domain knowledge into flood-driver weighting.

Empirical studies show that machine-learning models frequently outperform traditional statistical approaches in predictive accuracy for flood susceptibility mapping (Pham et al., 2020; Dano et al., 2023). Classroom applications allow students to generate flood-risk maps, compare AI-based and expert-weighted methods, and validate results using historical flood events, rainfall data, or spatial error matrices. These exercises support experiential learning while reinforcing critical assessment of data quality, spatial autocorrelation, and the ethical implications of hazard maps for land-use planning and marginalized communities.

Case Study 3: Drought in Agriculture

Drought remains a persistent threat to Philippine agriculture, particularly under climate-change conditions. Adaptation strategies such as afforestation, riparian buffers, agroforestry, and water-retention measures provide practical contexts for environmental modeling. Using drought and agricultural datasets, students can analyze soil-moisture dynamics through regression, spatial interpolation, or machine-learning models, predict drought indices such as the Standardized Precipitation Index (SPI) and Standardized Precipitation–Evapotranspiration Index (SPEI), and simulate the impacts of adaptation strategies through scenario analysis (Afan et al., 2024).

AI-enhanced drought forecasting models—including LSTM, Gaussian process regression, and boosting methods—improve predictive accuracy while offering hands-on opportunities to examine forecasting uncertainty, model validation, and scenario-based reasoning (Pande et al., 2024). These activities integrate statistical reasoning with climate science and agricultural risk management, illustrating how quantitative tools inform resilience planning.

Case Study 4: Dengue and Mpox Spatiotemporal Analysis

The Philippines experiences recurrent dengue outbreaks, and the recent detection of Mpox cases further underscores the importance of adaptable spatiotemporal surveillance systems. These public-health challenges provide rich datasets for teaching spatial and temporal modeling techniques. Students can conduct hotspot detection using Getis–Ord Gi* statistics or Kulldorff space–time scan methods, apply time-series decomposition to identify seasonal and long-term trends, and model disease risk factors using both regression-based and machine-learning classifiers.

AI-based disease prediction models, including random forests, XGBoost, and neural networks, have demonstrated improved outbreak-forecasting performance in Southeast Asia (Tian et al., 2024; Draidi Areed et al., 2025; Castro et al., 2023). Comparing these approaches with traditional epidemiological models allows students to critically examine issues of fairness, data sparsity, spatial representativeness, and interpretability in disease surveillance. Ongoing monitoring of Mpox cases in South Cotabato is particularly valuable for illustrating how emerging diseases require flexible statistical and AI tools capable of adapting to limited and evolving data.

Case Study 5: Disaster Preparedness Index (DPI)

The Disaster Preparedness Index (DPI) developed in the dissertation by Ceballos (2025) provides a comprehensive instructional framework that integrates expert elicitation, index construction, and simulation-based validation. Through this case, students can learn structured consensus-building via the Delphi method, derive expert-based weights using AHP, construct data-driven indices through Factor Analysis of Mixed Data (FAMD), and apply bootstrapping, Monte Carlo simulation, or jackknife methods for index validation.

Recent literature highlights the value of hybrid statistical–AI approaches in assessing disaster resilience and preparedness (Li & Mostafavi, 2025; Thekdi et al., 2023). The DPI framework aligns with international practices while grounding instruction in real disaster-risk-reduction and management (DRRM) contexts in the Philippines. Through these exercises, learners develop competence in multi-method modeling, robustness analysis, and ethical reflection—particularly in understanding how preparedness metrics influence resource allocation and decision-making at the community level.

Together, these case studies demonstrate how environmental statistics education can be anchored in real-world challenges that integrate statistical inference, AI-based modeling, and ethical responsibility. By engaging with Philippine-based applications, students not only strengthen their technical skills but also develop contextual awareness and critical judgment essential for responsible environmental decision-making.

7. PEDAGOGICAL STRATEGIES FOR MODERN ENVIRONMENTAL STATISTICS

Modern environmental statistics education must equip students not only with theoretical knowledge, but also with practical skills in computation, data handling, and ethical reasoning. As environmental decision-making increasingly relies on AI-augmented analytics, effective pedagogy must integrate real-world applications, computational tools, interdisciplinary collaboration, and open science practices. Together, these elements prepare learners to navigate complex environmental problems while maintaining statistical rigor, transparency, and social responsibility. The strategies discussed in this section offer a roadmap for teaching environmental statistics in the age of AI.

7.1 Integrating R, Python, and AI Tools

Hands-on coding is essential for developing computational literacy in environmental statistics. Integrating multiple analytical platforms allows students to build end-to-end workflows that mirror professional environmental data-science practice. R remains a powerful environment for statistical modeling, regression analysis, time-series analysis, data visualization, and reproducible reporting (Wickham et al., 2021). Python complements this ecosystem by supporting machine-learning workflows, neural-network implementation, and efficient data preprocessing (Geron, 2021). Spatial tools such as QGIS and cloud-based platforms like Google Earth Engine further enable geospatial analysis, geoprocessing, and integration of remote-sensing data.

By working across these tools, students gain experience moving from data acquisition and cleaning to modeling, validation, and visualization. This integrated approach reinforces conceptual understanding while building practical skills that are directly transferable to environmental research and professional practice.

7.2 Interdisciplinary Collaborations

Environmental challenges are inherently multidimensional, intersecting ecological, social, health, and governance domains. Pedagogical approaches that encourage collaboration across statistics, environmental science, public health, and disaster risk reduction and management (DRRM) promote holistic problem-solving and systems thinking. Through interdisciplinary projects, students encounter diverse data types, methodological perspectives, and epistemological traditions, which encourages flexibility in method selection and sensitivity to contextual factors (Tengö et al., 2021; Afan et al., 2024).

Such collaborations also help students appreciate that statistical and AI-based models are most effective when informed by domain expertise and grounded in real-world decision contexts. This perspective is particularly important for risk analysis, where technical outputs must be translated into actionable recommendations across disciplinary boundaries.

7.3 Ethical and Reflective Learning

Ethical reasoning is an essential component of AI-aware environmental statistics education. Students should be encouraged to reflect critically on uncertainty in hazard and exposure predictions, algorithmic fairness, ethical risk communication to communities and policymakers, and the potential impacts of AI-based decisions on vulnerable populations. These reflections help learners move beyond technical proficiency toward responsible analytical practice.

Structured ethical reflection can be embedded in project reports, classroom discussions, or reflective journals, providing a space for students to interrogate the assumptions, limitations, and societal consequences of their models. Such approaches foster awareness of how algorithmic bias, data gaps, and model misinterpretation can influence environmental outcomes, particularly in marginalized communities (Holstein et al., 2019; Shankar et al., 2017).

7.4 Open Science Practices

Adopting open science practices prepares students to become transparent, reproducible, and accountable researchers. Instruction that emphasizes the sharing of open datasets, the use of transparent and well-documented R or Python scripts, and version control systems such as GitHub supports reproducibility and collaborative learning. Encouraging the dissemination of preprints and working papers further strengthens scholarly communication, while adherence to FAIR principles—ensuring that data are Findable, Accessible, Interoperable, and Reusable—promotes ethical stewardship of environmental information (Wilkinson et al., 2016; Nosek et al., 2021).

Open science practices not only improve methodological rigor, but also reinforce values of collaboration, data literacy, and public accountability. In environmental domains where data and models directly influence policy and community outcomes, these practices are integral to responsible AI-enabled statistical education.

8. CONCLUSION: AI-ENABLED ENVIRONMETRICS FOR A RESILIENT FUTURE

Environmental hazards, climate-change impacts, and disaster risks are projected to intensify over the coming decades, particularly in vulnerable regions such as the Philippines (UNDRR, 2022; IPCC, 2023). In this context, preparing students to analyze, interpret, and critically evaluate environmental risks in an AI-enhanced analytical landscape is no longer optional but essential. Environmental statistics education must therefore evolve beyond isolated techniques to support informed decision-making under uncertainty, ethical responsibility, and societal complexity.

This chapter has demonstrated that environmental statistics pedagogy can be strengthened through the deliberate integration of classical statistical theory with modern AI-based tools, ethical reasoning, and community-centered perspectives. AI-enhanced modeling approaches—including machine learning, LSTM networks, and ensemble methods—offer powerful capabilities for forecasting hazards and pollutants, while spatiotemporal and probabilistic analyses provide structured ways to understand floods, droughts, and disease outbreaks. At the decision-making stage, multi-criteria and hybrid frameworks such as AHP and FAMD enable students to connect quantitative risk estimates with real planning and policy trade-offs. Equally important, embedding ethics and equity into instruction—through attention to bias, transparency, uncertainty communication, and Indigenous and local knowledge—ensures that analytical skills are aligned with principles of environmental justice and accountability (Holstein et al., 2019; Tengö et al., 2021).

Across the chapter, project-based learning, computational training, and open science practices have been presented as key pedagogical strategies for developing both technical competence and critical reflection. These approaches allow students to engage with authentic datasets, build reproducible workflows, and confront the limitations of models when applied to real-world environmental systems. By doing so, learners gain not only methodological proficiency but also the interpretive judgment necessary to assess when AI-based predictions are appropriate, trustworthy, and ethically defensible.

Environmental statistics education must therefore not merely keep pace with advances in AI, but actively shape their responsible use. Decisions derived from environmental data have direct consequences for human health, community resilience, and ecological sustainability. The fusion of statistical reasoning, risk analysis, and ethical AI thus represents not only a pedagogical challenge but a broader societal imperative, particularly as algorithmic systems increasingly influence environmental governance and disaster preparedness (Taddeo & Floridi, 2020; Roscher et al., 2020).

By embedding AI-aware, ethically grounded, and data-driven learning experiences into curricula, educators can cultivate a generation of statisticians and researchers capable of producing actionable, transparent, and equitable insights. Such training is critical for strengthening resilience, safeguarding ecosystems, and advancing sustainable development in an increasingly complex and AI-driven world.

REFERENCES

Afan, H. A., Almawla, A. S., Al-Hadeethi, B., Khaleel, F., AbdUlameer, A. H., Khan, M. M. H., Ma'arof, M. I. N., & Kamel, A. H. (2024). LSTM model integrated remote sensing data for drought prediction: A study on climate change impacts on water availability in the arid region. *Water (Basel), 16*(19), 2799. DOI: 10.3390/w16192799

Alam, A., Bhat, M. S., & Maheen, M. (2020). Using Landsat satellite data for assessing the land use and land cover change in Kashmir valley. *GeoJournal, 85*(6), 1529–1543. DOI: 10.1007/s10708-019-10037-x

Aljanabi, F., Dedeoğlu, M., & Şeker, C. (2024). Environmental monitoring of Land Use/Land Cover by integrating remote sensing and machine learning algorithms. *Journal of Engineering and Sustainable Development, 28*(4), 455-466. ttps://DOI: 10.31272/jeasd.28.4.4

Andersson, T. R., Markou, S., Requeima, J., Bruinsma, W. P., Vaughan, A., & Turner, R. E. (2023). Environmental sensor placement with convolutional Gaussian neural processes. *Environmental Data Science, 2*(e32), 1–16. DOI: 10.1017/eds.2023.22

Asif, M., Kuglitsch, M. M., Pelivan, I., & Albano, R. (2025). Review and intercomparison of machine learning applications for Short-term flood forecasting. *Water Resources Management, 39*(5), 1971–1991. DOI: 10.1007/s11269-025-04093-x

Babu, G. R., Maheswari, G., Parameshachari, B. D., & Ullo, S. L. (2020). PSO with LSTM deep learning model for land cover classification. *IEEE International Conference on Emerging Trends in Information Technology and Engineering*. https://arxiv.org/abs/2008.01635

Bogner, K., Bui, T., Gupta, H., Sharma, A., Nguyen, H., Khandelwal, A., Addanki, R., Saha, A., & Nemani, R. (2021). A global, operational, real-time flood forecasting system using machine learning and remote sensing. *Nature, 596*, 80–84. DOI: 10.1038/s41586-021-03600-2

Bonas, M., Datta, A., Wikle, C. K., Boone, E. L., Alamri, F. S., Hari, B. V., Kavila, I., Simmons, S. J., Jarvis, S. M., Burr, W. S., Pagendam, D. E., Chang, W., & Castruccio, S. (2024). Assessing predictability of environmental time series with statistical and machine learning models. *Environmetrics, 36*(1), e2864. DOI: 10.1002/env.2864 PMID: 40017797

Breiman, L. (2001). Statistical modeling: The two cultures (with comments and a rejoinder by the author). *Statistical Science, 16*(3), 199–231. DOI: 10.1214/ss/1009213726

Castro, I. K. G., Elquiero, N. M., & Fradejas, J. D. (2023). *Assessing machine learning methods in predicting dengue incidence using climatic factors in Region IV-A (CALABARZON), Philippines* (Bachelor's thesis). De La Salle University. Retrieved from https://animorepository.dlsu.edu.ph/etdb_bio/27

Ceballos, R. F., Gallano, R. C., & Visaya, L. D. (2024). Assessing the Relationship and Effect of Air Pollution [PM 2.5] on Child Respiratory Illness and Child Mortality in the Philippines. *Applied Environmental Research, 46*(3).

Cohen, A. J., Brauer, M., Burnett, R., Anderson, H. R., Frostad, J., Estep, K., Balakrishnan, K., Brunekreef, B., Dandona, L., Dandona, R., Feigin, V., Freedman, G., Hubbell, B., Jobling, A., Kan, H., Knibbs, L., Liu, Y., Martin, R., Morawska, L., & Forouzanfar, M. H. (2017). Estimates and 25-year trends of the global burden of disease attributable to ambient air pollution: An analysis of data from the Global Burden of Diseases Study 2015. *Lancet, 389*(10082), 1907–1918. DOI: 10.1016/S0140-6736(17)30505-6 PMID: 28408086

Dano, J. B., Cruz, R., & Tiburan, C. (2023). Machine learning approaches for flood susceptibility mapping in the Philippines. *Natural Hazards, 117*, 1885–1907.

Draidi Areed, W., Nguyen, T. T. T., Do, K. Q., Nguyen, T., Bui, V., Nelson, E., Warren, J. L., Doan, Q.-V., Sinh, N. V., Osborne, N. J., Richards, R., Tran, N. Q. L., Le, H., Pham, T., Hung, T. M., & Phung, D. (2025). A district-level ensemble model to enhance dengue prediction and control for the Mekong Delta Region of Vietnam. *PLoS Neglected Tropical Diseases, 19*(9), e0013571. DOI: 10.1371/journal.pntd.0013571 PMID: 41022038

Feng, L., Ma, D., Xie, M., & Xi, M. (2025). Review on the Application of Remote Sensing Data and Machine Learning to the Estimation of Anthropogenic Heat Emissions. *Remote Sensing (Basel), 17*(2), 200. DOI: 10.3390/rs17020200

Fischhoff, B., & Davis, A. L. (2014). Communicating scientific uncertainty. *Proceedings of the National Academy of Sciences of the United States of America, 117*(14), 7672–7675. DOI: 10.1073/pnas.131750411 PMID: 25225390

Gacu, J. G., Monjardin, C. E. F., Mangulabnan, R. G. T., Pugat, G. C. E., & Solmerin, J. G. (2025). Artificial intelligence (AI) in surface water management: A comprehensive review of methods, applications, and challenges. *Water (Basel), 17*(11), 1707. DOI: 10.3390/w17111707

Geron, A. (2021). *Hands-On Machine Learning with Scikit-Learn, Keras, and TensorFlow* (2nd ed.). O'Reilly Media.

Gruber, A., Gunzburger, M., Ju, L., Lan, R., & Wang, Z. (2023). Multifidelity Monte Carlo estimation for efficient uncertainty quantification in climate-related modeling. *Geoscientific Model Development*, *16*(4), 1213–1229. DOI: 10.5194/gmd-16-1213-2023

Guttikunda, S. K.. (2021). Air pollution in South and Southeast Asia: Science-based solutions. *Atmospheric Environment*, *246*, 118093.

Hassan, N., & Woo, C. S. (2021, August). Machine learning application in water quality using satellite data. [). IOP Publishing.]. *IOP Conference Series. Earth and Environmental Science*, *842*(1), 012018. DOI: 10.1088/1755-1315/842/1/012018

Hayes, K. R., Regan, H. M., & Burgman, M. A. (2021). Concepts and methods of uncertainty analysis in environmental risk assessment. In *Environmental Risk Assessment of Genetically Modified Organisms* (Vol. 3, pp. 189–206). CAB International., DOI: 10.1079/9781800621176.0028

Holstein, K., Wortman Vaughan, J., Daumé, H.III, Dudik, M., & Wallach, H. (2019, May). Improving fairness in machine learning systems: What do industry practitioners need? In *Proceedings of the 2019 CHI conference on human factors in computing systems* (pp. 1-16). DOI: 10.1145/3290605.3300830

Huser, R., Opitz, T., & Wadsworth, J. L. (2025). Modeling of spatial extremes in environmental data science: Time to move away from max-stable processes. *Environmental Data Science*, *4*, e3. DOI: 10.1017/eds.2024.54

Ispriyanti, D., Prahutama, A., & Taryono, A. P. (2018, May). Modelling space of spread Dengue Hemorrhagic Fever (DHF) in Central Java use spatial durbin model. [). IOP Publishing.]. *Journal of Physics: Conference Series*, *1025*(1), 012112. DOI: 10.1088/1742-6596/1025/1/012112

Jaiswal, R. K., Mukherjee, S., Raju, K. D., & Saxena, R. (2002). Forest fire risk zone mapping from satellite imagery and GIS. *International Journal of Applied Earth Observation and Geoinformation*, *4*(1), 1–10. DOI: 10.1016/S0303-2434(02)00006-5

Jaya, I. G. N. M., Andriyana, Y., Tantular, B., Pangastuti, S. S., & Kristiani, F. (2025). Spatiotemporal Dengue Forecasting for Sustainable Public Health in Bandung, Indonesia: A Comparative Study of Classical, Machine Learning, and Bayesian Models. *Sustainability (Basel)*, *17*(15), 6777. DOI: 10.3390/su17156777

Kiker, G. A., Bridges, T. S., & Varghese, A. (2021). Modernizing multi-criteria decision analysis in environmental management using AI-based decision support. *Journal of Environmental Management*, *293*, 112836.

Leal Filho, W., Kim, E., Borsatto, J. M. L. S., & Marcolin, C. B. (2025). Using artificial intelligence in sustainability teaching and learning. *Environmental Sciences Europe*, *37*(1), 124. DOI: 10.1186/s12302-025-01159-w

Li, X., & Mostafavi, A. (2025). Machine learning approach for disaster risk and resilience assessment in coupled human infrastructure systems performance. *npj. Npj Natural Hazards*, *2*(1), 56. DOI: 10.1038/s44304-025-00104-4

Lipič, N., & Ovsenik, M. (2020). The effect of statistical literacy on response to environmental change. *Organizacija*, *53*(2), 147–163. DOI: 10.2478/orga-2020-0010

Liu, W., Dugar, S., McCallum, I., Thapa, G., See, L., Khadka, P., Budhathoki, N., Brown, S., Mechler, R., Fritz, S., & Shakya, P. (2018). Integrated participatory and collaborative risk mapping for enhancing disaster resilience. *ISPRS International Journal of Geo-Information*, *7*(2), 68. DOI: 10.3390/ijgi7020068

Lundberg, S. M., & Lee, S. I. (2017). A unified approach to interpreting model predictions. *Advances in Neural Information Processing Systems*, •••, 30.

Majumder, R., & Reich, B. J. (2023). A deep learning synthetic likelihood approximation of a non-stationary spatial model for extreme streamflow forecasting. *Spatial Statistics*, *55*, 100755. DOI: 10.1016/j.spasta.2023.100755

McGovern, A., Ebert-Uphoff, I., Gagne, D. J., II, & Bostrom, A. (2021). The need for ethical, responsible, and trustworthy artificial intelligence for environmental sciences. *arXiv*. /arXiv.2112.08453DOI: 10.48550

Meresa, H., Murphy, C., Fealy, R., & Golian, S. (2021). Uncertainties and their interaction in flood hazard assessment with climate change. *Hydrology and Earth System Sciences*, *25*(9), 5237–5253. DOI: 10.5194/hess-25-5237-2021

Milojevic-Dupont, N., & Creutzig, F. (2021). Machine learning for geographically differentiated climate change mitigation in urban areas. *Nature Communications*, *12*, 4025.

Natural Hazards. (2024). Early warning system for floods at estuarine areas: Combining artificial intelligence with process-based models. *Natural Hazards, 121*, 4615–4638. DOI: 10.1007/s11069-024-06957-8

Necula, S. C., Hauer, I., Fotache, D., & Hurbean, L. (2025). Advanced Hybrid Models for Air Pollution Forecasting: Combining SARIMA and BiLSTM Architectures. *Electronics (2079-9292), 14*(3). DOI: 10.3390/electronics14030549

Nguyen, A., Kovyazin, V., & Pham, C. (2025). Application of Remote Sensing and GIS in Monitoring Forest Cover Changes in Vietnam Based on Natural Zoning. *Land (Basel)*, *14*(5), 1037. DOI: 10.3390/land14051037

Nosek, B. A., Ebersole, C. R., DeHaven, A. C., & Mellor, D. T. (2021). The preregistration revolution. *Proceedings of the National Academy of Sciences of the United States of America*, *118*(15), e2101233118. DOI: 10.1073/pnas.2101233118 PMID: 29531091

Oddo, D.. (2025). Harnessing artificial intelligence to address climate-induced challenges in water resources management. *Frontiers in Water*, *7*, 1637341. Advance online publication. DOI: 10.3389/frwa.2025.1637341

Otto, P., Doğan, O., & Taşpınar, S. (2022). A dynamic spatio-temporal stochastic volatility model with an application to environmental risks. *arXiv*. /arXiv.2211.03178DOI: 10.48550

Pande, C. B., Sidek, L. M., Varade, A. M., Elkhrachy, I., Radwan, N., Tolche, A. D., & Elbeltagi, A. (2024). Forecasting of meteorological drought using ensemble and machine learning models. *Environmental Sciences Europe*, *36*(1), 160. DOI: 10.1186/s12302-024-00975-w

Pandey, J. K., Rai, M., & Alam, E. (Eds.). (2025). *AI and ML in Early Warning Systems for Natural Disasters*. Bentham Science. DOI: 10.2174/97988988113891250101

Pathak, P., & Muralidharan, K. (2023). Bibliometric analysis and review of recent literature on flood susceptibility and trends in forecasting methods. *International Journal of Environmental Sciences & Natural Resources*, *32*(2). Advance online publication. DOI: 10.19080/IJESNR.2023.32.556337

Pham, B. T.. (2020). Flood susceptibility modelling using machine learning. *Water (Basel)*, *12*(4), 1138.

Pickering, E., Guth, S., Karniadakis, G. E., & Sapsis, T. P. (2022). *Discovering and forecasting extreme events via active learning in neural operators*. arXiv. / arXiv.2204.02488DOI: 10.48550

Prahutama, A., Hakim, A. R., Ispriyanti, D., Yasin, H., & Warsito, B. (2021). Geographically weighted negative bivariate binomial regression for modelling the number of dengue diseases and their mortality in East Nusa Tenggara, Indonesia. *Journal of Mathematical and Computational Science*, *11*(6), 7971–7990.

Purwitaningsih, L. M., & de Carvalho, A. C. (2022). Empowering local leaders in flood inundation mapping in Bagelen, Purworejo, Central Java. *Jàambá*, *14*(1), 1298. DOI: 10.4102/jamba.v14i1.1298 PMID: 36092748

Rana, I. A., & Routray, J. K. (2023). Integrating AI tools into disaster risk reduction education. *International Journal of Disaster Risk Reduction*, *96*, 103878.

Robin, J., Requena-Mesa, C., Benson, K., Alonso, L., Poehls, M., Carvalhais, N., & Reichstein, M. (2022). Space–time modeling of NDVI using ConvLSTM over sub-Saharan Africa. https://arxiv.org/abs/2210.13648

Roscher, R., Bohn, B., Duarte, M. F., & Garcke, J. (2020). Explainable machine learning for scientific insights and discoveries. *IEEE Access : Practical Innovations, Open Solutions*, *8*, 42200–42216. DOI: 10.1109/ACCESS.2020.2976199

Schenk, M., Drechsel-Grau, C., & Stefanek, M. (2024). Uncertainty, risk, and decision-making in science education. *Science & Education.* Advance online publication. DOI: 10.1007/s11191-024-00544-w

Shankar, S., Halpern, Y., Breck, E., Atwood, J., Wilson, J., & Sculley, D. (2017). No classification without representation: Assessing geodiversity issues in open data sets for the developing world. *arXiv preprint arXiv:1711.08536.* /arXiv.1711. 08536DOI: 10.48550

Taddeo, M., & Floridi, L. (2020). How AI can be a force for good. *Science*, *361*(6404), 751–752. DOI: 10.1126/science.aat5991 PMID: 30139858

Tengö, M., Hill, R., Malmer, P., Raymond, C. M., Spierenburg, M., Danielsen, F., & Folke, C. (2021). Weaving knowledge systems in IPBES, CBD and beyond—Lessons learned for sustainability. *Current Opinion in Environmental Sustainability*, *53*, 101016.

Thekdi, S., Tatar, U., Santos, J., & Chatterjee, S. (2023). Disaster Risk and Artificial Intelligence: A Framework to Characterize Conceptual Synergies and Future Opportunities. *Risk Analysis : An Official Publication of the Society for Risk Analysis*, *43*(8), 1641–1656. DOI: 10.1111/risa.14038 PMID: 36316234

Tian, N., Zheng, J.-X., Li, L.-H., Xue, J.-B., Xia, S., Lv, S., & Zhou, X.-N. (2024). Precision Prediction for Dengue Fever in Singapore: A Machine Learning Approach Incorporating Meteorological Data. *Tropical Medicine and Infectious Disease*, *9*(4), 72. DOI: 10.3390/tropicalmed9040072 PMID: 38668533

Tyralis, H., & Papacharalampous, G. (2024). A review of predictive uncertainty estimation with machine learning. *Artificial Intelligence Review*, *57*(4), 94. DOI: 10.1007/s10462-023-10698-8

UNDRR. (2022). *Global Assessment Report on Disaster Risk Reduction 2022: Our World at Risk.*

Wang, K., Ling, C., Chen, Y., & Zhang, Z. (2023). Spatio-temporal joint modelling on moderate and extreme air pollution in Spain. *Environmental and Ecological Statistics*, *30*(4), 601–624. DOI: 10.1007/s10651-023-00575-6

Wickham, H., Averick, M., Bryan, J., Chang, W., McGowan, L., François, R., Grolemund, G., Hayes, A., Henry, L., Hester, J., Kuhn, M., Pedersen, T., Miller, E., Bache, S., Müller, K., Ooms, J., Robinson, D., Seidel, D., Spinu, V., & Yutani, H. (2021). Welcome to the Tidyverse. *Journal of Open Source Software*, *4*(43), 1686. DOI: 10.21105/joss.01686

Wilkinson, M. D., Dumontier, M., Aalbersberg, I. J., Appleton, G., Axton, M., Baak, A., Blomberg, N., Boiten, J.-W., da Silva Santos, L. B., Bourne, P. E., Bouwman, J., Brookes, A. J., Clark, T., Crosas, M., Dillo, I., Dumon, O., Edmunds, S., Evelo, C. T., Finkers, R., & Mons, B. (2016). The FAIR Guiding Principles for scientific data management and stewardship. *Scientific Data*, *3*(1), 160018. DOI: 10.1038/sdata.2016.18 PMID: 26978244

Yang, J., Gong, P., Fu, R., Zhang, M., Chen, J., Liang, S., Xu, B., Shi, J., & Dickinson, R. (2013). The role of satellite remote sensing in climate change studies. *Nature Climate Change*, *3*(10), 875–883. DOI: 10.1038/nclimate1908

Yang, W., Wei, Y., Wei, H., Chen, Y., Huang, G., Li, X., Yao, N., Wang, X., Gu, X., Amin, M. B., & Kang, B. (2023). Survey on explainable AI: From approaches, limitations and applications aspects. *Human-Centric Intelligent Systems*, *3*(3), 161–188. DOI: 10.1007/s44230-023-00038-y

Zhang, X., Chen, G., Cai, L., Jiao, H., Hua, J., Luo, X., & Wei, X. (2021). Impact assessments of Typhoon Lekima on forest damages in subtropical China using machine learning methods and Landsat 8 OLI imagery. *Sustainability (Basel)*, *13*(9), 4893. DOI: 10.3390/su13094893

Chapter 2
Teaching Bayesian Estimation Through Interactive Learning:
Interactive and AI-Enhanced Approaches

Oya Ekici
http://orcid.org/0000-0001-5008-0238
Istanbul University, Turkey

ABSTRACT

Bayesian statistics, grounded in Bayes' theorem, has evolved into a central paradigm in modern data analysis. While its computational feasibility emerged after the 1950s, advances such as MCMC in the 1990s further accelerated its adoption across disciplines. Yet, teaching Bayesian reasoning remains challenging due to its conceptual complexity. This chapter introduces an interactive pedagogical model using RShiny visualizations and AI tools to teach Bayesian mean estimation. By enabling students to manipulate priors, explore posterior updates, and engage in AI-guided reflection, the approach fosters active, inquiry-based learning. It demonstrates how combining interactivity and AI support can make Bayesian reasoning more accessible, engaging, and conceptually meaningful.

1. INTRODUCTION

Although the Bayes' theorem, which underpins Bayesian analysis, is quite old, significant progress in this field only gained momentum after the 1950s, largely due to advancements in computing (Gelman et al., 2013). These developments have been

DOI: 10.4018/979-8-3373-6259-5.ch002

substantial enough to create an entirely alternative world to classical - frequentist statistics, all rooted in the same underlying Bayesian principle. This innovative approach, which has brought about a paradigm shift (Kruschke, 2015; Lindley, 2000), has now firmly established itself in the literature under the name Bayesian statistics. Nevertheless, widespread adoption by researchers across applied disciplines coincided with the onset of 'the replication crisis' in statistics. The growing interest in Bayesian methods has also made its way into statistics education (McElreath, 2020; Wagenmakers et al., 2018).

Bayesian statistics now features - either as a standalone course or, in programs less responsive to paradigm shifts, as a sub-topic within classical statistics - at the high school, undergraduate, and graduate levels of statistics education. Given its rising role in education, it becomes relevant to explore the pedagogical dimensions of Bayesian statistics.

Bayesian statistics offers a powerful framework for estimation under uncertainty, providing a natural way to incorporate prior knowledge and update beliefs with observed data. Despite its theoretical advantages, teaching Bayesian methods, requires attention, especially in traditional classroom settings where passive learning predominates (Ferrari, 2022; Pétrin-Pomerleau et al., 2023; Albert and Hu, 2019). The emergence of interactive tools like RShiny, combined with artificial intelligence (AI)-based supports (e.g., ChatGPT), presents novel opportunities to create dynamic, personalized, and engaging learning experiences for students.

In this rapidly evolving era of AI, excluding AI from the educational process is neither realistic nor pedagogically sound. Contemporary research consistently emphasizes that AI technologies are already reshaping how knowledge is accessed and constructed, making their integration into education both inevitable and necessary (Chen, Chen, and Lin, 2020; Reiss, 2021). Expecting students not to use AI is therefore neither realistic nor educationally productive. Particularly when students face challenges in a specific domain, their likelihood of turning to AI-based tools naturally increases (Johnston et al., 2024). This behavioral tendency highlights the importance of guiding rather than prohibiting AI use in academic contexts. At the current stage, considering the existing accuracy and genuine usefulness of AI technologies, the primary responsibility of educators is to provide guidance on how AI can be used critically, responsibly, and ethically. As Reiss (2021) and the European Network for Academic Integrity (Foltynek et al., 2023) argue, instructors play a crucial role in fostering students' ability to use AI tools while studying and engaging with subject matter, ensuring that they do so in accurate, discerning, reliable, and ethical ways. In this sense, the goal is not to prevent AI use, but to enable students to integrate AI meaningfully into their learning processes, supporting deeper understanding and authentic academic growth.

This chapter proposes a detailed pedagogical design that integrates RShiny applets and AI conversational agents to teach a topic from Bayesian statistics: Bayesian mean estimation effectively. By enabling students to actively explore likelihoods, priors, and posterior distributions, and interact with AI to clarify concepts and perform computations, this approach addresses key challenges in modern statistics education-bridging theory and practice with interactive, technology-enhanced learning.

The chapter aims to explain key concepts in Bayesian mean estimation and demonstrate how these concepts can be effectively emphasized through interactive RShiny applets. It also showcases the role of artificial intelligence tools, in supporting student inquiry, providing personalized feedback, and fostering critical thinking in the context of statistical learning. Furthermore, the chapter offers educators a replicable lesson plan that includes essential concepts, guiding questions, and hands-on activities. Finally, it discusses how pedagogical considerations can be meaningfully integrated into AI-supported Bayesian statistics education.

2. INTERACTIVE LESSON DESIGN

In the 2014 American Statistical Association (ASA) guidelines (ASA, 2014), recommendations were provided regarding course design, instructional tools, and foundational principles for undergraduate statistics education. However, an earlier ASA-endorsed framework, the Guidelines for Assessment and Instruction in Statistics Education (GAISE) College Report, originally published in 2005, was revised in 2016 to incorporate more contemporary pedagogical standards. Consequently, the principles and recommendations articulated in the 2016 GAISE Guidelines are adopted here. Accordingly, the core of this chapter presents a step-by-step lesson plan centered on the concept of Bayesian estimation of a mean.

2.1. Pedagogical Principles and Learning Goals

Teaching Bayesian estimation effectively requires moving beyond procedural instruction toward conceptual understanding. Grounded in constructivist and inquiry-based learning principles, this pedagogical model positions students as active participants in constructing probabilistic reasoning through exploration and reflection. Bayesian thinking itself, updating beliefs in light of new evidence, naturally aligns with iterative, inquiry-driven learning processes. Interactive tools such as RShiny applets and AI-based tutors serve as scaffolds that visualize abstract concepts (e.g., prior-posterior updating) and allow learners to test their intuitions dynamically. In this framework, interactivity is not an add-on but an intellectual mirror of Bayesian reasoning: learning proceeds by continual updating of understanding, informed by data, feedback, and prior knowledge.

The lesson is structured to guide students in understanding and applying the Bayesian approach to estimate a population mean. Students are introduced to key components such as prior distributions, likelihood, and posterior inference, and are expected to interpret these elements meaningfully. The instructional flow begins with a motivational segment -why use Bayesian methods? -which revisits conditional probability and the concept of belief updating. From there, the lesson proceeds through model setup (defining the data, prior, and likelihood), computational steps (posterior derivation), and culminates in interpretation and reflection.

2.2. Interactive Tools

Two main interactive components are used: RShiny applet and AI integration. RShiny is a framework that enables the development of interactive applications using the R programming language. It allows statistical analyses, data visualizations, and modeling results to be presented through user-friendly interfaces. With its client (ui) and server components, Shiny facilitates the dynamic sharing of data science outputs. Moreover, it integrates seamlessly with the R ecosystem, supporting reproducible, interactive, and visually rich data analysis workflows. In the context of this study, RShiny is employed to facilitate hands-on exploration of Bayesian inference. RShiny applet enables students to manipulate priors and data values dynamically and visualize resulting posterior distributions in real time. By enabling learners to manipulate data, visualize relationships, and instantly observe the effects of parameter changes, these tools promote deeper conceptual understanding and engagement (Chance et al., 2007; Cobb, 2015).

With AI Integration, students ask ChatGPT targeted questions to clarify theory, compute posteriors, and explore various hypothetical scenarios with AI assistance. This promotes autonomous exploration and supports learners at different levels of understanding. In essence, the role of artificial intelligence (AI) is multifaceted. Primarily, AI functions as an "intelligent learning companion," becoming an integral part of the interactive learning experience. At the same time, it also serves as an "intelligent teaching assistant," providing explanations, hints, and guidance to support students' conceptual understanding. In RShiny applets, students may occasionally encounter a lack of direction during data manipulation and model exploration. At this point, AI offers personalized guidance throughout the learning process, reformulating concepts when necessary and providing alternative examples for reinforcement. Furthermore, it can generate dynamic scenarios tailored to students' proficiency levels, thereby making the learning environment adaptable. In this way, AI operates as a multifunctional component within the system, supporting learning both cognitively and motivationally.

2.3. Lesson Flow

The ASA-endorsed GAISE Guidelines provide a comprehensive framework for statistics education, and the 2016 GAISE College Report (GAISE, 2016) remains one of the most current and influential documents in the field. Accordingly, this report can be regarded as a foundational resource for designing undergraduate statistics instruction. For this reason, the lesson structure and pedagogical flow presented in this chapter adhere closely to the principles articulated in the GAISE Guidelines. The lesson is organized into multiple stages of learning - including theoretical introduction, hands-on exploration, Bayesian computation, and reflective discussion supported by AI tools and RShiny applications - with the overarching goal of helping students develop a deep understanding of Bayesian concepts by applying them in both hypothetical and realistic contexts. These stages are outlined as follows:

1. **Motivation Phase:** Discussion of statistical inference and belief updating (aligned with GAISE Recommendations 1 and 2).
2. **Theoretical Background Phase:** Introduction to the theoretical foundations of Bayesian inference, including the role of the prior, likelihood, and posterior (aligned with Recommendations 2 and 4).
3. **Interactive Exploration Phase:** Hands-on exercises using RShiny applets to examine how priors and data jointly influence posterior estimation (aligned with Recommendations 3, 4, and 5).
4. **AI-enhanced Reflection Phase:** Students engage with AI tools to clarify concepts, discuss interpretations, and receive personalized feedback (aligned with Recommendations 1 and 4).
5. **Assessment Phase:** Students consolidate their understanding through reflective discussion on how different priors affect Bayesian estimates, supported by both interactive and AI-based exploration. (aligned with Recommendation 6)

3. INTERACTIVE LEARNING IN ACTION: BAYESIAN INFERENCE FOR A MEAN

This section illustrates how the proposed pedagogical model is implemented in practice, following the lesson flow outlined above. For each stage, the corresponding instructional content and activities are presented in detail, in the form in which they would be delivered directly during instruction.

3.1 Motivation Phase

This section presents the motivation underlying the lesson and constitutes the preparatory stage of the instructional design. The primary learning goal at this phase is to support students in developing statistical thinking. In particular, the aim is to help students understand how Bayesian inference can be used to manage uncertainty more effectively and how beliefs can be updated in the face of ambiguous situations commonly encountered in business settings, or more broadly, in the social sciences.

3.1.1 Motivation

How are decisions made in the real world when confronted with uncertainty and incomplete information? Consider, for example, a business evaluating whether to launch a new product and attempting to estimate its likelihood of success. The central challenge in such a context is the pervasive presence of uncertainty. Statistical analysis exists precisely to help address this challenge, yet the choice of inferential approach, or paradigm, matters greatly.

The Bayesian framework enables more informed decision-making by integrating prior knowledge or beliefs with newly observed data. In practice, Bayesian statistics can incorporate insights derived from earlier marketing studies or the performance of similar products, and then update the estimated probability of success as new market data become available. Thus, initial expectations grounded in past experience can be revised dynamically in response to new evidence. But how statistical concepts are taught is just as important as the inferential framework itself. Research shows that interactive, student-centered approaches lead to better conceptual understanding and more durable learning, particularly in quantitatively challenging subjects such as statistics (Theobald et al., 2020; Mayer, 2020). This provides strong pedagogical support for teaching Bayesian inference within an interactive learning environment.

In contrast, the frequentist approach relies solely on data collected after the research question is posed; that is, it bases inference exclusively on the newly obtained marketing data without incorporating prior experience. By combining previous knowledge with current information, the Bayesian approach offers more flexible and realistic estimates- making it not only a powerful inferential framework but also an engaging and conceptually rich learning experience.

3.2 Theoretical Background Phase: Foundation of Bayesian Reasoning and Conceptual Understanding

Empirical research on Bayesian pedagogy shows that structured probability training significantly improves students' ability to reason probabilistically and update beliefs in uncertain contexts, compared across different instructional designs (Steib et al., 2024). This section establishes the conceptual foundations of the lesson and constitutes the second preparatory stage of the instructional design. The primary learning goal at this phase is to help students understand statistical inference as a process of "belief updating". To this end, the fundamental principles of Bayesian reasoning are emphasized, accompanied by explanations aimed at strengthening conceptual understanding.

Furthermore, the roles of the key components of Bayesian inference -the prior, likelihood, and posterior- are discussed in relation to their function within the analytical process. Throughout these explanations, a single running example is used to enhance clarity and support coherent understanding. The relevant content and explanations are developed below.

Because Bayesian inference concepts are typically unfamiliar to students encountering statistics for the first time, the instructional design intentionally introduces priors, likelihoods, and posteriors first at a conceptual level and subsequently at a formal analytical level. This staged approach is not intended as repetition, but as a form of pedagogical support, allowing students to progressively integrate intuition with mathematical structure.

3.2.1 Bayesian Thinking as Belief Updating

Uncertainty regarding a characteristic of a population often motivates the need to model that uncertainty so it can be reduced or managed. When observing the entire population is infeasible or prohibitively costly, statistical reasoning is applied by drawing a sample from the population and using the resulting information to make inferences. This process is referred to as inference, and its foundations lie in probability theory. Through probability, uncertainty is not eliminated but rather constrained based on the information provided by the observed data. Within a parametric analysis framework, inference becomes possible because the data are assumed to follow a particular probabilistic pattern. In the frequentist approach, reasoning is based on the assumption of repeatable sampling: even though only a single sample is typically collected (and may not realistically be repeatable), inference is conceptually grounded in the distribution of all hypothetical samples that could have been drawn from the population. Thus, conclusions are derived from the theoretical distribution of these potential samples.

In contrast, Bayesian reasoning does not rely on the asymptotic behavior of samples. Rather than focusing on the "true" value of a population characteristic under uncertainty, it addresses the question of how plausible different values are given the information at hand. For example, consider a parameter of interest such as the average number of errors made by an employee on a production line, which we aim to estimate. In the Bayesian framework, the parameter is initially treated as uncertain, and reasoning proceeds as follows: prior knowledge- representing beliefs or expectations about the possible values of the parameter- is formally combined with the likelihood of the observed data under different hypothetical parameter values. This process yields "posterior beliefs", which provide the basis for inference under uncertainty (Kruschke and Liddell, 2017).

posterior $\propto$ *prior x likelihood*

As noted, the Bayesian approach also relies on probability, which forms the very essence of its reasoning. However, unlike the frequentist approach described earlier, Bayesian reasoning does not simply compute an estimate from a drawn sample -such as the average number of errors- and then examine how that estimate would vary across hypothetical repeated samples. In other words, it does not focus solely on the randomness of the data. In Bayesian reasoning, probability represents uncertainty and the degree of knowledge:

The prior expresses the belief or expectation regarding possible values of a parameter before observing the data. In the production line example, prior information about the average number of errors made by an employee could be derived from historical experience (audit reports, ERP records, etc.) or expert judgment. For instance, one might believe that employees typically make an average of 2 errors, and that this number could plausibly range between 0 and 5.

The likelihood represents the probability of the observed data under different hypothetical parameter values. It can be interpreted as a measure of how compatible the data are with each possible value of the parameter. Returning to the error count example, suppose observations are collected from 10 employees, and the average number of errors is 3. The likelihood then indicates how probable this observed data would be for different hypothetical averages. The data remain fixed, while the parameter varies; by evaluating which parameter values maximize the likelihood, one identifies the parameter most consistent with the observed data.

The posterior represents the updated belief after observing the data. Continuing the example, the posterior might indicate that, given the observed data, the average number of errors is approximately 2.7 with an 85% probability. This updated belief combines prior knowledge with the information contained in the data, providing a comprehensive summary of uncertainty under the Bayesian framework.

Therefore, in Bayesian reasoning, probability does not represent the long-run frequency of repeated trials, as in the frequentist perspective, but rather the degree of belief about a situation or a parameter under uncertainty. In other words, probability reflects the degree of certainty based on available information. This approach answers not the question "What is the true average number of errors?" but instead

"Given the observed data, how confident can we be that the average number of errors is approximately 2.7?" Consequently, Bayesian inference does not yield only a single point estimate; it provides a full distribution (the posterior) over the unknown parameter, offering the researcher a quantification of uncertainty.

From a computational perspective, the inference process fundamentally involves an updating operation to reach the posterior degree of belief. After observing data, the initial belief is revised and updated based on a core theoretical foundation: Bayes' theorem. This theorem, grounded in the multiplication rule of conditional probabilities, can be expressed as follows, where, θ is the parameter of interest and y represents the observed data. Given the prior distribution $p(\theta)$, the likelihood $p(y|\theta)$, and the posterior distribution $p(\theta|y)$, Bayes' theorem states that:

$$p(\theta|y) = \frac{p(\theta) \times p(y|\theta)}{p(y)}$$

which can equivalently be expressed as:

$$p(\theta|y) \propto p(\theta) \times p(y|\theta)$$

Here, the prior information about θ is updated by the information derived from the data via the likelihood. The denominator, $p(y)$, ensures normalization and is often referred to as the evidence or marginal likelihood (Spiegelhalter et al., 2004). Furthermore, once the posterior distribution is obtained, it can be naturally updated repeatedly as new data become available (Gelman et al., 2013). This iterative updating mechanism essentially constitutes a learning process.

3.2.2. Conceptual Roles of Priors, Likelihoods, and Posteriors

Bayes' theorem facilitates the interaction of these three key components, resulting in updated beliefs about the parameters of interest. Thus, understanding their conceptual roles is essential for both the theoretical foundation and practical application of Bayesian inference (Robert, 2007). To explore their conceptual roles in more depth, it is necessary to focus closely on each of these components, beginning with the prior.

Priors

The prior represents the knowledge or belief about the parameter of interest before any data are observed (Bernardo & Smith, 2009). Determining the distribution that encodes this prior knowledge is a crucial step. Although there are various classifications, priors are generally categorized into three main types: informative, weakly informative, and non-informative.

Informative priors contain strong prior information and are typically based on previous studies, reports, or expert opinion, allowing for well-founded assumptions about the parameter. For example, consider a manufacturing process where past quality control reports indicate that the defect rate averages around 0.03 with a standard deviation of 0.01. An informative prior for the defect rate of a randomly selected new batch could then be defined as follows: $\theta \sim \mathcal{N}(0.03, 0.01^2)$

Weakly informative priors contain enough information to guide the inference but are not so strong as to dominate the data after updating. Also referred to in the literature as vague or diffuse priors, these priors do not embody strong prior knowledge but provide a reasonable estimate of the plausible range for the parameter. For example, suppose we know the manufacturing process is relatively stable -meaning the defect rate usually remains within a consistent range- and production quality is generally steady, although past data may be inconsistent or limited. We expect the defect rate to be generally low but are uncertain about the exact value. In this case, a weakly informative prior could be specified as $\theta \sim \mathcal{N}(0.05, 0.05^2)$. Compared to an informative prior, this distribution has a larger standard deviation and thus a wider spread. Alternatively, a Beta distribution such as $\theta \sim Beta(2, 50)$ might be used to reflect a more natural bounded range. This Beta prior has a mean of approximately 0.04 and, again, a higher standard deviation (around 0.026) compared to an informative prior. Such priors provide guidance but do not express overly confident beliefs about the parameter.

Non-informative priors are used when there is little to no prior knowledge about the parameter (or when prior information is deliberately excluded). These priors represent distributions that carry minimal information, assigning equal weight to all possible values and thus encouraging inference driven entirely by the observed data. Typically, such priors reflect maximum uncertainty assumptions and are often specified as uniform distributions or distributions with very large variance. For example, if there is no prior knowledge about the manufacturing process except that the defect rate lies somewhere between 0 and 1, a non-informative prior such as $\theta \sim Uniform(0, 1)$ or equivalently $\theta \sim Beta(1, 1)$ may be assigned.

While the above classification reflects the information content of priors, another important dimension of prior selection concerns conjugate priors. Regardless of their information level, conjugate priors are frequently preferred in Bayesian analyses due to computational convenience. A conjugate prior is a prior distribution that, when multiplied by the likelihood function, results in a posterior distribution belonging to the same family as the prior (Gelman et al., 2013; Bernardo & Smith, 2009; DeGroot, 2004). This conjugacy is achieved because the kernel of the likelihood function "matches" the kernel of the prior distribution.

The choice of prior is critical in Bayesian inference and should be informed by problem-specific knowledge, the structure of the model, and the goals of the analysis. Careless or inappropriate specification of prior parameters can significantly affect the inference results.

Conditional Probabilities and Likelihood

In Bayesian inference, the likelihood can be understood as a bridge between the data and the parameters. It is important to emphasize that the likelihood is not a probability itself but a function based on probabilities. In the conditional probability function, the data is treated as the variable and the parameter as fixed, whereas in the likelihood function, the data is fixed and the parameter is treated as the variable. Thus, the data has been observed, but the parameters are unknown. The likelihood function $L(\theta|x) = f(x|\theta)$ helps answer the question of how well the observed data fits a particular parameter value (Gelman et al., 2013).

Mathematically, the likelihood has the same form as conditional probability (generally expressed as $P(data|parameter)$), but its interpretation differs: while conditional probability measures the probability of the data occurring given a parameter, likelihood assesses which parameter value is more plausible given the observed data.

In Bayesian inference, the likelihood function, which updates the prior with observed data, conveys information about both the accuracy and the variance of parameter estimates. The effect of sample characteristics can be directly observed in the likelihood function. For instance, sample size has a direct impact on the likelihood: as the sample size increases, uncertainty in parameter estimation decreases, the likelihood function develops a more pronounced peak, and plausible parameter values concentrate in a narrower range around the maximum likelihood estimate. Conversely, with a small sample, the likelihood is generally flatter and wider, reflecting greater parameter uncertainty. Moreover, sample statistics -such as the sample mean, variance, or sum- determine the shape of the likelihood function and serve as the fundamental units of information used in inference. The variance of the process generating the data also affects the likelihood. As the spread of the estimation errors increases, the likelihood becomes wider, indicating higher uncertainty about the parameter. When the spread (variance) of the estimation errors is small, the likelihood becomes narrower, providing relatively more information about the parameter.

Returning to the production line example, in the context of estimating the average number of errors made by employees over a given period, the error variance reflects the random fluctuations in employee performance- that is, even under the same conditions, there is a probability of making more or fewer errors in some periods. Sample size corresponds to the number of observed production days; as this number increases, uncertainty in the parameter estimate decreases and the likelihood function develops a sharper peak. Sample characteristics (e.g., mean, variance, or shape of the distribution of the error counts) reflect the overall statistical structure of the observed data. This structure directly influences the form and peak of the likelihood function, guiding parameter estimation. In other words, the shape of the likelihood function is determined by the data structure, which in turn directs the parameter estimates.

Posterior

According to the Bayesian principle, the posterior distribution is obtained by updating the prior with the likelihood. This distribution represents the part of the inference that answers questions about the parameter of interest. The posterior model of the parameter is essentially an outcome of the balance established between the prior and the likelihood (Bernardo & Smith, 2009; Robert, 2007). Estimates of parameters such as the mean, proportion, median, or variance, as well as uncertainty measures like credible intervals, can be derived from this distribution. When making predictions based on new observations, the posterior distribution is again used. Moreover, decision-making processes such as model comparison and hypothesis testing rely on information obtained from the posterior (Gelman et al., 2013; Robert, 2007). In the production line example, the posterior distribution can be used to predict the future performance of employees and to improve quality control processes. This allows quality control engineers to better understand the uncertainty and potential variation in error rates and to optimize the production process.

Since the posterior is a balanced combination of the prior and likelihood, the resulting inference depends on these components. When the sample size is large or the variance of the estimation error is small, the likelihood dominates, and the posterior approaches the data distribution. Conversely, with a small number of observations, the prior becomes more influential on the posterior (Robert, 2007). This effect can be observed analytically or graphically. In particular, with small samples, the differences created by different priors in the posterior can be clearly seen. Therefore, Bayesian inference should undergo a process known as sensitivity analysis (Spiegelhalter et al., 2004).

The posterior distribution cannot always be calculated analytically. This is often due to the computational difficulty of the marginal likelihood $p(y)$ in the denominator of Bayes' rule, which serves as a normalization constant. In such cases, simulation or approximation methods can be employed (Robert, 2007; Gelman et al., 2013). Even if the posterior cannot be computed exactly, samples drawn from the distribution can be used to calculate posterior summaries, make predictions, or compare models. Real world problems may also present situations where posterior sampling is challenging. For example, if the parameter space is high-dimensional, the posterior is multimodal, or complex hierarchical models are involved, sampling from the posterior can be difficult (Gelman et al., 2013; Robert, 2007). In such cases, alternative sampling methods must be employed.

3.3 Interactive Exploration Phase

This is the third phase of the course. Building on the foundation established during the motivation and conceptual exploration stages, this phase focuses on hands-on application. Consistent with applied Bayesian approaches in STEM education, this phase emphasizes hands-on Bayesian estimation using real student-generated data (Bertolini et al., 2023). Students gain practical experience in applying Bayesian estimation using real data of their own. This design choice is motivated by evidence showing that simulation-based and software-supported Bayesian instruction improves student engagement and conceptual understanding (Wang & Jin, 2024). The learning objective at this stage is to actively engage students in performing Bayesian estimation of means and interpreting the results.

Implementation Notes: An activity below is designed for classes of approximately 20 - 40 students and typically takes 2 - 3 hours to complete. Each student will need access to a computer with R and RStudio installed, along with the custom Shiny application. Internet access is only required if students will be interacting with AI features.

Assessment & Evaluation: We check understanding through quick quizzes, participation during class, and a small final project applying Bayesian concepts.

Example: Contextual Dataset: Screen Time Estimation

One such activity involves estimating the average smartphone screen time of their peers using a small sample dataset. Through the RShiny applet, students experiment with different prior assumptions, such as informative versus non-informative priors, and observe how these choices influence the resulting posterior estimates.

Suppose that students want to estimate the average smartphone screen time of second-year Business students at Istanbul University Faculty of Political Science, that is, their own classmates.

Assumption: Students' daily smartphone screen times are assumed to follow a normal distribution, with an unknown mean μ and a known standard deviation $\sigma = 30$ minutes.

Data Collection: The daily screen times (in minutes) for a randomly selected sample of 10 students are as follows:

115, 168, 364, 231, 211, 398, 327, 130, 348, 213.

Asking every student in the class to report their screen time would consume a significant portion of instructional time. Therefore, using a randomly selected sample of 10 students provides a practical and realistic scenario for applying a sample-based estimation process. Based on the smartphone screen times of this subset, students can practice estimating the average daily usage for the larger group.

Objective: The goal is to determine whether the average daily screen time exceeds 240 minutes. If it does, the students' screen time can be considered excessively high.

Perspective on Inference in this Problem

Bayesian inference is grounded in Bayes' theorem and, while applicable to a wide range of domains, can be directly applied to the problem at hand. In this context, the two approaches to inference can be contrasted as follows:

From a frequentist perspective, μ is treated as an unknown fixed parameter. According to frequentist inference, the observed data constitute just one of many possible datasets that could be obtained through repeated sampling from the population. This approach is based on interpreting probability as a long-run relative frequency. In this framework, an inference might be expressed as $p\left(\bar{y} = 250.5\backslash H_0{:}\mu \leq 240\right)$ where y denotes the observed values, $\bar{y}$ is the sample mean, and the null and alternative hypotheses are defined as $H_0{:}\mu \leq 240$ and $H_a{:}\mu > 240$.

In contrast, the Bayesian perspective treats μ as a random variable. Using Bayes' theorem, prior information about the parameter μ is updated with information from the observed data. Consequently, Bayesian inference relies not only on the likelihood but also on the prior distribution. This feature distinguishes Bayesian inference from its frequentist counterpart. In this context, an inference is expressed as $p\left(H_a{:}\mu > 240\backslash\bar{y} = 250.5\right)$

Bayesian Inference

1) **Specification of Prior Distribution:** Before collecting data from these 10 students, the prior distribution summarizes our knowledge about the parameter μ. Several approaches can be considered when specifying this distribution. After some discussion and reflection, a few possible priors can be outlined as follows:
    - **An informative prior:** Subjectively, it is considered unlikely that the average daily screen time exceeds 5 hours (i.e., 300 minutes). Statistically, this implies that the probability $p(\mu > 300)$ is small. A typical interpretation for "small" might be 5% or 10%. If 5% is chosen:

$$p(\mu > 300) \approx 0.05$$

a) **An informative prior (moderately):** Using the standard normal approximation,

$\mu = 300 - 1.645 \times 30 = 250.7.$

This yields the prior: $\mu \sim N(250.7, 30^2)$.

b) **A weaker prior:** If more uncertainty is assumed,

$\mu = 300 - 1.645 \times 60 = 201.3.$

Then the prior becomes: $\mu \sim N(201.3, 60^2)$.

c) **An informative prior (stronger prior, narrower distribution):** If prior knowledge is more confident,

$\mu = 300 - 1.645 \times 15 = 275.3.$

Then the prior is specified as: $\mu \sim N(275.3, 15^2)$.

- **An informative prior:** When reviewing the literature for typical screen times, one study reported that the average daily digital screen time for university students falls within the range of 4 - 6 hours (Kaewpradit et al., 2025). The midpoint of this range, 5 hours (i.e., 300 minutes), can be used as the prior mean: $\mu \sim N(300, 30^2)$.

The width of this interval can be interpreted as approximately a 95% credible range for the prior. Using the normal distribution rule $\mu \pm 2\sigma \approx 240 - 360$, and solving for σ (i.e., $300 - 2\sigma = 240$), we obtain $\sigma = 30$ minutes.

- **A weakly informative prior:** If the 4 - 6 hours range is known but there is greater uncertainty, a weaker prior can be specified: $\mu \sim N(300, 60^2)$.

In this case, the 95% interval is approximately 180 - 420 minutes. This prior reflects more uncertainty, making it less informative: using $\mu \pm 2\sigma \approx 180 - 420$ and solving $300 - 2\sigma = 180$, we find $\sigma = 60$ minutes.

- **A non-informative prior:** This can also be referred to as an objective prior. A fully non-informative prior can be defined as: $p(\mu) \propto 1$. Remaining objective, and without incorporating literature-based information, two alternative weak priors can be considered:

a) A vague or diffuse prior, which is related to the above but still weakly informative, can be defined. For example, a Uniform distribution over the interval (0, 960) minutes may be chosen (960 minutes accounts for 16 hours, assuming 8 hours of sleep). Although the uniform shape may give the impression of containing no information, limiting the parameter to the 0- 960 range provides a weak information.
b) Alternatively, a normal weakly informative prior can be specified as: $\mu \sim N(240, 120^2)$. Although the standard deviation is large ($\sigma = 120$), resulting in a wide distribution, this prior still encodes information. Its central value at 240 minutes provides a reference point, making it weakly informative rather than fully non-informative.

Selected Prior Distribution: Among the possible prior distributions, let us assume that the following prior has been chosen:

$$\mu \sim N(240, 120^2)$$

A normal prior was selected because the variable of interest -daily screen time- is continuous and thus naturally represented by a continuous distribution. At the same time, it offers practical mathematical advantages. Specifically, the normal distribution is conjugate to the likelihood in this setting: as a conjugate prior, it analytically combines with the kernel of the likelihood function while retaining the same functional form, ensuring that the posterior distribution remains in the same distributional family as the prior. This property allows Bayesian inference to be expressed in closed form and greatly simplifies the computational process. In summary, this conjugate prior provides the functional compatibility necessary for analytical derivation of the posterior. At the same time, with a very high standard deviation (covering roughly the range 100 - 300 minutes), it contributes very little information, making it a weakly informative prior.

2) **Likelihood Function:** Let Y denote the random variable representing daily smartphone screen time in a sample. Assuming a known standard deviation $\sigma = 30$, the likelihood function is given by:

$$Y \sim N(\mu, \sigma = 30)$$

3) **Posterior Distribution:** What are the parameters of the posterior distribution? That is,

$$\mu \backslash Y \sim N(\mu_1 = ?, \sigma_1 = ?)$$

Bayesian Calculation: For the Bayesian model specified as follows:
Prior: $\mu \sim N(\mu_0 = 240, \sigma_0^2 = 120^2)$
Likelihood: $Y \sim N(\mu, \sigma = 30)$
Posterior: $\mu \backslash Y \sim N(\mu_1, \sigma_1^2)$

The posterior estimate of the mean smartphone screen time, i.e., the parameters (μ_1, σ_1^2) can be calculated by combining the prior information with the data from the 10 observations using Bayes' theorem. The general rule for updating a normal prior with a normal likelihood is given below:

$$p(\mu|Y) = \frac{p(\mu) \times p(Y|\mu)}{\int p(\mu) \times p(Y|\mu)\, dy}$$

As previously discussed, Bayes' theorem provides the general framework for updating prior beliefs with observed data. Here, we explicitly write the marginal likelihood in the denominator, *p*(*Y*). Normally, computing this integral is required to normalize the posterior, but in many practical cases, evaluating this sum can be challenging. However, this difficulty can be overcome using simulation methods such as Markov Chain Monte Carlo (MCMC). On the other hand, when a conjugate prior is used, the posterior takes on a simpler form. Accordingly, the posterior parameters can be calculated as follows:

$$\mu_1 = \frac{\sigma^2/n}{\sigma_0^2 + \sigma^2/n} \times \mu_0 + \frac{\sigma_0^2}{\sigma_0^2 + \sigma^2/n} \times \bar{y}$$

$$\sigma_1 = \sqrt{\frac{1}{\frac{1}{\sigma_0^2} + \frac{n}{\sigma^2}}}$$

before proceeding with the calculations, the posterior mean μ_1 can be interpreted as a weighted average of the prior mean and the sample mean. The weights, given by $\frac{\sigma^2/n}{\sigma_0^2 + \sigma^2/n}$ and $\frac{\sigma_0^2}{\sigma_0^2 + \sigma^2/n}$ sum to 1. When the variance of the data is larger than the variance of the prior, $\frac{\sigma^2/n}{\sigma_0^2 + \sigma^2/n}$ becomes the larger weight. Consequently, the prior mean μ_0 is multiplied by a larger factor, and the prior exerts a stronger influence on the posterior. Conversely, if the prior variance is larger than the data variance, $\frac{\sigma_0^2}{\sigma_0^2 + \sigma^2/n}$ is larger, and the sample mean $\bar{y}$, receives a higher weight. In this case, the data have a more dominant effect on the posterior.

Substituting the actual values, it's obtained:

$$\mu_1 = \frac{30^2/10}{120^2 + 30^2/10} \times 240 + \frac{120^2}{120^2 + 30^2/10} \times 250.5 \approx 250.43$$

and

$$\sigma_1 = \sqrt{\frac{1}{\frac{1}{120^2} + \frac{10}{30^2}}} \approx \sqrt{89.44} \approx 9.46$$

In this example, the weights are

$$\frac{30^2/10}{120^2 + 30^2/10} \approx 0.0062 \text{and} \frac{120^2}{120^2 + 30^2/10} \approx 0.9938,$$

indicating that the weighted average is strongly influenced by the sample mean. Specifically, the sample mean $\bar{y}$ contributes about 99% to the posterior mean, while the prior mean μ_0 contributes only about 0.62%.

Similarly, for the posterior standard deviation, the precision of the data (given by n / σ^2) is much higher than the precision of the prior (given by $1 / \sigma_0^2$). As a result, the posterior standard deviation is largely determined by the variability of the data, reflecting the greater reliability of the observed sample.

The posterior distribution, with parameters calculated as above, can be expressed as

$$\mu \sim N\left(\mu_1 = 250.43, \sigma_1^2 = 9.46^2\right).$$

Given that the sample mean is 250.5 and the prior mean is 240, the posterior is almost entirely determined by the data. This is because the prior contains very little information, with a large standard deviation of 120, resulting in a posterior mean $\left(\mu_1 = 250.43\right)$ that is effectively equal to the sample mean ($\bar{y} = 250.5$).

Finally, it is possible to perform a calculation and provide a corresponding explanation regarding the initial objective. The probability $p(\mu > 240|\text{data}) = 0.8651$ represents the posterior probability that the true average daily screen time μ exceeds the critical threshold of 240 minutes, given the observed sample data. This value is computed using the posterior distribution of μ, which, under the conjugate Bayesian framework with a normal prior and known observation standard deviation, is also normal: $\mu \mid y \sim N\left(\mu_1, \sigma_1^2\right)$. Specifically, the posterior mean μ_1 and posterior standard deviation σ_1 are first calculated analytically. Then, the probability that $\mu > 240$ is obtained as the upper-tail probability of this normal distribution:

$$p(\mu > 240|y) = 1 - \Phi\left(\frac{240 - \mu_1}{\sigma_1}\right)$$

where Φ is the cumulative distribution function of the standard normal distribution. In this example, with $\mu_1 \approx 250.43$ and $\sigma_1 \approx 9.46$, the resulting probability is

0.8651. This indicates that, based on the observed sample of 10 students, there is an approximately 87% chance that the true average screen time exceeds 240 minutes. Although this is high, it is slightly below the commonly used threshold of 0.95 for deeming the average screen time excessively high.

RShiny Interaction

To enhance engagement and promote deeper understanding, the lesson plan incorporates practical, data-driven activities that allow students to apply Bayesian estimation to real or personally relevant datasets. Recent research indicates that multimodal, interactive, and actively structured instructional strategies enhance student engagement, learning outcomes, and satisfaction, particularly when such activities are fully integrated into the course design rather than offered as optional components (Huang, 2024; Van Wart et al., 2025). After introducing the Bayesian estimation example, explaining the priors, and performing the posterior calculation, students deepen their understanding through an interactive RShiny app, where they can manipulate parameters and observe the resulting changes in real time. This hands-on exploration helps bridge theoretical learning with real world application and encourages critical reflection on the assumptions and outcomes of Bayesian inference.

The RShiny applet (app) provides an interactive platform for Bayesian estimation of a normal mean with known variance. Specifically, it enables users to input a dataset (e.g., students' daily screen times), specify prior parameters (μ_0, σ_0), and visualize the prior, likelihood, and posterior distributions simultaneously. The app also reports analytical results, including the posterior mean (μ_1), posterior standard deviation (σ_1), 95% credible interval, and the probability that the mean exceeds a critical threshold.

Beyond these computational features, the app illustrates the conjugate Bayesian framework in a concrete and intuitive way. By allowing students to modify prior parameters, adjust the known observation variance, or alter the sample data, the tool makes the impact of different assumptions immediately observable. This dynamic exploration helps learners understand how prior beliefs and empirical evidence interact to shape the posterior distribution and the derived probabilities. For the purpose, students follow a structured exploration:

1. **Adjust prior parameters**: Experiment with different prior means and standard deviations to see how strongly prior beliefs influence the posterior.
2. **Observe the posterior**: Examine the posterior mean, standard deviation, credible interval, and the probability that μ exceeds a pre-defined threshold (e.g., 240 minutes).

3. **Visualize distributions**: Compare prior, likelihood, and posterior curves on the same plot to understand the interplay between prior information and observed data.
4. **Reflect critically**: Ask questions such as: How sensitive is the posterior to changes in the prior?

How does increasing sample size affect the posterior variance? What happens if the observed data are extreme compared to prior expectations? How do the posterior probabilities help us make decisions or interpret outcomes in context?

This step-by-step engagement encourages learners to actively link theoretical Bayesian concepts to observable results.

A) Interpreting the Default State of the App

In the Figure 1 below, you can see the app initialized with the default prior and sample settings. These defaults are intentionally selected to give students a clean, interpretable starting point before they begin exploring alternative assumptions. The app opens with a default prior defined as

$\mu \sim N(240, 120^2)$.

This prior has a very large standard deviation, meaning it is intentionally designed to be weakly informative. It expresses only a vague belief that the true mean is somewhere around 240 minutes but allows for a very broad range of plausible values - essentially giving the data substantial freedom to "speak for themselves". When you first encounter the app in this default state, here is how to interpret what you see:

The prior distribution, shown in green, is extremely wide because the default prior is specified with a very large standard deviation. This visual flatness signals substantial prior uncertainty: before seeing any data, we place very little weight on any particular value of the mean. As a result, the prior exerts only minimal influence on the posterior unless the sample size is extremely small.

The likelihood function, displayed in blue with a dashed line, is centered at the sample mean and is much more concentrated than the prior. It reflects the information contributed by the observed data. Because the prior is so diffuse, the posterior distribution -plotted in orange- ends up closely aligned with the likelihood. In other words, the posterior mean lies very near the sample mean, because the weakly informative prior contributes minimal pull toward the prior mean, and the posterior curve becomes substantially narrower than the prior. This visually demonstrates how weakly informative priors allow the data to dominate the updating process.

Since the prior is conjugate to the likelihood, the posterior remains a normal distribution. This allows the app to compute the posterior mean, posterior standard deviation, and credible intervals analytically. These quantities update instantly as the user modifies the prior parameters, sample size, or sample summary, giving students immediate intuition for how Bayesian updating works.

The graph also includes a vertical reference line at 240 minutes, representing a benchmark for daily screen time. The app reports the probability

$$p(\mu > 240|data)$$

which corresponds to the posterior area to the right of this line. This probability quantifies the strength of evidence, given both the prior and the data, that the true mean exceeds the specified benchmark. With a diffuse prior, this quantity is driven almost entirely by the observed sample mean and its associated uncertainty.

Overall, the default state is ideal for introducing Bayesian inference. The wide green prior highlights initial uncertainty, the blue likelihood represents the information supplied by the data, and the orange posterior clearly shows how the two combine - while making it visually obvious that, under a weakly informative prior, the data play the central role. This integrated display helps students grasp not only how the posterior is computed, but why its location and spread change as more information is introduced.

Figure 1. The RShiny app interface showing the prior, likelihood, and posterior distributions based on the initial prior settings and sample data.

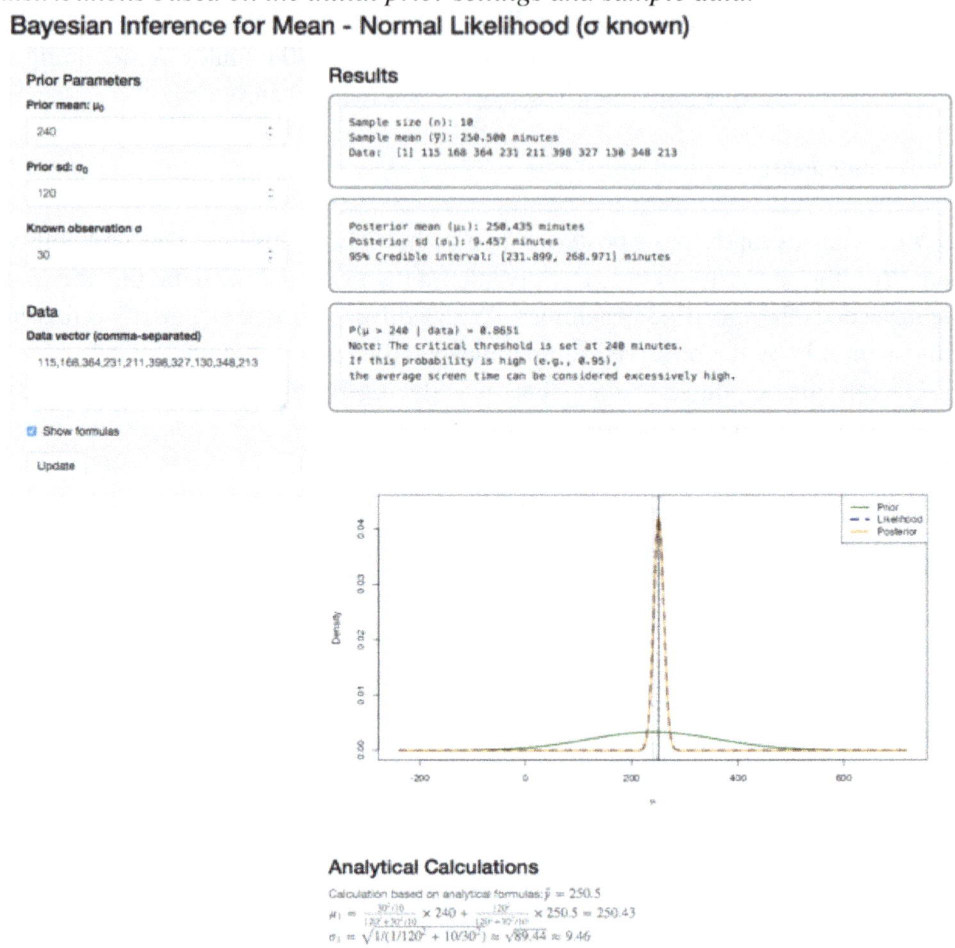

B) Interpreting the App with Alternative Prior Specifications

In Bayesian analysis, adjusting the prior is a critical aspect that significantly influences the resulting posterior distribution. This section explores the changes in the app's behavior and the corresponding outcomes from steps 1 to 4 when the prior is modified. Specifically, we examine the case where the prior is adjusted to $\mu_0 = 300$, $\sigma_0 = 30$ (i.e., $\mu \sim N(300, 30^2)$), while using the same sample data. Figure 2 shows the updated interface of the app, where you can observe how the prior curve shifts and narrows, and how the posterior distribution changes in response. First, the numeric results derived from the analytic conjugate update are represented and followed by an interpretation of these results in terms of the app's elements along with the four instructional steps. The numerical summary with the supplied data is as follows:

Sample mean $\bar{y} = 250.5$ (n = 10).

Posterior mean $\mu_1 \approx 255$.

Posterior standard deviation $\sigma_1 \approx 9.05$.

95% posterior credible interval $\approx [237.27, 272.73]$.

Posterior probability $p(\mu > 240|data) \approx 0.9514$.

Figure 2. The RShiny app interface showing how Bayesian estimation changes under an alternative prior specification: μ~$N(300, 30^2)$.

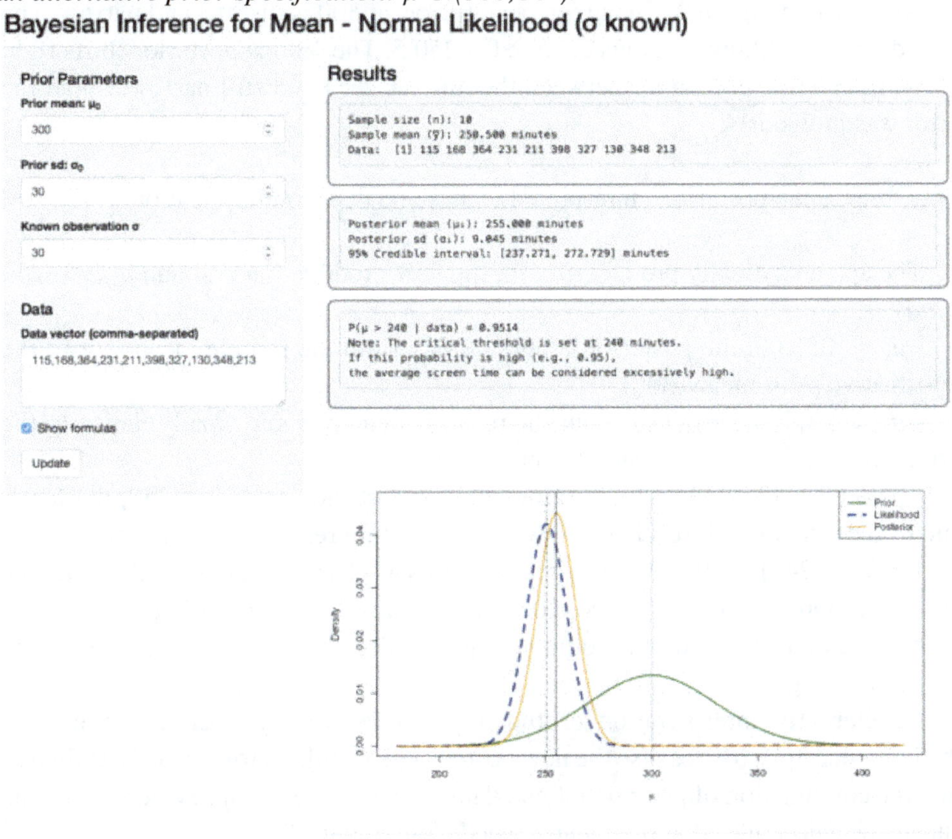

1) Adjust prior parameters - what changes and why?

With the prior set to $N(300, 30^2)$ you have moved from a very diffuse (weakly informative) prior to a reasonably informative prior centered at 300. In the app's plot this will be visible as the green prior curve becoming taller and much narrower, peaking at $\mu_0 = 300$ rather than being almost flat. Because this prior is relatively strong ($\sigma_0 = 30$ is small compared with the previous $\sigma_0 = 120$), it exerts a noticeable pull on the posterior. The posterior mean shifts upward from the data-driven value (approx. 250.5) toward the prior mean (300). Numerically this yield $\mu_1 \approx 255.00$ - a compromise between the prior (300) and the data (250.5). The posterior standard deviation also reflects both sources of information and is smaller than the likelihood's standard deviation (due to the combination of prior information and data), here ≈ 9.05.

As shown in Figure 2, The green peak (prior) at 300 is distinct and narrow. The blue dashed likelihood remains centered at 250.5. The orange posterior shifts right of the likelihood, ending up between them (near 255) and still narrower than the prior was previously.

2) Observe the posterior - interpreted values and decision implications

The app analytically produces μ_1, σ_1, the 95% credible interval and $p(\mu > 240 \mid data)$.

- $\mu_1 \approx 255.00$: the posterior is pulled away from the sample mean toward the informative prior mean (300).

- $\sigma_1 \approx 9.05$: uncertainty about the mean is moderate and small relative to the prior's $\sigma_0 = 30$ because the data add precision.

- 95% CI $\approx$ [237.27, 272.73]: although the posterior mean is >250, the lower end of the interval still reaches below 240, reflecting residual uncertainty.

- $p(\mu > 240) \approx 0.9514$: importantly, this probability exceeds 0.95. In the app's decision context (if you adopt 0.95 as the threshold for declaring "excessively high"), the updated posterior would now justify declaring the average screen time excessively high.

An alternative interpretation for students would be "the informative prior nudged the inference upward; because the new posterior probability crosses the 0.95 threshold, the combination of prior belief and data now provides strong evidence (per the chosen decision rule) that the mean exceeds 240 minutes".

3) Visualize distributions - what to look for in the plot

When users compare the three curves:

- Prior (green): now narrow and centered at 300; it clearly occupies a different location than the data's summary.

- Likelihood (blue, dashed): located at the sample mean (≈250.5) and represents the data's direct information.

- Posterior (orange): located between the prior and likelihood (≈255), visually narrower than the prior was and slightly narrower than the likelihood's effective curve for μ.

Key visual lessons to point out in the app:

- The posterior's peak (orange) is between the green and blue curves - that is the numerical compromise.

- The posterior's width (how concentrated the orange curve is) shows combined certainty: narrower than the prior alone, showing increased precision once data are included.

- The vertical reference line at 240 and the shaded right-tail area under the posterior (if you display it) correspond to the computed probability $p(\mu > 240)$. With the new prior this right-tail area becomes large enough to exceed the 0.95 cutoff.

4) Reflect critically

The "4) Reflect critically" phase involves asking key questions that encourage students to engage deeply with the results of their Bayesian analysis, such as the sensitivity of the posterior to prior changes, the effect of sample size on posterior variance, and the impact of extreme data points. These critical reflections provide an opportunity for deeper understanding and learning. This phase, however, can be significantly enriched with the use of AI tools. Guided AI prompts can help students explore these questions interactively and provide tailored feedback based on their responses. Therefore, the detailed exploration of this phase will be covered in Section 3.4, AI-enhanced Reflection Phase: Guided AI Prompts and Student Interaction.

3.4. AI-Enhanced Reflection Phase: Guided AI Prompts and Student Interaction

AI is specifically used for reflection. By definition, reflection involves students thinking about what they have learned, deepening their understanding, and analyzing their learning processes. Therefore, in this context, AI interacts as a collaborative tool that enhances students' active engagement in thinking, understanding, and learning (Peach et al., 2021).

Supported by AI tools, students can ask follow-up questions, validate their results, or simulate alternative scenarios, fostering a reflective and inquiry-based learning environment. These exercises encourage students to connect Bayesian thinking with everyday phenomena, allowing them to appreciate both the flexibility and the responsibility that come with making modeling choices under uncertainty. To further enhance this process, students can use the interactive RShiny apps at their disposal to conduct inquiries and explore their ideas. To deepen understanding and promote critical thinking, students can integrate AI tools (e.g., ChatGPT) with the RShiny app. recommended strategies include:

A. Generating Critical Prompts

Prompt 1: "Explain why the posterior mean shifts when the prior mean is changed.", or alternatively "How sensitive is the posterior to changes in the prior?" (critical thinking)

Prompt 2: "How does the posterior credible interval change with increasing sample size?", or "What happens if data are scarce and how does the model respond?", or alternatively "How does increasing sample size affect the posterior variance?" (critical thinking)

Prompt 3: "What happens if the observed data are extreme compared to prior expectations?" (critical thinking)

Prompt 4: "How do the posterior probabilities help us make decisions or interpret outcomes in context?" (critical thinking)

Prompt 5: "Calculate the posterior given these data and prior parameters." (computational)

Prompt 6: "What does the posterior represent in this context?", or "What distinguishes Bayesian estimation from frequentist estimation?" (conceptual)

Reflect critically - answers to the posed questions in this new configuration:

Answer 1: With an informative prior like $N(300, 30^2)$, the posterior is noticeably sensitive: the posterior mean moved from ≈250.5 (data) toward 255.0 (compromise). The sensitivity depends on the ratio of prior precision ($1/\sigma_0^2$) to data precision (n/σ^2). Here prior precision is nontrivial, so the prior mattering is expected. One can explore by varying σ_0: increase σ_0 to 120 → prior influence weakens and posterior returns closer to the sample mean; decrease σ_0 further → posterior moves closer to 300.

Answer 2: Increasing n increases the total data precision (n/σ^2), so the posterior variance $\sigma_1^2 = \frac{1}{\frac{1}{\sigma_0^2}+\frac{n}{\sigma^2}}$ shrinks. Practically: with a larger sample the data overwhelm even an informative prior, and the posterior concentrates more tightly around the data-determined value. In the app, increasing *n* (or adding more observations) will narrow the orange curve and reduce the influence of the green prior.

Answer 3: If data are far from the prior mean (e.g., sample mean << 300 or >> 300), the posterior will be a compromise; the degree of compromise depends on prior strength. With this $\sigma_0 = 30$ prior, moderate disagreements will still shift the posterior but not fully override the prior - the posterior will land between the two. If data are extremely far and sample size is large, the data will dominate. Visually, you'll see the navy likelihood peak far from the green prior; the orange posterior will settle between them, closer to whichever has much greater precision.

Answer 4: The posterior probability $p(\mu > 240|data)$ is a direct, probabilistic statement about the hypothesis of interest. In this configuration, $p(\mu > 240) \approx 0.9514$ by a decision criterion that uses 0.95 as a cutoff, this is strong evidence that the average daily screen time exceeds 240 minutes. You should learn to interpret this probabilistically ($\approx$95% chance under the model and prior that the mean exceeds 240), to consider sensitivity to the prior and sample size, and to connect that probability to concrete decisions (e.g., whether to flag the class's average as a concern).

B. Guided Reasoning With AI

In this phase, AI tools can guide students through the conceptual understanding of Bayesian analysis by prompting them to reflect on key relationships. For example, students can:

- ask AI to summarize the relationship between prior, likelihood, and posterior for different parameter settings or
- request explanations of how assumptions (normal likelihood, known variance) affect the posterior distribution

offering students deeper insights into the sensitivity of their results based on different modeling choices.

C. Reflective Comparison

In this phase, students engage with both Bayesian theory and practical analysis by toggling between different prior distributions and sample sizes to examine the impact on posterior estimates. For instance, students can explore the effects of switching from a diffuse prior to an informative prior, such as $\mu \sim N(275.3, 15^2)$, and compare the resulting posterior distribution both numerically and visually (see Figure 3). By doing so, students are tasked with recording changes in key Bayesian quantities such as the posterior mean ($\mu 1$), posterior standard deviation ($\sigma 1$), 95% CI, and posterior probability $p(\mu > 240)$, while varying the prior and sample size (n).

This exercise serves to highlight the sensitivity of the posterior to changes in prior beliefs and sample sizes, which is a core concept in Bayesian statistics. Students should observe that with a more informative prior, the posterior becomes more concentrated around the prior mean (275.3), and as the sample size increases, the posterior variance decreases. Through these comparisons, students will reflect on which combination of prior and sample size would allow them to confidently declare an "excessive" average screen time. For instance, they might argue that a larger sample size, in combination with a strongly informative prior, would provide a more reliable declaration of "excessive" screen time. Moreover, they are encouraged to critically assess the defensibility of their prior choice in real world contexts. A well-chosen prior should reflect reasonable beliefs based on available information and data, while minimizing biases. However, the choice of prior is often debated, especially when it is subjective or poorly justified. In some contexts, such as public health studies or educational assessments, the choice of prior may be relatively straightforward, while in others, it could be a contentious issue, requiring careful justification (Gelman et al., 2013; Kruschke, 2015).

Figure 3. The RShiny app interface showing how Bayesian estimation changes under an alternative prior specification: μ~N(275.3, 15²).

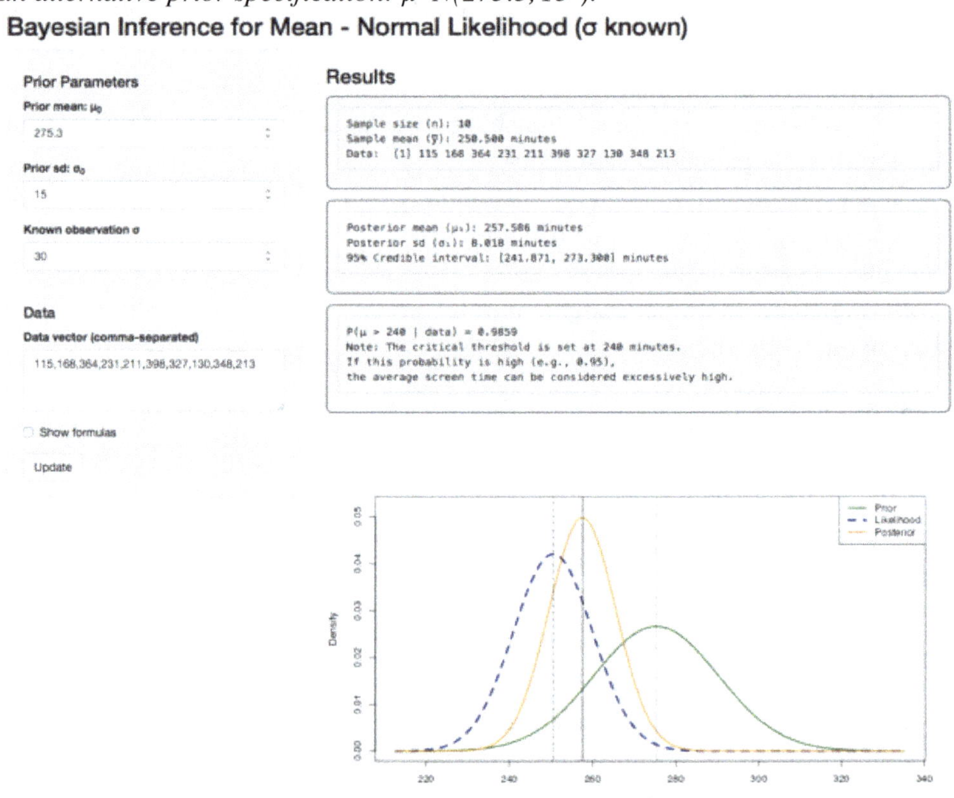

Following these explorations, students are asked to compare the AI's explanations of the Bayesian process with their own observations from the RShiny app. The AI may explain, for example, how changing priors influence the posterior distribution or how sample size adjustments affect precision. Students are encouraged to critically evaluate the AI's interpretations, questioning whether the AI's explanations align with the data visualizations they observe in the app. Are there assumptions the AI overlooks? Do the AI's conclusions seem reasonable given the context and the available data? This encourages a deeper level of reflection on the Bayesian methodology.

In this context, AI-supported tools enable students to evaluate their own understanding, generate questions, and receive feedback based on their existing knowledge and interpretations. Such an interactive process requires students to continually reassess both their own knowledge state and the feedback they receive. This ongoing, reciprocal updating aligns with approaches that model teacher–learner interaction within a hierarchical Bayesian framework and supports the probabilistic foundations of reflective learning (Chen et al., 2024). By combining interactive exploration with AI-assisted reflection, students not only learn to compute Bayesian quantities but also develop critical thinking skills to interpret, critique, and communicate these results effectively. This dual approach -computational and reflective- enhances their ability to make informed, data-driven decisions, a crucial skill in both academic and applied statistics.

3.5. Assessment Phase

The Assessment Phase aims to reinforce students' understanding of Bayesian inference by encouraging them to engage with reflective questions and participate in a mini-quiz. This phase serves as a critical checkpoint to ensure that students not only grasp the theoretical aspects of Bayesian analysis but also develop practical skills in its application. The mini-quiz includes questions such as: "Why did your choice of prior matter in your analysis?", "How would your conclusions change with a larger or more diverse dataset?", "How did the strength of your prior affect your results?", and "What limitations or assumptions did your model carry?" These questions are designed to prompt students to critically reflect on their own Bayesian models, fostering a deeper understanding of the process. Aligning assessment activities with active, reflective learning practices has been shown to support sustained improvements in student outcomes, particularly when such approaches are implemented consistently at the departmental level (Lau, Henderson, & Stains, 2024). To illustrate the nature of this assessment more concretely, an example of a short formative quiz is provided below.

Sample Mini-Quiz

To complement the reflective discussion and hands-on exploration, a short formative quiz can be used to consolidate key concepts. The purpose of this quiz is not to test procedural fluency alone, but to assess whether students can reason coherently about Bayesian inference.

Example quiz questions:

1. **Prior influence:** You analyze the same dataset using two different priors: one weakly informative and one strongly informative. Explain how and why the resulting posterior distributions differ. Under what conditions does the data dominate the prior?
2. **Interpretation of posterior output:** Suppose your analysis yields a posterior mean of 245 and a 95% credible interval of [238, 252]. Explain what this interval represents in plain language, and contrast it briefly with a frequentist confidence interval.
3. **Sensitivity and assumptions:** After increasing the sample size, you observe that the posterior becomes less sensitive to the choice of prior. Explain why this occurs and discuss what this implies about the role of prior assumptions in Bayesian inference.

These questions are intentionally open-ended and explanatory, encouraging students to articulate reasoning rather than simply report numerical results.

In addition to the quiz, students will engage in exercises that involve formula writing, prior justification, and posterior calculation. These activities help solidify their grasp of the core concepts of Bayesian statistics, from the specification of priors to the interpretation of posterior distributions. The comparison of weak versus strong priors is facilitated through AI-mediated interactions, where students can explore how their choices of prior impact the resulting posterior estimates. By manipulating the prior and observing the resulting changes in the posterior, students will gain practical insights into how prior knowledge can influence statistical conclusions.

For further assessment, students can be assigned a mini-project, in which they design their own Bayesian analysis. In this project, students will justify their choice of prior, compute the posterior, and critically evaluate the implications of their model. This process not only reinforces the computational aspects of Bayesian inference but also challenges students to consider the broader context of their assumptions and the real world applicability of their models.

Student responses to the quiz and mini-project can be evaluated using a concise rubric that emphasizes conceptual understanding and interpretive reasoning rather than procedural detail.

Short Assessment Rubric

Student responses can be evaluated using a concise rubric that prioritizes conceptual coherence over technical detail.

Table 1. Assessment Rubric for Evaluating Student Understanding in Bayesian Mean Estimation

Criterion	High Achievement	Satisfactory	Needs Improvement
Conceptual understanding	Clearly explains prior/ likelihood /posterior relationships using correct Bayesian logic	Demonstrates partial understanding with minor gaps or imprecise language	Explanations are vague, inconsistent, or conceptually incorrect
Interpretation of results	Accurately interprets posterior summaries in context	Interpretation is mostly correct but lacks depth or clarity	Misinterprets posterior quantities or reports results without explanation
Justification of modeling choices	Provides a clear and thoughtful justification for prior and assumptions	Justification is present but limited or generic	Little or no justification of modeling choices
Reflection and critical thinking	Thoughtfully reflects on assumptions, limitations, and sensitivity	Some reflection, but limited engagement with assumptions	Minimal or no reflection on assumptions or limitations

This rubric is designed to be lightweight and flexible, allowing instructors to adapt it to different class sizes and instructional contexts.

As to the learning outcomes, they are intentionally aligned with Bloom's taxonomy, progressing from conceptual understanding to analytical application. This structure supports students in moving from lower order cognitive processes (understanding Bayesian concepts) to higher order skills such as applying and interpreting probabilistic models, consistent with established educational frameworks (Bloom et al., 1956; Anderson & Krathwohl, 2001). By the end of this instructional sequence, students will be able to:

1. Specify and justify prior distributions for a normal mean under different informational assumptions.
2. Compute posterior distributions analytically for a normal–normal conjugate model.
3. Interpret posterior summaries (mean, credible interval, posterior probability) in context.
4. Evaluate sensitivity of posterior inferences to changes in prior assumptions and sample size.
5. Compare Bayesian and frequentist inferential statements for the same dataset.

6. Critically reflect on how modeling choices influence decision-making under uncertainty.

From an evaluation perspective, the effectiveness of the assessment phase can be examined through observable indicators such as students' ability to articulate prior - posterior relationships in written explanations, justify modeling choices in the mini-project, and correctly interpret posterior summaries across varying prior specifications. Improvements in conceptual coherence between students' prior assumptions, computational steps, and inferential conclusions would serve as evidence of meaningful learning. These indicators provide a basis for future empirical evaluation, even in the absence of formal experimental data.

4. LIMITATIONS AND RISKS OF AI-SUPPORTED BAYESIAN LEARNING

In the proposed instructional design, artificial intelligence is deliberately positioned as a reflective and dialogical support tool rather than as a computational authority or conceptual substitute for statistical reasoning. While AI-enhanced interaction offers clear pedagogical benefits, particularly in facilitating reflection, personalized feedback, and conceptual clarification, it also introduces a set of limitations and risks that must be acknowledged explicitly. Addressing these risks is essential not only for methodological transparency but also for ensuring that students develop robust statistical reasoning rather than procedural dependency.

4.1 Over-Reliance on AI Explanations

One potential risk concerns students' over-reliance on AI-generated explanations, particularly in computational or interpretive stages of Bayesian analysis. In the lesson design presented in this chapter, students interact extensively with an RShiny applet that dynamically updates priors, likelihoods, and posteriors as parameters change. This interactivity is intended to foreground conceptual relationships (such as the relative influence of prior precision and sample size) through visual and numerical feedback.

However, when AI tools are introduced as explanatory companions, there is a risk that students may externalize reasoning processes by deferring explanations to the AI rather than articulating them independently. For example, instead of reasoning through why a posterior mean shifts toward the prior under increased prior precision, a student may simply accept an AI-generated explanation without critically engaging with the underlying mechanism. This risk is particularly salient in quantitatively demanding topics such as Bayesian inference, where conceptual understanding must be actively constructed rather than passively received.

To mitigate this risk, AI interaction in the proposed design is intentionally restricted to the reflection phase, following hands-on exploration and analytical computation. Moreover, AI prompts are framed to elicit reasoning (e.g., "Explain why…" or "What happens if…") rather than provide direct answers. In this way, AI helps students put their reasoning into words and think more carefully about their understanding, instead of taking over the reasoning process itself.

4.2 Hallucination and Model Mismatch Risks

A second limitation arises from the possibility of AI hallucination or model mismatch. Large language models may generate explanations that are syntactically plausible but conceptually misaligned with the statistical assumptions of the model being used. In Bayesian mean estimation, such mismatches may include incorrect assumptions about known versus unknown variance, confusion between conjugate and non-conjugate settings, or inappropriate generalizations beyond the specified model.

This risk is particularly relevant in the present instructional context, where the Bayesian model is intentionally constrained (normal likelihood with known variance) to support analytical tractability and conceptual clarity. If an AI system implicitly assumes a different modeling framework such as unknown variance or hierarchical structure, it may provide explanations that conflict with the instructional model, potentially confusing learners.

To address this limitation, the pedagogical design emphasizes model transparency. Students are explicitly taught the assumptions underlying the Bayesian model before AI interaction is introduced, and AI is used primarily to interrogate consequences of those assumptions rather than to redefine them. In addition, students are encouraged to cross-check AI-generated explanations against the RShiny outputs, treating discrepancies as learning opportunities rather than errors to be ignored. This triangulation between theory, computation, and AI explanation reinforces knowledge-based caution and statistical rigor.

It should be noted, however, that the risk of hallucination and model mismatch is not inherent to AI on its own, but rather to the use of general-purpose large language models that are not explicitly aligned with the statistical framework being taught. In principle, this risk could be substantially reduced through the use of a domain-specific or pedagogically fine-tuned language model, trained on curated materials from Bayesian statistics education and constrained to operate within predefined modeling assumptions (e.g., known variance, conjugate priors). Such alignment would increase consistency between AI-generated explanations and the instructional model, thereby improving reliability. Nevertheless, even with specialized training, AI systems should not be treated as infallible sources of inference. From a pedagogical standpoint, maintaining a critical stance toward AI output remains essential, as the educational objective is not to eliminate uncertainty in explanations, but to cultivate students' ability to reason about uncertainty itself.

4.3 Conceptual Authority Shift

A more subtle but critical risk concerns the potential shift of authority from statistical reasoning to AI output. In such cases, students may justify conclusions by appealing to the AI ("because the AI says this is the posterior") rather than articulating why a posterior takes a particular form given the prior and likelihood, the pedagogical goal of fostering probabilistic reasoning is weakened. This risk directly contradicts the central pedagogical goal of Bayesian education, which is to cultivate disciplined reasoning under uncertainty.

Within the proposed framework, this risk is mitigated by embedding AI use within an explicit conceptual hierarchy. Bayesian theory and probabilistic modeling remain the primary sources of authority. The RShiny applet provides empirical and visual grounding. AI serves only as an interpretive aid. Assessment tasks further reinforce this hierarchy by requiring students to justify conclusions using posterior distributions, credible intervals, and sensitivity arguments, none of which can be validly answered by AI output alone without reference to the underlying model.

4.4 Surface-Level Understanding and Reporting Bias

Finally, AI-supported learning environments may inadvertently encourage surface-level understanding, where students focus on reporting posterior summaries (e.g., posterior mean or probability thresholds) rather than interpreting their meaning in context. For instance, students might report that

$$p(\mu > 240 \mid data) = 0.95$$

without reflecting on how this probability depends on prior choice, sample size or model assumptions. This risk is especially relevant in Bayesian statistics, where numerical results are inherently conditional on modeling decisions. To counteract this tendency, the lesson design explicitly integrates sensitivity analysis as a student task, requiring learners to vary prior parameters and sample sizes and to document how these changes affect posterior conclusions. AI is used here not to supply answers, but to prompt critical comparison across scenarios, reinforcing the idea that Bayesian inference is not a single outcome but a structured reasoning process.

Overall, these limitations underscore the necessity of pedagogically disciplined AI integration. When AI is framed as a reflective partner rather than an authoritative source, and when its use is embedded within a transparent modeling framework and guided assessment structure, its risks become manageable and pedagogically productive. Rather than weakening Bayesian understanding, careful acknowledgment and management of these limitations can strengthen students' statistical judgment, reflective judgement, and critical engagement with uncertainty.

4.5 Limited Evidence of Instructional Effectiveness

A natural limitation of the proposed instructional design is that, at this stage, evidence regarding its instructional effectiveness remains limited. The chapter does not claim that the RShiny - AI workflow has been empirically validated as superior to alternative approaches, nor does it attempt to establish causal learning gains. Rather, the design is presented as a pedagogically motivated model that builds on well-established principles of active learning, conceptual visualization, and formative feedback in statistics education.

The anticipated benefits of the approach are therefore grounded primarily in theoretical alignment with existing educational research, rather than in controlled experimental evaluation. While this alignment provides a strong rationale for the design, it also highlights the need for future empirical work. For example, subsequent studies could examine whether students exposed to AI-supported Bayesian instruction demonstrate deeper conceptual understanding of prior–posterior updating, improved interpretive skills, or greater sensitivity to modeling assumptions when compared to more traditional instructional formats.

Explicitly acknowledging this limitation is important. It situates the present contribution not as a final verdict on effectiveness, but as a structured and theoretically informed proposal that invites empirical testing and refinement. In this sense, the chapter aims to open a pedagogical pathway rather than to close a debate.

4.6 Reproducibility and Workflow Stability

A second limitation concerns the reproducibility of the proposed Shiny and AI supported workflow. On the one hand, the RShiny component of the design is highly reproducible, as it is based on fully specified statistical models, transparent assumptions, and deterministic computations. Any instructor with access to the applet and the underlying code can replicate the analytical and visual outputs shown to students.

The AI component, however, introduces a different level of variability. AI generated explanations may vary across model versions, system updates, or prompt formulations, potentially leading to differences in how concepts are articulated across instructional settings. This variability creates a reproducibility gap that is difficult to eliminate entirely in AI-supported learning environments.

To address this issue, the instructional design deliberately assigns AI a nonauthoritative role. Core explanations, modeling assumptions, and learning objectives are defined independently of AI interaction, and students are consistently directed back to the statistical model and the RShiny outputs as the primary sources of validation. In practice, reproducibility can be further strengthened by using standardized prompt templates, documenting AI usage guidelines, and clearly specifying the instructional boundaries within which AI is allowed to operate.

From an educational standpoint, this limitation also has a constructive dimension. Variability in AI output can be used to prompt discussion about interpretation, assumptions, and model dependence central themes in Bayesian reasoning itself. Nevertheless, for wider adoption and comparative evaluation across contexts, greater standardization and documentation will remain important considerations for future implementations.

5. DISCUSSION

This chapter contributes to the growing literature on Bayesian statistics education by proposing a pedagogically structured, technology-supported approach to teaching Bayesian estimation that prioritizes conceptual understanding over procedural fluency. Research on Bayesian learning has consistently shown that students struggle with the interpretation of priors, conditional probability, and the dynamic relationship between data and belief updating (Kruschke, 2015; Saldanha & Thompson, 2002). These difficulties often persist even when students can perform formal calculations, indicating a gap between computation and understanding.

Existing pedagogical approaches have addressed these challenges in different ways. Simulation-based Bayesian curricula emphasize learning through repeated data generation and visualization (Tintle et al., 2015; Zieffler et al., 2008), helping students develop intuition for posterior updating. Software environments such as JASP have further supported Bayesian learning by lowering technical barriers and allowing students to focus on model comparison and interpretation rather than coding (Wagenmakers et al., 2018). Similarly, Stan-based teaching environments promote principled probabilistic modeling and expose students to modern Bayesian workflows, particularly at the graduate level (Gelman et al., 2021).

The instructional design presented in this chapter builds on these developments while addressing a complementary pedagogical need: structured reflection on modeling assumptions and inferential consequences. By using a constrained RShiny applet focused on Bayesian mean estimation, students can directly observe how priors, likelihoods, and sample size jointly shape posterior distributions. This visual and interactive emphasis targets well-documented misconceptions about priors being either irrelevant or overly dominant, depending on sample size (Kruschke, 2015).

Within this environment, AI is intentionally positioned as a reflective aid rather than a source of statistical authority. Recent research in AI-supported learning suggests that the educational value of conversational agents lies primarily in their capacity to scaffold explanation, prompt self-explanation, and support metacognitive engagement, rather than to replace analytical reasoning (Holmes et al., 2019; Luckin et al., 2016). Consistent with this view, AI use in the proposed lesson is confined to guided reflection phases and is anchored to explicitly stated model assumptions, reducing the risk of conceptual drift or misplaced conceptual authority. These pedagogical choices are motivated not only by technological affordances, but also by conceptual difficulties in Bayesian learning.

In particular, the lesson design targets several recurring misconceptions that students commonly encounter when first learning Bayesian inference.

A central motivation behind the proposed instructional design is to address several well-documented misconceptions that students commonly bring to Bayesian statistics. One frequent misunderstanding is the perception that priors are inherently subjective and therefore arbitrary. In traditional instruction, priors are often introduced abstractly, which can reinforce the impression that they reflect personal belief rather than structured information. In this chapter, priors are consistently treated as model components that require explicit justification. Through the RShiny applet, students are invited to choose different prior centers and variances and immediately observe how these choices shape posterior inference. Seeing these effects unfold dynamically helps students recognize that priors encode information strength rather than opinion, and that their influence depends systematically on both prior precision and data.

Related to this, many students struggle with conditional probability, particularly by reversing the roles of the likelihood and the posterior. This confusion between $P(\mu |data)$ and $P(data|\mu)$, as discussed in Chapter 3, is a persistent obstacle in Bayesian learning. The instructional design addresses this difficulty by displaying the likelihood and posterior simultaneously and linking them to distinct roles within the model. By fixing the observed data and allowing the parameter to vary, the RShiny visualization makes it clear that the likelihood expresses how plausible the data are under different parameter values, whereas the posterior represents updated beliefs about the parameter itself. AI support at this stage is limited to prompting students to articulate, in their own words, why these two quantities represent fundamentally different conditional relationships.

Another common misconception concerns the role of the posterior distribution. Some students interpret the posterior primarily as a refined version of the prior, underestimating the contribution of the data. The lesson flow deliberately counters this tendency by encouraging students to vary sample size and sample mean while holding the prior fixed. In particular, scenarios with weak priors and increasing amounts of data highlight how posterior estimates can move substantially away from prior expectations. During the AI-supported reflection phase, students are asked to articulate when and why this shift occurs, reinforcing the idea that the posterior emerges from the interaction between prior information and observed evidence, rather than from prior belief alone.

Finally, students often find it difficult to grasp the interaction between sample size and prior strength. While this relationship can be derived algebraically, it is rarely intuitive at first encounter. In the proposed design, this interaction becomes visible through systematic comparison. Students explore parallel scenarios in which sample size increases under different prior precisions and observe how the influence of the prior diminishes as data accumulate. Here AI is used to prompt comparison across scenarios, asking students to explain observed differences rather than supplying conclusions. This shifts learning away from formula memorization toward causal reasoning about Bayesian updating.

These design choices, when considered collectively, illustrate how interactive visualization and carefully constrained AI support can help students confront and overcome persistent conceptual barriers in Bayesian inference. Rather than correcting misconceptions through exposition alone, the chapter emphasizes learning environments in which students can test assumptions, observe consequences, and reflect on their reasoning. This approach aligns naturally with the Bayesian view of learning itself as an iterative process of updating understanding in light of new evidence.

An additional contribution of this approach is its emphasis on intellectual responsibility in Bayesian inference. By requiring students to justify priors, conduct sensitivity analysis, and interpret posterior results conditionally, the lesson foregrounds the idea that Bayesian conclusions are not neutral outputs but reasoned judgments under uncertainty. This orientation aligns with broader calls in statistics education to emphasize interpretation, transparency, and critical reasoning alongside technical skill (GAISE, 2016).

As AI becomes increasingly embedded in data rich environments, equipping students with both the technical tools and the critical mindset to navigate such systems is essential. Ultimately, this chapter complements existing Bayesian teaching tools by offering a replicable pedagogical design rather than a new computational platform. When interactive visualization and AI-supported reflection are integrated within a disciplined instructional framework, Bayesian statistics becomes more accessible, conceptually coherent, and pedagogically robust.

REFERENCES

Albert, J., & Hu, J. (2019). *Probability and Bayesian modeling*. Chapman & Hall/ CRC., DOI: 10.1201/9781351030144

American Statistical Association. (2014). 2014 Curriculum Guidelines for Undergraduate Programs in Statistical Science, Alexandria, VA: Author. Available at https://www.amstat.org/education/curriculumguidelines.cfm

Bernardo, J. M., & Smith, A. F. M. (2009). *Bayesian Theory* (2nd ed.). John Wiley & Sons.

Bertolini, R., Finch, S. J., & Nehm, R. H. (2023). An application of Bayesian inference to examine student retention and attrition in the STEM classroom. *Frontiers in Education, 8*, 1073829. Advance online publication. DOI: 10.3389/feduc.2023.1073829

Chen, A. M., Palacci, A., Vélez, N., Hawkins, R. D., & Gershman, S. J. (2024). A hierarchical Bayesian model of adaptive teaching. *Cognitive Science, 48*(7), e13477. DOI: 10.1111/cogs.13477 PMID: 38980989

Chen, L., Chen, P., & Lin, Z. (2020). Artificial intelligence in education: A review. *IEEE Access : Practical Innovations, Open Solutions, 8*, 75264–75278. DOI: 10.1109/ACCESS.2020.2988510

DeGroot, M. H. (2004). *Optimal statistical decisions*. John Wiley & Sons. DOI: 10.1002/0471729000

Ferrari, D. (2022). Teaching Bayesian Statistics. *PS, Political Science & Politics, 55*(1), 230–235. DOI: 10.1017/S1049096521001244

Foltynek, T., Bjelobaba, S., Glendinning, I., Khan, Z. R., Santos, R., Pavletic, P., & Kravjar, J. (2023). ENAI Recommendations on the ethical use of Artificial Intelligence in Education. *International Journal for Educational Integrity, 19*(1), 12. Advance online publication. DOI: 10.1007/s40979-023-00133-4

GAISE College Report ASA Revision Committee (2016). "Guidelines for Assessment and Instruction in Statistics Education College Report 2016," [online]. Available at https://www.amstat.org/docs/default-source/amstat-documents/gaisecollege_full.pdf

Gelman, A., Carlin, J. B., Stern, H. S., Dunson, D. B., Vehtari, A., & Rubin, D. B. (2013). *Bayesian data analysis* (3rd ed.). CRC Press., DOI: 10.1201/b16018

Holmes, W., Bialik, M., & Fadel, C. (2019). *Artificial intelligence in education: Promises and implications for teaching and learning*. Center for Curriculum Redesign.

Huang, D. (2024). Innovative interactive instruction to enhance learning behaviors. *Journal of Innovation & Knowledge*, *10*(1), 100641. DOI: 10.1016/j.jik.2024.100641

Johnston, H., Wells, R. F., Shanks, E. M., Boey, T., & Parsons, B. N. (2024). Student perspectives on the use of generative artificial intelligence technologies in higher education. *International Journal for Educational Integrity*, *20*(1), 2. Advance online publication. DOI: 10.1007/s40979-024-00149-4

Kaewpradit, K., Ngamchaliew, P., & Buathong, N. (2025). Digital screen time usage, prevalence of excessive digital screen time, and its association with mental health, sleep quality, and academic performance among Southern University students. *Frontiers in Psychiatry*, *16*, 1535631. DOI: 10.3389/fpsyt.2025.1535631 PMID: 40195967

Kruschke, J. K. (2015). *Doing Bayesian Data Analysis: A Tutorial with R, JAGS, and Stan* (2nd ed.). Academic Press.

Kruschke, J. K., & Liddell, T. M. (2017). The Bayesian New Statistics: Hypothesis testing, estimation, meta-analysis, and power analysis from a Bayesian perspective. *Psychonomic Bulletin & Review*, *25*(1), 178–206. DOI: 10.3758/s13423-016-1221-4 PMID: 28176294

Lau, A. C., Henderson, C., Stains, M., Dancy, M., Merino, C., Apkarian, N., Raker, J. R., & Johnson, E. (2024). Characteristics of departments with high-use of active learning in introductory STEM courses: Implications for departmental transformation. *International Journal of STEM Education*, *11*(1), 10. Advance online publication. DOI: 10.1186/s40594-024-00470-x

Lindley, D. V. (2000). The philosophy of statistics. *The Statistician*, *49*(3), 293–337. DOI: 10.1111/1467-9884.00238

Luckin, R., Holmes, W., Griffiths, M., & Corcier, L. B. (2016). *Intelligence unleashed: An Argument for AI in Education*. Pearson.

Mayer, R. E. (2020). *Multimedia Learning* (3rd ed.). Cambridge University Press. DOI: 10.1017/9781316941355

McElreath, R. (2020). *Statistical rethinking: A Bayesian course with examples in R and Stan* (2nd ed.). Chapman & Hall/CRC., DOI: 10.1201/9780429029608

Peach, R. L., Greenbury, S. F., Johnston, I. G., Yaliraki, S. N., Lefevre, D. J., & Barahona, M. (2021). Understanding learner behaviour in online courses with Bayesian modelling and time series characterization. *Scientific Reports*, *11*(1), 2823. DOI: 10.1038/s41598-021-81709-3 PMID: 33531544

Pétrin-Pomerleau, P., Vincent, C., Mairena, P. M. G., Yilmaz, E., Charbonneau, A. T., Husereau, T., & Jacob, G. (2023). The Bayesian approach is intuitive conditionally to prior exposition to these examples. *The Quantitative Methods for Psychology, 19*(3), 244–253. DOI: 10.20982/tqmp.19.3.p244

Reiss, M. J. (2021). The use of AI in education: Practicalities and ethical considerations. *London Review of Education, 19*(1). Advance online publication. DOI: 10.14324/LRE.19.1.05

Robert, C. P. (2007). *The Bayesian Choice: From Decision Theoretic Foundations to Computational Implementation*. Springer.

Saldanha, L., & Thompson, P. (2002). Conceptions of sample and their relationship to statistical inference. *Educational Studies in Mathematics, 51*(3), 257–270. DOI: 10.1023/A:1023692604014

Spiegelhalter, D. J., Abrams, K. R., & Myles, J. P. (2004). *Bayesian Approaches to Clinical Trials and Health-Care Evaluation*. Wiley.

Steib, N., Büchter, T., Eichler, A., Binder, K., Krauss, S., Böcherer-Linder, K., Vogel, M., & Hilbert, S. (2024). How to teach Bayesian reasoning: An empirical study comparing four different probability training courses. *Learning and Instruction, 95*, 102032. DOI: 10.1016/j.learninstruc.2024.102032

Theobald, E. J., Hill, M. J., Tran, E., Agrawal, S., Arroyo, E. N., Behling, S., Chambwe, N., Cintrón, D. L., Cooper, J. D., Dunster, G., Grummer, J. A., Hennessey, K., Hsiao, J., Iranon, N., Jones, L.II, Jordt, H., Keller, M., Lacey, M. E., Littlefield, C. E., & Freeman, S. (2020). Active learning narrows achievement gaps for underrepresented students in undergraduate science, technology, engineering, and math. *Proceedings of the National Academy of Sciences of the United States of America, 117*(12), 6476–6483. DOI: 10.1073/pnas.1916903117 PMID: 32152114

Tintle, N., Chance, B., Cobb, G., Rossman, A., Roy, S., Swanson, T., & VanderStoep, J. (2015). *Introduction to statistical investigations: High school binding*. John Wiley.

Van Wart, M., McIntyre, M., Zhang, J., Medina, P., Ni, A., & Njualem, L. (2025). The perceived importance of active learning techniques in online STEM courses. *Computers and Education Open, 9*, 100309. DOI: 10.1016/j.caeo.2025.100309

Wagenmakers, E., Marsman, M., Jamil, T., Ly, A., Verhagen, J., Love, J., Selker, R., Gronau, Q. F., Šmíra, M., Epskamp, S., Matzke, D., Rouder, J. N., & Morey, R. D. (2018). Bayesian inference for psychology. Part I: Theoretical advantages and practical ramifications. *Psychonomic Bulletin & Review, 25*(1), 35–57. DOI: 10.3758/s13423-017-1343-3 PMID: 28779455

Wang, Y., & Jin, J. (2024). Research on Bayesian Statistics Teaching with R. *International Journal of Education and Humanities*, *12*(1), 39–40. DOI: 10.54097/5zh7f436

Weber, F., Ickstadt, K., & Glass, Ä. (2022). shinybrms: Fitting Bayesian regression models using a graphical user interface for the R package brms. *The R Journal*, *14*(2), 96–120. https://rjournal.github.io/. DOI: 10.32614/RJ-2022-027

Zieffler, A., Garfield, J., Delmas, R., & Reading, C. (2008). A framework to support research on informal inferential reasoning. *Statistics Education Research Journal*, *7*(2), 40–58. DOI: 10.52041/serj.v7i2.469

Chapter 3

AI as a Teaching Assistant: Intelligent Tutoring Systems in Statistics Education

Mustafa Kayyali
http://orcid.org/0000-0003-3300-262X
Maaref University of Applied Sciences, Syria

ABSTRACT

Artificial intelligence is no longer confined to research labs or industry; it has entered the classroom as both partner and provocateur. This chapter explores the role of AI as a teaching assistant in statistics education, with a particular focus on intelligent tutoring systems that adapt to learners' needs. By blending algorithmic precision with human-centered pedagogy, these systems offer individualized feedback, foster student engagement, and reduce the burden of repetitive instruction. Yet, the integration of AI in statistics teaching raises pressing questions about trust, equity, and the preservation of critical thinking. Drawing on global case studies, the chapter examines both the promise and the pitfalls of AI-driven tutoring, proposing a vision in which human educators and AI systems collaborate to create richer, more inclusive learning environments. The argument advanced here is not that machines should replace teachers, but that they can extend their reach and sharpen their effectiveness in transformative ways.

INTRODUCTION

Statistics has always been a discipline that sits uncomfortably between abstraction and application (Erduran Tekin, 2024). For students, it can feel like a thicket of

DOI: 10.4018/979-8-3373-6259-5.ch003

formulas, probabilities, and distributions that appear detached from lived experience, even though they underpin nearly every field of modern life—from public health to business analytics, from climate science to social research. Teachers of statistics have long confronted the challenge of bridging this gap: how to transform symbols on a page into tools of reasoning, judgment, and inquiry. The rise of artificial intelligence has reconfigured this challenge in ways that were scarcely imaginable a generation ago. AI is no longer just a subject of statistical modeling but has become an actor in the pedagogical process, shaping how learners encounter statistics and how teachers manage the complexity of instruction.

The notion of the "teaching assistant" provides a useful metaphor. Traditionally, teaching assistants were graduate students who supported professors by handling tutorials, grading, and offering supplementary explanations (Javed & O'Brien, 2024). Their role was both instructional and relational: they helped students who might have felt lost in the anonymity of a large lecture hall, creating spaces for dialogue and practice. When AI steps into this role, it disrupts the familiar balance. Intelligent tutoring systems are designed not simply to distribute workloads but to provide tailored feedback, instant clarification, and sometimes even emotional scaffolding through natural language interaction. The promise is seductive: a system that can attend to every student, every time, without fatigue or delay.

But educational history reminds us that technological promises are never neutral (Heath et al, 2022). Every new wave of tools—from blackboards to calculators, from learning management systems to MOOCs—has brought with it debates about what is gained and what is sacrificed (Joque, 2022). AI in statistics education raises similarly complex questions. Can algorithms truly grasp the nuance of statistical reasoning, where misunderstanding often lies not in the numbers themselves but in the conceptual framing of uncertainty? Will students come to rely on machine-generated hints rather than cultivating the intellectual patience required for problem-solving? And what of the teacher—does their role shrink as AI takes on more of the "hands-on" tutoring, or does it expand into new forms of mentorship and critical oversight?

This chapter situates these questions within the specific terrain of statistics pedagogy. Unlike narrative-based disciplines, where interpretive ambiguity is common, statistics demands precision in calculation but also sensitivity to context in application. It is precisely this duality—rigor and relevance—that makes it an ideal testbed for AI as a teaching assistant. Intelligent tutoring systems can provide drill-based practice in probability distributions just as easily as they can generate visualizations to illustrate regression models. Yet, if misapplied, they risk flattening statistics into a rote exercise, neglecting the reflective dimension that transforms a technique into an instrument of inquiry.

The global context adds further urgency. Across many countries, statistics education suffers from chronic under-enrollment and high dropout rates, often because students perceive it as alienating or excessively difficult (Desir, 2024). Teachers face large class sizes, limited resources, and an ever-growing demand for data literacy in an era where "evidence-based decision-making" has become a mantra across professions. Against this backdrop, AI presents itself as both a lifeline and a challenge: a lifeline because it can personalize learning at scale, and a challenge because its deployment requires infrastructure, ethical safeguards, and a willingness to rethink entrenched pedagogical models.

The introduction of AI-driven teaching assistants is not just a matter of convenience; it is a question of educational philosophy (Hossain & Islam, 2024). At its core, statistics education is not about memorizing formulas but about cultivating a way of thinking—a statistical literacy that allows students to interpret uncertainty, evaluate claims, and make reasoned choices in a world saturated with data. If AI can support this literacy, it will represent more than just a technical innovation; it will signify a pedagogical shift. But if it cannot, if it reduces statistics to automated feedback and mechanistic exercises, it may reinforce the very barriers it claims to dismantle.

This chapter, therefore, approaches the subject with both hope and caution. It examines the promise of intelligent tutoring systems in statistics education, not as a futuristic curiosity but as a present reality already reshaping classrooms across the world. It considers how these systems can relieve teachers of repetitive burdens, allow for more individualized student support, and even foster new forms of collaboration between human and machine. At the same time, it engages critically with issues of trust, equity, and pedagogical depth, recognizing that technology always reflects the values and assumptions of those who design and deploy it.

The pages that follow invite readers to consider AI not as a replacement for human teaching, but as a partner—one whose potential is vast but whose impact depends on how thoughtfully it is integrated. Statistics education, perhaps more than any other field, reveals the tension between precision and interpretation, between numbers and meaning. In this tension lies the opportunity to craft a vision of teaching where human and artificial intelligence together expand the boundaries of what learning can be.

DESIGNING INTELLIGENT TUTORING SYSTEMS FOR COMPLEX QUANTITATIVE LEARNING

Building an intelligent tutoring system for statistics isn't the same as automating vocabulary drills or labeling triangles; it's a stubborn, exhilarating craft that lives at the junction of inference, uncertainty, and human judgment. Quantitative learning—especially in probability, inference, and modeling—doesn't unfold in a straight line (Dvir & Ben-Zvi, 2023). Students don't simply acquire "the mean," then "the variance," then "the central limit theorem" as tidy, stackable blocks. They circle back, misapply, unlearn, and reframe. A system worth its salt must honor that nonlinear story: it has to see misconceptions early, treat them with nuance, and invite learners to move between symbolic manipulation, graphical sense-making, and narrative justification without yanking them through a one-size-fits-all pipeline. Harder still, it must do this while staying honest about what it knows and what it guesses.

At the core sits the learner model, that delicate portrait of a student that updates as work accumulates. Old-school rule-based profiles caught the obvious stuff—if the z-score is miscomputed three times, flag the formula; if samples are mixed up with populations, deploy a glossary nudge. The modern picture is livelier. Bayesian Knowledge Tracing and its descendants estimate latent mastery across skills; Item Response Theory (Item Response Theory) calibrates task difficulty and discrimination; deep knowledge tracing layers sequence models on top of practice streams to sense momentum, fatigue, and that curious phase where a student "almost gets it" but keeps tripping on edge cases (Šarić-Grgić et al, 2024). These are not ornaments; they're the difference between spamming hints and delivering the one question that unlocks a knot. The trick is restraint: a model that treats every pause as ignorance will drown the learner in interventions, while a model that waits for perfect evidence will miss the teachable minute entirely. The art—because this begins to look like art—is to balance sensitivity with patience.

Figure 1. Illustrative Functional Emphasis in an Intelligent Tutoring System for Statistics

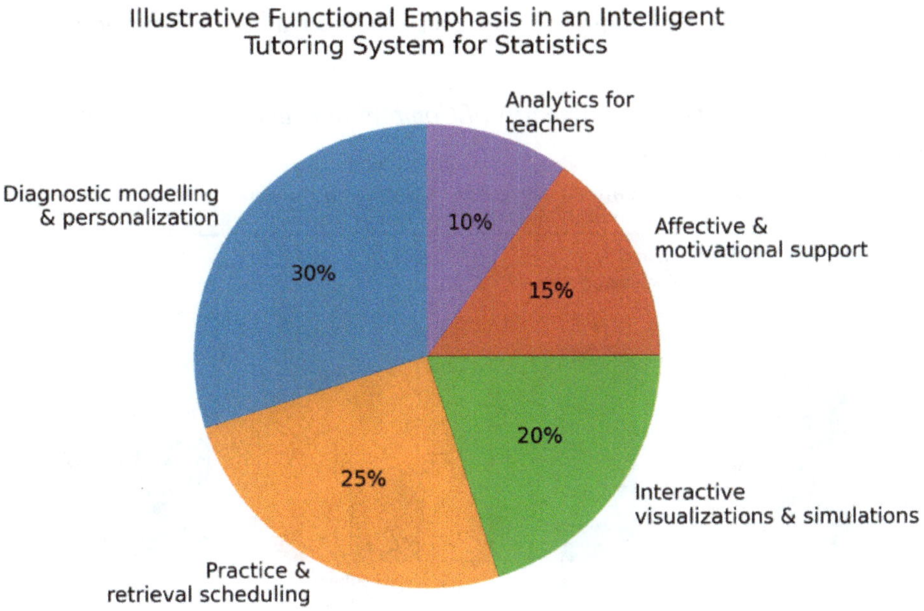

Representation is the system's second language. *Statistics is a chameleon; it speaks algebra, geometry, computation, and story.* When a student misreads a confidence interval as a probability statement about a fixed parameter, lecturing about coverage won't necessarily land; a simulated forest of intervals, some capturing the parameter and some missing by design, can shift intuition faster than a paragraph ever will. When linear regression turns slippery, a residual plot with live brushing can show how leverage and influence play their mischief; a student drags a single outlier and watches coefficients lurch, seeing in motion what a formula implies but does not dramatize. Intelligent tutoring here means multimodal translation. Text becomes dynamic visualization. Visualization becomes sandbox. Sandbox becomes plain language justification—because the point of learning statistics is not just doing it, but explaining what was done and why it was reasonable given the evidence.

Affective awareness matters more than we sometimes admit. Statistics is notorious for anxiety, and anxiety narrows cognitive bandwidth (Suzuki, 2021). The assistant can't become a therapist, and it shouldn't pretend, yet it can sense friction. Long pauses after an error, oscillation between two wrong strategies, abrupt session exits—these signals, handled gently, can trigger tone shifts: briefer prompts, optional "confidence sliders," celebratory feedback when a student revises a misconception on the second attempt. The language tilts from evaluative to invitational. “Looks like this concept is sticky; want to try a visual version first?” Those touches are small, but stacked across a semester they change a climate: students stop treating statistics as a hostile landscape and begin to experience it as a terrain with wayfinding.

Figure 2. Illustrative Learning Benefits of Combining Human Teaching with an AI Tutoring System in Statistics

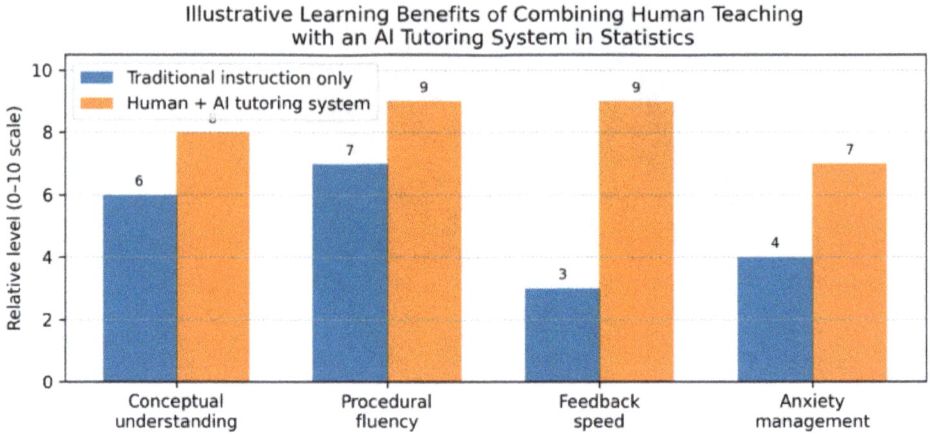

Authentic tasks keep the soul of the work intact. No one falls in love with p-values in the abstract. They care when a decision has a cost (Lakens, 2021). An intelligent tutoring system can stage small simulations where stakes are intelligible: you’re a city analyst allocating a limited vaccination budget, your Type I and Type II thresholds have downstream consequences, and every model assumption you break has a narrative cost—vulnerable neighborhoods miss coverage, or resources get misdirected. Now power analysis stops being a sterile table and becomes a planning instrument. The same holds for classification: precision and recall are no longer mystery metrics but choices with ethical weight when screening for a disease or triaging support services. Systems should let students “feel” these trade-offs by animating consequences rather than simply reporting metrics.

Collaboration is not an afterthought. Individualized tutoring can drift toward isolation if design isn’t intentional (McCaffery-Pomerleau, 2024). When the system detects a misconception blooming across many learners—say, confounding and Simpson’s paradox appearing together—it can recommend a synchronous mini-forum, with anonymized solution traces laid side by side and a prompt that asks, “Where did this line of reasoning begin to diverge from the data?” Students comment, upvote helpful explanations, and the teacher curates, highlighting two or three student-generated exemplars as "class notes." The assistant, in other words, becomes a facilitator of collective intelligence, not a whisperer of solitary answers.

Assessment should shed some of its punitive clothing. High-stakes, end-of-unit exams still have a place, but intelligent tutoring makes formative assessment ambient. Micro-insights aggregate into heatmaps that show conceptual shallows and depths without stapling a grade to each cell. Teachers see, for example, that multiple cohorts struggle with interpreting interaction terms in logistic regression when predictors are not centered. Next day's lesson shifts accordingly, with a live demo that toggles centering and rewrites coefficients in a way that brings interpretability home. Feedback loops get short enough to matter.

Then there's the messy belt of data governance—privacy, security, consent, fairness. Students deserve clarity: what signals are collected (keypresses, dwell time, revision counts), why they're collected (to tune difficulty, to schedule retrieval), and how long they're retained. Consent must be real, not "click-through theater." Auditing is non-negotiable: check for differential error rates in recommendations by linguistic background, device type, or access pattern; run counterfactual tests to ask whether the same student profile would receive the same hint sequence if their free-text explanation were terser or written in a different register. Fairness (algorithmic fairness) is not an abstraction in a statistics class; it's a living case study that the system itself can help teach by exposing anonymized audit results and inviting critique (Mitchell et al, 2021).

Content generation—especially with large language models in the loop—requires adult supervision. Automatically generated items should be validated against item banks with known psychometrics; distractors in multiple-choice questions should be plausible, not cartoonish; open-response rubrics must be transparent and, where possible, co-created. The system can even invite students to propose items after a unit, then run those suggestions through pilot testing with peers, turning assessment itself into a learning project about quality, bias, and clarity. Nothing cures cynicism about tests quite like designing one.

Table 1. Core ITS Components for Statistics Education

ITS Component	Role in statistics education	Representative features	Key risks if poorly designed
Learner model	Continuously estimates a student's mastery of core statistical concepts and procedures over time.	Bayesian knowledge tracing, deep knowledge tracing, item-response-based estimators.	Over- or under-estimates mastery, leading to boredom, confusion, or misplaced remediation.
Domain model (statistics content)	Encodes the structure of statistical ideas, skills, and misconceptions (e.g., sampling, inference, modeling).	Skill maps, concept hierarchies, tagged item banks, libraries of common misconceptions.	Misrepresents the structure of statistics and reinforces shallow procedural learning without conceptual depth.
Pedagogical model	Decides what task, hint, or explanation to present next based on learner state and pedagogical goals.	Mastery-based sequencing, hint policies, spaced retrieval timelines, adaptive challenge levels.	Over-intervenes or under-supports, collapsing productive struggle or leaving learners stuck and discouraged.
Representation & interface layer	Provides multimodal representations—formulas, graphs, simulations, and narratives—through which students interact with content.	Dynamic visualizations, interactive simulations, sandboxes, and explanation prompts.	Flattens statistics into static text or formula drills, missing chances to build intuition through visual and experiential learning.
Affective & engagement layer	Monitors behavioural signals and adapts tone, challenge, and support to reduce anxiety and sustain motivation.	Detection of frustration patterns, adaptive feedback language, encouragement and reflection prompts.	Misreads signals (e.g., pauses) and pathologises normal reflection, or ignores anxiety and disengagement entirely.
Teacher dashboard & analytics	Aggregates fine-grained data into interpretable insights that help teachers plan instruction and interventions.	Heatmaps of misconceptions, engagement trends, cohort comparison, and alert systems for at-risk students.	Overwhelms teachers with dashboards, or encourages surveillance rather than supportive, dialogic use of learner data.

One of the underrated design choices is latency. Instant feedback is celebrated, but a slight delay—half a breath—can prompt self-checks that deepen encoding. The assistant can say, "Hold your answer for 10 seconds; note one reason it might be wrong," then accept the submission. It's a tiny friction, a speed bump for meta-cognition, and it often pays for itself in error correction before the system utters a word. In a similar vein, periodic "no-help" windows—clearly labeled—invite productive struggle with the promise that any misunderstanding will be debriefed afterward with a layered explanation. Students learn that effort is not a punishment; it's the furnace where understanding is tempered.

For all the sophistication, the system should still sometimes shrug and say, "Not sure." Ambiguity is part of the discipline. A data set with missing not at random (MNAR) patterns might resist confident imputation advice; a causal question may be under-identified; a diagnostic may give mixed signals (Teegavarapu, 2024).

Rather than papering over uncertainty, the assistant can model scholarly humility: list competing approaches, note the trade-offs, and encourage justification tied to context. Students watch an expert stance in miniature and practice adopting it.

Implementation lives or dies on institutional scaffolds. Equity isn't a slogan here. Offline modes that sync later, device loans, accessible interfaces (screen reader compatibility, keyboard navigation, alt text for every visualization), multilingual glossaries aligned with domain usage—these are table stakes. Without them, the "intelligent" part of the system will simply amplify existing divides. When the basics are taken seriously, something hopeful happens: night-shift workers, commuters, and students learning in a second language start to experience statistics as attainable and even—on good days—intriguing.

Teachers remain the decisive variable. An intelligent tutor expands a classroom's surface area, but it doesn't confer purpose. Educators set norms ("Show your reasoning in words"), tell the stories that make methods matter, and name the ethical weight of seemingly technical choices (Akhter, 2025). The system's dashboards and diagnostics are instruments; teachers are the musicians. When those roles are respected, classes begin to feel different. Less triage, more inquiry. Less mystery about what went wrong, more shared language for fixing it. Students surprise themselves by becoming the kind of thinkers who can carry uncertainty without flinching and still make decisions when decisions must be made.

In the end, designing an intelligent tutoring system for complex quantitative learning is an exercise in intellectual hospitality (Yang et al, 2021). The goal isn't to outsmart students with clever hints or fence them in with surveillance-grade analytics. It's to build a place where reasoning can stretch, stumble, regroup, and finally stand on firmer ground. Numbers remain numbers—stubborn, elegant, sometimes unforgiving—but the relationship to them softens. The classroom becomes a studio for inference, not a gauntlet. And the assistant, when designed with care, keeps the air moving: less silence born of confusion, more quiet focused work punctuated by the occasional yes—that's it—when a hard idea finally clicks into place.

BALANCING HUMAN PEDAGOGY AND ALGORITHMIC GUIDANCE

There's a point in every statistics class where the room goes quiet in a particular way—the kind of quiet that isn't confusion exactly, but expectancy; students sense that the next move matters, that a definition will either unlock the path or send them in circles. In that moment, the difference between a human teacher's pause and an algorithm's prompt is not trivial. A person can hold silence with intention, sensing the mood, measuring the fragile courage of a student about to risk a partial answer;

an intelligent tutor, for all its precision, tends to fill gaps (Freire, 2025). Balancing these two dispositions—human spaciousness and algorithmic eagerness—is less a technical challenge than a pedagogical ethic. It requires asking, over and over, who should speak now and who should step back, what kind of help counts as help, and when a learner benefits more from sitting with uncertainty than from being ferried across it.

Human pedagogy is not simply warmth and anecdotes. It's a structured hospitality toward cognition: arranging tasks that feel just beyond reach, naming the logic beneath moves, locating ideas in a lineage so learners see how today's method grows out of yesterday's trouble (Kelly, 2024). Human teachers remember students in more than one dimension. Amal who writes in a second language and drafts luminous interpretations when given time; Rami who computes flawlessly but underestimates his own clarity; Lina who resists abstraction until a story pulls her in. Algorithms, on the other hand, hold a different memory—sharp, immediate, pattern-hungry. The assistant notices that a learner repeatedly mistakes standard error for standard deviation when sample sizes change, and it doesn't forget; it schedules a spaced retrieval (spaced retrieval) prompt three days later and again before the exam, with a new context to pressure-test transfer. Neither kind of memory is superior (Markham, 2021). The art is orchestration.

That orchestration begins with pacing. Teachers modulate tempo in a way that feels almost musical—accelerando during lively demonstrations, adagio when the class edges into hypothesis testing and the stakes rise because words like "significant" carry civic consequences outside the classroom (Cordovez, 2022). An intelligent system's pacing is more granular: micro-timings measured in keystrokes, dwell times, and revision loops. Designed well, those micro-signals can hand the teacher a portrait of class rhythm: a heatmap shows where attention sagged, which prompt caused collective hesitation, when fatigue set in after a long sequence of computation. Yet dashboards don't decide tone. A teacher can choose to slow the entire room, narrate a mistake, linger on a misinterpretation of confidence intervals until everyone hears the hinge click. The algorithm suggests; the human decides what matters.

Trust sits underneath the whole arrangement like bedrock—hard to see, essential for load-bearing. Students extend a different kind of trust to people than to systems. A teacher can say, "This is hard; it was hard for me, and here's where I tripped," and credibility rises, not falls. The algorithm cannot confess. It can disclose uncertainty (uncertainty disclosure): "I'm 62% confident this hint aligns with your goal," which is better than fake omniscience, yet not the same as vulnerability (Di Porto, 2023). This difference shapes consent. When students allow their clickstreams, partial attempts, and miniature essays to be analyzed for feedback, they are not consenting to a mere calculation; they are entering a compact where their data should be handled with dignity. Human teachers steward that compact; they put boundaries around collection, store only what instruction needs, and say out loud what will never be recorded. The algorithm, for its part, must earn trust by making its moves legible—no secret criteria, no invisible penalties for writing terse explanations or exploring an unusual path.

The central tension is not efficiency versus empathy; it's generalization versus particularity. Algorithms excel at detecting patterns across cohorts, across years—this misconception blossoms reliably after the sampling unit; power analysis goes sideways when base rates are lopsided; logistic regression coefficients get misread when predictors aren't centered. Teachers excel at the aberrations: the one student who has mastered mechanics but fears verbalization, the senior who distrusts any "black box" and needs a philosophical bridge, the pair whose collaborative rhythm hides that one person never touches the keyboard. Both vantage points are indispensable. An intelligent tutor that flags cohort-wide drift can free the teacher to spend time on the outliers; a teacher who names a non-technical barrier can program the system to back off in targeted ways—fewer interruptions, more space for drafting, optional visual-first modes for learners who think in pictures before formulas.

Figure 3. Illustrative Trajectories of Conceptual Mastery and Student Agency Across Levels of AI Integration in Statistics Education

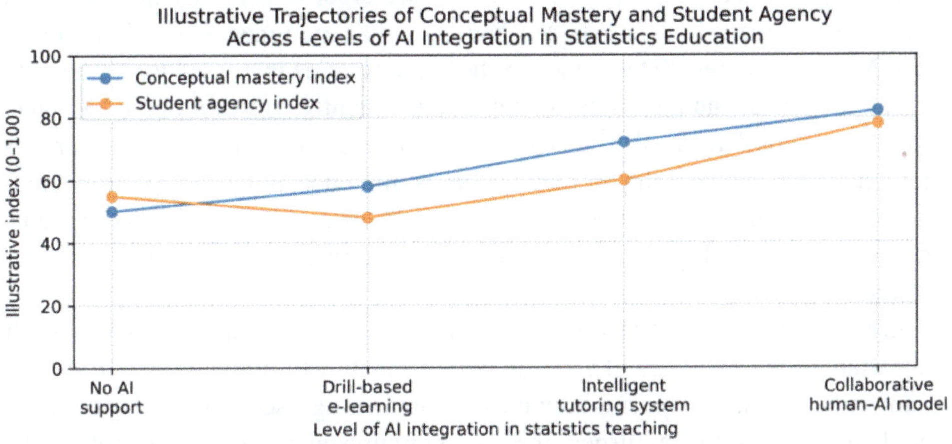

Feedback is where coordination either sings or sours. Algorithmic feedback is fast, tireless, and often right about local issues: a missing minus sign, a mistaken unit, an off-by-one error in an index. Human feedback is scarcer and strangely powerful; a single comment—"Your interpretation shows judgment, not just calculation, and that's the point of the method"—can change how a student approaches the rest of the term (Ananny, 2022). Striking the balance suggests a division of labor: let the system own the micro-corrections and the scheduling of retrieval, while the teacher owns the meaning-making and the cultivation of standards. A short rubric written by the class—"What makes an interpretation convincing?"—can be encoded as prompts the assistant deploys when students submit explanations, not as a score but as a mirror: "Have you named assumptions? Stated uncertainty? Addressed counter-interpretations?" The machine becomes a keeper of communal norms, not an umpire banging a gavel.

Another balance worth guarding concerns struggle. Productive struggle (productive cognitive struggle) is the engine of durable knowledge; unproductive struggle is a slow leak of motivation (Luby, 2022). An assistant will be tempted—chiefly because it can—to shorten every struggle. Yet some knots deserve time. When encountering Simpson's paradox for the first time, students benefit from wrestling with bafflement, because the resolution reorders intuition about conditioning and fairness. Here, design can force restraint: timed "no-hint" windows; a sequence that escalates from question framing to strategy cues before releasing any stepwise solution; reflective prompts inserted between attempts ("Name one reason your first strategy might be misleading"). Human teachers can stage the mood around this: call it a lab, not a test; invite speculation; foreground the idea that puzzlement is not a deficit but a sign that one's preconceptions are being renegotiated.

Language is another arena where human and algorithm must learn to dance. Statistics wears many dialects: terse algebra, visual grammar, story (Babu et al, 2023). A student writes, "The model predicts that salaries increase by 3 with every year of experience," and an assistant can nudge—gently—toward units: "3 what? dollars, thousands?" It can also catch hedging that smuggles certainty: "This proves that…" in contexts where the correct posture is inference, not proof. Yet tone matters. A teacher senses when precision policing stifles expression; the system must learn a similar tact—flag with suggestions, not citations; offer rewrites as optional, not mandatory.

Fairness in recommendation is where ethical rhetoric becomes engineering. If the assistant proposes remedial drills disproportionately to students writing shorter explanations, and those students happen to be navigating a second language or have limited time, the system has turned a proxy for circumstance into a marker of ability. Audits are mandatory. Teachers, not just vendors, must examine who gets which hints, how often, with what downstream effects. Counterfactual testing should be routine: feed two equivalent solution paths with different surface features—verbosity, order of operations, use of simulation versus closed-form—and confirm that recommendations remain consistent. When discrepancies surface, the fix is not merely technical; it includes explicit classroom conversations about algorithmic fairness (algorithmic fairness), with students invited to critique the very tool they use (Wang et al, 2022). Nothing matures statistical literacy like interrogating a live system with the same skepticism we ask them to bring to published models.

Assessment under the new regime benefits from plurality. An intelligent tutor can generate a stream of low-stakes checks, spotting conceptual slippage long before a midterm. But true balance means preserving spaces where a human reads a messy, thoughtful analysis and hears a voice. Oral defenses of small projects, quick whiteboard debates about model choice, reflective memos that narrate decision points—these are formats where nuance breathes. The machine can prep the ground—collating common confusions, picking representative cases—while the teacher adjudicates with human criteria: fairness, clarity, intellectual honesty. Grades are less the star than growth. A student moves from "Because R said so" to "Given heteroskedastic residuals and the goal of interpretability, we pivoted to robust standard errors and reported the sensitivity of conclusions to that choice," and everyone in the room hears the step change.

Table 2. Human Pedagogy, Algorithmic Guidance, and Collaborative Models

Dimension	Human pedagogy emphasised	Algorithmic guidance emphasised	Collaborative human–AI model
Pacing of instruction	Teacher adjusts tempo based on reading the room and individual histories.	Fine-grained pacing tuned to keystrokes, dwell time, and error patterns.	System surfaces pacing data; teacher uses it to fine-tune whole-class and individual tempo.
Feedback style and timing	Feedback is often slower but can be rich, narrative, and personally contextualised.	Instant, granular feedback on correctness, structure, and low-level misconceptions.	AI handles micro-corrections; teacher focuses on meaning-making, reasoning quality, and encouragement.
Design of productive struggle	Teachers intentionally hold silence and allow confusion to surface before intervening.	Automatic hints after a threshold of errors or inactivity, often with stepwise scaffolding.	Designers encode no-hint windows and reflection prompts; teacher frames struggle as intellectually valuable.
Context and authenticity of tasks	Examples are chosen to resonate with local cultures, disciplines, and lived experiences.	Pre-built, generic scenarios and datasets that scale across many institutions.	Teachers seed the system with locally relevant datasets and narratives that the AI reuses at scale.
Equity and access	Teachers advocate for devices, flexible modes, and human support for underserved learners.	Access shaped by infrastructure, licensing, and default design assumptions.	Institutions invest in infrastructure; teachers and students co-design policies for inclusive use.
Use of learner data	Data use is negotiated in class; teachers model ethical judgment about what should be tracked.	Large-scale logging and analysis of behaviour, often opaque to learners.	System makes its logic visible; teachers and students audit and debate data practices together.

continued on following page

Table 2. Continued

Dimension	Human pedagogy emphasised	Algorithmic guidance emphasised	Collaborative human–AI model
Assessment emphasis	Greater weight on open-ended projects, discussions, and interpretive writing.	High volume of low-stakes checks and mastery estimates across micro-skills.	Continuous formative analytics support richer human-designed summative tasks and oral defenses.
Trust and relational climate	Trust built through vulnerability, humour, shared stories, and visible care.	Trust tied to perceived accuracy and consistency of system recommendations.	Students see both teacher and system as accountable partners; disagreements are discussed openly as part of learning.

Cultural responsiveness deserves more than a paragraph tucked at the end. Statistics is not content-neutral; examples carry values (McCall, 2024). An assistant trained on generic corpora may default to datasets with cultural references that ring hollow for some students, or worse, to case studies that replicate stereotypes. Human pedagogy counters by curating contexts that matter locally: water usage in nearby districts, public transit delays that students actually experience, regional health surveys. Better yet, the system can be seeded with a teacher's dataset library and told to prioritize those; it can invite students to submit data stories from their communities and then scaffold analyses around them. Agency rises. Learners stop treating methods as hoops and start seeing them as tools to interrogate the world they inhabit.

We shouldn't forget the body in the room. Presence changes interpretation. A raised eyebrow can say, "Are you sure about that causal claim?" without humiliation. A teacher can read restlessness and decide to switch posture: stand, move, draw a diagram by hand, let the chalk squeak. Algorithms do not squeak. They hum, quietly, behind screens. That hum is powerful, but it misses the micro-rituals that compose classroom life: the way a shared laugh lowers the barrier to asking the "stupid" question; the way a minute of silence before revealing the bootstrap distribution invites everyone to imagine its shape. Balance means protecting those rituals from colonization by convenience.

Guardrails help, and they must be written down. A living "use policy," co-authored with students, can codify: when the assistant may give direct solutions (end-of-sequence mastery checks), when it must refrain (initial encounters with a big idea), what kind of data it collects, how long it keeps it, and what rights students have to view and delete their traces. Clear red lines: no surveillance beyond learning purpose, no behavioral scoring dressed up as analytics, no secret grading by machine. The presence of such rules is itself pedagogical; it teaches that technologies are governed, not given.

The workload question lurks nearby, a practical reality. Teachers already carry heavy plates; adding orchestration can feel like piling on. Balance here is merciful: start small. One unit with the assistant deeply integrated; one practice of weekly retrieval; one reflective prompt repeated until it becomes part of the course's heartbeat (Anderson, 2024). Let the system carry rote burdens—versioned practice sets, instant checkers, appointment scheduling—while teachers invest saved time in comments that only a person can write. Across a term, the trade begins to show. Less triage. More design.

If the measure of good balance is student agency, the signs are visible. Learners begin to ask better questions—not "Is this right?" but "Under what assumptions would this be defensible?" They use the assistant tactically, not compulsively: "Hide hints for now," "Show me a visualization," "Schedule a resurface in three days." They defend model choices to peers; they critique the system's recommendations with evidence; they see mistakes as information, not identity. Teachers, for their part, feel less like air-traffic controllers and more like mentors, less like graders of minutiae and more like cultivators of judgment. The algorithm becomes part of the furniture—useful, often elegant, occasionally annoying—but never the room itself.

There will be missteps. A hint arrives too early and short-circuits an insight. A model recommendation reflects bias from its training data (Zou et al, 2025). A dashboard measure seduces attention away from the difficult-to-quantify, like interpretive grace or ethical imagination. Balance forbids denial. Acknowledge, adjust, show the change. Let students see the patch notes. When the learning community watches a tool evolve in response to critique, confidence grows that the partnership is real.

In statistics, perhaps more than elsewhere, pedagogy is a stance toward uncertainty. Human teachers teach that stance with their faces and choices. Algorithms can support it by making patterns visible, by catching slippage before it hardens, by holding memory across a semester longer than any one person reasonably could. The balance we are after is not a 50–50 split so much as a covenant: the machine will be clear, patient, and bounded; the human will be present, brave, and generous. Between them, the classroom becomes a place where precision doesn't suffocate curiosity, where help doesn't erase struggle, and where students learn to carry risk with care—exactly the posture statistics demands when it meets the world.

CHALLENGES OF TRUST, EQUITY, AND PEDAGOGICAL INTEGRITY

Trust, once eroded in a classroom, is hard to recover (Lewicka, 2022). The arrival of algorithmic systems in statistics education unsettles trust in multiple directions at once: between students and their teachers, between teachers and the technology they are asked to rely upon, and between learners and the black-box machinery that interprets their keystrokes as signals of understanding or confusion. It is not paranoia to ask whether the system is truly "on your side." A student wonders if the data collected about them—the wrong answers, the hesitation before clicking, the poorly phrased explanation—will become evidence against their ability rather than evidence for what kind of help they need. A teacher wonders whether their role is being quietly diluted, reduced to an overseer of dashboards while the real instructional labor happens invisibly, line by line, in an algorithmic dialogue. These worries are not trivial side effects; they cut to the bone of educational integrity.

Building trust begins with transparency. Students deserve to know what is captured, how it is stored, and when it is discarded (Romano, 2024). But transparency, on its own, can feel clinical—like reading the small print on a contract. More powerful is intelligibility: a system that not only offers feedback but explains why it made a particular suggestion, what features in the student's work triggered its response, and how confident it is in that move. Without intelligibility, every nudge risks being read as arbitrary, every correction as a judgment handed down from nowhere. If the assistant tells a student, "Consider a nonparametric test," it must show the visual evidence—the skewed distribution, the failure of residuals to align with assumptions. Trust grows not from authority but from justification that feels both legible and fair.

Equity sits beside trust as its necessary sibling. Intelligent tutoring systems promise personalization, but personalization can quickly turn into stratification if access is uneven (Shoukat et al, 2025). Students with reliable devices, steady connectivity, and quiet spaces will reap more benefits than those working on old hardware, in crowded homes, or in languages that the system does not fully support. An equitable design must begin with infrastructure: offline modes, compatibility with assistive technologies, multilingual glossaries, and institutional provision of devices. But equity is not only about hardware; it is also about cultural responsiveness. The datasets and scenarios used to illustrate statistical principles must resonate with the lives of the learners. Otherwise, students learn that statistics belongs to someone else's world.

Consider a student in Damascus encountering a problem set built around American baseball statistics. The formulas translate fine; the cultural frame does not. Context matters. Equity in pedagogy means allowing teachers to seed the system with locally relevant data—water usage, regional climate shifts, neighborhood health surveys—so that the mathematics feels connected rather than transplanted (Roderick, 2023). When the examples carry meaning, students no longer experience statistics as a foreign tongue but as a dialect they can speak to describe their own world. Intelligent systems should amplify, not flatten, this cultural particularity.

Pedagogical integrity is perhaps the hardest challenge to name, because it lives in the fragile moments of instruction that often go unnoticed. Integrity is not only about avoiding shortcuts or resisting automation; it is about preserving the spirit of learning as a human encounter with difficulty, wonder, and doubt. If the assistant always provides the answer after two failed attempts, it risks teaching students that struggle is a defect to be eliminated. Yet any educator knows that some of the most durable learning emerges from the irritation of not-knowing, from sitting with a paradox until the pieces rearrange themselves into clarity. A system that interrupts too quickly violates pedagogical integrity by erasing the very texture of learning.

But there is an opposite danger too: if the assistant withholds support in the name of rigor, learners may disengage altogether, reading the silence as indifference. Balancing timely help with the value of productive struggle requires design decisions that are, in truth, pedagogical decisions wearing technological clothing. How long should the system wait before intervening? What counts as evidence of genuine effort? How should hints be sequenced so they lead toward insight without converting the task into paint-by-numbers? These questions are not technical puzzles alone; they are ethical commitments about what it means to respect the learner as an agent rather than a subject.

Teachers themselves live within this balancing act. Pedagogical integrity asks them not to outsource their judgment but to let technology extend it (Gallant & Rettinger, 2025). An intelligent system can map misconceptions across a cohort, showing that twenty students misapplied the central limit theorem in similar ways. That map is useful, but the teacher must still decide how to address it—whether to reteach with a new visualization, whether to let students debate the misinterpretation in small groups, whether to highlight the historical story of how statisticians themselves grappled with the same confusion. Integrity lies in refusing to let the map become the lesson, in using the data as a guide but keeping the pedagogy human.

There is also the matter of surveillance. Students can feel that every hesitation is being recorded, every misstep logged (Warner, 2025). This can easily shift the classroom atmosphere from experimentation to self-censorship. Who wants to try a bold strategy if it might be misread by an algorithm as incompetence? To guard against this, systems must embed opportunities for "safe failure"—spaces where students can work without permanent recording, or where they can delete attempts that were exploratory rather than performative. Without such zones, the promise of personalization may be bought at the price of intellectual risk-taking, and that is too high a cost.

The challenges multiply when considering bias. Algorithms trained on historical data often carry forward the inequities baked into those datasets (Jackson, 2021). A tutoring system might subtly offer more remedial tasks to students whose written explanations are shorter, even if those explanations are concise rather than confused. If those students happen to be navigating in a second language, bias masquerades as personalization. Teachers need access to the audit trail: what rules are being applied, what signals are driving interventions, and whether outcomes vary across demographic lines. Without auditing, bias remains invisible; without teacher oversight, it remains uncorrected. Equity in this sense demands vigilance, not trust.

A further complication arises around authority. Who holds the pedagogical voice when system and teacher disagree? If the algorithm insists on a nonparametric method while the teacher is deliberately pushing students to wrestle with parametric assumptions, confusion is inevitable. Students may not know which voice to trust. Pedagogical integrity requires that teachers remain the final authority, and systems must be designed to defer when contradictions appear. Better yet, the system can surface its recommendation as a suggestion, annotated with rationale, and then prompt the teacher to either endorse or override it in public view. That way, disagreement itself becomes a learning opportunity: students see that statistics, like pedagogy, is full of judgment calls, trade-offs, and debates rather than rigid rules.

The emotional texture of trust and equity should not be underestimated. Statistics has long carried a reputation as cold, abstract, intimidating. Intelligent tutoring systems risk amplifying this reputation if they come across as mechanical overseers. A well-designed system, however, can humanize statistics by lowering the stakes of error (Sajadi, 2024). Feedback can be framed as encouragement rather than verdict: "Many learners confuse these terms; let's try a visualization." The language matters. A phrase of empathy, even if generated by code, can change the affective climate of learning. But empathy must not be faked; systems that pretend to care when they cannot will quickly be unmasked. Pedagogical integrity lies in honesty: the system is not your friend, but it can be your ally.

Equity, finally, is not only about distribution of resources but about voice. Students should be invited to critique the system, to say when hints are unhelpful, when examples feel alien, when explanations confuse rather than clarify. That feedback should not vanish into a black hole; it should shape updates and modifications. In this way, students become co-designers of their learning environment, not passive recipients of someone else's pedagogical imagination. Such involvement deepens trust and models the very democratic spirit that statistics education ought to foster: decisions are evidence-based, but evidence is open to interpretation and revision.

The classroom where trust, equity, and integrity are pursued together feels different (Banwo et al, 2022). Students ask sharper questions, not "Is this right?" but "What does right mean here, given these assumptions?" Teachers worry less about being replaced and more about being amplified. Technology operates less like a secret judge and more like a transparent collaborator (George, 2024). And the subject itself—statistics, with all its abstractions and formulas—feels less like an obstacle course and more like a language for making sense of the world. Yet this is not an automatic outcome; it is the fragile product of careful choices, vigilance against bias, humility in design, and the courage to keep pedagogy human in an age enamored of algorithms.

To teach statistics with integrity in the company of intelligent tutors is to recognize that education is never just about answers. It is about cultivating judgment, skepticism, resilience, and a willingness to live with uncertainty. Machines can assist with some of this work, but they cannot carry the weight of trust, equity, or integrity alone. That responsibility remains in human hands (Mann, 2024). And perhaps that is how it should be.

TOWARD A FUTURE OF COLLABORATIVE HUMAN–AI TEACHING MODELS

The idea of collaboration between humans and machines in education has too often been framed in combative terms—replacement, competition, substitution (Monett & Paquet, 2025). It's a tired dichotomy, one that misses the more interesting horizon where human imagination and algorithmic capacity entangle in productive ways. The classroom of the future doesn't need to look like a battleground where one intelligence drives out the other; it can feel more like an ensemble, a shared rehearsal where each participant brings something indispensable. Human teachers carry intuition, empathy, narrative sense, and a capacity for improvisation that comes from living lives full of error and meaning. Machines carry memory at scale, patience that never frays, and the ability to crunch through probabilistic patterns at speeds the human mind cannot fathom. If education is to be both humane and effective in a world ruled by data, the challenge is not which voice wins but how to build a polyphony.

Statistics classrooms provide a telling stage for this future. They are messy, full of concepts that resist simple intuition—variance, confidence, likelihood, causality (Gatete, 2025). They require drill, yes, but also moments of conceptual unfreezing, those sudden shifts when a learner realizes that randomness is not noise but structure, that inference is less about certitude than about disciplined humility. Machines can handle the drill without boredom; teachers can handle the unfreezing with stories, with pauses, with the sideways gesture that says "look again." Collaborative models would not ask who owns the teaching but how the two kinds of intelligence share the load without suffocating each other.

One can imagine a scenario: a student, late at night, works through a dataset on hospital readmissions. The AI tutor notices repeated misinterpretation of odds ratios (Kim et al, 2022). Instead of simply correcting, it stages a tiny simulation—patients moving through bins of readmission and non-readmission, odds recalculated visually with every shuffle. The system then marks the misconception as "open" and prompts the teacher the next day with a gentle alert: three students tripped on odds ratios, perhaps design a collective intervention. The teacher takes this not as surveillance but as insight; during class, she tells a story of how misinterpretation of odds once distorted a public health policy, making clear that statistics is never just arithmetic but consequence. Together, the AI and the human have turned an error into a loop that connects practice, visualization, and ethical stakes. Neither could have done this alone.

Yet collaboration is not simply co-presence; it's negotiation of authority. Students are quick to pick up on contradictions. If the machine says one thing and the teacher another, trust can fray. The future demands explicit choreography. Machines must learn deference: to present recommendations as provisional, to acknowledge uncertainty, to signal when the final word rests with the human. Teachers, in turn, must practice a kind of humility: to accept when the system has surfaced a pattern they overlooked, to recognize that no human, however skilled, can track the micro-data of thirty learners simultaneously (Willis, 2023). Integrity comes from owning the partnership openly—telling students, "The system flagged a misconception, but I want us to examine it together and decide if it really holds." Transparency is not weakness; it is pedagogy.

The most exciting possibilities emerge when collaboration generates new pedagogical forms rather than simply accelerating the old. Imagine seminars where students debate not only the result of an analysis but the logic of the AI that offered feedback (Lee, 2023). They might critique the hint generation system, asking whether its interventions are fair or biased. They might re-train it with their own examples, seeding local datasets into the learning environment. In such classrooms, the line between tool-user and tool-designer blurs, and students begin to see statistical reasoning not only as computation but as an act of shaping systems of judgment. This meta-level awareness is crucial; the world students are entering will not only demand that they use models but that they evaluate, contest, and sometimes resist them.

Equity remains the nagging test of any vision. If collaborative human–AI models are available only to institutions with strong infrastructure, we risk creating an elite pedagogy for the few while leaving others with thin, mechanized versions (Sarkar, 2025). The very idea of collaboration collapses when access is uneven. A future worth working toward would ensure baseline provisions: devices on loan, bandwidth support, offline functionality, and the possibility of multimodal interaction for learners who think and express differently. Collaboration without equity is exploitation disguised as innovation. To keep integrity intact, educators and policymakers will need to insist that the tools are not mere imports from elsewhere but co-developed with local needs, languages, and cultural frames in mind.

Another tension is the role of failure. Machines like to tidy things up; they are built to minimize error. Humans, however, often learn most deeply from the sting of mistakes. A future of collaboration must design failure back into the process. AI tutors could withhold immediate correction, encouraging students to argue with their own misconceptions or compare answers with peers before a resolution is given (Shah, 2023). Teachers can then step in, not to sweep the errors away but to narrate them, to show how even experts misinterpret and recalibrate. In this model, the machine's precision and the human's fallibility combine not in contradiction but in complement: precision prevents errors from calcifying into habits, while fallibility teaches that imperfection is the ground of understanding.

The question of presence lingers. Teachers are bodies in a room, with voices that crack, eyes that wander, pauses that hold more meaning than any feedback button. AI tutors are disembodied, though some are wrapped in chat interfaces that mimic conversation. Collaboration does not require machines to fake humanity; it requires them to respect the distinctiveness of human presence (Cañas, 2022). The system can hum in the background, surfacing insights, suggesting tasks, visualizing data patterns, but it must leave space for the teacher to do the things only a human can: to comfort, to provoke, to connect learning with lived experience. The worst future would be one where human presence is hollowed out into proctoring, where the classroom becomes a showroom for algorithmic products. The better path insists that human warmth and machine sharpness remain distinct yet entangled.

Assessment, too, will need reimagining under collaboration. Machines are excellent at continuous formative checks, but summative judgments should never be ceded fully to code. The future will likely be hybrid: AI offering diagnostic maps, identifying weak spots, and predicting readiness, while teachers design authentic tasks—projects, presentations, debates—where human judgment about clarity, originality, and ethical awareness is decisive (George, 2023). Students deserve to be seen as whole people, not merely as statistical profiles of performance probabilities. Only human teachers can perceive that wholeness, but only machines can manage the day-to-day granularity of practice at scale. The partnership holds precisely because each side sees what the other cannot.

Looking ahead, one can imagine classrooms that feel less hierarchical, more like ecosystems. A teacher guides, a system supports, students contribute to the design of their own learning tools (Kim et al, 2022). Mistakes become data, but also stories. Interventions become suggestions, not verdicts. The rhythm alternates between the fast twitch of algorithmic feedback and the slow stretch of human reflection. Equity is guarded not by rhetoric but by deliberate structural choices. Pedagogical integrity is defended every time a teacher chooses to leave a silence open rather than letting a machine fill it.

Skeptics will ask: isn't this idealistic? Won't economic pressures push schools toward machine-heavy, human-light models, simply because they're cheaper? That risk is real, and perhaps inevitable in some contexts. But collaboration is not a default—it is a stance. It requires educators to argue, sometimes stubbornly, that teaching is not merely transmission but relationship, and that no machine can replace the alchemy of a well-timed story, a raised eyebrow, or a teacher admitting that even experts get confused. Collaborative models survive only if humans insist that their role is not ornamental but essential.

The future of human–AI teaching models is not utopian, nor is it dystopian (Longo, 2024). It is a field of tension, a set of choices, a continuing argument about what counts as education and who gets to shape it. Statistics, with its demand for rigor and its dance with uncertainty, offers a fitting proving ground. If collaboration can work there—if teachers and algorithms can together cultivate learners who are precise but not rigid, skeptical but not cynical, curious yet cautious—then perhaps it can work across the wider landscape of education.

The horizon is open. What is needed now is less talk of substitution and more practice of co-creation, less fixation on efficiency and more attention to meaning, less fear that machines will hollow out pedagogy and more resolve to craft pedagogies that harness what machines do well without forgetting what only humans can do. A collaborative future is not about balance in the sense of equal halves, but about complementarity: the joining of fallible, creative, embodied human beings with tireless, pattern-seeking, disembodied systems in the shared labor of helping students learn how to think in a world that will demand nothing less.

CONCLUSION

As we arrive at the close of this chapter, the central theme emerges with greater clarity: artificial intelligence as a teaching assistant in statistics education is neither a panacea nor a passing trend. It is, instead, an evolving companion to pedagogy—capable of amplifying human effort, accelerating personalized learning, and making statistical reasoning more approachable, yet also capable of unsettling established norms and raising profound ethical questions. The duality is inescapable, but it is also what makes this moment historically significant.

Intelligent tutoring systems demonstrate extraordinary capacity for adaptability. They can adjust explanations to the learner's pace, generate multiple representations of a problem, and offer feedback that might otherwise take a teacher days to provide. For students who struggle with foundational concepts, such systems can provide a bridge between confusion and understanding, offering second chances without stigma and repetition without judgment. For advanced learners, AI can create simulations, datasets, and visualizations that deepen engagement, extending beyond textbook exercises into exploratory learning. In these ways, AI is not just a tool but a pedagogical actor, shaping the rhythms of the classroom and the trajectory of students' intellectual growth.

Yet, to celebrate this potential without acknowledging the risks would be disingenuous. Overreliance on AI can inadvertently foster dependency, where students lean too heavily on machine-generated hints rather than grappling with uncertainty themselves. The risk of inequity also looms large: in contexts where access to reliable digital infrastructure is limited, the promise of intelligent tutoring systems may widen rather than narrow educational divides. Teachers, too, may experience unease—fearing that their expertise is being overshadowed, or that their professional identity is being subtly reshaped by algorithmic companions. The challenge is not only technical but existential: what does it mean to teach, to mentor, to inspire, in an age where machines can simulate aspects of those roles?

The conclusion, then, is not that AI should be embraced uncritically, nor that it should be resisted with suspicion, but that it should be engaged with deliberately. The task ahead for educators, policymakers, and developers is to craft frameworks that ensure AI's role remains supportive rather than substitutive. That means designing systems with transparency, embedding opportunities for reflection, and ensuring that human teachers retain their irreplaceable role as interpreters of meaning and cultivators of judgment.

For statistics education, the stakes are especially high. The discipline is foundational to how societies understand risk, interpret evidence, and make decisions in a world awash with data. If AI can help students not only calculate more efficiently but also reason more critically, it will strengthen the very fabric of democratic life and professional competence. But if it reduces statistical thinking to a sequence of automated prompts and shallow interactions, it risks producing learners who can perform procedures but cannot understand their implications.

The vision that emerges is one of partnership. AI as a teaching assistant is most powerful when it frees teachers from mechanical tasks so they can focus on the uniquely human work of mentorship, empathy, and inspiration. It is most valuable when it democratizes access to quality tutoring, giving every student the chance to receive tailored guidance. It is most transformative when it fosters collaboration—between student and machine, between teacher and technology, and ultimately, between knowledge and society.

As educators, we stand at a threshold. The classroom of the near future will not look like the classroom of the past. Screens, simulations, and intelligent systems will be present, often invisibly, shaping how students encounter knowledge. The question is whether we will guide this transformation with intentionality or allow it to unfold haphazardly. The future of statistics education—and, by extension, the cultivation of data-literate citizens—depends on making that choice wisely.

In closing, one might say that the ultimate measure of success for AI in statistics education is not how well it can replicate a teacher's voice, but how effectively it can help students find their own. If intelligent tutoring systems can be harnessed to encourage curiosity, foster resilience, and deepen statistical reasoning, then they will indeed have earned their place in the pedagogical landscape. If not, they risk becoming another layer of noise in an already noisy educational environment. The responsibility rests with us—not the machines—to decide which of these futures becomes reality.

REFERENCES

Akhter, E. (2025). AI IN THE CLASSROOM: EVALUATING THE EFFECTIVENESS OF INTELLIGENT TUTORING SYSTEMS FOR MULTILINGUAL LEARNERS IN SECONDARY EDUCATION. ASRC Procedia. *Global Perspectives in Science and Scholarship*, *1*(01), 532–563. DOI: 10.63125/gcq1qr39

Ananny, M. (2022). Seeing like an Algorithmic Error: What Are Algorithmic Mistakes, Why Do They Matter, How Might They Be Public Problem? *Yale JL & Tech.*, *24*, 342.

Anderson, M. (2024). *Rekindle Your Professional Fire: Powerful Habits for Becoming a More Well-balanced Teacher*. ASCD.

Babu, K. S., Nagaraju, M. V., & Johnson, G. (2023). *Mathematics in everyday life: The hidden language of the world*. Shineeks Publishers.

Banwo, B. O., Khalifa, M., & Seashore Louis, K. (2022). Exploring trust: Culturally responsive and positive school leadership. *Journal of Educational Administration*, *60*(3), 323–339. DOI: 10.1108/JEA-03-2021-0065

Cañas, J. J. (2022). AI and ethics when human beings collaborate with AI agents. *Frontiers in Psychology*, *13*, 836650. DOI: 10.3389/fpsyg.2022.836650 PMID: 35310226

Cordovez, E. M. (2022). Teaching and Learning Music Technologically.

Desir, S. W., Jr. (2024). High School Acceleration and First-Year College Student Success: Do Advanced Placement or Dual Enrollment Influence College Persistence Differently (Doctoral dissertation, University of South Florida).

Di Porto, F. (2023). Algorithmic disclosure rules. *Artificial Intelligence and Law*, *31*(1), 13–51. DOI: 10.1007/s10506-021-09302-7

Dvir, M., & Ben-Zvi, D. (2023). Fostering students' informal quantitative estimations of uncertainty through statistical modeling. *Instructional Science*, *51*(3), 423–450. DOI: 10.1007/s11251-023-09622-y

Erduran Tekin, Ö. (2024). Academic self-discipline as a mediating variable in the relationship between social media addiction and academic achievement: Mixed methodology. *Humanities & Social Sciences Communications*, *11*(1), 1–9. DOI: 10.1057/s41599-024-03633-x

Freire, P. (2025). *Pedagogy of freedom: Ethics, democracy, and civic courage*. Bloomsbury Publishing USA.

Gallant, T. B., & Rettinger, D. A. (2025). *The Opposite of Cheating: Teaching for Integrity in the Age of AI* (Vol. 4). University of Oklahoma Press.

Gatete, D. O. (2025). Statistics: The Art and Science of Learning from Data. *International Journal of Research and Innovation in Social Science*, *9*(7), 285–301. DOI: 10.47772/IJRISS.2025.90700021

George, A. S. (2023). Preparing students for an AI-driven world: Rethinking curriculum and pedagogy in the age of artificial intelligence. *Partners Universal Innovative Research Publication*, *1*(2), 112–136.

George, A. S. (2024). Technology Tension in Schools: Addressing the Complex Impacts of Digital Advances on Teaching, Learning, and Wellbeing. [PUMRJ]. *Partners Universal Multidisciplinary Research Journal*, *1*(3), 49–65.

Heath, M., Asim, S., Milman, N., & Henderson, J. (2022). Confronting tools of the oppressor: Framing just technology integration in educational technology and teacher education. *Contemporary Issues in Technology & Teacher Education*, *22*(4), 754–777.

Hossain, M. E., & Islam, M. A. (2024). AI and the Future of Education: Philosophical Questions about the Role of Artificial Intelligence in the Classroom. *International Journal of Research and Innovation in Social Science*, *8*(IIIS, 3s), 5541–5547. DOI: 10.47772/IJRISS.2024.803419S

Jackson, M. C. (2021). Artificial intelligence & algorithmic bias: The issues with technology reflecting history & humans. j. Bus. &. *Tech. l.*, *16*, 299.

Javed, T., & O'Brien, A. (2024). Teaching Together: A Cross-Cultural Analysis of Graduate Teaching Assistant Experiences and Pedagogy. Postgraduate Pedagogies, 4(1).

Joque, J. (2022). *Revolutionary mathematics: Artificial intelligence, statistics and the logic of capitalism.* Verso Books.

Kelly, A. N. (2024). Whole Human Pedagogy: A Novel Framework for Education Abroad Praxis.

Kim, J., Lee, H., & Cho, Y. H. (2022). Learning design to support student-AI collaboration: Perspectives of leading teachers for AI in education. *Education and Information Technologies*, *27*(5), 6069–6104. DOI: 10.1007/s10639-021-10831-6

Kim, J. H., Kim, M., Kwak, D. W., & Lee, S. (2022). Home-tutoring services assisted with technology: Investigating the role of artificial intelligence using a randomized field experiment. *JMR, Journal of Marketing Research*, *59*(1), 79–96. DOI: 10.1177/00222437211050351

Lakens, D. (2021). The practical alternative to the p value is the correctly used p value. *Perspectives on Psychological Science : A Journal of the Association for Psychological Science*, *16*(3), 639–648. DOI: 10.1177/1745691620958012 PMID: 33560174

Lee, A. V. Y. (2023). Supporting students' generation of feedback in large-scale online course with artificial intelligence-enabled evaluation. *Studies in Educational Evaluation*, *77*, 101250. DOI: 10.1016/j.stueduc.2023.101250

Lewicka, D. (2022). Building and rebuilding trust in higher education institutions (HEIs). Student's perspective. *Journal of Organizational Change Management*, *35*(6), 887–915. DOI: 10.1108/JOCM-02-2022-0037

Longo, A. (2024). The dystopian threat of AI in primary education. School Children and the Challenge of Managing AI Technologies, 47.

Luby, K. E. (2022). Strategies for Teachers that Reduce Anxiety and Promote Productive Struggle for Students in Secondary Mathematics Classes (Doctoral dissertation, Northeastern University).

Mann, H. (2024). *Artificial Integrity: The paths to leading AI toward a human-centered future*. John Wiley & Sons.

Markham, A. (2021). The limits of the imaginary: Challenges to intervening in future speculations of memory, data, and algorithms. *New Media & Society*, *23*(2), 382–405. DOI: 10.1177/1461444820929322

McCaffery-Pomerleau, K. A. (2024). Unlocking the Power of Co-Collaboration: The Impact of Educator Involvement in Educational Technology Development (Doctoral dissertation, Northeastern University).

McCall, S. A. (2024). *A Troubling Inheritance: Reworking Problematic Curricula*. Rowman & Littlefield. DOI: 10.5040/9798216431817

Mitchell, S., Potash, E., Barocas, S., D'Amour, A., & Lum, K. (2021). Algorithmic fairness: Choices, assumptions, and definitions. *Annual Review of Statistics and Its Application*, *8*(1), 141–163. DOI: 10.1146/annurev-statistics-042720-125902

Monett, D., & Paquet, G. (2025). Against the Commodification of Education—If harms then not AI. *Journal of Open, Distance, and Digital Education*, *2*(1).

Roderick, T. (2023). *Teach for climate justice: A vision for transforming education*. Harvard Education Press.

Romano, L. (2024). *The Transparency Problem in Higher Education Administration: Using a Grounded Theory to Create a Model for Rebuilding Trust*. St. John's University.

Sajadi, A. (2024). Optimizing Data Input Interfaces Through User Error Analysis: A Statistical and HCI-Driven Approach. *International Journal of Advanced Human Computer Interaction*, *2*(2), 67–77.

Šarić-Grgić, I., Grubišić, A., & Gašpar, A. (2024). Twenty-Five Years of Bayesian knowledge tracing: A systematic review. *User Modeling and User-Adapted Interaction*, *34*(4), 1127–1173. DOI: 10.1007/s11257-023-09389-4

Sarkar, A. (2025). Bridging the Divide: A Systems Thinking Approach to Inclusivity in AI Development and Education. Available at *SSRN* 5097669. DOI: 10.2139/ssrn.5097669

Shah, P. (2023). *AI and the Future of Education: Teaching in the Age of Artificial Intelligence*. John Wiley & Sons.

Shoukat, W., Rizwan, N., & Khan, M. T. (2025). The role of artificial intelligence (AI) tutors in personalized learning: Benefits and challenges. *Journal of Social Signs Review*, *3*(4), 1–13.

Suzuki, W. (2021). *Good Anxiety: Harnessing the Power of the Most Misunderstood Emotion*. Simon and Schuster.

Teegavarapu, R. S. (2024). *Imputation Methods for Missing Hydrometeorological Data Estimation*. Springer International Publishing AG. DOI: 10.1007/978-3-031-60946-6

Wang, X., Zhang, Y., & Zhu, R. (2022). A brief review on algorithmic fairness. *Management System Engineering*, *1*(1), 7. DOI: 10.1007/s44176-022-00006-z

Warner, B. (2025). *Edtech for Multilingual Learners: 48 Fun and Flexible Activities for Every Classroom*. ASCD.

Willis, A. S. (2023). Teachers' cultural, social and emotional capabilities: How teacher compassion and humility is an antecedent to student confidence. *Pedagogy, Culture & Society*, *31*(1), 91–108. DOI: 10.1080/14681366.2021.1884122

Yang, C., Chiang, F. K., Cheng, Q., & Ji, J. (2021). Machine learning-based student modeling methodology for intelligent tutoring systems. *Journal of Educational Computing Research*, *59*(6), 1015–1035. DOI: 10.1177/0735633120986256

Zou, T., Shi, J., Wang, M., & Lin, C. (2025). Inverse Design of Structured Electrodes in Lithium Metal Batteries: Integrated High-Throughput Phase-Field Modeling and Machine Learning. *Advanced Functional Materials*, , 12788.

KEY TERMS AND DEFINITIONS

Intelligent Tutoring System (ITS): an AI-driven learning environment that models students' understanding and delivers adaptive tasks, hints, and feedback in real time.

Learner Model: a dynamic representation of a student's evolving mastery, misconceptions, and behaviour used by an ITS to personalize statistics instruction.

Multimodal Representation: the use of formulas, graphs, simulations, and narrative explanations in tandem to deepen conceptual understanding of statistical ideas.

Affective Tutoring: ITS features that sense and respond to learner emotions (e.g., anxiety, frustration) to sustain engagement in statistics learning.

Productive Struggle: deliberately managed difficulty that pushes learners to grapple with statistical concepts without tipping into discouraging failure.

Algorithmic Guidance: the set of AI-generated recommendations, hints, and task selections that shape how students progress through statistics content.

Collaborative Human–AI Teaching Model: a classroom design where human pedagogy and intelligent tutoring systems are explicitly orchestrated to complement rather than replace each other

Chapter 4
Assessment and Evaluation Strategies Using AI Technologies in Statistical Education

Ahmad Solih Darmawan
http://orcid.org/0009-0000-5189-6570
Universitas Esa Unggul, Indonesia

Binastya Anggara Sekti
http://orcid.org/0000-0001-5489-4888
Universitas Esa Unggul, Indonesia

Mohammad Norman Gaza Laksono
http://orcid.org/0009-0005-2863-5483
Uppsala Universitet, Sweden

ABSTRACT

The rapid integration of Artificial Intelligence (AI) technologies into educational environments has significantly transformed assessment practices, particularly in the field of statistical education. Traditional evaluation methods—often rigid, summative, and limited in scope—fail to capture the depth of conceptual understanding and reasoning required in statistics. This chapter explores how AI-powered tools such as natural language processing, intelligent tutoring systems, machine learning, and learning analytics can foster more personalized, responsive, and equitable assessment strategies. Grounded in theoretical frameworks including constructivism, cognitive load theory, and formative assessment principles, the chapter proposes a multi-layered

DOI: 10.4018/979-8-3373-6259-5.ch004

framework for AI-based statistical evaluation. It further analyzes international case studies from South Korea, Finland, the United States, and Indonesia, revealing the contextual factors influencing successful AI adoption.

1. INTRODUCTION

1.1 Background and Context

Statistical education has long faced challenges in fostering deep conceptual understanding among learners. Traditional assessment models, such as standardized tests and static quizzes, often fall short in capturing the nuances of students' reasoning and problem-solving processes in statistics. This issue becomes more pressing as the demand for statistical literacy increases globally, not only among data science students but also across disciplines such as social sciences, business, and healthcare. In this evolving landscape, educators must rethink how assessments are designed and delivered to accommodate diverse learning styles and better support student success. Statistical education at university level faces significant challenges, particularly with the rapid advancements in technology and evolving teaching methods (Quiñones et al., 2024).

At the same time, technological advances—particularly in Artificial Intelligence (AI)—are rapidly transforming the educational sector. AI technologies, such as machine learning, natural language processing (NLP), and learning analytics, have introduced new possibilities for dynamic, personalized, and data-driven assessment strategies. In contrast to traditional models, AI-powered systems can adapt to individual learning trajectories, identify misconceptions in real time, and provide targeted feedback. These capabilities have the potential to redefine the purpose and practice of assessment, especially in subjects as cognitively demanding as statistics. Many students have integrated generative AI tools into their work and have highlighted their advantages in coursework activities (Al Labadi & Ly, 2025).

Statistics, by its nature, involves abstract reasoning, probabilistic thinking, and multidimensional data interpretation. These competencies are often difficult to evaluate using fixed-format assessments. AI tools offer a means to operationalize more authentic evaluations—such as open-ended problem-solving, exploratory data analysis, and concept mapping—while maintaining scalability and efficiency. Thus, the integration of AI in statistical assessment is not just a matter of technological enhancement; it is a pedagogical necessity that aligns with 21st-century learning goals. Teaching ability, innovative pedagogical ideas, and contributions to statistical education resources have benefited many, demonstrating expertise and generosity (Davies & MacGillivray, 2024).

Recent global events, including the COVID-19 pandemic, have also accelerated the shift toward online and hybrid learning models, further necessitating innovation in assessment practices. Traditional invigilation and pen-and-paper formats are no longer sufficient or feasible in many contexts. AI-based assessment systems provide scalable solutions that support remote learning while ensuring academic integrity and consistent standards. These systems are increasingly being adopted by universities and online platforms worldwide, signaling a paradigm shift in educational assessment.

This chapter sets the stage for a comprehensive exploration of how AI technologies are reshaping assessment and evaluation in statistical education. It outlines the motivations, challenges, and opportunities inherent in this transformation, with an emphasis on aligning AI capabilities with pedagogical integrity. The chapter argues that AI is not a replacement for human educators but a powerful ally in designing fairer, more responsive, and more effective assessment ecosystems.

1.2 Purpose and Significance of the Chapter

The primary aim of this chapter is to examine the intersection of AI technologies and statistical pedagogy through the lens of assessment and evaluation. By doing so, it addresses a critical gap in the current literature, where much of the discussion around AI in education remains general or limited to cognitive tutoring systems without sufficient focus on domain-specific challenges. This chapter contributes to the growing body of knowledge by contextualizing AI applications within the unique demands and intricacies of statistical instruction.

More specifically, the chapter seeks to:

- Illuminate the limitations of traditional statistical assessments and the pedagogical challenges they present;
- Explore emerging AI-based tools and frameworks that support more adaptive, valid, and inclusive evaluation practices;
- Discuss ethical considerations, such as fairness, bias mitigation, and transparency in AI assessments;
- Present real-world case studies where AI has been successfully integrated into statistical evaluation;
- Offer recommendations for educators, researchers, and policymakers on implementing AI-enhanced assessments in statistical curricula.

The significance of this inquiry lies in its potential to influence educational practice at multiple levels—from classroom implementation to institutional policy. By bridging the gap between AI research and statistical pedagogy, the chapter aspires to serve as both a conceptual guide and a practical resource for stakeholders aiming to enhance student learning outcomes through intelligent assessment.

Additionally, this chapter contributes to broader conversations on educational equity and innovation. AI, when applied responsibly, can help level the playing field by providing customized support to learners with varied backgrounds, abilities, and access levels. It can also democratize data-driven decision-making in education, enabling instructors to make informed interventions based on robust learning analytics.

By foregrounding statistical education—a field essential to data literacy and scientific reasoning—this chapter underscores the importance of aligning AI capabilities with disciplinary goals. It posits that thoughtful integration of AI into assessment practices can not only improve learning outcomes but also enrich the overall educational experience.

1.3 Structure of the Chapter

This chapter is structured to provide a logical progression from foundational context to focused exploration. Section 1.1 establishes the background and urgency for reforming statistical assessment in light of AI innovations. It presents the pedagogical, technological, and contextual motivations that drive the integration of AI into educational evaluation.

Section 1.2 clarifies the objectives, scope, and potential impact of the chapter, explaining why this topic matters and how it aligns with current academic and policy interests. It highlights the novelty and importance of focusing on statistical education—a field where traditional assessments often fail to capture the depth of student understanding.

Subsequent sections of the chapter will delve into theoretical frameworks, technological taxonomies, implementation models, and case studies to provide a comprehensive understanding of AI-enhanced assessment. These sections will draw on interdisciplinary research, empirical findings, and practitioner insights to offer a balanced and in-depth perspective.

Finally, the chapter concludes by synthesizing key insights and outlining actionable recommendations. It reflects on the broader implications of AI integration in education, particularly in enhancing fairness, validity, and responsiveness in assessment. Readers are encouraged to consider how these insights can inform their own practices, research, and institutional strategies.

In sum, this chapter lays the groundwork for a detailed inquiry into how AI technologies can elevate the standards and practices of assessment in statistical education. It positions itself as both an academic contribution and a practical guide for navigating the complexities and potentials of AI-driven educational transformation.

2. THEORETICAL FOUNDATIONS OF AI-DRIVEN ASSESSMENT IN STATISTICAL EDUCATION

2.1 Constructivism and Personalized Learning

At the core of contemporary educational theory is constructivism, which posits that learners actively construct knowledge based on their prior experiences and interactions with new information. This theory challenges traditional didactic instruction and assessment models that treat learners as passive recipients of knowledge. In statistical education, where learners must grapple with abstract concepts like variability, probability distributions, and inferential reasoning, constructivism calls for assessments that measure more than rote memorization or procedural execution. Effective undergraduate statistical education requires training using real-world data (Bennie & Erickson, 2024).

Artificial Intelligence (AI) technologies resonate with constructivist principles because they support active learning through immediate feedback, adaptive content delivery, and individualized learning pathways (Sekti, 2025a). For example, intelligent tutoring systems (ITS) simulate personalized instruction by adjusting statistical problem difficulty based on student performance. These systems align with the constructivist belief that learners benefit most when instruction is tailored to their current level of understanding and cognitive load.

Moreover, personalized learning environments—powered by AI—allow students to engage with statistical content at their own pace, revisit foundational concepts, and receive hints when they struggle. This dynamic support system enhances students' ability to build mental models and connect statistical theory to real-world contexts. Personalized feedback, in particular, facilitates reflection, self-regulation, and metacognitive growth, all of which are hallmarks of effective statistical learning.

Thus, the synergy between AI capabilities and constructivist ideals provides a compelling theoretical foundation for reimagining assessment practices. By leveraging AI to support personalization, educators can move beyond standardized evaluation and create assessment experiences that are formative, supportive, and cognitively aligned with how learners construct statistical understanding. Enhance the teaching of statistics for engineering students, potentially leading to deeper learning outcomes and a stronger understanding of statistical applications in engineering (Díaz Palencia, 2024).

Figure 1. Application Areas of AI in Statistical Education

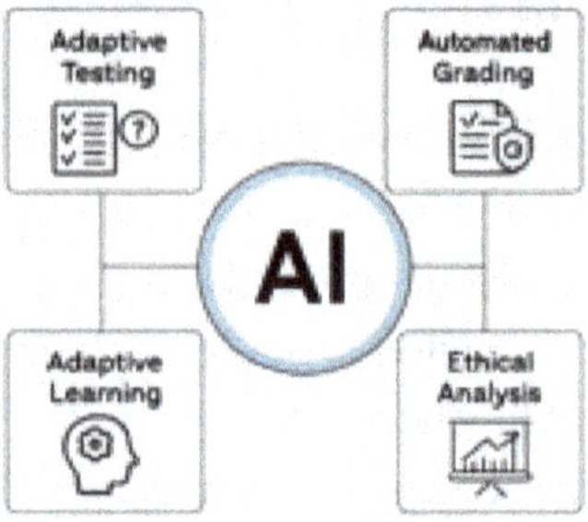

Figure 1 illustrates the core application domains of AI in statistical education, including adaptive testing, automated grading, ethical analysis, case study generation, and adaptive learning systems. Each domain connects back to a central AI engine responsible for intelligent data processing and personalized decision-making.

2.2 Cognitive Load Theory and Adaptive Testing

Cognitive Load Theory (CLT) provides another crucial lens through which to design AI-driven assessments. CLT asserts that instructional materials must consider the limitations of working memory and the mental effort required to process new information. In statistical education, where concepts often involve multistep procedures, abstract symbols, and complex datasets, poorly designed assessments can easily overwhelm learners. Cognitive load theory has been in development since the 1980s. Much of the impetus for that development has come from firstly, replication failures using randomised controlled trials and secondly, from the incorporation of other theories into cognitive load theory (Sweller, 2023).

AI-powered adaptive testing systems address these challenges by dynamically adjusting the difficulty, format, and sequencing of assessment items. Rather than exposing all students to the same set of questions, adaptive algorithms analyze performance in real time and curate question paths that optimize cognitive load. Students who struggle with basic concepts receive more scaffolding, while advanced learners are challenged with higher-order problems, such as interpreting confidence intervals or designing sampling strategies.

These mechanisms reduce extraneous cognitive load and maximize germane load—effort that contributes directly to learning. Additionally, adaptive assessments powered by AI can incorporate multimedia resources (e.g., interactive simulations, animated charts) to reinforce statistical concepts without increasing cognitive burden. For example, a student struggling with hypothesis testing might be directed to a brief animation before answering the next question. Table 1 below illustrates comparative characteristics of leadership models in higher education, illustrating shifts in decision-making orientation, data usage, and analytical capacity across different institutional phases

Table 1. Comparative characteristics of leadership models in higher education

Cognitive Load Type	Traditional Assessment	AI-Driven Assessment
Intrinsic Load	Fixed problem difficulty	Matches difficulty to learner's prior knowledge
Extraneous Load	Unclear instructions, irrelevant content	Streamlined UI, clear prompts, supportive scaffolding
Germane Load	Rarely optimized	Encouraged via reflection prompts and targeted feedback

Through these mechanisms, AI does not simply make assessments more efficient—it makes them more pedagogically sound. CLT-informed adaptive testing creates opportunities for deeper engagement and better retention of statistical concepts. According to cognitive load theory, learning can only be successful when instructional materials and procedures are designed in accordance with human cognitive architecture (Krieglstein, Beege, Rey, Sanchez-Stockhammer, & Schneider, 2023).

In the evolving landscape of AI-enabled statistical systems, several emerging paradigms have the potential to redefine how data is modeled, processed, and interpreted. One such paradigm is neuromorphic computing, which mimics the human brain's architecture and computation mechanisms to perform complex pattern recognition tasks with greater efficiency. Unlike traditional von Neumann architectures, neuromorphic chips can handle noisy, incomplete, or high-dimensional data — scenarios common in real-world educational and social statistics. These chips enable edge AI systems to perform low-power, high-speed analytics, a significant advantage in field-based educational research in underserved regions (Sekti, 2025d).

Furthermore, the adoption of probabilistic AI models is becoming increasingly important in addressing uncertainty and bias in statistical inferences. Traditional deterministic models may provide high accuracy but often fail to communicate confidence intervals or distributional variability — critical aspects in social science contexts. Probabilistic graphical models (PGMs), Bayesian networks, and Gaussian processes are now being integrated into AI platforms to allow educators and policymakers to better understand the range of possible outcomes rather than fixed predictions. These models help to avoid overfitting and support adaptive curriculum planning based on regional, demographic, or linguistic variations.

Another emerging technique is the implementation of continual learning and online adaptation within AI statistical platforms. In many educational environments, statistical patterns evolve rapidly due to curriculum changes, social events, or disruptions such as pandemics. AI models that rely on static training data quickly become obsolete. Continual learning architectures allow models to update incrementally, incorporating new statistical observations without catastrophic forgetting. For example, adaptive AI-based assessment platforms can update student profiling metrics in real time, adjusting learning pathways dynamically without requiring full retraining.

Moreover, federated learning frameworks are revolutionizing the way statistical data can be shared and utilized while maintaining privacy. In education systems where student data is sensitive and fragmented across institutions, federated learning allows for decentralized training of models without raw data ever leaving its original source. This is especially relevant for large-scale policy evaluations across school networks, where a shared statistical model can be co-created without violating student privacy or institutional data policies. Blockchain can be used to coordinate updates to these models, ensuring transparency, version control, and auditability.

The combination of these paradigms—neuromorphic edge computing, probabilistic AI, continual adaptation, and federated analytics—presents a new frontier for AI-powered statistical systems. Together, they promote scalability, resilience, and fairness while maintaining the rigor expected from scientific data analysis. These developments mark a shift from centralized, static statistical methods to decentralized, dynamic, and context-aware learning frameworks. The future of AI in statistics lies not only in prediction accuracy but also in epistemic transparency and socio-technical adaptability.

2.3 Assessment for Learning: Formative Evaluation and Feedback Loops

While summative assessments serve to measure final outcomes, formative assessments aim to improve learning as it happens. AI-based assessment tools are especially suited for formative purposes because they provide continuous, actionable feedback to both students and instructors. In statistics education, this capability is invaluable for identifying misconceptions in real time, such as misinterpreting p-values or assuming causality from correlation. This educational innovation learning activity aims to describe the application of a game-based learning platform such as Kahoot, a formative evaluation tool to assess students' learning (Cadet, 2023).

AI-enabled platforms can detect patterns in student responses and behaviors to generate diagnostic insights. For example, a system might alert an instructor that several students frequently confuse standard deviation with standard error. This enables timely instructional intervention and avoids the perpetuation of misunderstanding. Moreover, formative analytics can suggest personalized practice problems, explanatory videos, or interactive exercises tailored to individual learning gaps.

Feedback loops are critical in reinforcing learning, and AI technologies can make these loops more responsive and precise. Natural Language Processing (NLP) tools, for instance, can evaluate written responses to statistical problems and provide feedback that goes beyond correctness—addressing reasoning, clarity, and use of terminology. Unlike traditional grading, which may take days, AI feedback is instantaneous and can be received multiple times during the learning process.

These dynamic feedback mechanisms support metacognition and foster a growth mindset among learners. They also reduce reliance on high-stakes testing by providing multiple, lower-pressure opportunities to demonstrate learning. Ultimately, AI-driven formative assessment transforms evaluation from a judgmental act into a continuous dialogue that enhances understanding.

2.4 Data-Driven Decision Making and Learning Analytics

The fourth theoretical pillar underpinning AI-based assessment is the use of learning analytics and educational data mining. These approaches apply statistical and computational techniques to analyze vast amounts of learner data and extract patterns that inform instructional decisions. In the context of statistical education, learning analytics can provide rich insights into how students interact with content, respond to different question types, and progress through a course.

AI technologies enable real-time data visualization for instructors through dashboards that display metrics such as concept mastery, time on task, error types, and learning trajectory. These analytics allow educators to identify at-risk students, refine instructional materials, and personalize assessments. For example, an instructor may notice that students consistently underperform on questions involving Bayes' Theorem and subsequently revise both instruction and practice items.

Furthermore, AI can automate the classification of student behaviors into categories such as guessing, confusion, or disengagement. These classifications inform proactive interventions and enhance student support. Educational institutions can also aggregate analytics across courses and semesters to inform curriculum development, program evaluation, and accreditation efforts. Table 2 is overview of AI applications in higher education, highlighting functional domains, analytical approaches, and potential institutional implications.

Table 2. Overview of AI applications in higher education.

Metric	Description	Instructional Use
Time on Task	Average time spent per activity or question	Detects engagement and content difficulty
Error Pattern Analysis	Frequency of common misconceptions	Guides targeted review and clarification
Concept Mastery Score	Cumulative understanding per topic	Identifies areas for re-teaching or enrichment
Learning Trajectory	Progression over time	Informs pacing and course adjustments

These data-driven strategies support more responsive, inclusive, and effective assessment design. They also exemplify how statistical principles can be applied within educational practice—a powerful meta-message for students studying the discipline.

2.5 Summary and Implications for Practice

This chapter has outlined four theoretical foundations that justify and inform the use of AI in assessment within statistical education: constructivism, cognitive load theory, formative evaluation, and learning analytics. Each provides a distinct rationale for integrating AI technologies to enhance the validity, responsiveness, and personalization of assessment practices.

The convergence of these frameworks highlights a critical shift: from assessment as a static measure of knowledge to assessment as an active contributor to learning. AI makes this shift possible by enabling real-time feedback, adaptive content, and predictive analytics. Together, these capabilities help educators move toward a more holistic, learner-centered model of statistical instruction.

For practitioners, these theories offer guiding principles for selecting and implementing AI tools. Rather than adopting technology for its novelty, educators are encouraged to align tool functionalities with pedagogical goals. A deep understanding of these theoretical foundations can also help educators critically evaluate vendor claims and design interventions that are not only technologically sophisticated but also educationally meaningful.

As AI becomes increasingly embedded in education, grounding its use in theory is essential to ensure ethical, effective, and equitable applications. In the context of statistics—a discipline rooted in evidence and reasoning—this theoretical grounding is particularly important. Future chapters will build upon these foundations to explore specific technologies, implementation frameworks, and global case studies that illustrate the practical application of these ideas in diverse educational settings.

3. TAXONOMY OF AI TECHNOLOGIES IN EDUCATIONAL ASSESSMENT

3.1 Introduction to AI Taxonomies in Education

As the integration of Artificial Intelligence (AI) into educational contexts becomes increasingly widespread, it is essential to develop a structured understanding of the diverse types of AI technologies and their roles in assessment. A taxonomy serves as an organized framework that classifies AI tools according to their functions, underlying techniques, and pedagogical applications. In the context of statistical education, such a taxonomy helps educators and developers choose appropriate tools aligned with instructional objectives and learner needs.

AI in educational assessment typically falls into four broad categories: Natural Language Processing (NLP), Machine Learning (ML), Intelligent Tutoring Systems (ITS), and Learning Analytics. Each category encompasses specific tools and techniques designed to automate, personalize, and enhance the assessment process. While these categories are often interrelated, distinguishing their core characteristics is vital for understanding their strengths, limitations, and implementation requirements.

This chapter presents a detailed taxonomy of AI technologies relevant to statistical assessment. It outlines each category, discusses their contributions to educational evaluation, and provides examples of their application in both formative and summative contexts. This structured overview enables stakeholders to navigate the AI landscape more effectively and make informed decisions about adoption and integration.

3.2 Natural Language Processing (NLP)

Natural Language Processing (NLP) refers to a branch of artificial intelligence that enables machines to understand, interpret, and generate human language. In educational assessment, NLP plays an important role in evaluating open-ended responses, generating feedback, and supporting dialogic interaction between learners and AI systems. In statistical education, NLP tools are particularly useful for assessing students' written explanations of concepts such as hypothesis testing, the distinction between correlation and causation, and the interpretation of confidence intervals. One prominent application of NLP is automated essay scoring (AES), which evaluates the quality and content of student writing using predefined rubrics or machine-learned criteria. These systems analyze features such as coherence, grammatical correctness, vocabulary usage, and argument structure, enabling more consistent and scalable evaluation compared to manual grading. Large Language Models (LLMs) recently demonstrated extraordinary capability in various natural language processing (NLP) tasks including language translation, text generation, question answering, etc (Raiaan et al., 2024).

In addition, NLP supports the development of chatbots and virtual teaching assistants capable of responding to student inquiries in natural language. For example, a student seeking clarification about the interpretation of a p-value can receive immediate feedback through a conversational interface. NLP techniques can also be applied to text mining in student discussion forums to identify common misconceptions and inform instructional improvements. Through these applications, NLP helps bridge qualitative and quantitative assessment by transforming narrative responses into structured, actionable insights, thereby enhancing both the depth and scalability of evaluation in statistical education.

3.3 Machine Learning (ML)

Machine Learning (ML) encompasses algorithms that enable systems to learn from data, recognize patterns, and make predictions or decisions without explicit programming. In educational assessment, ML is used to identify learning trends, classify performance levels, and personalize content delivery based on student profiles. In statistical education, ML models are commonly applied to predict student performance, for example in identifying learners who may struggle with topics such as Bayesian inference or multivariate analysis. These predictions can support early intervention and targeted assistance. ML also underpins adaptive testing systems that dynamically adjust the sequence and difficulty of questions in response to students' prior answers. In addition, anomaly detection techniques can identify irregular response patterns that may indicate guessing, disengagement, or potential academic misconduct, while clustering methods group learners based on shared characteristics to support differentiated instruction. Despite these capabilities, ML systems require sufficiently large and representative datasets and must address issues related to bias, transparency, and interpretability, particularly when used in high-stakes educational decisions (Sekti, 2025c).

Beyond algorithmic considerations, the implementation of ML in statistical education depends on robust and interoperable infrastructure. Educational systems often face challenges related to data integration across institutions, as differences in platforms, standards, and access protocols can limit the exchange of analytical insights. Emerging interoperability frameworks, such as Ed-Fi and the Experience API (xAPI), aim to enable standardized and modular data sharing across heterogeneous systems. At the same time, ensuring the auditability and transparency of ML-driven decisions is increasingly important. Approaches such as verifiable logging mechanisms, including blockchain-based solutions, can support traceability of model inputs, processes, and outputs. Infrastructure must also accommodate hybrid learning environments that combine online, offline, and low-bandwidth contexts, requiring adaptive systems capable of local processing and periodic synchronization. Finally, scalable and resilient architectures, often combining centralized coordination with distributed execution, are essential to support the broader integration of ML into statistical education ecosystems.

3.4 Intelligent Tutoring Systems (ITS)

Intelligent Tutoring Systems are AI-powered platforms that simulate human tutoring by offering personalized instruction, feedback, and assessment. ITS are designed to mimic one-on-one human interaction, adjusting content delivery in response to learner inputs. In statistics education, ITS can guide students through complex problem-solving processes, offering hints, explanations, and questions tailored to their level of understanding. Intelligent Tutoring Systems (ITSs) have a great potential to effectively transform teaching and learning (Wang et al., 2023).

For example, an ITS might present a student with a sampling distribution problem and, upon detecting hesitation, provide a step-by-step breakdown or visual aids to support comprehension. As the student progresses, the system tracks performance metrics and updates the learner model to refine future interactions.

ITS typically integrate multiple AI components, including NLP for understanding student queries, ML for predictive modeling, and rule-based systems for instructional sequencing. They are most effective when combined with robust domain models that encapsulate the conceptual structure of the subject matter.

The strength of ITS lies in their ability to offer scaffolded learning experiences that adapt in real time. In assessments, ITS can generate performance data that reflect not just correctness but also process, persistence, and cognitive strategies. These insights are invaluable for formative evaluation and instructional planning.

3.5 Learning Analytics and Educational Data Mining

Learning Analytics (LA) and Educational Data Mining (EDM) refer to the collection, analysis, and interpretation of data generated during the learning process. These fields provide powerful tools for assessment by uncovering trends, predicting outcomes, and visualizing learning behaviors. LA and EDM use techniques from statistics, AI, and information science to turn raw educational data into actionable knowledge. Educational data mining is capable of producing useful data-driven applications (e.g., early warning systems in schools or the prediction of students' academic achievement) based on predictive models (Wongvorachan, He, & Bulut, 2023).

In statistical education, learning analytics dashboards allow instructors to monitor student engagement, mastery of concepts, and time spent on specific tasks. For instance, heatmaps may reveal which questions generate the most errors, while trajectory graphs show how students improve over time. These tools support real-time and longitudinal evaluation of learning progress.

Educational data mining enables more granular insights, such as identifying which types of questions lead to the fastest learning gains or detecting patterns in how students transition between conceptual topics. EDM techniques include clustering, classification, regression analysis, and sequential pattern mining.

Together, LA and EDM shift assessment from episodic to continuous. They empower educators to make data-informed decisions and personalize learning at scale. Furthermore, these tools embody the very statistical thinking that the curriculum aims to develop, offering a meta-level application of statistics in its own pedagogy.

3.6 Summary of the Taxonomy

The taxonomy of AI technologies presented in this chapter highlights the multifaceted nature of AI's contributions to educational assessment. NLP enables the evaluation of open-ended responses and natural dialogue. ML supports prediction, personalization, and anomaly detection. ITS provides adaptive, scaffolded instruction and assessment. LA and EDM offer continuous insights into learning behaviors and outcomes. Table 3 below summarizes the core features, educational functions, and sample applications of each AI category.

Table 3. Summarizes the core features, educational functions, and sample applications of each AI category.

AI Category	Core Functions	Assessment Applications	Example Use Case
NLP	Language understanding, text generation	Essay scoring, chatbots, feedback generation	Automated scoring of statistical concept explanations
ML	Pattern recognition, prediction	Adaptive testing, student modeling	Forecasting difficulty with probability distributions
ITS	Personalized tutoring and interaction	Formative feedback, learning path adjustment	Guided support through hypothesis testing exercises
LA/EDM	Data aggregation and analysis	Dashboard insights, intervention triggers	Heatmaps of student errors in regression analysis

Understanding this taxonomy allows educators, developers, and policymakers to make strategic decisions about adopting and integrating AI tools. Rather than viewing AI as a monolithic solution, this classification reveals a rich ecosystem of technologies, each with distinct affordances and implications for assessment.

Future chapters will explore how these tools can be implemented in practice and the conditions necessary for their successful adoption in statistical education environments.

4. FRAMEWORK FOR AI-BASED STATISTICAL EVALUATION

4.1 Introduction to Framework Design

As Artificial Intelligence (AI) becomes increasingly embedded in statistical education, there is a growing need for coherent frameworks to guide the design and implementation of AI-based assessment systems. Such frameworks ensure that AI tools function not merely as technological additions, but as integral components of pedagogical strategies. A robust framework aligns AI capabilities with learning objectives, assessment goals, instructional scaffolding, and ethical considerations, enabling more structured and meaningful integration into educational practice.

A multi-layered approach can integrate AI technologies such as adaptive testing systems, automated feedback tools, learner analytics dashboards, and intelligent tutoring modules into a cohesive assessment ecosystem. This approach supports both formative and summative purposes, allowing real-time engagement while maintaining validity and fairness in outcomes. Effective frameworks are iterative, data-informed, and learner-centered, adapting to student needs, providing actionable feedback, and promoting statistical reasoning, while also addressing issues of privacy, transparency, and instructional autonomy..

4.2 Components of the AI-Driven Assessment Framework

The implementation of hybrid AI–statistical tools in classrooms across different countries reveals significant variation in effectiveness and infrastructure readiness. Comparative experiences from Indonesia and South Korea illustrate how cultural, technological, and pedagogical contexts shape the design and use of AI-based assessment systems. In Indonesia, the expansion of digital education platforms such as Rumah Belajar and Merdeka Mengajar has incorporated AI-driven assessment modules to support student pacing and feedback. However, limitations in internet connectivity and device availability have required the use of computationally efficient models, such as logistic regression and k-means clustering, which can operate effectively on low-end devices. In contrast, South Korean classrooms have leveraged advanced infrastructure to implement high-resolution analytics through platforms like AI Tutee and ClassNote AI, utilizing models such as Bayesian networks and probabilistic decision trees to generate real-time feedback and predictive insights.

These differences highlight the importance of contextual design in AI-driven assessment frameworks. While high-capacity environments can support real-time analytics and affective computing, resource-constrained settings prioritize system resilience and accessibility. In both contexts, emerging innovations such as blockchain-linked gradebooks have been explored to enhance transparency and trust in assessment processes. These systems enable secure, time-stamped recording of grades and peer evaluations, reducing the risk of manipulation and improving accountability. Additionally, hybrid classrooms increasingly employ AI-generated visual analytics, including heatmaps, learning trajectory graphs, and performance dashboards, to make statistical insights more accessible to both students and educators.

Despite these advancements, the integration of AI in statistical assessment presents challenges related to inclusivity, interpretability, and alignment with curriculum goals. AI systems may introduce unintended biases or reinforce existing inequalities if not carefully designed and monitored. To address these concerns, there is growing emphasis on developing teacher capacity, particularly in statistical literacy and the interpretation of AI-generated outputs. Educators are encouraged to treat AI recommendations as probabilistic insights rather than definitive judgments, ensuring that human judgment remains central in decision-making processes.

The proposed framework comprises five core components:

1. Diagnostic Baseline Assessment – Students begin with an adaptive placement test that evaluates their prior statistical knowledge and identifies strengths and weaknesses.
2. Adaptive Testing Engine – Machine learning algorithms adjust question difficulty and type based on student responses in real time, ensuring alignment with individual readiness.
3. Formative Feedback Loop – Through NLP and ITS, students receive instant, personalized feedback on their performance, including explanations, visual aids, and hints.
4. Learning Trajectory Mapping – Analytics track student progress across statistical competencies, enabling longitudinal insight and personalized learning plans.
5. Summative Evaluation Integration – Final assessments incorporate all previous learning data to provide a comprehensive, fair, and validated measure of student performance.

4.3 Application in a Course Setting

To illustrate the framework in action, consider a foundational statistics course at the undergraduate level. The course begins with an AI-powered diagnostic that categorizes students into learning profiles. Based on this, each student receives a tailored learning plan and adaptive quizzes. As the course progresses, ITS modules scaffold complex tasks like ANOVA, regression analysis, and confidence interval construction.

Formative assessments occur weekly, with NLP tools providing feedback on student justifications and explanations. For instance, students who repeatedly misuse the term "significance" are directed to a micro-lesson clarifying statistical terminology. Learning trajectory dashboards allow instructors to monitor progress and intervene when students deviate from expected growth paths.

At the course's end, a capstone assessment synthesizes data from all previous activities to provide a holistic performance profile. This profile includes not only final test scores but also metrics on engagement, improvement, and conceptual mastery. The framework thereby supports a comprehensive evaluation of both product and process.

4.4 Framework Evaluation Criteria

For the framework to be pedagogically sound and practically viable, it must meet several criteria:

- Validity: Does the framework measure the intended statistical skills and reasoning?
- Reliability: Are results consistent across contexts and populations?
- Transparency: Are the algorithms and outputs interpretable by instructors and students?
- Adaptivity: Can the system personalize learning and evolve with the student?
- Scalability: Is the framework feasible across different class sizes and delivery modes?
- Ethical Soundness: Does it respect privacy, agency, and diversity?

Table 4 presents how each component of the framework aligns with these evaluation criteria.

Table 4. The Component of the framework aligns with these evaluation criteria.

Framework Component	Validity	Reliability	Transparency	Adaptivity	Scalability	Ethical Soundness
Diagnostic Baseline	✓	✓	✓	✓	✓	✓
Adaptive Testing Engine	✓	✓	Partial	✓✓	✓✓	Partial
Formative Feedback Loop	✓✓	Partial	✓✓	✓✓	✓	✓✓
Learning Trajectory Map	✓	✓	✓	✓✓	✓✓	✓✓
Summative Integration	✓✓	✓✓	Partial	✓	✓✓	✓

(✓ = Meets, ✓✓ = Strongly Meets, Partial = Conditional)

4.5 Summary and Transition

This chapter presented a comprehensive framework for AI-based assessment tailored to the demands of statistical education. It emphasized the interconnectedness of diagnostic tools, adaptive engines, feedback mechanisms, and trajectory mapping in creating a responsive and inclusive evaluation environment.

By grounding the framework in pedagogical and ethical principles, educators can ensure that AI supports—not supplants—effective teaching. In the next chapter, we will examine real-world case studies that demonstrate the successful implementation of these principles across diverse educational settings.

5. CASE STUDIES FROM GLOBAL CLASSROOMS

5.1 Introduction to Global Implementation

One of the most pressing ethical concerns in AI-driven statistical systems is algorithmic bias, particularly in socio-educational contexts where statistical predictions can have direct consequences on student outcomes, funding decisions, or policy implementations. Statistical models trained on imbalanced or historically biased datasets can inadvertently reinforce existing inequalities. For example, an AI system predicting student dropout risks may overestimate risk for students from certain socioeconomic backgrounds due to embedded historical bias in past datasets.

This challenge is compounded when decision-makers assume the statistical outputs of AI systems are neutral or objective. As studies have shown, the "myth of neutrality" surrounding algorithms can lead to over-reliance on flawed models. This is especially dangerous in education and public services, where AI-generated statistical insights could influence access to scholarships, placement in programs, or targeted interventions. The ethical implication here is not only about fairness in data but also about epistemic responsibility—acknowledging how knowledge is constructed and acted upon in statistical systems.

To address such issues, researchers and practitioners are increasingly turning to decentralized ethics mechanisms, such as blockchain-based voting or audit trails. In experimental implementations, decisions made by statistical-AI models are not automatically enforced. Instead, they are logged into transparent ledgers and subject to peer or expert review. For instance, in an AI-enabled grading system, teachers or quality assurance staff can review the model's grading rationale before finalizing results. Each decision point is logged immutably, ensuring traceability and accountability. This model allows for "human-in-the-loop ethics", where statistical outputs become inputs for dialogue rather than endpoints for action.

Moreover, there is a growing movement toward explainable AI (XAI) in statistical systems. Explainability techniques—such as LIME (Local Interpretable Model-Agnostic Explanations) and SHAP (SHapley Additive exPlanations)—enable users to understand the statistical logic behind a model's decision. In educational applications, these tools can help instructors interpret why a student was flagged as at risk, or how particular variables (e.g., attendance, test scores, engagement metrics) contributed to a statistical inference.

Ethical considerations also extend to data ownership and consent. Many AI-statistical platforms harvest large volumes of personal and behavioral data. However, students, teachers, and parents are often unaware of how their data is used in statistical modeling. Ethical frameworks now propose "statistical data sovereignty", where individuals or institutions retain partial control over how their data is used and by whom. Blockchain smart contracts can encode such rules, enabling consent-based data sharing and even monetization in academic research contexts.

Finally, educational institutions must consider the long-term ethical impact of statistical AI integration. As these tools become embedded into teaching, learning, and assessment, there is a risk that the human elements of judgment, empathy, and contextual awareness are sidelined in favor of algorithmic reasoning. Ethically-informed statistical AI must therefore be designed not just for accuracy or efficiency, but for pedagogical alignment, cultural sensitivity, and social justice. Ongoing dialogue between technologists, educators, ethicists, and students is essential to navigate this evolving terrain responsibly.

The application of AI in assessment is not a theoretical concept alone—it is actively shaping classrooms around the world. As diverse educational institutions adopt AI technologies, their approaches and outcomes vary based on contextual factors such as technological infrastructure, educator training, curriculum alignment, and cultural attitudes toward data and automation. This chapter presents comparative case studies from four countries—South Korea, Finland, the United States, and Indonesia—each of which has pioneered distinct approaches to AI-driven statistical assessment.

The case studies offer insights into both the opportunities and challenges associated with implementation. They examine how AI tools are selected, integrated, and evaluated; how teachers and students respond to them; and what measurable outcomes have been observed. Through these comparative narratives, we gain a better understanding of how local contexts influence the success and scalability of AI-enhanced evaluation.

5.2 Case Study 1: Adaptive Testing at Seoul National University (South Korea)

Seoul National University (SNU), one of South Korea's top institutions, implemented an AI-driven adaptive testing platform in its undergraduate statistics program. The goal was to personalize student assessments and improve retention of core concepts such as descriptive analysis and hypothesis testing (Yodplob & Ketsuwan, 2025).

The adaptive system used machine learning algorithms to analyze student responses and dynamically select subsequent questions based on difficulty and topical relevance. For instance, if a student showed proficiency in frequency distributions but struggled with variance calculations, the system adjusted the pathway accordingly. Effective classroom instruction requires monitoring student participation and interaction during class, identifying cues to simulate their attention (Trabelsi, Alnajjar, Parambil, Gochoo, & Ali, 2023).

Results from the pilot semester showed:

- A 20% increase in final exam performance compared to previous cohorts.
- Higher engagement levels during assessments, as measured by completion rates and time-on-task.
- Positive student feedback regarding fairness and clarity of assessment.

One challenge reported was the need for extensive question banks tagged with metadata, which required significant initial investment in instructional design. Nevertheless, the system was retained for future use and expanded to other quantitative disciplines.

5.3 Case Study 2: Real-Time Analytics at University of Helsinki (Finland)

The University of Helsinki adopted a learning analytics dashboard for its blended learning statistics courses. The platform tracked key metrics such as login frequency, time spent on exercises, response accuracy, and improvement trends (Alabi, Elmusrati, Leivo, Almangush, & Mäkitie, 2023).

Heatmaps and trajectory graphs enabled instructors to identify students at risk and intervene early. Weekly reports generated by the AI system were used to personalize feedback emails, recommend resources, and adjust pacing for tutorials.

Outcomes included:

- A 22% reduction in dropout rates for introductory statistics.
- Increased participation in discussion forums and peer review activities.
- Enhanced satisfaction among instructors, who reported better situational awareness.

Ethical considerations were carefully addressed by anonymizing data and allowing students to opt out. Students who opted in were able to view their own analytics, fostering self-regulation.

5.4 Case Study 3: NLP-Based Feedback in MIT OpenCourseWare (United States)

Massachusetts Institute of Technology (MIT) integrated Natural Language Processing (NLP) tools into its open-access statistics courses. These tools were designed to evaluate short written explanations of statistical reasoning tasks (Dede & Lidwell, 2023).

Students were asked to justify their answers to problems involving correlation, standard error, and p-value interpretation. The NLP system analyzed grammatical structure, terminology use, and conceptual clarity to provide immediate formative feedback.

Key findings from the deployment:

- 60% reduction in manual grading time for teaching assistants.
- Improved quality of student explanations, as seen in successive assignment iterations.
- Positive feedback from students who appreciated the immediate and detailed nature of the AI feedback.

Limitations included difficulty in interpreting non-standard or multilingual responses, which the development team addressed in subsequent versions with multilingual NLP models.

5.5 Case Study 4: Mobile Assessment Tools in Indonesian Public Universities

In Indonesia, where internet infrastructure varies greatly, a consortium of public universities introduced a lightweight AI-based mobile app for assessing statistical knowledge. The app focused on concepts frequently tested in national exams, such as central tendency, sampling methods, and data interpretation (Sari, Astrada, Septiana, & Pamungkas, 2025).

The app incorporated adaptive quizzes, interactive visualizations, and offline access. Students received weekly feedback reports and badges for learning milestones.

Impact assessment revealed:

- 30% increase in student quiz participation compared to traditional LMS.
- Enhanced engagement in rural and under-resourced areas.
- Cost-effective implementation, supported by a partnership with a local EdTech startup.

Cultural factors, such as student hesitation to challenge AI-generated feedback, highlighted the need for socio-technical training as part of the rollout.

5.6 Comparative Analysis and Lessons Learned

Table 5 below summarizes key features, challenges, and outcomes across the four case studies.

Table 5. below summarizes key features, challenges, and outcomes across the four case studies.

Country	AI Tool Used	Main Impact	Key Challenge
South Korea	Adaptive Testing	+20% in exam scores	Building high-quality question bank
Finland	Learning Analytics	-22% dropout rate	Privacy and consent management
United States	NLP Feedback Engine	-60% grading time, better explanations	Handling non-standard responses
Indonesia	Mobile AI App	+30% quiz participation in rural areas	Cultural adaptation and training needs

The diversity of these implementations underscores that there is no one-size-fits-all approach to AI in assessment. Local adaptation, stakeholder involvement, and continuous evaluation are critical success factors. Institutions must not only invest in technology but also in the pedagogical and cultural groundwork that enables effective use.

5.7 Summary and Implications for Adoption

This chapter illustrated the real-world application of AI-based assessment strategies through international case studies. Each example demonstrated the potential for AI to improve personalization, reduce workload, enhance fairness, and expand access. However, they also revealed implementation barriers that must be acknowledged and addressed.

Educators considering AI adoption should conduct needs assessments, pilot studies, and ethical reviews before full deployment. They should also provide training for teachers and students, especially in interpreting AI-generated insights. Flexibility, transparency, and collaboration with stakeholders will increase the likelihood of successful and sustainable integration.

In the next chapter, we will explore how these case study findings inform best practices for aligning AI tools with assessment principles such as validity, reliability, and fairness.

6. PEDAGOGICAL ALIGNMENT—ENSURING VALIDITY, RELIABILITY, AND FAIRNESS IN AI-BASED ASSESSMENT

6.1 Introduction to Pedagogical Alignment

For AI-powered assessment tools to be effective and ethically sound in statistical education, they must align with foundational principles of pedagogical quality—namely, validity, reliability, and fairness. While AI can offer advanced personalization and real-time feedback, these advantages are meaningless if the assessment outcomes do not accurately reflect what students are expected to know and be able to do. This chapter explores how AI-based assessment systems can and must be designed to uphold these core educational values (Galan & Kotze, 2024).

Pedagogical alignment ensures that technology enhances, rather than disrupts, the integrity of instruction and evaluation. In the context of statistical education, where conceptual reasoning and data interpretation are paramount, misaligned assessments can easily misrepresent student learning. Therefore, any AI assessment initiative must be evaluated against clear standards for content validity, internal consistency, and equity across diverse learner populations.

This chapter unpacks each of these principles in detail, discusses potential risks and mitigation strategies, and presents design considerations to help ensure AI assessments support pedagogical goals.

6.2 Validity in AI-Based Statistical Assessment

Validity refers to the extent to which an assessment measures what it purports to measure. In statistical education, this involves capturing students' ability to reason with uncertainty, interpret data, apply appropriate methods, and explain their thinking.

AI assessment tools may compromise validity if their scoring algorithms emphasize surface features (e.g., grammar, speed, or keyword frequency) rather than conceptual understanding. For example, an NLP tool that rewards verbose answers without evaluating statistical logic would yield inflated scores that don't reflect actual comprehension.

To ensure validity:

- Item design must be grounded in curricular goals and statistical competencies.
- AI systems must be trained and validated on data representing diverse problem-solving approaches.
- Human oversight is essential for evaluating borderline or novel responses that deviate from expected patterns.

6.3 Reliability in AI Systems

Reliability concerns the consistency of assessment results over time, across different users, and in various contexts. In traditional settings, reliability is often assessed via test-retest consistency or inter-rater agreement. In AI-based systems, reliability hinges on algorithmic stability, data quality, and model generalizability.

Sources of unreliability in AI assessments may include:

- Bias in training data, leading to inconsistent performance across demographic groups.
- Overfitting, where the AI model performs well on training data but poorly in new contexts.
- Technical variability, such as server load affecting processing speed or system availability.

To address these risks:

- Validation protocols (e.g., cross-validation, holdout testing) must be applied during model development.
- Periodic recalibration of algorithms should occur based on new data.
- User interface design must ensure consistent experiences across devices and settings.

Reliability is critical in statistical education, where students' future coursework or careers may depend on accurate evaluations of their analytical skills.

6.4 Fairness and Equity in AI-Driven Assessment

Fairness addresses whether all students are evaluated equitably, regardless of their background, learning style, or access to resources. AI systems can unintentionally perpetuate or amplify existing inequities if not carefully designed.

Risks to fairness include:

- Cultural bias in question phrasing or examples.
- Differential item functioning, where certain questions are harder for some groups despite equal ability.
- Digital divide, where students in low-connectivity areas face disadvantages in using online AI tools.

Strategies to enhance fairness:

- Bias audits on training datasets to detect demographic imbalances.
- Inclusive item development, incorporating diverse perspectives and contexts.
- Offline or low-bandwidth versions of assessment tools to expand accessibility.

Ethical AI design must be intersectional—accounting not just for technical performance but for social consequences. Equity in assessment is both a moral imperative and a legal responsibility.

6.5 Integrated Strategies for Pedagogical Alignment

Effective AI-based assessment systems are those that embed validity, reliability, and fairness into every layer of design and implementation. Table 6.1 outlines practical strategies and their corresponding pedagogical alignment dimensions.

Table 6. practical strategies and their corresponding pedagogical alignment dimensions

Strategy	Validity	Reliability	Fairness
Human-in-the-loop Review	✓✓	✓	✓
Bias-Aware Model Training	✓	✓✓	✓✓
Curriculum-Aligned Item Design	✓✓	✓✓	✓
Interface Consistency Testing	-	✓✓	✓
Multimodal Feedback Options	✓	-	✓✓
Student Data Transparency	✓	✓	✓✓

(✓ = Supports, ✓✓ = Strongly Supports, – = Not Applicable)

These strategies reinforce the principle that technology should support, not distort, educational meaning-making. Pedagogical alignment is not a static checklist but an ongoing process of review, reflection, and revision.

6.6 Summary and Design Implications

Pedagogical alignment is the backbone of trustworthy AI assessment. Without attention to validity, systems may misrepresent what students know. Without reliability, results become unstable and untrustworthy. Without fairness, we risk widening the very gaps education is meant to close.

Educators, developers, and policymakers must collaborate to embed these principles at every stage—from data collection and model training to user experience and reporting. AI offers unprecedented power to personalize learning and scale quality assessment, but only if grounded in rigorous educational design.

The next chapter will translate these principles into future-focused recommendations, including professional development, policy frameworks, and research agendas needed to sustain ethical AI adoption in statistical education.

7. FUTURE DIRECTIONS AND RECOMMENDATIONS

7.1 Overview of Emerging Trends

As the landscape of education continues to evolve alongside technological innovation, the integration of Artificial Intelligence (AI) in statistical assessment is poised for substantial transformation. Emerging trends point toward greater sophistication, increased accessibility, and tighter alignment with pedagogical and ethical imperatives. This chapter synthesizes key developments on the horizon and proposes strategic recommendations to guide educators, institutions, and policymakers in responsibly scaling AI-based assessment practices in statistical education.

Major trends include the rise of explainable AI (XAI), expanded multilingual AI capabilities, greater attention to data privacy regulations, and the incorporation of AI into lifelong learning pathways. Each of these developments holds the potential to enhance educational equity, learner autonomy, and assessment personalization—if applied with care and rigor.

7.2 Strategic Recommendations for Educators

Educators play a pivotal role in shaping how AI tools are interpreted, contextualized, and embedded within the learning environment. For AI to be pedagogically meaningful and ethically responsible, educators must be equipped with both technical fluency and pedagogical foresight. The following recommendations are directed at instructors and academic leaders:

1. Professional Development in AI Literacy: Offer continuous training to help educators understand AI functionalities, limitations, and interpretive strategies, especially around learning analytics and adaptive assessments.
2. Collaborative Tool Selection: Involve educators in evaluating and selecting AI tools to ensure alignment with curricular goals and instructional values.
3. Co-Designing Feedback Loops: Work with AI developers to design feedback systems that complement, rather than replace, human insight. Prioritize formative over summative outputs.
4. Championing Inclusivity: Advocate for tools that are accessible, linguistically diverse, and sensitive to student diversity in cognition, language, and culture.

Ultimately, empowering educators is the cornerstone of ethical and effective AI deployment.

7.3 Policy Recommendations for Institutions

At the institutional level, policies must support the infrastructure, governance, and evaluative frameworks needed for sustainable AI integration. Key recommendations include:

1. Institutional AI Governance Policies: Develop clear guidelines on AI adoption, including ethical use, data security, algorithmic transparency, and equity standards (Sekti, 2025b).
2. Assessment Innovation Grants: Provide funding and support for departments experimenting with AI-enhanced assessment models, especially in foundational courses like statistics.
3. Inclusive Data Collection Frameworks: Ensure institutional data used in training AI systems are representative of student diversity and regularly audited for bias.
4. AI-Education Ethics Committees: Establish cross-disciplinary committees to review AI implementations, monitor unintended consequences, and provide oversight.

These policy shifts position institutions not just as consumers of educational AI but as stewards of its responsible evolution.

7.4 Recommendations for EdTech Developers

EdTech companies developing AI assessment tools must engage in transparent, user-centered design processes grounded in evidence-based pedagogy. Developers are advised to:

1. Prioritize Explainability: Build models with interpretable outputs so that users (students, teachers) understand the basis of AI decisions.
2. Design for Interoperability: Ensure tools integrate with existing Learning Management Systems (LMS), dashboards, and institutional data platforms.
3. Collaborate with Domain Experts: Partner with statisticians and educational researchers to develop content-appropriate scoring rubrics and training datasets.
4. Embed Ethics by Design: Incorporate bias detection, user consent, and audit trails from the early stages of product development.

This ensures that AI tools enhance, rather than disrupt, educational ecosystems.

7.5 International Collaboration and Research Agendas

The global scope of AI adoption in education calls for increased cross-national collaboration. Future research should focus on:

- Comparative effectiveness studies of AI assessment across different cultural, linguistic, and educational systems.

- Longitudinal impact research tracking how AI assessment affects learning outcomes, motivation, and equity over time.
- Global AI Literacy Initiatives that promote ethical and informed use of AI among students and teachers.

Institutions can partner on joint research projects, share open datasets for training and validation, and co-develop multilingual AI models that reflect global diversity.

7.6 Concluding Reflections

AI technologies have ushered in a new era of possibilities for statistical education assessment. From adaptive testing and real-time feedback to predictive analytics and personalized pathways, the tools available today are more powerful and scalable than ever before. However, their value is not inherent—it must be actualized through thoughtful design, pedagogical alignment, and ongoing reflection.

This chapter has laid out a roadmap for future innovation grounded in ethical responsibility and pedagogical integrity. Whether in the classroom, the policy boardroom, or the development lab, stakeholders must collaborate to ensure that AI advances serve the core mission of education: to cultivate understanding, equity, and human potential.

The final chapter will summarize the book's key insights and re-emphasize the central thesis: that AI, when wielded wisely, can become a transformative force in statistical education—not by replacing educators, but by empowering them to assess, support, and inspire learners in more meaningful ways.

8. CONCLUSION AND FINAL REFLECTIONS

8.1 Revisiting the Central Thesis

This book has explored how Artificial Intelligence (AI) can redefine assessment and evaluation strategies in statistical education. Grounded in pedagogical theory, technological taxonomies, practical case studies, and global perspectives, our central argument has remained consistent: AI, when ethically and thoughtfully deployed, can empower educators to create more responsive, inclusive, and meaningful assessments that foster true statistical understanding.

We began by identifying the limitations of traditional assessments—rigidity, time constraints, inconsistency—and outlined the potential of AI tools such as NLP, adaptive testing engines, ITS, and learning analytics to address these challenges.

A robust framework was presented, showing how AI systems can be holistically integrated into the assessment cycle, from diagnosis to summative evaluation.

Through international case studies, we examined how different institutions have navigated implementation in contextually unique ways. These narratives underscored the need for localization, stakeholder engagement, and continuous improvement. We then addressed the core pedagogical concerns of validity, reliability, and fairness, offering strategies to ensure alignment between technological innovation and instructional integrity.

Finally, our recommendations aimed to guide diverse stakeholders—educators, institutions, EdTech developers, and policymakers—in forging responsible, collaborative pathways for AI adoption in education.

8.2 Key Takeaways Across Chapters

The following points summarize the essential insights from each chapter:

- **Chapter 1:** Highlighted the urgency of reforming statistical assessment through AI, given changing learner needs and technological capacities.
- **Chapter 2:** Mapped theoretical underpinnings such as constructivism, cognitive load theory, and formative evaluation, linking them to AI's pedagogical potential.
- **Chapter 3:** Defined a taxonomy of AI tools and their assessment functions, helping demystify the ecosystem of AI technologies.
- **Chapter 4:** Proposed an actionable framework for integrating AI in statistical assessment, with emphasis on feedback, adaptivity, and personalization.
- **Chapter 5:** Showcased real-world implementations and highlighted contextual nuances through global case studies.
- **Chapter 6:** Critically analyzed AI alignment with educational principles—validity, reliability, and fairness—and provided corrective design strategies.
- **Chapter 7:** Outlined future directions and cross-sector recommendations to support ethical, pedagogically grounded AI innovation.

Together, these chapters offer a blueprint for reimagining statistical assessment in ways that are both technologically advanced and human-centered.

8.3 Limitations and Considerations

While the promise of AI in assessment is vast, this book acknowledges several limitations. The rapid pace of AI development may outstrip the capacity of institutions to adapt. Disparities in infrastructure and expertise could widen gaps in educational equity. Moreover, ethical concerns—particularly regarding algorithmic bias and student data privacy—require ongoing scrutiny and transparent governance.

Furthermore, the pedagogical success of AI tools is heavily contingent on thoughtful integration. Poorly designed systems may lead to misinterpretation of student abilities or overreliance on automation. Therefore, AI should be viewed not as a replacement for human judgment but as an augmentation of it.

8.4 Final Reflections

AI offers an opportunity not just to digitize existing practices, but to reimagine them entirely. In statistical education, where understanding data, uncertainty, and inference is vital to modern citizenship, the quality of assessment matters profoundly. When AI is used to enhance personalization, provide timely feedback, and empower reflective learning, it becomes a tool for equity and engagement.

But achieving this requires a balance of innovation and introspection—a commitment to centering pedagogy, ethics, and student well-being in every AI-driven solution. This book serves as both a call to action and a roadmap for realizing this vision.

The future of AI in statistical assessment is not predetermined. It is shaped, in every classroom and every institution, by the choices we make. Let those choices be guided by purpose, informed by evidence, and inspired by the promise of truly transformative education.

REFERENCES

Al Labadi, L., & Ly, A. (2025). Enhancing statistics education through Project-Based Learning (PBL) and the emergence of ChatGPT. *Teaching Statistics*, *47*(3), 200–218. DOI: 10.1111/test.12405

Alabi, R. O., Elmusrati, M., Leivo, I., Almangush, A., & Mäkitie, A. A. (2023). Machine learning explainability in nasopharyngeal cancer survival using LIME and SHAP. *Scientific Reports*, *13*(1), 8984. Advance online publication. DOI: 10.1038/s41598-023-35795-0 PMID: 37268685

Bennie, B., & Erickson, R. A. (2024). Obtaining and Applying Public Data for Training Students in Technical Statistical Writing: Case Studies with Data from U.S. Geological Survey and General Ecological Literature. *Journal of Statistics and Data Science Education : An Official Journal of the of the American Statistical Association*, *32*(2), 217–226. DOI: 10.1080/26939169.2023.2195459

Cadet, M. J. (2023). Application of game-based online learning platform: Kahoot a formative evaluation tool to assess learning. *Teaching and Learning in Nursing*, *18*(3), 419–422. DOI: 10.1016/j.teln.2023.03.009

Davies, N., & MacGillivray, H. (2024). Tribute to Peter Holmes and his statistical education achievements. *Teaching Statistics*, *46*(3), 122–126. DOI: 10.1111/test.12376

Dede, C., & Lidwell, W. (2023). Developing a Next-Generation Model for Massive Digital Learning. *Education Sciences*, *13*(8), 845. Advance online publication. DOI: 10.3390/educsci13080845

Díaz Palencia, J. L. (2024). Applying the anthropological theory of didactics to enhance a multicultural approach to statistics education for engineering students. *Journal for Multicultural Education*, *18*(4), 435–446. DOI: 10.1108/JME-04-2024-0043

Galan, J., & Kotze, D. J. (2024). Pedagogy of Planning Studios for Multidisciplinary, Research-Oriented, Personalized, and Intensive Learning. *Journal of Planning Education and Research*, *44*(3), 1096–1108. DOI: 10.1177/0739456X221082502

Krieglstein, F., Beege, M., Rey, G. D., Sanchez-Stockhammer, C., & Schneider, S. (2023). Development and Validation of a Theory-Based Questionnaire to Measure Different Types of Cognitive Load. *Educational Psychology Review*, *35*(1), 9. Advance online publication. DOI: 10.1007/s10648-023-09738-0

Quiñones, D., Ruz, F., Díaz-Arancibia, J., Paz, F., Osega, J., & Rojas, L. F. (2024). Innovating Statistics Education: The Design of a Novel App Using Design Thinking. *Applied Sciences (Basel, Switzerland)*, *14*(18), 8515. Advance online publication. DOI: 10.3390/app14188515

Raiaan, M. A. K., Mukta, M. S. H., Fatema, K., Fahad, N. M., Sakib, S., Mim, M. M. J., Ahmad, J., Ali, M. E., & Azam, S. (2024). A Review on Large Language Models: Architectures, Applications, Taxonomies, Open Issues and Challenges. *IEEE Access : Practical Innovations, Open Solutions*, *12*, 26839–26874. DOI: 10.1109/ACCESS.2024.3365742

Sari, W., Astrada, A., Septiana, V., & Pamungkas, R. A. (2025). Screen Time and Emotional Development Among Indonesian Preschoolers: A Comparative Study Across Socioeconomic Contexts in Jakarta. *Media Publikasi Promosi Kesehatan Indonesia*, *8*(9), 1001–1012. DOI: 10.56338/mppki.v8i9.7879

Sekti, B. A. (2025a). AI Technology Management Concepts and Strategies. In *AI Technology Management and Value Creation* (pp. 1–32). DOI: 10.4018/979-8-3373-2497-5.ch001

Sekti, B. A. (2025b). IT Service Information Security Management. In *Cases on Information Systems Service Management* (pp. 61–93). DOI: 10.4018/979-8-3373-2352-7.ch003

Sekti, B. A. (2025c). Machine learning and artificial intelligence (AI) in manufacturing. In *Integrating Digital Innovation and Integrated Frameworks in Manufacturing* (pp. 255–292). DOI: 10.4018/979-8-3373-1082-4.ch011

Sekti, B. A. (2025d). Machine Learning vs. AI: Key Concepts. In *Implementing Enterprise Cybersecurity With AI* (pp. 1–27). DOI: 10.4018/979-8-3373-2252-0.ch001

Sweller, J. (2023). The Development of Cognitive Load Theory: Replication Crises and Incorporation of Other Theories Can Lead to Theory Expansion. *Educational Psychology Review*, *35*(4), 95. Advance online publication. DOI: 10.1007/s10648-023-09817-2

Trabelsi, Z., Alnajjar, F., Parambil, M. M. A., Gochoo, M., & Ali, L. (2023). Real-Time Attention Monitoring System for Classroom: A Deep Learning Approach for Student's Behavior Recognition. *Big Data and Cognitive Computing*, *7*(1), 48. Advance online publication. DOI: 10.3390/bdcc7010048

Wang, H., Tlili, A., Huang, R., Cai, Z., Li, M., Cheng, Z., Yang, D., Li, M., Zhu, X., & Fei, C. (2023). Examining the applications of intelligent tutoring systems in real educational contexts: A systematic literature review from the social experiment perspective. *Education and Information Technologies*, *28*(7), 9113–9148. DOI: 10.1007/s10639-022-11555-x PMID: 36643383

Wongvorachan, T., He, S., & Bulut, O. (2023). A Comparison of Undersampling, Oversampling, and SMOTE Methods for Dealing with Imbalanced Classification in Educational Data Mining. *Information (Basel)*, *14*(1), 54. Advance online publication. DOI: 10.3390/info14010054

Yodplob, T., & Ketsuwan, C. (2025). Modified Seoul National University Renal Stone Complexity Scoring System for Predicting Stone-Free Status After Extracorporeal Shock Wave Lithotripsy. *Research and Reports in Urology*, *17*, 279–286. DOI: 10.2147/RRU.S534829 PMID: 40800736

ADDITIONAL READING

Bonino, D., & Pastrone, C. (2015). Smart cities and the Internet of Things. In *Enabling Things to Talk* (pp. 259–276). Springer.

Gaur, A., Scotney, B., Parr, G., & McClean, S. (2015). Smart city architecture and its applications based on IoT. *Procedia Computer Science*, *52*, 1089–1094. DOI: 10.1016/j.procs.2015.05.122

Islam, S. M. R., Kwak, D., Kabir, M. H., Hossain, M., & Kwak, K.-S. (2015). The Internet of Things for health care: A comprehensive survey. *IEEE Access : Practical Innovations, Open Solutions*, *3*, 678–708. DOI: 10.1109/ACCESS.2015.2437951

Liao, Y., Deschamps, F., Loures, E., & Ramos, L. F. P. (2017). Past, present and future of Industry 4.0—A systematic literature review and research agenda proposal. *International Journal of Production Research*, *55*(12), 3609–3629. DOI: 10.1080/00207543.2017.1308576

Lin, J., Yu, W., Zhang, N., Yang, X., Zhang, H., & Zhao, W. (2017). A survey on Internet of Things: Architecture, enabling technologies, security and privacy, and applications. *IEEE Internet of Things Journal*, *4*(5), 1125–1142. DOI: 10.1109/JIOT.2017.2683200

Xu, X., Yu, H., & Ren, J. (2021). Blockchain-based trustworthy edge computing service provision in smart cities. *IEEE Internet of Things Journal*, *8*(17), 13963–13975.

Zubair, M., Bedi, J., & Wani, A. R. (2022). Ethical implications of artificial intelligence: A framework for responsible adoption in digital governance. *AI & Society*, *37*, 625–640.

Chapter 5
Epistemic Stewardship and Pedagogies of Reasoning in AI-Mediated Statistics Classrooms:
Integrating Causal Identification Fairness Metrics

Ashraf Alam
http://orcid.org/0000-0001-6178-1187
Department of Education, National Institute of Technology, Calicut, India

ABSTRACT

This chapter advances a conceptual-theoretical blueprint for statistics education in AI-adjacent learning ecologies, where predictive pipelines and generative synthesis can amplify computation yet erode epistemic agency. Centering variability, transnumeration, and validity-bounded inference, it reframes competence as disciplined judgment under uncertainty, not procedural throughput or platform fluency. AI is positioned as scaffold, simulator, and critic, while learners retain accountability for assumption articulation, calibration, robustness under distribution shift, and harm-aware thresholding. The chapter specifies a tiered curriculum architecture, orchestration routines, and integrity-by-design assessment, integrating equity-of-opportunity, privacy-by-design, and contestability as pedagogical constraints. Five internally coherent tables operationalize big ideas, competency progressions, tool-phase guardrails, analytic rubrics, and multi-source evidence ecologies, yielding an audit-ready, globally portable design for academics, policymakers, and learning technologists.

DOI: 10.4018/979-8-3373-6259-5.ch005

1. INTRODUCTION

1.1 Epistemic Re-Armament for Algorithmic Societies

Statistics education now operates inside algorithmic infrastructures where predictive scores, automated classification, and generative synthesis mediate access to credit, schooling, employment, health triage, climate adaptation resources, and public services. In such environments, procedural software fluency is a weak proxy for competence because computational outputs can be produced without conceptual accountability, while decisions still demand defensible reasoning under uncertainty (Cukurova, 2025; Lee et al., 2024; Tahir et al., 2024). A modern statistics curriculum must therefore cultivate *statistical literacy*, *statistical reasoning*, and *statistical thinking* as layered capacities for interpreting claims, interrogating variability, and sustaining inquiry cycles that remain coherent when automation accelerates production of analyses. The core pedagogical mandate becomes disciplined judgment, including explicit assumptions, inferential warrants, error-cost reasoning, and validity scrutiny, with AI treated as a probabilistic hypothesis generator rather than an epistemic authority. This positioning restores accountability by making learners responsible for the logic of evidence, the semantics of measurement, and the governance implications of decision rules.

1.2 Audience, Scope, and Cross-Sector Transfer Architecture

This chapter is designed for instructors, curriculum leaders, workforce development professionals, and digital learning technologists who must align statistics education with real decision ecologies across STEM and non-STEM programs. The intended scope spans foundational and intermediate statistics, with selective integration of prediction workflows where they concretize core ideas rather than substituting them, ensuring that simulation, resampling, model checking, and uncertainty communication remain central. Transfer is treated as an instructional design problem, not an incidental outcome, so the chapter uses sector-neutral epistemic invariants such as variability, sampling, measurement validity, confounding, calibration, and robustness as organizing constructs that travel across health screening, climate risk management, business analytics, governance, and education systems. Delivery constraints are treated as constitutive, covering high-resource compute environments and low-resource settings with intermittent connectivity, where offline-first simulations, paper-based randomization, and lightweight analytic pipelines must preserve conceptual fidelity. This scope positions statistics as a universal interpretive technology for model-mediated societies, while keeping curricular boundaries tight enough to protect coherence.

1.3 Central Thesis, Normative Stance, and Pedagogical Ethics of Assistance

The thesis is that AI-adjacent tools can strengthen statistics education when they are engineered into pedagogy as scaffold, simulator, and critic, while statistical reasoning retains epistemic primacy as the standard for accepting or rejecting claims. As scaffold, AI can support contrastive explanation, misconception refutation, and adaptive representational translation, yet the learner must still articulate assumptions and justify inferential moves (Leong et al., 2024; Yim & Su, 2025). As simulator, AI-enabled generation can operationalize sampling variability, bootstrap intuition, missingness mechanisms, and distribution shift, permitting rapid stress-testing of conclusions under counterfactual perturbations and adversarial scenarios. As critic, AI can be constrained into structured interrogation that pressures learners to surface hidden defaults, diagnose overfitting, examine calibration, and test validity threats through sensitivity reasoning. The normative stance prioritizes augmentation over automation, baseline transparency before black-box dependence, and explicit disclosure of assistance as part of professional ethics. Within this stance, competence is demonstrated through auditable reasoning and decision accountability, not through prompt virtuosity or superficial output fluency.

1.4 Systemic Design Problems in Teaching, Assessment, and Governance

The primary instructional risk is epistemic deference, where learners outsource sense-making to persuasive synthesis and thereby lose the cognitive habits needed for uncertainty reasoning, diagnostic skepticism, and principled decision thresholds. Statistics education must therefore preserve productive struggle without romanticizing friction, using carefully staged constraints that require learners to generate preliminary models, anticipate failure modes, and defend representational choices before any automated summary is treated as plausible. At the curriculum level, a common failure is a tool-first bootcamp trajectory that inflates computational spectacle while eroding conceptual depth, especially around sampling distributions, confounding logic, and model checking. Assessment design becomes an integrity and validity problem because generative assistance can mimic competent prose and code, so evidence must be built from process traces, oral micro-defenses, version histories, and reproducible analytic workflows that reveal reasoning quality. Governance problems are inseparable from pedagogy because privacy constraints, procurement rules, fairness expectations, and auditability requirements shape what can be taught, what data can be used, and what claims can be responsibly made in institutional contexts.

1.5 Terminological Framework and Chapter Roadmap

Key terms are used with operational precision throughout the chapter to maintain conceptual control across disciplines. *Statistical inquiry* denotes an iterative cycle of problem formulation, data production, analysis, interpretation, and communication, with explicit attention to uncertainty, error structures, and decision consequences. *Variability* functions as the unifying conceptual nucleus linking descriptive summaries, probability, sampling, inference, and model diagnostics, while *transnumeration* denotes principled movement among raw data, representations, and summaries to support meaning-making. *Model-based reasoning* is treated as disciplined simplification that demands assumption articulation, diagnostic checking, and robustness evaluation under plausible perturbations. *AI* denotes learning systems that generate predictions, classifications, or content, while *AutoML* denotes pipeline automation that can conceal evaluation choices and default priors, thereby requiring governance-aware scrutiny. The chapter proceeds from theoretical foundations in Section 2 to curriculum architecture in Section 3, classroom routines and tooling in Section 4, equity-ethics-integrity design in Section 5, and assessment-evaluation research design in Section 6, culminating in an implementation synthesis in Section 7.

2. THEORETICAL FOUNDATIONS FOR STATISTICS EDUCATION IN AI-ADJACENT CONTEXTS

2.1 Variability-Centric Ontologies for Uncertainty Reasoning

Statistics education is most defensible when it is organized around *variability* as the primary cognitive object, because variability unifies descriptive summarization, probabilistic modeling, sampling logic, and inferential warranting under a single epistemic grammar of uncertainty. Learners must acquire distributional reasoning as a form of population-level cognition that resists case-based anecdotalism, including sensitivity to tail behavior, heteroscedasticity, multimodality, and outlier-generating mechanisms that often masquerade as signal (Airaj, 2024; Ramirez & Esparrell, 2024; Alam, 2022). Core constructs such as *sampling variability*, *measurement error*, *selection effects*, and *distribution shift* should be treated as first-order explanatory primitives rather than afterthoughts appended to procedures. Inferential competence then becomes the ability to translate observed data into contingent claims that remain stable under plausible perturbations, with explicit separation of estimation uncertainty and decision uncertainty. This section-level architecture anticipates the operational alignment in Table 1, where conceptual nuclei are coupled to AI affordances and failure modes that threaten epistemic agency.

2.2 Cognitive-Developmental Learning Progressions and Representational Fluency

Robust statistics education requires an explicit developmental progression from informal inferential reasoning to formal inference, guided by progressive formalization rather than abrupt symbolization. The pedagogical aim is to stabilize intuitive notions of randomness, long-run behavior, and signal-to-noise discrimination, then consolidate them into representational fluency across raw data, summaries, visualizations, and model parameters, a process often described as *transnumeration* (Farooqi et al., 2024; Tang, 2024; Edwards-Fapohunda & Adediji, 2024). Conceptual bottlenecks commonly arise when learners conflate probability with certainty, interpret variability as error rather than information, and treat summary statistics as causal explanations, so instruction must engineer contrastive cases that surface these misconceptions without collapsing into rote correction. Cognitive architecture considerations matter because high-assistance environments can offload computation while inflating superficial confidence, so learning design must preserve metacognitive monitoring through confidence calibration, error anticipation, and revision planning. When these progressions are mapped against tool-mediated workflows, Table 1 provides a concrete design check that prevents representational automation from substituting for conceptual consolidation.

2.3 Instructional Theories for Inquiry, Argumentation, and Epistemic Agency

A conceptually coherent statistics curriculum operationalizes *inquiry-based learning* as a disciplined cycle of problem formulation, data production, analysis, interpretation, and communication, where each phase includes explicit epistemic obligations. Task design should prioritize reasoning-centered performance, requiring learners to justify measurement choices, articulate assumptions, compare competing explanations, and defend inferential claims under uncertainty, thereby embedding *argumentation theory* into routine classroom discourse (Almasri, 2024; Perkins et al., 2024). *Cognitive apprenticeship* strengthens this architecture by externalizing expert moves such as diagnostic checking, sensitivity reasoning, and baseline-first modeling, then fading scaffolds to transfer agency to learners. *Variation theory* can be used to orchestrate carefully designed contrasts, near-miss datasets, and counterexamples that make the boundaries of concepts visible, while *conceptual change* mechanisms support refutation of stable misconceptions through structured confrontation with anomalies. Table 1 is invoked here as a governance-aware instructional blueprint that links these theories to tool affordances without allowing tool fluency to eclipse inferential accountability.

2.4 Validity, Epistemology, and Boundary Conditions of Statistical Claims

Statistical epistemology becomes operational, not philosophical, when analytic pipelines can conceal defaults, because claims are only as defensible as their validity conditions. A rigorous framework distinguishes internal validity threats such as confounding, selection bias, and measurement distortion, from external validity constraints such as transportability failure under distribution shift, and from statistical conclusion validity risks such as multiple testing, model misspecification, and miscalibrated uncertainty (Guo et al., 2024; Alam, 2023c). Inferential pluralism is pedagogically useful when it clarifies warrant structures, with frequentist reasoning emphasizing long-run error control, Bayesian reasoning emphasizing coherent updating under explicit priors, and likelihood reasoning emphasizing comparative evidential support, yet all three converge on the obligation of model checking and sensitivity analysis. The practical boundary between prediction and explanation must be made explicit, because predictive adequacy does not license causal interpretation, and causal claims require counterfactual discipline and design logic. The operational mapping in Table 1 is placed here to translate validity threats into instructional countermeasures and AI guardrails that keep learners accountable for warrants rather than outputs.

Table 1. Mapping Statistical Big Ideas to AI Pedagogical Guardrails

Foundational Anchor Construct	High-Leverage Statistical Idea	AI Affordance Modality	Predictable Epistemic Failure Mode	Pedagogical Countermove and Governance Safeguard
Variability Ontology	Distributional thinking with tail-risk awareness and heterogeneity detection	Synthetic data generation for controlled shifts, perturbations, and rare-event amplification	Overgeneralization from plausible-looking samples, neglect of tail behavior and subgroup dispersion	Require pre-specified distributional diagnostics, mandate uncertainty statements, enforce baseline comparison using transparent summaries
Sampling Logic	Sampling distributions, resampling inference, and repeated-sampling intuition	Rapid simulation of bootstrap and randomization regimes with parameter toggles	Deterministic interpretation of simulated outputs, confusion between variability and error	Use constrained prompts that demand repeated-sampling narratives, require manual sanity checks with small-sample analogs, log workflow provenance
Association and Confounding	Covariation reasoning with confounder detection and selection effect critique	Counterexample generation that flips associations under stratification and collider conditioning	Correlation-to-causation slippage, spurious narrative coherence, omission of selection mechanisms	Enforce causal language restrictions, require explicit DAG-like assumption articulation in prose, include structured confounding audit checklist
Model-Based Reasoning	Bias-variance trade-off, overfitting detection, calibration, and robustness	Automated model comparison with cross-validation templates and calibration visual summaries	Metric fixation, silent reliance on defaults, unexamined optimization objectives	Require declaration of target function and error costs, obligate calibration verification, restrict AutoML to post-baseline phase with documentation

continued on following page

Table 1. Continued

Foundational Anchor Construct	High-Leverage Statistical Idea	AI Affordance Modality	Predictable Epistemic Failure Mode	Pedagogical Countermove and Governance Safeguard
Validity and Decision Accountability	Uncertainty communication, threshold choice, and harm-aware decision rules	Scenario-based critique prompts that force stakeholder-specific error asymmetry analysis	Epistemic deference to authoritative tone, threshold choice without utility rationale	Mandate decision memos with explicit utility assumptions, require contestability narrative, implement disclosure norms and reproducibility checks
Representational Fluency	Transnumeration across raw data, graphs, summaries, and parameters	Multimodal explanation and representation translation across tables, plots, and narratives	Representation laundering, acceptance of persuasive visualizations without design justification	Require justification of representational choices, include graph-audit protocol, enforce version history review and oral micro-defense

The table operationalizes a governance-ready linkage between core statistical ideas and tool-mediated affordances, while foregrounding predictable epistemic breakdowns that arise when automation is mistaken for understanding. Each row is intentionally phrased as a design specification that can be enacted as classroom policy, assignment architecture, and assessment evidence, thereby converting abstract validity concerns into concrete instructional constraints. The countermeasures emphasize baseline transparency, provenance logging, diagnostic routines, and structured justification, which together form an integrity-preserving ecology suited to both high-resource and low-resource environments. Table 1 also functions as a coherence instrument across this section, since the constructs in 2.1 and 2.2 are connected to the discourse norms in 2.3 and the validity boundary conditions in 2.4 through a single, auditable mapping. This mapping can later be expanded into curriculum progression logic and tool-selection heuristics without introducing new conceptual primitives, thereby reducing curricular fragmentation while preserving epistemic rigor.

2.5 Cross-Disciplinary Critical Dimensions for Global Statistical Literacy

Statistics education must incorporate cross-disciplinary critical dimensions because statistical claims are socially consequential artifacts embedded in institutions, infrastructures, and governance regimes. *Critical statistical literacy* extends beyond numeracy by requiring scrutiny of categorization practices, proxy variables, aggregation choices, and measurement regimes that can produce epistemic harm through misclassification, invisibilization, or unjust resource allocation (Sperling et al., 2024). A global outlook demands attention to *data asymmetries* across regions, including uneven measurement capacity, differing legal constraints on data use, and context collapse when models trained in one socio-technical ecology are transported into another. Ethical framing should be grounded in *relational accountability* and harm-based reasoning, where fairness is treated as an ongoing responsibility tied to error asymmetries and contestability rather than as a single metric target. Policy and workforce relevance follow when learners can produce decision-grade communication, including calibrated uncertainty language, threshold rationales, and auditable workflows aligned to governance constraints. Table 1 is referenced here as the integrating instrument that makes these critical dimensions actionable, because it translates sociotechnical risks into concrete classroom guardrails and evidence expectations.

3. CURRICULUM REDESIGN AND PROGRAM ARCHITECTURE FOR STATISTICS EDUCATION

3.1 Epistemic Competency Targets and Program-Level Outcome Grammars

A statistics curriculum that remains coherent in AI-adjacent environments must be written as an outcomes grammar of epistemic competencies, not as a catalog of topics, because competence is demonstrated through warrants, diagnostics, and accountability rather than through procedural throughput. Program outcomes should explicitly encode *statistical literacy*, *statistical reasoning*, and *statistical thinking* as layered capacities, progressing from interpretation of claims to explanation of variability and finally to inquiry-driven decision making under uncertainty (Alam, 2023b; Iqbal et al., 2024; Davis et al., 2024). This outcomes grammar is best operationalized through *constructive alignment* and *backward design*, where assessments privilege assumption articulation, uncertainty quantification, and validity critique, thereby preventing a drift into tool-centric performativity. The governance alignment established in Table 1 should remain a standing constraint, so every outcome is paired with integrity-preserving evidence modalities such as reproducible workflows, decision memos, and defensible threshold rationales. The vertical coherence of these outcomes is consolidated in Table 2, which functions as the program's competency spine and the audit lens for curriculum drift.

3.2 Spiral Competency Progressions across Tiers and Credential Bands

A spiral architecture is necessary because statistics concepts exhibit cumulative abstraction, where early intuitions about variability and randomness must be repeatedly re-contextualized into more formal inferential warrants, diagnostic checks, and robustness reasoning. The introductory tier should stabilize distributional cognition and *transnumeration*, training learners to move among raw data, summaries, and representations without mistaking any representation for reality (Sharma et al., 2024; Robert et al., 2024; Bukar et al., 2024). The intermediate tier should deepen model-based reasoning through residual logic, cross-validation habits, calibration awareness, and sensitivity to confounding, while explicitly separating predictive adequacy from explanatory legitimacy. The advanced tier should consolidate decision-grade competence by integrating causal logic constraints, transportability reasoning under *distribution shift*, fairness-aware error decomposition, and monitoring practices aligned to deployment realities. This tiering should be expressed through a competency progression matrix rather than through content lists, so that each tier has observable evidence artifacts and non-negotiable epistemic moves, as specified in Table 2. Table 2 also functions as a portability instrument across institutions, enabling low-resource and high-resource implementations to converge on the same inferential standards.

Table 2. Competency Progression for AI-Ready Statistics Curricula

Competency Strand	Introductory Tier Performance Signature	Intermediate Tier Performance Signature	Advanced Tier Performance Signature	Misconception Risk and Corrective Scaffold
Variability and Distribution	Learner narrates center-spread-shape, flags tail-risk, and justifies representation choices with uncertainty language.	Learner models heteroscedasticity, distinguishes noise from structure, and uses diagnostic plots to refine interpretive claims.	Learner stress-tests distributional assumptions under shift, quantifies tail sensitivity, and defends robustness boundaries.	Determinism bias is countered through constrained simulation, contrastive cases, and explicit variability-as-information reframing.
Sampling and Inferential Warranting	Learner explains repeated-sampling intuition, uses resampling logic, and states what a statistic can and cannot claim.	Learner selects inference frameworks by question type, checks assumptions, and interprets intervals as uncertainty envelopes.	Learner performs sensitivity analysis for missingness, selection, and transportability, articulating validity conditions and limits.	Pseudo-certainty is disrupted via small-sample analogs, bootstrap narratives, and mandatory uncertainty statements in memos.
Association, Confounding, and Causal Boundaries	Learner distinguishes association from causation, identifies plausible confounders, and avoids causal verbs in interpretations.	Learner critiques selection effects, stratifies analyses, and explains Simpson-type reversals as structural artifacts.	Learner applies counterfactual discipline, evaluates identification plausibility, and specifies causal assumptions in audit prose.	Correlation-to-causation slippage is corrected by causal language constraints, confounding audits, and counterexample generation.
Model-Based Reasoning and Validation	Learner compares baselines, interprets residuals, and treats models as provisional simplifications with assumptions.	Learner manages bias-variance trade-offs, uses cross-validation, checks calibration, and documents evaluation design choices.	Learner monitors drift, interrogates objective functions, and defends model acceptance through decision-cost reasoning.	Metric fixation is corrected through baseline-first rules, calibration checks, and explicit optimization-objective declarations.

continued on following page

Table 2. Continued

Competency Strand	Introductory Tier Performance Signature	Intermediate Tier Performance Signature	Advanced Tier Performance Signature	Misconception Risk and Corrective Scaffold
Uncertainty Communication and Decision Governance	Learner writes stakeholder-aware summaries, states uncertainty explicitly, and avoids overclaiming from point estimates.	Learner justifies thresholds using asymmetric error costs, interprets calibration, and writes decision memos with constraints.	Learner integrates harm analysis, contestability narratives, and governance constraints into decision-rule documentation.	Narrative overreach is reduced through structured claim-evidence-uncertainty templates and mandatory limitation statements.
Integrity, Reproducibility, and Sociotechnical Accountability	Learner maintains workflow traces, discloses assistance, and produces reproducible notebooks or equivalent artifacts.	Learner documents data provenance, checks leakage risks, and uses version control norms for auditability.	Learner aligns artifacts to policy constraints, privacy minimization, and fairness accountability with reproducibility safeguards.	Opaque reliance is mitigated via disclosure norms, process evidence requirements, and oral micro-defenses of key choices.

Table 2 operationalizes a tiered competency spine that keeps conceptual depth intact while allowing flexible local implementation, because it specifies epistemic performance signatures rather than mandating particular platforms. The strands make *validity* and *accountability* teachable objects, not peripheral compliance concerns, thereby aligning curriculum structure with decision-grade reasoning demands. The misconception column functions as an instructional control system, translating predictable cognitive failure modes into corrective scaffolds that can be embedded in tasks, rubrics, and classroom routines. The progression also preserves coherence with Table 1 by ensuring that AI affordances remain subordinate to inferential warrants, provenance discipline, and governance constraints, preventing tool-driven curricular drift. In subsequent sections, Table 2 can be used as a calibration device for task design, micro-credential stacking, and capstone assessment architecture, while maintaining parity across high-resource and low-resource environments.

3.3 Prediction Touchpoints without Epistemic Eclipse and Automation Myopia

Embedding machine-learning touchpoints is defensible only when they are subordinated to inferential logic, validity constraints, and interpretability-first sequencing, because otherwise curricula drift into automation myopia where predictive scores are mistaken for understanding. A baseline-first doctrine should be mandatory, so learners must justify incremental value over transparent benchmarks before accessing more complex pipelines, thereby protecting epistemic humility and diagnostic habits (Sana et al., 2024; Nguyen et al., 2024; Obidovna, 2024). Prediction modules should be framed as an extension of statistical modeling, emphasizing error decomposition, calibration, cross-validation design, and robustness under *covariate shift*, with explicit separation of predictive adequacy from causal interpretation. Task requirements should force decision accountability, including threshold rationales tied to asymmetric error costs, subgroup error audits, and sensitivity checks for missingness and leakage, aligning directly to the governance countermeasures articulated in Table 1 and the tiered performance signatures in Table 2. This approach prevents conceptual displacement by making predictive tooling a context for rehearsing statistical ideas, not a spectacle of hyperparameter optimization, and it produces artifacts that remain auditable for workforce and policy contexts.

3.4 Global Context Ecologies, Data Provenance, and Curricular Transferability

Curriculum architecture gains global relevance when contexts are treated as epistemic infrastructures that shape interpretive plausibility, validity threats, and harm profiles, rather than as decorative case studies. Health screening tasks should foreground base-rate reasoning, calibration, and asymmetric error costs, climate risk tasks should foreground non-stationarity and tail exposure, governance tasks should foreground selection bias and measurement politics, and business tasks should foreground strategic behavior and feedback loops, while keeping the same conceptual nucleus of variability, sampling, and model checking (Amdan et al., 2024; Alqahtani & Wafula, 2025). Data provenance must be curricular infrastructure, so learners routinely document sampling frames, missingness mechanisms, label construction, and proxy risks, thereby turning *construct validity* into an everyday analytic practice. Low-resource equivalence should be designed in advance through offline-first simulations, small-data inference tasks, and paper-based randomization, ensuring that Table 2 competencies can be evidenced without high-bandwidth dependence. This context ecology approach strengthens transfer because learners practice invariant reasoning moves across heterogeneous domains, while remaining accountable to local constraints and governance realities.

3.5 Micro-Credential Stacking, Capstone Architectures, and Change-Management Realism

A sustainable program architecture requires stackable micro-credentials and capstone pathways that operationalize competency claims as auditable artifacts, thereby translating Table 2 from a curriculum spine into a credentialing logic that workforce systems can interpret. Micro-credentials should certify narrowly defined performance signatures such as uncertainty communication, reproducible analysis, validity critique, fairness-aware error analysis, and governance-ready documentation, with assessment designs that privilege process evidence and oral defense rather than polished outputs (Abuhassna et al., 2024; Alam, 2023a). Capstones should be staged as multi-phase inquiry systems, beginning with problem framing and measurement design, moving through baseline modeling and robustness checks, and culminating in stakeholder decision memos that include threshold justification, contestability pathways, and disclosure norms aligned with Table 1 guardrails. Change management must be treated as a design constraint, with faculty communities of practice, rubric moderation, workload-aware assessment templates, and secure data environments that prevent inequitable access and policy noncompliance. This architecture makes the curriculum durable under tool volatility by anchoring competence in epistemic practices and governance literacy rather than in transient platform affordances.

4. CLASSROOM ROUTINES, TASK DESIGN, AND TOOLING IN STATISTICS EDUCATION

4.1 Epistemic Interaction Routines for Agency-Preserving Sensemaking

An AI-adjacent statistics classroom must institutionalize routines that encode epistemic agency as the default posture, so learners treat computational outputs as provisional hypotheses that require interrogation, not as authoritative conclusions. High-leverage routines include data-sensemaking colloquia where claims are articulated before analysis, diagnostic studios where residual reasoning and calibration are discussed as epistemic evidence, and critique seminars where alternative representations compete under explicit validity constraints (Afzaal et al., 2024; Rabiatu & Shehu, 2024; Lérias et al., 2024). These routines operationalize *cognitive apprenticeship* through modeled expert moves, scaffolded rehearsal, and gradual release, while preventing epistemic drift into answer-seeking. Productive struggle is preserved through phase constraints that defer automation until learners have articulated assumptions, specified uncertainty expectations, and predicted plausible failure modes. The governance alignment in Table 1 remains a standing constraint, and the competency spine in Table 2 provides progression targets, while Table 3 later translates these routines into tool-permitted phases and verification artifacts that make integrity and auditability instructionally routine.

4.2 Task Archetypes, Didactic Transpositions, and Disciplinary Transfer

Task design should be treated as didactic engineering, where statistical ideas are transposed into executable learning episodes that elicit reasoning about variability, sampling, and validity rather than rote computation. High-yield task archetypes include compare-groups investigations that foreground distributional overlap, association tasks that force confounding critique, and modeling tasks that require baseline-first justification and diagnostic checking (Zhou et al., 2024; Fitrianto et al., 2024; Forero-Corba & Bennasar, 2024). Each archetype should embed *transnumeration* demands, requiring learners to justify representational choices, interrogate aggregation effects, and translate outputs into decision-grade narratives with calibrated uncertainty language. Transfer across disciplines is stabilized by maintaining invariant epistemic moves, such as stating assumptions, checking sensitivity, and articulating boundary conditions, while contexts vary across health, climate, governance, and business. In AI-mediated environments, tasks must include structured skepticism prompts that require counterexample generation and robustness checks, with Table 3 serving as a classroom-level control system that couples task intent to permissible tooling and mandatory verification evidence.

4.3 Tool-Orchestrated Learning Episodes and Integrity-Grade Evidence Capture

Operational orchestration should be designed as a three-phase learning episode, beginning with low-tech elicitation that surfaces priors and misconceptions, moving to tool-supported exploration for simulation and hypothesis refinement, and culminating in an AI-restricted defense phase where learners must justify claims using transparent reasoning. This sequencing mitigates automation-induced complacency by forcing learners to articulate model purpose, specify evaluation design, and pre-commit to diagnostic checks before any generated narrative is admitted as plausible (Al-Zahrani & Alasmari, 2024; Alam & Mohanty, 2022). Evidence capture is a non-negotiable instructional substrate, including workflow traces, version histories, and decision memos that make reasoning auditable without resorting to surveillance-heavy practices. Tool selection must be tied to epistemic intent, permitted phase, and predictable failure modes, which is operationalized in Table 3. Table 3 also preserves alignment with Table 2 by ensuring that each tool-mediated episode produces evidence that corresponds to tiered competency signatures rather than to superficial output quality.

Table 3. Task-Tool-Guardrail for Epistemic Goal Alignment in Classrooms

Instructional Intent Vector	Tool Archetype Band	Permitted Learning Phase Boundary	Predictable Epistemic Risk Profile	Required Verification and Evidence Artifact
Data Elicitation Studio	Lightweight survey-logic tools, local spreadsheets, and offline randomization generators	Pre-tool phase, followed by minimal computation for transparency	Construct drift, proxy contamination, and category reification through premature summarization	Operational definition memo, sampling plan sketch, and provenance note with disclosure norms
Simulation Inference Laboratory	Resampling engines, local notebooks, and controlled synthetic data generators	Exploration phase only, with constrained prompts for uncertainty narration	Deterministic reading of stochastic outputs, and overconfidence from dense simulation traces	Repeated-sampling narrative, sanity-check with small-n analog, and logged parameter perturbations
Model Critique Clinic	Interpretable modeling toolkits, baseline comparators, and calibration check utilities	Post-baseline phase, after explicit objective declaration	Metric fixation, default dependence, and leakage blindness under convenience evaluation	Baseline comparison report, calibration statement, and validation design justification with version history
Representation Audit Seminar	Visualization systems, linked views, and automated chart suggestion modules	Interpretation phase, after representational choice rationale is drafted	Representation laundering, axis manipulation, and aggregation concealment of subgroup structure	Graph audit protocol, alternative representation appendix substitute within memo, and uncertainty annotation
Fairness and Harm Walkthrough	Subgroup evaluation tools, threshold analysis utilities, and scenario-based critique prompts	Decision phase, after explicit harm model articulation	Fairness metric fetishism, threshold arbitrariness, and moral outsourcing to dashboards	Error asymmetry matrix, threshold rationale tied to utilities, and contestability narrative for stakeholders
Oral Micro-Defense Colloquium	AI-restricted environment, whiteboard reasoning, and peer critique scripts	Defense phase, with computation frozen and prompts disabled	Performative fluency without conceptual ownership, and post-hoc rationalization	Live justification transcript, assumption articulation checklist, and reproducibility pledge with assistance disclosure

Table 3 functions as a classroom-level governance instrument that converts abstract pedagogical intent into enforceable orchestration constraints, thereby stabilizing epistemic agency under high-assistance conditions. The matrix also operationalizes integrity as design, not policing, because it specifies verification artifacts that reveal reasoning quality, assumption discipline, and decision accountability without requiring invasive monitoring. Each row encodes a predictable risk profile, enabling instructors to pre-empt failure modes through phase boundaries and evidence requirements, while maintaining alignment with Table 1 guardrails and Table 2 competency progression signatures. Because the tool archetypes are specified as bands rather than brands, the matrix remains portable across institutions and resource levels, including offline-first settings that can implement equivalent verification through local notebooks and structured memos. This portability sustains a globally relevant instructional architecture while preserving conceptual rigor and audit-ready defensibility.

4.4 Sociotechnical Guardrails, Risk Controls, and Robustness Engineering

Tooling must be embedded within a sociotechnical control layer that treats privacy, security, and reliability constraints as pedagogical design parameters rather than as administrative afterthoughts. Guardrails should include access controls, data minimization routines, sandboxed environments for sensitive datasets, and disclosure norms that make assistance transparent and auditable, while avoiding coercive surveillance (Joel Augustus et al., 2025; Abbasi et al., 2025). Robustness engineering should become an instructional habit, requiring learners to perform sensitivity checks under missingness, scaling changes, alternative binning, and plausible distribution shifts, thereby converting fragility into a teachable diagnostic object. Visualization governance is especially critical because persuasive graphics can launder weak reasoning, so students should justify transformation choices, subgroup splits, and exclusion rules using validity language and uncertainty annotations, consistent with Table 3 representation-audit requirements. These guardrails connect directly to Table 1 by translating validity threats into operational constraints, and they connect to Table 2 by ensuring that competence is evidenced through diagnostic reasoning and reproducibility rather than through polished outputs.

4.5 Teacher Professional Cognition, Normative Classroom Culture, and Durable Implementation

Teacher development must prioritize professional cognition in statistical epistemology, diagnostic pedagogy, and tool-failure literacy, because instruction collapses when educators treat platforms as infallible authorities rather than as fallible instruments. Effective professional learning is structured as communities of practice with task rehearsals, rubric calibration, prompt-log moderation, and shared libraries of failure cases that make misconceptions and validity threats predictable rather than surprising (Grájeda et al., 2024; Dieterle et al., 2024; Jatileni et al., 2024). Classroom culture should institutionalize norms that treat AI outputs as hypotheses, require assistance disclosure, and reward uncertainty-aware reasoning, with explicit sanctions for opacity that undermines auditability and fairness. The hidden curriculum must be managed deliberately, because repeated exposure to automated answers can cultivate dependency and epistemic passivity, so teachers should systematically engineer gradual transfer of responsibility through constrained phases and oral defenses aligned to Table 3. This culture also supports workforce and policy relevance by producing learners who can justify decision rules, communicate calibrated uncertainty, and document analytic workflows that remain contestable, secure, and governance-ready across sectors.

5. EQUITY, ETHICS, AND INTEGRITY AS STATISTICS EDUCATION DESIGN PRINCIPLES

5.1 Equity-of-Opportunity Architectures in Algorithmically Mediated Learning Ecologies

Equity in AI-adjacent statistics education must be engineered as equity-of-opportunity, not merely as device access, because opportunity is shaped by interface scaffolds, feedback timing, linguistic register, and differential exposure to high-cognitive-demand argumentation tasks. A defensible design stance treats *UDL* as a statistical pedagogy heuristic, enabling multiple representational pathways for *variability* and *uncertainty* while preserving invariant epistemic standards for inference, validity critique, and decision accountability (Alam & Mohanty, 2023; Lye & Lim, 2024; Xia et al., 2024). Low-resource constraints should be accommodated through offline-first simulation, small-data resampling, and paper-based randomization, ensuring conceptual parity rather than a bifurcated curriculum where privileged learners practice diagnosis and others practice keystrokes. Equity also requires mitigation of automation-induced stratification, where confidence, fluency, and polished prose can obscure shallow reasoning, a risk that is operationally countered through process-evidence requirements and oral micro-defenses. Table 4 is later used as the equity-preserving scoring grammar that rewards warrant quality, transparency, and harm-aware reasoning independent of stylistic sophistication.

5.2 Ethical Reasoning across the Statistical Inquiry Cycle and the Data Lifecycle

Ethics in statistics education should be operationalized across the full inquiry cycle, because ethical harm is often created upstream in problem framing and measurement, then laundered downstream through aggregation and optimization. Problem framing must include stakeholder enumeration, harm modeling, and constraint specification, so that the analytic objective is treated as a value-laden choice rather than a neutral technicality (Mahmoud & Sørensen, 2024; Karakose & Tülübas, 2024; Yue et al., 2024). Data practices must encode *data minimization*, *purpose limitation*, and storage discipline, alongside construct validity scrutiny that interrogates proxies, label formation, and omission patterns, especially in sensitive domains such as education, health, and social protection. Model training and evaluation must be framed as trade-off governance, balancing accuracy, calibration, subgroup error asymmetries, interpretability, and contestability, with threshold selection justified by utilities and rights-sensitive constraints rather than by convenience defaults. Synthetic data and generated explanations should be treated as epistemically non-neutral, demanding leakage checks, plausibility audits, and uncertainty disclosure. Table 4 later stabilizes these ethical requirements by embedding them into performance descriptors that convert abstract ethics into assessable reasoning moves.

5.3 Critical Statistical Literacy, Power-Aware Measurement, and Sociotechnical Accountability

Statistics education gains global legitimacy when it integrates *critical statistical literacy* as a disciplined practice of questioning whose categories, whose measurements, and whose aggregation rules become institutional reality, because classification systems can produce epistemic harm through invisibilization, misrecognition, and distributive inequity. Learners should be trained to treat categorization as a governance act, to interrogate proxy variables as socio-technical compromises, and to recognize that fairness metrics can be mutually incompatible, requiring context-bound justification rather than metric shopping (Rane, 2024; Ezeoguine & Eteng-Uket, 2024; Ng et al., 2025; Schwab-McCoy, 2019). A power-aware curriculum also treats the communication layer as consequential, since persuasive narratives and polished visualizations can normalize weak warrants, therefore representational choices must be justified through validity language, uncertainty annotation, and subgroup legibility. Accountability should be framed through *algorithmic impact assessment* logic, where decision rules, data provenance, and monitoring obligations are made explicit and contestable, aligning classroom practice with policy-grade documentation habits. Table 4 later provides the scoring architecture that rewards measurement justice, contestability narratives, and harm-aware threshold reasoning, thereby making sociotechnical accountability a concrete learning target rather than a rhetorical add-on.

5.4 Integrity-by-Design Assessment Architecture and Analytic Rubric Formalization

Academic integrity in AI-adjacent statistics education should be treated as an assessment architecture problem, because output correctness is no longer diagnostic of understanding when generative systems can produce plausible prose, code, and visualizations at scale. Integrity-by-design relies on task structures that require local adaptation, intermediate artifacts, and defensible reasoning traces, including decision memos, annotated diagnostics, and reproducible workflows that reveal warrant construction rather than aesthetic polish (Wang & Li, 2024; Lim, 2024; Legaki et al., 2020). The evaluative center should shift from answer possession to epistemic process, rewarding assumption articulation, uncertainty calibration, validity critique, and harm-aware decision justification, while penalizing opacity, untraceable transformations, and post-hoc rationalization. Assistance disclosure should be normalized as professional practice, not framed as moral failure, enabling transparent differentiation between scaffolding and outsourcing. Table 4 operationalizes this architecture as a multi-dimensional analytic rubric, so scoring becomes an explicit epistemic contract that aligns student effort with defensible statistical judgment, equity-aware interpretation, and audit-ready accountability.

Table 4. Rubric for Statistical Reasoning, Equity, and Integrity

Rubric Dimension Strand	Emergent Performance Signature	Developing Performance Signature	Proficient Performance Signature	Advanced Performance Signature
Uncertainty and Assumption Discipline	Uses point claims with minimal uncertainty language, assumptions remain implicit and unstable.	States uncertainty qualitatively, identifies some assumptions yet does not test their consequences.	Quantifies uncertainty appropriately, articulates assumptions clearly, links assumptions to inference limits.	Performs sensitivity reasoning under plausible perturbations, defends boundary conditions with calibrated confidence and humility.
Data Provenance and Measurement Justice	Describes data superficially, treats categories as natural, omits sampling and labeling constraints.	Notes provenance partially, recognizes missingness, begins to question proxies and construct validity.	Documents provenance, sampling frame, missingness logic, critiques proxies using validity and equity language.	Designs measurement choices to reduce harm, anticipates category-induced bias, justifies inclusions and exclusions as governance acts.
Model Choice, Validation, and Robustness	Selects models by convenience, validation is minimal, defaults are accepted without scrutiny.	Uses basic validation, compares limited alternatives, notices overfitting signals without robust mitigation.	Chooses baselines first, validates with sound design, checks calibration, interprets diagnostics as epistemic evidence.	Stress-tests under shift and leakage risk, justifies objective functions, defends robustness with transparent limitations and trade-offs.
Fairness, Harm, and Threshold Accountability	Treats fairness as a slogan, thresholds are arbitrary, harms are unexamined.	Reports subgroup metrics mechanically, acknowledges trade-offs, provides weak threshold rationale.	Analyzes subgroup errors, links metrics to harm narratives, chooses thresholds using utility and constraint reasoning.	Constructs contestable decision rules, anticipates downstream externalities, justifies fairness choices under metric incompatibilities.

continued on following page

Table 4. Continued

Rubric Dimension Strand	Emergent Performance Signature	Developing Performance Signature	Proficient Performance Signature	Advanced Performance Signature
Communication, Stakeholder Legibility, and Contestability	Produces descriptive summaries, reasoning chain is opaque, limitations are absent or generic.	Communicates results with partial clarity, includes some limitations, stakeholder framing remains thin.	Writes decision-grade narratives, states limitations concretely, aligns claims to stakeholder needs and risk tolerance.	Produces contestability-ready documentation, enables challenge pathways, balances technical precision with accessible uncertainty communication.
Reproducibility, Disclosure, and Process Integrity	Workflow is not reproducible, assistance is undisclosed, artifacts lack traceability.	Partial traceability exists, some disclosure is provided, reproducibility is fragile and incomplete.	Maintains reproducible workflow, discloses assistance transparently, preserves version history and verification steps.	Demonstrates audit-ready provenance, integrates verification checkpoints, documents assistance as controlled scaffolding within integrity norms.

Table 4 functions as a scoring and learning contract that makes integrity and equity operational, because it converts abstract ideals into observable performance signatures that can be taught, practiced, and verified. The rubric also mitigates automation-driven distortions by decoupling evaluation from stylistic polish and anchoring judgment in process evidence, diagnostic reasoning, and harm-aware decision justification. Each strand is intentionally framed as a cross-disciplinary competence, enabling alignment with workforce expectations for auditability, policy expectations for accountability, and instructional expectations for conceptual mastery. Table 4 also reinforces coherence with earlier foundations by treating *variability*, *validity*, and *robustness* as assessable reasoning objects, not as optional reflections. In later sections, the rubric can be integrated into task architectures and evaluation blueprints without introducing new constructs, thereby stabilizing curriculum implementation across diverse institutional constraints and resource regimes.

5.5 Institutional Governance, Policy Coherence, and Contestable Accountability Mechanisms

Institutional governance must be designed to support equity, ethics, and integrity at scale, because classroom norms collapse when platform procurement, data governance, and acceptable-use policies are misaligned with pedagogical intent. Acceptable-use regimes should define differentiated assistance categories, requiring disclosure and traceability for generative support while protecting legitimate scaffolding for accessibility and language mediation (Sarwar & Ms Saima, 2024; Dai & Liu, 2024; Cheah et al., 2025; Legaki & Hamari, 2020). Data governance should implement privacy-by-design through deidentification discipline, access control, retention limits, and vendor logging constraints, ensuring that instructional analytics do not become covert surveillance. Oversight structures should treat *contestability* as a learner right, establishing pathways to challenge automated feedback, grading analytics, and model-driven recommendations, with documentation standards that make rationales inspectable and corrigible. Table 4 should be adopted as a common evaluation grammar across courses, enabling moderation, auditability, and equity checks through consistent performance descriptors rather than ad hoc judgments. This governance coherence transforms statistics education into a decision-grade capability, producing graduates who can justify models, defend thresholds, and communicate uncertainty in ways that remain accountable to law, policy, and public trust.

6. ASSESSMENT, EVALUATION, AND RESEARCH DESIGNS IN STATISTICS EDUCATION

6.1 Evidence-Centered Assessment Architectures for Epistemic Performance

Assessment in AI-adjacent statistics education must be engineered through *evidence-centered design*, where the competency claim, the elicited evidence, and the scoring inference are tightly coupled so that polished outputs cannot masquerade as conceptual mastery. The primary target is epistemic performance, including assumption articulation, uncertainty calibration, validity critique, and decision accountability, which are better captured through composite artifacts than through isolated answers (Liu et al., 2024; Alam & Mohanty, 2024; Karataş et al., 2025; Romero-Rodríguez et al., 2024). These artifacts should integrate reproducible analytic traces, annotated representations, and decision memos that make reasoning legible under audit, aligning scoring with the integrity logic formalized in *Table 4*. The assessment system should explicitly discriminate between procedural execution, interpretive justification, and governance awareness, ensuring that assistance remains disclosed and bounded rather than covert and outcome-only. The blueprint logic in *Table 5* is referenced here as the coordination layer that links each outcome claim to an evidence portfolio and a defensible scoring mechanism, thereby preventing construct underrepresentation and automation-induced validity erosion.

6.2 Validity, Reliability, and Fairness as Measurement Governance

Validity must be treated as a governance argument rather than a psychometric afterthought, because a score in high-assistance environments can drift toward measuring fluency, access, or rhetorical polish rather than statistical reasoning. A robust validity architecture integrates *content alignment*, *response-process integrity*, and *consequential validity*, ensuring that tasks actually elicit uncertainty reasoning, diagnostic skepticism, and harm-aware threshold justification (Bender, 2024; Topaz et al., 2025; Watson & Smith, 2022). Reliability should be stabilized through moderation routines consistent with *generalizability theory*, including benchmark portfolios, rubric calibration, and inter-rater coherence checks that reduce idiosyncratic scoring variance. Fairness should be operationalized as *measurement invariance* and opportunity parity, with attention to language mediation, accessibility, and differential tool access that can distort performance evidence. These constraints align naturally with the analytic rubric in *Table 4* and should be instantiated through the mitigation safeguards specified in *Table 5*, which embeds equity checks, validity-threat detection, and audit-ready documentation as non-negotiable scoring conditions rather than optional compliance add-ons.

6.3 Multilevel Evidence Ecologies

Program evaluation must be designed as a multilevel evidence ecology that integrates task-level artifacts, course-level portfolios, and program-level claims into a coherent inference chain, preventing simplistic metrics from substituting for defensible judgments. The evaluation logic should privilege triangulation across modalities, including written argumentation, reproducible analytic workflows, oral micro-defenses, and representation audits, because no single channel remains robust under pervasive generative assistance. Learning analytics can be used as a diagnostic layer, not as a summative oracle, with interpretation constrained by confound sensitivity, prior-preparation heterogeneity, and access variance that can create spurious performance narratives. Aggregation rules should be explicitly declared, with defensible weighting of evidence types and explicit rules for handling missing artifacts, ensuring that the system remains auditable and contestable. This subsection culminates in *Table 5*, which functions as a comprehensive blueprint aligning outcome claims, evidence portfolios, analytic scoring, validity threats, and mitigation safeguards across the full assessment-evaluation stack.

Table 5. Comprehensive Blueprint for Assessment, Evaluation, and Research Evidence

Outcome Claim Construct	Evidence Artifact Portfolio	Analytic and Scoring Mechanism	Validity and Equity Threat Vector	Mitigation and Audit Safeguard Protocol
Uncertainty Reasoning and Assumption Discipline	Decision memo with explicit assumptions, uncertainty statements, and sensitivity narrative tied to a reproducible trace.	Rubric-scored warrant quality, calibrated uncertainty language checks, and cross-artifact coherence verification.	Rhetorical inflation, deterministic interpretation, and stylistic privilege masking shallow reasoning.	Mandatory oral micro-defense, disclosure verification, and consistency checks between trace outputs and narrative claims.
Sampling and Inferential Warranting	Resampling notebook, repeated-sampling explanation, and annotated representation of sampling variability.	Structured scoring of inferential warrant, simulation sanity checks, and representational justification evaluation.	Simulation determinism, procedure mimicry, and access-based computational advantage.	Offline-equivalent protocol option, parameter-logging requirement, and small-n analog verification checkpoint.
Model Validation, Calibration, and Robustness	Baseline comparison report, calibration statement, diagnostic annotations, and versioned evaluation design rationale.	Multi-dimensional scoring using *Table 4* strands, validation-design audit, and leakage-risk screening.	Metric fixation, default dependence, and hidden objective-function drift.	Baseline-first rule enforcement, calibration verification requirement, and documented objective-function declaration with change log.
Fairness, Harm, and Threshold Accountability	Subgroup error analysis, harm narrative, threshold rationale tied to utilities, and contestability statement.	Rubric-scored harm reasoning, threshold defensibility assessment, and subgroup error-parity interpretation check.	Fairness metric fetishism, moral outsourcing to dashboards, and language barriers in harm articulation.	Standardized harm-model template, peer critique protocol, and equity review of subgroup definitions and exclusions.
Data Provenance and Measurement Justice	Provenance sheet, construct definition note, proxy-risk critique, and missingness mechanism statement.	Validity critique scoring, construct coherence checks, and evidence of category governance reasoning.	Category reification, proxy laundering, and omission bias invisibilizing vulnerable groups.	Required provenance disclosures, representation-audit gate, and explicit inclusion-exclusion justification review.
Reproducibility, Disclosure, and Process Integrity	Version history, assistance disclosure, reproducible workflow, and verification checklist completion.	Audit scoring for trace completeness, reproducibility run-check, and disclosure consistency evaluation.	Opaque assistance, untraceable transformations, and surveillance-driven chilling effects.	Privacy-respecting trace policy, minimal-necessary logging, and reproducibility pledge with verification sampling.

Table 5 converts evaluation into a coherent, audit-ready inference system by binding each outcome claim to a portfolio of evidence artifacts that remain informative even when generative assistance is ubiquitous. The blueprint also operationalizes validity and fairness by naming predictable threat vectors and embedding mitigation protocols as required checkpoints, thereby reducing construct contamination and opportunity distortion. Its structure harmonizes with *Table 4* by ensuring that rubric dimensions are instantiated through concrete evidence modalities, not aspirational language, while remaining portable across resource contexts through offline-equivalent protocols and minimal-necessary logging. The table further strengthens governance readiness by making contestability and disclosure part of the evaluative substrate, enabling transparent challenge pathways and reproducible verification without punitive surveillance. In later implementation, this blueprint can be used as a program-level contract among instructors, technologists, and policy stewards, aligning assessment labor, analytic tooling, and integrity norms to a single defensible logic.

6.4 Research Design Logics for Iterative Optimization

A conceptual-theoretical chapter can still specify rigorous research design logics as an implementation guide, emphasizing inference discipline and mechanism plausibility without claiming empirical results. *Design-based research* provides a cycle structure for iterative refinement of tasks, scaffolds, and discourse routines, using theory-driven conjectures about how representational fluency, diagnostic reasoning, and metacognitive calibration develop under constrained tool orchestration. When institutions require impact verification, quasi-experimental logic can be specified as a defensible option, including *propensity-score* alignment, *difference-in-differences* contrasts, and multilevel specification to handle classroom clustering, instructor effects, and context heterogeneity. Process-level analysis can be framed through *sequence analysis* and *process mining* of workflow traces, interpreted cautiously as indicators of strategy patterns rather than as direct proxies for understanding. These designs should treat *Table 5* as an a priori schema for dependent constructs and evidence channels, ensuring that measurement aligns to competencies rather than to platform telemetry convenience.

6.5 Ethics, Open-Practice Constraints, and Cost-Aware Deployability

Ethics must be integrated into assessment and evaluation as *privacy-by-design* and proportionality, because instructional trace data can become sensitive behavioral dossiers if governance is weak. Data minimization, retention limits, and purpose limitation should be embedded into evaluation workflows, with transparent learner-facing disclosures that preserve trust while maintaining auditability. Open-practice aspirations should be framed as reproducibility norms rather than as indiscriminate sharing, using deidentified exemplars, reusable task shells, and platform-agnostic scoring templates that respect legal constraints and contextual sensitivities. Cost-aware deployability is a systems constraint, so programs should model total cost of ownership, including moderation labor, rubric calibration time, secure infrastructure, and opportunity costs of over-instrumentation. Hybrid strategies can balance feasibility and rigor, combining local notebooks, constrained tool use, and selective procurement aligned to governance requirements, with *Table 5* guiding which evidence modalities are non-negotiable and which can be adapted. This approach yields a globally portable evaluation architecture that is technically robust, ethically grounded, and operationally sustainable.

7. CONCLUSION

7.1 Integrative Synthesis of Epistemic Commitments and Design Coherence

This chapter consolidates a coherent epistemic contract for statistics education in AI-adjacent societies, where the central deliverable is disciplined judgment under uncertainty rather than procedural throughput or platform fluency. The integrative spine is variability-centric reasoning, representational fluency through *transnumeration*, and validity-aware inference that treats models as provisional instruments bounded by assumptions, data provenance, and transportability constraints. AI is positioned as scaffold, simulator, and critic, yet never as an epistemic sovereign, because accountability for claims, thresholds, and harms remains irreducibly human. Coherence is stabilized through the internal design instruments, *Table 1* aligns statistical big ideas with AI affordances and guardrails, *Table 2* encodes tiered competency signatures that preserve conceptual depth, *Table 3* operationalizes classroom orchestration and verification artifacts, *Table 4* formalizes equity-ethics-integrity scoring as a learning contract, and *Table 5* binds outcomes to evidence ecologies with validity safeguards. Together these constructs create an audit-ready educational architecture that is portable across disciplines and resource contexts, while sustaining contestability, reproducibility, and decision-grade uncertainty communication.

7.2 Phased Implementation Priorities for Institutional Realism and Scalability

Sustainable implementation requires phased adoption that privileges epistemic routines and assessment architecture before expanding tool complexity, because early missteps can normalize dependency, opacity, and metric fetishism. Initial phases should institutionalize baseline-first modeling, constrained tool orchestration, and disclosure norms, using *Table 3* phase boundaries and verification artifacts to prevent automation myopia. Concurrently, programs should adopt the analytic rubric in *Table 4* as a common scoring grammar, enabling moderation, measurement coherence, and fairness checks across courses, while aligning evidence capture to the blueprint in *Table 5* with minimal-necessary logging and privacy-by-design. Mid-phase scaling should focus on faculty communities of practice, calibration protocols, and shared task libraries grounded in *Table 2* progression signatures, ensuring that curricular spirals deepen inferential warrants rather than proliferate disconnected techniques. Later phases can introduce more sophisticated tool bands and governance mechanisms, including contestability pathways, secure sandboxes, and procurement constraints that preserve auditability and equity. This phased strategy reduces institutional fragility, distributes workload realistically, and maintains alignment between pedagogy, governance, and workforce relevance.

7.3 Future-Oriented Research and Global Collaboration Agendas for Durable Impact

A durable global agenda for statistics education requires shared conceptual infrastructures that enable cross-institutional coherence without imposing platform monocultures, beginning with validated learning progressions for uncertainty reasoning, diagnostic skepticism, and AI-specific misconception patterns. Priority constructs include competence in calibration language, robustness under distribution shift, confounding critique without causal overreach, and disclosure-normalized integrity, all measurable through portfolio evidence architectures consistent with *Table 5*. International collaboration should focus on interoperable repositories of high-leverage tasks, misconception-triggering contrasts, rubric-anchored exemplars, and offline-equivalent simulations, enabling low-resource and high-resource settings to converge on the same epistemic standards. Governance-oriented collaboration should advance contestability protocols and learner rights in analytics-embedded ecosystems, ensuring that educational data practices remain proportionate, transparent, and corrigible. Long-horizon impact depends on sustaining *epistemic agency* as the central educational virtue, so future work should prioritize instructional designs that keep learners as authors of arguments, stewards of assumptions, and accountable decision reasoners, even as AI tooling evolves in capability, persuasiveness, and ubiquity.

REFERENCES

Abbasi, B. N., Wu, Y., & Luo, Z. (2025). Exploring the impact of artificial intelligence on curriculum development in global higher education institutions. *Education and Information Technologies, 30*(1), 547–581.

Abuhassna, H., Awae, F., Adnan, M. A., Daud, M., & Almheiri, A. S. (2024). The information age for education via artificial intelligence and machine learning: A bibliometric and systematic literature analysis. *International Journal of Information and Education Technology (IJIET), 14*(5), 700.

Afzaal, M., Shanshan, X., Yan, D., & Younas, M. (2024). Mapping artificial intelligence integration in education: A decade of innovation and impact (2013–2023): A bibliometric analysis. *IEEE Access.*

Airaj, M. (2024). Ethical artificial intelligence for teaching-learning in higher education. *Education and Information Technologies, 29*(13), 17145–17167.

Alam, A. (2022). Impact of university's human resources practices on professors' occupational performance: Empirical evidence from India's higher education sector. In *Inclusive businesses in developing economies: Converging people, profit, and corporate citizenship* (pp. 107–131). Springer.

Alam, A. (2023a). Media multitasking with M-learning technology in real-time classroom learning: Analysing the dynamics in formal educational settings for the future of E-learning in India. In *Proceedings of the 2023 2nd International Conference on Smart Technologies and Systems for Next Generation Computing (ICSTSN)* (pp. 1–6). IEEE.

Alam, A. (2023b). The secret sauce of student success: Cracking the code by navigating the path to personalized learning with educational data mining. In *Proceedings of the 2023 2nd International Conference on Smart Technologies and Systems for Next Generation Computing (ICSTSN)* (pp. 1–8). IEEE.

Alam, A. (2023c). Intelligence unleashed: An argument for AI-enabled learning ecologies with real world examples of today and a peek into the future. In *AIP Conference Proceedings* (Vol. 2717, No. 1, Article 030001). AIP Publishing.

Alam, A., & Mohanty, A. (2022, December). Facial analytics or virtual avatars: Competencies and design considerations for student-teacher interaction in AI-powered online education for effective classroom engagement. In *Proceedings of the International Conference on Communication, Networks and Computing* (pp. 252–265). Springer Nature.

Alam, A., & Mohanty, A. (2023, January). Learning on the move: A pedagogical framework for state-of-the-art mobile learning. In *Proceedings of the International Conference on Data Management, Analytics and Innovation* (pp. 735–748). Springer Nature.

Alam, A., & Mohanty, A. (2024). Integrated constructive robotics in education (ICRE) model: A paradigmatic framework for transformative learning in educational ecosystem. *Cogent Education, 11*(1), 2324487.

Almasri, F. (2024). Exploring the impact of artificial intelligence in teaching and learning of science: A systematic review of empirical research. *Research in Science Education, 54*(5), 977–997.

Alqahtani, N., & Wafula, Z. (2025). Artificial intelligence integration: Pedagogical strategies and policies at leading universities. *Innovative Higher Education, 50*(2), 665–684.

Al-Zahrani, A. M., & Alasmari, T. M. (2024). Exploring the impact of artificial intelligence on higher education: The dynamics of ethical, social, and educational implications. *Humanities & Social Sciences Communications, 11*(1), 1–12.

Amdan, M. A. B., Janius, N., & Kasdiah, M. A. H. B. (2024). Concept paper: Efficiency of artificial intelligence (AI) tools for STEM education in Malaysia. *International Journal of Science and Research Archive, 12*(2), 553–559.

Bender, S. M. (2024). Awareness of artificial intelligence as an essential digital literacy: ChatGPT and Gen-AI in the classroom. *Changing English, 31*(2), 161–174.

Bukar, U. A., Sayeed, M. S., Razak, S. F. A., Yogarayan, S., & Sneesl, R. (2024). Decision-making framework for the utilization of generative artificial intelligence in education: A case study of ChatGPT. *IEEE Access : Practical Innovations, Open Solutions, 12*, 95368–95389.

Cheah, Y. H., Lu, J., & Kim, J. (2025). Integrating generative artificial intelligence in K–12 education: Examining teachers' preparedness, practices, and barriers. *Computers and Education: Artificial Intelligence, 8*, 100363.

Cukurova, M. (2025). The interplay of learning, analytics and artificial intelligence in education: A vision for hybrid intelligence. *British Journal of Educational Technology, 56*(2), 469–488.

Dai, K., & Liu, Q. (2024). Leveraging artificial intelligence (AI) in English as a foreign language (EFL) classes: Challenges and opportunities in the spotlight. *Computers in Human Behavior, 159*, 108354.

Davis, C., Bush, T., & Wood, S. (2024). Artificial intelligence in education: Enhancing learning experiences through personalized adaptation. *International Journal of Cyber and IT Service Management*, *4*(1), 26–32.

Dieterle, E., Dede, C., & Walker, M. (2024). The cyclical ethical effects of using artificial intelligence in education. *AI & Society*, *39*(2), 633–643. PMID: 36185064

Edwards-Fapohunda, M. O., & Adediji, M. A. (2024). Sustainable development of distance learning in continuing adult education: The impact of artificial intelligence. *Iconic Research and Engineering Journals*, *8*(1), 113–114.

Ezeoguine, E. P., & Eteng-Uket, S. (2024). Artificial intelligence tools and higher education student's engagement. *Edukasiana: Jurnal Inovasi Pendidikan*, *3*(3), 300–312.

Farooqi, M. T. K., Amanat, I., & Awan, S. M. (2024). Ethical considerations and challenges in the integration of artificial intelligence in education: A systematic review. *Journal of Excellence in Management Sciences*, *3*(4), 35–50.

Fitrianto, I., Setyawan, C. E., & Saleh, M. (2024). Utilizing artificial intelligence for personalized Arabic language learning plans. *International Journal of Post Axial: Futuristic Teaching and Learning*, 30–40.

Forero-Corba, W., & Bennasar, F. N. (2024). Techniques and applications of machine learning and artificial intelligence in education: A systematic review. *RIED-Revista Iberoamericana de Educación a Distancia, 27*(1).

Grájeda, A., Burgos, J., Córdova, P., & Sanjinés, A. (2024). Assessing student-perceived impact of using artificial intelligence tools: Construction of a synthetic index of application in higher education. *Cogent Education*, *11*(1), 2287917.

Guo, S., Zheng, Y., & Zhai, X. (2024). Artificial intelligence in education research during 2013–2023: A review based on bibliometric analysis. *Education and Information Technologies*, *29*(13), 16387–16409.

Iqbal, M., Khan, N. U., & Imran, M. (2024). The role of artificial intelligence (AI) in transforming educational practices: Opportunities, challenges, and implications. *Qlantic Journal of Social Sciences*, *5*(2), 348–359.

Jatileni, C. N., Sanusi, I. T., Olaleye, S. A., Ayanwale, M. A., Agbo, F. J., & Oyelere, P. B. (2024). Artificial intelligence in compulsory level of education: Perspectives from Namibian in-service teachers. *Education and Information Technologies*, *29*(10), 12569–12596.

Joel Augustus, D., Asiegbu Victor, I., & Obinna, E. (2025). Leveraging artificial intelligence (AI) for educational development in Nigeria: Examining the challenges and opportunities. *Journal of Social Science*, *2*(2).

Karakose, T., & Tülübas, T. (2024). School leadership and management in the age of artificial intelligence (AI): Recent developments and future prospects. *Educational Process: International Journal*, *13*(1), 7–14.

Karataş, F., Eriçok, B., & Tanrikulu, L. (2025). Reshaping curriculum adaptation in the age of artificial intelligence: Mapping teachers' AI-driven curriculum adaptation patterns. *British Educational Research Journal*, *51*(1), 154–180.

Lee, Y. J., Davis, R. O., & Ryu, J. (2024). Korean in-service teachers' perceptions of implementing artificial intelligence (AI) education for teaching in schools and their AI teacher training programs. *International Journal of Information and Education Technology (IJIET)*, *14*(2), 214–219.

Legaki, N. Z., Xi, N., Hamari, J., Karpouzis, K., & Assimakopoulos, V. (2020). The effect of challenge-based gamification on learning: An experiment in the context of statistics education. *International Journal of Human-Computer Studies*, *144*, 102496. PMID: 32565668

Legaki, Z., & Hamari, J. (2020). Gamification in statistics education: A literature review. In *Proceedings of the International GamiFIN Conference* (pp. 41–51). CEUR Workshop Proceedings.

Leong, W. Y., Leong, Y. Z., & San Leong, W. (2024, October). Artificial intelligence in education. In *Proceedings of the IET International Conference on Engineering Technologies and Applications (ICETA 2024)* (pp. 183–184). IET.

Lim, E. M. (2024). Metaphor analysis on pre-service early childhood teachers' conception of AI (artificial intelligence) education for young children. *Thinking Skills and Creativity*, *51*, 101455.

Liu, R., Zenke, C., Liu, C., Holmes, A., Thornton, P., & Malan, D. J. (2024, March). Teaching CS50 with AI: Leveraging generative artificial intelligence in computer science education. In *Proceedings of the 55th ACM Technical Symposium on Computer Science Education*, Volume 1 (pp. 750–756). Association for Computing Machinery.

Lye, C. Y., & Lim, L. (2024). Generative artificial intelligence in tertiary education: Assessment redesign principles and considerations. *Education Sciences*, *14*(6), 569.

Mahmoud, C. F., & Sørensen, J. T. (2024). Artificial intelligence in personalized learning with a focus on current developments and future prospects. *Research and Advances in Education*, *3*(8), 25–31.

Ng, D. T. K., Chan, E. K. C., & Lo, C. K. (2025). Opportunities, challenges and school strategies for integrating generative AI in education. *Computers and Education: Artificial Intelligence*, 100373.

Nguyen, A., Kremantzis, M., Essien, A., Petrounias, I., & Hosseini, S. (2024). Enhancing student engagement through artificial intelligence (AI): Understanding the basics, opportunities, and challenges. *Journal of University Teaching & Learning Practice*, *21*(6), 1–13.

Obidovna, D. Z. (2024). The pedagogical-psychological aspects of artificial intelligence technologies in integrative education. *International Journal of Literature and Languages*, *4*(3), 13–19.

Perkins, M., Furze, L., Roe, J., & MacVaugh, J. (2024). The artificial intelligence assessment scale (AIAS): A framework for ethical integration of generative AI in educational assessment. *Journal of University Teaching & Learning Practice*, *21*(6), 49–66.

Rabiatu, M. M., & Shehu, S. A. (2024). Adopting artificial intelligence (AI) in education: Challenges and possibilities. *Asian Journal of Advanced Research and Reports*, *18*(2), 106–111.

Ramirez, E. A. B., & Esparrell, J. A. F. (2024). Artificial intelligence (AI) in education: Unlocking the perfect synergy for learning. *Educational Process: International Journal*, *13*(1), 35–51.

Rane, N. (2024). Enhancing the quality of teaching and learning through Gemini, ChatGPT, and similar generative artificial intelligence: Challenges, future prospects, and ethical considerations in education. *TESOL and Technology Studies*, *5*(1), 1–6.

Robert, A., Potter, K., & Frank, L. (2024). The impact of artificial intelligence on students' learning experience. *Wiley Interdisciplinary Reviews: Computational Statistics*, *2*(1), 75–84.

Romero-Rodríguez, M. E., Rodríguez-Donate, M. C., & Nieto-González, I. L. (2024). Improving active learning: Innovation in statistics education. In *Teaching innovations in economics: Towards a sustainable world* (pp. 371–384). Springer Nature.

Sana, E., Fitriani, A., Soetarno, D., & Yusuf, M. (2024). Analysis of user perceptions on interactive learning platforms based on artificial intelligence. *Journal of Computer Science and Technology Application*, *1*(1), 26–32.

Sarwar, M. A., & Ms Saima, A. G. (2024). The role of artificial intelligence in shaping the future of education at higher secondary level. *Journal of Education and Social Studies*, *5*(1), 34–45.

Schwab-McCoy, A. (2019). The state of statistics education research in client disciplines: Themes and trends across the university. *Journal of Statistics Education : An International Journal on the Teaching and Learning of Statistics*, *27*(3), 253–264.

Sperling, K., Stenberg, C. J., McGrath, C., Åkerfeldt, A., Heintz, F., & Stenliden, L. (2024). In search of artificial intelligence (AI) literacy in teacher education: A scoping review. *Computers and Education Open*, *6*, 100169.

Tahir, M., Hassan, F. D., & Shagoo, M. R. (2024). Role of artificial intelligence in education: A conceptual review. *World Journal of Advanced Research and Reviews*, *22*(1), 1469–1475.

Tang, K. H. D. (2024). Implications of artificial intelligence for teaching and learning. *Acta Pedagogia Asiana*, *3*(2), 65–79.

Topaz, M., Peltonen, L. M., Michalowski, M., Stiglic, G., Ronquillo, C., Pruinelli, L., & Fukahori, H. (2025). The ChatGPT effect: Nursing education and generative artificial intelligence. *The Journal of Nursing Education*, *64*(6), e40–e43. PMID: 38302101

Wang, J., & Li, J. (2024). Artificial intelligence empowering public health education: Prospects and challenges. *Frontiers in Public Health*, *12*, 1389026. PMID: 39022411

Watson, J., & Smith, C. (2022). Statistics education at a time of global disruption and crises: A growing challenge for the curriculum, classroom and beyond. *Curriculum Perspectives*, *42*(2), 171–179.

Xia, Q., Weng, X., Ouyang, F., Lin, T. J., & Chiu, T. K. (2024). A scoping review on how generative artificial intelligence transforms assessment in higher education. *International Journal of Educational Technology in Higher Education*, *21*(1), 40.

Yim, I. H. Y., & Su, J. (2025). Artificial intelligence (AI) learning tools in K–12 education: A scoping review. *Journal of Computers in Education*, *12*(1), 93–131.

Yue, M., Jong, M. S. Y., & Ng, D. T. K. (2024). Understanding K–12 teachers' technological pedagogical content knowledge readiness and attitudes toward artificial intelligence education. *Education and Information Technologies*, *29*(15), 19505–19536.

Zhou, X., Zhang, J., & Chan, C. (2024). Unveiling students' experiences and perceptions of artificial intelligence usage in higher education. *Journal of University Teaching & Learning Practice*, *21*(6), 126–145.

Chapter 6
Integrating AI Tools Into Statistics Education
From Intelligent Tutors to Automated Modeling

Anupam Pareek
http://orcid.org/0000-0002-6166-659X
Poornima University, Jaipur, India

Nikhil Kumar Goyal
http://orcid.org/0009-0007-4532-8033
Noida International University, Greater Noida, India

ABSTRACT

This chapter examines how artificial intelligence (AI) has transformed the teaching and learning processes in modern statistics through discussions of the intelligent tutoring systems and automated modeling algorithms that are redefining modern statistical education. Conventional methods of statistics may pose a challenge to learners especially in abstract conceptualization, interpretation, and application of models to real data. Using AI-managed tools, teachers will be able to deliver personalized learning experiences, feedback, and intelligent guidance that support a variety of learning styles. The intelligent tutoring systems provide customized routes to the probability, hypothesis testing and data analysis mastery, and the automated modeling platforms represent by AI simplify the tasks involved in model selection, validation and interpretation. The chapter also points to pedagogical advantages of these technologies, such as increased engagement, better conceptual understanding, and better accessibility by learners of various levels of proficiency.

DOI: 10.4018/979-8-3373-6259-5.ch006

1. INTRODUCTION

This chapter explores the growing role of artificial intelligence in statistics learning with special attention to three main functions, namely artificial intelligence as a learning support system, artificial intelligence as an automated analysis support system, and artificial intelligence as a creative educational partner. The chapter relies on the theories of learning, statistical reasons, and collaboration between humans and AI, as well as studies these technologies considering the possibility of conceptual learning, personalization, and accessibility.

By mentioning intelligent tutoring systems, automated modeling platforms, and AI-based visualization tools, the chapter mentions the opportunities and challenges of pedagogy, such as excessive use of automation, a lack of transparency, ethical issues of privacy and bias of information. The case studies in classrooms show how AI may be utilized in design in case of incorporation of reflective activities and instructor guidance.

The chapter wraps up with suggestions of assessment redesign, support of student readiness, and scalable implementation models where the successful application of AI in statistics learning involves the alignment of technological innovation with the existing theoretical assumptions of the principles of statistical literacy and ethical responsibility.

1.1 Evolving Landscape of Statistics Education

Statistics has never left and will always remain an essential part of decision-making on data and information in various health-related and business-related, engineering and social sciences. Nevertheless, instructing statistics has always been very difficult. Students tend to find it abstract and formula-heavy, and they have trouble with such things as probability distributions, inferential logic, and interpretation of models. In addition, the distance between the theory and practical application often makes the learners uninterested. As artificial intelligence (AI) and machine learning are becoming a reality, the pedagogical landscape is radically changing. It is not that AI-based learning resources are just auxiliary services, but those tools transform the way statistical concepts are taught, practiced, and applied (Andinasari et al., 2019).

Figure 1. Changing Landscape Of Education

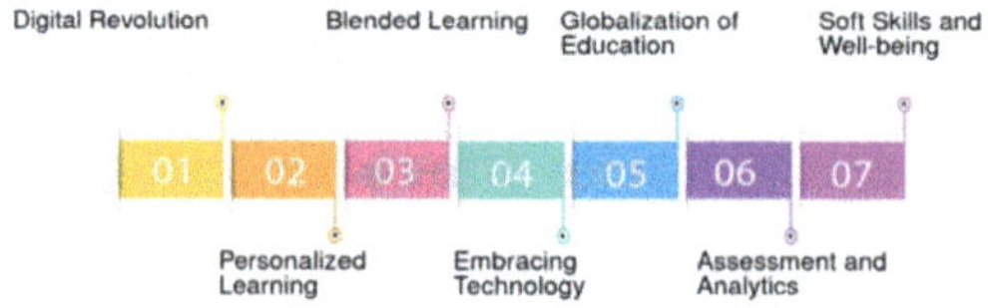

Lectures and problem sets were oftentimes used in traditional classrooms, which restricted the level of individualization. Although these approaches can help several learners, there are those whose education and mathematical ability are different, and this creates a gap between them. The AI tools solve this gap by providing adaptive learning platforms that tailor the delivery of content based on their performance. As an example, an AI-controlled tutor can tell that a student has a problem with hypothesis testing and gives adaptive exercises or simplified explanations until they have mastered the problem. This allows a more accommodative learning process to be generated where faster and slower learners both have increased individualized attention.

Moreover, with the big data and data science taking leading positions in the contemporary industries, the need to be statistically literate is increasing exponentially. Not only are students now required to solve problems in textbooks, but also analyze complex and unstructured data, interpret the outputs of machine learning programs and make evidence-based choices. The AI-enhanced tools fill this gap by modeling real world scenarios, automate a portion of the modeling process, and visually present results in a way that is not dogmatic to understand. Such pedagogical-technological synergy puts AI as an inseparable partner in training the learners to live in the information era (Ashofteh & Bravo, 2021).

1.2 Role of AI in Enhancing Pedagogy

There is no recent advent of artificial intelligence in education, as intelligent tutoring systems were studied since the 1980s. Nevertheless, with the current developments in the natural language processing (NLP), machine learning, and adaptive analytics, they have become much more effective and available. AI in statistics education can carry out tasks that were previously restricted to human instructors: identifying misconceptions, providing immediate feedback, and providing alternative problem solving approaches.

Figure 2. Role of AI in education

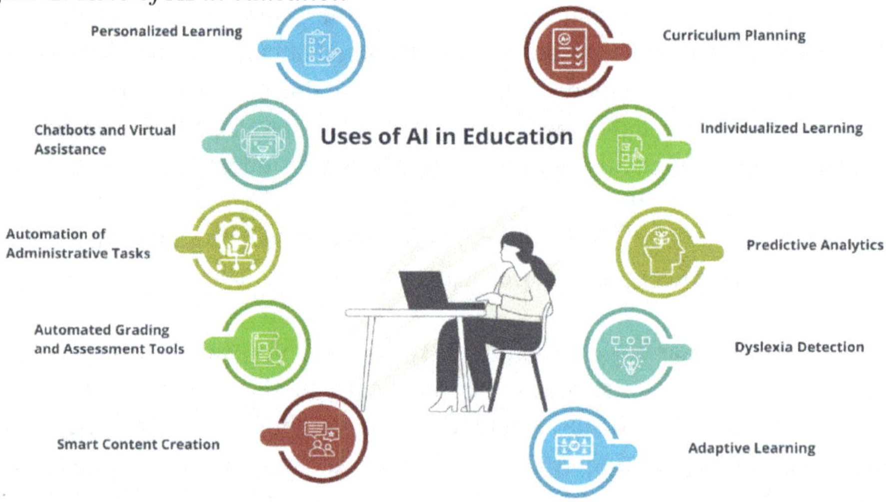

To illustrate, smart tutors will be able to monitor the manner in which a student tackles a probability problem. Provided that the error is the same one, i.e. the learner systematically misses the rule of addition to overlapping events, the system identifies the error pattern and interferes with context examples that help the learner understand the difference between disjoint and independent events. This corrective intervention in situ helps in forestalling the gnosisification of misperceptions which would otherwise remain undetected at a classroom level (Bargagliotti & Franklin, 2015).

Also, AI helps to use the time in the classroom more effectively. Automated grading of assignments and modeling exercises unloads teachers, thereby enabling them to address more advanced teaching activities, including facilitating discussions or mentoring research projects. Another tool that teachers have access to is the analytics dashboard that summarizes performance trends across students and allows taking proactive action to mitigate the issue in at-risk students. In this way, AI is not going to eliminate teachers; it will improve their ability to deliver effective and personalized teaching.

1.3 Intelligent Tutors to Automated Modeling

One of the advantages of AI in statistics education is the duality of the tool to begin the journey of gaining knowledge of the fundamentals of the field but also assist in higher-level analytical tasks. The primary role of intelligent tutors is that of adaptive mentors whereby students are made to have good conceptual bases. However, automated modeling tools will help the application of those concepts to real-world datasets, closing the gap between learning in the classroom and practice in the real world (Sharma et al., 2026).

The shift can be represented by automated modeling systems like AutoML (Automated Machine Learning). In traditional environments, model selection, parameter tuning and validation commonly have students overwhelmed and they do not focus on conceptual learning. Automation based on the AI enables the learner to concentrate on interpreting the results and why some models are more effective instead of losing in the technical loop. As an example, an AutoML system may be capable of executing a number of regression models, assessing them based on statistical measures, and rendering the most precise one, in addition to providing justification of the choice.

This two-pronged strategy will make sure that students not only understand statistical theory but will also acquire practical skills that are pertinent to industry. They also get to know how to critically assess the outputs of AI, interpret the models assumptions, and how to detect the possibilities of bias, which are also invaluable tools in a world where more and more decisions are made based on automated tools (Ben-Zvi & Makar, 2016).

1.4 Pedagogical Considerations

Although the integration of AI may be associated with opportunities that have never been observed before, the integration has also brought up issues that cannot be ignored. Excessive use of automated tools will also jeopardize the capacity of the students to learn how to do manual calculations or produce intuition. When learners continuously rely on AI systems to make their decisions, they might not be able to think critically and challenge the erroneous results or when the assumptions are being made.

Back-sight is another issue. AI models, particularly those based on deep learning, are often black-box and it is not easy to learners to have a feel of the reasoning behind some of the predictions or suggestions. This inability to explain things can pose a barrier to learning in the pedagogical context since the students can accept the results without necessarily understanding the principles behind them. That way, explainable AI (XAI) stands out as a crucial element of statistics education, as it makes sure that a student does not just operate AI tools, but also learns how they work and what their limitations are (Biehler et al., 2024).

Lastly, ethical issues like privacy of data, bias in the algorithms, and fair access should be also incorporated in the curriculum. The learners ought to be informed on how biased training data may distort results or how personal information should be used in statistical modeling. The consideration of these discussions in form of embedding is a way that will make future data professionals not only technically qualified but also morally sound.

1.5 Typology of AI Use in Statistics Education

There are three key roles of AI in statistics education that come to mind to make the concept more understandable. To start with, AI can be used as a learning aid, including an intelligent tutoring system, adaptive quizzes, or a learning analytics dashboard, where the primary aim is to facilitate the process of student learning. Second, AI may be used as a statistical analysis and modeling aid, such as by automated model selection, parameter tuning, and visualization generation in which the aim is to aid data analysis work and not teaching. Third, recent developments in generative AI allow AI to become a content generation partner to generate the explanations, examples, datasets, formative feedback in real time.

In being frequently used synonymously, the only way in which it becomes possible to distinguish them analytically is to assist in clarifying the pedagogical goals and risks associated with the use of ICT and proper assessment strategy. This chapter is divided into the following sections that follow these functional groupings to give a logical flow of topic of learning support, to analytical automation, and to newly emerging generative abilities.

2. THEORETICAL FOUNDATIONS OF AI IN EDUCATION AND STATISTICS

2.1 Learning Theories and AI-Enhanced Education

Introducing AI in statistics education is not only a technological-level innovation, but also a pedagogical development based on traditional theories of learning. Classroom methods of teaching statistics tended to follow the principles of behaviorism, with focus on drills and problems to practice, and encouragement of correct answers. Although this model proved useful in memorization, it often did not lead to more in-depth perception of abstract statistical ideas. Intelligent tutoring systems based on AI are an extension of behaviorist theories in that they give immediate feedback and rewards, yet they also integrate more sophisticated paradigms of learning (Goyal et al., 2025a).

In constructivist terms, learners develop their own knowledge through an active process of working with issues, datasets, and simulations. AI facilitates this strategy by means of dynamic platforms enabling the students to control variables, see real-time results, and run hypotheses in interactive settings. As an example, in the context of sampling distributions, AI-based simulators can create thousands of random samples, allowing a student to watch the central limit law in action and not just memorize its definition. These practical experiences are beneficial to conceptual understanding, which is consistent with the constructivist philosophy that knowledge is developed when a person takes an active part.

The other theory with an impact is the cognitive load theory whereby the complexity in what is being taught to students overloads the working memory making learning impossible. Bayesian inference or regression analysis In statistics, the abstraction involved in concepts like Bayesian inference or regression analysis may add several layers of abstraction at once, causing cognitive overload. Combating this issue, AI tools help to decompose multifaceted problems, transforming them into small and solvable parts. Adaptive tutors are able in the case where the student is not following a particular step like calculating a posterior probability, the tutor can detect and offer specific guidance to the student before proceeding. This scaffolding does not cause any cognitive load and maintains the integrity of learning (Boels, 2023).

2.2 Artificial Intelligence in the Context of Statistical Thinking

In its most basic form, statistics is the reasoning under uncertainty, the ability to make inferences using data and to detect the signal versus the noise. Information AI, especially machine learning, is similar in purpose but frequently pursues it by optimising algorithms instead of hard probabilistic logic. The introduction of AI to statistics instruction provides consequential inquiries as to the connection between conventional statistical cognition and contemporary AI practices.

The focus of statistical inference has traditionally been on transparency, which means that learners should be able to interpret p-values, confidence intervals, and derive estimators and have an understanding of their assumptions. In contrast, AI systems can make very precise predictions with no clear explanations, which can be frequently criticized as the so-called black box problem. This poses a challenge and an opportunity to the educators. The difficulty is in making sure that the students do not necessarily trust AI outputs blindly. The chance, though, is that AI enables learners to experiment with the practical constraints of models, e.g., overfitting, multicollinearity or sample bias, in a way that real-world textbook examples do not display (Boels et al., 2023).

Integrating AI devices in coursework, students acquire the ability to balance between probabilistic thinking and the results of machine learning. They learn to value that although AI provides computing power and pattern recognition, the interpretative and ethical aspects of data analysis still need to have a foundational base on statistical logic (Callingham & Watson, 2017).

2.3 Theories of Human–AI Collaboration in Learning

The other theoretically grounded area that applies to AI in statistics education is the emerging science of human-AI collaboration. AI is not a passive tool as the traditional software tools are; it is a partner that adjusts to the human input. This demands that the role of the learner, the teacher and the machine in the educational ecosystem be re-evaluated.

This is especially practical in terms of the distributed cognition model. It implies that cognitive processes do not exist in individual minds only, but are shared among individuals, instruments and environments. Cognition may be shared among students, teachers, and artificial intelligence in a statistics classroom. To illustrate, an AI platform can do some mundane computations, which leaves cognitive resources to be used in interpretation and reasoning. This type of division of labor does not weaken learning but makes it more effective as collaboration with machines optimizes human and machine advantages: AI offers computational power and pattern recognition, and human beings offer situational judgment and moralism (Kumari et al., 2026).

The concept of the Zone of Proximal Development (ZPD) of the Vygotskian theory is relevant to AI-enhanced learning, as well. The difference between what a learner is capable of doing without assistance and what he/she can do with assistance is what the ZPD is all about. AI tutors serve the ZPD as a scaffold, that is, when they are required, supporting and when they are not needed, abandoning. In statistics, this may be assisting a learner in understanding residual plots in regression until he/she has sufficient experience to do this independently. Due to the adaptability of AI, the scaffolding role is singular to it such that the instruction is neither too simple nor too challenging (Ellis & Slade, 2023).

2.4 Epistemological Foundations

Theoretical thought is not limited to the pedagogy but also to ethics and epistemology. Transparency, replicability and accountability have long been the focus of statistics, which do support the scientific method. AI, nevertheless, is commonly trained with opaque algorithms on massive data, posing the issue of fairness, bias, and explainability. To incorporate AI into statistics education, it is necessary to incorporate these ethical debates into the curriculum according to which learners need to know the strength and weaknesses of AI systems.

Epistemologically, the two have some differences in terms of the methods used to come up with knowledge in statistics and AI. Statistical models can place a premium on being interpretable, and can provide causal relationships and uncertainty. Deep learning and other AI models can offer truthful predictions without clear understanding of how and why something works. Students should be taught to critically assess these differences with an eye to creating an effective practitioner who is able to strike a balance between predictive and interpretive clarity (Engel, 2017).

To illustrate this point, in an instance where an AI model forecasts traffic movement in a very precise and accurate way, but fails to provide transparency concerning contributing factors, students should be provided with the ability to ask themselves whether such a model can be used in making decisions in urban planning. The integration of explainable AI (XAI) in statistics education will make sure the trade-offs between accuracy, transparency, and accountability are valued by the learners.

2.5 Foundations of Statistical Thinking and Literacy

Research in the field of statistics education highlights the idea that it is not possible to learn statistics only as a means of learning successfully computational processes, but to learn how to think about variability, uncertainty, and how to make decisions when dealing with data. Garfield and Ben-Zvi refer to statistical reasoning being the skill to examine, relate, and even justify statistical ideas, whereas Moore lays an emphasis on statistics as an investigative technique instead of a set of formulas. Likewise, the statistical inquiry cycle by Wild and Pfannkuch has shown that problem formulation, data collection and analysis and interpretation are elements of a single reasoning process as opposed to single skills.

In this view, AI tools not just due to improved efficiency but also out of their capability to help the key aspects of statistical thought: perceiving variability, connecting context to data, interpreting models, and expressing conclusions should be considered. Because of this, say the automated modeling tools will be more productive in technical terms, but unless explicitly taught as an instructional medium they might tend to skip crucial steps in the process: model justification, model checking (Fleischer et al., 2022).

Thus, the successful application of AI must also be matched by the existing models of statistical literacy and inquiry where automation is able to complement the chances of interpretation, criticism, and reflection, but not to supplant them. This consistency has been fundamental in averting the problem of surface exposure to the statistical product and ensuring the epistemological underpinnings of statistics training.

3. INTELLIGENT TUTORING SYSTEMS IN STATISTICS EDUCATION

3.1 Evolution of Intelligent Tutoring Systems (ITS) in Education

Intelligent Tutoring Systems (ITS) can be described as an extension of the shortcomings of conventional teaching techniques, which usually fail to meet the needs of all the students within a classroom. Computer-assisted-instruction was originally presented as simple, pre-programmed lessons, which were not adaptive. With the advent of ITS, this picture changed as systems that could be used to diagnose student knowledge and track progress and provide individualized feedback were introduced (Goyal, 2025b).

ITS has over the years developed into machine learning and natural language processing (NLP) based systems rather than rule-based systems. Early ITS were fixed on hard-decision trees, and were less adaptable. However, the present-day AI-based tutors are able to read responses of students in natural language, assessing argumentation patterns and even participate in discussions. This has rendered ITS specifically appropriate to statistics, where the interpretation of results can be at least as important as the accuracy of the computation (Fleischer et al., 2024).

3.2 Core Components of Intelligent Tutoring Systems for Statistics

ITS is developed on a number of interlinked components that collaborate to offer personalized learning. These are the components of ITS that need to be understood in order to appreciate the way in which ITS aids in teaching and learning statistics.

The domain model is the object of interest - statistical concepts, methods and problem-solving strategies. It encompasses probability distributions, hypothesis testing, regression analysis and data visualization in statistics. An effective domain model would mean that the tutor would be in a position to assign problems of different complexity and direct learners through hierarchical stages that are consistent with curricular requirements.

The student model is also important. It serves as a dynamic map of what the learner knows, can and cannot do and what he or she is not doing well. As an example, when a student has a problem that relates to the understanding of assumptions in a t-test, the student model takes note of the problem. It can evolve over time to represent the student progress in order to allow the system to provide a more customized information. This is essential in statistics, since mastery has been in many cases been based on developing layered knowledge; variability can only be understood before testing a hypothesis, and a poor understanding of one concept can cripple the subsequent one (Frischemeier, 2020).

3.3 Benefits of ITS in Statistics Education

The integration of ITS into statistics classrooms offers several pedagogical and practical benefits. Personalization is one of the greatest benefits. Conventional classrooms tend to support the average student and leave the high achievers and challenged students unattended. ITS, however, follows the learning pace of the individual learner giving remedial practice to a learner as needed and progressively challenging the learner as necessary. This will make sure that the students are in a position to move towards mastery (Gal, 2002).

Another strength is instant feedback. In traditional contexts, students can wait days or weeks to get graded assignments but by that time the wrong beliefs would have set in. ITS provides real-time feedback, which gives students an opportunity to rectify errors in the process. As an example, a mistake in interpreting a p-value can be often corrected in real time, but the system can quickly correct it and avoid the dissemination of the wrong perception.

ITS improves interaction and drive as well. Statistics is frightening to many students because it is mathematically rigorous. The learning process is more interactive with the help of gamified ITS settings, adaptive quizzes, and interactive simulations. Students gain confidence and encouragement when they can see in real time their progress, e.g. the increased accuracy in prediction during a regression modeling exercise (Gal & Ograjenšek, 2017).

3.4 Limitations and Challenges of ITS Implementation

ITS in statistics education is not without its challenges even though they are beneficial. Over reliance on automation is one of the big problems. Students can get accustomed to system guidance and fail when it is necessary to work alone and solve problems. As an answer to this, ITS needs to be made to support the gradual demise of scaffold, prompting students to solve problems independently (Garfield et al., 2008).

The other problem is that AI-driven ITS is a black box. Although such systems can be adapted successfully, not all teachers and learners can comprehend the logic of some recommendations or interventions. This obscurity may take away the confidence in the system in statistics education, where interpretability is the most important thing.

There are also barriers in practice. Creation of domain-specific ITS needs a lot of resources such as proper statistical models, pedagogical plans and technical infrastructure. Most institutions, especially those operating in low resources setting, might be unable to roll out ITS at large scale. Also, it is important to make sure that access is not unfair; students who lack access to a consistent internet connection or access to modern devices might be left behind in terms of the advantages of AI-powered tutoring (Farooqi et al., 2026).

4. AUTOMATED STATISTICAL MODELING WITH AI TOOLS

4.1 Emergence of Automated Statistical Modeling

The history of automated statistical modeling has been influenced by the increasing complexity of data, and the need to provide analysis quickly and accurately. Conventional statistical modeling can involve skill in likely choice of methodology, assumption checking, and interpretation of outcome. Yet not all learners- or even professionals- have the time or experience to learn these steps in detail. This introduced the necessity of the systems capable of automating much of the process without affecting reliability.

This is now met by AI-driven modeling tools commonly known as AutoML (Automated Machine Learning) or Automated Statistical Modeling System. The tools help in pre-processing data, selection of models, parameter tuning and validation. As an example, systems such as Google AutoML or IBM Watson Studio can automatically run a variety of regression models, pick the most suitable model and give feedback on the accuracy scores all without the user writing a lot of code (Gonda et al., 2022).

This automation is especially radical in the area of statistics teaching. Students find it difficult, not only to learn statistical theory, but also technical implementation. The advantage of automated systems is that they decrease the cognitive load, which is focused on the routine computational tasks and provides students with more opportunities to understand the concepts and interpret the results. As an example, rather than becoming bogged down in calculating residuals by hand, a student can use automated software to compute the residuals and devote additional time to interpreting what the residuals tell us about model fit.

4.2 Key Features of Automated Modeling Tools

Handling of missing values, encoding of categorical variables or scaling data are some of the tasks that many students find tedious. With automated tools, these processes are made easier by identifying the patterns of missing data, suggesting possible methods of imputation, and making sure data is in a correct format to be used in statistical models. As an example, in the analysis of a dataset of survey responses the system can automatically propose filling in missing demographic values with group averages, thereby making the dataset ready to be analyzed (Koga, 2022).

Model selection and comparison is also another important feature. Under traditional statistics, the appropriate model depends on profound knowledge to be selected: it is either linear regression, logistic regression, ANOVA or some other more advanced models. Multiple models are run simultaneously by automated systems and their performance is compared to each other by using a statistical measure such as R2, AIC (Akaike Information Criterion) or cross-validation scores. Students are thus able to know not only the model to work best but also the reasons why a given model is better than the other thereby solidifying their conceptual learning.

Another field in which automation is useful is hyperparameter tuning. Many models, such as decision trees or neural networks, rely heavily on fine-tuned parameters for optimal performance. The optimisation techniques that are automated modeling tools apply the parameters to high-quality results by running rapidly through the optimization algorithms provided by artificial intelligence. When the number of parameter sets to be evaluated manually is dozens, an automated system can do so in minutes (Goyal et al., 2025c).

4.3 Pedagogical Benefits of Automated Modeling in Statistics Education

Automation allows students to work with the real world-data sooner in their education. They will no longer have to wait weeks to learn coding or to test models manually: they can dive directly into the analysis of datasets related to healthcare, economics, or social sciences. This style renders statistics relevant and interesting because it demonstrates that statistics can be applied in the resolution of practical problems.

Second, conceptual learning is supported by automated modeling. With less time on mechanical calculations, students have the opportunity to concentrate on the interpretation of results and have an extended implication. As an example, once an automated system produces a regression output, the instructor can host a discussion about how to interpret coefficients, confidence intervals, and p-values in practice. This transition is in line with the pedagogical concept of focusing on critical thinking at the expense of rote processes (Koga, 2025).

Third, automation enhances accessibility and inclusivity. Even students who might be deficient in programming or mathematical calculation have exposure to higher-order statistical techniques. An example of this is a student who is taking a business analytics course and has a weak background in math, who can still use automated tools to analyze data on consumer behavior and learn something which they would not have otherwise.

4.4 Limitations and Challenges of Automated Modeling

Using automated tools as a whole, students are likely not to grasp the assumptions and workings of the statistical approaches. Say, an automated system can choose a logistic regression model, but unless students are taught this, they will not realise that it assumes linearity in the log-odds. This fact may deprive them of critical evaluation of models in professional settings.

The other difficulty is interpretability. Automated modeling systems can offer very precise results but with no clear explanations on how models were constructed and why some decisions were made. Such a black-box disposition can be counter-productive to learning, particularly in statistics education where it is necessary to have knowledge about assumptions and limitations. It is important that teachers have automation accompanied with clear explanation of interpretation and critical analysis (Kuiper & Sturdivant, 2015).

We have also technical and equity related challenges. Automated modeling tools usually need sophisticated software or cloud environment, which is not always affordable and accessible to every institution. Moreover, high dependence on the internet connectivity may lock out learners in low-resource areas, resulting in increased educational inequities.

5. AI-ENHANCED DATA VISUALIZATION IN STATISTICS EDUCATION

5.1 Role of Visualization in Learning Statistics

The use of visualization during the teaching and learning of statistics has never been a stranger. Theories such as distributions, variability, correlation and regression are abstract until the learner can see an example of them in the form of a graph. An example of this is that a histogram can intuitively give the attention to skewness in a dataset by just looking at it than rows of numerical frequency tables. Likewise, scatterplots give learners a chance to see the relationship between variables way before they are mathematically aware of correlation coefficients (Goyal et al., 2025d).

AI-based tools enhance this function by turning visualizations into more dynamic, interactive and context-sensitive. Conventional static graphs may depict data distributions, whereas AI-based systems may change visualisations dynamically as students tweak parameters or as they test hypotheses. To illustrate, in case a student would vary the sample size in a dataset, the AI tool would automatically update the confidence interval graph, and thus the student would gain insight into the concept of variability.

In addition to simple graphs, AI systems are now able to provide a way of placing complex statistical models into more understandable visuals. As an example, regression surfaces, multidimensional scaling, and time-series forecasting can all be presented in interactive dashboards, with learners controlling them and seeing results. This practical experimentation helps to render abstract ideas into reality, particularly among the visual learners who have a hard time with formulas.

5.2 AI-Driven Personalization in Data Visualization

One of the most powerful contributions of AI to visualization lies in personalized learning experiences. All learners receive information differently; some like numerical summaries whereas others understand information through the use of graphs. AI-supported interfaces leverage machine learning methods to monitor the behavior of learners and adjust the visualization styles.

An example is that when an AI tutor notices that a learner is using longer hours to interpret scatterplots than regression tables, it may focus on graphical regression lines and residual plotting and reduce textual contents. On the other hand, a student, who works better with numeric output, may be given more tabular displays and few visuals. This individualization guarantees that the visualization is made to suit the cognitive style of the student and lessens frustration and increases understanding (Leavy et al., 2024).

Learning can also be scaffolds by AI by progressive visualization. New users may start with plain bar graphs to learn about proportions, and more experienced users slowly learn interactive multivariate plots or three-dimensional visualizations. This progressive complexity will avoid cases of cognitive overloading where the learner gains confidence to handle complicated concepts first (Lee, 2020).

5.3 Advanced Visualization Techniques Enabled by AI

In contrast to the static graphs, AI-based dashboards enable learners to control variables, use samples of the data, and immediately visualize their results. As an example, within a public health dataset students might be able to filter by region or age, to view the change in disease prevalence, and hence data analysis becomes very interactive and exploratory (Li, 2022).

The other innovation is dimensionality reduction visualization that is quite proficient in multivariate statistics. Principal Component Analysis (PCA) or t-SNE AI algorithms are capable of compressing high-dimensional datasets to two or three dimensions to plot. The students can then see the formation of clusters, distribution of variance, or the outliers. This makes them understand the concepts of multicollinearity, latent variables and clustering without being distracted with equations.

Lastly, AI-based visualization includes explanation through natural language with graphics. A student may encounter a scatterplot with an AI-based explanation of the form: This dataset has a moderate positive correlation ($r = 0.62$). The dependent variable tends to increase with the increase in the independent variable albeit with a moderate variance. Such hybrid of images and text analysis enriches and makes the learning process more multidimensional.

6. PEDAGOGICAL, AND PRACTICAL CONSIDERATIONS IN AI-ENHANCED STATISTICS EDUCATION

6.1 Data Privacy, Bias, and Transparency

The introduction of AI in statistics education brings several ethical issues, which need to be firmly resolved by educators, learners, and policymakers. The most noticeable issue is the privacy of data. Most AI-based solutions are based on the data gathering of learners to provide personalized experience and produce adaptive feedback and monitor progress. Although such insights might be pedagogically useful, they also prompt the question of how data about students is stored and accessed as well as whether informed consent is appropriately obtained. The institutional obligation of implementing AI tools should therefore be ensuring that they do not violate the data protection frameworks like GDPR or the local laws protecting privacy (Luptakova, 2023).

Another ethical issue is that of algorithmic bias. Artificial intelligence is as fair as the data and algorithms that drive them. In case the information on which an intelligent tutoring system is trained is skewed, such as only representing a particular demographic group of learning styles, the advice that will be given will not benefit those who belong to other cultural or cognitive groups. The result in a heterogeneous classroom might be different, as some students might be more advantaged through AI-driven support than others. Instructional practitioners will have to be careful and keep on auditing AI tools to make sure that they are fair, inclusive, and culturally sensitive.

6.2 Pedagogical Implications: Balancing Technology with Human Instruction

Although AI has the potential to transform, its introduction in statistics education has to be accompanied by meaningful pedagogy. The risk of excessive dependence on automation is one of the biggest implications. To provide an example, in the case when AI systems automatically create regression models or p-values, students can start accepting the output without learning the background statistical reasoning. This runs the danger of creating learners that can use tools but not meaningfully interpret outcomes- which is a critical drawback in a data based world (Goyal et al., 2025e).

To prevent this trap, teachers need to use a hybrid learning model in which AI is used to assist and not substitute critical thinking. An example is, an AI platform can serve to give a student an automated visualization of data, though the instructor must instruct the student to ask questions to the validity of the model: Do the assumptions of normality hold? Does correlation mean causation? What happens with change in parameters? This kind of directed inquiry makes sure that students take AI outputs as a source of reflection and not as a matter of fact (Mike & Hazzan, 2022).

Equity of access is another pedagogical consideration. Not every learner is going to be equally familiar with AI tools. Others can be school-based or those with minimal exposure to higher digital platforms, and some can be digital natives. Teachers should be able to create learning exercises that consider such differences to structure the use of AI devices in a way that allows all students, regardless of their previous exposure to the tool, to interact in meaningful ways.

6.3 Practical Challenges in Classroom Implementation

In addition to ethical and pedagogical issues, the practical implementation of AI in statistics education has a few challenges. The former is infrastructure requirements. Numerous AI-based applications require large quantities of computational resources, a robust internet connection, and up-to-date hardware. This in underfunded schools or digitally disadvantaged regions creates obstacles that may lead to the lack of an equal opportunity to utilize AI-enhanced learning. Institutions and governments should therefore invest in digital infrastructure such that AI does not enhance available educational inequalities (Pan & Gu, 2023).

Teacher preparedness is another practical difficulty. A lot of teachers are statisticians who do not train in AI technologies. Unless educated correctly, the educators can be intimidated by the complexity of AI-led platforms or even fail to utilize their potential. The empowerment of teachers to effectively and even confidently apply AI tools in their teaching methods requires training programs, workshops, and continuous technical support.

There is also the issue of cost. Some of the AI platforms are free or open-source, whereas some of them are expensive to obtain the licensing. These costs should be balanced by institutions with the pedagogical advantages and guarantees sustainable funding models. Moreover, use of commercial AI systems could put schools at the mercy of vendor ecosystems, reducing flexibility and casting long-term cost-effectiveness doubt.

6.4 Redesigning Assessment in AI-Enhanced Statistics Courses

Statistical AI tools require actual shifts in the assessment design in statistics classrooms. Conventional tests that focus on procedural computation are increasingly becoming subject to automation and as such is no longer reliable in assessing student knowledge. Instead, judgement must be made more focused on interpretive argument, model criticism, and context exposition.

The interpretive assignments which are the situation when students get the model outputs produced by the AI systems and must justify the assumptions, determine the adequacy of the models, and discuss the findings in a practical setting are also one of the solutions. Such assignments in the form of rubrics have the ability to evaluate clarity of argument, justification of any conclusion, and understanding of uncertainly, not just the correctness of numerical outcomes (Kumari & Goyal, 2026).

The use of project-based assessments is also quite useful in AI-mediated settings. Students may be assigned the task to choose suitable variables, explain the modeling options, and talk about ethical aspects associated with the use of data. The addition of the oral defenses, reflective reports and peer-review activities also enhance academic integrity as well as peer-review activities which support conceptual learning.

6.5 Student Readiness and Psychological Engagement

People can interact with AI-enhanced learning via technical and psychological preparedness to engage in learning. The most effectively documented obstacle to the study of quantitative courses is statistics anxiety (fear of mathematical failure and low self-efficacy). Whereas AI tutors can offer encouraging feedback and can decrease the amount of pressure placed on performance, poorly conceived systems can also develop dependence or fear of independent problem solving.

Also, learners differ in their faith and belief in AI recommendations. Others can be too dependent on automated results and others just do not believe in algorithmic feedback at all. The instructional approaches should thus contain clear talks of AI weaknesses, affordances of autonomous problem solving, and guided significant consideration of AI-assisted decision making.

Technical competence as well as confidence can be developed, through orientation, low-stakes exploratory activities and through guided experimentation. Students will be more inclined to discuss and use AI tools in a critical and productive manner instead of passive consumption of automatic responses once they get to know more about how and why such tools work. Solving both emotional and cognitive aspects of the learning process is therefore required in the successful integration of AI in statistics education.

7. CASE STUDIES OF AI IN STATISTICS CLASSROOMS

7.1 Intelligent Tutoring Systems for Introductory Statistics

One of the most significant applications of AI in statistics teaching has been in the development of intelligent tutoring systems (ITS) to assist learners in learning the basic statistical concepts such as probability distributions, hypothesis testing and regression analysis. One of the most well-known is Carnegie Learning's MATHia, an AI algorithm that analyzes live student inputs and delivers adaptive hints based on each learner's pace. In practice, the systems provide some of the one-to-one interaction a student might get from a personal tutor and help close the gap between classroom instruction and individual learning needs.

I present a case study of an undergraduate introductory statistics course in which an ITS was implemented in conjunction with traditional lectures. Using the platform, students were required to solve problems on probability and descriptive statistics. The AI system assessed their progress, identified misconceptions (such as mixing up standard deviation and variance) and gave guided practice to bring the learners to mastery. At the end of the semester, surveys indicated that students who used the ITS on a regular basis had not only higher exam scores but also more confidence in the application of statistical reasoning to real-life problems (Ridgway, 2016).

There were also some limitations pointed out in the case. For instance, some students would tend to follow suggestions too mechanically, coming to the correct answer, but not really understanding how to come to it. While effective in terms of error identification, this led to questions as to whether AI tutors, on their own, might cause surface or shallow learning without being coupled with activities for reflection. Instructors countered by embedding reflection questions following the AI-based exercises by asking students why a given solution was right. This hybrid design of artificial intelligence assistance and instructor-led reflection was used to ensure greater conceptual understanding.

7.2 Automated Modeling in Advanced Statistics Courses

Another interesting case study is from graduate applied statistics courses, where AI tools for automated modeling are being used more and more to simplify complex analysis. In one such course, students were introduced to AutoML platforms such as Google Cloud AutoML and H2O.ai that can automatically preprocess data, choose the right model, and tune hyperparameters. These platforms were incorporated into a project-based task for students analyzing a big dataset on how people move in cities.

Traditionally, a manual process of building a model - selecting between logistic regression, decision trees, or random forests, then tuning model parameters - took weeks of manual labor. With the help of AI-powered AutoML the students were able to create baseline models in hours. This opens valuable classroom time for higher-order activities, such as reflection on model assumptions, interpretation and the ethical aspects of automated decision making in real-world domains such as traffic management or healthcare (Schwarz, 2025).

Interestingly, the use of AutoML moved the focus of learning away from how to compute and toward how to critique. Students started posing deeper questions about model performance: why did the automated system place emphasis on accuracy and not interpretability? Is a less accurate, but simpler, model of the regression more transparent for the decision-makers? This was a paradigm shift in pedagogy - from instructing construction of manual models to developing critical data literacy and decision making skills.

7.3 AI-Driven Learning Analytics for Classroom Insights

Third case study is from a high school statistics elective course, where teachers used AI-fuelled learning analytics to monitor student progress and tailor instruction. The system gathered data from quizzes, assignments and in-class exercises, and created dashboards of which students didn't grasp certain concepts-say, conditional probability or chi-square tests. Using predictive analytics, the platform was even able to predict which students were at risk of falling behind based on patterns of their engagement.

The teacher made use of these insights to apply differentiated instruction. For example, if the system identified a group of students who were persistently under-performing on hypothesis testing, the teacher devised a special workshop session for them; at the same time, high-ability learners were given enrichment problems involving real data. This data-driven information gave the teacher the ability to use classroom time more effectively and meet the needs of students at various levels without compromising standards (Goyal, 2025f).

Students also had access to their own progress reports. By visualizing their strengths and weaknesses, they would be able to assume greater ownership of their learning. Counsellors have also said that they found seeing the physical changes on their graphs to be motivating, whilst others have said they liked early warnings that allowed them to get help before they fell too far behind.

However, implications disguised as ethics were raised. Other students complained about being uncomfortable with the level of surveillance, worrying that they were marked as “weak” learners if they cannot get away from eyes. The school's response was to create transparent policies that were focused on using learning analytics for formative purposes rather than punitive grading. Teachers also described the process of how the data was anonymized and locked away to help build trust among students and their parents.

8. FUTURE DIRECTIONS FOR AI IN STATISTICS EDUCATION

8.1 Generative AI as a Teaching Partner

One of the most promising statistical teaching paths for the future is the emergence of generative AI tools like large language models (LLMs). Unlike previous uses of AI that were limited either to tutoring or analytics, generative AI is able to produce personalized instructional materials on the fly. For example, a teacher can request that an AI system produce a sample problem set concerning regression analysis that is customized for the students' existing skill levels, complete with hints and step-by-step explanations. Similarly, students could engage in conversation with AI conversational agents to help explain concepts or ensure that they received instant feedback about their interpretations of statistical findings.

The generative AI can also pave the way for individualized learning journeys. Rather than having fixed textbooks or standard assignments, learners would be served dynamically generated materials that would vary not just in individual mastery of the subject, but also in their own personal interests. A student interested in sports could be given data sets about player statistics, whereas another with an interest in environmental science could investigate climate data. This contextualized individualization personalizes abstract concepts and makes them more interesting and relevant.

However, there are dangers to this future direction. "Generative AI models can generate hallucinations - inaccurate or misleading information that sounds real. In a statistical learning environment, such mistakes can have dramatic repercussions if students inadvertently learn incorrect reasoning or formulas. Moreover, educators will have to implement safeguards, in the form of fact-checking procedures and assignments that critically analyze, rather than passively consume, AI-generated content. This provides a learning environment in which AI is both a tool and a thing to be challenged, learning students to treat automated knowledge with healthy skepticism.

8.2 Multimodal and Immersive Learning with AI

Another direction in the future is to use AI to provide multimodal learning environments that are beyond text and numbers. In statistics education, for example, this could take the form of integrating visual, auditory and interactive simulations in order to deepen conceptual understanding. For example, AI-powered virtual labs could enable students to play around with datasets in real-time and instantly understand the implications for regression lines, probability distributions or confidence intervals. Such immersive experiences facilitate the translation of theoretical knowledge to practical knowledge.

AI augmented with virtual and augmented reality (VR/AR) may also have a growing impact. For example, imagine a VR classroom where students are immersed in a "data landscape" with data correlations represented as slopes or clusters of data points represented as physical groupings in space. Such an embodied experience can have a potential to make statistical concepts more intuitive, particularly for learners who are especially challenged by the abstract mathematical representations. AI systems can adjust these experiences in real-time, based on student reactions, to ensure a learning experience that is neither too easy nor too difficult for the individual.

Another connectivity element of multimodality is speech and natural language understanding. Future AI tools could even be used to give students the opportunity to verbally describe a statistical concept, after which the system would provide corrective feedback or probing questions. Interactive dialogue leads to critical thinking and helps students develop the ability to express their understanding of concepts, a skill that is frequently absent in more traditional statistics courses (Wahba et al., 2024).

As these multimodal ways of working develop, teachers will be challenged to ensure accessibility and equity. High-tech VR and AI resources may be expensive, potentially exacerbating the divide between institutions with ample resources and those with fewer resources. To counter this, developers and policy makers need to consider open source solutions and scalable platforms that democratize access to immersive statistical learning.

8.3 AI for Global Collaboration and Accessibility

A third emerging trend is the use of AI to enable statistics education collaboration on a global scale. With cloud-based AI platforms, students from other countries could collaborate on data-driven studies, analyzing the collective datasets with AI-mediated feedback. For instance, a class in India and a class in Germany might work together on data related to climate change, using AI tools to compare local trends and simultaneously pick up on cross-cultural perspectives on environmental policy.

AI-powered language translation and accessibility solutions will have a major role in this global transition. Statistics education is dominated by English-language resources, yet future AI platforms could automatically translate lectures, textbooks and datasets into many languages in real time. This would enable high quality statistical training to reach a much larger cross section of the population, particularly in developing areas where language has been an obstacle. AI can be used for building adaptive learning materials for students with disabilities, for example, using statistical graphs and converting them into audio description for visually challenged learners (Xing, 2024).

There are also ethical issues in global accessibility. Will AI be used to support the dominant cultural values of statistics or to support diverse ways of thinking? The issue is that if a generative AI system is trained mainly on Western academic sources, it could underestimate local knowledge systems or other methodologies. Educators, therefore, need to critically evaluate how AI filters and presents statistical knowledge, so that the future classrooms are inclusive in addition to being culturally sensitive.

In educational institutions with low resources, full-scale AI systems can be impractical because of poor connectivity and low hardware. These are, however, replaced by scalable options, such as lightweight mobile-based tutoring applications, offline simulation tools, and open-source statistical applications, which can be locally hosted, like CODAP or jupyter-based notebooks. Combined solutions that introduce elements of teacher-based learning with periodic AI-assisted learning might offer economical options to adoption.

The policy makers and curriculum designers must then focus on modular and interoperable AI solutions that are capable of operating under variety of infrastructural environments. Collaborations between schools, non-governmental organizations and open source communities will further ease access impediments and will encourage the development of culturally sensitive material.

CONCLUSION

The incorporation of Artificial Intelligence (AI) for statistics learning is a groundbreaking change for the way learners are taught to think about data, learn how to think analytically, and apply statistical reasoning in the real world. Unlike traditional analog teaching methods where the learning process is heavily dependent on static textbooks, preset examples, and homogenized assignments, AI brings out a dynamic, adaptive, and interactive element for learning. This chapter has discussed the various ways AI is transforming statistics education, from intelligent tutoring systems to automated model building and reconstruction, to generative AI-enabled personalised content creation, multimodal simulations, and global collaborative platforms.

At its heart, the use of AI in statistics education speaks to one of the oldest and most enduring challenges for teaching quantitative courses: the diversity of student learning styles and paces. Intelligent tutors are capable of tracking learners in real time, identifying misconceptions and offering immediate, personalised feedback. Automated modeling software makes complex analytical tasks easy, so students can spend less time with the mechanics of procedures and more time focusing on the interpretation and critical evaluation of results. These features enhance understanding and instill confidence and interest, making statistics less intimidating and more accessible and meaningful.

In conclusion, the incorporation of AI into statistics education provides opportunities and responsibilities. It delivers a pledge to make learning more personal, engaging, and globally accessible - while preparing students for a world where statistical reasoning and AI-powered analytics are a Siamese twinning. But to make this promise a reality, educators, technologists, and policymakers must shift to a collaborative approach that ensures that AI tools are used fairly, transparently, and with integrity. The long game isn't just about better learners but about creating a new generation of critical thinkers and responsible data citizens who can use AI to improve our society. If this balance can be attained, statistics education can become not only a highly technological field, but a thoroughly humanistic one.

REFERENCES

Andinasari, Z., Zulkardi, , Somakim, , & Wasiran, Y. (2019). Learning design of reciprocal proportionality using airplanes context. *Journal of Physics: Conference Series, 1166*(1), 012018. DOI: 10.1088/1742-6596/1166/1/012018

Ashofteh, A., & Bravo, J. M. (2021). Data science training for official statistics: A new scientific paradigm of information and knowledge development in national statistical systems. *Statistical Journal of the IAOS, 37*(3), 771–789. DOI: 10.3233/SJI-210841

Bargagliotti, A., & Franklin, C. (2015). The statistical education of teachers: Preparing teachers to teach statistics. *Chance, 28*(3), 19–27. DOI: 10.1080/09332480.2015.1099362

Ben-Zvi, D., & Makar, K. (2016). International perspectives on the teaching and learning of statistics. In Ben-Zvi, D., & Makar, K. (Eds.), *The teaching and learning of statistics* (pp. 1–10). Springer., DOI: 10.1007/978-3-319-23470-0_1

Biehler, R., Frischemeier, D., Gould, R., & Pfannkuch, M. (2024). Impacts of digitalization on content and goals of statistics education. In Pepin, B., Gueudet, G., & Choppin, J. (Eds.), *Handbook of digital resources in mathematics education* (pp. 547–583). Springer. DOI: 10.1007/978-3-031-45667-1_20

Boels, L. (2023). Reflections on gaze data in statistics education. *Teaching Statistics, 45*(S1), 40–51. DOI: 10.1111/test.12340

Boels, L., Lyford, A., Bakker, A., & Drijvers, P. (2023). Assessing students' interpretations of histograms before and after interpreting dotplots: A gaze-based machine learning analysis. *Frontline Learning Research, 11*(2), 1–30. DOI: 10.14786/flr.v11i2.1139

Callingham, R., & Watson, J. M. (2017). The development of statistical literacy at school. *Statistics Education Research Journal, 16*(1), 181–201. DOI: 10.52041/serj.v16i1.223

Ellis, A. R., & Slade, E. (2023). A new era of learning: Considerations for ChatGPT as a tool to enhance statistics and data science education. *Journal of Statistics and Data Science Education : An Official Journal of the of the American Statistical Association, 31*(2), 128–133. DOI: 10.1080/26939169.2023.2223609

Engel, J. (2017). Statistical literacy for active citizenship: A call for data science education. *Statistics Education Research Journal, 16*(1), 44–49. DOI: 10.52041/serj.v16i1.213

Farooqi, A., Das, D., Tripathi, M., Dutta, R., Goyal, N. K., & Sheikh, M. F. (2026). Navigating ethical frontiers in AI-driven geriatric care. In Stolakis, K., & Efthymiou, I. (Eds.), *AI for geriatric care in an aging society: Ethical, clinical, and policy challenges* (pp. 243–266). IGI Global Scientific Publishing., DOI: 10.4018/979-8-3373-5462-0.ch009

Fleischer, Y., Biehler, R., & Schulte, C. (2022). Teaching and learning data-driven machine learning with educationally designed Jupyter notebooks. *Statistics Education Research Journal, 21*(2), 1–25. DOI: 10.52041/serj.v21i2.61

Fleischer, Y., Podworny, S., & Biehler, R. (2024). Teaching and learning to construct data-based decision trees using data cards as the first introduction to machine learning in middle school. *Statistics Education Research Journal, 23*(1), 1–24. DOI: 10.52041/serj.v23i1.450

Frischemeier, D. (2020). Building statisticians at an early age: Statistical projects exploring meaningful data in primary school. *Statistics Education Research Journal, 19*(1), 39–56. DOI: 10.52041/serj.v19i1.118

Gal, I. (2002). Adults' statistical literacy: Meanings, components, responsibilities. *International Statistical Review = Revue Internationale de Statistique, 70*(1), 1–25. DOI: 10.1111/j.1751-5823.2002.tb00336.x

Gal, I., & Ograjenšek, I. (2017). Official statistics and statistics education: Bridging the gap. *Journal of Official Statistics, 33*(1), 79–100. DOI: 10.1515/jos-2017-0005

Garfield, J. B., Ben-Zvi, D., Chance, B., Medina, E., Roseth, C., & Zieffler, A. (2008). *Developing students' statistical reasoning: Connecting research and teaching practice*. Springer.

Gonda, D., Pavlovičová, G., Ďuriš, V., & Tirpáková, A. (2022). Implementation of pedagogical research into statistical courses to develop students' statistical literacy. *Mathematics, 10*(11), 1793. DOI: 10.3390/math10111793

Goyal, N. K. (2025a). Security and privacy in IoT, fog, and blockchain networks. In Sathio, A., Rind, M., Awan, S., & Junejo, A. (Eds.), *Energy-efficient deep learning approaches in IoT, fog, and green blockchain revolution* (pp. 371–398). IGI Global Scientific Publishing., DOI: 10.4018/979-8-3373-0300-0.ch015

Goyal, N. K. (2025b). Weaponizing misinformation and cyberattacks on supply chains. In Bukhari, S., & Zafar, I. (Eds.), *Mass media and impact of fake news on supply chains* (pp. 177–210). IGI Global Scientific Publishing., DOI: 10.4018/979-8-3373-2175-2.ch007

Goyal, N. K., Dandotiya, M., Kumari, M., Kaloria, S., & Anushya, A. (2025c). AI-powered haptic devices for patient rehabilitation. In Mamodiya, U., Kalam, A., Bossoufi, B., Awad, M., & Somwanshi, D. (Eds.), *Integrating AI with haptic systems for smarter healthcare solutions* (pp. 143–170). IGI Global Scientific Publishing., DOI: 10.4018/979-8-3373-2307-7.ch007

Goyal, N. K., Dandotiya, M., Kumari, M., Sheikh, M. F., & Sharma, S. (2025d). Emerging job roles in the tourism sector leveraging artificial intelligence. In Silic, M., Luthia, M., Ahmad, F., & Chakraborty, P. (Eds.), *Empowering sustainable performance and competitive advantage in tourism* (pp. 89–126). IGI Global Scientific Publishing., DOI: 10.4018/979-8-3373-4546-8.ch004

Goyal, N. K., Dandotiya, M., Qurashi, J. A., Kumari, M., & Sharma, S. (2025e). AI-driven predictive analytics for disease management. In Ouaissa, M., Ouaissa, M., Imad, M., Qurashi, J., & Farooq, M. (Eds.), *Utilizing AI of medical things for healthcare security and sustainability* (pp. 231–276). IGI Global Scientific Publishing., DOI: 10.4018/979-8-3373-0690-2.ch008

Goyal, N. K., Kumari, M., Kushwah, V., Dandotiya, M., & Vijay, A. (2025f). Evaluating blockchain security: Trade-offs in consensus mechanisms. *IET Conference Proceedings,* 2024(38), 80–88. https://doi.org/DOI: 10.1049/icp.2025.0775

Koga, S. (2022). Characteristics of statistical literacy skills from the perspective of critical thinking. *Teaching Statistics, 44*(2), 59–67. DOI: 10.1111/test.12302

Koga, S. (2025). Lessons to demonstrate statistical literacy skills: A case study of Japanese high school students on reading statistical reports. *Journal of Statistics and Data Science Education : An Official Journal of the of the American Statistical Association, 33*(1), 77–89. DOI: 10.1080/26939169.2024.2334903

Kuiper, S., & Sturdivant, R. X. (2015). Using online game-based simulations to strengthen students' understanding of practical statistical issues in real-world data analysis. *The American Statistician, 69*(4), 354–361. DOI: 10.1080/00031305.2015.1075421

Kumari, M., & Goyal, N. K. (2026). Artificial intelligence in the cryptocurrency ecosystem: Crime mechanisms, detection strategies, and legal perspectives. In Lin, L. (Ed.), *Innovations in cryptocrime and financial fraud* (pp. 245–282). IGI Global Scientific Publishing., DOI: 10.4018/979-8-3373-0675-9.ch007

Kumari, M., Kumawat, R., Tripathi, M., Suganthi, K., Goyal, N. K., & Sheikh, M. F. (2026). Blockchain for transparency and traceability in supply chains. In Khan, M., Mehmood, T., & Rao, M. (Eds.), *Maximizing operational efficiency at the intersection of supply chain management and marketing* (pp. 35–64). IGI Global Scientific Publishing., DOI: 10.4018/979-8-3373-3109-6.ch002

Leavy, A. M., Hourigan, M., & Fitzpatrick, M. (2024). Exploring the plight of the honeybee: Using data sensors and CODAP to support emerging bilingual learners in reasoning about big statistical ideas. *Statistics Education Research Journal*, *23*(2), 1–24. DOI: 10.52041/serj.v22i2.706

Lee, D. (2020). Teaching statistics online to prepare educators for evidence-based practice. *Journal of Education for Teaching*, *46*(3), 424–429. DOI: 10.1080/02607476.2020.1766303

Li, K. W. (2022). An empirical study on integrating technology into statistics classroom practice. *Journal of Pedagogical Research*, *6*(3), 112–136. DOI: 10.33902/JPR.202212339

Luptakova, I. D. (2023). Using a selected machine learning method in the R language in statistics learning. In *ICETA 2023 – 21st International Conference on Emerging eLearning Technologies and Applications* (pp. 348–352). IEEE. https://doi.org/DOI: 10.1109/ICETA61311.2023.10344171

Mike, K., & Hazzan, O. (2022). Machine learning for non-major data science students: A white box approach. *Statistics Education Research Journal*, *21*(2), 1–22. DOI: 10.52041/serj.v21i2.45

Pan, Y., & Gu, J. (2023). Empowering education: ChatGPT's role in teaching and learning statistics and data analytics. *International Journal of Technology in Teaching and Learning*, *19*(1), 34–51. DOI: 10.37120/ijttl.2023.19.1.02

Ridgway, J. (2016). Implications of the data revolution for statistics education. *International Statistical Review = Revue Internationale de Statistique*, *84*(3), 528–549. DOI: 10.1111/insr.12110

Schwarz, J. (2025). The use of generative AI in statistical data analysis and its impact on teaching statistics at universities of applied sciences. *Teaching Statistics*, *47*(2), 118–128. DOI: 10.1111/test.12398

Sharma, P., Kumawat, R., Jain, G., Keswani, G., Goyal, N. K., & Sheikh, M. F. (2026). Machine learning-based intrusion detection systems for healthcare Internet of Things (HIoT). In Shieh, C., Goel, P., Horng, M., & Pandey, H. (Eds.), *Resilient healthcare Internet of Things systems: Architectures, security, and trust* (pp. 185–214). IGI Global Scientific Publishing., DOI: 10.4018/979-8-3373-7610-3.ch007

Wahba, F., Ajlouni, A. O., & Abumosa, M. A. (2024). The impact of ChatGPT-based learning statistics on undergraduates' statistical reasoning and attitudes toward statistics. *Eurasia Journal of Mathematics, Science and Technology Education*, *20*(7), 1–14. DOI: 10.29333/ejmste/14726

Xing, Y. (2024). Exploring the use of ChatGPT in learning and instructing statistics and data analytics. *Teaching Statistics*, *46*(2), 95–104. DOI: 10.1111/test.12367

Chapter 7
Faculty Development for AI-Integrated Statistics Teaching

C. Fowmina
http://orcid.org/0000-0002-0684-8729
Vinayaka Mission's Research Foundation, Chennai, India

R. Saravanan
http://orcid.org/0009-0009-9189-3740
Vinayaka Mission's Research Foundation, Chennai, India

Mamta Mishra
http://orcid.org/0009-0005-0701-5760
Sinhgad College of Engineering, Pune, India

Anagha Bhope
Sri Balaji University, Pune, India

P. Selvakumar
http://orcid.org/0000-0002-3650-4548
Department of Science and Humanities, Nehru Institute of Technology, Coimbatore, India

T. C. Manjunath
http://orcid.org/0000-0003-2545-9160
Rajarajeswari College of Engineering, Bengaluru, India

ABSTRACT

Artificial Intelligence (AI) is revolutionizing education across disciplines, and its impact on statistics education is especially profound. As a field rooted in data interpretation, quantitative reasoning, and analytical thinking, statistics benefits uniquely from AI's capabilities in data processing, pattern recognition, and adaptive learning. The integration of AI in statistics education is not merely a trend but a transformative shift that redefines how students learn statistical concepts, how educators teach them, and how both groups interact with data. By leveraging AI tools, intelligent tutoring systems, predictive analytics, and interactive platforms, educators can create more personalized, engaging, and effective learning experiences. This comprehensive examination explores the multifaceted role of AI in statistics

DOI: 10.4018/979-8-3373-6259-5.ch007

education, highlighting its benefits, applications, challenges, and future potential. Intelligent Tutoring Systems (ITS): AI-powered intelligent tutoring systems simulate human-like guidance by interpreting student input and offering instant feedback.

THE ROLE OF AI IN ENHANCING STATISTICS EDUCATION

Artificial Intelligence (AI) is revolutionizing education across disciplines, and its impact on statistics education is especially profound. As a field rooted in data interpretation, quantitative reasoning, and analytical thinking, statistics benefits uniquely from AI's capabilities in data processing, pattern recognition, and adaptive learning. The integration of AI in statistics education is not merely a trend but a transformative shift that redefines how students learn statistical concepts, how educators teach them, and how both groups interact with data. By leveraging AI tools, intelligent tutoring systems, predictive analytics, and interactive platforms, educators can create more personalized, engaging, and effective learning experiences. This comprehensive examination explores the multifaceted role of AI in statistics education, highlighting its benefits, applications, challenges, and future potential. Intelligent Tutoring Systems (ITS): AI-powered intelligent tutoring systems simulate human-like guidance by interpreting student input and offering instant feedback. In the context of statistics education, ITS can be especially useful for solving problems that involve formulas, reasoning, or stepwise logic. Examples: A tutoring system might guide a student through constructing a confidence interval or conducting a chi-square test, offering hints at each step. Virtual agents can simulate real-life statistical problems, encouraging critical thinking and application. Benefits: Supports students outside classroom hours. Offers consistent, nonjudgmental assistance. Enables instructors to track student progress and intervene when necessary. Enhanced Data Visualization and Interaction: Statistics is a visual discipline that relies on interpreting charts, graphs, and numerical patterns. AI enhances this experience through interactive and dynamic data visualization tools. Examples: AI platforms like Tableau with embedded machine learning suggest the most relevant charts based on data structure. Educational tools can simulate real-world data scenarios, allowing students to interact with datasets and apply statistical techniques. Augmented reality (AR) and virtual reality (VR) combined with AI can create immersive learning environments for understanding distributions, sampling, and variability. Outcomes: Improves students' ability to make sense of complex data. Encourages exploratory data analysis (EDA). Bridges the gap between theoretical knowledge and real-world application.

Simulation and Modeling: AI can generate complex, real-time simulations that help students grasp abstract statistical principles through experiential learning. These simulations allow learners to model hypotheses, manipulate variables, and observe outcomes. Applications: Monte Carlo simulations to teach concepts of probability and randomness. Bootstrap sampling methods for inference. Regression modeling simulations using real or synthetic datasets. Educational Value: Makes abstract concepts tangible. Reinforces learning through active experimentation. Develops students' critical thinking and data literacy skills. Predictive Analytics for Student Success: AI algorithms can analyze student performance and engagement data to predict academic outcomes. In statistics education, this can help instructors identify at-risk students early and implement timely interventions. Indicators Monitored: Time spent on learning platforms. Frequency of access to materials. Assignment and quiz performance trends. Implications: Enhances academic advising and support services. Promotes a proactive rather than reactive approach to student performance. Facilitates targeted remediation efforts. Challenges and Ethical Considerations: Despite its advantages, the integration of AI in statistics education is not without challenges. Issues of accessibility, data privacy, and algorithmic bias must be addressed to ensure equitable and ethical implementation. Concerns: Students in under-resourced schools may lack access to AI tools. AI algorithms may reflect biases present in training data. Overreliance on AI may reduce human interaction and critical thinking. Solutions: Promote inclusive design and accessibility in educational technologies. Educate students and teachers about AI ethics and data responsibility. Balance AI integration with human mentorship and pedagogical support. Artificial Intelligence is not just a supplement to traditional statistics education—it is a catalyst for transforming how students engage with data, how educators deliver instruction, and how learning outcomes are assessed and optimized. From adaptive learning systems to intelligent tutors, from dynamic simulations to predictive analytics, AI empowers a more personalized, interactive, and practical approach to teaching statistics. As the demand for data-literate professionals grows across all sectors, integrating AI into statistics education becomes both a pedagogical necessity and an opportunity for innovation. However, successful implementation requires thoughtful design, ethical considerations, and ongoing collaboration between educators, technologists, and learners. Embracing AI in statistics education promises not only to improve understanding but to inspire a new generation of statisticians, data scientists, and informed citizens in a data-driven world.

INCORPORATING AI AND MACHINE LEARNING INTO STATISTICS COURSES

The intersection of Artificial Intelligence (AI), Machine Learning (ML), and statistics represents one of the most transformative educational shifts in contemporary data-driven disciplines. As the demand for professionals skilled in both statistical reasoning and AI technologies continues to surge, integrating AI and ML concepts into statistics courses has become not only beneficial but essential. This integration equips students with the ability to analyze large and complex datasets, develop predictive models, and apply statistical reasoning to real-world problems—skills that are increasingly required in sectors such as healthcare, finance, marketing, manufacturing, and scientific research. Consequently, incorporating AI and ML into statistics courses enhances the relevance, applicability, and effectiveness of statistical education in the modern era (Boutilier & Chan, 2023). Curricular Enhancements: Topics and Skills to Include: Incorporating AI and ML into statistics courses involves the careful inclusion of both conceptual understanding and practical skill development. A reimagined statistics curriculum might include: Key Topics: Fundamentals of machine learning: regression, classification, clustering, decision trees, neural networks. Statistical learning theory and model evaluation (e.g., bias-variance trade-off, overfitting, cross-validation). Feature engineering, data preprocessing, and exploratory data analysis using AI tools. Introduction to natural language processing, computer vision, or reinforcement learning in advanced courses. Essential Skills: Proficiency in Python or R for data manipulation and modeling. Use of libraries such as Scikit-learn, TensorFlow, PyTorch, or caret. Data visualization and interpretation of AI model outputs. Critical evaluation of model performance and ethical implications. By grounding these topics in solid statistical theory, students not only learn to use AI tools but also understand how and why they work, promoting deeper learning and better application (Al-Labadi L., et al., 2025). Using AI Tools to Enhance Statistical Understanding: AI tools themselves can be used not just as content but as teaching aids in statistics education. Intelligent tutoring systems, automated feedback tools, and AI-driven simulation environments can help students grasp abstract statistical concepts. AI-Assisted Teaching Enhancements: Interactive simulations: Tools like TensorFlow Playground or Google Teachable Machine allow students to visualize how AI models learn from data. Automated feedback systems: Help students debug code, understand modeling errors, and receive instant corrections. Adaptive learning platforms: AI systems personalize content delivery based on a learner's progress, strengthening their understanding of statistics and AI simultaneously. By using AI as both subject and tool, instructors create a more immersive and personalized learning environment. Benefits for Students and Lifelong Learning: The integration of AI and ML into statistics education dramatically enhances students' readiness for the workforce, graduate studies, and interdisciplinary research (Gandomi A H., et al., 2023). Benefits for Learners: Future-proofing: Learners acquire skills that are expected to remain in demand for years to come. Data fluency: Students become confident in interpreting AI outputs and making data-informed decisions. Critical thinking: Exposure to both algorithmic thinking and statistical reasoning cultivates a balanced analytical mindset. Portfolio building: Capstone projects involving AI applications provide evidence of applied skills for future employers. In addition, students develop the agility to continuously learn and adapt as AI tools and statistical methodologies evolve. Assessing Learning in AI-Enhanced Statistics Courses: Assessment practices must evolve alongside curriculum content. Traditional exams can be supplemented with project evaluations, coding assignments, and peer-reviewed model analysis. Assessment Methods: Model-building projects: Students create and evaluate AI models using statistical reasoning. Code notebooks: Submissions using Jupyter or R Markdown that combine narrative, code, and analysis. Data storytelling: Students interpret model outcomes and communicate findings to non-technical audiences. Ethics reflections: Short essays or discussions on the implications of AI and data bias. These assessments help evaluate both conceptual understanding and technical proficiency, ensuring holistic learning outcomes (Mehra J., et al., 2025). Conclusion: Transforming Statistics Education for the AI Era: Incorporating AI and machine learning into statistics courses is a forward-looking response to the evolving landscape of data analysis, technological innovation, and workforce expectations. This integration not only enriches the content and relevance of statistical education but also empowers students to become adaptive, analytical., and ethically responsible practitioners. By reimagining the curriculum, embracing hands-on learning, and supporting both educators and students through training and resources, institutions can create a new generation of learners who are well-equipped to thrive in AI-powered environments. Ultimately, integrating AI and ML into statistics is not just a curricular enhancement—it is a transformative shift that positions statistics education at the heart of the data revolution.

USING AI FOR DATA ANALYSIS AND MODELING

Artificial Intelligence (AI) has emerged as a revolutionary force in the realm of data analysis and modeling, transforming how data is processed, interpreted, and used to inform decisions across sectors. In an age defined by exponential data growth and increasing complexity, traditional analytical tools often fall short in their ability to handle vast datasets, uncover subtle patterns, and generate actionable insights in real time. AI—through techniques such as machine learning (ML), deep learning, and natural language processing (NLP)—offers powerful solutions for automating data analysis, enhancing model accuracy, and enabling predictive and prescriptive analytics (Banala S., et al., 2025). The integration of AI into data workflows not only accelerates the speed of analysis but also empowers organizations and researchers to make smarter, evidence-based decisions that were previously unattainable with conventional statistical methods alone. Types of AI Techniques Used in Data Analysis and Modeling: A broad range of AI methodologies supports diverse analytical needs, each offering unique capabilities depending on the data type and analysis objectives. Machine Learning (ML): Supervised Learning: Algorithms (e.g., linear regression, support vector machines, random forests) are trained on labeled data to predict outcomes or classify data points. Unsupervised Learning: Techniques like clustering (K-means, DBSCAN) and dimensionality reduction (PCA, t-SNE) are used for exploratory analysis of unlabeled data. Semi-supervised and Reinforcement Learning: Applied in scenarios with limited labeled data or dynamic decision environments. Deep Learning: Neural networks, particularly Convolutional Neural Networks (CNNs) and Recurrent Neural Networks (RNNs), excel in handling complex data such as images, audio, and sequences. Used for advanced modeling tasks like image recognition, speech processing, and time-series forecasting (Qayyum F., et al., 2022). Natural Language Processing (NLP): Enables the analysis of unstructured text data, extracting meaning through sentiment analysis, topic modeling, or summarization. Widely applied in customer feedback analysis, social media monitoring, and document classification. Generative AI: Techniques like Generative Adversarial Networks (GANs) and Large Language Models (LLMs) generate new data instances or synthesize narratives based on input patterns. Used in data augmentation, synthetic dataset creation, and report generation. By leveraging these techniques, analysts can move beyond surface-level insights to extract a nuanced, multi-dimensional understanding from diverse datasets.

Applications of AI-Based Data Modeling Across Domains: AI's impact on data modeling spans multiple sectors, enabling unprecedented analytical capabilities: Healthcare: Predictive models for disease outbreaks, patient readmissions, and treatment outcomes. AI-driven analysis of genomic data, medical imaging, and electronic health records. Finance: Fraud detection through anomaly detection algorithms. Credit scoring models using alternative data and deep learning. Portfolio optimization and real-time risk assessment. Marketing and Retail: Customer segmentation and behavior prediction (Cabrera et al., 2023). Personalization engines based on recommender systems. Sentiment analysis of consumer reviews and social media. Manufacturing and IoT: Predictive maintenance using sensor data. Process optimization and quality control. Supply chain forecasting and anomaly detection. Education and Social Sciences: Student performance prediction and adaptive learning systems. Content recommendation and behavioral analytics. In each of these domains, AI not only enhances the accuracy and depth of insights but also democratizes access to powerful analytical tools for non-expert users. Challenges and Considerations: Despite its strengths, AI-based data analysis comes with several challenges: Data Quality and Bias: Poor-quality or biased data can lead to inaccurate and unethical outcomes. Interpretability: Some AI models, particularly deep learning, are "black boxes" and lack transparency. Overfitting: High model complexity can result in overfitting to training data, harming generalizability. Ethical and Legal Concerns:

Privacy, consent, and data ownership must be considered when using AI on sensitive datasets. Skill Gaps: Effective use of AI requires interdisciplinary skills in programming, statistics, domain knowledge, and ethics (Hariyanti F., et al., 2025). Addressing these challenges requires robust governance, explainable AI tools, and a commitment to ethical data practices. The integration of AI into data analysis and modeling represents a paradigm shift that redefines how data is understood, leveraged, and acted upon. No longer confined to static reports or linear models, modern analytics powered by AI delivers dynamic, adaptive, and predictive insights with unmatched precision and speed. While challenges remain, the benefits—ranging from enhanced efficiency and scalability to deeper, more actionable insights—are undeniable. Organizations, researchers, and educators must therefore embrace AI not only as a tool but as a transformative analytical partner. When thoughtfully implemented with attention to ethics, transparency, and continuous learning, AI has the potential to revolutionize decision-making and drive innovation across every domain reliant on data.

TEACHING AI-DRIVEN STATISTICAL METHODS AND TOOLS

The integration of Artificial Intelligence (AI) into statistical education is reshaping how statistical methods are taught, understood, and applied. AI-driven statistical methods and tools offer unprecedented opportunities for enhancing traditional curricula, providing students with hands-on experience in analyzing complex data, and fostering critical thinking and innovation. As the demand for data literacy and AI competence rises across disciplines, educators are increasingly tasked with equipping students not only with foundational statistical knowledge but also with the ability to utilize modern AI techniques effectively (Rocha-Feregrino G., et al., 2025). Teaching AI-driven statistical methods requires a careful balance of theory and application, merging classical inferential statistics with machine learning, deep learning, and other AI methodologies that are now integral to real-world data analysis. The Evolving Landscape of Statistical Education: Traditional statistics education has focused on descriptive and inferential techniques such as hypothesis testing, confidence intervals, regression analysis, and probability distributions. While these remain foundational., they are often limited in handling massive, unstructured, or high-dimensional data sets common in today's digital world. AI-driven statistical methods expand this scope, enabling predictive analytics, pattern recognition, natural language understanding, and automated decision-making. AI transforms statistical education by: Introducing algorithms that learn from data (e.g., supervised/unsupervised learning). Offering tools for high-dimensional data modeling. Enabling real-time analytics and visualization. Teaching students to critically assess model assumptions, fairness, and bias. This shift calls for a curriculum that bridges classical methods with contemporary AI approaches while maintaining statistical rigor. Tools and Platforms for Teaching AI-Driven Statistics: A wide array of software platforms and tools support the teaching of AI-driven statistical methods (Xie X., 2023). Programming Languages: Python: With libraries such as NumPy, pandas, scikit-learn, TensorFlow, Keras, and PyTorch, Python is ideal for both traditional statistics and AI. R: Suitable for statistical analysis, R also integrates AI tools like caret, mlr, keras, and tidymodels. Visualization Tools: Matplotlib, Seaborn, Plotly (Python), and ggplot2 (R) support advanced data visualization and model interpretation. AutoML Platforms: Tools like Google AutoML, H2O.ai, and Azure Machine Learning help students automate model selection, tuning, and deployment. Jupyter Notebooks and R Markdown: Interactive platforms that combine code, analysis, and commentary for reproducible teaching and learning experiences.

AI Simulators and Cloud-Based Labs: Platforms such as IBM Watson Studio, Google Colab, and Kaggle Kernels enable hands-on experience without requiring high-end hardware. Introducing these tools into coursework ensures students gain practical skills in working with real datasets using industry-standard software. Challenges in Teaching AI-Driven Statistics: While the benefits of AI integration are substantial., educators face several challenges: Curriculum Overload: Balancing statistical theory and AI topics within limited course time. Technical Barriers: Students may lack sufficient programming or mathematical background (Ouyang & Zhang, 2024). Rapidly Changing Field: AI tools and methodologies evolve quickly, requiring constant curriculum updates. Access to Resources: Not all institutions have infrastructure for high-performance computing or cloud platforms. Ethical Literacy: Many courses focus on tools and performance, neglecting fairness and societal impact. Overcoming these challenges requires institutional support, interdisciplinary collaboration, and continuous faculty development. Future Directions in AI-Driven Statistics Education: The future of AI-enhanced statistics education is dynamic and promising. Personalized Learning: AI-powered educational platforms can adapt content to individual student needs. Virtual Labs and Simulations: Immersive environments allow students to test models and visualize data in real time. Interdisciplinary Courses: Combine statistics with AI, data science, ethics, and domain-specific knowledge. Lifelong Learning and Microcredentials: Stackable certificates and online courses provide continuous upskilling opportunities. Research and Innovation Hubs: Educational institutions are developing AI research centers that blend teaching with active inquiry (Limbore N V., et al., 2025). These trends point toward a more interactive, accessible, and forward-thinking model of statistical education. As AI continues to transform the data landscape, teaching AI-driven statistical methods and tools becomes not only relevant but essential. Educators must prepare students to move beyond rote analysis and engage deeply with data through

AI-enhanced techniques. This involves cultivating a hybrid skillset—statistical literacy, computational thinking, ethical awareness, and domain knowledge. By integrating machine learning, deep learning, NLP, and other AI approaches into the statistics curriculum, educators can empower students to thrive in the era of big data and intelligent systems. The ultimate goal is not just to teach students how to use AI tools, but to foster a mindset of curiosity, critical thinking, and responsible innovation in the pursuit of knowledge and societal progress.

ACTIVE LEARNING STRATEGIES FOR AI-INTEGRATED STATISTICS

The integration of Artificial Intelligence (AI) into statistics education presents a transformative opportunity to shift from passive, lecture-based instruction to dynamic, student-centered learning. Active learning, characterized by student engagement through collaboration, problem-solving, experimentation, and reflection, complements AI technologies by fostering deeper conceptual understanding, critical thinking, and real-world application. As statistical analysis increasingly intersects with AI-driven tools and algorithms, active learning strategies become essential for cultivating students who are not just proficient in using AI but are capable of interpreting and questioning the outcomes these tools produce. By embedding AI into active learning pedagogies, educators can create enriched, interactive learning environments that mirror the data-driven world students will encounter in their academic and professional careers (Lokhande M., et al., 2025). The Synergy Between Active Learning and AI in Statistics: Active learning and AI integration are inherently synergistic. AI tools such as automated feedback systems, data visualization platforms, predictive modeling environments, and intelligent tutoring systems can elevate the effectiveness of active learning by providing real-time insights, personalized learning paths, and scalable instructional support. Conversely, active learning strategies ensure that the use of AI is not superficial or mechanistic but becomes part of a critical., reflective learning process. In statistics courses, students must not only learn how to perform calculations but also interpret data, question assumptions, and understand context. AI can process vast datasets and perform complex computations, while active learning encourages students to ask "why" and "how," developing interpretative and analytical skills that are essential in modern data science. Flipped Classroom with AI-Enhanced Pre-Class Activities: The flipped classroom model, where students engage with instructional content before class and spend class time in collaborative, problem-solving tasks, aligns well with AI integration. AI can support this model through: AI-Powered Videos and Tutorials: Platforms like Khan Academy, edX, or custom LMSs with embedded AI can deliver tailored lessons and track comprehension. Intelligent Questioning Systems: Tools like Squirrel AI or Knewton adapt content based on a learner's strengths and weaknesses, preparing them better for in-class work (Yixuan Z., et al., 2025). In-class sessions can then focus on activities like peer teaching, data exploration, simulation experiments, or debates on model selection and ethical AI use, fostering critical thinking and cooperative learning. Data Challenges and AI Hackathons: Hosting mini-hackathons or data challenges within a statistics course allows students to compete or collaborate in solving analytical problems using AI. These time-bound events enhance engagement and motivation, reinforce technical skills, and simulate real-world conditions. Instructors can use public datasets (from Kaggle, UCI Machine Learning Repository, or government portals) and define challenges such as predicting stock trends, diagnosing medical conditions, or detecting fake news. Students must preprocess data, apply machine learning models, evaluate outcomes, and explain their approach—developing both statistical and AI literacy.

Figure 1. Benefits of AI in education

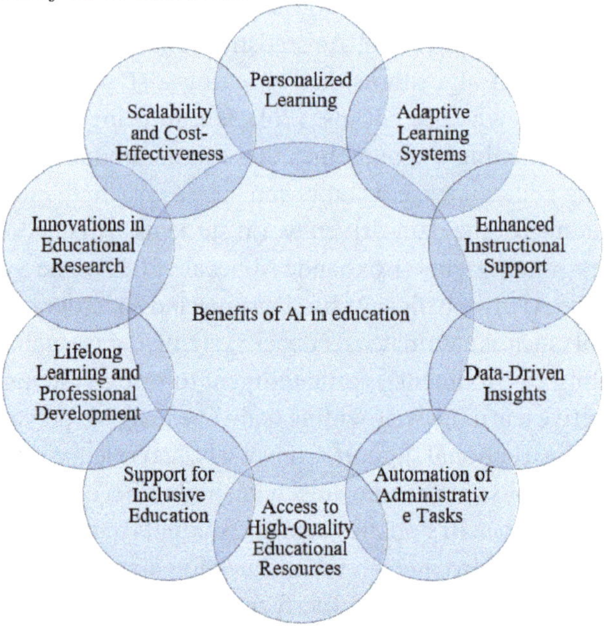

Collaborative Learning Through AI Platforms: Collaboration is central to active learning. AI platforms can facilitate and enhance group work by: Tracking Participation and Contribution: AI can monitor collaborative documents, forums, or code repositories to ensure equitable participation. Recommending Peer Matches: Based on learning patterns or preferences, AI can suggest optimal student groupings.

Automated Peer Feedback: AI systems can analyze peer feedback for quality and sentiment, helping students improve their evaluation skills. Such systems allow for dynamic, data-informed group activities and improve student accountability and learning outcomes (Kurniawan D., et al., 2025). Ethics and Critical Discussions on AI Use: Active learning is not just about doing—it's also about thinking. Courses should include structured discussions on the ethical and societal implications of AI in statistics. Students can be assigned to analyze a controversial AI model (e.g., facial recognition, predictive policing) and discuss its statistical foundations, limitations, biases, and real-world consequences. These activities promote metacognition, civic awareness, and cross-disciplinary dialogue—skills vital for responsible data scientists and statisticians. Gamification and AI-Enhanced Learning Environments: Incorporating game elements into statistics education—such as points, levels, or AI-driven challenges—boosts motivation and engagement. AI can adjust game difficulty, provide real-time coaching, or generate novel statistical scenarios for students to analyze. For example, a game might involve exploring a dataset through a "choose-your-own-adventure" interface, where each decision affects the outcome and requires statistical justification. AI can track pathways, offer feedback, and log performance for analysis. Conclusion: Empowering Statistical Thinkers through Active AI Learning: Active learning strategies, when paired with AI, transform the statistics classroom into a dynamic lab of inquiry, discovery, and innovation (Kurtz G., et al., 2024). Rather than passively absorbing statistical procedures, students engage with real-world data, leverage intelligent tools, and reflect on the impact of their analyses. This pedagogical approach not only improves conceptual mastery but also fosters essential 21st-century skills—critical thinking, collaboration, ethical reasoning, and adaptability. By empowering students to actively construct knowledge through AI-enhanced experiences, educators prepare them for careers where statistics and machine learning are not just tools but lenses through which to understand and shape the world. As we enter an era defined by data and automation, integrating active learning with AI ensures that statistics education remains relevant, rigorous, and profoundly human-centered.

USING REAL-WORLD EXAMPLES AND CASE STUDIES IN STATISTICS EDUCATION AND AI INTEGRATION

Incorporating real-world examples and case studies into statistics education, particularly in the context of Artificial Intelligence (AI) integration, is a highly effective pedagogical strategy that bridges the gap between theoretical learning and practical application. It enhances student engagement, facilitates deeper understanding, and cultivates essential analytical and problem-solving skills. Real-world data and scenarios not only make abstract statistical concepts more tangible and relevant but also foster critical thinking as students encounter the ambiguity, variability, and complexity inherent in authentic datasets (Bayaga A., 2025). When these examples are augmented with AI tools and applications, learners gain firsthand experience with how statistical methods are deployed in data-driven decision-making, automation, and innovation across industries. The Pedagogical Value of Real-World Examples: Statistics is fundamentally a tool for understanding the world through data. Teaching it in isolation—detached from real-world contexts—can limit students' appreciation of its value and reduce motivation. Real-world examples contextualize statistical methods, showing students how regression, hypothesis testing, clustering, or time-series analysis are applied to address tangible problems such as predicting consumer behavior, diagnosing diseases, detecting fraud, or assessing climate trends. These examples resonate more with learners because they connect to familiar domains, stimulate curiosity, and reveal the societal relevance of statistics and AI. Examples from Healthcare: AI and Predictive Analytics: Healthcare provides a rich context for teaching statistics using AI-enhanced real-world examples. One such example is predicting patient readmissions using electronic health records (EHRs) (Yang Y., et al., 2021). Instructors can provide anonymized datasets that include patient demographics, diagnoses, treatments, and outcomes. Students can apply descriptive statistics, correlation analysis, and classification algorithms (e.g., random forest, logistic regression) to model the likelihood of readmission. Beyond modeling, students must interpret confusion matrices, understand sensitivity and specificity, and evaluate ethical concerns such as bias in data or model transparency. By tackling such real-world health problems, learners gain exposure to the high-stakes nature of statistical decisions supported by AI tools. Environmental Data and Climate Modeling: Environmental science offers numerous examples for integrating statistics and AI, from modeling pollution levels to forecasting natural disasters. A classroom case study might focus on predicting air quality indices (AQI) based on weather patterns and emission data. Students use regression techniques, time-series analysis, and AI-based forecasting models like LSTM neural networks. These exercises reveal how statistical thinking supports sustainability and public health. They also highlight the limitations of models and the importance of considering external factors, uncertainty, and data quality in environmental decision-making.

Public Policy and Societal Impact Analysis: In the domain of public policy, case studies can illustrate how data and AI are used to assess programs or predict social outcomes. For example, students can explore how statistical and AI tools are used to predict school dropout rates or evaluate poverty reduction initiatives. Datasets from governments or NGOs often contain rich demographic and socioeconomic variables. Students can analyze these datasets using linear or logistic regression, decision trees, or ensemble methods, followed by interpreting results in the context of policy decisions, social justice, and ethical AI use (Ding A C E., et al., 2024). These examples broaden students' perspectives and show the power and responsibility that come with statistical modeling. Business Operations and Customer Analytics: Real-world examples from marketing and operations—like customer segmentation, sales forecasting, or supply chain optimization—demonstrate how statistics and AI drive strategic decisions. Students might analyze e-commerce data to recommend personalized marketing strategies using clustering algorithms and association rule mining. They can compare statistical models with AI tools such as recommendation engines to understand trade-offs between interpretability and accuracy. These activities reflect the role of statistics in modern business intelligence and encourage students to think strategically. Ethical Dimensions in Real-World AI Applications: Real-world examples provide opportunities to explore ethical dimensions of statistics and AI. Whether it's bias in hiring algorithms, surveillance technologies, or unequal access to predictive healthcare, students can analyze how statistical decisions influence equity and justice (Chowdhary S., et al., 2025). By critically examining case studies with known biases or unintended consequences, students learn to assess fairness metrics, identify proxy variables, and consider the human impact of data-driven systems. Conclusion: Transforming Education Through Real-World Relevance: Embedding real-world examples and case studies in AI-integrated statistics education is vital for preparing students to tackle complex, data-rich challenges across domains. It transforms statistics from an abstract academic subject into a living discipline, empowering learners to become critical thinkers, ethical decision-makers, and skilled analysts. By situating statistical methods within authentic contexts and enhancing them with AI tools, educators cultivate a generation of data-literate citizens who can understand, evaluate, and contribute to the data-driven world around them. Through consistent engagement with real-world problems, students not only grasp the mechanics of statistical modeling but also appreciate its relevance, complexity, and impact—leading to more meaningful learning and lasting knowledge.

COLLABORATIVE LEARNING AND PROJECT-BASED LEARNING IN AI-INTEGRATED STATISTICS EDUCATION

Collaborative learning and project-based learning (PBL) represent two powerful pedagogical approaches that significantly enrich the teaching and learning of statistics, particularly when integrated with Artificial Intelligence (AI). These learner-centered strategies emphasize cooperation, real-world relevance, and active engagement, which are essential for developing 21st-century skills such as critical thinking, problem-solving, digital fluency, and data literacy. In the context of AI-integrated statistics education, collaborative learning and PBL empower students to explore complex datasets, apply statistical techniques and AI tools, and co-construct knowledge through shared inquiry and experimentation (Upadhyaya A N., et al., 2025). These methods foster not only academic understanding but also personal development, ethical reasoning, and professional readiness. Project-Based Learning (PBL): A Contextual Framework for Deep Learning: Project-based learning (PBL) places students in the driver's seat of their education by engaging them in sustained, inquiry-based investigations of complex questions, problems, or challenges. In AI and statistics education, PBL might involve semester-long tasks such as building predictive models, conducting hypothesis testing on community data, designing AI-based recommender systems, or simulating decision-making scenarios using statistical inference. PBL transforms theoretical instruction into hands-on exploration. Students take ownership of their learning by setting goals, identifying resources, collecting and analyzing data, and presenting their findings to authentic audiences—be it their peers, instructors, or industry mentors. These projects require integration of multiple skill sets, including coding, statistical analysis, domain-specific knowledge, collaboration, communication, and ethical reasoning. The iterative nature of projects—characterized by feedback, revision, and refinement—mirrors the professional research and development process (Rahmaty M., 2023). Designing Effective Collaborative and Project-Based Experiences: Clear Learning Objectives: Projects should be aligned with curriculum goals and designed to develop both statistical and AI competencies. Whether the focus is on exploratory data analysis, model building, or ethical implications, instructors should articulate the expected outcomes from the start. Meaningful Problem Contexts: Authentic, open-ended problems engage students and promote deeper learning. These may include local community issues, global challenges (e.g., disease outbreaks), or industry-specific scenarios like market analysis or risk prediction. Team Formation and Role Assignment: Diverse teams bring varied perspectives and skill sets. Assigning roles—such as data analyst, coder, quality controller, and presenter—ensures participation and accountability. Roles can rotate to provide comprehensive exposure.

Scaffolding and Support: Instructors should provide checkpoints, milestones, and feedback throughout the project. Mini-lessons, curated resources, and peer review sessions help maintain focus and improve quality. Integration of AI Tools: Students should be introduced to tools such as scikit-learn, TensorFlow, Tableau, Orange, or IBM Watson Studio. These tools enhance statistical analysis and allow for more advanced AI applications like image recognition, natural language processing, or predictive modeling. Communication and Reflection: Students should present findings through reports, dashboards, posters, or video pitches. Reflective writing and debriefing sessions help them internalize their learning and articulate how statistics and AI contributed to solving the problem (Muhammad A., 2024). Challenges and Strategies for Implementation: Implementing collaborative PBL in

AI-integrated statistics courses comes with challenges such as uneven group participation, varied skill levels, time management, and assessment complexity. Effective strategies include: Setting up group contracts and peer evaluation systems to ensure an equitable workload. Offering coding workshops or tutorials to bridge technical gaps. Incorporating interim progress reports and instructor feedback. Designing rubrics that assess both individual and team contributions. Creating cross-disciplinary collaborations (e.g., pairing statistics students with computer science or domain-specific peers). Conclusion: Building Collaborative Problem Solvers for the AI Age: Collaborative learning and project-based learning are transformative strategies that align perfectly with the goals of AI-integrated statistics education. By engaging in real-world projects, collaborating with peers, and utilizing cutting-edge AI tools, students move beyond rote memorization to become adaptive problem-solvers and ethical data practitioners (Diaz Pratiwi M., et al., 2025). These approaches foster not only statistical literacy but also teamwork, creativity, empathy, and digital fluency—skills essential for navigating the complexities of the AI-driven world. Educators who adopt collaborative and PBL frameworks help create inclusive, dynamic, and impactful learning environments that prepare students not just to understand data, but to use it meaningfully and responsibly. In doing so, they cultivate a generation of statisticians, data scientists, and educators who can think critically, act collaboratively, and lead innovations that serve society.

ASSESSING STUDENT LEARNING OUTCOMES IN AI-INTEGRATED STATISTICS EDUCATION

Assessment in AI-integrated statistics education plays a pivotal role in evaluating students' mastery of both foundational statistical concepts and advanced data-driven skills enabled by artificial intelligence (AI) technologies. With the infusion of AI tools, methodologies, and real-world applications into statistics curricula, the traditional methods of assessment must evolve to capture the multifaceted nature of student learning (Alkhater & Danish, 2024). Effective assessment must measure not only content knowledge but also computational thinking, problem-solving abilities, ethical reasoning, data interpretation, and collaboration skills. Designing robust and comprehensive assessment strategies in such a hybridized learning environment ensures that students are prepared to apply statistics and AI meaningfully and responsibly in academic, professional., and societal contexts. Key Learning Outcomes in AI-Integrated Statistics: Assessments should be purposefully aligned with specific learning outcomes. Some key outcomes include: Statistical literacy: Understanding statistical measures, data distribution, hypothesis testing, and inferential logic. AI fluency: Grasping AI concepts like supervised/unsupervised learning, neural networks, classification, and clustering. Data handling: Cleaning, transforming, and visualizing data using tools such as Python, R, or Excel. Programming proficiency: Writing code for statistical analysis or AI models using libraries such as scikit-learn, TensorFlow, or pandas (AlDhaen & Danish, 2024). Interpretation and communication: Translating data insights into clear, accessible narratives and visualizations. Ethical reasoning: Assessing algorithmic bias, data privacy, and the societal impact of AI applications. Collaboration and project management: Demonstrating teamwork, communication, and organizational skills. Each of these outcomes should be directly linked to measurable assessment tasks that reflect student growth in both knowledge and skills.

Rubrics and Criteria for Assessment: Clear and detailed rubrics are essential to ensure transparency and consistency in grading. Rubrics for AI-integrated statistics courses might include criteria such as: Technical accuracy: Correct use of statistical and AI models. Code quality: Efficiency, readability, and documentation of programming work. Data literacy: Appropriate handling, analysis, and interpretation of datasets. Communication skills: Clarity in writing, visualizations, and oral presentations. Creativity and problem-solving: Innovation in applying statistical and AI techniques to complex challenges (Dai X., et al., 2025). Ethical awareness: Consideration of fairness, bias, and societal impact. Rubrics help students understand expectations and guide instructors in providing consistent feedback. Challenges in Assessing AI-Enhanced Learning and How to Overcome Them: Technical disparities: Not all students may have equal access to hardware, software, or prior coding experience. Instructors should provide scaffolding, tutorials, and access to cloud-based tools. Assessment overload: Complex projects may overwhelm students. Breaking them into manageable milestones and providing ongoing feedback can mitigate this. Plagiarism and AI misuse: With the rise of generative AI tools (e.g., ChatGPT, GitHub Copilot), educators must design assessments that require originality and personalized responses, such as oral defenses or code walk-throughs. Measuring group work: Assessing individual contributions in group projects can be difficult. Using peer assessments and rotating roles helps ensure accountability. Conclusion: Toward a Holistic and Future-Ready Assessment Paradigm: Assessing student learning in AI-integrated statistics requires a shift from traditional exam-centric approaches to a more nuanced and holistic framework (Nisha Angeline M., et al., 2025). By embracing a blend of formative, summative, performance-based, and reflective assessments, educators can capture the full range of competencies needed in the data-driven world. Such assessments not only measure what students know but also how they think, collaborate, create, and reflect. Moreover, effective assessment fosters lifelong learning habits and prepares students for the ethical and technical challenges of applying AI in real-world contexts. With thoughtful design, transparency, and adaptability, assessment can become a powerful tool for both measuring and enhancing student learning in the era of AI-integrated statistics education.

EVALUATING THE EFFECTIVENESS OF AI-INTEGRATED STATISTICS CURRICULUM

The integration of artificial intelligence (AI) into statistics education is revolutionizing how statistical concepts are taught, understood, and applied. As institutions and educators redesign curricula to reflect this technological shift, it becomes essential to systematically evaluate the effectiveness of AI-integrated statistics programs. Such evaluation ensures that the curriculum not only aligns with academic goals but also prepares students with the necessary skills for real-world data science, analytics, and AI-driven decision-making environments. A comprehensive evaluation framework encompasses both formative and summative assessment techniques, quantitative and qualitative data analysis, stakeholder feedback, and continuous curriculum improvement (Coates J M., et al., 2025). The goal is to identify strengths, address gaps, and refine instructional practices to foster student achievement and engagement in this interdisciplinary field. Core Components of an Evaluation Framework: An effective evaluation strategy for AI-integrated statistics curricula typically includes the following components: Input Evaluation: Focuses on resources, faculty expertise, student preparedness, and technological infrastructure. Key questions include: Are faculty adequately trained in AI tools and pedagogy? Do students have access to appropriate hardware, software, and datasets? Are there sufficient teaching materials and lab support systems? Process Evaluation: Monitors how the curriculum is implemented in the classroom. This includes: Teaching methods (e.g., project-based learning, flipped classrooms). AI tool integration (e.g., use of Jupyter notebooks, Python, R, ML libraries). Classroom dynamics and student engagement. Challenges faced by instructors and learners. Output Evaluation: Assesses the immediate results of curriculum implementation, such as Student performance on assessments (Suharyo S., et al., 2024). Improvement in data analysis, coding, and critical thinking skills. Quality of student projects and presentations. Student feedback and satisfaction levels. Outcome Evaluation: Examines the long-term impact, including: Retention of statistical and AI concepts. Career readiness and placement in data science roles. Transferability of learned skills to new tools and domains. Lifelong learning attitudes toward technology and data.

Student Learning Outcome (SLO) Evaluation: Measuring learning outcomes requires the development of well-defined, observable, and measurable goals that reflect both statistical and AI competencies. For instance: Cognitive domain: Understanding probability distributions, model fitting, AI algorithms (e.g., regression, classification). Psychomotor domain: Using coding platforms to preprocess data, train models, and visualize results. Affective domain: Demonstrating ethical reasoning, collaboration, curiosity, and persistence. Rubrics can be developed for each project or task to assess how well students meet these outcomes. Regular benchmarking across semesters helps track curriculum effectiveness longitudinally (Dong L., et al., 2025). Faculty Evaluation and Development: Faculty readiness and instructional quality are critical components of successful AI integration. Evaluation here includes: Self-assessment surveys on confidence in teaching AI topics. Peer observations and reviews of teaching practices. Analysis of faculty-student interaction, mentorship, and responsiveness. Participation in professional development workshops and training. Encouraging a culture of reflective teaching and continuous learning supports sustained curriculum effectiveness. Ethics, Inclusion, and Equity Evaluation: Incorporating AI into education must be done with attention to fairness and inclusion. Evaluators should assess: Representation of diverse datasets in teaching examples. Opportunities for all students regardless of prior coding experience. Awareness of algorithmic bias and ethical dilemmas. Support mechanisms for disadvantaged students. Equity-focused evaluation ensures that AI integration empowers all learners, not just those with pre-existing technical advantages. Conclusion: Building a Sustainable and Effective AI-Integrated Curriculum: Evaluating the effectiveness of an AI-integrated statistics curriculum is a multifaceted endeavor that requires thoughtful planning, robust data collection, and collaborative engagement (Tu Y., et al., 2025). By using diverse evaluation strategies—ranging from student performance data to faculty reflections and industry feedback—educators can create a curriculum that is both rigorous and responsive. This process not only strengthens the curriculum's instructional design but also prepares students to be critical thinkers and ethical practitioners in a world increasingly shaped by AI and data. As AI continues to evolve, so too must our methods of teaching and evaluation. A well-evaluated curriculum becomes a dynamic ecosystem—one that adapts to new technologies, reflects the needs of diverse learners, and fosters a culture of excellence in data-driven education.

EMERGING TRENDS IN AI AND STATISTICS EDUCATION

Artificial Intelligence (AI) is reshaping the landscape of education, and its impact is particularly profound in the teaching and learning of statistics. As the demand for data literacy and computational thinking grows across disciplines, AI is not only enhancing traditional statistics instruction but also transforming pedagogical models, curricular structures, assessment strategies, and faculty development initiatives. In this dynamic context, several emerging trends are shaping the future of AI-integrated statistics education, reflecting both technological innovations and evolving educational philosophies. These trends highlight the increasing convergence of automation, interactivity, personalization, and ethics within statistics classrooms (Siddiqui M T., et al., 2025). Integration of Generative AI in Teaching and Learning: One of the most significant emerging trends is the integration of generative AI tools, such as ChatGPT, Bard, Claude, and Copilot, into statistics education. These tools can assist both educators and students in tasks ranging from problem-solving to data interpretation, natural language explanation of statistical concepts, and even code generation for statistical computing. Educators are using generative AI to create dynamic learning content such as quizzes, practice problems, and simulations. Provide real-time, AI-driven tutoring or feedback to students. Simplify complex statistical ideas using natural language interfaces. Generate visual aids and charts automatically based on user prompts. For students, these tools foster independent learning and exploration, allowing them to test hypotheses or visualize data patterns with AI support. However, effective integration requires critical literacy to evaluate AI outputs, understand model limitations, and uphold academic integrity. Personalized and Adaptive Learning Systems: AI-driven personalization is a game-changer in education. Adaptive learning platforms, powered by machine learning algorithms, now enable customized instruction paths for statistics students (Meinlschmidt G., et al., 2025). These systems monitor learner behavior, performance trends, and engagement levels to deliver tailored feedback, dynamically adjust content difficulty, and suggest supplementary resources. Key aspects of this trend include: Learning analytics dashboards: Allow educators to track student progress, identify struggling learners, and intervene proactively. Skill mapping: Systems identify gaps in statistical understanding and adapt instructional content accordingly. AI chatbots: Provide 24/7 support by answering statistics queries, explaining concepts, or troubleshooting coding issues in R, Python, or SAS. Such platforms democratize learning by catering to individual student needs and learning styles, making statistical education more inclusive and effective.

AI-Augmented Assessment and Feedback Systems: Assessment strategies in statistics education are evolving with AI's ability to analyze student work, detect learning gaps, and provide instantaneous feedback. AI-enabled assessment tools offer: Automated grading, particularly for programming-based assignments, statistical analyses, or multiple-choice questions. Plagiarism detection: Ensuring academic integrity in AI-rich environments. Constructive feedback: Students receive detailed feedback on their logical reasoning, interpretation of statistical results, and report writing. Furthermore, educators can use AI-generated insights to redesign course materials or adjust teaching strategies based on aggregate student performance data. Collaborative Learning via AI-Powered Platforms: AI is also enhancing collaborative learning environments (Burrill & Pfannkuch, 2024). Tools like GitHub Copilot, JupyterHub with AI integrations, and collaborative data science platforms enable students to work in teams, co-write code, analyze datasets, and interpret results. Emerging practices include: Peer review systems powered by AI that evaluate collaborative contributions. Automated version control that tracks individual student edits or code inputs. Shared notebooks with embedded AI assistants to guide statistical modeling. Such platforms promote teamwork, accountability, and communication skills while maintaining analytical rigor. Faculty Development and AI Literacy Programs: To support these changes, institutions are investing in continuous faculty development. Emerging trends in faculty training include: AI boot camps and micro-credentials: Short, intensive programs that prepare educators to integrate AI into teaching. Communities of Practice: Peer-led initiatives where educators co-develop AI-rich curricula and share experiences. AI pedagogical toolkits: Ready-to-use templates, sample lesson plans, and annotated code repositories to ease implementation. This trend ensures that educators remain at the forefront of technological innovation and can model digital fluency for their students (Matos T., et al., 2025). Conclusion: Preparing for the Future of AI-Driven Statistics Education: The convergence of AI and statistics education is not just a technological advancement—it marks a pedagogical transformation. Emerging trends reflect a shift from rote memorization and procedural learning to inquiry-based, collaborative, and personalized education. As AI continues to evolve, educators must remain adaptive, ethically grounded, and committed to continuous learning. By embracing these trends, institutions can prepare students not just to use AI tools, but to critically engage with the statistical foundations that underpin intelligent systems. The future of statistics education lies in a seamless blend of computational power, human insight, and societal relevance. Educators who align with these trends will be at the forefront of training the next generation of data-literate citizens, scientists, and innovators.

CONCLUSION

As artificial intelligence (AI) continues to redefine the contours of modern education, its integration into statistics teaching is no longer a future ambition but a present necessity. The convergence of AI and statistics has triggered a significant pedagogical shift, demanding not only new tools and methods but also a fundamental rethinking of educators' roles, responsibilities, and capabilities. In this evolving educational ecosystem, faculty development emerges as the cornerstone of successful AI-integrated statistics instruction. Without well-prepared, knowledgeable, and confident educators, even the most advanced technologies and well-designed curricula cannot achieve their intended impact. This conclusion underscores the central role of faculty development in ensuring the sustainability, scalability, and equity of AI-enhanced statistics education. Moreover, faculty development fosters pedagogical innovation. Integrating AI into statistics teaching is not simply about incorporating new tools but about transforming the way students learn, engage, and apply statistical thinking. Educators must learn to design interdisciplinary learning experiences, align AI applications with learning objectives, and employ active learning strategies that encourage critical thinking and problem-solving. Faculty development workshops, mentorship programs, and communities of practice provide a fertile ground for such pedagogical experimentation and collaboration. In these settings, educators share best practices, adapt to diverse student needs, and co-create teaching materials that reflect real-world complexity and ethical nuance. Additionally, faculty development serves as a bridge between academic knowledge and industry relevance. With AI transforming nearly every sector—from healthcare and finance to marketing and social sciences—statistics instructors must understand how AI is applied outside academia. By staying connected to real-world trends and use cases, educators can contextualize classroom content, incorporate authentic datasets, and prepare students for the practical demands of the AI-powered job market. Development initiatives such as industry-academic collaborations, guest lectures from AI professionals, and externships help faculty stay attuned to the evolving expectations of employers and researchers. Sustainability is another critical dimension. Faculty trained in AI integration are more likely to develop scalable, adaptable teaching practices that can be maintained and improved over time. As faculty turnover, institutional changes, and curriculum reforms occur, having a strong foundation of AI-literate instructors ensures continuity and resilience in educational delivery. Ongoing development programs—offered through professional learning communities, MOOCs, certification programs, and institutional centers for teaching and learning—create an infrastructure of support that sustains innovation across cohorts and generations of educators. In this context, mentorship becomes an invaluable complement to formal development programs. Experienced faculty who have successfully integrated AI can mentor their peers, offering guidance, feedback, and moral support. Peer mentorship not only accelerates the learning curve for newcomers but also fosters a sense of community, trust, and shared purpose. This relational dimension of development ensures that AI integration is not perceived as an individual burden but as a collective endeavor. In summary, faculty development is not a peripheral concern but a central pillar of AI-integrated statistics education. It ensures technological fluency, pedagogical agility, ethical grounding, and institutional sustainability. By investing in faculty development, institutions not only enhance the quality of teaching but also amplify the long-term success of their students, the relevance of their programs, and their contribution to the broader data-driven society. The future of statistics education in the AI era will be shaped not by technology alone, but by the educators who wield it wisely and inspire the next generation to do the same.

REFERENCES

Al-Labadi, L., Jazi, O. A., Ataei, M., Bao, K., & Yu, R. (2025). AI meets academia: Enhancing statistics education with ChatGPT in undergraduate courses. *TechTrends*, *69*(2), 143–154. DOI: 10.1007/s11528-025-01112-x

AlDhaen, E., & Danish, F. (2024). Exploring the role of artificial intelligence in education: A survey-based study at University of Technology and Applied Science. In *Business Sustainability with AI* (Vol. 1, pp. 63–74). Springer., DOI: 10.1007/978-3-031-56345-4_7

Alkhater, N., & Danish, F. (2024). "The impact of artificial intelligence on students' learning experience." In Business Sustainability with Artificial Intelligence (AI). *Challenges and Opportunities, Springer*, *1*, 75–84. DOI: 10.1007/978-3-031-56345-4_8

Banala, S., Panyaram, S., & Selvakumar, P. (2025). Artificial intelligence in software testing. In Chelliah, P., Venkatesh, R., Natraj, N., & Jeyaraj, R. (Eds.), *Artificial intelligence for cloud-native software engineering* (pp. 237–262). IGI Global Scientific Publishing., DOI: 10.4018/979-8-3693-9356-7.ch009

Bayaga, A. (2025). Leveraging AI-enhanced and emerging technologies for pedagogical innovations in higher education. *Education and Information Technologies*, *30*(1), 1045–1072. DOI: 10.1007/s10639-024-13122-y

Boutilier, J. J., & Chan, T. C. Y. (2023). Introducing and integrating machine learning in an operations research curriculum: An application-driven course. *Transactions on Education*, *23*(2), 64–83. DOI: 10.1287/ited.2021.0256

Burrill, G., & Pfannkuch, M. (2024). Emerging trends in statistics education. *ZDM Mathematics Education*, *56*(1), 19–29. DOI: 10.1007/s11858-023-01501-7

Cabrera, Á. A., Tulio Ribeiro, M., Lee, B., & Deline, R. (2023). What did my AI learn? How data scientists make sense of model behavior. *ACM Transactions on Interactive Intelligent Systems*, *13*(4), 44. DOI: 10.1145/3609565

Chowdhary, S., Selvakumar, P., Sangeetha, B., Sarvaani, V. V., Anute, N., & Sharma, M. (2025). The role of social capital in entrepreneurial development. In Martínez-Falcó, J., Sánchez-García, E., & Marco-Lajara, B. (Eds.), *Support networks for entrepreneurs: Social capital and strategic collaborations* (pp. 311–338). IGI Global Scientific Publishing., DOI: 10.4018/979-8-3693-9836-4.ch013

Coates, J. M., Santhanalakshmi, K., Dinesh, N., Gandhimathi, S., & Chandel, P. S. Mohit, (2025). "Assessment and evaluation in transnational staff development." In Morris G, Ye J (Eds.), Training and development in transnational higher education (pp. 387-406). IGI Global Scientific Publishing. DOI: DOI: 10.4018/979-8-3373-1897-4.ch019

Dai, X., Zhang, Y., & Li, M. (2025). "How students use AI feedback matters: Experimental evidence on physics achievement and autonomy." arXiv preprint, arXiv:2505.08672v2. DOI: /arXiv.2505.08672DOI: 10.48550

Diaz Pratiwi, M., Hernawan, A. H., & Fadillah, A. F. (2025). "Coding and Artificial Intelligence (AI) learning in teachers' perspective." Curricula: Journal of Curriculum Development, 4(1), 215–228. DOI: DOI: 10.31227/osf.io/8rj2m

Ding, A. C. E., Shi, L., Yang, H., & Choi, I. (2024). Enhancing teacher AI literacy and integration through different types of cases in teacher professional development. *Computers and Education Open*, *5*, 100178. Advance online publication. DOI: 10.1016/j.caeo.2024.100178

Dong, L., Tang, X., & Wang, X. (2025). Examining the effect of artificial intelligence in relation to students' academic achievement in classroom: A meta-analysis. *Computers and Education: Artificial Intelligence*, *6*, 100185. DOI: 10.1016/j.caeai.2025.100185

Gandomi, A. H., Chen, F., & Abualigah, L. (2023). Big data analytics using artificial intelligence. *Electronics (Basel)*, *12*(11), 2455. DOI: 10.3390/electronics12112455

Hariyanti, F., Budayasa, I. K., & Setianingsih, R. (2025). The role of AI in enhancing statistical literacy: A systematic review in education. *Multidisciplinary Reviews*, *8*(1), 145–157. DOI: 10.31893/multirev.2025376

Kurniawan, D., Masitoh, S., & Bachri, B. S. (2025). Integrating AI in digital project-based blended learning to enhance critical thinking and problem-solving skills. *Multidisciplinary Reviews*, *8*(2), 334–348. DOI: 10.4081/mr.2025.312

Kurtz, G., Amzalag, M., Shaked, N., Zaguri, Y., Kohen-Vacs, D., Gal, E., Zailer, G., & Barak-Medina, E. (2024). Strategies for integrating generative AI into higher education: Navigating challenges and leveraging opportunities. *Education Sciences*, *14*(5), 503. DOI: 10.3390/educsci14050503

Limbore, N. V., Anute, N., Ahluwalia, G. K., Chordiya, P. B., & Kalshetti, P. (2025). Ethical leadership and corporate responsibility. In Harriott, S. (Ed.), *Innovative approaches to managing conflict and change in diverse work environments* (pp. 193–218). IGI Global Scientific Publishing., DOI: 10.4018/979-8-3693-9556-1.ch009

Lokhande, M., John Deva Prasanna, D. S., Ragupathi, T., Vaissnave, V., & Manjunath, T. C. (2025). “Novel ML algorithms for healthcare.” In Ajibesin A, N G, Thangavel S (Eds.), Synergizing data envelopment analysis and machine learning for performance optimization in healthcare (pp. 113-134). IGI Global Scientific Publishing. DOI: DOI: 10.4018/979-8-3373-0081-8.ch005

Matos, T., Santos, W., Zdravevski, E., Coelho, P. J., & Pires, I. M. P. (2025). “A systematic review of artificial intelligence applications in education: Emerging trends and challenges.” Decision Analytics Journal., 12. *Article*, *100441*, 1–20. DOI: 10.1016/j.dajour.2025.100441

Mehra, J., Madaan, S., & Balu, N. Mohit, Manjunath T C, (2025). “The ubiquitous internet and smart computation available 24/7 for anyone and anywhere.” In Babulak E (Ed.), Educational AI humanoid computing devices for cyber nomads (pp. 247-270). IGI Global Scientific Publishing. DOI: DOI: 10.4018/979-8-3693-8985-0.ch010

Meinlschmidt, G., Koc, S., Boerner, E., Tegethoff, M., Simacek, T., Schirmer, L., & Schneider, M. (2025). “Enhancing professional communication training in higher education through artificial intelligence (AI)-integrated exercises: Study protocol for a randomised controlled trial.” BMC Medical Education, 25(1). *BMC Medical Education*, *307*(1), 1–9. DOI: 10.1186/s12909-025-07307-3 PMID: 40448046

Muhammad, A. (2024). Combining symbolic AI and deep neural networks for robust real-time autonomous decision systems. *International Journal of Hybrid AI Systems*, *3*(2), 55–68. DOI: 10.13140/RG.2.2.23456.78901

Nisha Angeline, M., Gupta, M. K., Nazar, N., Elumalai, D., & Bhattacharya, S. (2025). Emerging materials for energy storage and environmental applications. In Muduli, K., Moharana, B., Ales, S., & Biswal, D. (Eds.), *Using computational intelligence for sustainable manufacturing of advanced materials* (pp. 53–72). IGI Global Scientific Publishing., DOI: 10.4018/979-8-3693-7974-5.ch003

Ouyang, F., & Zhang, L. (2024). AI-driven learning analytics applications and tools in computer-supported collaborative learning: A systematic review. *Educational Research Review*, *41*, 100620. DOI: 10.1016/j.edurev.2024.100616

Qayyum, F., Kim, D. H., Bong, S. J., Chi, S. Y., & Choi, Y. H. (2022). A survey of datasets, preprocessing, modeling mechanisms, and simulation tools based on AI for material analysis and discovery. *Materials (Basel)*, *15*(4), 1434. DOI: 10.3390/ma15041434 PMID: 35207974

Rahmaty, M. (2023). Machine learning with big data to solve real-world problems. *Journal of Data Analytics*, *2*(1), 9–16. DOI: 10.59615/jda.2.1.9

Rocha-Feregrino, G., & Sánchez, G. S. (2025). "Transforming the teaching of probability and statistics: The impact of AI-driven contextualization on architecture students' motivation." **Proceedings of the 2025 IEEE International Conference for the Future of Education*, 198–206. DOI: DOI: 10.1109/IFE63672.2025.11024621

Siddiqui, M. T., Mansoori, M. V., & Yadav, A.Mohammad Talha Siddiqui. (2025). AI-enabled pedagogy: Advancing education through innovative teaching tools and the AI-TEACH model. *Journal of Informatics Education and Research*, *5*(1), 1–20. DOI: 10.52783/jier.v5i1.2261

Suharyo, S., Nugroho, A., & Wibowo, H. (2024). Artificial intelligence in the context of curriculum design for primary and secondary education. *Humanika*, *30*(2), 208–217. DOI: 10.14710/humanika.v30i2.60563

Tu, Y., Chen, J., & Huang, C. (2025). Empowering personalized learning with generative artificial intelligence: Mechanisms, challenges and pathways. *Frontiers of Digital Education*, *2*(19), 1–18. DOI: 10.1007/s44366-025-0056-9

Upadhyaya, A. N., Debnath, P., Rani, P., Selvakumar, P., Manjunath, T. C., & Bhattacharya, S. (2025). AI-based disaster prediction and early warning systems. In Mobo, F. (Ed.), *AI and emerging technologies for emergency response and smart cities* (pp. 55–74). IGI Global Scientific Publishing., DOI: 10.4018/979-8-3693-9770-1.ch003

Xie, X. (2023). Influence of AI-driven inquiry teaching on learning outcomes. *International Journal of Emerging Technologies in Learning*, *18*(21), 23–38. DOI: 10.3991/ijet.v18i23.45473

Yang, Y., Zhuang, Y., & Pan, Y. (2021). Multiple knowledge representation for big data artificial intelligence: Framework, applications, and case studies. *Frontiers of Information Technology & Electronic Engineering*, *22*(12), 1551–1558. DOI: 10.1631/FITEE.2100463

Yixuan, Z., & Xiaohua, Z. (2025). "Research and design of an AI-integrated online learning system." **Proceedings of the 2025 7th International Symposium on Educational Technology*, 211–220. DOI: DOI: 10.1109/ISCBI64586.2025.11015364

Chapter 8
Redesigning Curricula to Align With AI and Data Science Trends

Shiney Chib
http://orcid.org/0000-0001-7648-9963
Datta Meghe Institute of Management Studies, India

Pallapati Ravi ravi Kumar
http://orcid.org/0009-0008-7217-4081
Koneru Lakshmaiah Education Foundation, India

Arvinder Kour Mehta
http://orcid.org/0000-0002-7428-0346
Yeshwantrao Chavan College of Engineering, Nagpur, India

Sumit Kushwaha
http://orcid.org/0000-0002-3830-1736
Chandigarh University, India

P. Nehru
http://orcid.org/0009-0002-5689-2792
B.S. Abdur Rahman Crescent Institute of Science and Technology, India

P. Selvakumar
http://orcid.org/0000-0002-3650-4548
Department of Science and Humanities, Nehru Institute of Technology, Coimbatore, India

ABSTRACT

The integration of Artificial Intelligence (AI) and Data Science into education marks a transformative shift in the way teaching and learning are conceptualized, delivered, and assessed. These technologies are reshaping educational environments at every level, from primary classrooms to higher education and lifelong learning platforms. By harnessing the power of AI and data analytics, educators and institutions can personalize learning experiences, improve administrative efficiency, enhance student engagement, and make data-driven decisions that lead to improved academic outcomes. AI, through machine learning algorithms and natural language processing, enables the creation of intelligent tutoring systems, adaptive learning platforms, and automated grading tools that cater to the unique needs and learning paces of

DOI: 10.4018/979-8-3373-6259-5.ch008

individual students. These tools can identify knowledge gaps, suggest tailored content, and even provide real-time feedback, thereby fostering a more inclusive and student-centered educational approach.

INTRODUCTION: THE IMPACT OF AI AND DATA SCIENCE ON EDUCATION

The integration of Artificial Intelligence (AI) and Data Science into education marks a transformative shift in the way teaching and learning are conceptualized, delivered, and assessed. These technologies are reshaping educational environments at every level, from primary classrooms to higher education and lifelong learning platforms. By harnessing the power of AI and data analytics, educators and institutions can personalize learning experiences, improve administrative efficiency, enhance student engagement, and make data-driven decisions that lead to improved academic outcomes. AI, through machine learning algorithms and natural language processing, enables the creation of intelligent tutoring systems, adaptive learning platforms, and automated grading tools that cater to the unique needs and learning paces of individual students. These tools can identify knowledge gaps, suggest tailored content, and even provide real-time feedback, thereby fostering a more inclusive and student-centered educational approach. One of the most significant impacts of AI in education is the facilitation of personalized learning. Traditional classroom models often struggle to meet the diverse needs of all students due to rigid curricula and fixed pacing. AI-driven systems, however, can analyze individual learning styles, historical performance data, and engagement levels to deliver customized content and recommend activities that align with each learner's strengths and weaknesses. For instance, platforms like Coursera, Khan Academy, and Duolingo use AI to track learner progress and suggest resources that support continuous improvement. These adaptive learning technologies help bridge the gap between struggling and advanced learners by offering differentiated instruction without the constraints of classroom time or teacher bandwidth.

Moreover, AI is contributing to the development of intelligent learning environments and smart campuses. Educational institutions are leveraging AI and data analytics to manage resources, monitor campus security, enhance energy efficiency, and streamline administrative operations. In classrooms, AI-integrated tools such as augmented reality (AR), virtual reality (VR), and intelligent whiteboards are creating immersive and interactive learning experiences that stimulate curiosity and deeper understanding. These smart technologies are reshaping the physical and digital spaces in which learning occurs, making them more dynamic, responsive, and aligned with 21st-century educational demands. The impact of AI and data science also extends to curriculum development and teacher training. As these technologies become increasingly embedded in educational systems, there is a growing need to redesign curricula that include AI and data literacy as core competencies. Equipping students with the skills to understand, interact with, and critically evaluate AI systems prepares them for future careers in a technology-driven world. Simultaneously, educators must receive ongoing professional development to effectively integrate AI tools into their pedagogy, interpret data insights, and navigate the evolving digital landscape. In conclusion, the impact of AI and data science on education is profound and multifaceted. These technologies are not only transforming how we teach and learn but are also reshaping the roles of educators, the design of learning environments, and the structure of educational systems. While challenges related to equity, ethics, and implementation remain, the opportunities presented by AI and data science offer a compelling vision for a more personalized, efficient, and inclusive education system. By embracing these tools with a balanced approach—rooted in human-centered values and ethical safeguards—education can evolve to meet the complex demands of the digital age and empower learners across the globe to thrive in the knowledge economy.

THE NEED FOR CURRICULUM REDESIGN IN THE AGE OF AI

In the rapidly evolving landscape shaped by artificial intelligence (AI), the traditional educational curriculum is increasingly being recognized as outdated and insufficient to prepare learners for the demands of the 21st-century workforce and society. The emergence of AI, along with its integration into various sectors—healthcare, finance, transportation, manufacturing, education, and more—has underscored an urgent need to rethink, revise, and redesign existing curricula to remain relevant, inclusive, and future-ready. A curriculum developed in an industrial-age context, focused heavily on rote learning, standardized testing, and rigid subject divisions, no longer meets the multifaceted competencies required in a world increasingly driven by automation, data, and intelligent systems (Karataş F., et al, 2025). Thus, the call for curriculum redesign in the age of AI is not merely a matter of educational enhancement but a fundamental imperative for societal transformation, economic sustainability, and personal empowerment. One of the primary drivers of curriculum redesign is the growing demand for new skill sets that AI and automation technologies necessitate. The World Economic Forum and other global think tanks have repeatedly emphasized the importance of equipping students with "21st-century skills" such as critical thinking, creativity, collaboration, digital literacy, emotional intelligence, and problem-solving. These are precisely the skills that AI currently cannot replicate easily and are projected to become even more vital in a workforce where machines and humans increasingly coexist. Traditional curricula often prioritize factual recall and procedural knowledge, whereas future-ready curricula must emphasize cognitive flexibility, interdisciplinary understanding, and the ability to adapt to rapidly changing environments. Embedding such skills into the core of educational content demands not just new subjects but also novel pedagogical approaches, assessment models, and learner engagement strategies. Another important aspect driving curriculum change is the changing nature of jobs and the economy (Luckin R., 2025). According to numerous labor market studies, a significant percentage of today's students will enter jobs that do not yet exist or that will be significantly reshaped by AI and automation. As repetitive and routine tasks become automated, jobs will increasingly require uniquely human attributes—like empathy, judgment, cultural understanding, and complex decision-making. Therefore, a redesigned curriculum must focus not just on technical proficiency but also on fostering holistic human development. Education must move toward nurturing the whole person—integrating cognitive, social, emotional, and ethical dimensions. Subjects like philosophy, media studies, entrepreneurship, and environmental sustainability must be reimagined and positioned alongside STEM to create well-rounded learners capable of critical engagement in AI-driven societies.

In terms of pedagogy, the integration of AI into educational processes offers both challenges and opportunities for curriculum innovation. AI-powered tools such as intelligent tutoring systems, adaptive learning platforms, and predictive analytics can support personalized instruction and real-time feedback. A reimagined curriculum must therefore leverage these tools not as external supplements but as integral components of the learning process. This integration requires curricula to be flexible and iterative, allowing for continuous feedback loops where student performance data informs instructional adjustments (Jeon I S., et al, 2024). The traditional model of static syllabi and uniform content delivery must give way to dynamic curricula that evolve in response to learner needs, technological advancements, and societal developments. Teacher training and professional development play a critical role in the successful implementation of an AI-informed curriculum. Educators need support not only in understanding AI tools and their classroom applications but also in shifting their instructional philosophies. Teachers must become facilitators of learning, guiding students in inquiry-based, collaborative, and technology-enhanced environments. A redesigned curriculum must therefore include structured opportunities for teacher engagement, co-creation, and reflection. Furthermore, education policy must ensure that teachers have access to the resources, time, and professional communities needed to navigate the complex transition toward AI-integrated education effectively. In conclusion, the need for curriculum redesign in the age of AI is not optional but essential. The acceleration of AI technologies presents unprecedented challenges and opportunities for education systems worldwide (Upadhyaya A N., et al, 2025). A forward-looking curriculum must be dynamic, inclusive, interdisciplinary, and deeply attuned to the realities of a digitally mediated world. It must equip students with the knowledge, skills, and values needed to thrive as ethical, competent, and empowered citizens in an AI-driven future. This transformation calls for bold vision, thoughtful planning, and collective action among educators, policymakers, technologists, parents, and students. Only by fundamentally reimagining what we teach and how we teach it can education fulfill its promise of shaping a just, sustainable, and intelligent society in the AI era.

INTEGRATING AI AND DATA SCIENCE FUNDAMENTALS INTO EDUCATION

The integration of Artificial Intelligence (AI) and Data Science fundamentals into educational curricula represents a pivotal step toward preparing learners for the demands of the 21st-century digital economy. As AI and data-driven technologies reshape industries, societies, and everyday life, it becomes increasingly essential that education systems evolve to include foundational knowledge of these domains. Embedding AI and Data Science into mainstream education is not just about teaching coding or programming; it involves cultivating a comprehensive understanding of how intelligent systems work, how data is generated and analyzed, and how these technologies impact the world (Nisha Angeline M., et al, 2025). Equipping students with such literacy from an early age ensures that they can navigate, contribute to, and critically assess a world dominated by algorithms, automation, and vast amounts of digital information. To begin with, the fundamentals of AI encompass a range of concepts, including machine learning, neural networks, natural language processing, robotics, computer vision, and intelligent decision-making systems. These areas are increasingly central to technological advancement and innovation. Teaching AI fundamentals involves not just theoretical knowledge but also practical applications—helping students understand how recommendation systems work on social media, how virtual assistants process speech, or how autonomous vehicles make navigation decisions. By integrating such real-world contexts into the classroom, educators can make AI tangible and relevant to students' lives. Moreover, AI literacy encourages interdisciplinary learning, blending computer science with mathematics, linguistics, psychology, and ethics to provide a well-rounded perspective on intelligent technologies. The integration of AI and Data Science into education should be staged and age-appropriate (Karakozov S D., et al, 2024). In primary education, this may involve introducing pattern recognition, logical thinking, simple algorithms, and visual data representation through games and interactive activities. At the middle and secondary levels, students can progress to understanding how AI systems learn, analyzing real-world datasets, and exploring the societal implications of algorithmic decision-making. By the time students reach higher education, they should be equipped to engage with more complex topics such as supervised vs. unsupervised learning, clustering, regression models, deep learning architectures, and ethical frameworks for responsible AI use. Modular, scaffolded learning pathways ensure that students build their knowledge progressively and with confidence.

One of the critical challenges in integrating AI and Data Science fundamentals into education is teacher preparation and capacity-building. Many current educators were trained in eras where AI and big data were either emerging or non-existent. To effectively teach these subjects, educators need robust professional development opportunities, including access to training programs, teaching resources, mentorship networks, and hands-on practice. Teacher education institutions must also revise their curricula to prepare future teachers with both content knowledge and pedagogical strategies for teaching AI and data science (Olatunde-Aiyedun T G., 2024). Partnerships between educational institutions, technology companies, and research organizations can facilitate this transformation by offering certification programs, online courses, and in-service training. Ethics and social responsibility are equally important components of AI and Data Science education. As students learn to design, develop, and use intelligent systems, they must also grapple with questions around data privacy, algorithmic bias, surveillance, automation-related job displacement, and the societal impacts of AI decisions. Teaching these issues alongside technical content helps foster responsible innovation and civic consciousness. Case studies, debates, and ethical simulations can serve as effective tools to engage students in these critical conversations. The goal is to cultivate not only technically skilled individuals but also ethically aware, socially responsible digital citizens. In conclusion, integrating AI and Data Science fundamentals into education is a strategic imperative for preparing students to thrive in a complex, data-rich, and technologically advanced world (Aldoseri A., et al, 2023). It is essential not only for future employment but also for active participation in democratic societies, ethical decision-making, and lifelong learning. The integration process requires systemic changes—curriculum redesign, teacher training, equitable access, pedagogical innovation, and sustained policy support. When done thoughtfully and inclusively, AI and Data Science education can empower learners to become innovators, problem-solvers, and leaders in shaping a future where technology serves humanity's best interests. As education systems embrace this transformation, they lay the foundation for a new generation of thinkers and creators who will drive progress in the age of intelligent machines and big data.

DEVELOPING INTERDISCIPLINARY AND PROJECT-BASED LEARNING IN THE AGE OF AI

In a world characterized by rapid technological advancement, global interconnectivity, and complex societal challenges, traditional educational models that isolate subjects into rigid silos are proving inadequate for preparing students for the demands of the 21st century. The integration of interdisciplinary and project-based learning (PBL) into modern curricula represents a transformative response to this inadequacy, promoting a holistic, contextual, and application-oriented approach to knowledge acquisition. These pedagogies encourage learners to explore connections across disciplines, apply their knowledge in real-world contexts, and develop essential skills such as critical thinking, collaboration, creativity, and communication (Shi & Wang, 2025). With the advent of artificial intelligence (AI), data science, sustainability concerns, and evolving workforce requirements, education systems globally are recognizing the need to move beyond fragmented content delivery to integrated, inquiry-based, and experiential learning environments. The integration of AI and data science has elevated the urgency and relevance of interdisciplinary and project-based approaches. AI technologies intersect with nearly every domain—healthcare, transportation, media, law, art, and education—requiring students to engage with multiple perspectives to understand and responsibly use these tools. For instance, a student project on facial recognition technology might involve learning the technical underpinnings of AI (computer science), analyzing statistical performance (mathematics), considering societal implications (social studies), exploring ethical concerns (philosophy), and evaluating regulatory frameworks (civics/law). This comprehensive engagement helps students develop not only technical skills but also moral and civic literacy, preparing them to make informed decisions in AI-influenced societies. Educators play a crucial role in facilitating this shift (Ekizer & Yıldırım, 2023). Teaching in interdisciplinary and project-based environments demands new pedagogical strategies, curriculum planning approaches, and assessment methods. Teachers must act as facilitators, coaches, and co-learners, guiding students in formulating questions, accessing resources, making connections, and reflecting on their process. Professional development programs must therefore equip educators with the tools to design and implement effective interdisciplinary projects, assess student learning in authentic ways, and create inclusive classrooms where all students feel empowered to contribute. Collaborative teaching models—where educators from different subject areas co-plan and co-teach units—can also enhance the depth and coherence of interdisciplinary instruction.

Technology and digital platforms have significantly expanded the possibilities for implementing interdisciplinary and project-based learning. Tools such as collaborative online workspaces (e.g., Google Workspace, Microsoft Teams), design software (e.g., Canva, Tinkercad), coding environments (e.g., Scratch, Python), and data visualization platforms (e.g., Tableau, Jupyter Notebooks) enable students to engage in complex projects regardless of physical boundaries. AI-enhanced tools can provide real-time feedback, recommend resources, and personalize learning pathways, making projects more adaptive to individual student needs (Posekany A., 2025). Virtual labs, simulations, and augmented reality (AR) environments also allow for immersive learning experiences that were previously difficult to achieve in traditional classrooms. However, implementing interdisciplinary and project-based learning is not without challenges. It requires a fundamental shift in school culture, curriculum structures, time allocation, and assessment policies. Teachers often face constraints in terms of subject boundaries, standardized testing pressures, and a lack of planning time. Additionally, resources and infrastructure may be limited, especially in underfunded schools. To address these challenges, school leaders and policymakers must advocate for flexible curricula, provide planning time for collaborative teaching, invest in teacher training, and allocate resources to support project work. Curriculum frameworks should emphasize essential questions and transferable skills rather than rigid content coverage, allowing room for integration and innovation. In conclusion, developing interdisciplinary and project-based learning is essential for modernizing education and preparing students for an unpredictable and interconnected world (Coates J M., et al, 2025). These approaches break down artificial barriers between subjects, encourage holistic understanding, and promote real-world problem-solving. They align naturally with the demands of the digital age, where AI, climate change, globalization, and social justice require integrated thinking and action. By embedding interdisciplinary and project-based learning into curricula, schools can cultivate empowered learners who are capable of thinking critically, collaborating effectively, and acting ethically. This paradigm shift holds the potential not only to improve academic outcomes but also to create more just, creative, and sustainable futures for individuals and societies alike.

FOSTERING CRITICAL THINKING AND PROBLEM-SOLVING SKILLS IN 21ST-CENTURY EDUCATION

In the face of rapidly changing technologies, complex global challenges, and an ever-evolving job market, the ability to think critically and solve problems has emerged as a cornerstone of modern education. Traditional rote learning and memorization-focused curricula are no longer sufficient to prepare students for the intricacies of the 21st-century world. Instead, fostering critical thinking and problem-solving skills has become a fundamental goal of educational systems worldwide. These skills are not just academic assets; they are life competencies that empower individuals to navigate uncertainty, make informed decisions, collaborate effectively, and innovate responsibly (Chowdhary S., et al, 2025). As artificial intelligence, automation, and data-driven technologies continue to reshape industries and societies, learners must be equipped with the cognitive tools to interpret information, evaluate evidence, challenge assumptions, and design solutions to real-world problems. To effectively nurture these competencies, education must undergo a pedagogical transformation that reorients instruction from passive reception to active exploration. Inquiry-based learning, project-based learning, and experiential learning are among the most effective instructional strategies to support critical thinking and problem-solving. These approaches encourage students to formulate questions, investigate phenomena, develop hypotheses, experiment with ideas, and reflect on their outcomes. Rather than being told what to learn, students learn how to learn—an essential distinction in a world where knowledge is abundant and rapidly changing. Equally important is the role of assessment in fostering these skills (Ammann et al, 2025). Traditional assessments—like multiple-choice tests—often fail to capture students' capacity for deep thinking and complex problem-solving. Instead, educators should utilize performance-based assessments, including open-ended questions, research projects, case studies, simulations, and design challenges. These assessment formats allow students to demonstrate their analytical reasoning, creativity, and strategic thinking. Rubrics that assess criteria such as evidence use, clarity of argument, depth of insight, and innovation are essential in evaluating critical thinking and problem-solving fairly and comprehensively.

Furthermore, curriculum design must be intentional in embedding opportunities for critical thought and problem-solving across all subjects—not just in STEM or humanities but also in the arts, physical education, and vocational training. Every discipline offers unique ways of thinking and problem-solving. For example, art classes can explore visual literacy and symbolism, music can involve composition challenges, and physical education can emphasize strategy and teamwork (Sindakis S., 2023). When students see that critical thinking is not confined to a particular subject but is a life-wide competence, they are more likely to apply it flexibly and consistently. At the policy level, educational systems and curriculum frameworks must prioritize and mandate the development of these competencies. National education policies, such as the New Education Policy (NEP) 2020 in India, emphasize the importance of 21st-century skills and experiential learning. Global frameworks like UNESCO's Education for Sustainable Development (ESD) and the OECD Learning Compass 2030 also advocate for critical thinking as a key learning outcome. Governments and educational leaders must ensure that funding, curriculum guidelines, teacher training, and assessment reforms align to make critical thinking and problem-solving central to education. In conclusion, fostering critical thinking and problem-solving skills is not a peripheral educational objective—it is a central mission for cultivating informed, capable, and ethical individuals ready to face the complexities of the contemporary world (Wardani I S., et al, 2023). As automation replaces routine tasks, the uniquely human ability to reason, evaluate, and innovate becomes the most valuable asset students can acquire. By transforming pedagogy, assessments, curricula, and teacher preparation, education systems can embed these vital skills into the heart of learning. In doing so, we empower the next generation not only to succeed in the workforce but also to contribute meaningfully to society, shape democratic discourse, and address the pressing issues of our time with intelligence, empathy, and purpose.

MACHINE LEARNING AND DEEP LEARNING COURSE MODULES: A COMPREHENSIVE FRAMEWORK FOR MODERN EDUCATION

As artificial intelligence (AI) increasingly permeates every sector of society—from healthcare and finance to agriculture, transportation, education, and beyond—developing a robust understanding of Machine Learning (ML) and Deep Learning (DL) has become imperative for students, professionals, and researchers alike. These two domains represent the core engines of modern AI applications. In response to this rising demand, academic institutions and training platforms around the world are introducing structured Machine Learning and Deep Learning course modules aimed at equipping learners with both theoretical foundations and hands-on skills. These modules serve to demystify complex algorithms and empower learners to design, implement, and optimize intelligent systems capable of learning from data (Abe & Birabil, 2022). Whether offered as part of undergraduate computer science curricula, postgraduate AI programs, technical diplomas, or online certification tracks, these modules are essential components of future-ready education. A well-structured Machine Learning course typically begins with foundational concepts to build a strong theoretical base. This includes topics such as supervised and unsupervised learning, classification, regression, clustering, model evaluation, and overfitting/underfitting. Students are introduced to common algorithms like linear regression, logistic regression, k-nearest neighbors (KNN), decision trees, naive Bayes, and support vector machines (SVMs). These fundamental techniques are taught not just through theoretical exposition, but through programming exercises in languages like Python, using libraries such as Scikit-learn and Pandas. Emphasis is placed on understanding data preprocessing, feature selection, and the importance of model interpretability. Learners explore the full machine learning pipeline—from data collection and cleaning to training, testing, and evaluation. A major highlight of these courses is the transition into Deep Learning, a specialized and highly impactful subset of machine learning. Deep Learning modules typically begin with the basics of neural networks, including perceptrons, activation functions (sigmoid, ReLU, tanh), loss functions, and the backpropagation algorithm. Students learn how deep neural networks can model complex, non-linear relationships in data (Musa N S., et al, 2024). This stage includes hands-on implementation of multi-layer perceptrons (MLPs) and the use of deep learning frameworks such as TensorFlow and PyTorch, which offer scalable, production-ready tools for developing AI systems. Another key component of deep learning education is recurrent neural networks (RNNs) and their variants, such as Long Short-Term Memory (LSTM) and Gated Recurrent Units (GRU), which are designed to handle sequential data. These models are foundational for natural language processing (NLP) tasks, such as sentiment analysis, language translation, speech recognition, and chatbot development. Students explore the dynamics of time-series data, attention mechanisms, and sequence-to-sequence models. Real-world projects might include building language models, machine translation systems, or even generating text with recurrent models.

A comprehensive course in ML and DL also introduces learners to unsupervised and self-supervised learning, reinforcement learning, and generative models such as Generative Adversarial Networks (GANs). GANs are particularly emphasized in applications involving synthetic data generation, art creation, and deepfakes. Reinforcement learning modules explore the reward-punishment paradigm used in training agents for games, robotics, and autonomous decision-making. Tools like OpenAI Gym are used for hands-on reinforcement learning experiments. To support diverse learners, course modules are increasingly designed to be interdisciplinary and application-driven. Students from non-computer science backgrounds—such as business, healthcare, biology, linguistics, and environmental science—can engage with tailored ML/DL modules that apply to their domains (Razzaq S., et al, 2023). For example, bioinformatics students may study protein structure prediction using deep learning, while journalists may use NLP to analyze misinformation and sentiment trends. This accessibility is enhanced through visual programming tools, modular content, and collaborative projects. As the landscape of AI evolves, continuous updates to ML/DL course content are necessary. Emerging trends such as federated learning, edge AI, quantum machine learning, and responsible AI are gradually being incorporated into advanced modules. Moreover, institutions are placing increasing emphasis on ethics and AI governance, encouraging learners to question the broader impacts of deploying intelligent systems and consider guidelines for transparency, accountability, and fairness. In conclusion, well-designed Machine Learning and Deep Learning course modules serve as essential building blocks for equipping learners with the skills and mindset needed to thrive in the AI-driven era (Deng D., et al, 2022). These courses foster not just technical proficiency but also creativity, ethical awareness, and domain-specific expertise. By combining rigorous theoretical instruction with experiential, project-based learning, these modules prepare students to innovate responsibly and solve complex problems across industries. Whether as part of formal degree programs or standalone certifications, ML and DL education is indispensable for shaping the next generation of data scientists, AI engineers, researchers, and informed digital citizens. As AI continues to reshape the future, education must lead the way in ensuring that its power is harnessed thoughtfully, inclusively, and for the benefit of all.

DATA ANALYSIS AND VISUALIZATION TECHNIQUES: EMPOWERING INSIGHT-DRIVEN DECISION MAKING

In an increasingly data-driven world, the ability to extract meaningful insights from complex datasets has become a foundational skill across virtually every industry and academic discipline. From business strategy and scientific research to public policy, education, and healthcare, data analysis and visualization techniques enable individuals and organizations to make informed decisions, identify patterns, predict trends, and communicate findings effectively. As the volume, variety, and velocity of data continue to grow exponentially, so does the need for a well-structured educational foundation in data analysis and visualization techniques (Kumar & Renuka, 2023). These techniques lie at the heart of data science and analytics, serving as essential tools for transforming raw data into actionable knowledge. Following data cleaning, analysts engage in exploratory data analysis (EDA)—a critical step that involves summarizing the main characteristics of the data, often using visual methods. EDA helps uncover initial patterns, spot anomalies, test assumptions, and check for correlations among variables. Common techniques include calculating descriptive statistics (mean, median, standard deviation), plotting histograms, boxplots, scatterplots, and correlation matrices. EDA enables analysts to develop hypotheses and choose appropriate models for deeper analysis. In the era of big data and machine learning, algorithmic data analysis is gaining prominence. Students and analysts are increasingly being trained to apply algorithms for classification, clustering, and predictive modeling. Techniques such as k-means clustering, decision trees, random forests, and logistic regression are commonly introduced. While these algorithms are often associated with AI and data science, their core function lies in uncovering complex relationships within large and high-dimensional datasets—offering more nuanced insights than traditional methods (Mavropoulos T., et al, 2021). Understanding these algorithms also helps analysts choose the best model for a given data scenario and interpret the results responsibly. Tools for data visualization range from basic platforms like Microsoft Excel and Google Sheets to advanced programming environments such as Python (Matplotlib, Seaborn, Plotly), R (ggplot2, Shiny), and business intelligence (BI) tools like Tableau, Power BI, and QlikView. These tools allow users to create interactive, dynamic visualizations that not only display data but also enable exploration and manipulation. Dashboards built with these tools are widely used in organizations to monitor key performance indicators (KPIs), track progress, and support real-time decision-making.

Figure 1. Challenges and Future Directions of Big Data and AI in Education

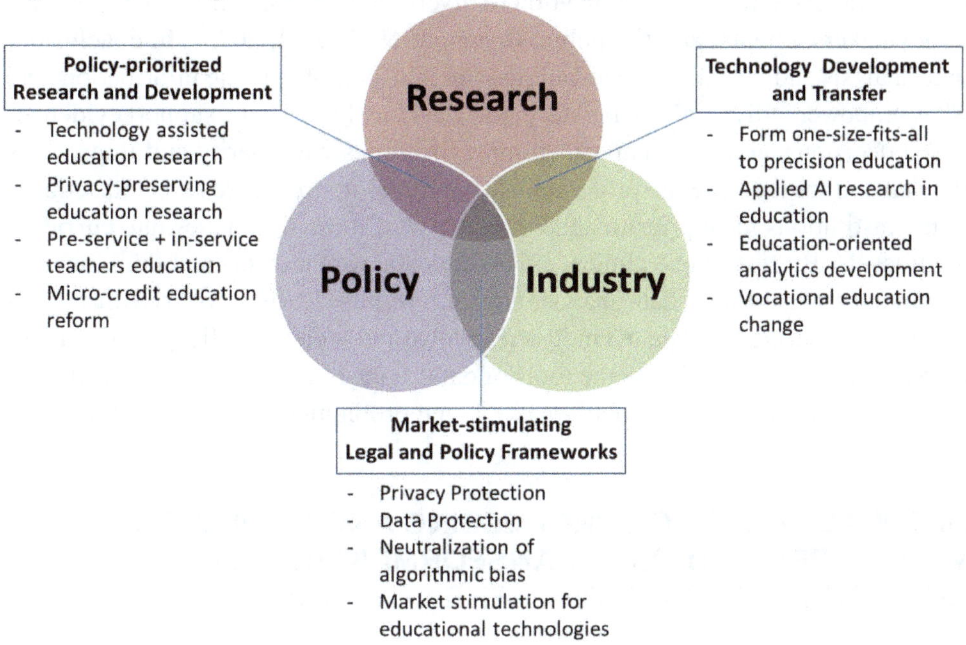

A key focus of contemporary education in this field is data literacy—the ability to read, work with, analyze, and communicate data. Data literacy extends beyond technical proficiency; it includes ethical reasoning, contextual understanding, and effective communication. Learners must be able to critically assess data sources, understand limitations, recognize biases, and question assumptions. In an era where misinformation and data manipulation are prevalent, cultivating a strong sense of data ethics is essential. This includes respecting privacy, securing sensitive information, and ensuring fairness and transparency in data use and interpretation (Ding Z., et al, 2024). Collaborative data analysis is emphasized in team-based learning environments. Projects are often conducted in groups, simulating real workplace scenarios where teams must combine technical, analytical, and communication skills. Students learn version control (e.g., using Git), collaborative documentation, and agile workflows—skills that are invaluable in data analytics professions. Peer feedback, presentations, and stakeholder engagement activities further enhance learning outcomes and prepare students for interdisciplinary roles. The importance of storytelling with data is another central element in data analysis education. Even the most accurate and complex analysis can fail to make an impact if not communicated effectively. Data storytelling combines narrative techniques with visuals and insights to create compelling messages. Students are taught to structure their findings with a clear beginning, middle, and end—identifying the "so what" of the data and tailoring their communication to diverse audiences, including executives, policymakers, clients, and the public (Limbore N V., et al, 2025). In conclusion, data analysis and visualization techniques are indispensable in the information age. They empower individuals to transform raw data into knowledge, support evidence-based decisions, and communicate complex findings with clarity and impact. As the demand for data-literate professionals continues to grow across sectors, educational institutions must prioritize the integration of these techniques into curricula at all levels. By fostering technical skills, ethical awareness, critical thinking, and communication abilities, data analysis education equips learners to thrive in a world increasingly defined by data. As industries evolve and societal challenges grow more complex, those equipped with the tools of data analysis and visualization will be at the forefront of innovation, policy-making, and problem-solving in the digital era.

NATURAL LANGUAGE PROCESSING AND COMPUTER VISION APPLICATIONS: TRANSFORMING HUMAN-COMPUTER INTERACTION IN THE AGE OF AI

Natural Language Processing (NLP) and Computer Vision are two of the most dynamic and transformative subfields of Artificial Intelligence (AI), enabling machines to interpret, understand, and respond to human language and visual information. These technologies play a pivotal role in revolutionizing how we interact with digital systems, bridging the gap between human communication and computational intelligence. With the proliferation of text, images, and video data across the internet, the need for systems that can process, analyze, and derive meaning from such content has never been greater. NLP and computer vision applications are now deeply embedded in education, healthcare, business, security, and numerous other sectors, driving innovation, automation, and personalization at unprecedented scales (Mehra J., et al, 2025). Natural Language Processing deals with the interaction between computers and human (natural) languages. It enables machines to read, decipher, understand, and make sense of human language in a valuable way. Core NLP tasks include language modeling, tokenization, part-of-speech tagging, named entity recognition, syntactic parsing, sentiment analysis, machine translation, text summarization, and question answering. These tasks are critical for building applications such as chatbots, virtual assistants, language translation tools, grammar correction systems, and intelligent search engines. In business and customer service, NLP enables sentiment analysis and opinion mining, helping companies understand customer feedback and public perception. Chatbots and virtual agents like Siri, Alexa, and Google Assistant rely on NLP for speech recognition and conversational responses, making human-machine interaction more natural and efficient (Devi & Naved, 2021). NLP is also instrumental in automating document processing in sectors such as finance, law, and insurance, where large volumes of unstructured text data need to be analyzed for decision-making. Computer Vision, on the other hand, focuses on enabling computers to interpret and process visual data from the world—images, videos, and live camera feeds—similar to how human vision works. Fundamental computer vision tasks include image classification, object detection, image segmentation, facial recognition, optical character recognition (OCR), and motion tracking. These capabilities form the backbone of applications ranging from medical imaging diagnostics and autonomous vehicles to industrial automation and augmented reality.

One of the most impactful areas of computer vision is facial recognition. This technology is now widely used in security and authentication systems, unlocking phones, granting building access, and verifying identities at airports. However, it has also raised ethical concerns about privacy, surveillance, and algorithmic bias, prompting discussions about the need for regulation and responsible AI practices (McNamara D S., et al, 2022). The intersection of NLP and computer vision, often referred to as multimodal AI, is giving rise to even more advanced applications. For example, systems like Google Lens allow users to point their phone cameras at objects to get contextual information—combining image recognition with text generation. Caption generation systems use computer vision to analyze images and NLP to generate descriptive text, enabling accessibility tools for the visually impaired. Video content analysis platforms use both vision and language processing to tag, summarize, and recommend video clips in entertainment and education. Despite their potential, both NLP and computer vision face significant challenges. In NLP, understanding context, sarcasm, and cultural nuances remains difficult. For computer vision, varying lighting conditions, image quality, and occlusion can affect recognition accuracy. Moreover, both fields struggle with algorithmic bias, where models trained on biased data produce unfair or inaccurate outcomes. Addressing these issues requires diverse and representative datasets, rigorous model evaluation, and human oversight in high-stakes applications (Afzaal M., et al, 2021). In conclusion, Natural Language Processing and Computer Vision are reshaping the digital landscape by enabling machines to understand and interpret the world as humans do—through language and vision. Their applications span nearly every domain, offering solutions that are faster, more accurate, and increasingly intelligent. As these technologies evolve and converge, they open new possibilities for communication, learning, creativity, and interaction. However, with great power comes great responsibility, and we must deploy these systems ethically, inclusively, and transparently. By integrating NLP and computer vision into education, research, and industry, we pave the way for a future where human-AI collaboration is not only possible but profoundly transformative.

ASSESSING STUDENT LEARNING OUTCOMES IN AI AND DATA SCIENCE

In the evolving educational landscape driven by Artificial Intelligence (AI) and Data Science, traditional assessment models are increasingly inadequate for capturing the breadth and depth of student learning. These fields demand a mix of theoretical understanding, technical skill, interdisciplinary knowledge, ethical reasoning, and real-world application—qualities that cannot be comprehensively evaluated through rote exams or standard multiple-choice tests. As a result, assessing student learning outcomes in AI and data science requires a multifaceted, dynamic, and competency-based approach that aligns with both academic goals and industry expectations (García-Martínez I., et al, 2023). Effective assessment in this context not only measures knowledge acquisition but also gauges problem-solving capabilities, practical application, collaboration, and the ability to adapt to rapidly changing technological environments. Project-based assessments are central to evaluating learning outcomes in AI and data science programs. In such assessments, students are often asked to complete capstone projects, case studies, or industry collaborations over an extended period. These projects assess a range of competencies, including technical proficiency in tools like Python, R, TensorFlow, or scikit-learn; data handling using SQL and cloud services; and model evaluation through metrics like precision, recall, F1-score, or ROC-AUC. More importantly, they test soft skills such as time management, collaboration, ethical decision-making, and presentation ability. A well-structured project rubric should evaluate the clarity of problem definition, quality of data wrangling, justification of model selection, experimentation methodology, reproducibility, and clarity in communication. Another important dimension of assessment in AI and data science is formative assessment, which refers to continuous, low-stakes evaluations intended to guide learning rather than simply judge it (Owan V J., et al, 2023). Examples include quizzes, in-class exercises, discussion participation, peer reviews, notebook submissions, and feedback loops on code. Formative assessment helps students identify misconceptions early, receive timely guidance, and develop confidence in their problem-solving process.

In AI and data science education, where the learning curve can be steep and topics such as neural networks or natural language processing may be conceptually dense, formative assessments ensure that students stay engaged and are not overwhelmed.

Automated assessment systems also play a growing role in AI and data science education, particularly in large-scale or online courses. Platforms like Coursera, edX, DataCamp, and Google Colab facilitate the auto-grading of coding assignments using test cases or predefined outputs. These systems can efficiently evaluate thousands of submissions, provide instant feedback, and reinforce mastery learning. However, care must be taken to balance automation with qualitative assessment methods to ensure a comprehensive evaluation of student understanding, especially in complex or open-ended tasks (Ramachandran K K., 2024). Another increasingly relevant approach is the use of learning analytics and AI-driven assessment tools. These tools use data collected from student interactions within learning platforms to assess performance trends, predict risk of failure, and personalize feedback. For example, if a student consistently struggles with certain machine learning algorithms or coding patterns, an AI system can highlight this and suggest targeted practice. Educators can use dashboards that visualize student engagement, submission history, and progress over time to support tailored mentoring and intervention. In some institutions, competency-based education (CBE) frameworks are being adopted, where students advance upon mastering specific competencies instead of completing a fixed curriculum within a predefined timeline. For graduate and doctoral-level education in AI and data science, assessment expands further into research output, including literature reviews, publication of papers, development of novel algorithms, and contributions to open-source projects (Avalekar U A., et al, 2025). The ability to formulate research questions, design experiments, interpret results critically, and engage in scholarly communication becomes central to assessment at this level. In conclusion, assessing student learning outcomes in AI and data science requires an evolving, multidimensional strategy that reflects the interdisciplinary, practical, and ethical demands of the field. A combination of authentic, formative, summative, automated, peer-reviewed, and portfolio-based assessments ensures that students are not only acquiring knowledge but are also able to apply it responsibly and creatively. With thoughtful design, continuous feedback, and alignment to real-world competencies, assessment becomes a powerful tool not just for measuring learning, but for enhancing it—preparing students to thrive in the data-driven world of tomorrow.

EMERGING TRENDS AND FUTURE DIRECTIONS IN AI AND DATA SCIENCE EDUCATION

As artificial intelligence (AI) and data science continue to reshape nearly every aspect of modern life—from healthcare and finance to transportation, agriculture, and governance—the education sector must evolve to prepare learners for a future dominated by intelligent technologies. The rapid pace of innovation, coupled with the interdisciplinary nature of AI and data science, has triggered a transformation in how educational institutions approach curriculum design, teaching methods, assessment strategies, and faculty development. As we look toward the future, several emerging trends and strategic directions are defining the next generation of AI and data science education (Chib S., et al, 2025). These trends reflect not only advancements in technology but also a growing emphasis on ethical considerations, practical applications, inclusivity, and lifelong learning. Another significant trend is the adoption of personalized and adaptive learning technologies powered by AI itself. AI-enabled educational platforms can now analyze students' learning behaviors, identify gaps in understanding, and deliver customized content at an individual pace. Intelligent tutoring systems, recommendation engines, and automated feedback tools enhance student engagement and improve learning outcomes. These technologies are especially useful in large-scale or online learning environments, where personalized attention is difficult to achieve through traditional methods. As these systems evolve, we can expect them to become more sophisticated in interpreting complex learner data and offering more nuanced support, making education more inclusive and learner-centric. Project-based and experiential learning is also gaining momentum as a dominant pedagogical strategy. Instead of relying solely on theoretical lectures, educators are engaging students through real-world projects, capstone experiences, and collaborations with industry partners (Srivathsa B S., et al, 2025). These projects help students apply theoretical concepts to practical challenges, build portfolios, and develop skills such as teamwork, communication, and critical thinking. In the future, we can expect more institutions to adopt challenge-based learning models, where students tackle open-ended problems sourced from industry, government, or local communities. Competitions like hackathons, data-thons, and innovation challenges will continue to grow in popularity, providing students with opportunities to demonstrate their abilities in authentic contexts.

As AI systems become more multimodal and advanced, educational institutions are also beginning to emphasize new subfields such as natural language processing (NLP), computer vision, reinforcement learning, and generative AI. Courses and modules dedicated to chatbots, language models, image recognition, video analysis, and autonomous systems are being added to curricula. For example, students are now building AI systems that can generate art, compose music, write essays, or interact in human-like conversations. These emerging topics expand the boundaries of AI education and prepare students to work on cutting-edge problems. Shortly, the curriculum is expected to become more modular and rapidly adaptive, with institutions continuously updating course content to reflect the latest developments in AI research and applications. Another trend is the globalization and democratization of AI and data science education (McFarland D A., et al, 2021). Through online platforms and international collaborations, learners from around the world can now access world-class instruction in AI and data science regardless of geographical location. Initiatives like AI4ALL, DataCamp Donates, and university-led MOOC programs are helping bridge the digital divide. Cross-border research partnerships, student exchange programs, and virtual labs foster global perspectives and cultural exchange. As AI challenges and opportunities are inherently global—ranging from climate change and pandemics to cybersecurity and misinformation—future education will emphasize international cooperation and global problem-solving. The future of AI and data science education also lies in lifelong and modular learning models. The rapid pace of technological change means that knowledge quickly becomes outdated. Consequently, professionals across all sectors will need to continuously update their skills. Micro-credentials, online certificates, modular courses, and flexible learning formats will dominate adult and continuing education. Institutions must respond by offering stackable credentials, industry-aligned short courses, and hybrid models that allow learners to upskill while balancing work and life commitments (Haber E., et al, 2025). Industry-academic partnerships will play a central role in ensuring the relevance and responsiveness of lifelong learning initiatives. In conclusion, AI and data science education are evolving into a dynamic, interdisciplinary, and inclusive field that prioritizes ethical responsibility, practical relevance, and lifelong adaptability. Emerging trends such as personalized learning, ethical AI, interdisciplinary integration, global access, sustainability, and continuous upskilling are shaping a future in which education empowers learners not only to use AI tools but to shape their development and societal impact. Educational institutions that embrace these trends and invest in agile, forward-thinking strategies will be best positioned to prepare students for the complexities and possibilities of the AI-powered world.

CONCLUSION

Redesigning the curriculum for AI and data science education is both a pressing necessity and a complex endeavor, as these disciplines rapidly evolve and integrate across domains. While artificial intelligence and data science offer transformative potential in education, industry, healthcare, governance, and countless other sectors, equipping students with the necessary knowledge, skills, and ethical frameworks to harness these technologies presents a unique set of challenges. Simultaneously, there are immense opportunities to rethink how education can be delivered, how interdisciplinary learning can be fostered, and how institutions can better prepare students for the demands of the 21st-century workforce. The process of curriculum redesign, therefore, must not only respond to emerging technological capabilities but also anticipate future societal needs, ensuring that education remains relevant, inclusive, and forward-thinking. Another significant challenge is the shortage of qualified faculty and instructors capable of teaching both the technical and ethical dimensions of AI and data science. Many universities struggle to attract faculty with industry experience and cutting-edge research expertise in deep learning, computer vision, natural language processing, or responsible AI practices. This shortage is exacerbated by the high demand for such professionals in the private sector, where compensation packages far exceed academic salaries. To address this issue, institutions must invest in faculty development programs, promote collaborative teaching models that include practitioners, and create opportunities for existing faculty to reskill through sabbaticals, training workshops, and research partnerships. Further complicating curriculum redesign is the diversity of student backgrounds entering AI and data science programs. Students may come from fields such as mathematics, computer science, biology, psychology, business, or the humanities. This diversity is an asset for interdisciplinary learning but also poses challenges for curriculum coherence and instructional design. Some students may lack programming skills, while others may struggle with abstract mathematical concepts or statistical reasoning. Curriculum developers must design flexible learning pathways, offer bridge courses, and provide differentiated instruction to accommodate various entry points while maintaining academic rigor. Competency-based learning models, diagnostic assessments, and adaptive learning technologies can play a crucial role in this regard.

Another major opportunity lies in leveraging open educational resources (OERs), cloud platforms, and collaborative tools to make AI and data science education more accessible and affordable. High-quality resources such as online tutorials, GitHub repositories, MOOCs, and open datasets democratize learning and enable institutions to rapidly incorporate contemporary content without incurring significant costs. Tools like Jupyter Notebooks, Google Colab, and Microsoft Azure Notebooks offer students practical experience in coding, data visualization, and model deployment, while platforms like Kaggle foster a global community of learners engaged in competitive problem-solving. By embedding these tools into coursework, educators can create an engaging and interactive learning environment. A forward-looking opportunity is to incorporate personalized and adaptive learning strategies powered by AI itself. Intelligent tutoring systems, learning analytics dashboards, and recommendation engines can support differentiated instruction, identify at-risk students, and provide real-time feedback. By embedding these technologies into AI and data science courses, educators can create a meta-learning environment where students not only learn about AI but also experience its application in their learning journey. This recursive approach reinforces understanding and prepares students to work on educational technologies, an expanding field within AI. Another strategic opportunity is the alignment of AI and data science education with sustainability and the UN Sustainable Development Goals (SDGs). By focusing on how these technologies can address challenges such as poverty, hunger, health, clean energy, and climate change, educators can inspire students to pursue purpose-driven innovation. Courses can include modules on sustainable AI, responsible data practices, green computing, and ethical AI design. Institutions can also establish partnerships with NGOs, governments, and international organizations to co-develop curriculum materials and real-world projects aimed at social impact. In conclusion, while redesigning AI and data science curricula presents significant challenges—such as keeping pace with technological change, addressing faculty shortages, integrating ethics, and meeting diverse learner needs—it also offers transformative opportunities. By embracing interdisciplinary collaboration, real-world engagement, ethical reflection, inclusivity, sustainability, and technological innovation, institutions can build forward-looking programs that prepare students not just for today's jobs, but for tomorrow's societal challenges. Curriculum redesign, when approached strategically and inclusively, is a powerful lever to shape the future of education and ensure that the benefits of AI and data science are widely shared and responsibly harnessed.

REFERENCES

Abe, E. C., & Birabil, S. T. (2022). Fostering creativity and critical thinking in 21st century classroom. *Innovare Journal of Education, 10*(1), 8–16. DOI: 10.22159/ijoe.2022v10i3.44671

Afzaal, M., Nouri, J., Zia, A., Papapetrou, P., Norqvist, L., & Nilsson, M. (2021). Explainable AI for data-driven feedback and intelligent action recommendations to support students self-regulation. *Frontiers in Artificial Intelligence, 4*, 715143. Advance online publication. DOI: 10.3389/frai.2021.723447 PMID: 34870183

Aldoseri, A., Al-Khalifa, K. N., & Hamouda, A. M. (2023). Re-thinking data strategy and integration for artificial intelligence: Concepts, opportunities, and challenges. *Applied Sciences (Basel, Switzerland), 13*(9), 8792. DOI: 10.3390/app13127082

Ammann, P. J. L., Golde, J. M., & Akbik, A. (2025). "Question decomposition for retrieval-augmented generation." *Proceedings of the 63rd Annual Meeting of the Association for Computational Linguistics (ACL)*, 497–507. DOI: DOI: 10.18653/v1/2025.acl-srw.32

Avalekar, U. A., Mehta, V., Mishra, B. R., Prasanna, L., Rajlakshmi, P. V., & Manjunath, T. C. (2025). The current advances in AI-driven education. In Babulak, E. (Ed.), *Educational AI humanoid computing devices for cyber nomads* (pp. 173–196). IGI Global Scientific Publishing., DOI: 10.4018/979-8-3693-8985-0.ch008

Chib, S., Mehta, A. K., Selvakumar, P., Saravanan, A., Mishra, B. R., & Manjunath, T. C. (2025). Mental health challenges and solutions in high-pressure work environments. In Harriott, S. (Ed.), *Innovative approaches to managing conflict and change in diverse work environments* (pp. 247–272). IGI Global Scientific Publishing., DOI: 10.4018/979-8-3693-9556-1.ch011

Chowdhary, S., Selvakumar, P., Sangeetha, B., Sarvaani, V. V., Anute, N., & Sharma, M. (2025). The role of social capital in entrepreneurial development. In Martínez-Falcó, J., Sánchez-García, E., & Marco-Lajara, B. (Eds.), *Support networks for entrepreneurs: Social capital and strategic collaborations* (pp. 311–338). IGI Global Scientific Publishing., DOI: 10.4018/979-8-3693-9836-4.ch013

Coates, J. M., Santhanalakshmi, K., Dinesh, N., Gandhimathi, S., & Chandel, P. S. Mohit, (2025). "Assessment and evaluation in transnational staff development." In Morris G, Ye J (Eds.), Training and development in transnational higher education (pp. 387-406). IGI Global Scientific Publishing. DOI: DOI: 10.4018/979-8-3373-1897-4.ch019

Deng, D., Wu, A., Qu, H., & Wu, Y. (2022). DashBot: Insight-driven dashboard generation based on deep reinforcement learning. *IEEE Transactions on Visualization and Computer Graphics*, *28*(1), 907–917. DOI: 10.1109/TVCG.2022.3209468 PMID: 36179003

Devi, V. A., & Naved, M. (2021). Dive in deep learning: computer vision, natural language processing, and signal processing. In Prakash, S., Parveen, R., & Ahmad, T. (Eds.), *Machine Learning in Signal Processing* (pp. 43–68). Taylor & Francis., DOI: 10.1201/9781003107026-5

Ding, Z., Ji, Y., Gan, Y., Wang, Y., & Xia, Y. (2024). Current status and trends of technology, methods, and applications of human–computer intelligent interaction (HCII): A bibliometric research. *Multimedia Tools and Applications*, *83*(7), 12095–12114. DOI: 10.1007/s11042-023-18096-6

Ekizer, F. N., & Yıldırım, S. S. (2023). 21st century skills and learning environments: ELT students' perceptions. *Educational Research Review*, *18*(6), 114–128. DOI: 10.5897/ERR2023.4332

García-Martínez, I., Fernández-Batanero, J. M., Fernández-Cerero, J., & León, S. P. (2023). Analysing the impact of artificial intelligence and computational sciences on student performance: Systematic review and meta-analysis. *Journal of New Approaches in Educational Research*, *12*(1), 1–17. DOI: 10.7821/naer.2023.1.1240

Haber, E., Jemielniak, D., & Kurasiński, A. (2025). Future trends and emerging tools. In Haber, E., Jemielniak, D., & Kurasiński, A. (Eds.), *AI in Writing and Research: A Roadmap for Higher Education* (pp. 187–202). Springer., DOI: 10.1007/978-3-031-91705-9_7

Jeon, I. S., Kang, S. J., & Kang, S. J. (2024). A staged framework for computer vision education: Integrating AI, data science, and computational thinking. *Applied Sciences (Basel, Switzerland)*, *14*(2), 235–250. DOI: 10.3390/app14219792

Karakozov, S. D., Natal'ya, I., Samylkina, N. N., & Samokhvalova, E. A. (2024). Variable teaching of artificial intelligence and data analysis basics in computer science general education course: Integrative approach and key components. *Siberian Pedagogical Journal*, *6*(6), 9–23. DOI: 10.15293/1813-4718.2406.01

Karataş, F., Eriçok, B., & Tanrikulu, L. (2025). Reshaping curriculum adaptation in the age of artificial intelligence: Mapping teachers' AI-driven curriculum adaptation patterns. *British Educational Research Journal*, *51*(1), 112–129. DOI: 10.1002/berj.4068

Kumar, L. A., & Renuka, D. K. (2023). Deep learning approach for natural language processing, speech, and computer vision: techniques and use cases. In Singh, P., Ramos, J., & Khurana, M. (Eds.), *Machine Learning in Signal Processing* (pp. 215–235). Taylor & Francis., DOI: 10.1201/9781003286670-10

Limbore, N. V., Anute, N., Ahluwalia, G. K., Chordiya, P. B., & Kalshetti, P. (2025). Ethical leadership and corporate responsibility. In Harriott, S. (Ed.), *Innovative approaches to managing conflict and change in diverse work environments* (pp. 193–218). IGI Global Scientific Publishing., DOI: 10.4018/979-8-3693-9556-1.ch009

Luckin, R. (2025). Nurturing human intelligence in the age of AI: Rethinking education for the future. *Development and Learning in Organizations*, *39*(4), 8–11. DOI: 10.1108/DLO-04-2024-0108

Mavropoulos, T., Symeonidis, S., Tsanousa, A., & Zikos, G. (2021). Smart integration of sensors, computer vision and knowledge representation for intelligent monitoring and verbal human-computer interaction. *Journal of Intelligent & Robotic Systems*, *101*(2), 67–85. DOI: 10.1007/s10846-021-01377-z PMID: 34127879

McFarland, D. A., Khanna, S., Domingue, B. W., & Pardos, Z. A. (2021). Education data science: Past, present, future. *AERA Open*, *7*(1), 23328584211052055. DOI: 10.1177/23328584211052055

McNamara, D. S., Arner, T., Butterfuss, R., Basu Mallick, D., Lan, A., Roscoe, R., Roediger, H., & Baraniuk, R. (2022). Situating AI (and big data) in the learning sciences: Moving toward large-scale learning sciences. In Ouyang, F., Jiao, P., McLaren, B., & Alavi, A. (Eds.), *Artificial Intelligence in STEM Education: The Paradigmatic Shifts in* (pp. 427–449). Taylor & Francis., DOI: 10.1201/9781003181187-23

Mehra, J., Madaan, S., & Balu, N. Mohit, Manjunath T C, (2025). "The ubiquitous internet and smart computation available 24/7 for anyone and anywhere." In Babulak E (Ed.), Educational AI humanoid computing devices for cyber nomads (pp. 247-270). IGI Global Scientific Publishing. DOI: DOI: 10.4018/979-8-3693-8985-0.ch010

Musa, N. S., Mirza, N. M., Rafique, S. H., Abdallah, A. M., & Murugan, T. (2024). Machine learning and deep learning techniques for distributed denial of service anomaly detection in software defined networks—Current research solutions. *IEEE Access : Practical Innovations, Open Solutions*, *12*, 60521–60537. DOI: 10.1109/ACCESS.2024.3360868

Nisha Angeline, M., Selvakumar, P., Gupta, M. K., Nazar, N., Elumalai, D., & Bhattacharya, S. (2025). Emerging materials for energy storage and environmental applications. In Muduli, K., Moharana, B., Ales, S., & Biswal, D. (Eds.), *Using computational intelligence for sustainable manufacturing of advanced materials* (pp. 53–72). IGI Global Scientific Publishing., DOI: 10.4018/979-8-3693-7974-5.ch003

Olatunde-Aiyedun, T. G. (2024). Artificial intelligence (AI) in education: Integration of AI into science education curriculum in Nigerian universities. *International Journal of Artificial Intelligence for Digital Education*, *1*(1), 1–14. DOI: 10.2139/ssrn.4633644

Owan, V. J., Abang, K. B., Idika, D. O., Etta, E. O., & Bassey, B. A. (2023). Exploring the potential of artificial intelligence tools in educational measurement and assessment. *Eurasia Journal of Mathematics, Science and Technology Education*, *19*(10), em2367. Advance online publication. DOI: 10.29333/ejmste/13428

Posekany, A. (2025). Project-based learning connecting robotics and artificial intelligence. *Lecture Notes in Networks and Systems*, *1280*, 319–326. DOI: 10.1007/978-3-031-83523-0_30

Ramachandran, K. K. (2024). Data science in the 21st century: Evolution, challenges, and future directions. *International Journal of Business and Data Analytics*, *7*(3), 201–219. DOI: 10.4018/IJBDA.20240703

Razzaq, S., Shah, B., Iqbal, F., Ilyas, M., Maqbool, F., & Rocha, A. (2023). DeepClassRooms: A deep learning based digital twin framework for on-campus class rooms. *Neural Computing & Applications*, *35*(11), 49815–49833. DOI: 10.1007/s00521-021-06754-5 PMID: 35017794

Shi, X., & Wang, B. (2025). "Exploration of interdisciplinary project-based teaching driven by generative AI." *Proceedings of the 4th International Conference on Educational Innovation and Multimedia Technology*, 454–465. DOI: DOI: 10.2991/978-94-6463-750-2_45

Sindakis, S. (2023). "Promoting creativity and critical thinking: Fostering 21st-century skills in education." Academia World News, 1–6. DOI: DOI: 10.13140/RG.2.2.34567.89123

Srivathsa, B. S., Pandey, H., & Naganandini, G. (2025). Future trends in education: The impact of AI, data science, and immersive technologies. In Naganandini, G. (Ed.), *Future Prospects of AI and Data Science* (pp. 115–132). IGI Global., DOI: 10.4018/979-8-3693-8292-9.ch007

Upadhyaya, A. N., Debnath, P., Rani, P., Manjunath, T. C., & Bhattacharya, S. (2025). AI-based disaster prediction and early warning systems. In Mobo, F. (Ed.), *AI and emerging technologies for emergency response and smart cities* (pp. 55–74). IGI Global Scientific Publishing., DOI: 10.4018/979-8-3693-9770-1.ch003

Wardani, I. S., & Fiorintina, E. (2023). Building critical thinking skills of 21st century students through problem based learning model. [Jurnal Pendidikan Indonesia]. *JPI*, *12*(1), 45–54. DOI: 10.23887/jpiundiksha.v12i3.58789

Chapter 9
Teaching Statistical Inference in the AI Era:
Interactive Tools and Critical Questioning With Confidence Intervals

Merve Samioğlu
http://orcid.org/0000-0003-1401-1379
Istanbul University, Turkey

ABSTRACT

Artificial intelligence (AI) is rapidly transforming the landscape of data literacy and redefining how statistical concepts are learned, understood, and applied in educational settings. As data-driven technologies increasingly influence decision-making across fields, it has become essential for learners to understand statistical reasoning and develop the ability to critically interpret AI-generated analyses. This chapter explores how the teaching of confidence intervals (CIs) can serve as an effective platform for fostering both statistical and AI literacy. Building on decades of research showing that students develop a deeper grasp of inferential reasoning through interactive visualization and guided inquiry, this chapter proposes a pedagogical model that integrates dynamic simulation tools with AI-assisted questioning. The central goal of this instructional approach is twofold: first, to strengthen students' conceptual understanding of statistical inference, and second, to cultivate their capacity to interrogate and evaluate AI-generated explanations.

DOI: 10.4018/979-8-3373-6259-5.ch009

INTRODUCTION

Artificial intelligence (AI) is expeditiously changing how students encounter, interpret, and use data. Statistical literacy is no longer optional – it is essential for understanding, critiquing, and applying the outputs of AI systems. Among the many concepts in statistics education, confidence intervals (CIs) provide a natural entry point for teaching uncertainty, inference, and trade-offs in estimation. Yet, students often misinterpret confidence intervals, perceiving them as deterministic "probability statements" rather than as long-run coverage properties.

In this chapter, we propose a classroom strategy that combines interactive visualization tools with AI-assisted inquiry to deepen students' conceptual understanding of CIs while simultaneously cultivating their skills in questioning and critiquing AI. The approach is rooted in two ideas: (1) students grasp concepts more effectively when they manipulate dynamic, visual representations, and (2) the meaningful use of AI in education requires learning to ask precise, critical questions. By integrating these elements, the chapter offers a pedagogical model that addresses both statistical and AI literacy.

In order to address these aims, this chapter is structured into six main sections. The first section provides an overview of the evolution and growing influence of Artificial Intelligence in the 21st century, highlighting its transformative role in education, research, and everyday life. This section sets the stage for understanding how AI technologies shape the ways we learn and think statistically. The second section focuses on the importance of *critical questioning* in engaging effectively with AI systems. It examines how fostering inquiry-oriented thinking and crafting thoughtful prompts can enhance human–AI collaboration and promote deeper conceptual understanding. The third section discusses the teaching and learning of *statistical inference*, addressing common conceptual challenges, pedagogical difficulties, and the potential benefits of integrating AI-driven tools into the learning process. The fourth section outlines the *methodology* adopted in the study, describing the instructional design, the interactive tools developed, and the pedagogical framework used during classroom implementation. The fifth section presents the *findings*, which are based on students' feedback and reflections collected after the classroom implementation. Rather than reporting empirical data, this section synthesizes qualitative insights into how students perceived the interactive tools and the role of critical questioning in their understanding of confidence intervals. Finally, the sixth section provides a *discussion* of the findings, drawing broader conclusions about the pedagogical implications of integrating AI and critical thinking into statistical inference education, as well as suggestions for future research and practice.

1. ARTIFICIAL INTELLIGENCE IN THE 21ST CENTURY: IMPLICATIONS AND APPLICATIONS IN EDUCATION

Artificial intelligence (AI) refers to a technological field developed with the aim of enabling computer systems to perform processes such as learning, comprehension, problem-solving, decision-making, creativity, and autonomy by imitating human intelligence (Russell & Norvig, 2021; Haenlein & Kaplan, 2019). According to McCarthy et al. (1956) classical definition, AI is "the science and engineering of making intelligent machines." This definition is based on the idea not only of imitating human intelligence but also modeling it algorithmically and transferring it to computer systems. Contemporary definitions increasingly formalise AI in terms of *systems* that generate outputs for human-defined objectives. For example, the ISO/IEC terminology standard defines an AI system as an engineered system that generates outputs such as content, forecasts, recommendations, or decisions for a given set of human-defined objectives (ISO/IEC, 2022). Similarly, the OECD's updated definition characterises an AI system as a machine-based system that, for explicit or implicit objectives, infers from inputs how to generate outputs (including predictions, content, recommendations, or decisions) that can influence real or virtual environments, with varying levels of autonomy and adaptiveness (OECD, 2023). These more recent formulations complement influential textbook definitions that emphasise intelligent agents acting in an environment to achieve goals (Russell & Norvig, 2021) and historical accounts of AI as the pursuit of machine capabilities typically associated with human intelligence (Nilsson, 2009).

1.1 Historical Development of Artificial Intelligence

The technology of AI has evolved from being an experimental field limited to research laboratories to reaching wide user communities, especially over the past decade, through free or low-cost tools and open-access models. For example, the opening of AI research environments and the public release of "foundation models" have marked a new era since the 2010s. Historically, AI emerged as a scientific field in the 1950s with the coining of the term "artificial intelligence" during the Dartmouth Summer Research Project on Artificial Intelligence (McCarthy et al., 1956). Today, AI is not only an engineering field but also an interdisciplinary area of research situated at the intersection of cognitive psychology, linguistics, philosophy, ethics, statistics, and educational sciences (Ng et al., 2021).

The historical development of AI is directly linked to technological capacity. This process, which began in the 1950s with systems based on symbolic reasoning, evolved into expert systems in the 1980s, machine learning in the 2000s, and deep learning models in the 2010s. The proliferation of big data, the widespread use of graphical processing units (GPUs), and the development of open-source libraries (e.g., TensorFlow, PyTorch) have allowed AI to move beyond laboratory settings and become accessible to the public (Russell and Norvig, 2021). Particularly, the public release of ChatGPT and similar large language models at the end of 2022 brought AI to the center of everyday life on a global scale. This turning point transformed AI from a research tool into a learning instrument interacted with by a wide range of users, from students to teachers (Bozkurt et al., 2021).

The open accessibility of AI has led to the democratization of technology. The ability of users to access information by asking questions in natural language has introduced the concept of the "prompt" and highlighted its pedagogical importance. Knowledge production is now related not only to access to data but also to the formulation of the right questions (Haugsbaken and Hagelia, 2024). The widespread adoption of AI in this manner has increased access to information and services while simultaneously raising risks of misuse. Therefore, AI literacy which includes individuals' understanding of how AI works, how it can be used, what its limitations are, and what ethical responsibilities it entails, is now considered a new fundamental competency area (Long and Magerko, 2020).

AI is currently used in a wide range of fields such as healthcare, finance, transportation, art, law, and education. Applications such as disease diagnosis and drug discovery in healthcare; risk analysis and algorithmic trading in finance; autonomous vehicles in transportation; and visual and musical production in art demonstrate that AI has permeated nearly all aspects of human activity (Brynjolfsson and McAfee, 2017). However, education is a field where the pedagogical and ethical implications of AI are particularly complex. In education, AI both facilitates knowledge production or work efficiency and it directly affects the nature of learning, the teacher-student relationship, and the way knowledge itself is perceived (Zawacki-Richter et al., 2019).

1.2 Applications of Artificial Intelligence in Education

As discussed in the previous section, Artificial Intelligence has become deeply integrated into many aspects of modern life, and education is no exception. From personalized instruction to automated assessment, AI technologies are increasingly shaping how learning processes are designed and experienced. In educational contexts, AI is a supplementary tool and a transformative element that supports both teaching and learning in dynamic ways. The applications of AI in education can be broadly categorized into four key dimensions:

1. Personalized learning: Systems that provide dynamic content according to students' individual pace, prior knowledge levels, and learning styles are among the most common applications of AI. For example, intelligent learning management

systems can suggest specific exercises based on the questions a student has answered incorrectly (Holmes, 2021). This makes the idea of "individualized instruction for every student" technologically feasible.

2. Assessment and feedback: AI can analyze students' conceptual errors in open-ended responses using natural language processing techniques and provide instant feedback. This not only reduces teachers' workload—especially in large classrooms—but also enables students to learn quickly from their mistakes (Vashishth et al., 2024).
3. Accessibility and inclusivity: AI-supported solutions such as voice assistants, caption generators, and text-to-speech systems are designed for students with special needs, such as visual or hearing impairments. UNESCO (2023) emphasizes that such applications "strengthen inclusivity and equality of opportunity in education."
4. Interactive and exploratory learning: AI-based simulations in which students ask questions, engage in discussions, and explore concepts through trial and error are particularly effective in teaching abstract concepts in subjects such as statistics, physics, and economics (Amlasri, 2022). Interaction between students and AI serves not only as a means of obtaining information but also as a way of developing ways of thinking.

These dimensions are critically important in terms of how AI personalizes learning, transforms the role of teachers, and strengthens data-driven decision-making processes in education. However, the full realization of this potential depends on how users (both students and teachers) understand and interpret AI.

The importance of AI in education lies not merely in providing new tools but in redefining learning processes themselves. Zawacki-Richter et al. (2019) describe the role of AI in education as "the reconfiguration of the learning ecosystem." This ecosystem turns teachers into interpreters of data and students into active producers of knowledge. For example, in a statistics course, when students use a "confidence interval applet" to observe sample distributions and then ask questions to an AI system, they not only experience the concept practically but also make their thinking processes visible by questioning the answers generated by the AI. This method increases metacognitive awareness (Lin et al., 2025).

In AI-based learning environments, the teacher is no longer a transmitter of knowledge but a facilitator who guides students' modes of thinking. This necessitates a rethinking of instructional design. Bozkurt et al. (2021) define the teacher's role in the age of AI as that of a "guide, ethical evaluator, and critical thinking developer." Therefore, AI literacy should encompass not only technical knowledge but also pedagogical and ethical awareness.

1.3 The Relationship Between Artificial Intelligence and Statistics Education

Statistics education occupies a special position in understanding the modes of thinking that underlie AI. AI systems fundamentally operate through statistical methods: they recognize patterns in large datasets, make predictions based on these patterns, and optimize themselves over time. Therefore, the science of statistics constitutes the mathematical backbone of AI. The use of AI in statistics instruction thus provides a dual learning opportunity: students learn statistics while also gaining insight into how AI functions (Lin et al., n.d.). This establishes a natural connection between statistics education and AI. Cukurova (2025) notes that AI "lies at the intersection of statistical modeling and cognitive modeling." Understanding this relationship allows students to develop a deeper comprehension of both statistics and AI.

For instance, the concept of a confidence interval is an abstract statistical construct and therefore often difficult for students to grasp. A student who visualizes the distribution of sample means with the help of an applet learns the concept of uncertainty experientially. When this student subsequently asks the AI questions such as "Why do some samples deviate so much from the mean?", "What changes when I increase the confidence level?", or "Why does the interval widen when I raise the confidence level from 95% to 99%?", their conceptual understanding is reinforced. This process enhances both statistical thinking and inquiry skills. While evaluating the AI's response, the student recognizes the probabilistic nature of the model and learns to approach information critically. At the same time, such interactions allow students to statistically evaluate the responses generated by AI and to refine their own reasoning processes.

However, the information provided by AI is not always accurate or unbiased. Since AI models are trained on human-generated data, they may also reflect the biases present in those data (Bender et al., 2021). This makes it necessary for students to question the responses they receive from AI and to ask, "On what source is this information based?" Lim et al. (2025) emphasize that ethical awareness must be an integral component of AI-based learning environments. Ethical awareness in education requires that students understand the limitations of AI, issues of data privacy, and algorithmic bias. In this context, teachers should cultivate students not only as users of technology but also as digital citizens.

Interaction with AI also requires the skill of *critical prompting*. For a student, asking the right questions is a prerequisite for receiving accurate answers (Altınpulluk and Alptekin, 2025). This skill represents not only a request for information but also a mode of thinking. A poorly formulated question may lead to misleading information from the AI. Therefore, *prompt literacy* is recognized as a new domain of metacognitive competence in education (Haugsbaken and Hagelia, 2024).

1.4 The Cognitive and Ethical Significance of Artificial Intelligence in Education

Artificial intelligence (AI) has been transformed into a technology that not only imitates human intelligence but also collaborates with it (Russell & Norvig, 2021). This transformation generates both opportunities and responsibilities within the field of education (Luckin et al., 2016). Students can now access knowledge by interacting with AI through natural language, while teachers can monitor their students' learning processes in data-driven and adaptive ways (Holmes & Porayska-Pomsta, 2023). However, these possibilities gain meaning through technical skills, critical thinking, ethical awareness, and statistical literacy (Long & Magerko, 2020; Floridi & Cowls, 2021).

AI facilitates access to information but simultaneously necessitates critical thinking (Dignum, 2019). Students must learn how to use technology and how to understand it, question it, and manage it ethically (Mata, 2022). In this respect, the integration of statistics instruction with AI-based tools offers a powerful model for future learning environments (Baker et al., 2019). The significance of AI in education is not merely instrumental but cognitive: it makes learning deeper, inquiry more structured, and thinking more visible (Holmes & Porayska-Pomsta, 2023). Especially in abstract domains such as statistics education, the use of AI strengthens both conceptual understanding and the culture of inquiry (Garfield & Ben-Zvi, 2008).

Statistical thinking represents reasoning based on data (Wild & Pfannkuch, 1999), while AI represents the technological infrastructure that supports and automates such reasoning (Janssen et al., 2022). The shared foundation of both domains is the ability to cope with uncertainty, a key component of decision-making in both human cognition and machine learning (Gigerenzer, 2010; Jordan & Mitchell, 2015). Therefore, a learning environment in which students understand both statistical concepts and the nature of AI both produces knowledge and contributes to the development of conscious, critical., and ethical individuals (Williamson & Eynon, 2020). In this respect, AI is not merely the technology of the future but also a fundamental component of the learning philosophy of the future (Selwyn, 2019).

2. THE IMPORTANCE OF ASKING THE RIGHT QUESTIONS TO ARTIFICIAL INTELLIGENCE

Artificial intelligence (AI) systems today have become powerful tools for a wide range of purposes such as information access, creativity, and problem solving (Luckin et al., 2016). These systems are used across diverse domains from education and business to scientific research and personal development. However, the potential of AI largely depends on how users interact with it, and in particular, on the quality of the questions they ask. As conversational AI and large language models (LLMs) have become more widespread in educational and professional settings, the ability to ask critical and well-structured questions has emerged as a fundamental form of digital literacy and pedagogical competence (Holmes & Porayska-Pomsta, 2023). When this skill is lacking, users may misinterpret AI outputs, accept incomplete or biased answers, and even propagate misinformation (Floridi & Chiriatti, 2020).

At their core, large language models do not possess true comprehension; rather, they generate responses through probabilistic predictions derived from massive datasets, instead of deliberate reasoning (Bender et al., 2021). For example, a model produces answers by estimating which sequence of words is most likely to occur in a given context, yet it performs no pedagogical or conceptual evaluation in doing so. Consequently, the accuracy and usefulness of AI-generated responses are closely linked to the clarity and quality of user input. This phenomenon has increased the significance of the concept known as "prompt engineering" in education and knowledge acquisition processes. Prompt engineering refers to the intentional design of prompts that guide AI models toward relevant, accurate, and contextually meaningful outputs (Reynolds & McDonell, 2021). When a user successfully frames their intent, the likelihood that the AI will produce pedagogically valuable and accurate responses increases substantially.

In traditional learning processes, inquiry is at the heart of cognitive engagement. Asking good questions enables students to explore ideas, clarify concepts, and construct knowledge (Chin & Osborne, 2008). This principle also applies to AI-mediated learning, although with an added layer of complexity. When a student asks a question to a human teacher, the teacher can interpret the student's intent, identify misconceptions, and adjust explanations accordingly. In contrast, an AI model lacks such awareness; it interprets only the linguistic form of the input rather than the pedagogical intent behind it (Holmes & Porayska-Pomsta, 2023). This underscores the importance of formulating clear, contextually grounded questions.

For instance, a student studying confidence intervals in statistics might ask, "Why are some sample means very different from the population mean?" A well-designed prompt of this kind clarifies the context by specifying factors such as sample size, confidence level, and distribution type. Conversely, a vague question like "Why is my data different?" may generate responses unrelated to the statistical concept the student seeks to understand (Van der Linden & Glas, 2010). Similarly, in disciplines such as history or philosophy, questions posed without context can result in responses that are limited in both accuracy and depth.

Prompt design is not merely a technical skill; it is also a cognitive and metacognitive process. The learner must clarify what they seek to learn, situate that goal within a conceptual framework, and anticipate possible interpretations or responses

(Guo, 2022). In this sense, critical questioning functions both as a learning strategy and as a safeguard against misinformation. AI systems do not "know" in the human sense; they simulate knowledge through linguistic prediction. As a result, their responses can appear coherent and confident even when they are factually incorrect or logically inconsistent (Bender et al., 2021). This phenomenon, which is sometimes referred to as "AI hallucination", can lead to serious errors when combined with a lack of critical thinking, emphasizing the danger of uncritical trust in AI-generated information (Marcus & Davis, 2019).

2.1 Critical Evaluation and Artificial Intelligence Literacy

When prompts are vague or insufficiently specific, AI models may generate responses that sound plausible but are in fact inaccurate or misleading. In educational contexts, this can lead to subtle conceptual misunderstandings that are difficult to detect. For instance, a student might ask, "What does a 95% confidence interval mean?" The AI may respond with a technically phrased explanation but fail to clarify that the interval pertains to the *method*, not to a single estimate. As a result, the student may adopt a common misconception, believing that there is a 95% probability that the true mean lies within the calculated interval (Gigerenzer, 2004; Nickerson, 2000).

Such cases illustrate that critical questioning must be paired with critical evaluation. Users should verify the accuracy of AI-generated outputs by consulting multiple sources, comparing data, and reflecting on the reasoning process. In doing so, AI becomes less a static authority and more a dynamic partner in learning and inquiry (Luckin, 2018). The emergence of publicly accessible AI systems, especially since the release of conversational large language models such as ChatGPT in late 2022, has dramatically transformed global patterns of information-seeking behavior (Kasneci et al., 2023). Previously, information retrieval occurred primarily through search engines and curated content, but it is now becoming increasingly conversational and generative. Rather than searching for existing answers, users are co-creating new ones through interaction.

This transformation has also expanded the notion of literacy itself. Traditional digital literacy involved the ability to locate, evaluate, and synthesize information (Gilster, 1997). AI literacy, however, adds a new dimension: the ability to design effective prompts that produce reliable, context-sensitive information outputs (Long & Magerko, 2020; Ng et al., 2021). This is not only about understanding technology, but about learning to communicate effectively with it.

From this perspective, prompt design can be compared to hypothesis formulation in scientific inquiry. The user constructs a mental model of what the AI "knows," specifies relevant constraints, and tests how different formulations of the same question yield different outcomes. This iterative process develops epistemic awareness of how knowledge is generated and represented within algorithmic systems (Henrickson & Meroño-Peñuela, 2025). Such awareness is crucial for preventing the passive consumption of AI-generated content and fostering active, reflective engagement.

In educational practice, encouraging critical inquiry in AI use is key to promoting higher-order thinking. Students should not view AI as a source of ready-made answers, but rather as a thinking partner that requires guidance and framing (Holmes & Porayska-Pomsta, 2023). Teachers can design classroom activities in which students test different prompt formulations, compare resulting outputs, and observe how variations in wording influence interpretation and reasoning. Through this reflective experimentation, learners not only deepen their conceptual understanding but also internalize the principles of meaningful and responsible inquiry (Chin & Osborne, 2008).

2.2 Pedagogical Integration and Ethical Dimensions

In the teaching of statistical inference, students can be encouraged to ask increasingly precise questions to an AI system regarding sampling error or confidence intervals. In this iterative process, it becomes evident that vague questions tend to produce superficial explanations, whereas more detailed prompts elicit deeper reasoning and conceptually robust responses. Such experiences foster not only conceptual understanding but also metacognitive control: students do not merely learn statistics—they also learn the structure of meaningful inquiry itself. This dual process aligns with the objective of this section, which is further elaborated in Section 4.

Additionally, incorporating *AI-prompt reflection tasks* (activities in which students analyze why certain outputs were misleading or incomplete) can strengthen skepticism and evaluative skills (Zawacki-Richter et al., 2019). This approach resonates with the principles of *critical pedagogy*, which encourages learners to question the sources of knowledge and authority (Freire, 1970). In the age of AI, this principle acquires a new dimension; questioning both the machine and oneself.

Critical inquiry also intersects with the ethics of AI use. When users fail to contextualize their questions, AI models may inadvertently reinforce biases or stereotypes embedded in their training data (Caliskan et al., 2017). For instance, an uncritical question such as "What are the typical traits of successful people?" might yield culturally biased responses that reflect societal or algorithmic prejudices. Awareness of such risks requires users to anticipate the ethical implications of their own prompts—considering how the assumptions, categories, and social meanings embedded in their questions frame the resulting knowledge (Buolamwini & Gebru, 2018).

Thus, "teaching how to ask" becomes an ethical practice in itself. It reminds users that technology is not neutral and that the way a question is formulated carries both moral and epistemological weight. Framing determines what becomes visible and what remains hidden, what counts as knowledge and what is excluded (Winner, 2017). Encouraging reflective questioning helps prevent the automation of bias and the uncritical perpetuation of skewed information (Crawford, 2021).

Integrating critical inquiry into AI literacy education requires a shift from *tool-centered* pedagogy to *dialogue-centered* approaches (Blikstein & Worsley, 2016). Students should not only learn the technical structure of prompts but also discuss why certain formulations succeed or fail. This process can be supported through guided reflection, collaborative experimentation, and explicit instruction on question typologies (e.g., descriptive, explanatory, evaluative, or speculative questions).

Instructors can also model the process of debugging a poor prompt: demonstrating how an ambiguous question leads to unreliable results, much like an invalid statistical model yields misleading inferences (Yang et al., 2024). By linking AI prompting to familiar scientific practices such as hypothesis testing or data validation, students can internalize the logic of rigorous inquiry. Over time, this practice cultivates epistemic humility and a deeper awareness of how both human and machine cognition co-construct meaning (Chen, 2025).

2.3 Critical Inquiry as the Bridge Between Human and Machine Intelligence

Critical inquiry represents a fundamental bridge between human cognitive capacity and the algorithmic functioning of artificial intelligence (AI) systems. As AI becomes increasingly integrated into education, research, and professional domains, the ways in which users not only access but also question and interpret information are being transformed. In this context, the ability to ask well-structured, context-sensitive, and ethically informed questions is a decisive factor in the quality of human–AI interaction.

Asking the right question is not merely an act of information retrieval but a form of epistemic control, it defines the boundaries of AI's generative capacity and imposes a conscious framework upon its probabilistic nature (Floridi & Chiriatti, 2020; Marcus & Davis, 2019). Conversely, poorly formulated, shallow, or biased prompts do not just diminish the usefulness of AI, they also risk amplifying misinformation and reproducing existing social and cultural biases embedded in training data (Bender et al., 2021; Buolamwini & Gebru, 2018). In contrast, prompts that are critically and reflectively constructed can transform AI from a passive generator of responses into an *active participant* in the learning process. Such prompts encourage users to recognize the model's limitations, question the accuracy of its outputs, and, when necessary, generate alternative perspectives (Long & Magerko, 2020).

Within educational contexts, cultivating this capacity can be viewed as a digital extension of critical pedagogy. As Freire (1970) asserted in *Pedagogy of the Oppressed*, genuine learning is not about passively receiving information but about continuously questioning and reconstructing it. In the age of AI, this principle gains renewed significance: critical inquiry becomes the epistemological tool for remaining human within automated systems. By moving beyond "What does the AI say?" to "Why does the AI say this?", learners and professionals alike deepen their cognitive awareness and ethical sensitivity (Holmes & Porayska-Pomsta, 2023). Thus, critical inquiry is not only a technological competency but one of the defining modes of thinking in the digital age.

2.4 Examples for Effective and Ineffective Prompts in the Context of Confidence Intervals

One of the main objectives of this chapter is to design an interactive learning process that integrates AI into the teaching of confidence intervals. This approach not only utilizes AI as an informational tool but also encourages students to formulate effective prompts to guide their own learning and deepen their conceptual understanding. When interacting with large language models such as ChatGPT, students begin to realize that the way they formulate their questions directly affects the quality, depth, and accuracy of the responses they receive.

Therefore, the table below presents examples of "bad" and "good" prompts related to the topic of confidence intervals, illustrating how well-crafted prompt design enhances both statistical reasoning and pedagogical outcomes. Through these examples, students learn that the quality of AI-generated responses is closely tied to the clarity, scope, and contextual precision of their questions.

Table 1. Comparison of Bad and Good Prompts on Confidence Intervals

Bad Prompt	Why It Is Bad	Good Prompt (Correct Version)
What is a confidence interval?	Too general; scope and target audience are unclear.	Explain the concept of confidence interval in a way suitable for a beginner statistics student; illustrate what a 95% confidence interval means with an example.
Calculate a 95% confidence interval.	Required data (mean, standard deviation, sample size) are missing.	Step by step, calculate the 95% confidence interval for n=30, mean=80, standard deviation=10, and interpret the result.
Why is a confidence interval important?	Context (survey, experiment, research?) is not specified.	Write a 150-word paragraph explaining why confidence intervals are important when evaluating the generalizability of survey results.
What is confidence level, and what does coverage rate mean?	Type of answer (theoretical or example-based) is unclear.	Statistically define confidence level and coverage rate; explain the difference with formulas and examples.
Write a text about confidence intervals.	Tone, length, detail level, and target audience are not specified.	Write approximately 400 words as a undergraduate-level statistics lecture note, explaining confidence intervals with formulas, interpretation, and examples.
What happens to confidence intervals when sample size increases?	Too broad; does not specify the mechanism or statistical reasoning involved.	Explain how increasing the sample size affects the width of a 95% confidence interval and why this happens in terms of the standard error.
Why do some confidence intervals miss the true mean?	Does not explicitly connect the question to sampling variability or repeated sampling.	Using the idea of repeated sampling, explain why some confidence intervals in a simulation fail to contain the population mean even when the confidence level is 95%.
Explain confidence intervals better.	Unclear objective and level of explanation.	Explain confidence intervals to an introductory statistics student and describe how they relate to sampling variability and repeated sampling.

As shown in the table, good prompts clearly specify the content, context, and purpose of the statistical concept, enabling the AI system to produce more accurate and meaningful responses. For instance, simply asking *"Calculate a 95% confidence interval"* may lead the model to generate a random or incomplete result, whereas specifying the sample size, mean, and standard deviation allows the model to correctly apply the formula and explain each step of the computation. This distinction highlights the educational significance of critical questioning and prompt engineering in AI-supported learning environments.

Effective prompt design transforms students from passive recipients of information into active thinkers who guide their own learning process. In statistics education, this shift enables students to move beyond surface-level memorization and toward meaningful understanding through constructivist learning experiences. Furthermore, when students observe inconsistencies or errors in AI-generated responses resulting from poorly formulated prompts, they develop stronger critical thinking and meta-cognitive awareness.

Ultimately, the goal of integrating AI into statistics education is not merely to introduce technological innovation, but to strengthen students' ability to ask precise and meaningful questions, critically evaluate the reliability of information, and understand the contextual limits of knowledge. Since concepts such as confidence intervals inherently involve uncertainty and probability, crafting accurate prompts serves as a key strategy for fostering deeper learning and making AI use pedagogically meaningful.

3. CHALLENGES IN TEACHING STATISTICAL INFERENCE

Perhaps, one of the most important applications of statistics is statistical inference. Whether driven by academic curiosity or commercial concerns, when conducting any research, we aim to obtain information about the phenomenon or situation of interest. However, reaching the entire population to gather this information is often impossible. For example, if we suspect that the amount of liquid in a soft drink bottle is less than the amount stated on the bottle, or even that the beverage company intentionally fills the bottles with less liquid, what we should do is to measure the liquid in the relevant bottle. However, measuring just a single bottle would be insufficient to conclude that the company intentionally fills the bottles with less liquid. To make such an inference, all bottles produced by the company would need to be measured. As mentioned earlier, this is an impossible method. Even if there were a method sufficient to measure all bottles produced at that moment, the population of interest here is the amount of liquid in all bottles the company has produced in the past and will produce in the future. Therefore, reaching the entire population is impossible.

However, the impossibility of reaching the population does not prevent us from making an inference about it. Instead of accessing the entire population, a subset considered to represent it well can be selected. Analyses are then conducted on this subset, called a sample, and by assuming that the information obtained is valid for the population as well, an inference about the population is made. This widely used method is called *statistical inference*. In summary, statistical inference is the process of drawing conclusions about a population based on information obtained from a sample. Statistical inference is not concerned with all numerical values that make up the population, but rather with the numbers summarizing these values. These values summarizing the population are called *population parameters*, generally denoted by the symbol Θ. Some commonly used population parameters include the mean (μ), standard deviation (σ) or variance (σ^2), and proportion (p). The counterparts of population parameters in the sample are called *sample statistics*.

This process, which forms a significant part of statistical theory, is traditionally considered in two main areas: Estimation and Hypothesis Testing. In the estimation process, inferences are made about the numerical values that population parameters can take, and the estimation process is addressed in two stages: point estimation and interval estimation.

Point estimation is expressing the estimate of a population parameter as a single numerical value based on information obtained from the sample. In other words, the sample statistic obtained from the sample is used as the estimate of the population parameter. However, the probability that a point estimation equals the population parameter is theoretically zero ($P[\theta = \Theta] = 0$). In other words, confidence in a point estimation is zero. Therefore, expressing a population parameter with a point estimation does not constitute a reliable inference. To make a reliable estimate for the parameter of interest, an error margin (e) is accepted, and an error range is created around the point estimation ($\theta \pm e$). Such an interval ($\theta - e, \theta + e$) is called an interval estimation of the population parameter Θ. The probability that Θ falls within the interval ($\theta - e, \theta + e$) depends on the value of e and can be calculated if the necessary assumptions are met

While confidence in a point estimation is zero ($P[\theta = \Theta] = 0$), the confidence in the estimate increases due to the error interval around it. Mathematically, this can be expressed as:

$$P\left[\hat{\theta} - e \leq \Theta \leq \hat{\theta} + e\right] = 1 - \alpha$$

In this equation, $(1 - \alpha)$ represents the probability that Θ falls within the interval $(\hat{\theta} - e, \hat{\theta} + e)$. When the expression inside the parentheses is arranged for the point estimation θ ($\theta - e \leq \Theta \leq \theta + e$), a $100(1 - \alpha)\%$ confidence interval for Θ is obtained. $(1 - \alpha)$ indicates the confidence level in the interval estimate ($\theta - e, \theta + e$).

Ideally, in a confidence interval., the confidence level $(1 - \alpha)$ should be maximized, and the error (e) should be minimized. However, these two factors are directly proportional; if a small error is desired, the confidence level will be low, and a high confidence level requires a larger error. In other words, if a high confidence level is desired, the error will also increase. With a fixed sample size, increasing the confidence level requires increasing the error. To achieve both a small error and a high confidence level, the sample size should be increased.

One of the most common misunderstandings about confidence intervals is thinking that the confidence level represents the probability that the population parameter is within the confidence interval., just because the confidence level is a probability. This misunderstanding can be clarified when the concept of coverage rate is correctly understood. When a sample of n observations is selected, it is unknown whether the confidence interval obtained from this sample contains the population parameter, but the confidence level in this interval is $1 - \alpha$. If the sampling process is repeated, for example, 100 times, and the confidence level is 95%, it can be predicted that approximately 95 of these 100 intervals will contain the population parameter. Each of the 100 intervals has a 95% confidence level, but approximately about 5 of them will not contain the population parameter.

Expressing confidence intervals in terms of concrete ratios rather than abstract probabilities makes them easier for students to grasp and conceptually understand. However, when explained traditionally in class, the concept of coverage rate is not adequately internalized by students. Furthermore, when selecting a sample to make an inference about the population for solving a concrete problem, it is not possible to repeat the "select a sample of n observations" process multiple times, so the concept of coverage rate is not fully understood.

One of the best ways to address this deficiency is using interactive tools during lessons. Virtual manipulatives are digital., interactive, and visual representations of physical mathematics materials. These tools allow students to model, explore, and understand mathematical concepts via computers or other digital devices (Moyer et al., 2002). Moyer, Bolyard, and Spikell (2002) define virtual manipulatives as "dynamic and interactive learning objects that can be manipulated via computer and include visual representations of mathematical concepts." They are also defined as "computer-based renditions of common mathematics manipulatives and tools" (Dorward, & Heal., 1999). These tools support students' conceptual understanding by concretizing abstract mathematical concepts (Clements & McMillen, 1996; Moyer-Packenham & Westenskow, 2013). An applet designed to improve understanding of confidence intervals in statistical inference is a type of virtual manipulative. Reinforcing confidence intervals with an applet after explaining them using traditional methods is an effective way for students to better understand both the topic and the related concepts. For this purpose, an applet is designed by the author. Below is a figure of the applet illustrating the confidence interval for the mean.

Figure 1. Output of the applet illustrating a sample confidence interval that contains the population mean under the specified parameters

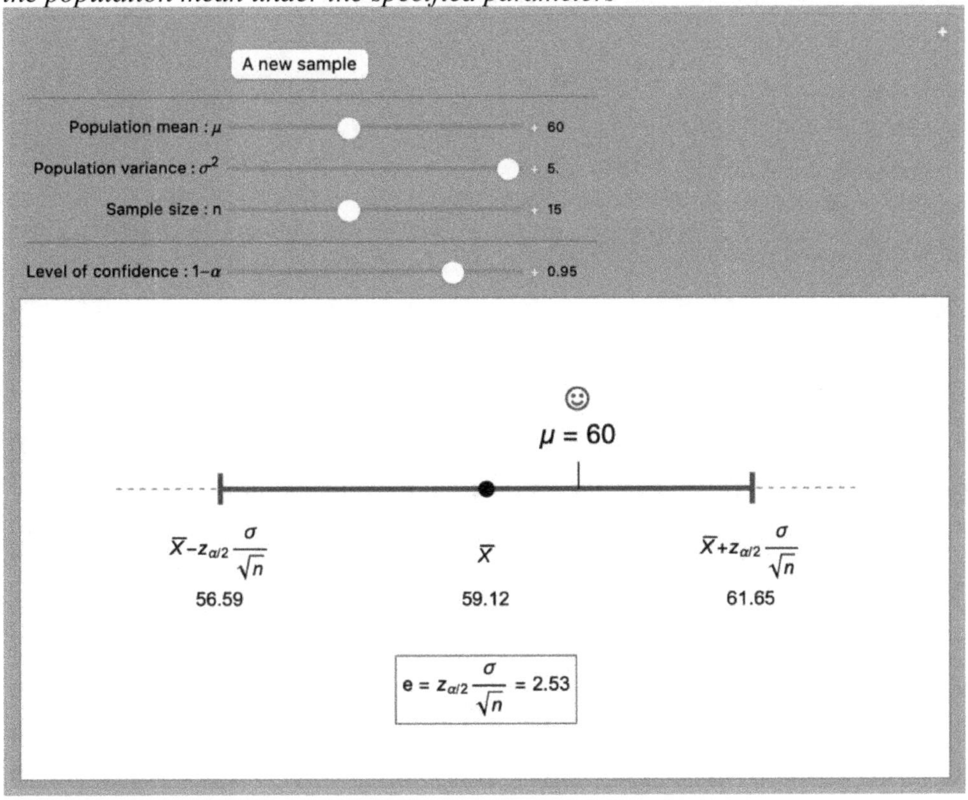

The applet, designed with the assumption of the population is normally distributed and the population variance is known, allows the user to set the population mean, population variance, sample size, and confidence level using sliders. Each time the “a new sample” button is clicked, a new sample is selected based on the specified criteria. On the main screen of the applet, a visual representation displays the sample mean, the confidence interval at the chosen confidence level, and an indication of whether the confidence interval includes the population mean. When the “a new sample” button is clicked repeatedly without changing any of the variables, new confidence intervals are generated, showing whether or not each interval contains the population mean. In Figure 1, the population mean lies within the confidence interval., while in Figure 2, the confidence interval does not include the population mean.

Figure 2. Output of the applet illustrating a sample confidence interval that does not contain the population mean under the specified parameters

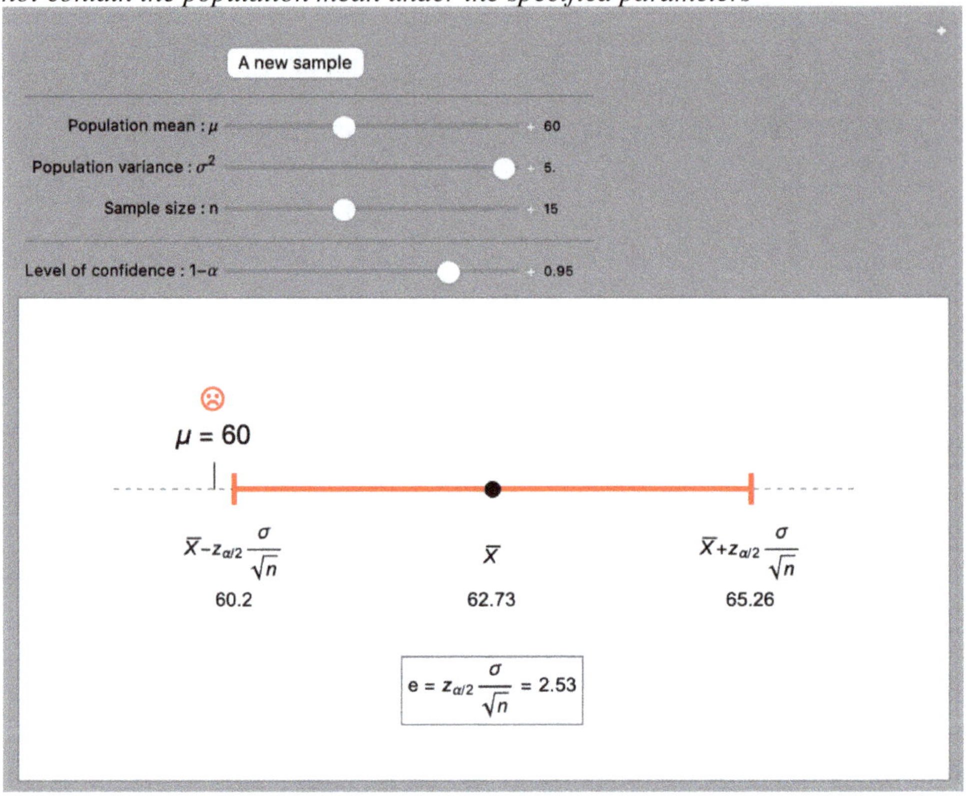

It is important to note that since all variables determining the margin of error are the same in both figures, the lengths of the confidence intervals are equal; however, while one of the confidence intervals formed by different samples includes the population mean, the other does not.

4. INSTRUCTIONAL DESIGN

After the confidence intervals are explained to students using the traditional method, several critical questions are asked to assess whether they understand certain key distinctions. The first question is "What is the confidence level?", the second is "What is the coverage rate?", and another is "What is the difference between the confidence level and the coverage rate?". After collecting students' answers, they are asked to pose the same questions to an AI program, as creating the prompt as follows: "Statistically define confidence level and coverage rate; explain the difference with formulas and examples." When this prompt is asked to ChatGPT, it provides the following definitions in order:

"1. Confidence Level (CL)

Definition:

In statistics, the confidence level is the probability that a confidence interval (CI) calculated from a random sample contains the true population parameter. It reflects the reliability of the estimation method, not the probability that the specific interval contains the parameter.

- *Usually expressed as a percentage (e.g., 90%, 95%, 99%).*

Formula:

For a population mean μ (assuming known variance σ^2):

$$CI = \bar{x} \pm z_{\alpha/2} \frac{\sigma}{\sqrt{n}}$$

where:

- $\bar{x}$ = sample mean
- $z_{\alpha/2}$ = critical value from the standard normal distribution for significance level ($CL = 1 - \alpha$)
- n = sample size
- σ = population standard deviation

Interpretation:

If we construct 100 confidence intervals using this method from 100 independent samples, about CL% of these intervals will contain the true population mean μ.

Example:

- Sample size: $n = 50$
- Sample mean: $\bar{x} = 100$
- Population standard deviation: $\sigma = 15$
- Confidence level: 95% $\left(\alpha = 0.05,\ z_{0.025} \approx 1.96\right)$

$$CI = 100 \pm 1.96 \frac{15}{\sqrt{50}} \approx 100 \pm 4.15$$

So the 95% confidence interval is [95.85, 104.15]. If we repeated this many times, ~95% of such intervals would include the true mean μ.

2. Coverage Rate (CR)

Definition:

The coverage rate is the actual proportion of times that a confidence interval contains the true parameter in repeated sampling. It is an empirical measure of how well the interval estimation method works.

- *If you simulate many samples, the coverage rate can differ slightly from the nominal confidence level.*

Formula:

Suppose you perform N independent experiments and construct confidence intervals CI_i for $i = 1, 2, \ldots N$. Let $I_i = 1$ if CI_i contains μ, 0 otherwise. Then:

$$Coverage\ Rate\ (CR) = \frac{1}{N}\sum_{i=1}^{N} I_i$$

Example:

- *You simulate 1000 samples and construct 95% CIs for each.*
- 947 of these intervals contain the true mean μ.

$$CR = \frac{947}{1000} = 0.947 \approx 94.7\%$$

Here, the nominal confidence level is 95%, but the actual coverage rate is 94.7%.

3. Difference Between Confidence Level and Coverage Rate

Table 2.

Aspect	*Confidence Level (CL)*	*Coverage Rate (CR)*
Type	*Theoretical / nominal*	*Empirical / actual*
Meaning	*Probability that the CI procedure contains the true parameter*	*Proportion of intervals that actually contain the true parameter*
Formula	$CL = 1 - \alpha$	$CR = \frac{1}{N}\sum_{i=1}^{N} I_i$
Example	*95% CI method is designed so 95% of intervals contain* μ	*In simulation, 947/1000 intervals contain* μ *94.7% coverage*

Key idea:

- Confidence level is the intended reliability before sampling.
- Coverage rate is the realized reliability after repeated sampling or simulation.
- In practice, for small samples or non-normal data, CR may differ from CL."

After obtaining these responses from ChatGPT, these concepts are demonstrated to the students again using the applet While the confidence level remains fixed at 95%, each time the "new sample" button is clicked, a new sample is drawn, and it is observed whether the sample's confidence interval contains the population mean. At this point, students are asked how many times they expect the sample intervals not to contain the population mean after pressing the "new sample" button a certain number of times. Students observe that if the button is pressed 100 times, approximately 5 of those intervals will not include the population mean. The confidence level theoretically indicates that 95 out of 100 intervals will contain the population mean, while the coverage rate shows how many actually do in practice.

After this stage, another critical question is asked: *"What is the importance of the sample size (n) in the confidence interval?"* Theoretically, as the sample size increases, the error decreases, which in turn shortens the length of the confidence intervals. In other words, increasing the sample size reduces the margin of error without changing the confidence level. While increasing the sample size does not alter the coverage rate, it results in narrower confidence intervals. After this topic is explained using the traditional method, students are once again asked to pose the same question to an AI program. When this question is asked to ChatGPT, the following answer is obtained:

"As the sample size increases, the confidence interval becomes narrower — meaning our estimate becomes more precise (accurate).

1. General Formula of a Confidence Interval

For a mean (when the population standard deviation is unknown and the sample is large), the confidence interval is generally written as:

$$\overline{X} \pm z_{\alpha/2} \times \frac{S}{\sqrt{n}}$$

Where;

- $\overline{X}$: sample mean
- S: sample standard deviation
- n: sample size

- $z_{\alpha/2}$: critical value from the standard normal distribution corresponding to the chosen confidence level (e.g., ≈1.96 for 95%)

2. Effect of Sample Size

Notice that the sample size n appears in the denominator under a square root:

$$\frac{S}{\sqrt{n}}$$

This term is known as the standard error.
Therefore:

- As n increases, $\sqrt{n}$ increases
- $\frac{S}{\sqrt{n}}$ decreases
- Hence, the half-width of the confidence interval (the margin of error) decreases

Result: Larger sample → Narrower confidence interval → More precise estimate

3. What Happens When n Increases?

In the formula, notice that n is under the square root in the denominator:

- As n increases, $\sqrt{n}$ increases.
- Therefore, $\frac{S}{\sqrt{n}}$ decreases.
- So the confidence interval becomes narrower.

Result: A larger sample → smaller margin of error → narrower confidence interval → more precise estimate.

4. What if n is Small?
   - With a small sample, estimates are more uncertain.
   - The margin of error increases, and the confidence interval widens.
   - This means you have less reliable information about the true population parameter.
5. Example

Suppose we have the same data but different sample sizes:

- $n = 25 \rightarrow$ margin of error: $\frac{S}{\sqrt{25}} = \frac{S}{5}$

- $n = 100 \rightarrow$ margin of error: $\frac{s}{\sqrt{100}} = \frac{s}{10}$

So, when the sample size increases fourfold, the margin of error is cut in half."

After obtaining these responses from ChatGPT, the applet is shown to the students once again. In the applet, while the population mean is set to 30, the population variance to 3, and the confidence level to 95%, the sample size is first set to 10. For this sample size, the margin of error is 1.86. Each time a new sample is selected, the sample mean changes, and therefore the confidence intervals also change; however, the length of the confidence interval ($\bar{x} \pm e$) remains constant. Next, the sample size is successively increased to 15, 20, and 30. When the sample size is 15, the margin of error is 1.52; when it is 20, the margin of error is 1.31; and when it is 30, the margin of error decreases to 1.07. This demonstrates that increasing the sample size, while keeping the confidence level constant, reduces the margin of error, in other words, it narrows the confidence interval. Screenshots of the applet for sample sizes of 10 and 30 are shown in Figures 3 and 4.

Figure 3. Output of the applet illustrating the confidence interval for a sample size of 10, demonstrating a wider interval due to a larger margin of error

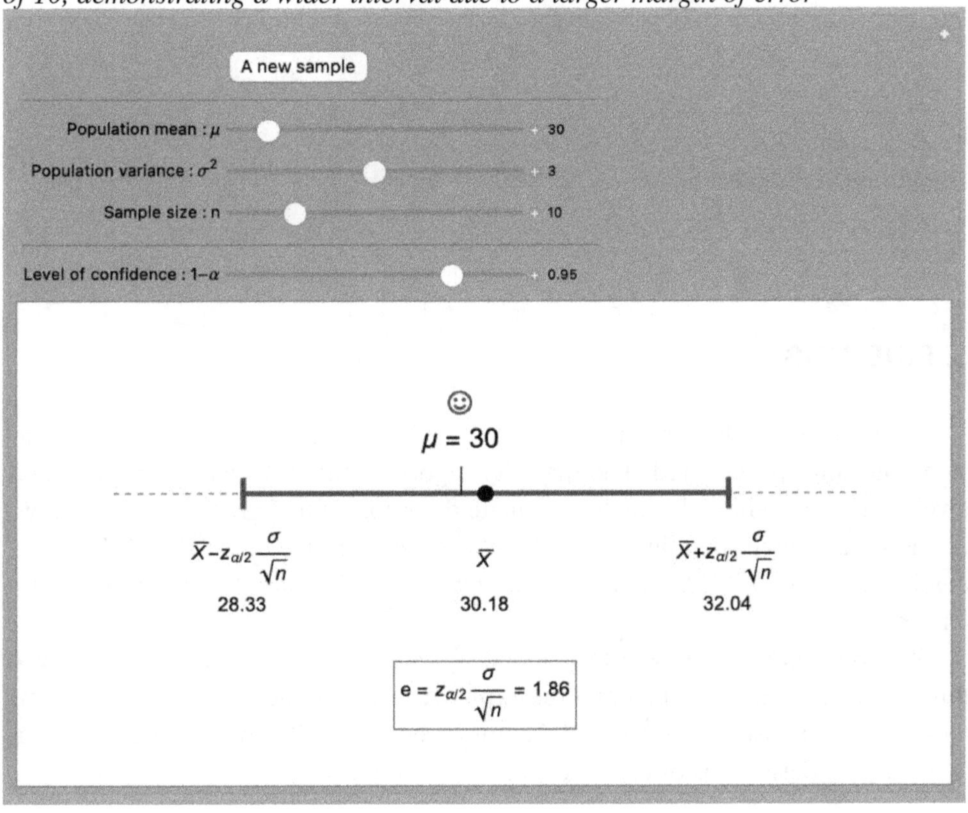

Figure 4. Output of the applet illustrating the confidence interval for a sample size of 30, demonstrating a narrower interval as the margin of error decreases

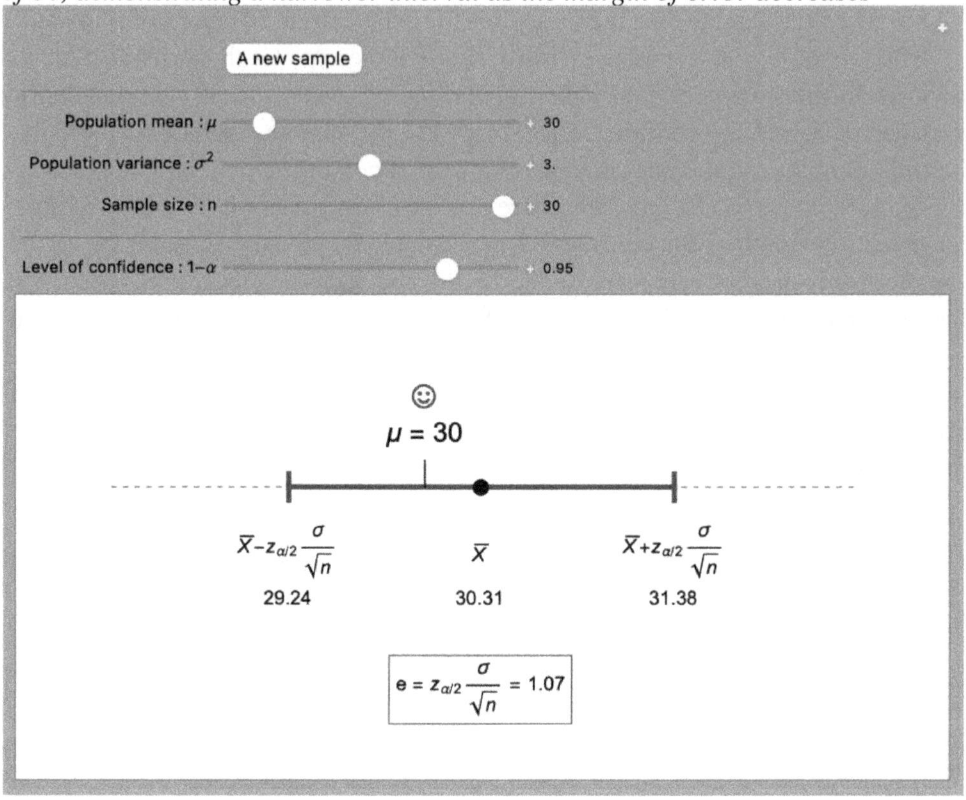

5. FINDINGS

At the end of the lesson, students were asked to reflect on how well they understood the concepts covered. The majority reported that they had achieved a good level of understanding. To further evaluate their conceptual grasp, several follow-up questions were posed, including: "*What is a confidence interval?*", "*What is a confidence level?*", "*What does coverage rate mean?*", and "*Why is sample size important?*"

Students were encouraged to respond by integrating what they had observed through the interactive applet and the explanations they had received from the AI tool. Their responses demonstrated that they were generally able to articulate clear and accurate definitions of these key statistical concepts.

A particularly noteworthy outcome was that students appeared to develop a solid understanding of the distinction between the confidence level and the coverage rate. They recognized that while the confidence level represents an abstract probability statement, the coverage rate gains meaning only through repeated sampling. This distinction, which often causes confusion in traditional instruction, was clearly grasped by most students after the interactive and AI-supported learning experience.

Furthermore, when asked about the importance of sample size, students correctly reasoned that, holding all other variables constant, increasing the sample size reduces the sampling error and consequently narrows the width of the confidence interval. This understanding indicated that students could link conceptual knowledge with visual and computational evidence derived from both the applet and AI-based explanations.

Overall, the feedback and student responses suggest that the integration of interactive tools and AI-supported questioning contributed positively to conceptual clarity and engagement in learning about confidence intervals.

6. DISCUSSION

The main purpose of this chapter is to emphasize the importance of using artificial intelligence (AI) consciously and pedagogically in statistics education. Especially for abstract and conceptually challenging topics such as the *confidence interval.,* students' interaction with AI can make the learning process more profound. When students ask AI the right questions, they not only acquire information but also test their own understanding, recognize their misconceptions, and reorganize their conceptual frameworks. Therefore, interaction with AI can be regarded as a learning tool that stimulates both cognitive and metacognitive processes (Zawacki-Richter et al., 2019).

However, in this process, *how* a question is asked, that is, the quality of the *prompt*, directly determines the quality of learning outcomes. When students fail to formulate appropriate questions for AI, or in other words, when they do not use effective prompts, the responses obtained from the system may be superficial., incomplete, or conceptually inaccurate. This, in turn, may reinforce common misconceptions in statistics, such as confusing confidence intervals with probabilities (Bender et al., 2021). Therefore, in order for AI interaction to be educationally effective, formulating accurate, clear, and context-appropriate prompts is a critical skill.

Maximizing the benefits of AI thus requires more than technological familiarity; it demands critical thinking and digital literacy. The process of prompt formulation enables students to identify what they know about a topic, what they wish to understand, and what kind of explanation they expect. In this sense, writing an effective prompt is not simply about asking for information but about constructing a learning goal. This self-questioning process enhances cognitive depth and fosters self-regulation skills (Chin & Osborne, 2008).

The comparison between ineffective and effective prompts in this chapter illustrates that AI can function not as a passive source of information but as an interactive learning partner. Nevertheless, teacher guidance remains central. Instructors need both technological pedagogical content knowledge (TPACK) and AI literacy (Bozkurt et al., 2021) to ensure that AI integration strengthens conceptual reasoning rather than replacing it.

In addition to its pedagogical implications, the approach outlined here also carries practical relevance for educational leaders and programme coordinators. In this respect, a number of actionable implications may be identified. At the curricular level, departments can articulate explicit AI-literacy outcomes within statistics and research-methods courses, including prompt formulation, verification of outputs, and ethical awareness. At the level of instructor support, institutions can provide structured professional development that helps instructors integrate generative AI and interactive tools into instructional design in pedagogically coherent ways. At the level of assessment and institutional policy, evaluation practices should emphasize conceptual interpretation and critical reasoning rather than procedural reproduction. In parallel, institutions should establish clear guidelines for responsible AI use, including transparency, academic integrity, and data privacy. When such structural alignment is achieved, generative AI is more likely to function as a scaffold for statistical reasoning and uncertainty thinking rather than as an unexamined authority.

Taken together, these findings suggest that integrating AI into statistics education should be understood not as a technological addition but as a strategic redesign of instructional practice. Learning to ask precise and critical questions strengthens students' statistical reasoning and their capacity to navigate uncertainty responsibly in digital environments. In this respect, the chapter contributes a practical model for combining interactive visualization and AI-supported inquiry in the teaching of confidence intervals.

The present work also opens several avenues for future research. Further studies may investigate how prompt formulation skills develop across educational levels, how AI-supported inquiry interacts with different instructional models (e.g., collaborative or project-based learning), and how the quality of students' prompts relates to measurable learning outcomes. Empirical comparisons between traditional instruction and AI-supported interactive approaches would provide stronger evidence regarding effectiveness. Additionally, future research should explore how AI literacy relates to ethical sensitivity and data-awareness competencies in quantitative education.

Ultimately, ensuring the effective and responsible integration of AI requires a coherent learning ecosystem. Educators must guide students not only in using AI tools but in questioning them critically. Institutions, in turn, must support this transformation through policy frameworks, professional development, and curriculum alignment. In this way, AI can serve not as a shortcut to answers, but as a catalyst for deeper statistical understanding and reflective inquiry.

REFERENCES

Altınpulluk, H., & Alptekin, G. (2025). AI Literacy in Distance Learning: Analyzing Graduate Students' Competencies Across Key Variables. In *Proceedings of the World Conference on Education and Teaching* (Vol. 4, No. 1, pp. 48-60). DOI: 10.33422/etconf.v4i1.1058

Amlasri, F. (2022). Simulations to teach science subjects: Connections among students; engagement, self-confidence, satisfaction, and learning styles. *Education and Information Technologies*, *27*(5), 7161–7181. DOI: 10.1007/s10639-022-10940-w PMID: 35153535

Baker, T., Smith, L., & Anissa, N. (2019). Educ-AI-tion rebooted? Exploring the future of artificial intelligence in schools and colleges.

Bender, E. M., Gebru, T., McMillan-Major, A., & Shmitchell, S. (2021). On the dangers of stochastic parrots: Can language models be too big? *Proceedings of the 2021 ACM Conference on Fairness, Accountability, and Transparency (FAccT '21)*, 610–623. DOI: 10.1145/3442188.3445922

Blikstein, P., & Worsley, M. (2016). Multimodal learning analytics and education data mining: Using computational technologies to measure complex learning tasks. *Journal of Learning Analytics*, *3*(2), 220–238. DOI: 10.18608/jla.2016.32.11

Bozkurt, A., Karadeniz, A., Baneres, D., Guerrero-Roldán, A. E., & Rodríguez, M. E. (2021). Artificial intelligence and reflections from educational landscape: A review of AI studies in half a century. *Sustainability (Basel)*, *13*(2), 800. DOI: 10.3390/su13020800

Brynjolfsson, E., & McAfee, A. (2017). *Machine, platform, crowd: Harnessing our digital future*. W. W. Norton & Company.

Buolamwini, J., & Gebru, T. (2018, January). Gender shades: Intersectional accuracy disparities in commercial gender classification. In *Conference on fairness, accountability and transparency* (pp. 77-91). PMLR.

Caliskan, A., Bryson, J. J., & Narayanan, A. (2017). Semantics derived automatically from language corpora contain human-like biases. *Science*, *356*(6334), 183–186. DOI: 10.1126/science.aal4230 PMID: 28408601

Chen, B. (2025). Beyond tools: Generative AI as epistemic infrastructure in education. *arXiv preprint arXiv:2504.06928*.

Chin, C., & Osborne, J. (2008). Students' questions: A potential resource for teaching and learning science. *Studies in Science Education*, *44*(1), 1–39. DOI: 10.1080/03057260701828101

Clements, D. H., & McMillen, S. (1996). Rethinking "concrete" manipulatives. *Teaching Children Mathematics*, *2*(5), 270–279. DOI: 10.5951/TCM.2.5.0270

Crawford, K. (2021). *The atlas of AI: Power, politics, and the planetary costs of artificial intelligence*. Yale University Press.

Cukurova, M. (2025). The interplay of learning, analytics and artificial intelligence in education: A vision for hybrid intelligence. *British Journal of Educational Technology*, *56*(2), 469–488. DOI: 10.1111/bjet.13514

Dignum, V. (2019). *Responsible Artificial Intelligence: Developing and Using AI in a Responsible Way*. Springer. DOI: 10.1007/978-3-030-30371-6

Dorward, J., & Heal, R. (1999). National library of virtual manipulatives for elementary and middle level mathematics. In *WebNet World Conference on the WWW and Internet* (pp. 1510-1511). Association for the Advancement of Computing in Education (AACE).

Floridi, L., & Chiriatti, M. (2020). GPT-3: Its nature, scope, limits, and consequences. *Minds and Machines*, *30*(4), 681–694. DOI: 10.1007/s11023-020-09548-1

Floridi, L., & Cowls, J. (2021). *The Ethics of Artificial Intelligence: Principles, Challenges, and Opportunities*. Oxford University Press.

Freire, P. (1970). Pedagogy of the oppressed (MB Ramos, Trans.). *New York: Continuum, 2007.*

Garfield, J., & Ben-Zvi, D. (2008). *Developing Students' Statistical Reasoning: Connecting Research and Teaching Practice*. Springer Science & Business Media.

Gigerenzer, G. (2004). Mindless statistics. *Journal of Socio-Economics*, *33*(5), 587–606. DOI: 10.1016/j.socec.2004.09.033

Gigerenzer, G. (2010). *Rationality for Mortals: How People Cope with Uncertainty*. Oxford University Press.

Gilster, P. (1997). *Digital literacy*. Wiley Computer Pub.

Guo, L. (2022). Using metacognitive prompts to enhance self-regulated learning and learning outcomes: A meta-analysis of experimental studies in computer-based learning environments. *Journal of Computer Assisted Learning*, *38*(3), 811–832. DOI: 10.1111/jcal.12650

Haenlein, M., & Kaplan, A. (2019). A brief history of artificial intelligence: On the past, present, and future of artificial intelligence. *California Management Review*, *61*(4), 5–14. DOI: 10.1177/0008125619864925

Haugsbaken, H., & Hagelia, M. (2024). A New AI Literacy For The Algorithmic Age: Prompt Engineering Or Eductional Promptization? In *2024 4th International Conference on Applied Artificial Intelligence (ICAPAI)* (pp. 1-8). IEEE.

Henrickson, L., & Meroño-Peñuela, A. (2025). Prompting meaning: A hermeneutic approach to optimising prompt engineering with ChatGPT. *AI & Society*, *40*(2), 903–918. DOI: 10.1007/s00146-023-01752-8

Holmes, W. (2021). *Artificial intelligence in education: Promises and implications for teaching and learning*. Center for Curriculum Redesign.

Holmes, W., & Porayska-Pomsta, K. (2023). The ethics of artificial intelligence in education. *Lontoo: Routledge*, 621-653.

ISO/IEC. (2022). *ISO/IEC 22989:2022—Information technology—Artificial intelligence—Artificial intelligence concepts and terminology*. International Organization for Standardization.

Janssen, M., Hartog, M., Matheus, R., Yi Ding, A., & Kuk, G. (2022). Will algorithms blind people? The effect of explainable AI and decision-makers' experience on AI-supported decision-making in government. *Social Science Computer Review*, *40*(2), 478–493. DOI: 10.1177/0894439320980118

Jordan, M. I., & Mitchell, T. M. (2015). Machine learning: Trends, perspectives, and prospects. *Science*, *349*(6245), 255–260. DOI: 10.1126/science.aaa8415 PMID: 26185243

Kasneci, E., Seßler, K., Küchemann, S., Bannert, M., Dementieva, D., Fischer, F., Gasser, U., Groh, G., Günnemann, S., Hüllermeier, E., Krusche, S., Kutyniok, G., Michaeli, T., Nerdel, C., Pfeffer, J., Poquet, O., Sailer, M., Schmidt, A., Seidel, T., & Kasneci, G. (2023). ChatGPT for good? On opportunities and challenges of large language models for education. *Learning and Individual Differences*, *103*, 102274. DOI: 10.1016/j.lindif.2023.102274

Lim, T., Gottipati, S., & Cheong, M. (2025). What students really think: Unpacking AI ethics in educational assessments through a triadic framework. *International Journal of Educational Technology in Higher Education*, *22*(1), 56. DOI: 10.1186/s41239-025-00556-8

Lin, T., Zhang, J., & Xiong, B. (2025). Effects of Technology Perceptions, Teacher Beliefs, and AI Literacy on AI Technology Adoption in Sustainable Mathematics Education. *Sustainability (Basel)*, *17*(8), 3698. DOI: 10.3390/su17083698

Long, D., & Magerko, B. (2020). What is AI literacy? Competencies and design considerations. *Proceedings of the 2020 CHI Conference on Human Factors in Computing Systems (CHI '20)*, 1–16. DOI: 10.1145/3313831.3376727

Luckin, R. (2018). *Machine Learning and Human Intelligence. The future of education for the 21st century*. UCL institute of education press.

Luckin, R., Holmes, W., Griffiths, M., & Forcier, L. B. (2016). *Intelligence Unleashed: An Argument for AI in Education*. Pearson Education.

Marcus, G., & Davis, E. (2019). *Rebooting AI: Building artificial intelligence we can trust*. Vintage.

Mata, L. (Ed.). (2022). *Ethical Use of Information Technology in Higher Education*. DOI: 10.1007/978-981-16-1951-9

McCarthy, J., Minsky, M. L., & ML, N. (1956). Rochester, and CE Shannon (1955). *Proposal for the 1956 Dartmouth Summer Research Project on Artificial Intelligence*.

Moyer, P. S., Bolyard, J. J., & Spikell, M. A. (2002). What are virtual manipulatives? *Teaching Children Mathematics*, *8*(6), 372–377. DOI: 10.5951/TCM.8.6.0372

Moyer-Packenham, P. S., & Westenskow, A. (2013). Effects of virtual manipulatives on student achievement and mathematics learning. [IJVPLE]. *International Journal of Virtual and Personal Learning Environments*, *4*(3), 35–50. DOI: 10.4018/jvple.2013070103

Ng, D. T. K., Leung, J. K. L., Chu, K. W. S., & Qiao, M. S. (2021). AI literacy: Definition, teaching, evaluation and ethical issues. *Proceedings of the Association for Information Science and Technology*, *58*(1), 504–509. DOI: 10.1002/pra2.487

Nickerson, R. S. (2000). Null hypothesis significance testing: A review of an old and continuing controversy. *Psychological Methods*, *5*(2), 241–301. DOI: 10.1037/1082-989X.5.2.241 PMID: 10937333

Nilsson, N. J. (2009). *The quest for artificial intelligence: A history of ideas and achievements*. Cambridge University Press. DOI: 10.1017/CBO9780511819346

OECD. (2023). *Recommendation of the Council on Artificial Intelligence* (OECD Legal Instrument OECD/LEGAL/0449). Organisation for Economic Co-operation and Development.

Reynolds, L., & McDonell, K. (2021, May). Prompt programming for large language models: Beyond the few-shot paradigm. In *Extended abstracts of the 2021 CHI conference on human factors in computing systems* (pp. 1-7).

Russell, S., & Norvig, P. (2021). *Artificial intelligence: A modern approach* (4th ed.). Pearson.

Selwyn, N. (2019). *Should Robots Replace Teachers? AI and the Future of Education*. John Wiley & Sons.

UNESCO. (2023). *Guidance for generative AI in education and research*. UNESCO.

Vashishth, T. K., Sharma, V., Sharma, K. K., Kumar, B., Panwar, R., & Chaudhary, S. (2024). AI-driven learning analytics for personalized feedback and assessment in higher education. In *Using traditional design methods to enhance AI-driven decision making* (pp. 206–230). IGI Global Scientific Publishing. DOI: 10.4018/979-8-3693-0639-0.ch009

Wild, C. J., & Pfannkuch, M. (1999). Statistical thinking in empirical enquiry. *International Statistical Review = Revue Internationale de Statistique*, *67*(3), 223–248. DOI: 10.1111/j.1751-5823.1999.tb00442.x

Williamson, B., & Eynon, R. (2020). Historical threads, missing links, and future directions in AI in education. *Learning, Media and Technology*, *45*(3), 223–235. DOI: 10.1080/17439884.2020.1798995

Winner, L. (2017). Do artifacts have politics? In *Computer ethics* (pp. 177–192). Routledge. DOI: 10.4324/9781315259697-21

Yang, S., Zhao, H., Xu, Y., Brennan, K., & Schneider, B. (2024, August). Debugging with an AI tutor: Investigating novice help-seeking behaviors and perceived learning. In *Proceedings of the 2024 ACM Conference on International Computing Education Research-Volume 1* (pp. 84-94). DOI: 10.1145/3632620.3671092

Zawacki-Richter, O., Marín, V. I., Bond, M., & Gouverneur, F. (2019). Systematic review of research on artificial intelligence applications in higher education—Where are the educators? *International Journal of Educational Technology in Higher Education*, *16*(1), 39. DOI: 10.1186/s41239-019-0171-0

Chapter 10
Machine Learning for Earthquake Detection and Characterization: A Statistical and Seismological Perspective

Aries P. Valeriano
http://orcid.org/0000-0003-4029-0666
University of Southeastern Philippines, Philippines

Victor Paul J. dela Cruz
http://orcid.org/0009-0007-8717-516X
University of Southeastern Philippines, Philippines

Roel F. Ceballos
http://orcid.org/0000-0001-8267-6482
University of Southeastern Philippines, Philippines

Fe F. Largo
http://orcid.org/0009-0004-2274-4614
University of Southeastern Philippines, Philippines

Anthony F. Capili
http://orcid.org/0000-0001-6018-1948
University of Southeastern Philippines, Philippines

John Riz V. Bagnol
http://orcid.org/0009-0004-9952-4310
Université de Technologie de Compiègne, France

ABSTRACT

Earthquake detection provides a compelling context for rethinking statistics pedagogy through the integration of classical inference and artificial intelligence (AI). Traditional techniques such as STA/LTA and matched filtering illustrate key statistical principles like signal processing and interpretability but rely on assumptions (e.g., stationary noise) and handcrafted features that limit performance in complex environments. AI-driven models, including CNNs, EQTransformer, and CRED, improve sensitivity by learning hierarchical patterns, yet introduce challenges in

DOI: 10.4018/979-8-3373-6259-5.ch010

interpretability, domain generalization, and uncertainty quantification. These issues are amplified in data-sparse settings like the Philippines. This chapter advocates an integrative pedagogical approach that combines statistical reasoning with AI, using strategies such as transfer learning and uncertainty-aware modeling to develop robust, explainable, and context-sensitive analytical skills.

1. INTRODUCTION

Earthquake detection is typically formulated as a statistical signal processing problem, wherein the observed waveform, $x(t) = s(t) + n(t)$, consists of the seismic signal $s(t)$ combined with the background noise $n(t)$. Classical methods such as short-term average (STA), long term average (LTA) and matched filtering convert waveforms into decision statistics and compare them with fixed thresholds. These methods are computationally efficient and easy to interpret (Allen, 1978; Gibbons & Ringdal, 2006). However, they assume stable noise and rely on predefined features, which limits their use in complex seismic environments (Lay & Wallace, 1995; Kanamori & Brodsky, 2004). Machine learning (ML) approaches treat earthquake detection as a data driven problem, where models learn a mapping $\hat{y} = f_\theta(x)$ from labeled waveform data $D = \{(x_i, y_i)\}_{i=1}^{N}$. Deep learning models such as convolutional neural networks, PhaseNet, and EQTransformer can learn useful features directly from raw waveforms and improve detection under noisy conditions (Perol et al., 2018; Zhu & Beroza, 2019; Mousavi et al., 2020). Recent overviews have shown the rapid growth of ML in seismology, including its applications in detection, phase picking, and cataloging (Kubo, Naoi, & Kano, 2024; Hu et al., 2025). Despite their advantages, ML models are sensitive to limited training data, labeling errors, and changes in data conditions across regions. These challenges are common in areas with few seismic records, such as the Philippines, where limited data can increase uncertainty and reduce model reliability. Unlike classical methods, ML models are often complex and harder to interpret. Explainable AI methods can help identify which parts of the input influence predictions, but full transparency remains difficult in high-risk applications (Adadi & Berrada, 2018; Arrieta et al., 2020). This chapter addresses these challenges by providing a statistical view of earthquake detection with a focus on data limited settings. Specifically, it aims to:

1. Compare classical and ML methods in handling noise, limited data, and uncertainty;
2. Examine the limits of deep learning models, including sensitivity to limited data and changing conditions across regions;

3. Assess the role of uncertainty quantification and explainable AI in improving interpretation; and
4. Discuss implications for statistics education by combining traditional inference with data driven learning.

By linking classical statistical methods with modern ML, this chapter provides guidance for applying statistical learning to important and data limited seismic problems.

2. CLASSICAL STATISTICAL METHODS IN EARTHQUAKE DETECTION

2.1 Statistical Foundations of Classical Seismic Detection

Classical earthquake detection is grounded in statistical signal detection theory, where a recorded seismic waveform is modeled as the combination of an underlying earthquake signal and background noise. This relationship is commonly expressed as $x(t) = s(t) + n(t)$, where $x(t)$ denotes the observed ground motion, $s(t)$ represents the earthquake-generated signal, and $n(t)$ represents environmental and anthropogenic noise recorded at the seismic station. This additive signal–noise assumption forms the basis of both classical detection theory and modern data-driven seismic analysis frameworks (Bergen et al., 2019; Mousavi & Beroza (2022)). Earthquake detection is typically formulated as a binary hypothesis testing problem:

$$H_0{:}x(t) = n(t), H_1{:}x(t) = s(t) + n(t)$$

In modern seismic monitoring systems, this decision problem is increasingly implemented through ML classifiers that learn mappings between waveform inputs and event/no-event outputs, effectively approximating statistical decision boundaries derived from classical detection theory (Zhu & Beroza, 2019; Bergen et al., 2019). The primary objective under this framework is to reliably distinguish weak earthquake signals from background noise. In practice, seismic noise exhibits strong temporal variability influenced by ocean microseisms, atmospheric forcing, and human activity, making strict stationarity assumptions unrealistic in operational settings. This motivates the use of adaptive and data-driven methods in seismic analysis pipelines (Bergen et al., 2019). Recent advances in earthquake seismology demonstrate that deep learning-based methods significantly improve detection performance, particularly for small-magnitude earthquakes and dense seismic networks. These models learn discriminative representations directly from waveform data, reducing reliance on manually engineered statistical features while preserving the fundamental objective of separating signal from noise (Zhu & Beroza, 2019; Mousavi et al., 2020).

2.2 STA/LTA as a Sequential Statistical Detector

The Short-Term Average/Long-Term Average (STA/LTA) method is one of the most widely used classical seismic detection algorithms in operational monitoring systems, originally developed for automated detection of transient seismic signals in continuous waveform data (Allen, 1978). It remains a standard baseline method in seismic monitoring workflows and is widely documented in observational and operational seismology literature (Withers et al., 1996; Trnkoczy, 2009). The STA/LTA method is defined through two time-dependent signal energy estimators. The short-term average is given by

$$STA\left(t\right) = \frac{1}{N_s}\sum_{i=t-N_s+1}^{t} |\ x(i)\ | \tag{1}$$

where $x(i)$ denotes the seismic waveform amplitude at discrete time index i, and N_s represents the short-time window length controlling sensitivity to transient signal changes. The long-term average is defined as

$$LTA\left(t\right) = \frac{1}{N_l}\sum_{i=t-N_l+1}^{t} |\ x(i)\ | \tag{2}$$

where $N_l \gg N_s$, ensuring that the long-term window captures background noise characteristics rather than transient seismic events. The detection statistic is defined as

$$R\left(t\right) = \frac{STA(t)}{LTA(t)} \tag{3}$$

which measures short-term deviations relative to background noise levels. An event is declared when $R(t) > \lambda$, where λ is a predefined detection threshold that controls the trade-off between sensitivity and false alarms. In this framework, the STA component captures rapid increases in signal energy associated with seismic arrivals, while the LTA component provides a reference baseline of ambient noise levels. The ratio therefore acts as a normalized detector of transient seismic events (Allen, 1978). Despite its simplicity and computational efficiency, subsequent studies have shown that STA/LTA performance depends strongly on parameter selection and noise conditions. In noisy and non-stationary environments, more advanced detection approaches such as waveform cross-correlation and template matching have been shown to improve detection sensitivity (Withers et al., 1996; Trnkoczy, 2009; Gibbons & Ringdal, 2006).

2.3 Matched Filtering and Cross-Correlation Detection

Matched filtering is a statistically optimal detection method under additive white Gaussian noise and a known signal template, achieving optimality in the Neyman–Pearson sense for signal detection problems. In earthquake seismology, it is widely used to detect weak or emergent seismic events by comparing observed waveforms with previously recorded template events (Gibbons & Ringdal, 2006). The matched filtering operation is expressed through the cross-correlation function:

$$C(\tau) = \int x(t)\, s^*(t-\tau)\, dt \tag{4}$$

where $x(t)$ denotes the observed seismic waveform, $s(t)$ represents a reference template waveform from a previously recorded earthquake, and τ is the time shift applied to align the template with the observed signal. The symbol * denotes the complex conjugate, which reverses the sign of the imaginary part of a signal; for real-valued seismic data, this operation does not change the signal. In practice, discrete-time implementations are used due to sampled waveform data. This measure quantifies waveform similarity and is widely used in template-based earthquake detection systems. Detection is performed by identifying the time shift that maximizes the correlation:

$$\hat{\tau} = \arg\max_{\tau} C(\tau) \tag{5}$$

An event is declared when the maximum correlation exceeds a predefined threshold:

$$\max_{\tau} C(\tau) > \lambda$$

where λ is a detection threshold that controls the trade-off between sensitivity and false alarms. This procedure is equivalent to a maximum likelihood decision rule under Gaussian noise assumptions, making matched filtering one of the most sensitive techniques for detecting small earthquakes embedded in noise (Gibbons & Ringdal, 2006). However, its effectiveness depends strongly on the availability and representativeness of waveform templates. Performance may degrade when observed events do not closely match existing templates, particularly in regions with incomplete seismic catalogs or evolving fault systems. This limitation motivates the use of complementary data-driven approaches for generalized detection (Mousavi

& Beroza, 2022). Recent developments in earthquake detection show that template-based methods remain highly effective for dense seismic networks and repeating earthquakes, but are often complemented by ML approaches that generalize beyond fixed template libraries (Mousavi & Beroza, 2022).

2.4 Frequency-Domain Detection Methods

Frequency-domain seismic analysis is based on the Fourier transform, which converts a time-domain seismic waveform into its frequency-domain representation:

$$X(f) = \int_{-\infty}^{\infty} x(t)\, e^{-j2\pi ft}\, dt \tag{6}$$

where $x(t)$ is the recorded seismic waveform in the time domain and $X(f)$ represents its spectral decomposition in the frequency domain. This transformation allows seismic signals to be analyzed in terms of their frequency components, which is useful for distinguishing earthquake signals from background noise with overlapping time-domain characteristics (Bergen et al., 2019; Lay & Wallace, 1995). In the frequency domain, seismic signal processing is commonly performed using a linear filtering operation defined as:

$$X_{\text{filtered}}(f) = H(f)X(f) \tag{7}$$

where $H(f)$ is the frequency response function of a linear time-invariant filter that controls the attenuation or amplification of specific frequency bands. This approach is widely used in seismic preprocessing workflows to enhance signal detectability by attenuating frequency bands dominated by noise such as microseisms and anthropogenic noise (Lay & Wallace, 1995). Frequency-domain filtering can improve signal-to-noise ratio by emphasizing frequency regions where earthquake energy is relatively stronger. However, filters with non-linear phase responses may distort waveform phase characteristics, which are critical for seismic phase identification and arrival-time estimation in earthquake detection systems (Zhu & Beroza, 2019). These limitations reflect the trade-off between noise suppression and signal preservation in frequency-domain seismic analysis, particularly for weak or low-magnitude earthquake events.

2.5 Multi-Scale and Hybrid STA/LTA Extensions

Multi-scale STA/LTA methods extend classical seismic detection by incorporating multiple temporal resolutions into a unified detection statistic. The approach generalizes the standard STA/LTA formulation by computing detection ratios across different window lengths, expressed as:

$$R_{\text{multi}}\left(t\right) = \sum_{k=1}^{K} w_k \frac{STA_k(t)}{LTA_k(t)}, \sum_{k=1}^{K} w_k = 1, \ w_k \geq 0 \tag{8}$$

where K represents the number of temporal scales, w_k denotes weighting coefficients, and $STA_k(t)$ and $LTA_k(t)$ represent short-term and long-term averages computed using scale-specific window lengths $N_s^{(k)}$ and $N_l^{(k)}$. Each scale corresponds to a different temporal resolution. Short windows increase sensitivity to abrupt energy changes associated with seismic phase arrivals, while longer windows provide more stable estimates of background noise levels. This multi-resolution behavior is consistent with established properties of STA/LTA detectors in non-stationary seismic noise environments (Withers et al., 1996; Trnkoczy, 2009). Although classical in formulation, multi-scale extensions can be interpreted as an ensemble-type aggregation of detection statistics across different temporal resolutions. This perspective aligns conceptually with modern data-driven seismic detection frameworks, where multi-resolution feature representations are used to improve robustness under low signal-to-noise conditions (Mousavi & Beroza, 2022).

2.6 Unified Interpretation of Classical Methods

Across classical seismic detection methods, a unified mathematical structure can be described in which raw waveform data $x(t)$ is transformed into a decision statistic through a mapping $T(x(t))$, followed by a classification decision:

$x(t) \rightarrow T(x(t)) \rightarrow$ decision

In this framework, $T(x(t))$ may correspond to STA/LTA ratios, cross-correlation functions, or spectral energy measures depending on the detection strategy employed. Despite methodological differences, classical earthquake detection approaches share a common pipeline consisting of feature extraction from raw seismic waveforms, transformation into scalar or low-dimensional decision statistics, and application of threshold-based classification rules (Trnkoczy, 2009). These systems are generally non-adaptive in the sense that their detection rules are predefined and rely on fixed statistical assumptions rather than being learned from data. As a result, their performance is sensitive to parameter selection and to the validity of underlying noise assumptions in the seismic environment (Withers et al., 1996). In modern seismic monitoring, classical detection pipelines are often discussed alongside data-driven approaches in which seismic waveforms are processed using machine learning models that learn representations directly from data, reducing reliance on manually engineered features (Bergen et al., 2019; Mousavi & Beroza, 2022). Despite these developments, classical methods remain widely used due to their interpretability, computational efficiency, and robustness in real-time seismic monitoring systems. Consequently, hybrid workflows combining classical statistical detectors with machine learning-based post-processing or classification components have been explored in recent seismic research to improve performance under low signal-to-noise conditions (Mousavi & Beroza, 2023).

2.7 Summary of Classical Seismic Detection Methods

Table 1 summarizes classical seismic detection approaches in terms of strengths and limitations. STA/LTA is fast, interpretable, and low-cost, but its sensitivity to non-stationary noise and thresholds can reduce reliability. Matched filtering excels at detecting weak or repeating events but depends on complete template databases and is computationally intensive. Frequency-domain methods enhance signal-to-noise ratio and provide spectral insight, though they may introduce phase distortions and reduce temporal accuracy. Multi-scale STA/LTA improves robustness under variable noise conditions but adds tuning complexity. Each method has its ideal use: STA/LTA for rapid detection under stable noise, matched filtering for weak or repeating events, frequency-domain methods for spectral analysis, and multi-scale STA/LTA for balancing sensitivity and robustness. Hybrid approaches can combine these advantages to maximize detection reliability.

Table 1. Classical Seismic Detection Methods Overview

Method	Mathematical Formulation	Statistical Interpretation	Strengths	Limitations
STA/LTA	$R(t) = \frac{STA(t)}{LTA(t)}$	Energy-ratio based change detection under noise	Real-time, interpretable, low computational cost	Sensitive to non-stationary noise and threshold selection
Matched Filtering	$C(\tau) = \int x(t)\, s^*(t - \tau)\, dt$	Optimal similarity detector under Gaussian noise assumption	Highly sensitive to weak or repeating events	Requires complete template database; computationally expensive
Frequency Filtering	$X(f) = \int_{-\infty}^{\infty} x(t)\, e^{-j2\pi ft}\, dt$, $X_{\text{filtered}}(f) = H(f)X(f)$	Spectral decomposition for signal–noise separation	Improves SNR; enables frequency-based interpretation	Phase distortion; reduced temporal resolution
Multi-scale STA/LTA	$R_{\text{multi}}(t) = \sum_{k=1}^{K} w_k \frac{STA_k(t)}{LTA_k(t)}$	Ensemble energy-ratio detector across multiple time scales	Robust under non-stationary noise	High tuning complexity

Following the tabular comparison, Figure 1 illustrates the classical seismic detection workflow as a deterministic signal-processing pipeline. Raw waveform data $x(t)$ is first subjected to preprocessing steps such as filtering and normalization to enhance signal quality and reduce noise effects. The processed signal is then transformed into detection statistics, including STA/LTA ratios, cross-correlation measures, and spectral energy representations. Finally, a threshold-based decision rule is applied to classify segments of the waveform as either seismic events or non-events.

Figure 1. Classical Seismic Detection Pipeline

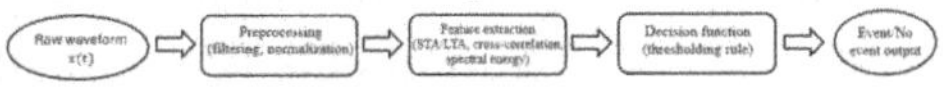

Although effective and computationally efficient, this pipeline is inherently non-adaptive because detection rules are fixed and not learned from data. This limitation motivates the development of modern ML approaches, which replace handcrafted statistical features with learned representations, improving adaptability in complex and non-stationary seismic environments.

3. ML APPROACHES FOR SEISMIC DETECTION

3.1 Deep Learning Architectures for Seismic Detection

Machine learning reframes earthquake detection as a supervised pattern recognition problem in which seismic waveforms are mapped to detection labels through flexible nonlinear functions. Given a dataset $D = \{(x_i, y_i)\}_{i=1}^{N}$, where x_i represents a seismic waveform segment and $y_i \in \{0,1\}$ denotes the absence or presence of an earthquake signal, the objective is to learn a function $f_\theta(x)$, parameterized by θ, that minimizes empirical risk. This formulation departs from classical hypothesis testing by replacing explicit probabilistic assumptions with data-driven function approximation (Goodfellow et al., 2016; Mousavi & Beroza, 2022). Early applications of deep learning in seismology demonstrated that convolutional neural networks (CNNs) can effectively extract hierarchical representations from raw waveform data (Perol et al., 2018). More recent studies have shown that deep neural architectures significantly improve detection accuracy and robustness, particularly in low signal-to-noise environments (Ross et al., 2018). A convolutional neural network layer is defined as:

$$h^{(l)} = \sigma(W^{(l)} * h^{(l1)} + b^{(l)}) \tag{9}$$

where $h^{(l)}$ denotes the feature map at layer l, $W^{(l)}$ represents convolutional filters, $*$ denotes the convolution operation, $b^{(l)}$ is a bias term, and $\sigma(\cdot)$ is a nonlinear activation function such as ReLU. The input is defined as $h^{(0)} = x(t)$, corresponding to the raw seismic waveform. In this formulation, convolutional filters learn localized time-dependent features directly from waveform data. Early layers capture simple oscillatory patterns that help distinguish noise from signal, while deeper layers encode more complex waveform characteristics such as P-wave and S-wave arrivals. This hierarchical feature learning enables CNNs to approximate nonlinear mappings between waveform inputs and detection outputs, improving performance in noisy and heterogeneous seismic environments (Perol et al., 2018; Ross et al., 2018). Deep CNN architectures further enhance performance by modeling more complex representations of seismic signals, improving sensitivity to weak events and generalization across different seismic regions and network configurations (Ross et al., 2018).

Recent advances in seismic detection incorporate attention mechanisms to model global dependencies in seismic waveforms. The Earthquake Transformer (EQTransformer) integrates convolutional layers with self-attention modules to jointly perform earthquake detection and phase picking, enabling end-to-end learning directly from raw waveform data (Mousavi et al., 2020). The attention mechanism is defined as:

$$Attention\left(Q, K, V\right) = softmax\left(\frac{QK^{\top}}{\sqrt{d_k}}\right)V \tag{10}$$

where Q(queries), K(keys), and V(values) are learned representations derived from the input, and d_k is the dimensionality of the key vectors (Vaswani et al., 2017). In seismic applications, these matrices encode relationships between different temporal segments of the waveform. This mechanism enables the model to dynamically assign weights to different portions of the signal, focusing on relevant seismic phases while suppressing noise. Unlike convolutional neural networks, which primarily capture local patterns, attention mechanisms explicitly model long-range temporal dependencies through pairwise interactions across the entire waveform. This improves detection accuracy and phase identification in complex seismic environments (Ross et al., 2018). Hybrid architectures such as the CRED model combine convolutional and recurrent neural networks to capture both spatial and temporal dependencies in seismic waveforms. The recurrent component is typically expressed as:

$$h_t = RNN\left(x_t, h_{t-1}\right) \tag{11}$$

where x_t is the input at time step t, and h_t represents the hidden state encoding temporal context. This formulation allows the model to retain information from previous waveform segments, which is particularly important for detecting long-duration or emergent seismic events. By integrating CNN-based feature extraction with recurrent temporal modeling, CRED captures both localized waveform patterns and sequential dependencies, improving detection performance in continuous seismic data streams (Mousavi et al., 2019).

3.2 Advantages Over Classical Methods

ML approaches offer substantial advantages over classical statistical detection methods. First, they replace handcrafted feature extraction with automated representation learning, enabling models to discover optimal features directly from raw waveform data (Perol et al., 2018; Mousavi et al., 2019). This eliminates the need for manually tuned descriptors such as STA/LTA ratios or spectral thresholds. Second, deep learning models significantly improve detection sensitivity, particularly for low-magnitude events embedded in noise. Empirical studies demonstrate that convolutional and similarity-based methods outperform traditional detectors under low signal-to-noise ratio conditions (Yoon et al., 2015; Perol et al., 2018; Ross et al., 2018). Third, these models scale effectively to modern real-time seismic workflows by learning complex waveform representations and enabling integrated tasks such as detection and phase picking within unified frameworks (Zhu & Beroza, 2019;

Mousavi & Beroza, 2022). Finally, ML models adapt to complex and non-stationary noise environments by implicitly learning noise characteristics from data, in contrast to classical approaches that rely on fixed assumptions of stationarity and often degrade under varying noise conditions (Mousavi et al., 2019; Mousavi & Beroza, 2023).

3.3 Statistical and Methodological Limitations

Despite their strong empirical performance, ML models introduce important statistical challenges. A key limitation is dependence on labeled datasets, typically represented as $D = \{(x_i, y_i)\}_{i=1}^{N}$. These labels are often generated through expert interpretation or legacy algorithms, which may introduce systematic biases. As a result, models can inherit annotation bias, leading to overly optimistic performance estimates (Mousavi & Beroza, 2022). Another major issue is domain shift, where the joint distribution of training data differs from deployment conditions, $P_{train}(X, Y) \neq P_{test}(X, Y)$. Seismic signals vary across geographic regions due to differences in geology, instrumentation, and noise environments. Consequently, models trained in one region may not generalize well to another, revealing limitations in model transferability (Mousavi & Beroza, 2023). Additionally, most deep learning models produce deterministic predictions, $\hat{y} = f_\theta(x)$, without calibrated uncertainty estimates. This limits their applicability in hazard-sensitive systems, where confidence quantification is critical. Methods such as deep ensembles provide practical approaches for improving predictive uncertainty estimation in such settings (Lakshminarayanan et al., 2017). Interpretability also remains a challenge. Unlike classical methods with clear statistical meaning, deep models operate as complex nonlinear systems. Techniques such as Grad-CAM provide partial insights into model behavior, but do not fully resolve the black-box nature of these models (Selvaraju et al., 2017; Adadi & Berrada, 2018; Jobin et al., 2019). Finally, improved predictive accuracy does not guarantee reliability under distributional uncertainty, particularly in safety-critical applications such as earthquake monitoring. This underscores the need for robust validation and uncertainty-aware modeling frameworks (Mousavi & Beroza, 2022).

3.4 Synthesis: Statistical Perspective of ML in Seismology

From a statistical perspective, ML fundamentally transforms seismic detection by replacing explicit hypothesis testing with empirical risk minimization. Classical methods rely on predefined statistical models and threshold-based decisions, whereas ML approaches learn flexible decision boundaries directly from data. This transformation can be summarized as

$$x(t) \rightarrow f_\theta(x) \rightarrow \hat{y}$$

where f_θ represents a learned nonlinear mapping. While this approach improves predictive performance, it introduces trade-offs in interpretability, calibration, and robustness. Consequently, classical statistical principles remain essential for understanding and evaluating ML-based seismic detection systems (Kanamori & Brodsky, 2004; Lay & Wallace, 1995; Mousavi & Beroza, 2022).

3.5 Summary of ML-Based Seismic Detection Methods

Table 2 summarizes key ML models for seismic detection, presenting their mathematical formulation, strengths, and limitations. Convolutional neural networks (CNNs) excel at hierarchical feature extraction and are robust to noise but require large labeled datasets. EQTransformer models capture global dependencies using attention mechanisms, enabling the integration of long-range context, though they are computationally intensive. Temporal sequence models such as CRED leverage recurrent architectures to model waveform dynamics over time, but training complexity can be high. PhaseNet provides CNN-based probabilistic phase picking, achieving accurate arrival detection, though its performance can degrade under domain shifts. Each model offers distinct advantages: CNNs are effective for local feature learning, EQTransformer for global context, CRED for temporal dependencies, and PhaseNet for precise phase picking. The choice of model depends on dataset size, computational resources, and the specific detection or phase-picking task, and hybrid approaches may combine these strengths to achieve more robust and generalizable performance.

Table 2. ML-Based Seismic Detection Methods

Model	Mathematical Basis	Strengths	Limitations
CNN	$h^{(l)} = \sigma(W^{(l)} * h^{(l-1)} + b^{(l)})$	Hierarchical feature learning, robust to noise	Requires large labeled data
EQTransformer	$softmax\left(\frac{QK^{T}}{\sqrt{d_k}}\right)V$	Captures global dependencies	Computationally intensive
CRED	$h_t = RNN(x_t, h_{t-1})$	Models temporal sequences	Training complexity
PhaseNet	CNN-based probabilistic phase picking	Accurate arrival detection	Sensitive to domain shift

Figure 2 illustrates the corresponding ML detection pipeline. Raw waveform data $x(t)$is first preprocessed through normalization and segmentation, and then input into a neural network model $f_\theta(x)$. Within this model, feature learning and representation extraction are performed automatically through convolutional, recurrent, or attention-based architectures, depending on the specific network design. The model produces predictive outputs $\hat{y}$, which typically represent probabilities or confidence scores for event detection or phase picking.

Figure 2. ML-Based Seismic Detection Pipeline

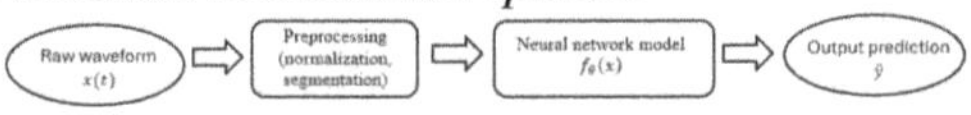

In many applications, $\hat{y}$ directly serves as the final prediction. When probabilistic outputs are used, a decision rule (e.g., thresholding) may be applied to convert $\hat{y}$into discrete event or no-event classifications. This pipeline mirrors classical seismic detection workflows but replaces handcrafted feature extraction with learned, data-driven representations embedded within the model. Its effectiveness depends strongly on high-quality and representative training data and highlights the importance of domain adaptation, uncertainty quantification, and statistical validation in real-world deployment (Perol et al., 2018; Zhu & Beroza, 2019; Mousavi & Beroza, 2022).

4. SEISMIC DETECTION IN DATA-SPARSE ENVIRONMENTS

4.1 Methodological Implications in Sparse Data

Earthquake detection in data-sparse environments introduces additional statistical and methodological challenges that significantly affect both classical and machine learning (ML) approaches. In regions such as the Philippines, seismic monitoring systems are often characterized by limited station density, heterogeneous sensor quality, irregular data availability, and scarcity of labeled waveform datasets.

In classical seismic detection, sparse or discontinuous data primarily affects the stability of background noise statistics. For example, the STA/LTA detector relies on a stable estimation of long-term background noise levels; when data coverage is limited or irregular, the long-term average becomes unstable, increasing false triggers and missed detections (Allen, 1978; Gibbons & Ringdal, 2006).

In contrast, ML and deep learning models trained on large labeled seismic datasets have demonstrated substantial improvements over classical algorithms in event detection and phase-picking tasks (Perol et al., 2018; Ross et al., 2018; Zhu & Beroza, 2019). However, these models require extensive labeled data for effective training, such as those provided by datasets like the Stanford Earthquake Dataset (STEAD), and their performance degrades when trained on limited, unevenly distributed, or regionally biased records (Yoon et al., 2015; Mousavi & Beroza, 2022).

When training data are limited relative to model complexity in sparse observational settings, the empirical risk minimization (ERM) objective is still well-defined but exhibits increased variance and reduced generalization performance. This is expressed as:

$$\hat{\theta} = \arg\min_{\theta} \frac{1}{N} \sum_{i=1}^{N} l(f_{\theta}\left(x_i\right), y_i) \tag{12}$$

In such regimes, small sample sizes Nrelative to model capacity can lead to unstable parameter estimates and degraded performance on unseen data. Broader studies in seismic machine learning further show that sparse, heterogeneous, or unevenly labeled datasets can significantly limit model robustness, predictive generalization, and uncertainty quantification across regions (Mousavi & Beroza, 2022; Kubo et al., 2024).

4.2 Algorithmic Strategies for Sparse Data

To address challenges in sparse seismic data environments, several algorithmic strategies have been proposed in recent literature:

i. Transfer Learning Framework - A model pretrained on a large external dataset is adapted to a target region with limited labeled data. This is typically implemented through a joint optimization of source and target losses, expressed as:

$$\hat{\theta} = \arg\min_{\theta} \left[\sum_{(x_i, y_i) \in D_{source}} l\left(f_{\theta}\left(x_i\right), y_i\right) + \lambda \sum_{(x_j, y_j) \in D_{target}} l\left(f_{\theta}\left(x_j\right), y_j\right) \right] \tag{13}$$

Here, D_{source} represents a large external dataset, D_{target} denotes the limited local dataset, and λ controls the contribution of target-domain adaptation. Transfer learning has been shown to improve detection performance in regions with scarce labeled seismic data (Zhu et al., 2023).

ii. Data Augmentation – This approach increases the effective sample size by generating perturbed or synthetic waveforms:

$$x_i' = x_i + \epsilon_i \tag{14}$$

where ϵ_i represents noise perturbations or simulated seismic signal variations. This strategy exposes models to diverse signal conditions and improves robustness to noise and waveform variability (Mousavi & Beroza, 2022).

iii. Semi-Supervised Learning – This approach incorporates both labeled and unlabeled data to enhance model training:

$$L = L_{supervised} + \gamma L_{unsupervised} \tag{15}$$

where γ controls the contribution of the unsupervised component. This approach is particularly useful in seismic settings where labeled data are limited and costly to obtain (Mousavi & Beroza, 2022).

iv. Uncertainty-Aware Learning - Predictive uncertainty estimation is critical in sparse-data regimes. Deep ensembles approximate predictive distributions by averaging outputs from multiple independently trained models:

$$p\left(y \mid x\right) \approx \frac{1}{M}\sum_{m=1}^{M} p(y \mid x, \theta_m\Big) \tag{16}$$

where M is the number of models. This approach improves reliability and robustness under limited or heterogeneous data conditions (Lakshminarayanan et al., 2017).

4.3 Summary of Seismic Detection in Data-Sparse Environments

Table 3 summarizes key strategies for improving seismic detection in data-sparse environments such as the Philippines, where limited training data can lead to unstable parameter estimates and reduced generalization. Transfer learning leverages large external datasets to reduce variance and improve performance but can introduce bias if source and target distributions differ. Data augmentation increases the effective sample size and robustness to noise, though unrealistic synthetic signals may mislead the model. Semi-supervised learning exploits abundant unlabeled data, making it useful when labeling is costly, but performance depends on pseudo-label quality. Deep ensembles provide reliable uncertainty estimates, enhancing prediction confidence, though at higher computational cost. No single method is sufficient on its own; combining these strategies in hybrid approaches often achieves the best balance of robustness, generalization, and uncertainty for seismic detection in sparse-data settings.

Table 3. Seismic Detection Strategies in Data-Sparse Environments

Approach	Mathematical Basis	Strengths	Limitations
Transfer Learning	Weighted empirical risk minimization	Leverages global datasets	Domain mismatch risk
Data Augmentation	$x_i' = x_i + \epsilon_i$	Increases effective sample size	May introduce unrealistic signals
Semi-Supervised Learning	Combined loss function	Uses unlabeled data	Sensitive to pseudo-label quality
Deep Ensembles	Model averaging	Provides uncertainty estimates	Computational cost

Figure 3 illustrates a conceptual pipeline for seismic detection in sparse-data environments. Raw waveform data $x(t)$are first processed using a pretrained feature extractor, which embeds prior knowledge from large-scale seismic datasets. A fine-tuning stage then adapts the model to local seismic conditions, addressing domain shifts between global and regional data. The final output includes both the predicted output and an uncertainty estimate, enabling more informed decision-making under limited data conditions. This pipeline emphasizes adaptation, robustness, and uncertainty-aware prediction rather than purely deterministic outputs.

Figure 3. Sparse-Data Seismic Detection Pipeline

5. STATISTICAL COMPARISON OF CLASSICAL AND ML METHODS

5.1 Interpretability

A fundamental distinction between classical and ML approaches to earthquake detection lies in interpretability. Classical methods such as STA/LTA and matched filtering rely on explicitly defined decision statistics, where the mapping from the seismic waveform $x(t)$to a detection outcome is transparent and analytically tractable (Gibbons & Ringdal, 2006). These quantities correspond directly to physical signal properties, particularly abrupt amplitude changes associated with seismic phase arrivals, making such methods interpretable and physically grounded. In contrast, ML-based detectors define a nonlinear mapping $\hat{y} = f_\theta(x(t))$,

where $x(t)$ is the input waveform, $\hat{y}$ is the predicted output (e.g., event probability), $f_\theta(\cdot)$ is a neural network, and θ denotes its parameters. Deep learning models such as PhaseNet, CRED, and EQTransformer learn hierarchical representations directly from waveform data and achieve high detection and phase-picking performance. PhaseNet demonstrates accurate probabilistic phase picking (Zhu & Beroza, 2019). CRED captures temporal dependencies in seismic signals (Mousavi et al., 2019). EQTransformer uses attention mechanisms to model long-range dependencies and jointly perform detection and phase picking (Mousavi et al., 2020). Despite their performance advantages, these models distribute information across many parameters, making direct physical interpretability difficult. This limitation becomes more pronounced in data-sparse environments, where small training datasets can lead to unstable feature learning and reduced generalization (Mousavi & Beroza, 2022; Mousavi & Beroza, 2023). To improve understanding of model behavior, explainable AI methods are used. SHAP values quantify the contribution of each input feature to the model output, defined as

$$\phi_i = \sum_{S \subseteq F \setminus \{i\}} \frac{|S|!(|F| - |S| - 1)!}{|F|!} [f(S \cup \{i\}) - f(S)], \tag{17}$$

where ϕ_i represents the contribution of feature i, F is the set of all features, and S is a subset excluding i (Lundberg & Lee, 2017). Gradient-based attribution methods estimate feature importance by computing

$$\frac{\partial f_\theta(x)}{\partial x},$$

which measures the sensitivity of model outputs to input perturbations (Selvaraju et al., 2017). Attention mechanisms assign normalized weights

$$\alpha_i = \frac{\exp(e_i)}{\sum_j \exp(e_j)} \tag{18}$$

where α_i represents the importance weight of the i-th time segment. These weights provide insight into which portions of the waveform influence model predictions (Vaswani et al., 2017). Although these approaches often identify regions corresponding to P- and S-wave arrivals, they remain associative rather than causal, describing model behavior without revealing underlying physical mechanisms (Adadi & Berrada, 2018). Their reliability may also degrade under distributional changes, such as heterogeneous network conditions or limited data, because the explanations themselves can shift when the data distribution differs from training conditions (Mousavi & Beroza, 2022; Mousavi & Beroza, 2023). Consequently, interpretability remains an active area of research in ML-based seismic detection.

5.2 Uncertainty Quantification

Uncertainty plays a central role in earthquake detection because misclassification can have serious consequences. Classical detectors encode uncertainty implicitly through threshold-based decision rules such as $R(t) > \lambda$. In this setting, uncertainty is not modeled probabilistically but is instead managed through parameter tuning. In machine learning frameworks, uncertainty is modeled explicitly using predictive distributions

$$p(y \mid x, D) = \int p(y \mid x, \theta)\, p(\theta \mid D)\, d\theta, \tag{19}$$

where y is the label, x is the waveform input, D is the dataset, and θ represents model parameters. This formulation follows Bayesian principles but is generally intractable for deep neural networks, requiring approximation methods. Monte Carlo (MC) dropout approximates Bayesian inference by performing stochastic forward passes at inference time, producing the estimate

$$\hat{y} = \frac{1}{T}\sum_{t=1}^{T} f_{\theta_t}\left(x\right), \tag{20}$$

where T is the number of stochastic passes and θ_t denotes sampled network parameters induced by dropout (Gal & Ghahramani, 2016). Deep ensembles provide another approximation by averaging predictions from independently trained models, as in Equation 16. This approach captures variability across models and provides both mean predictions and uncertainty estimates, particularly for epistemic uncertainty. Recent studies in seismology show that uncertainty-aware models maintain strong predictive performance while producing meaningful confidence estimates. For example, Bayesian and dropout-based convolutional neural networks assign higher uncertainty to misclassified or out-of-distribution seismic signals, allowing low-confidence predictions to be identified or rejected (Zhang et al., 2025). These approaches improve robustness in tasks such as phase detection and source localization, especially under low signal-to-noise conditions. Epistemic uncertainty, arising from limited data and incomplete model knowledge, is particularly significant in data-sparse environments. This motivates the use of Bayesian and ensemble-based methods to improve reliability. Explicit uncertainty modeling provides a more principled measure of confidence than threshold-based rules alone, especially when data limitations affect generalization.

5.3 Generalization and Domain Shift

A key limitation of machine learning–based seismic detection is sensitivity to domain shift, formally expressed as:

$$P_{\text{train}}(X,Y) \neq P_{\text{test}}(X,Y) \tag{21}$$

where P_{train} and P_{test} denote the joint distributions of the training and deployment (test) data, and X and Y represent the input features and corresponding labels, respectively. This discrepancy violates the assumption that training and deployment data are independently and identically distributed (i.i.d.) from the same underlying distribution, often resulting in degraded model performance when applied to out-of-distribution data. This motivates the use of domain adaptation and transfer learning techniques designed to reduce distributional discrepancies between source and target domains (Gholamzadeh Khoee et al., 2024).

In seismic applications, domain shift can arise from differences in geological structures, sensor types, acquisition settings, and ambient noise conditions. Studies have shown that models trained in one region often exhibit reduced performance when deployed in another without adaptation. To address this, transfer learning approaches have been applied to improve ground motion prediction and seismic intensity estimation in regions with limited labeled data (Jozinović et al., 2022; Zhu et al., 2023). This issue is particularly pronounced in low-resource seismic regions, where training datasets may not adequately represent the variability of real-world seismic signals. Empirical findings in earthquake engineering and structural analysis further confirm that machine learning models trained on specific datasets often fail to generalize across different spatial or environmental conditions (Hu et al., 2025). In contrast, classical seismic analysis methods rely more on physically interpretable features and established geophysical principles rather than purely learned representations. This reliance on domain knowledge can provide more stable and consistent performance across varying conditions, although often at the cost of reduced adaptability compared to data-driven approaches (Lay & Wallace, 1995).

5.4 Decision-Theoretic Perspective

Earthquake detection can be formulated as a statistical decision problem where the optimal action $a \in \{0,1\}$ (e.g., signal or no signal) minimizes the expected cost given observed data x:

$$a^*(x) = \arg\min_{a\in\{0,1\}} \mathbb{E}_{y|x}\left[C(a,y)\right] \tag{22}$$

where y denotes the true state and $C(a, y)$ is a cost function that quantifies the penalty of choosing action $a$when the true state is y. This formulation corresponds to the Bayesian decision rule, which minimizes posterior expected risk. Classical seismic detection methods can be interpreted as approximate implementations of this framework. In particular, decision thresholds applied to signal statistics (e.g., STA/LTA ratios or waveform correlation measures) act as proxies for likelihood-ratio–based or signal-to-noise–driven decision rules derived under assumed or simplified models of noise distributions and stationarity. Although not always explicitly formulated in Bayesian terms, these methods implicitly encode assumptions about signal and noise behavior as well as detection costs. Modern machine learning approaches instead learn decision functions by minimizing empirical risk over labeled datasets, which serves as a sample-based approximation of the expected cost under the training distribution. This enables models to learn complex nonlinear decision boundaries directly from data rather than relying on handcrafted detection statistics. While machine learning models can approximate near-optimal decision rules when sufficient and representative training data are available, their performance may degrade in data-sparse or non-stationary environments. In such cases, limited labeled examples and distributional shifts can lead to unreliable probability estimates, increased uncertainty, and suboptimal decision-making (Gamboa-Chacón et al., 2025). In the broader deep learning literature, it is well recognized that poorly calibrated models may produce overconfident predictions under uncertainty or dataset shift (Gawlikowski et al., 2023).

This decision-theoretic perspective aligns with classical detection theory in seismology, which relies on assumed or explicit statistical models of noise processes and signal characteristics to derive robust decision rules under simplified or stationary conditions. Such formulations provide stable performance without requiring large labeled datasets, making them particularly effective in traditional seismic monitoring systems (Kanamori & Brodsky, 2004)

5.5 Statistical Comparison of Classical and ML Methods Summary

Table 4 summarizes the key statistical differences between classical and machine learning (ML) approaches for earthquake detection, particularly in data-sparse environments. Classical methods such as STA/LTA and matched filtering are highly interpretable and physically grounded, offering robust performance across different regions. In these approaches, uncertainty is handled implicitly through thresholding rules derived from assumed signal-to-noise characteristics and statistical properties of seismic noise. Machine learning methods, in contrast, learn nonlinear decision boundaries directly from data and provide explicit or approximate uncertainty estimates using methods such as Bayesian neural networks, Monte Carlo dropout, and deep ensembles. While this enables flexible modeling and richer probabilistic outputs, interpretability is generally lower and often requires post-hoc explainability techniques such as SHAP or attention-based visualization methods. Machine learning performance is also sensitive to domain shifts and limited training data, making calibration and validation essential for reliable deployment in heterogeneous seismic environments.

This comparison reflects a trade-off between interpretability and flexibility. Classical approaches are transparent, robust, and data-efficient, whereas machine learning approaches offer adaptive modeling and uncertainty quantification but require additional mechanisms to ensure reliability under changing conditions.

Table 4. Statistical Comparison of Classical and ML Methods

Aspect	Classical Methods	ML Methods
Interpretability	High (transparent STA/LTA or matched filtering)	Low (requires XAI such as SHAP, attention)
Uncertainty	Implicit (threshold-based)	Explicit (Bayesian inference, MC dropout, deep ensembles)
Generalization	Physically grounded, robust across regions	Data-dependent, sensitive to domain shift
Decision Rule	Fixed threshold	Learned nonlinear boundary, may degrade in sparse data

6. UNCERTAINTY AND EXPLAINABLE AI IN SEISMOLOGY

6.1 Types of Uncertainty

Uncertainty in seismic detection can be decomposed into aleatoric and epistemic components. Aleatoric uncertainty represents the inherent variability in seismic signals and noise that cannot be reduced even with infinite data, while epistemic uncertainty arises from limited knowledge of model parameters and can be reduced with additional data (Kendall & Gal, 2017; Hüllermeier & Waegeman, 2021). This decomposition can be expressed mathematically as

$$Var\left(y \mid x\right) = \underbrace{E_{\theta}\left[Var(y \mid x,\theta)\right]}_{\text{aleotoric}} + \underbrace{Var_{\theta}\left[E(y \mid x,\theta)\right]}_{\text{epistemic}}, \tag{23}$$

where the first term captures noise-induced variability and the second term captures model uncertainty. In seismic applications, aleatoric uncertainty arises from inherent measurement noise and variability in the seismic signals. Epistemic uncertainty reflects limited knowledge about model parameters, which is especially significant in regions with sparse seismic data where training samples are limited. This can lead to elevated model uncertainty and reduced reliability of learned representations in ML models (Mousavi & Beroza, 2023). Explicit modeling of these uncertainties allows ML methods to quantify confidence in predictions, guide data collection, and improve decision-making under data-sparse conditions, complementing classical physically grounded approaches that rely on fixed thresholds and implicit uncertainty modeling.

6.2 Explainability Methods

Explainable AI (XAI) methods aim to improve the transparency of machine learning–based seismic detection systems. SHAP provides feature attribution based on Shapley values, enabling interpretation of model predictions in terms of input contributions (Lundberg & Lee, 2017). Grad-CAM extends gradient-based attribution methods by producing gradient-weighted activation maps that highlight important time-frequency regions associated with model predictions (Selvaraju et al., 2017). Attention mechanisms are sometimes used to support interpretability by assigning weights to different parts of the input, as in Equation 18. Despite these advances, XAI methods remain limited in their ability to provide causal explanations. They primarily function as diagnostic tools that describe model behavior without revealing underlying physical mechanisms (Adadi & Berrada, 2018). Their reliability may decrease under distribution shifts or when applied to out-of-sample data, so combining XAI with physically informed and uncertainty-aware models is important (Arrieta et al., 2020).

Figure 4. XAI-Enhanced Seismic Detection Pipeline

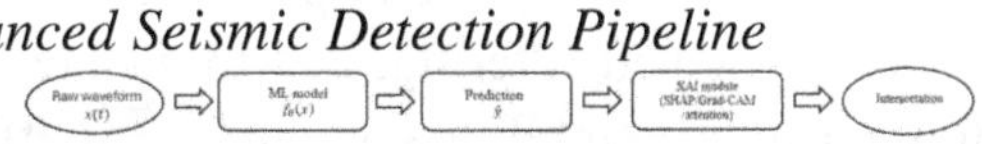

7. IMPLICATIONS FOR STATISTICS PEDAGOGY IN THE AI ERA

The integration of ML into seismology necessitates a transformation in statistical education. Traditional curricula emphasize analytical solutions and parametric inference, whereas modern applications require the integration of statistical theory with computational modeling and data-driven learning (Hardin et al., 2015; Donoho, 2017). A unified framework can be expressed as

$$\textit{Statistical Learning} = \textit{Inference} + \textit{Prediction} + \textit{Uncertainty} + \textit{Interpretability}, \tag{25}$$

where each component represents a core competency. In this formulation, inference corresponds to hypothesis testing and model-based reasoning, prediction refers to ML and function approximation, uncertainty encompasses probabilistic reasoning and calibration, and interpretability involves explainable AI methods. This perspective aligns with modern views of statistics as a discipline integrating modeling, computation, and data-driven decision-making (Donoho, 2017).

Earthquake detection serves as an effective pedagogical example because it involves real-time decision-making under uncertainty, noisy and incomplete data, and high-stakes outcomes. These characteristics reflect broader challenges in modern data science applications, where heterogeneous data and uncertainty must be systematically addressed (Hardin et al., 2015). Recent educational and ethical AI frameworks emphasize that statistical training must incorporate computational methods, uncertainty quantification, interpretability, and responsible AI principles (Jobin et al., 2019; Arrieta et al., 2020). In high-risk applications such as earthquake monitoring, models must be not only accurate but also interpretable, reliable, and aligned with domain knowledge.

8. CONCLUSION

This chapter examined earthquake detection and characterization through a comparison of classical statistical methods and modern machine learning approaches, with emphasis on their statistical behavior and pedagogical relevance. Classical methods such as STA/LTA, matched filtering, and frequency domain techniques remain valuable due to their interpretability, computational efficiency, and strong statistical grounding. However, they rely on fixed assumptions and handcrafted features, which limit their adaptability in complex and non-stationary seismic environments. Machine learning models such as CNNs, EQTransformer, and CRED offer improved performance by learning directly from waveform data and capturing complex patterns, particularly for low magnitude events. However, these gains come with challenges in interpretability, calibration, and sensitivity to limited and non-representative training data. These issues become more pronounced in data sparse environments such as the Philippines, where domain shift and data scarcity can significantly affect model reliability. Uncertainty quantification and explainable AI play an important role in bridging these gaps. Classical approaches handle uncertainty implicitly through threshold-based decisions, while ML methods provide explicit probabilistic estimates using Bayesian approximations, Monte Carlo dropout, and ensemble techniques. Explainable AI methods such as SHAP, Grad CAM, and attention mechanisms offer partial interpretability, although they do not fully recover the underlying physical mechanisms and may be sensitive to distributional changes. From a pedagogical perspective, the comparison highlights the importance of integrating classical statistical reasoning with modern data driven approaches in statistics education. Earthquake detection provides a meaningful context for teaching key concepts such as inference, prediction, uncertainty, and interpretability in a unified framework that reflects real world data science practice. Classical and machine learning approaches should be viewed as complementary rather than competing paradigms. Classical methods provide transparency and strong statistical grounding, while machine learning methods provide flexibility and predictive strength. Their integration, supported by uncertainty aware and explainable AI techniques, offers a more robust and educationally valuable framework for modern seismic analysis

REFERENCES

Adadi, A., & Berrada, M. (2018). Peeking inside the black-box: A survey on explainable artificial intelligence (XAI). *IEEE Access : Practical Innovations, Open Solutions*, *6*, 52138–52160. DOI: 10.1109/ACCESS.2018.2870052

Allen, R. V. (1978). Automatic earthquake recognition and timing from single traces. *Bulletin of the Seismological Society of America*, *68*(5), 1521–1532. DOI: 10.1785/BSSA0680051521

Arrieta, A. B., Díaz-Rodríguez, N., Del Ser, J., Bennetot, A., Tabik, S., Barbado, A., & Herrera, F. (2020). Explainable artificial intelligence (XAI): Concepts, taxonomies, opportunities and challenges toward responsible AI. *Information Fusion*, *58*, 82–115. DOI: 10.1016/j.inffus.2019.12.012

Bergen, K. J., Johnson, P. A., de Hoop, M. V., & Beroza, G. C. (2019). Machine learning for data-driven discovery in solid Earth geoscience. *Science*, *363*(6433), eaau0323. Advance online publication. DOI: 10.1126/science.aau0323 PMID: 30898903

Donoho, D. L. (2017). 50 years of data science. *Journal of Computational and Graphical Statistics*, *26*(4), 745–766. DOI: 10.1080/10618600.2017.1384734

Gal, Y., & Ghahramani, Z. (2016). Dropout as a Bayesian approximation: Representing model uncertainty in deep learning. *In Proceedings of the 33rd International Conference on Machine Learning* (Proceedings of Machine Learning Research, Vol. 48, pp. 1050–1059). https://proceedings.mlr.press/v48/gal16.html

Gamboa-Chacón, S., Meneses, E., & Chaves, E. J. (2025). Analysis of earthquake detection using deep learning: Evaluating reliability and uncertainty in prediction methods. *Computers & Geosciences*, *197*, 105877. Advance online publication. DOI: 10.1016/j.cageo.2025.105877

Gawlikowski, J., Tassi, C. R. N., Ali, M., Lee, J., Humt, M., Feng, J., Kruspe, A., Triebel, R., Jung, P., Roscher, R., Shahzad, M., Yang, W., Bamler, R., & Zhu, X. X. (2023). A survey of uncertainty in deep neural networks. *Artificial Intelligence Review*, *56*(S1, Suppl 1), 1513–1589. DOI: 10.1007/s10462-023-10562-9

Gholamzadeh Khoee, A., Yu, Y., & Feldt, R. (2024). Domain generalization through meta-learning: A survey. *Artificial Intelligence Review*. https://link.springer.com/article/10.1007/s10462-024-10922-z

Gibbons, S. J., & Ringdal, F. (2006). The detection of low magnitude seismic events using array-based waveform correlation. *Geophysical Journal International, 165*(1), 149–166. DOI: 10.1111/j.1365-246X.2006.02865.x

Goodfellow, I., Bengio, Y., & Courville, A. (2016). *Deep learning.* MIT Press.

Hardin, J., Hoerl, R., Horton, N. J., Nolan, D., Baumer, B., Hall-Holt, O., Murrell, P., Peng, R., Roback, P., Temple Lang, D., & Ward, M. D. (2015). Data science in statistics curricula: Preparing students to "think with data.". *The American Statistician, 69*(4), 343–353. DOI: 10.1080/00031305.2015.1077729

Hu, S., Guo, T., Alam, M. S., Koetaka, Y., Ghafoori, E., & Karavasilis, T. L. (2025). Machine learning in earthquake engineering: A review on recent progress and future trends in seismic performance evaluation and design. *Engineering Structures, 340,* 120721. DOI: 10.1016/j.engstruct.2025.120721

Hüllermeier, E., & Waegeman, W. (2021). Aleatoric and epistemic uncertainty in machine learning: An introduction to concepts and methods. *Machine Learning, 110*(2), 457–506. DOI: 10.1007/s10994-021-05946-3

Jobin, A., Ienca, M., & Vayena, E. (2019). The global landscape of AI ethics guidelines. *Nature Machine Intelligence, 1*(9), 389–399. DOI: 10.1038/s42256-019-0088-2

Jozinović, D., Lomax, A., Štajduhar, I., & Michelini, A. (2022). Transfer learning: Improving neural network-based prediction of earthquake ground shaking for an area with insufficient training data. *Geophysical Journal International, 229*(1), 704–721. https://academic.oup.com/gji/article/229/1/704/6447541. DOI: 10.1093/gji/ggab488

Kanamori, H., & Brodsky, E. E. (2004). The physics of earthquakes. *Reports on Progress in Physics, 67*(8), 1429–1496. DOI: 10.1088/0034-4885/67/8/R03

Kendall, A., & Gal, Y. (2017). What uncertainties do we need in Bayesian deep learning for computer vision? *Advances in Neural Information Processing Systems,* 30. https://papers.nips.cc/paper/7141-what-uncertainties-do-we-need

Kubo, H., Naoi, M., & Kano, M. (2024). Recent advances in earthquake seismology using machine learning. *Earth, Planets, and Space, 76*(1), 36. DOI: 10.1186/s40623-024-01982-0

Lakshminarayanan, B., Pritzel, A., & Blundell, C. (2017). Simple and scalable predictive uncertainty estimation using deep ensembles. *In Proceedings of the 31st International Conference on Neural Information Processing Systems (NeurIPS 2017)* (pp. 6405–6416). Curran Associates, Inc.

Lay, T., & Wallace, T. C. (1995). *Modern global seismology.* Academic Press.

Lundberg, S. M., & Lee, S.-I. (2017). A unified approach to interpreting model predictions. In *Advances in Neural Information Processing Systems 30 (NeurIPS 2017)* (pp. 4765–4774). Curran Associates, Inc.

Mousavi, S. M., & Beroza, G. C. (2022). Deep-learning seismology. *Science, 377*(6607), eabm4470. Advance online publication. DOI: 10.1126/science.abm4470 PMID: 35951699

Mousavi, S. M., & Beroza, G. C. (2023). Machine learning in earthquake seismology. *Annual Review of Earth and Planetary Sciences, 51*(1), 105–129. DOI: 10.1146/annurev-earth-071822-100323

Mousavi, S. M., Ellsworth, W. L., Zhu, W., Chuang, L. Y., & Beroza, G. C. (2019). CRED: A deep residual network of convolutional and recurrent units for earthquake signal detection. *Scientific Reports, 9*(1), 10267. DOI: 10.1038/s41598-019-45748-1 PMID: 31311942

Mousavi, S. M., Sheng, Y., Zhu, W., & Beroza, G. C. (2020). Earthquake Transformer—An attentive deep-learning model for simultaneous earthquake detection and phase picking. *Nature Communications, 11*(1), 3952. DOI: 10.1038/s41467-020-17591-w PMID: 32770023

Perol, T., Gharbi, M., & Denolle, M. (2018). Convolutional neural network for earthquake detection and location. *Science Advances, 4*(2), e1700578. DOI: 10.1126/sciadv.1700578 PMID: 29487899

Ross, Z. E., Meier, M.-A., Hauksson, E., & Heaton, T. H. (2018). Generalized seismic phase detection with deep learning. *Bulletin of the Seismological Society of America, 108*(5A), 2894–2901. DOI: 10.1785/0120180080

Selvaraju, R. R., Cogswell, M., Das, A., Vedantam, R., Parikh, D., & Batra, D. (2017). Grad-CAM: Visual explanations from deep networks via gradient-based localization. *Proceedings of the IEEE International Conference on Computer Vision*, 618–626. https://doi.org/DOI: 10.1109/ICCV.2017.74

Trnkoczy, A. (2009). Understanding and parameter setting of STA/LTA trigger algorithm. *In New manual of seismological observatory practice (NMSOP)*. GFZ German Research Centre for Geosciences. https://api.semanticscholar.org/CorpusID: 145040868

Vaswani, A., Shazeer, N., Parmar, N., Uszkoreit, J., Jones, L., Gomez, A. N., Kaiser, Ł., & Polosukhin, I. (2017). Attention is all you need. *In Proceedings of the 31st International Conference on Neural Information Processing Systems (NeurIPS 2017)* (pp. 6000–6010). Curran Associates, Inc.

Withers, M. M., Aster, R. C., Young, C. J., & Chael, E. P. (1996). High-frequency analysis of seismic background noise as a function of wind speed and shallow depth. *Bulletin of the Seismological Society of America*, *86*(5), 1507–1515. DOI: 10.1785/BSSA0860051507

Yoon, C. E., O'Reilly, O., Bergen, K. J., & Beroza, G. C. (2015). Earthquake detection through computationally efficient similarity search. *Science Advances*, *1*(11), e1501057. DOI: 10.1126/sciadv.1501057 PMID: 26665176

Zhang, Y.-L., Yu, Z.-C., & He, C. (2025). Uncertainty-aware neural networks with manual quality control for hydraulic fracturing downhole microseismic monitoring: From automated phase detection to robust source location. *Petroleum Science*, *22*(11), 4520–4537. DOI: 10.1016/j.petsci.2025.07.017

Zhu, J., Li, S., Wei, Y., & Song, J. (2023). On-site instrumental seismic intensity prediction for China via recurrent neural network and transfer learning. *Journal of Asian Earth Sciences*. https://www.sciencedirect.com/science/article/abs/pii/S1367912023000718

Zhu, W., & Beroza, G. C. (2019). PhaseNet: A deep-neural-network-based seismic arrival time picking method. *Geophysical Journal International*, *216*(1), 261–273. DOI: 10.1093/gji/ggy423

Chapter 11
Reproducibility, Transparency, and Open Science in AI-Driven Statistical Education

Victor Paul Jungco dela Cruz
http://orcid.org/0009-0007-8717-516X
University of Southeastern Philippines, Philippines

Fe Monique Musni Tagaytay
http://orcid.org/0000-0001-7667-2346
University of Southeastern Philippines, Philippines

ABSTRACT

Rapid integration of artificial intelligence into statistical education presents critical risks to the scientific values of reproducibility, transparency, and openness. This chapter examines how AI tools can generate polished yet unverifiable outputs, fostering an illusion of competence that undermines genuine statistical understanding. Grounded in the open science movement and the broader reproducibility crisis, the chapter advocates for embedding reproducible computational workflows using R, Python, Quarto, and Git into statistics curricula. It presents the Transparency, Reproducibility, Openness, and Provenance (TROPE) framework for aligning classroom practices with core scientific values. Strategies for teaching critical evaluation of AI-generated results, FAIR data principles, and ethical AI attribution are also discussed. The chapter argues that teaching students to document, verify, and openly share their analytical workflows is a foundational obligation for producing trustworthy researchers.

DOI: 10.4018/979-8-3373-6259-5.ch011

INTRODUCTION

The unprecedented rise of artificial intelligence (AI) in statistical education has introduced powerful tools for simulation, automated feedback, and data exploration. These systems allow users to generate outputs with a single prompt. It is now common for students to present papers wholly generated by or heavily assisted by AI, for employees to generate complex data analyses without directly examine data, and programmers for programmers to generate functional code without writing it themselves. The power and convenience afforded by AI are undeniable.

However, this ease comes at a considerable cost. Polished AI-generated outputs can create a dangerous illusion of competence, bypassing the learning, struggle, and reasoning that traditionally accompany human effort. Amid this rapid technological acceleration, we face a growing threat to fundamental scientific values specifically, reproducibility, transparency, and openness, when the appearance of high-quality results takes precedence over genuine understanding the skill.

This concern is especially acute in AI-driven statistics education. One of the primarily aims of statistics education is to prepare future researchers and data analysts. That objective may be undermined when AI tools increasingly replace foundational learning rather than support it. When students rely on AI-powered platforms, dynamic applets, or large language model (LLM) assistants without understanding the underlying computational workflows, they risk producing results that cannot be verified, replicated, or critically evaluated (National Academies of Sciences, Engineering, and Medicine [NASEM], 2019).

The consequences of this gap extend beyond the classroom. When these students later analyze medical data or inform economic policy, the illusion of competence becomes a liability. In an environment saturated with automated answers, true expertise is not simply the ability to generate results, but the capacity to reason deeply, evaluate uncertainty, and understand methods without relying on AI as a crutch.

Growing dependence on AI to bypass foundational learning amplifies the problem of reproducibility in science. Across disciplines, several published findings cannot be successfully replicated. The problem labeled as a reproducibility crisis in the psychology, biomedicine, economics, and the social sciences. Researchers have called for more robust practices, including preregistration, open data, and transparent statistical workflows (Baker, 2016; Nosek et al., 2015; Open Science Collaboration, 2015).

Parallel to this crisis, advances in deep learning and natural language processing, have transformed how students learn statistics, design experiments, write code, and interpret results (Zhai, 2023). Tools such as ChatGPT, GitHub Copilot, and automated machine learning (AutoML) platforms have expanded opportunities for rapid learning, but also raise concerns about opacity, reliability, and the reproducibility of AI-supported analyses (Peng & Hicks, 2021; van Dis et al., 2023).

Integrating reproducibility and transparency into the statistics education should not be treated as optional enrichment but a foundational responsibility of the curriculum (Stodden et al., 2014; Wilkinson et al., 2016). Yet many programs continue to emphasize classical inference, data visualization, and programming skills without explicit instruction in reproducible workflows. Many students graduate without experience in version control, containerization, literate programming tools, or formal documentation practices (Horton, 2023; Mendez-Carbajo & Dellachiesa, 2023). As AI systems increasingly participate in knowledge production, sometimes generating entire analytic pipelines, statistics education must evolve. Educators must reassert the core scientific values of transparency, accountability, and methodological rigor in an era of automated reasoning.

RESEARCH GAPS: EXISTING FRAMEWORKS, EMPIRICAL EVIDENCE, AND THE NEED FOR TROPE

The rapid spread of AI tools in education has outpaced research on how open science principles apply when AI mediates statistical learning. Although reproducibility and transparency are widely endorsed, few studies examine how these norms are enacted in educational contexts where AI supports statistics instruction (Ball, 2023; Hosseini et al., 2024). Existing guidance is largely aimed at professional researchers and provides limited direction for classrooms, leaving students and instructors without clear procedures for documenting, sharing, or verifying AI-assisted analyses. As a result, students often produce technically polished outputs that cannot be readily checked, reproduced, or extended, undermining core epistemic goals of statistics education (Gundsen et al., 2024).

A related gap concerns students' capacity to critically evaluate AI outputs. While student use of AI tools is now widespread, many users report limited understanding of how these systems generate results or how reliable those outputs are. In statistical work, this poses risks: uncritical acceptance of AI-generated analyses can lead to the use of incorrect methods, hallucinated values, or fabricated references. Empirical evidence indicates that lower AI literacy is associated with reduced critical scrutiny of AI outputs, highlighting the need for pedagogy that prioritizes verification, interpretation, and systematic error detection (Clerc et al., 2025; Pitts et al., 2025; Sun et al. 2024 as cited in Shoufan & Esmaeil, 2026).

Further gaps arise around transparency and accountability in AI-assisted statistical work. Despite well-documented concerns about opacity and inconsistency in AI-generated outputs, there is little pedagogical guidance on documenting AI contributions, assigning epistemic responsibility, or ensuring analytical transparency. Foundational issues of provenance, accountability, and equitable access remain underexplored in statistics education research (Bender et al., 2021; Lund et al., 2023; Mitchell et al., 2019; UNESCO, 2023).

These challenges are compounded by limitations in dominant AI-in-education frameworks. Although evidence shows that AI-assisted learning can improve short-term outcomes such as efficiency and performance, particularly in higher education and STEM contexts (Kasneci et al., 2023; Lund et al., 2023), prevailing frameworks remain largely outcome-focused. They position AI as a pedagogical aid rather than as a contributor to scientific workflow production and therefore provide little guidance on how AI-generated analyses should be documented, verified, or reproduced. This omission is consequential, as learning quality depends on whether students engage with AI outputs analytically or procedurally.

Importantly, these gaps reflect classroom realities, particularly in under-resourced contexts where access to paid software, stable infrastructure, and formal training is limited, yet pressure to adopt AI tools persists. In such settings, AI can either exacerbate inequities or support open, low-cost, and transparent scientific practice, depending on how it is pedagogically framed. The Transparency, Reproducibility, Openness, and Provenance in Education (TROPE) framework addresses this need by offering a tool-agnostic, scalable approach that embeds AI use within reproducible and provenance-aware statistical workflows aligned with the epistemic standards of scientific practice.

1. THE REPRODUCIBILITY CRISIS AND THE OPEN SCIENCE IMPERATIVE

1.1 Traditional Definitions

Reproducibility is often defined as the ability of an independent researcher to recompute results using the same data, code, and methods. It safeguards the trustworthiness of a scientific claim by ensuring that original calculations were performed correctly and mitigates the risk of computational error, data manipulation, or honest mistakes. A related but distinct concept to this is replicability, which refers to achieving consistent results using new data but similar methods (NASEM, 2019; Peng, 2011). Reproducibility checks if the computation meets mathematical and code rigor, while replicability checks if the findings apply to broader populations or other settings. Both reproducibility and replicability are necessary as standards of verification. They are achieved through transparency, which ensures that all analytic steps, data transformations, and decision rules are accessible and clearly documented (Stodden et al., 2016). At its core, reproducibility is the practice of inviting others to verify and challenge scientific results. It is what makes a claim scientific in the first place, aligning squarely with Karl Popper's philosophy of falsifiability (Popper, 1959).

1.2 Understanding the Reproducibility Crisis

Beginning in the 2010s, a wave of high-profile replication failures exposed that many published findings could not be independently reproduced.

The Open Science Collaboration (2015) attempted to replicate 100 psychological studies and found that only approximately 39% produced statistically significant results consistent with the originals. Similar findings emerged in cancer biology (Errington et al., 2021), economics (Camerer et al., 2016), and neuroscience (Poldrack et al., 2017).

Baker (2016) found that more than 70% of 1,576 scientists published in Nature had failed to reproduce another researcher's work, and over 50% failed to reproduce their own. The causes identified were selective reporting, inadequate documentation of methods, underpowered studies, analytic flexibility, and the unavailability of data and code. Each of these causes has direct implications for statistical education. Students who are not taught to document their analytical decisions, share their data and code, and pre-register their analyses are implicitly learning practices that contribute to the crisis.

These incidents emphasize how computational reproducibility should be prioritized as a baseline standard in the classroom and clearly distinguished as equally necessary as replicability and generalizability. While Replicability focuses on whether the same findings emerge with different data collected under the same conditions, and Generalizability is concerned with whether findings extend to new populations and contexts, Reproducibility addresses whether the results can be reproduced given the same data and code (Plesser, 2018; Rasmussen et al., 2023). Statistics education must address all three, but computational reproducibility is the most tractable starting point because it is entirely within the researcher's or the student's control.

1.3 Open Science as a Framework for Education

Open science is a broad movement that encompasses open access publishing, open data sharing, open-source software, pre-registration of research hypotheses, and transparent reporting of methods (Vicente-Saez & Martinez-Fuentes, 2018). While initiatives like the Berlin Declaration on Open Access to Knowledge in the Sciences and Humanities (2003) and subsequent frameworks have advocated for free, online access to scientific knowledge as a global public good, modern standards focus heavily on how data itself is managed. Today, funding agencies and research institutions worldwide increasingly adopt the Findable, Accessible, Interoperable and Reusable (FAIR) data principles.

In education, open science translates to teaching students how to produce analyses that others can inspect, reproduce, and verify. However, AI tools complicate this process by introducing untraceable reasoning steps, proprietary systems, and opaque training data (Mitchell et al., 2019). In statistics education, open science principles translate into specific pedagogical commitments. Students should be taught to share their analysis code alongside their reports; to use publicly available datasets or to document data collection procedures fully; to employ version control so that analytical decisions are traceable; and to write reports in literate programming formats that interweave code, output, and narrative. These practices develop concrete professional competencies that are increasingly demanded by employers in data science, public health, social research, and policy analysis (Wilson et al., 2017).

Nosek et al. (2015) proposed a set of guidelines known as the Transparency and Openness Promotion (TOP) guidelines, which specify eight standards for transparent research: citation standards, data transparency, analytic methods (code) transparency, research materials transparency, design and analysis transparency, pre-registration, pre-registration of replication, and replication. While these standards were designed for professional researchers, they provide an excellent curriculum scaffold for statistics educators. Teaching students to meet even the lower tiers of TOP guidelines instills practices that reduce bias and increase the credibility of their analyses.

1.4 Implications for AI-Driven Statistical Instruction

The integration of AI into statistics education heightens the need for open science pedagogy. When a student uses an AI assistant such as ChatGPT, Claude, or Gemini to generate statistical analyses such as fitting regression models, interpreting output, or suggesting analytical strategies, the transparency of that workflow is fundamentally at risk. Unlike code executed in an R or Python script, a conversational AI exchange may not be documented, version-controlled, or reproducible. The student cannot guarantee that asking the same question tomorrow will produce the same answer, because large language models exhibit stochastic behavior and are subject to model updates (Bender et al., 2021; Marcus & Davis, 2019).

Beyond reproducibility issues, AI-generated statistical outputs may contain errors that are difficult for novices to detect. LLMs have been documented to produce incorrect statistical formulas, misinterpret output, and confabulate references (Alkaissi & McFarlane, 2023; Halaweh, 2023). Without a foundational understanding of reproducible workflows and critical evaluation skills, students may introduce such errors into their work because they lack a mechanism to detect them. This creates what Bender et al. (2021) termed the 'stochastic parrot' problem in an educational register. AI outputs appear authoritative and coherent but lack genuine grounding.

Open science education provides a critical counterweight to over-reliance on AI outputs. When students are trained to document their analytical decisions in literate programming notebooks, commit their code to version control, and situate AI assistance within an accountable workflow, they develop the habits of mind necessary for both scientific integrity and informed AI use. They cannot simply copy and paste AI-generated output; instead, they are forced to treat AI as an assistant capable of error and subject to the scrutiny of a competent human.

2. TEACHING REPRODUCIBLE WORKFLOWS: R, PYTHON, AND LITERATE PROGRAMMING

Reproducible workflows are the backbone of modern data science. At the most basic level, they are about making sure that the work is grounded not just in producing the answer but more importantly, showing how the answer was reached so that others can use the work meaningfully. They enable analysts, students, and researchers to systematically organize their work, track changes, validate findings, and communicate analyses transparently and clearly to others.

2.1 The Case for Computational Literacy in Statistics Education

One of the biggest changes that statistics education has seen recently is the shift from hand-calculation and point-and-click software toward code-based statistical analysis (Baumer et al., 2014; Çetinkaya-Rundel & Rundel, 2018). This is not just a technical shift. If in the past students completed statistical analyses by simply following what comes next in the procedure, now they are increasingly expected to make their reasoning visible through code. This means that the work is no longer result-oriented but thinking oriented. The shift is more towards a change in the way students think about statistics and by extension, also creates a shift in how statistics is taught and learned.

Programming languages such as R and Python are now dominant tools in data science, academic research, and industry practice. In a statistical classroom, they offer clear advantages. They make each step of the analytical process visible, allowing results to be reproduced exactly and they support simulation and visualization in ways that would otherwise be difficult to achieve manually. They also integrate naturally with literate programming environments that combine explanation and computation.

When students write code, they cannot skip steps because they have to specify the decisions they made to arrive at an analysis. Decisions made throughout the process from data import, cleaning, transformation, modeling, to visualization must not only be correct but they also have to make the reasoning behind it clear.

Learning R or Python is not only about learning analytic tools. Computational literacy in this context does not equate to tool proficiency but to using these tools to understand what their code is doing, follow the sequence of their analysis and explain the choices they made along the way. Learning R or Python changes how students engage with their own work and naturally cultivates more ownership and accountability for the analyses they produce. This is vastly different from menu-driven interfaces such as SPSS or early versions of Minitab where the decisions made during the process tend to be made by default without the student's awareness (Pruim et al., 2017).

In teaching, this implies the need for teachers to focus on more than the final answers when examining student work. Teachers can also place more emphasis on how students approached the problem, where their reasoning may have gone wrong, and whether they understand the decisions they made throughout the analysis. This makes statistical learning more visible and allows teachers to give deeper feedback.

2.2 R and the Tidyverse: A Pedagogical Ecosystem

R is an open-source programming language and environment for statistical computing and graphics, first developed by Ross Ihaka and Robert Gentleman at the University of Auckland in the 1990s and now maintained by the R Core Team (R Core Team, 2024). Its ecosystem has expanded enormously with the development of the *tidyverse*, a collection of R packages designed for data science that share a common philosophy, grammar, and data structure (Wickham et al., 2019). The *tidyverse* packages, including ggplot2 for visualization, *dplyr* for data manipulation, *tidyr* for data tidying, and *readr* for data import, provide a coherent and pedagogically accessible framework for teaching data analysis. Rather than confronting students with disconnected tools, this framework allows them to move through the steps of an analysis in a way that is more structured and easier to follow. This helps students focus more on the logic of the process rather than feeling that they need to learn a new system for every task.

The *mosaic* package (Pruim et al., 2017) has been specifically designed for introductory statistics instruction in R, offering simplified functions for common statistical operations that allow beginners to engage with real data without being overwhelmed by programming complexity. More recently, the infer package provides a tidy framework for statistical inference grounded in simulation-based methods (Bray et al., 2021). These tools collectively support a pedagogical approach that grounds statistical concepts in computation and data exploration before introducing formal theoretical frameworks. This helps students encounter statistical ideas through practice and exploration first, before moving into more abstract formalization. This is particularly important for student who struggle with the technical demands of programming before they can fully engage with the statistical ideas themselves.

Example: Confidence Intervals in R with Literate Programming

Students are given a dataset of exam scores and asked to construct a 95% confidence interval for the population mean using both the theoretical t-distribution approach and bootstrapping. In doing so, they are not only asked to produce an answer, but also to document the steps used to arrive at it. In an R Markdown document, they load the data with *readr*, compute summary statistics with *dplyr*, generate bootstrap samples with infer, and visualize the bootstrap distribution with *ggplot2*. The final rendered report includes the code, the output, and a written interpretation, demonstrating what a full reproducible workflow looks like in practice.

2.3 Python for Statistical Analysis: NumPy, pandas, and SciPy

Python has emerged as the *lingua franca* of data science and machine learning, and its use in statistics education is growing rapidly, particularly at the interface with AI and deep learning (VanderPlas, 2016; McKinney, 2017). This makes it an increasingly important language for students to encounter, not only because of its technical capabilities but also because of its growing prominence in research and professional practice. The core scientific Python ecosystem includes *NumPy* for numerical computation, pandas for tabular data manipulation, *SciPy* for statistical functions, and Matplotlib and Seaborn for visualization. For machine learning and AI applications, *scikit-learn* provides a comprehensive set of algorithms with a consistent API, and *TensorFlow* and *PyTorch* support deep learning workflows.

For statistics education specifically, the *statsmodels* library provides a wide range of statistical models, including ordinary least squares, generalized linear models, and time series analysis. Its output also resembles that of more traditional statistical software, which can make it easier for students transitioning from point-and-click environments to follow. The *pingouin* package offers a more accessible interface for common statistical tests and presents results in a form that is easier to read and interpret (Seabold & Perktold, 2010; Vallat, 2018).

Choosing between R and Python for statistics instruction depends on curricular context. R has a stronger tradition in statistics and biostatistics, while Python is more prevalent in computer science, engineering, and industry data science roles. Ideally, statistics curricula should expose students to both languages, emphasizing that the choice of tool is less important than the habits of reproducible, documented, and transparent analysis (Çetinkaya-Rundel & Rundel, 2018). From a teaching standpoint, the more important goal is not commitment to one language but helping students develop habits of analysis that they can carry across tools and contexts. Some institutions have adopted a bilingual approach, teaching core statistical concepts in R and introducing Python in applied or capstone courses.

2.4 Literate Programming: R Markdown, Quarto, and Jupyter Notebooks

Literate programming, introduced by Donald Knuth (1984), refers to the integration of code and natural language within a single document. The goal is to produce analytical workflows that are both executable and human readable. In statistics education, this approach has been widely implemented through tools: R Markdown, Quarto, and Jupyter Notebooks. These tools make statistical reasoning more transparent and easier to follow.

One influential study by Baumer et al. (2014), identified a common weakness in introductory statistics workflows: students often copying from statistical software into word documents or presentation slides. This practice not only introduced the errors but also disconnected results from the code that produced them. The authors demonstrated how R Markdown enables fully reproducible analyses that are feasible even in introductory courses.

R Markdown, introduced by Yihui Xie and colleagues at RStudio (now Posit), allows users to combine R code chunks with Markdown with a single .Rmd file that can be rendered to HTML, PDF, or Word output (Xie et al., 2020). R Markdown documents embed the analysis code alongside the results, ensuring that the reported output is traceable. This allows the document to function as self-contained record that can be rerun, verified or extended by others.

Quarto, released by Posit in 2022, extends this model by supporting multiple programming languages, including R, Python, Julia, and Observable Javascript (Allaire et al., 2022). Quarto documents use the .qmd extension and can be rendered into a broad range of outputs, including interactive web applications, books, and presentations. This flexibility makes Quarto particularly well suited for courses that span multiple languages or incorporate AI-assisted coding workflows.

Figure 1. Inputs in Reproducible Analysis in Quarto (Python chunk)

```
# Example: Reproducible Analysis in Quarto (Python chunk)
import pandas as pd
import seaborn as sns
from scipy import stats

# Load data
df = pd.read_csv('student_scores.csv')

# Compute 95% CI
n = len(df['score'])
mean = df['score'].mean()
se = stats.sem(df['score'])
ci = stats.t.interval(0.95, df=n-1, loc=mean, scale=se)

print(f'Mean: {mean:.2f}, 95% CI: ({ci[0]:.2f}, {ci[1]:.2f})')

# Visualize
sns.histplot(df['score'], kde=True)
# All output is embedded in the rendered .qmd document
```

Jupyter Notebooks, originally developed for Python, provide an interactive browser-based environment where code, output, and explanatory text are organized in executable cells (Kluyver et al., 2016). Jupyter supports dozens of programming languages and is widely used data science, machine learning education, and research computing. Cloud-based platforms such as Google Colab and Binder further lower technical barriers by allowing students to run notebooks without local installation, enable to focus more directly on analytical reasoning.

Literate programming environments play an established role in statistics education by supporting transparency and reproducibility. Marwick et al. (2018) demonstrate that research compendiums developed in tools such as R Markdown significantly improve the reproducibility of published analyses. Incorporating these tools into statistics courses aligns with instructional practice with contemporary expectations for open and reproducible research.

Pedagogically, literate programming also strengthens students' analytical communication skills. Beckman et al. (2021) argue that integrating code, output, and explanation helps students articulate their reasoning more clearly, while Dogucu and Çetinkaya-Rundel (2022) emphasize the importance of introducing modern data science tools early in instruction. Early exposure normalizes computation as part of statistical reasoning, reduces hesitation around programming, and allows students to focus more directly on understanding analytical concepts.

2.5 Environment management as a condition of reproducibility

Literate programming tools create documents that combine prose, code, and output into a single narrative. This supports reproducibility by keeping code and results together, allowing analyses to be rerun more easily, and making analytic choices visible within the document itself.

One part of reproducibility that is commonly overlooked is software environment management, or the need to specify the exact versions of programming languages, packages, and dependencies used in an analysis. Package updates can introduce breaking changes or produce different numerical results. This means that an analysis that is reproducible today may not remain reproducible in the future if it is run under a different software environment (Gentleman & Temple Lang, 2007).

In R, the *renv* package (Ushey, 2023) provides a project-level environment management system that records the exact version of every package used in a project and allows those versions to be restored on any machine. The equivalent in Python is a combination of virtual environments (*venv* or *conda*) and a requirements.txt or environment.yml file that specifies package versions. Docker containers provide a further layer of reproducibility by encapsulating not just the software environment but the entire operating system and system-level dependencies (Boettiger, 2015). This reinforces the idea that a reproducible analysis is not only one that is documented well, but one that can still be run under the same conditions.

Teaching students to use *renv* or *conda*, to include a requirements file in every project, and to document their software environment in their reports is a concrete and immediately practicable open science skill. These habits also prepare students for collaborative data science work, where team members may use different machines and need to ensure that their analyses produce identical results.

Rule et al. (2018) and Stodden et al. (2016) argue that computational work should be conducted and evaluated using reproducible notebook-based workflows, with emphasis on clarity of narrative, the ability to regenerate results from the same data and code, transparent documentation, and appropriate use of version control. More recent pedagogical guidance has extended these criteria to include explicit documentation of AI assistance when used in coursework.

3. VERSION CONTROL AND TRANSPARENCY: TEACHING GIT AND GITHUB IN THE STATISTICS CLASSROOM

3.1 What is Version Control and Why Does It Matter in Education?

Data analysis, statistical research, and teaching statistics have at least one thing in common. These activities all produce many files, such as data files, source code, figures, tables, and prepared reports (Bryan & Hester, 2021). Without explicit and structured management, project organization can become difficult to maintain, taking time away from the primary work and reducing the quality of the final product.

Version control is foundational to reproducible science because it provides an audit trail for data, code, and documents. It is a system that records changes to files over time, allowing users to recall specific versions later. Originally developed for software engineering, version control is now recognized as an essential tool for reproducible research and open science (Wilson et al., 2017). Git, created by Linus Torvalds in 2005, is the most widely used version control system. GitHub, GitLab, and Bitbucket are web-based platforms that host Git repositories and provide additional tools for collaboration, documentation, and continuous integration.

In statistics education, version control serves several interconnected purposes. First, it provides a complete, auditable history of all changes to an analysis, so that edits to the data, code, or interpretation are recorded with a timestamp and a message explaining the change. Second, it enables multiple students to work on the same analysis simultaneously without overwriting each other's contributions. Third, it facilitates transparency. By hosting a repository publicly on GitHub, students share not just their outputs and results, but also their broader analytical journey, including processes, mistakes, corrections, and deliberate changes of direction. Lastly, it provides a natural structure for the iterative process of data analysis by encouraging students to commit frequently, write informative commit messages, and maintain a clear record of how the analysis evolved (Bryan & Hester, 2021; Bryan et al., 2021).

3.2 Integrating Git and GitHub into Statistics Courses

Bryan et al. (2021) provides a comprehensive and pedagogically oriented introduction to Git and GitHub for R users in her freely available resource 'Happy Git and GitHub for the useR,' which has become a standard reference in data science education. She argues that Git, although initially intimidating, becomes more natural with practice. In statistics courses, this matters because it helps students see their analyses as work that develops over time and needs to be managed deliberately. As Bryan (2018, p. 3) notes, “If you are in data science, you need to get comfortable with Git”.

Several pedagogical strategies have been proposed for introducing version control in statistics courses. Beckman et al. (2021) recommend beginning with GitHub Classroom, which allows instructors to create assignment repositories for each student, automatically collect submissions, and provide feedback through pull requests. This helps students encounter version control not as an abstract technical exercise, but as part of the ordinary process of submitting, revising, and improving their work. The value of this approach is that it forms habits of rigor early, so that careful analytical practice becomes part of how students work by default.

Baumer et al. (2014) describe how Git and GitHub were integrated from the first week of the curriculum, with students creating repositories for all assignments and using pull requests for peer review. They argue that this not only teaches version control, but also models professional data science practice and emphasizes collaboration, revision, and documentation as a normal part of serious analytical work. A seven-phase summary of a git workflow for statistics assignments is shown on table 1,

Table 1. Git workflow for statistics assignments

Phase	Actor	Action	Tool	Purpose
1	Instructor	**Create assignment** Example: Instructor creates a GitHub Classroom assignment with a template repository containing data, an empty R Markdown or Quarto file, and a README.	GitHub Classroom	Distribute template repository
2	Student	**Accept & clone** Example: Students clone the repository to their local machines (or work in a cloud environment such as Posit Cloud or JupyterHub).	Git / browser	Obtain local working copy
3	Student	**Initialize environment**	renv / conda	Document software dependencies
4	Student	**Iterative commits** Example: Students commit their work at each major analytical step with informative commit messages.	Git commit	Record analytical decisions
5	Student	**Push to GitHub** Example: Students push their final analysis to GitHub and share the repository link as their submission.	Git push	Back up and share progress
6	Instructor	**Review & feedback**	GitHub Issues / PR	Formative assessment on process
7	Student	**Final push & tag**	Git tag	Mark submission version

Note: For phases 6 and 7, instructor and student-peers can review the full commit history to evaluate the analytical process, not just the final product.

3.3 Open Repositories and FAIR Data in Student Projects

The FAIR principles, which stand for Findable, Accessible, Interoperable, and Reusable, were outlined by Wilkinson et al. (2016) as a framework for improving how scientific data is managed and shared. FAIR does not automatically mean that data must be fully open. Proprietary or sensitive data can still follow FAIR principles if they are accompanied by clear metadata and instructions for access. In educational settings, however, students working with non-sensitive datasets can be encouraged to share their data and code under open licenses such as Creative Commons CC-BY or MIT, so that others can inspect, reuse, and build on their work.

Zenodo, an open repository operated by CERN, allows students to deposit datasets and analysis code and receive a Digital Object Identifier (DOI), which makes their work citable. The Open Science Framework (OSF), developed by the Center for Open Science, provides a free platform for preregistering analyses, sharing data and code, and documenting research workflows (Foster & Deardorff, 2017). Introducing students to these platforms, even through course projects, helps them become familiar with how open science is practiced and encourages them to see their work as something that can be shared, cited, and used by others.

3.4 Preregistration and Registered Reports as Educational Tools

Preregistration is the practice of specifying hypotheses, methods, and analysis plans before collecting or analyzing data. It is widely regarded as one of the most powerful tools for reducing researcher degrees of freedom and the associated risk of false positive findings (Wagenmakers et al., 2012; Chambers, 2013). The registered reports format, developed by the journal Cortex and subsequently adopted by over 300 journals, takes preregistration further by providing in-principle acceptance of a paper before data collection, based on the quality of the research question and methods rather than the significance of the results.

In educational settings, asking students to preregister their analysis plans, even informally through an OSF registration or a brief written statement submitted before data analysis begins, helps them learn to distinguish between confirmatory and exploratory analysis. Nosek et al. (2018) argue that one of the most important skills for modern data analysts is the ability to distinguish between hypotheses that were specified before analysis (confirmatory) and patterns that were identified during analysis (exploratory). Teaching this distinction through preregistration exercises can actively shape how students approach data analysis and statistical inference.

4. AI-GENERATED RESULTS AND REPRODUCIBILITY CONCERNS

4.1 The Nature of AI-Generated Statistical Output

Large language models such as GPT-4, Claude, Gemini, and their successors are increasingly used by students to assist with statistical analysis. Students commonly use AI for generating code, interpreting output, suggesting analytical approaches, and even producing written summaries of statistical results. These tools can be genuinely helpful in teaching and learning by providing instant explanations, scaffolding code for beginners, and helping students who are stuck continue making progress. However, they also raise reproducibility concerns that differ in important ways from those associated with conventional computational tools (Alkaissi & McFarlane, 2023).

First, LLMs are stochastic, which means that the same prompt may produce different outputs across sessions, across model versions, and even within the same session if the temperature parameter is nonzero. Unlike an R or Python script that produces the same output when given the same input, AI-generated analysis cannot be assumed to be reproducible in the same way. Second, LLMs are periodically updated, and these updates can substantially change how they respond to statistical tasks. A code snippet generated by GPT-3.5 may behave differently in GPT-4, and a code snippet generated by Claude 2 may differ from one generated by Claude 3. Third, LLMs can produce outputs that appear statistically sound but are still incorrect by using the wrong formulas, misinterpreting assumptions, or fabricating references (Bender et al., 2021; Halaweh, 2023). This is where the illusion of competence becomes especially dangerous. The output may look polished and convincing even when the reasoning behind it is flawed.

4.2 Documented Cases of AI Statistical Errors

The literature on AI errors in academic and professional contexts is growing rapidly. Alkaissi and McFarlane (2023) demonstrated that ChatGPT fabricated plausible but entirely fictitious references in response to queries about medical research, a phenomenon termed 'hallucination' in AI research. In the statistical domain, Peng (2022) noted that AI tools can produce code that runs without errors but performs logically incorrect analyses, such as computing a correlation on variables that have not been properly cleaned, or fitting a linear model without checking required assumptions.

Firat (2023) analyzed a series of statistical tasks submitted to ChatGPT and found that while the model performed well on standard textbook problems, it struggled with more nuanced tasks such as selecting appropriate tests for complex research designs, interpreting interaction effects, and handling missing data appropriately. Importantly, the model's outputs were often presented with a high level of confidence, making it difficult for novice users to identify errors without independent domain knowledge.

These findings have direct implications for statistics education. Students who uncritically accept AI-generated statistical analyses may produce incorrect results, misinterpret their data, and develop a false sense of competence. They believe they have learned to do statistics because they have obtained output, without understanding whether that output is correct (Kasneci et al., 2023). In this sense, AI can easily become a crutch rather than a support for learning. This is the equivalent of copying answers without understanding the underlying reasoning, a long-standing concern in education that AI now enables at unprecedented scale and sophistication. The danger is not only that the tool may be wrong, but that its polished output can make that wrongness harder to detect. This deepens the illusion of competence by making students feel more capable than they are.

4.3 Strategies for Teaching Critical Evaluation of AI Statistical Output

Teaching students to critically evaluate AI-generated statistical output means helping them develop their own expectations about what results are plausible before they turn to AI for help and helping them use those expectations to judge whether the AI's output makes sense. This may be understood as a form of statistical calibration, similar to what physics and engineering often describe as a back-of-the-envelope calculation, where an approximate estimate is used as a check on more detailed results.

Several teaching strategies can support this kind of judgment. Instructors can assign 'AI debugging' exercises where students are given AI-generated statistical code or output that contains deliberate errors and asked to identify and correct them using their own knowledge. This reverses the typical dependency pattern, placing the student in the expert role and treating AI output as an object of critical analysis rather than a source of authority (Kasneci et al., 2023; Yang et al., 2024).

Another classroom strategy is to require students to reproduce AI-generated results using their own code in R or Python. This engages students in verifying the accuracy of the AI's output and developing independent computational competence. This "trust but verify" approach is similar to the peer review process in academic publishing, where claims are expected to be checked rather than accepted simply because they appear plausible.

Instructors can also introduce students to 'prompt documentation' as a reproducibility practice. This requires students to record the exact prompts submitted to an AI tool, the model and version used, the date of the query, and the response obtained. This creates an auditable record of AI assistance much like the citation of sources in traditional scholarship. While not equivalent to full computational reproducibility, prompt documentation represents a meaningful transparency measure for AI-augmented analyses (Lund et al., 2023).

These strategies frame the role of AI in statistical education differently. They train students not to surrender judgment to AI, but to approach its outputs with scrutiny and responsibility. Rather than treating AI as an authority, students learn to see themselves as the ones responsible for evaluating whether results are correct. They also reinforce the central role of the analyst as the authority and the importance of genuine statistical understanding.

4.4 AI Transparency Tools and Model Cards

The AI research community has developed several tools and frameworks to improve the transparency and accountability of AI systems. Model cards, introduced by Mitchell et al. (2019), are short documents that accompany machine learning models and provide standardized information about their intended use, performance characteristics, limitations, and ethical considerations. Datasheets for datasets, proposed by Gebru et al. (2021), serve a similar purpose for training datasets. Teaching students to read and evaluate model cards and datasheets develops their capacity to assess AI tools critically rather than treating them as opaque oracles.

In the classroom, this can be operationalized through a structured activity in which students read the model card or documentation for an AI tool they are using, such as Anthropic's documentation for Claude or OpenAI's documentation for GPT-4, and evaluate what information is and is not provided about the model's statistical capabilities, training data, known limitations, and evaluation benchmarks. This activity connects open science principles of transparency and documentation directly to AI literacy, reinforcing the thematic integration of the chapter.

5. A PEDAGOGICAL FRAMEWORK FOR OPEN SCIENCE IN AI-DRIVEN STATISTICS COURSES

5.1 Principles of the Framework

This chapter proposes a pedagogical framework based on Transparency, Reproducibility, Openness, and Provenance in Education (TROPE) to bring open science practices into AI-driven statistics courses. Its four principles are as follows:

1. **Transparency**. Analytical choices such as data preparation, model selection, handling outliers, and interpreting results should be visible in the code and explained in the written account. When AI is used, the prompts, model, and version should also be documented.
2. **Reproducibility**. Analyses should be carried out in literate programming environments such as R Markdown, Quarto, or Jupyter, with environment management tools such as renv or conda and version control through Git, so that others with access to the repository can reproduce the results exactly.

3. **Openness**. When privacy allows, data and code should be shared publicly under open licenses, ideally through repositories such as Zenodo, OSF, or GitHub. Analysis plans should be preregistered or clearly identified as exploratory.
4. **Provenance**: Sources of data, code, and AI-generated content should be documented. This includes citing data sources, package versions, and AI tools used, along with maintaining a Git history that shows how the analysis developed.

Figure 2. Open Science as a Framework for Education in AI-Driven Statistics

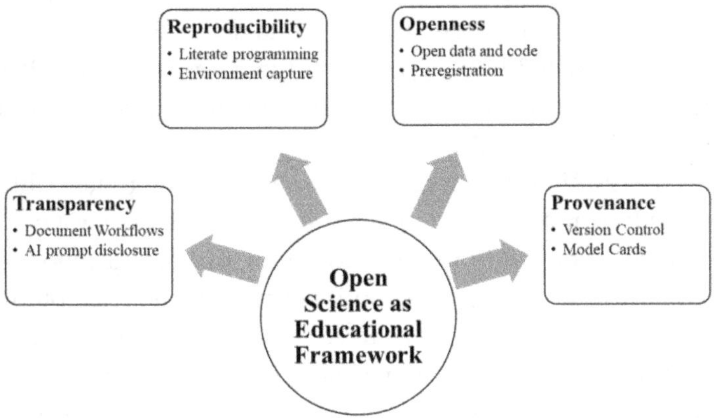

5.2 Scaffolded Implementation Across Course Levels

The TROPE framework can be implemented across introductory, intermediate, and advanced statistics courses. At the introductory level, the emphasis should be on literate programming (R Markdown or Jupyter Notebooks) and the basic Git workflow (commit, push, share). Students at this level should learn to produce self-contained reproducible reports and to distinguish between AI assistance and their own understanding.

At the intermediate level, students should be introduced to environment management, GitHub Classroom for collaborative projects, and the distinction between confirmatory and exploratory analysis. They should practice documenting AI assistance as a transparency measure and should critically evaluate AI-generated code by running it independently and checking results against alternative implementations.

At the advanced level, students should engage with FAIR data principles, preregistration on OSF, and the creation of full research compendiums, or self-contained repositories that include the data, code, and documentation needed to reproduce a published or course-based analysis. They should also learn to read model cards and datasheets critically and to explain the specific reproducibility limits of any AI tools used in their analyses.

5.3 Assessment Strategies for Reproducibility and Open Science

Traditional assessment in statistics courses often focuses on whether the final answer is correct and whether the right statistical test was used. An open science approach asks instructors to assess more than the final result. It also asks whether the workflow is clear and reproducible: Is the analysis documented in a literate programming environment? Is the code stored in a version-controlled repository with informative commit messages? Is the software environment documented? Are AI tools properly acknowledged?

Beckman et al. (2021) propose rubrics for assessing reproducibility in student data analyses that look not only at statistical correctness, but also at clarity of code, quality of documentation, and the accessibility of the shared repository. Several institutions have also adopted reproducibility checklists modeled on those used in peer-reviewed journals, asking students to confirm before submission that an independent reader could reproduce their analysis (Stodden & Miguez, 2014).

Portfolio-based assessment, where students build a GitHub portfolio of analyses across a course or curriculum, can provide a clearer record of how they are developing as data analysts and give employers or graduate programs visible evidence of their computational and open science skills (Baumer et al., 2014; Dogucu & Çetinkaya-Rundel, 2022). It also reinforces the idea that sharing work openly can be a normal part of serious analytical practice.

5.4 Ethical Dimensions: AI Attribution and Academic Integrity

The integration of AI tools into student statistical analyses raises complex questions of academic integrity and attribution. If a student uses an AI tool to generate the code for a statistical analysis, what does this mean for the learning outcomes of the course? How should AI assistance be disclosed? What counts as the student's own work in an era of generative AI? These questions do not have simple answers and remain the subject of ongoing debate in higher education (Eaton, 2023; Cotton et al., 2023).

The open science framework offers one principled approach to these questions: transparency about AI use. Rather than treating AI assistance as inherently problematic, instructors can require students to document all AI interactions as part of their analytical workflow by noting the tool used, the prompt submitted, and the response obtained, and by demonstrating their own understanding through interpreting and extending the AI-generated content. This approach treats transparency about AI use as part of normal analytical practice rather than an optional disclosure, and it aligns with emerging professional norms in data science and research (Lund et al., 2023; Hosseini & Horbach, 2023).

UNESCO's Guidance for Generative AI in Education and Research (2023) recommends that institutions develop clear policies for AI use in academic work that balance the legitimate educational benefits of AI tools with the need to ensure that students develop genuine competencies. Embedding open science practices into statistics courses, where AI use is documented as part of standard procedure rather than simply prohibited, represents one practical way to respond to this recommendation.

6. DISCUSSION: IMPLICATIONS FOR THE FUTURE OF STATISTICS EDUCATION

6.1 Reconceptualizing Statistical Competence in the AI Era

The competencies required of students in statistics are changing rapidly as AI becomes more common in the work of analysis. Where statistical education once focused primarily on selecting appropriate tests, computing test statistics, and interpreting p-values, statistical competence now also includes the ability to design and carry out reproducible workflows, critically evaluate AI-generated analyses, work with open data, and contribute to collaborative and transparent forms of analysis. In other words, responsible practice is no longer peripheral to statistical training. It is part of what statistical competence now requires.

The TROPE framework proposed in this chapter offers one way to organize these expectations for teaching. It is grounded in practical tools of reproducible data science such as R, Python, Git, and literate programming environments, while also emphasizing the values of transparency, documentation, and accountability in open science. That combination matters. Tools without these values can produce technically competent but shallow work, while values without the tools to support them are difficult to carry out in practice.

6.2 Challenges and Limitations

This framework also comes with real challenges. First, teaching reproducible workflows and version control requires instructors who have experience with these practices and feel prepared to teach them. That remains a professional development challenge because many statistics instructors were trained before these practices became standard (Donoho, 2017).

Second, the cognitive load of learning R or Python, Git, and literate programming at the same time may overwhelm beginning students, especially those without prior programming experience. This is why careful sequencing and scaffolding, as described in Section 5.2.

Third, institutional constraints may also limit implementation. Learning management systems may not support GitHub-based submission, library policies may not make data sharing easy, and assessment frameworks may still be built around final answers rather than workflow quality. Institutional change, along with the use of flexible platforms such as Posit Cloud, JupyterHub, and OSF, may help instructors work within these constraints.

Fourth, AI tools are changing so quickly that specific guidance about platforms and capabilities can become dated very fast. The principles emphasized in this chapter, transparency, reproducibility, openness, and provenance, are meant to last longer than any particular tool recommendation. Instructors will need to keep adapting to changes in AI while keeping these principles in view.

6.3 Future Research Directions and Open Gaps

Several directions for future research follow from this chapter. First, more empirical work is needed on the effectiveness of reproducibility-focused teaching in statistics courses. Do students who learn in open science-oriented classrooms develop stronger statistical reasoning, better judgment, and more durable habits of responsible practice than those in more conventional courses? The evidence base here is still thin. In the recent scoping review by Dudda et al. (2025), which examined 105 empirical studies of open-science and reproducibility interventions across disciplines, only 15 directly measured effects on reproducibility itself, with most relying on proxy outcomes. Randomized or quasi-experimental studies comparing different teaching approaches would be valuable.

Second, more research is needed on how students develop, or fail to develop, the ability to critically evaluate AI-generated statistical output. We still do not understand enough about how students judge AI-generated claims, including the role of prior statistical knowledge, confidence, and beliefs about what counts as trustworthy knowledge. Qualitative studies that examine student reasoning during AI-assisted analysis tasks would offer useful insight.

Third, more research is needed on the equity implications of open science education. Open-source tools such as R, Python, and Git are free, but learning to use them still depends on reliable internet access, adequate hardware, and time. Instructors should consider how these demands may place a heavier burden on students from lower-resource backgrounds and should advocate for institutional support, including computer labs, cloud computing access, and technical assistance, that makes open science education more accessible.

A further area for research concerns instructors' readiness to teach in ways that align with reproducibility, open science, and responsible AI use. If statistics courses are expected to make workflows, documentation, verification, and AI transparency part of normal practice, then more needs to be understood about whether instructors feel prepared to teach and assess these skills. Research could examine teachers' own computational confidence, their familiarity with reproducible workflows, and the kinds of professional development and institutional support that make this kind of teaching sustainable.

CONCLUSION

Reproducibility, transparency, and open science are not add-ons to statistics education. They are part of its ethical and intellectual foundation. In an era when AI tools can generate persuasive but potentially incorrect statistical output so easily, the ability to critically evaluate, document, and reproduce analytical workflows is more important than ever. This chapter has argued for bringing reproducible computational tools such as R, Python, R Markdown, Quarto, and Jupyter Notebooks, version control systems such as Git and GitHub, and open science practices such as FAIR data, preregistration, and open repositories into statistics courses at all levels.

The Transparency, Reproducibility, Openness, and Provenance (TROPE) framework offers one way to organize this work by connecting specific classroom practices to broader scientific values. By teaching students to document their AI use, commit their code to version-controlled repositories, and share their work openly, statistics educators can help make responsible practice part of statistical competence.

The reproducibility crisis has shown the cost of a scientific culture that prioritizes publication over accountability, novelty over rigor, and output over process. Statistics education has a chance to model something different: a culture in which the process of analysis matters, transparency is built into ordinary practice, and students learn that polished output is never a substitute for understanding. The teacher's role in this process is not simply to permit or restrict AI use, but to help students build the habits of judgment, verification, and documentation that make statistical work trustworthy. In the AI era, that culture of openness, documentation, and accountability is essential to trustworthy statistical work.

REFERENCES

Alkaissi, H., & McFarlane, S. I. (2023). Artificial hallucinations in ChatGPT: Implications in scientific writing. *Cureus, 15*(2), e35179. DOI: 10.7759/cureus.35179 PMID: 36811129

Allaire, J. J., Teague, C., Scheidegger, C., Xie, Y., & Dervieux, C. (2022). *Quarto* (Version 1.0) [Computer software]. DOI: 10.5281/zenodo.5960048

Baker, M. (2016). 1,500 scientists lift the lid on reproducibility. *Nature, 533*(7604), 452–454. DOI: 10.1038/533452a PMID: 27225100

Ball, P. (2023). Is AI leading to a reproducibility crisis in science? *Nature, 624*(7990), 22–25. DOI: 10.1038/d41586-023-03817-6

Baumer, B. S., Kaplan, D. T., & Horton, N. J. (2014). R Markdown: Integrating a reproducible analysis tool into introductory statistics. *Technology Innovations in Statistics Education, 8*(1).

Beckman, M. D., Çetinkaya-Rundel, M., Horton, N. J., Rundel, C. W., Sullivan, A. J., & Tackett, M. (2021). Implementing version control with Git and GitHub as a learning objective in statistics and data science courses. *Journal of Statistics and Data Science Education, 29*(sup1), S132–S144.

Bender, E. M., Gebru, T., McMillan-Major, A., & Shmitchell, S. (2021). On the dangers of stochastic parrots: Can language models be too big? *Proceedings of the 2021 ACM Conference on Fairness, Accountability, and Transparency (FAccT '21)*, 610–623. DOI: 10.1145/3442188.3445922

Berlin Declaration on Open Access to Knowledge in the Sciences and Humanities. (2003). *Max Planck Society*. https://openaccess.mpg.de/Berlin-Declaration

Boettiger, C. (2015). An introduction to Docker for reproducible research. *Operating Systems Review*, *49*(1), 71–79. DOI: 10.1145/2723872.2723882

Bray, A., Çetinkaya-Rundel, M., & Hardin, J. (2021). *infer: An R package for tidyverse-friendly statistical inference*. https://infer.netlify.app

Bryan, J., & Hester, J. (2021). *What they forgot to teach you about R: The stuff you need to know about R beyond data analysis.* https://rstats.wtf

Bryan, J., Hester, J., & the The Stat 545 Tas. (2021). *Happy Git and GitHub for the useR*. https://happygitwithr.com

Camerer, C. F., Dreber, A., Forsell, E., Ho, T.-H., Huber, J., Johannesson, M., & Hung, H. (2016). Evaluating replicability of laboratory experiments in economics. *Science*, *351*(6280), 1433–1436. DOI: 10.1126/science.aaf0918 PMID: 26940865

Çetinkaya-Rundel, M., & Rundel, C. (2018). Infrastructure and tools for teaching computing throughout the statistical curriculum. *The American Statistician*, *72*(1), 58–65. DOI: 10.1080/00031305.2017.1397549

Chambers, C. D. (2013). Registered reports: A new publishing initiative at *Cortex*. *Cortex; A Journal Devoted to the Study of the Nervous System and Behavior*, *49*(3), 609–610. DOI: 10.1016/j.cortex.2012.12.016 PMID: 23347556

Clerc, O., Abdelghani, R., Desvaux, C., Poisson, E., Oudeyer, P. Y., & Sauzéon, H. (2026). *Teaching students to question the machine: An AI literacy intervention improves students' regulation of LLM use in a science task*. arXiv (Cornell University). https://doi.org/10.48550/arxiv.2604.01955

Cotton, D. R. E., Cotton, P. A., & Shipway, J. R. (2023). Chatting and cheating: Ensuring academic integrity in the era of ChatGPT. *Innovations in Education and Teaching International*, *61*(2), 228–239. DOI: 10.1080/14703297.2023.2190148

Dogucu, M., & Çetinkaya-Rundel, M. (2022). Tools and recommendations for reproducible teaching. *Journal of Statistics and Data Science Education : An Official Journal of the of the American Statistical Association*, *30*(3), 251–260. DOI: 10.1080/26939169.2022.2138645

Donoho, D. (2017). 50 years of data science. *Journal of Computational and Graphical Statistics*, *26*(4), 745–766. DOI: 10.1080/10618600.2017.1384734

Dudda, L., Kormann, E., Kozula, M., DeVito, N. J., Klebel, T., Dewi, A. P. M., Spijker, R., Stegeman, I., Van den Eynden, V., Ross-Hellauer, T., & Leeflang, M. M. G. (2025). Open science interventions to improve reproducibility and replicability of research: A scoping review. *Royal Society Open Science*, *12*(4), 242057. DOI: 10.1098/rsos.242057 PMID: 40206851

Eaton, S. E. (2023). *Plagiarism in higher education: Tackling tough topics in academic integrity*. ABC-CLIO.

Errington, T. M., Mathur, M., Soderberg, C. K., Denis, A., Perfors, A., Ioannidis, J. P. A., & Nosek, B. A. (2021). Investigating the replicability of preclinical cancer biology. *eLife*, *10*, e71601. DOI: 10.7554/eLife.71601 PMID: 34874005

Firat, M. (2023). How Chat GPT can transform autodidactic experiences and open education? *Theory and Practice in Language Studies*, *13*(3).

Foster, E. D., & Deardorff, A. (2017). Open science framework (OSF). *Journal of the Medical Library Association: JMLA*, *105*(2), 203. DOI: 10.5195/jmla.2017.88

Gebru, T., Morgenstern, J., Vecchione, B., Vaughan, J. W., Wallach, H., Daumé, H.III, & Crawford, K. (2021). Datasheets for datasets. *Communications of the ACM*, *64*(12), 86–92. DOI: 10.1145/3458723

Gentleman, R., & Temple Lang, D. (2007). Statistical analyses and reproducible research. *Journal of Computational and Graphical Statistics*, *16*(1), 1–23. DOI: 10.1198/106186007X178663

Halaweh, M. (2023). ChatGPT in education: Strategies for responsible implementation. *Contemporary Educational Technology*, *15*(2), ep421. DOI: 10.30935/cedtech/13036

Horton, N. J. (2023). Teaching reproducibility and responsibility workflows. *Journal of Statistics and Data Science Publication.* (Invited perspective / conference-linked publication). https://www.prodabi.de/wpcontent/uploads/Slides_Nick_Horton_Teaching_Reproducibility_and_responsible_Workflows.pdf

Hosseini, M., & Horbach, S. P. J. M. (2023). Fighting AI-facilitated research misconduct: The importance of involving multiple stakeholders. *Publications*, *11*(3), 43.

Hosseini, M., Horbach, S. P. J. M., Holmes, K. L., & Ross-Hellauer, T. (2024). Open science at the generative AI turn: An exploratory analysis of challenges and opportunities. *Quantitative Science Studies*. Advance online publication. DOI: 10.1162/qss_a_00337 PMID: 40124128

Kasneci, E., Seßler, K., Küchemann, S., Bannert, M., Dementieva, D., Fischer, F., Gasser, U., Groh, G., Günnemann, S., Hüllermeier, E., Krusche, S., Kutyniok, G., Michaeli, T., Nerdel, C., Pfeffer, J., Poquet, O., Sailer, M., Schmidt, A., Seidel, T., & Kasneci, G. (2023). ChatGPT for good? On opportunities and challenges of large language models for education. *Learning and Individual Differences*, *103*, 102274. DOI: 10.1016/j.lindif.2023.102274

Kluyver, T., Ragan-Kelley, B., Pérez, F., Granger, B., Bussonnier, M., Frederic, J., & Willing, C. (2016). Jupyter Notebooks—A publishing format for reproducible computational workflows. In Loizides, F., & Schmidt, B. (Eds.), *Positioning and Power in Academic Publishing: Players, Agents and Agendas* (pp. 87–90). IOS Press. DOI: 10.3233/978-1-61499-649-1-87

Knuth, D. E. (1984). Literate programming. *The Computer Journal*, *27*(2), 97–111. DOI: 10.1093/comjnl/27.2.97

Lund, B. D., Wang, T., Mannuru, N. R., Nie, B., Shimray, S., & Wang, Z. (2023). ChatGPT and a new academic reality: Artificial intelligence-written research papers and the ethics of the large language model publishing landscape. *Journal of the Association for Information Science and Technology*, *74*(5), 570–581. DOI: 10.1002/asi.24750

Marcus, G., & Davis, E. (2019). *Rebooting AI: Building artificial intelligence we can trust*. Vintage.

Marwick, B., Boettiger, C., & Mullen, L. (2018). Packaging data analytical work reproducibly using R (and friends). *The American Statistician*, *72*(1), 80–88. DOI: 10.1080/00031305.2017.1375986

McKinney, W. (2017). *Python for data analysis: Data wrangling with Pandas, NumPy, and IPython* (2nd ed.). O'Reilly Media.

Mendez-Carbajo, D., & Dellachiesa, A. (2023). Data citations and reproducibility in the undergraduate curriculum. *Harvard Data Science Review*, *5*(3). Advance online publication. DOI: 10.1162/99608f92.c2835391

Mitchell, M., Wu, S., Zaldivar, A., Barnes, P., Vasserman, L., Hutchinson, B., & Gebru, T. (2019). Model cards for model reporting. *Proceedings of the Conference on Fairness, Accountability, and Transparency (FAT* '19)*, 220–229. DOI: 10.1145/3287560.3287596

Nosek, B. A., Alter, G., Banks, G. C., Borsboom, D., Bowman, S. D., Breckler, S. J., Buck, S., Chambers, C. D., Chin, G., Christensen, G., Contestabile, M., Dafoe, A., Eich, E., Freese, J., Glennerster, R., Goroff, D., Green, D. P., Hesse, B., Humphreys, M., & Yarkoni, T. (2015). Promoting an open research culture. *Science*, *348*(6242), 1422–1425. DOI: 10.1126/science.aab2374 PMID: 26113702

Nosek, B. A., Ebersole, C. R., DeHaven, A. C., & Mellor, D. T. (2018). The preregistration revolution. *Proceedings of the National Academy of Sciences of the United States of America*, *115*(11), 2600–2606. DOI: 10.1073/pnas.1708274114 PMID: 29531091

Open Science Collaboration. (2015). Estimating the reproducibility of psychological science. *Science*, *349*(6251), aac4716. DOI: 10.1126/science.aac4716 PMID: 26315443

Pitts, G., Rani, N., Mildort, W., & Cook, E. (2025). *Students' reliance on AI in Higher Education: Identifying contributing factors*. ArXiv.org. https://doi.org/10.48550/arxiv.2506.13845

Peng, R. D. (2011). Reproducible research in computational science. *Science, 334*(6060), 1226–1227. DOI: 10.1126/science.1213847 PMID: 22144613

Peng, R. D. (2022). *Mastering software development in R.* Leanpub.

Peng, R. D., & Hicks, S. C. (2021). Reproducible research: A retrospective. *Annual Review of Public Health, 42*(1), 79–93. DOI: 10.1146/annurev-publhealth-012420-105110 PMID: 33467923

Plesser, H. E. (2018). Reproducibility vs. replicability: A brief history of a confused terminology. *Frontiers in Neuroinformatics, 11*, 76. DOI: 10.3389/fninf.2017.00076 PMID: 29403370

Poldrack, R. A., Baker, C. I., Durnez, J., Gorgolewski, K. J., Matthews, P. M., Munafò, M. R., Nichols, T. E., Poline, J.-B., Vul, E., & Yarkoni, T. (2017). Scanning the horizon: Towards transparent and reproducible neuroimaging research. *Nature Reviews. Neuroscience, 18*(2), 115–126. DOI: 10.1038/nrn.2016.167 PMID: 28053326

Popper, K. R. (1959). *The logic of scientific discovery*. Hutchinson.

Pruim, R., Kaplan, D. T., & Horton, N. J. (2017). The mosaic package: Helping students to 'think with data' using R. *The R Journal, 9*(1), 77–102. DOI: 10.32614/RJ-2017-024

R Core Team. (2024). *R: A language and environment for statistical computing*. R Foundation for Statistical Computing. https://www.R-project.org

Rasmussen, L. V., Whitley, E. W., & Welty, L. J. (2023). Pragmatic reproducible research: Improving the research process from raw data to results, bit by bit. *The Journal of Clinical Investigation, 133*(16), e173741. DOI: 10.1172/JCI173741 PMID: 37581309

Seabold, S., & Perktold, J. (2010). Statsmodels: Econometric and statistical modeling with Python. *Proceedings of the 9th Python in Science Conference*, 57–61. DOI: 10.25080/Majora-92bf1922-011

Shoufan, A., & Esmaeil, A. (2026). *AI Hallucination from Students' Perspective: A Thematic Analysis.* arXiv (Cornell University). https://doi.org/10.48550/arxiv.2602.17671

Stodden, V., Leisch, F., & Peng, R. D. (Eds.). (2014). *Implementing reproducible research.* CRC Press. DOI: 10.1201/b16868

Stodden, V., McNutt, M., Bailey, D. H., Deelman, E., Gil, Y., Hanson, B., Heroux, M. A., Ioannidis, J. P. A., & Taufer, M. (2016). Enhancing reproducibility for computational methods. *Science, 354*(6317), 1240–1241. DOI: 10.1126/science.aah6168 PMID: 27940837

Stodden, V., & Miguez, S. (2014). Best practices for computational science: Software infrastructure and environments for reproducible and extensible research. *Journal of Open Research Software*, *2*(1), e21. DOI: 10.5334/jors.ay

UNESCO. (2023). *Guidance for generative AI in education and research*. UNESCO Publishing., DOI: 10.54675/EWZM9535

Ushey, K. (2023). *renv: Project environments for R* (Version 1.0.3) [R package]. https://rstudio.github.io/renv

Vallat, R. (2018). Pingouin: Statistics in Python. *Journal of Open Source Software*, *3*(31), 1026. DOI: 10.21105/joss.01026

van Dis, E. A., Bollen, J., Zuidema, W., van Rooji, R., & Bockting, C. L. (2023). ChatGPT: Five priorities for research. *Nature*, *614*(7947), 224–226. DOI: 10.1038/d41586-023-00288-7 PMID: 36737653

VanderPlas, J. (2016). *Python data science handbook: Essential tools for working with data*. O'Reilly Media.

Vicente-Saez, R., & Martinez-Fuentes, C. (2018). Open science now: A systematic literature review for an integrated definition. *Journal of Business Research*, *88*, 428–436. DOI: 10.1016/j.jbusres.2017.12.043

Wagenmakers, E.-J., Wetzels, R., Borsboom, D., van der Maas, H. L. J., & Kievit, R. A. (2012). An agenda for purely confirmatory research. *Perspectives on Psychological Science : A Journal of the Association for Psychological Science*, *7*(6), 632–638. DOI: 10.1177/1745691612463078 PMID: 26168122

Wickham, H., Averick, M., Bryan, J., Chang, W., McGowan, L., François, R., Grolemund, G., Hayes, A., Henry, L., Hester, J., Kuhn, M., Pedersen, T., Miller, E., Bache, S., Müller, K., Ooms, J., Robinson, D., Seidel, D., Spinu, V., & Yutani, H. (2019). Welcome to the tidyverse. *Journal of Open Source Software*, *4*(43), 1686. DOI: 10.21105/joss.01686

Wilkinson, M. D., Dumontier, M., Aalbersberg, I. J., Appleton, G., Axton, M., Baak, A., Blomberg, N., Boiten, J.-W., da Silva Santos, L. B., Bourne, P. E., Bouwman, J., Brookes, A. J., Clark, T., Crosas, M., Dillo, I., Dumon, O., Edmunds, S., Evelo, C. T., Finkers, R., & Mons, B. (2016). The FAIR guiding principles for scientific data management and stewardship. *Scientific Data*, *3*(1), 160018. DOI: 10.1038/sdata.2016.18 PMID: 26978244

Wilson, G., Bryan, J., Cranston, K., Kitzes, J., Nederbragt, L., & Teal, T. K. (2017). Good enough practices in scientific computing. *PLoS Computational Biology*, *13*(6), e1005510. DOI: 10.1371/journal.pcbi.1005510 PMID: 28640806

Xie, Y., Allaire, J. J., & Grolemund, G. (2020). *R Markdown: The definitive guide*. CRC Press. https://bookdown.org/yihui/rmarkdown

Yang, S., Zhao, H., Xu, Y., Brennan, K., & Schneider, B. (2024). Debugging with an AI tutor: Investigating novice help-seeking behaviors and perceived learning. *Proceedings of the 2024 ACM Conference on International Computing Education Research*, 84–94. DOI: 10.1145/3632620.3671092

Chapter 12
Statistics Pedagogy in the Age of AI: Analyzing Its Challenges, Strategies, and Global Case Studies

S. Ghiri
http://orcid.org/0009-0001-0032-4967
ITM Skills University, India

David C. Gray
http://orcid.org/0009-0004-4000-5583
Univeristy of Liberia, Liberia

ABSTRACT

In an era defined by the rapid integration of artificial intelligence (AI), the discipline of statistics and its pedagogical approaches face a critical inflection point. This chapter explores this transformative landscape, examining the profound challenges and opportunities for statistics education. In response, this chapter presents a comprehensive set of pedagogical strategies designed to foster deep data literacy and computational thinking. These strategies include leveraging generative AI as a learning partner, implementing simulation-based inference to enhance conceptual understanding, and redesigning assessment methods for the modern data ecosystem. Ultimately, this chapter provides a forward-looking framework for educators, curriculum designers, and academic leaders seeking to equip students with the essential statistical competencies required to navigate a data-centric, AI-driven future.

DOI: 10.4018/979-8-3373-6259-5.ch012

1. INTRODUCTION

Statistics education is being reshaped by the convergence of ubiquitous data, powerful computational systems, and increasingly capable AI tools that operate as co-pilots for analysis rather than mere calculators. In this environment, data literacy and statistical thinking have become foundational competencies for civic participation and workforce readiness. Yet the same technologies that promise personalization and efficiency also raise new questions about equity, ethics, and the nature of statistical understanding when machines can generate analyses and explanations on demand. (Zhang, 2025; Grassini et al., 2025; Büscher, 2022; Sharma, 2017)

1.1 The Unprecedented Data Firehose

Contemporary societies generate vast streams of digital trace data from transactions, sensors, social media, and institutional systems, far exceeding the curated datasets traditionally used in statistics classrooms. This high-volume, high-velocity, and high-variety data landscape makes AI indispensable for pattern detection, forecasting, and anomaly identification, but it also foregrounds issues of data quality, bias, and representativeness that are often muted in textbook examples. Preparing students to reason statistically in this data deluge requires moving beyond procedural calculation toward critical engagement with data sources, transformations, and modeling assumptions.(Penn GSE, n.d.; Akintunde et al., 2025; The Academic, 2025; Ridsdale et al., 2015)

1.2 The Analyst's New Partner: AI as Co-Pilot

Where earlier software functioned primarily as a programmable calculator, contemporary AI systems can propose models, generate code, and draft narrative interpretations in response to natural language prompts. Studies of generative AI–supported tools such as show that students increasingly approach statistical tasks through iterative prompting, using AI to scaffold coding, graphing, and explanation while still needing prior statistical knowledge to interpret outputs meaningfully. This shift compels a redefinition of the human analyst's role from operator of computational procedures to strategic and ethical commander of the inquiry—formulating questions, interrogating assumptions, judging appropriateness of methods, and scrutinizing results.(Grassini et al., 2025; Rao et al., 2026; Rao et al., 2026)

1.3 Core Thesis: An Urgent Call for Pedagogical Reinvention

The central claim of this chapter is that statistics pedagogy must be reinvented for an AI-saturated world rather than merely augmented with new tools. Existing instructional patterns that emphasize hand computation and isolated techniques risk becoming obsolete as AI automates routine procedures. Instead, curricula must foreground statistical thinking problem formulation, data critique, modeling judgment, and communication under uncertainty coupled with AI literacy, including understanding AI capabilities, limitations, and ethical implications. This reinvention requires re-conceptualizing teacher knowledge (AASPK), redesigning assessments to value higher-order reasoning, and building policies that safeguard privacy and equity while enabling innovation.(Wild & Pfannkuch, 1999; UNESCO, 2019; Pane et al., 2015; Zhang, 2025)

2. Theoretical Frameworks for AI-Enhanced Statistics Pedagogy

2.1 From SPK to AI-Aware Statistical Pedagogical Knowledge (AASPK)

Burgess's work on Statistical Pedagogical Knowledge (SPK) adapts Shulman's broader theory of pedagogical content knowledge to the specific demands of teaching statistics, highlighting common content knowledge, specialized statistical content knowledge, knowledge of content and students, and knowledge of content and teaching. Classroom studies show that gaps in SPK lead to "missed opportunities," where teachers fail to capitalize on moments to deepen students' statistical reasoning about variation, data, and inference. However, SPK was formulated prior to the widespread availability of AI tools that can automatically compute statistics, fit models, and produce visualizations.(Burgess, 2007; Koehler et al., 2013)

To address this gap, the chapter proposes AI-Aware Statistical Pedagogical Knowledge (AASPK) as a framework that adds AI-specific dimensions to SPK. AASPK is conceptualized primarily as a competency model for teachers, while also functioning as a diagnostic framework for identifying strengths and weaknesses in AI-enhanced practice and as a curriculum design lens for aligning tasks, tools, and assessments.

AASPK is organized into five interrelated dimensions:

AI-augmented statistical content knowledge – understanding how AI systems implement statistical procedures, which approximations they employ, and where their outputs may be misleading.

AI-aware pedagogical design knowledge – designing tasks that require students to make and justify choices about when and how to enlist AI support.

AI-mediated assessment and feedback knowledge – using AI for formative assessment and feedback while preserving opportunities for students to display independent reasoning.

Data ethics and governance knowledge – understanding privacy, consent, bias, and regulatory frameworks (e.g., GDPR) relevant to student data and algorithmic decision-making.(8allocate, 2025; AI4EDU, 2025)

Learning analytics interpretation knowledge – interpreting dashboards, predictive models, and engagement metrics in ways that respect uncertainty and avoid deficit labeling of students.(The Academic, 2025; Lukarov et al., 2018)

These AASPK dimensions map explicitly onto both teacher actions and student outcomes (Table 1).

Table 1. Conceptual comparison of SPK, TPACK, and AASPK

Framework	Core Focus	Key Dimensions	Application in Statistics Teaching
SPK *(Statistical Pedagogical Knowledge)*	Statistical content knowledge and pedagogy; pre-AI frameworks	Common statistical content knowledge; specialized content knowledge; knowledge of content and students; knowledge of content and teaching	Identifying and capitalizing on moments to deepen students' reasoning about variation, data, and inference; avoiding missed opportunities in discussion
TPACK *(Technological Pedagogical Content Knowledge)*	Integration of technology with pedagogy and content; emphasizes how technology affords or constrains instruction	Technological knowledge (TK); pedagogical knowledge (PK); content knowledge (CK); and their intersections: TPK, TCK, PCK, and TPACK	Using dynamic applets, simulations, and statistical visualisation tools; understanding how software design shapes learner engagement with data
AASPK *(AI-Aware Statistical Pedagogical Knowledge)*	AI-enhanced statistical pedagogy with explicit attention to ethics, algorithmic transparency, and human judgment	AI-augmented statistical content knowledge; AI-aware pedagogical design; AI-mediated assessment and feedback; data ethics and governance; learning analytics interpretation	Designing tasks requiring critical AI engagement; prompting students to formulate questions before consulting AI; scrutinising AI-generated analyses; integrating privacy and bias discussions into statistical inquiry

In practice, an AASPK lens prompts questions such as: *Does this activity require students to formulate questions before consulting AI? How are students asked to critique and cross-check AI-generated analyses? How are privacy and bias discussed as part of the statistical investigation cycle?* These questions re-locate pedagogical attention from simply using tools to cultivating human judgment in AI-rich environments.

2.2 Constructivist and Social Constructivist Foundations

Constructivist theories, drawing on Piaget, posit that learners actively construct knowledge by reconciling new experiences with prior conceptions. Social constructivism, rooted in Vygotsky, emphasizes that cognitive development is mediated by interaction with more knowledgeable others within cultural and historical contexts, with concepts such as the Zone of Proximal Development (ZPD) and scaffolding central to instructional design. In statistics education, constructivist approaches have long advocated for inquiry-based tasks, real data, and opportunities for students to articulate and refine their reasoning.(EdTech Books, n.d.; McLeod, 2024)

AI-enhanced environments reconfigure, but do not replace, these foundations. Generative AI tutors can function as "more knowledgeable others" within a student's ZPD, offering hints, explanations, and alternative representations, yet empirical work shows that prior statistical understanding remains crucial for interpreting AI suggestions and for noticing when outputs are nonsensical or inconsistent. From a constructivist perspective, AI tools should be positioned as resources within collaborative problem-solving, not as authoritative oracles, and instructional designs must include structured opportunities for students to negotiate meaning, challenge AI, and compare AI explanations with peer and teacher reasoning.(Rao et al., 2026)

2.3 Extending TPACK for AI Integration

The TPACK framework formalizes the intersecting domains of technological, pedagogical, and content knowledge required for effective technology integration, arguing that high-quality teaching with technology involves nuanced understandings of how technology affords or constrains particular pedagogical moves in specific content areas. In the context of statistics, TPACK has supported research on teachers' use of dynamic applets, simulations, and visualization tools.(Mishra & Koehler, 2006; Educational Technology, n.d.; Koehler et al., 2013)

AI integration, however, introduces at least three additional complexities. First, many AI systems are probabilistic and opaque, making their behavior less predictable than conventional tools and raising transparency and explainability concerns. Second, AI systems often collect and process learner data at scale, intertwining technology integration with institutional data governance and privacy policies. Third, AI systems can generate content (e.g., hints, questions, rubrics) rather than merely presenting pre-authored materials, shifting teacher roles toward curation, verification, and orchestration. An "AI-extended TPACK" thus requires teachers to understand not only what AI tools can do, but how their algorithmic nature interacts with pedagogy and statistical content, and how to exercise professional judgment when AI outputs conflict with disciplinary norms.(IJTLE, 2024; AI4EDU, 2025; 8allocate, 2025; Zhang, 2025)

2.4 Data Literacy and Statistical Literacy Frameworks

Data literacy frameworks from library and higher education communities conceptualize competencies across the data lifecycle: establishing data culture, providing and managing data, analyzing and evaluating data, interpreting results, and publishing or communicating findings. In parallel, statistical literacy frameworks in statistics education highlight the ability to interpret, critically evaluate, and communicate about statistical information in everyday contexts, including awareness of missing information and underlying assumptions.(Akintunde et al., 2025; Ridsdale et al., 2015; Büscher, 2022; Carlson & Johnston, 2015; Sharma, 2017)

Integrating these lenses suggests that AI-era statistics pedagogy should cultivate data-informed citizenship—students who can question how data were collected, recognize the interests of data producers, understand limitations of algorithmic classifications, and communicate uncertainty clearly. Classroom tasks that require students to interrogate AI-generated graphs, summaries, or predictive scores against raw data and contextual knowledge directly enact these frameworks.(UNESCO, 2019; Akintunde et al., 2025)

2.5 AI-Driven Learning Analytics as a Theoretical Lens

AI-powered learning analytics extend traditional data collection on attendance and grades to fine-grained traces of clickstreams, problem attempts, and textual interactions, enabling predictive models of engagement, success, and risk. Programmes such as learning analytics degrees and institutional initiatives demonstrate how algorithmic analyses are increasingly used to guide interventions, resource allocation, and curriculum redesign. For statistics pedagogy, learning analytics both provide rich data for formative assessment and raise critical questions about measurement, fairness, and interpretability.(Lukarov et al., 2018; Higher Ed Dive, 2023; Penn GSE, n.d.; The Academic, 2025)

A theoretical stance informed by AASPK and data literacy treats learning analytics dashboards not as objective truth but as statistical models subject to sampling error, modeling assumptions, and potential bias. Teachers and students must therefore be supported to read, question, and act on these analytics in ways consistent with sound statistical practice asking what variables are omitted, what outcomes are being predicted, and how false positives or false negatives in early-warning systems might differentially affect student subgroups.(Ridsdale et al., 2015; The Academic, 2025)

Section Summary

Together, SPK, AASPK, constructivism, extended TPACK, data literacy, and learning analytics frameworks provide a multi-layered theoretical foundation for understanding how AI alters, and can potentially enrich, statistics pedagogy. They foreground teacher competencies, student reasoning, technological affordances, and ethical governance as mutually constitutive dimensions rather than isolated concerns.(Burgess, 2007; Akintunde et al., 2025; The Academic, 2025; Mishra & Koehler, 2006)

3. CURRENT CHALLENGES IN AI-ENHANCED STATISTICS EDUCATION

3.1 Digital Divide and Global Equity Concerns

Persistent digital divides threaten to make AI-enhanced statistics education an accelerant of inequality rather than a vehicle for inclusion. In the United States, an estimated 24 million people lack access to high-speed internet, with low-income households and rural communities disproportionately affected, limiting their ability to engage with AI-driven platforms outside school. In India, recent UDISE Plus data indicate that only about 57 percent of schools have functional computers and around 54 percent have internet access, underscoring substantial infrastructure gaps that constrain implementation of AI-based tools in mathematics and statistics classrooms.(Global Citizen, 2023; Giving Compass, 2023; Business Standard, 2025; Kearney, n.d.; India Today, 2025)

Equity challenges are even more pronounced in parts of Africa, Latin America, and Southeast Asia, where many schools contend with intermittent electricity, limited device access, and under-resourced teaching staff. Case studies from Rwanda and experimental trials of low-bandwidth AI math tutors in Ghana show that mobile-first and offline AI solutions can yield statistically significant learning gains, but they also depend on donor funding, pilot scale, and fragile connectivity arrangements. Without deliberate policy commitments to prioritize underserved regions, AI risks deepening what some authors describe as cognitive disenfranchisement, where only a subset of students gain access to the epistemic tools needed to shape and critique algorithmic systems.(Uwineza et al., 2025; Uwineza et al., 2025; Jukes et al., 2024; Jukes et al., 2024; DRCLAS ReVista, 2024)

3.2 Privacy, Security, and Ethical Considerations

AI systems used in statistics education often require access to sensitive student data—performance histories, behavioral logs, and sometimes biometric indicators—to drive personalization and predictive models. Regulatory frameworks such as the EU's General Data Protection Regulation (GDPR) and sector-specific laws like FERPA in the United States establish legal obligations around consent, data minimization, and rights of access and erasure, yet many institutions lack robust governance structures for AI deployments.(AI4EDU, 2025; 8allocate, 2025; The Academic, 2025)

Recent policy analyses highlight the need for Data Protection Impact Assessments (DPIAs) when AI systems profile learners or process children's data at scale, emphasizing risks of re-identification, discriminatory outcomes, and misuse of predictive labels. Finnish initiatives that combine GDPR-aligned anonymization, algorithmic transparency requirements, and explicit digital citizenship education offer emerging models of responsible practice, but they require substantial investment in technical infrastructure and staff expertise. For statistics pedagogy, these issues are not merely administrative: they are opportunities to integrate real cases of data governance, consent, and algorithmic auditing into curricular discussions of sampling, bias, and inference.(Nucamp, 2025; 8allocate, 2025; AI4EDU, 2025)

3.3 Teacher Preparation, Competencies, and Resistance

Despite growing enthusiasm for AI, many educators express skepticism, anxiety, or resistance to adopting AI tools in their teaching. A recent systematic review of barriers to educator acceptance of AI identifies insufficient training, opaque alignment with pedagogical goals, infrastructure limitations, and ethical concerns as recurrent obstacles, with differences across regions: resource constraints dominate in low-income contexts, while concerns about professional identity and academic integrity are more salient in higher-income systems. Surveys in multiple countries suggest that a substantial share of teachers feel unprepared to evaluate AI tools, interpret learning analytics, or redesign assessments in ways that reflect AI-mediated learning.(CIDDL, 2024; UNESCO, 2024; IJLTER, 2024)

UNESCO's AI competency frameworks for teachers and students articulate multi-dimensional profiles that include human-centred mindsets, ethics of AI, AI techniques and applications, and AI system design, with progressive levels from understanding to applying and creating. However, embedding these competencies into pre-service preparation and in-service professional development for statistics teachers remains nascent. Professional development programs often focus on tool demonstration rather than on cultivating AI pedagogical reasoning—teachers' capacity to decide *when* to allow AI assistance, *how* to frame AI outputs as conjectures rather than answers, and *how* to scaffold students' critique of AI-mediated analyses. (UNESCO, 2024; CIDDL, 2024)

3.4 Assessment, Academic Integrity, and LLM Hallucinations

The rapid diffusion of large language models capable of generating code, explanations, and full statistical reports challenges traditional assessment designs that rely on take-home problem sets or unproctored written assignments. Studies of hallucinations in educational uses of LLMs show that these systems can confidently produce fabricated references, incorrect numerical results, or superficially plausible but conceptually flawed explanations, posing risks for students who may lack the expertise to detect errors. At the same time, over-reliance on AI-generated content detection tools has been shown to misclassify non-native writers, raising equity concerns around false accusations of misconduct.(Athaluri et al., 2024; IJTLE, 2024; Grassini et al., 2025)

These dynamics necessitate a rethinking of what constitutes acceptable collaboration with AI in statistics courses. Some institutions are experimenting with in-class, AI-assisted assessments where students document prompts, critique AI outputs, and justify revised solutions, shifting emphasis from raw answers to meta-cognitive reasoning. Others maintain AI-free assessment zones to ensure that foundational reasoning skills are evaluated independently. In all cases, the presence of hallucination-prone tools underscores the importance of teaching verification practices—manual recalculation, triangulation across tools, and comparison with domain knowledge—as core statistical competencies.(Grassini et al., 2025; Rao et al., 2026)

3.5 Student-Centred Challenges: Dependence, Uncertainty, and Self-Regulation

From the learner's perspective, AI co-pilots can lower barriers to entry in coding and analysis but may also reduce productive struggle and tolerance for uncertainty, which are important for developing deep statistical understanding. Qualitative studies of students using generative AI for graphing and analysis reveal a tension: AI can scaffold step-by-step reasoning and encourage iterative refinement, yet students sometimes delegate too much agency to the system, accepting outputs without fully interrogating assumptions or considering alternative models.(D'Mello, 2017; Rao et al., 2026)

Self-regulated learning research indicates that effective use of AI requires goal setting, monitoring, and reflection: students must decide when AI is appropriate, evaluate its suggestions against task goals, and adjust strategies when inconsistencies arise. Without explicit guidance, there is a risk that students will form misconceptions (e.g., equating statistical significance with practical importance) that are reinforced by AI explanations, or that they will perceive uncertainty as a defect rather than an inherent feature of inferential reasoning. Addressing these challenges requires embedding AI usage norms, reflection prompts, and uncertainty-focused discussions directly into course design.(Schwartz et al., 2023; Grassini et al., 2025)

Section Summary

Digital inequities, privacy and ethical risks, incomplete teacher preparation, assessment disruptions, and student self-regulation challenges collectively illustrate that integrating AI into statistics education is not a neutral technology upgrade but a multi-dimensional transformation that can both mitigate and exacerbate existing systemic issues.(IJLTER, 2024; DRCLAS ReVista, 2024; IJTLE, 2024)

4. INNOVATIVE STRATEGIES FOR AI INTEGRATION

4.1 Personalized Learning Pathways in Statistics

Personalized learning systems use diagnostic assessments and adaptive algorithms to tailor content, pacing, and representations to individual learners' evolving profiles. Meta-analyses of personalized and adaptive learning in mathematics report positive, though heterogeneous, effects on achievement, with some studies showing substantial gains when diagnostic assessments drive targeted practice. For example, analyses of personalized learning initiatives in U.S. schools suggest that students in schools implementing such practices can make greater progress in mathematics and reading over two years than matched peers, with especially notable gains for initially lower-performing students.(Sharma, 2024; Herold, 2017; Pane et al., 2015; Zhang, 2025)

In statistics, AI-driven systems can ensure that students have mastered foundational ideas (variation, distribution, sampling) before advancing to inference, dynamically adjusting tasks based on patterns of errors and response times. However, the evidence base remains context-dependent: vendor-funded evaluations may report dramatic percentage gains that do not always replicate in independent studies or at scale. Thus, personalization should be adopted with realistic expectations and ongoing local evaluation rather than as a universal solution.(BusinessWire, 2023; WWC, 2013; Pham et al., 2022)

4.2 Intelligent Tutoring Systems for Statistics and Algebraic Foundations

Intelligent tutoring systems (ITS) provide step-wise feedback, hints, and problem sequencing approximating one-to-one human tutoring. Carnegie Learning's MATHia, for instance, has been examined using large longitudinal datasets, with analyses indicating that increased completion of MATHia workspaces in middle grades predicts stronger Algebra I performance, particularly for students who started with lower test scores. These findings suggest that ITS can help close preparation gaps, though they primarily establish predictive relationships rather than randomized causal effects and may be sensitive to implementation fidelity.(BusinessWire, 2021; Carnegie Learning, n.d.)

Beyond algebra, ITS have been deployed in probability and introductory statistics, sometimes combined with affect-sensitive components that detect boredom or confusion and adapt feedback accordingly. Meta-analytic work on ALEKS, a widely used adaptive system for mathematics and statistics, finds that learning outcomes with ALEKS are on average comparable to traditional instruction, with more substantial benefits when ALEKS supplements rather than replaces teacher-led instruction (Hedges g around 0.43 in supplemental use). These results underscore that AI tutors are most effective when embedded in blended models where human teachers interpret analytics, contextualize concepts, and address misconceptions that automated systems may miss.(D'Mello, 2017; Pham et al., 2022)

4.3 AI-Powered Assessment and Feedback

AI-assisted assessment platforms such as Gradescope use machine learning to group similar responses, support rubric-based grading, and generate detailed analytics on item performance, enabling faster and more consistent evaluation of open-response statistics tasks. Studies of Gradescope adoption in engineering and quantitative courses report substantial reductions in grading time, improved transparency about point allocation, and positive student perceptions of fairness and feedback detail, though they also note the need for careful rubric design and oversight to avoid codifying instructor biases.(University of Miami, n.d.; Baral et al., n.d.)

Natural language processing is increasingly used to evaluate short-answer explanations, statistical reasoning in written form, and even argumentation quality, providing near-immediate formative feedback. Singapore's Short Answer Feedback Assistant and Authoring Copilot exemplify this trend, helping teachers construct and mark short-answer items while retaining pedagogical control. However, current systems still struggle with nuanced reasoning and may reward formulaic phrasing over genuine insight, making human review essential for high-stakes decisions. (MOE Singapore, 2023)

4.4 Collaborative AI Learning Environments

AI can also serve as a catalyst for collaborative learning rather than just individualized tutoring. Platforms that automatically form heterogeneous groups based on complementary skill profiles, generate multiple contextualized datasets for parallel inquiry, or provide conversational agents that facilitate group reflection create new opportunities for peer-to-peer engagement in statistics. For instance, adaptive systems can assign different but structurally similar datasets to small groups, prompting students to compare sampling variability or model fit across contexts, thereby deepening their understanding of generalizable patterns.(The Academic, 2025; Lukarov et al., 2018)

Cross-border collaborations—where students in different countries analyze local datasets and then exchange interpretations—are increasingly feasible through AI-mediated matching and translation tools. Such designs can foreground cultural dimensions of data, such as how economic indicators or health statistics are defined and contested in different settings, nurturing global statistical literacy alongside technical skills.(DRCLAS ReVista, 2024; UNESCO, 2019)

4.5 A Framework for AI-Modified Instruction–Assessment–Feedback Loops

To clarify how AI changes core pedagogical cycles in statistics, this chapter proposes a descriptive model comprising three phases—design, orchestration, and interpretation—each of which is reshaped by AI.

Design phase – Teachers specify learning objectives (e.g., reasoning about sampling distributions), select or create tasks, and configure AI supports (tutors, hints, analytics, generative prompts). AASPK guides choices about which components of the statistical investigation cycle should be automated (e.g., simulation runs) and which must remain student-driven (e.g., formulating informal hypotheses).(Mishra & Koehler, 2006; Burgess, 2007)

Orchestration phase – During instruction, AI systems personalize task difficulty, provide immediate feedback, and surface real-time analytics about misconceptions or disengagement. Teachers monitor dashboards, decide when to intervene, and facilitate peer discussion that problematizes AI outputs (e.g., "Why might the model's prediction be unreliable here?").(D'Mello, 2017; The Academic, 2025)

Interpretation phase – After activities, AI aggregates evidence of learning (concept inventories, performance trajectories, written explanations). Teachers and students jointly interpret this evidence, contextualizing scores, reflecting on AI reliability, and planning next steps. Learning analytics are treated as *statistical estimates*—with uncertainty bounds and potential bias—rather than definitive labels.(Ridsdale et al., 2015; The Academic, 2025)

This framework makes explicit that AI does not simply "speed up" existing processes; it redistributes cognitive and ethical responsibilities across humans and machines. It also provides a structure for designing professional development and curriculum materials that target specific AASPK competencies at each phase.

4.6 Supporting Student Self-Regulation With AI Co-Pilots

Emerging meta-analyses on generative AI in education suggest moderate positive effects on learning outcomes, particularly for autonomous learning and self-regulation, when tools are embedded in structured tasks that require planning, monitoring, and reflection. In statistics, this translates to assignments where students must document their AI prompts, justify why they trusted or overruled AI suggestions, and articulate how AI changed their understanding of concepts such as sampling variability or model fit.(Rao et al., 2026; Grassini et al., 2025)

Design strategies include:

Prompt-journaling: Students maintain a log of AI interactions, tagging each with goals (e.g., "clarify concept," "debug code") and post-hoc evaluations of usefulness.

Uncertainty annotations: Students annotate AI outputs with statements of confidence, questions, and proposed verification steps.

AI-free checkpoints: Critical milestones (e.g., formulating research questions, deciding on modeling strategy) are initially completed without AI, with AI consulted only after initial reasoning is articulated.

These practices help students internalize norms of critical engagement rather than passive consumption of AI outputs, aligning with long-standing goals in statistics education to foster reflective, autonomous thinkers.

Section Summary

Innovative uses of AI in personalized learning, tutoring, assessment, collaboration, and self-regulation demonstrate substantial potential to enhance statistics learning, but effectiveness depends on careful design, blended implementation, and explicit attention to human judgment at each phase of the instructional cycle.(Pane et al., 2015; Zhang, 2025; Grassini et al., 2025)

5. GLOBAL CASE STUDIES AND CONTEXTUAL CONSTRAINTS

Finland has positioned itself as a leader in ethical, human-centred AI for public services, including education, through its AuroraAI programme and pilots with adaptive platforms such as Eduten. Short-term evaluations report additional gains in mathematics achievement and engagement in schools that adopt these tools, and Finland has coupled pilots with strong GDPR-aligned governance, algorithmic transparency requirements, and digital citizenship education (e.g., the open *Elements of AI* course). At the same time, these pilots often involve motivated and relatively well-resourced schools, and the costs of scaling sophisticated infrastructure while preserving local control and privacy remain active points of debate.

Singapore's EdTech Masterplan 2030 similarly illustrates a coordinated, policy-driven approach to AI integration. The national Student Learning Space (SLS) embeds AI-enabled recommendation engines and tools such as the Short Answer Feedback Assistant and Authoring Copilot to support formative assessment in mathematics and statistics. Internal evaluations suggest improved feedback timeliness and more differentiated instruction, yet public reports also highlight the need for substantial ongoing teacher professional development and careful auditing of automated scoring to ensure alignment with curricular standards and to avoid narrowing conceptions of acceptable reasoning.

In the United States, AI-enhanced statistics and quantitative education is shaped by a heterogeneous mix of institutional initiatives and commercial platforms. Georgia Tech's long-running Jill Watson virtual teaching assistant demonstrates how conversational agents can answer routine questions and strengthen teaching presence in large online courses, freeing human staff to focus on complex conceptual support. Community colleges such as Ivy Tech have used predictive learning analytics to identify at-risk students early in a term and trigger timely interventions, with reported reductions in D/F rates. At the same time, there are concerns about how predictive labels may stigmatize students, how accurate models are for minoritized groups, and how faculty can meaningfully contest algorithmic recommendations.

Across North America and Europe, commercial adaptive platforms such as MATHia, DreamBox, Khan Academy, ALEKS, CENTURY Tech, and similar systems are widely used in mathematics and statistics-related courses. Randomized trials and meta-analyses generally report moderate positive effects on achievement, particularly when platforms are used in blended models that combine automated practice with teacher facilitation, and when students engage regularly over multiple weeks. However, impact estimates vary across contexts, some studies are vendor-commissioned or quasi-experimental, and outcome measures often emphasize standardized test scores rather than longer-term statistical reasoning, transfer, or ethical judgment. Educators and policymakers therefore need to interpret vendor-reported percentage gains cautiously and attend to local implementation data.

In India and South Asia, AI-driven mathematics and statistics platforms are being deployed at scale amid large class sizes, multilingual classrooms, and uneven infrastructure. Trials of Khan Academy and related tools show that when access, connectivity, and structured lab time are in place, students can realize meaningful gains in achievement and confidence; when these conditions are absent, effects are modest or null. Mobile-first and low-bandwidth designs, including WhatsApp-based micro-lessons and offline-capable tutors, have emerged as pragmatic responses, but persistent gaps in device access (especially for girls and rural learners) and high-stakes exam pressures constrain the extent to which AI can support exploratory statistical inquiry.

China's Squirrel AI illustrates how adaptive learning systems can be scaled through extensive learning-centre networks, using fine-grained knowledge graphs to diagnose micro-skills and personalize instruction. Case reports describe significant improvements in test performance and retention for underperforming students, particularly when AI tutors are combined with human mentors who provide socio-emotional support. Yet independent, peer-reviewed evaluations remain relatively limited compared to vendor and media accounts, and questions persist about data intensity, algorithmic opacity, and the degree to which curricula become optimized for testable micro-skills at the expense of broader statistical literacy.

In Sub-Saharan Africa, emerging initiatives in countries such as Rwanda, Ghana, Kenya, Nigeria, and South Africa are experimenting with AI-supported tutoring, multilingual interfaces, and analytics-enabled open schooling. Pilot projects with low-bandwidth or offline-capable AI math tutors have reported statistically significant learning gains and improved engagement, even in contexts with intermittent electricity and limited hardware. However, these projects frequently depend on donor funding, operate at small scale, and face challenges sustaining infrastructure and technical support once external funding ends. Without broader investments in connectivity, teacher training, and local content development, there is a risk that AI tools primarily serve better-resourced urban or private schools.

Latin American experiences with AI-enhanced mathematics and statistics learning highlight similar tensions. Randomized and quasi-experimental studies of Khan Academy and related platforms in Brazil and El Salvador indicate that when schools provide adequate infrastructure, structured time, and teacher facilitation, students can improve test scores and attitudes toward mathematics. New pilots of generative-AI–based tutors such as Khanmigo in Brazilian public schools report promising engagement and perceived usefulness, but evidence so far comes from small samples and early implementation stages. Persistent regional inequalities in connectivity, school funding, and teacher professional development mean that only a subset of learners currently benefit from these innovations.

Taken together, these global case studies suggest that AI can support meaningful improvements in statistics and mathematics learning when embedded within coherent policy frameworks, adequate infrastructure, and teacher-centred implementation strategies. At the same time, they show that gains are often context-specific, dependent on sustained support, and constrained by broader political-economic conditions. Effectiveness claims must therefore be interpreted with attention to study designs, sample characteristics, and institutional capacity, and AI-enhanced statistics pedagogy should be approached as a long-term systems transformation rather than a quick technological fix.

6. IMPACT ON CAREER PREPARATION

6.1 Evolving Labour Market Demands

Labour market analyses consistently emphasize the growing demand for workers who can combine domain expertise with data analysis, statistical reasoning, and AI literacy. Employers seek graduates able to formulate data-driven questions, select appropriate analytical methods, interpret probabilistic outputs, and communicate uncertainty and limitations to diverse stakeholders. AI-enhanced tools are becoming standard in sectors such as finance, healthcare, logistics, and public policy, making familiarity with AI-supported statistical workflows a prerequisite rather than a niche skill.(Zhang, 2025; Penn GSE, n.d.; Akintunde et al., 2025; The Academic, 2025)

For statistics education, this implies that courses must prepare students not only to perform procedures but to operate within socio-technical systems where algorithmic outputs influence high-stakes decisions (e.g., credit scoring, risk prediction, resource allocation). Curricula that integrate authentic datasets, ethical case analyses, and AI-mediated investigations better approximate the kinds of tasks students will encounter in the workplace.

6.2 Non-Negotiable Human Competencies vs Delegable Skills

In an AI-rich labour market, it is crucial to distinguish between competencies that can be delegated to machines and those that remain essentially human. Delegable skills include routine computation, standard visualization, basic code generation, and initial model fitting—tasks that AI systems increasingly perform accurately and efficiently. Non-negotiable human competencies include:

Problem formulation and question design – deciding what to measure, which comparisons matter, and how to define success or harm in a given context.(Wild & Pfannkuch, 1999; Akintunde et al., 2025)

Contextual and ethical judgment – evaluating whether available data appropriately represent populations of interest, anticipating disparate impacts, and weighing trade-offs between predictive accuracy and fairness.(AI4EDU, 2025; UNESCO, 2019)

Interpretation and argumentation – constructing coherent narratives that link quantitative evidence to substantive claims, acknowledging uncertainty and alternative explanations.(Büscher, 2022; Sharma, 2017)

Collaboration and communication – working across disciplinary, organizational, and cultural boundaries to explain statistical insights and negotiate actions.(Penn GSE, n.d.; UNESCO, 2019)

Statistics pedagogy must therefore prioritize these human competencies, using AI to offload low-level tasks so that instructional time and cognitive effort can be redirected toward higher-order reasoning, ethical deliberation, and collaborative sense-making.

6.3 Credentialing and Recognition of AI-Enhanced Competencies

Traditional degree transcripts often fail to capture fine-grained competencies in AI-enhanced statistical practice (e.g., ability to audit models, design responsible dashboards, or lead data-ethics deliberations). Blockchain-based micro-credentialing systems have been proposed as one way to recognize modular achievements, including AI literacy and data ethics, in verifiable and portable formats. Such systems could record evidence of students' performance on authentic projects involving AI-supported analysis, making skills visible to employers while reducing incentives for credential fraud.(Zhang, 2025)

However, implementing blockchain credentials raises its own challenges, including interoperability across institutions, governance of credential standards, and ensuring that assessment tasks used to confer micro-credentials adequately assess the non-negotiable human competencies identified above. For now, the primary implication is that programmes should design cumulative experiences—capstones, portfolios, internships—where students demonstrate integrated AI-enhanced statistical skills, even if formal credentialing systems remain conventional.(UNESCO, 2023; Zhang, 2025)

Section Summary

AI is reconfiguring labour market expectations around statistics and data work, but it does not eliminate the need for human statistical thinkers. Instead, it elevates the importance of problem formulation, ethical judgment, interpretation, and communication, while shifting computation and routine coding toward automated systems.(Akintunde et al., 2025; UNESCO, 2019; Zhang, 2025)

7. FUTURE DIRECTIONS AND EMERGING TRENDS

7.1 Advances in Natural Language Processing and Generative Tutors

Rapid progress in large language models is enabling conversational tutoring systems that can parse student questions, generate tailored explanations, and even co-construct statistical code and visualizations. Studies of generative AI tutors integrated with tools like R show that students appreciate the ability to iterate on prompts and receive context-sensitive feedback, though current systems still struggle with domain-specific nuances and occasionally produce erroneous or inappropriate advice.(Grassini et al., 2025; Rao et al., 2026)

Future systems are likely to integrate multi-modal capabilities (e.g., interpreting uploaded graphs, handwritten work, or spoken explanations) and to draw on course-specific knowledge bases, potentially reducing hallucinations and aligning responses more closely with instructor expectations. Nonetheless, maintaining human oversight, establishing transparent boundaries on AI authority, and designing interaction protocols that foreground student reasoning will remain central pedagogical concerns. (IJTLE, 2024; Grassini et al., 2025)

7.2 Immersive and Virtual/Augmented Reality Applications

Virtual and augmented reality (VR/AR) environments are beginning to be used to visualize complex statistical objects and processes—allowing students to "walk through" distributions, manipulate sample sizes in three dimensions, or experience simulations of random processes in embodied ways. When combined with AI that adapts scenarios in real time based on student actions, such environments can provide highly engaging learning experiences, particularly for learners who benefit from spatial and kinaesthetic representations.(Zhang, 2025)

However, VR/AR deployments in statistics education remain experimental and resource-intensive, raising concerns about scalability and equity. Without careful design, they may privilege well-resourced institutions and consume budgets that might otherwise support broadband access, teacher training, or accessible low-tech materials. Evaluating VR/AR applications should therefore include not only engagement metrics but also comparisons of conceptual understanding and transfer relative to less costly interventions.(DRCLAS ReVista, 2024)

7.3 Learning Analytics and Curriculum Co-Design

As AI-powered learning analytics become more sophisticated, there is growing interest in using aggregated data to inform curriculum design, sequencing, and resource development in statistics. For instance, analyses of item difficulty, error patterns, and time-on-task across thousands of learners can reveal which concepts (e.g., conditional probability, sampling distributions) consistently pose challenges, suggesting where additional scaffolds or alternative representations are needed. (Lukarov et al., 2018; The Academic, 2025)

Participatory learning analytics approaches advocate involving teachers and students in interpreting analytics dashboards and co-designing responses, rather than treating analytics as top-down instruments for accountability. In statistics courses, this might involve student-led inquiries into their own performance data—calculating confidence intervals around class averages, examining correlations between study behaviours and outcomes, and debating the ethics of predictive risk scores—connecting meta-learning about AI and analytics with core curricular goals. (The Academic, 2025)

7.4 Ethical AI Development and Global Governance

Global organizations such as UNESCO and the OECD have issued guidance on AI and education, emphasizing human rights, equity, transparency, and teacher empowerment. The Beijing Consensus on AI and Education, for example, calls for AI integration that enhances human capacities, supports lifelong learning, and safeguards against new forms of exclusion, including algorithmic discrimination. UNESCO's more recent policy guidance reiterates these themes while providing practical recommendations on governance, capacity building, and research priorities. (MOE China, 2019; UNESCO, 2019; UNESCO, 2023)

For statistics pedagogy, these frameworks underscore the need to align AI adoption with broader social goals: fostering statistically literate citizens who can scrutinize AI-mediated evidence, not merely operate tools. They also highlight the importance of international cooperation in developing open, culturally inclusive resources and in sharing evidence on effective, ethical AI-enhanced teaching practices.

Section Summary

Future trajectories for AI in statistics education will be shaped not only by technical advances in generative models, VR/AR, and analytics but also by governance frameworks, equity considerations, and the extent to which stakeholders position AI as a partner in human learning rather than as a replacement for human judgment. (UNESCO, 2019; UNESCO, 2023; Grassini et al., 2025)

8. POLICY IMPLICATIONS

8.1 National Policy Frameworks

National policies on AI in education play a critical role in setting expectations, allocating resources, and defining safeguards. The Beijing Consensus and UNESCO's guidance documents call for whole-of-government approaches that integrate AI planning into broader education strategies, including teacher empowerment, infrastructure development, and ethical governance. Countries like Finland have translated these principles into national programmes such as AuroraAI, which link public services and emphasize human-centric design and GDPR-compliant data practices.(Ministry of Finance Finland, n.d.; GovInsider, 2023; MOE China, 2019; UNESCO, 2023; UNESCO, 2019)

For statistics education, national frameworks should explicitly address AI's role in developing data and statistical literacy for all learners, not just those in specialized tracks. This includes supporting open, high-quality datasets and tools for classroom use, funding longitudinal research on AI-enhanced pedagogy, and ensuring that curricular standards highlight critical engagement with AI-generated information.

8.2 Institutional Governance and Implementation Guidelines

At the institutional level, AI adoption requires governance structures that balance innovation with safeguards. Recommendations from privacy and AI-ethics literature emphasize establishing AI ethics committees, conducting DPIAs for high-risk applications, and developing clear policies on acceptable AI use by students and staff. Institutions should articulate principles for AI in assessment (e.g., when AI-assisted work is permissible), set criteria for selecting and reviewing AI tools (including transparency about training data and performance across subgroups), and provide mechanisms for students and teachers to contest automated decisions.(8allocate, 2025; AI4EDU, 2025)

In statistics departments and programmes, governance should include processes for reviewing vendor claims, scrutinizing evaluation studies for methodological rigour, and piloting new tools in small-scale trials before scaling. Institutional support for integrating AI-related case studies into statistics courses—such as algorithmic bias incidents or data breaches—can simultaneously advance governance goals and enrich pedagogy.

8.3 Professional Development and AI Competency Frameworks

Policy documents increasingly highlight teacher professional development as a linchpin of responsible AI integration. For statistics educators, professional development needs to extend beyond tool training to encompass AASPK dimensions: understanding AI-implemented statistical procedures, designing AI-aware tasks and assessments, interpreting learning analytics, and facilitating ethical discussions about data and algorithms.(UNESCO, 2024; CIDDL, 2024; UNESCO, 2019)

Effective strategies include:

Embedding AI and data-ethics modules into pre-service statistics teacher education programmes.

Creating communities of practice where teachers share AI-enhanced lesson designs, reflect on challenges, and co-develop assessment rubrics.

Partnering with learning analytics and computer science experts to offer joint workshops that bridge technical and pedagogical perspectives.(Penn GSE, n.d.; The Academic, 2025)

8.4 Research and Evaluation Priorities

Given the rapid pace of AI innovation and the heterogeneity of contexts, ongoing research is essential. Recent meta-analyses demonstrate overall positive but highly variable effects of AI interventions on learning outcomes, underscoring the importance of examining moderating factors such as subject domain, educational level, intervention duration, and implementation fidelity. Priorities for statistics education research include longitudinal studies of conceptual understanding and transfer, investigations of equity impacts (e.g., for linguistically diverse or marginalized students), and comparative studies of different human–AI orchestration models. (Grassini et al., 2025; Zhang, 2025)

Policymakers and funders should support mixed-methods research that combines experimental or quasi-experimental designs with qualitative work capturing students' and teachers' experiences, as in case studies from Rwanda, Ghana, and other emerging contexts. Transparent reporting of methods, including sample sizes, attrition, and potential conflicts of interest, is critical for building a trustworthy evidence base.(Uwineza et al., 2025; Jukes et al., 2024)

Section Summary

Effective policy responses to AI in statistics education must operate at national and institutional levels, centring teacher capacity, ethical governance, and sustained research rather than assuming that technology alone will deliver improved outcomes. (UNESCO, 2023; AI4EDU, 2025; UNESCO, 2019)

9. CHALLENGES AND LIMITATIONS

9.1 Technical Limitations, Reliability, and Bias

Despite impressive capabilities, current AI systems remain prone to errors, hallucinations, and biased outputs, which can be particularly problematic in statistics education where precision and interpretive nuance matter. Black-box models obscure the reasoning behind recommendations or assessments, making it difficult for teachers and students to identify why a particular hint was given or why an answer was marked incorrect. Training data that under-represent certain languages, dialects, or educational contexts can lead to systematic under-performance or misinterpretation for specific student groups.(IJTLE, 2024; Grassini et al., 2025; DRCLAS ReVista, 2024)

These limitations mean that AI outputs must be treated as *hypotheses* rather than ground truth, and that curricula should explicitly teach students how to test AI-generated claims using statistical tools—recalculating, resampling, or comparing with alternative models—as part of standard practice.

9.2 Pedagogical Risks and Unintended Consequences

Integrating AI may inadvertently undermine the development of core statistical thinking if students come to view AI as an infallible authority or if assessments reward superficial engagement with AI explanations. Studies of students' statistical thinking with generative AI indicate that while AI can scaffold step-wise reasoning, it does not eliminate the need for students to understand underlying concepts, and it sometimes encourages a "prompt-and-accept" mentality.(Rao et al., 2026)

A particular concern is the potential reinforcement of misconceptions. For instance, if generative models produce oversimplified or inaccurate explanations of p-values, confidence intervals, or regression assumptions, and if students repeatedly encounter these explanations during unsupervised study, misconceptions may become entrenched. Empirical work on hallucinations in educational contexts underscores the importance of designing tasks where students must compare AI explanations with textbook definitions, instructor notes, or empirical simulations, rather than relying on AI alone.(Athaluri et al., 2024; IJTLE, 2024)

9.3 Scaling, Sustainability, and Political Economy

Scaling AI-enhanced statistics education involves substantial costs in infrastructure, licensing, teacher training, and support. Vendor-driven models may lock institutions into proprietary ecosystems, raising concerns about long-term affordability, interoperability, and local control over data. In low- and middle-income countries, reliance on donor-funded pilots can lead to cycles of innovation and abandonment when funding ends, undermining trust and continuity.(CENTURY Tech, 2024; Uwineza et al., 2025; Nucamp, 2025; DRCLAS ReVista, 2024)

Furthermore, high-stakes assessment cultures may pressure schools to deploy AI primarily for test preparation, narrowing the curriculum to exam-aligned items and sidelining broader goals of statistical literacy, ethical reasoning, and critical engagement with data. Political debates about surveillance, automation, and labour may also shape public perceptions of AI in schools, influencing adoption decisions irrespective of pedagogical evidence.

Section Summary

Technical unreliability, potential reinforcement of misconceptions, and structural constraints around cost and assessment cultures limit what AI can realistically achieve in statistics education and highlight the necessity of sustained human oversight and critical reflection.

10. CONCLUSION

10.1 Reframing Statistics Pedagogy in the Age of AI

The evidence reviewed in this chapter indicates that AI can significantly enhance aspects of statistics education—personalization, formative assessment, access to authentic data, and support for struggling learners—when implemented thoughtfully and in concert with robust pedagogical frameworks. At the same time, AI introduces new risks related to equity, privacy, hallucinations, and policy capture, and it cannot substitute for the human capacities that underlie meaningful statistical reasoning. (Pane et al., 2015; Grassini et al., 2025; Zhang, 2025)

Reframing statistics pedagogy for the age of AI involves three interlocking commitments: (1) centring statistical thinking, data literacy, and ethical judgment as primary learning outcomes; (2) developing AASPK among teachers so they can orchestrate productive human–AI collaborations; and (3) embedding AI-related case studies and tools within curricula in ways that expose, rather than conceal, uncertainty, bias, and the constructed nature of models.(Burgess, 2007; Akintunde et al., 2025; UNESCO, 2019)

10.2 Principles for Human–AI Partnership in Statistics Education

Based on the analysis, several guiding principles emerge for delineating non-negotiable human competencies and appropriately delegated tasks:

Humans define questions; AI assists with execution. Students and teachers retain responsibility for formulating research questions, defining variables, and choosing what to measure; AI can then support data collection, transformation, and preliminary modeling.(Wild & Pfannkuch, 1999; Akintunde et al., 2025)

Humans interpret and judge; AI proposes. AI may suggest models, visualizations, or interpretations, but humans must evaluate fit, plausibility, and ethical implications, particularly when decisions affect people's opportunities or well-being.(Sharma, 2017; AI4EDU, 2025)

Humans manage values; AI manages volume. Value-laden trade-offs—such as balancing false positives and false negatives in risk prediction or deciding how to weigh fairness criteria—are human responsibilities, whereas AI can manage large-scale computation and search.(UNESCO, 2019; Zhang, 2025)

Humans teach uncertainty; AI exposes variability. Statistics educators should leverage AI-driven simulations and visualizations to make variability and uncertainty salient, while explicitly teaching that models are simplifications and that predictive accuracy does not equal truth.

These principles can be translated into course policies, assessment designs, and professional development agendas, ensuring that AI augments rather than erodes the human capacities that statistics education seeks to cultivate.

11. IMPLICATIONS FOR PRACTICE

11.1 For Teachers

Statistics teachers should approach AI integration as an opportunity to reallocate instructional time from routine computation to higher-order reasoning, while remaining vigilant about the limitations and biases of AI systems. Practical steps include designing tasks that require students to justify when they use AI, explain how they verified AI outputs, and compare AI-generated analyses with manual or alternative approaches.(IJTLE, 2024; Rao et al., 2026)

Teachers also need structured support to build AASPK: collaborative lesson study focused on AI-enhanced tasks, workshops on learning analytics interpretation, and access to exemplars of AI-informed formative assessment. Engaging with research literature and local evaluation data can strengthen teachers' capacity to critically appraise vendor claims and to adapt tools to their own pedagogical goals.(IJLTER, 2024; The Academic, 2025)

11.2 For Students: Self-Regulating AI Use

Students should be explicitly taught how to self-regulate their use of AI in statistics learning. This entails:

Setting clear learning goals before consulting AI.

Using AI to probe understanding (e.g., asking for alternative explanations or counterexamples) rather than merely obtaining answers.

Cross-checking AI outputs through manual calculation, simulations, or consultation of trusted resources.

Reflecting on episodes where AI was misleading and articulating strategies to avoid similar pitfalls in the future.(Grassini et al., 2025; Rao et al., 2026)

Such practices can be embedded in course syllabi, with guidelines on acceptable AI use and reflection prompts attached to assignments, reinforcing that AI is a tool to be interrogated, not a source of unquestioned authority.

11.3 For Curriculum Designers and Assessment Leaders

Curriculum designers should revise learning outcomes and syllabi to explicitly incorporate AI literacy, data ethics, and critical engagement with AI-generated evidence into statistics programmes. This includes designing sequences of tasks where students move from AI-free exploration to AI-supported refinement, and where assessments value interpretation, critique, and communication as much as computational accuracy.(Pane et al., 2015; UNESCO, 2019)

Assessment leaders should develop rubrics that separate evaluation of conceptual reasoning from evaluation of tool usage, ensuring that students are neither penalized for responsible AI use nor rewarded for uncritical dependence. New assessment formats—such as oral defenses of AI-assisted analyses, portfolios of prompt-response cycles, or group projects auditing AI models—can surface the human competencies that matter for professional practice.

11.4 For Policymakers and Leaders

Educational leaders and policymakers must ensure that AI investments in statistics education are guided by evidence, equity, and ethical considerations rather than by technological hype. This involves funding infrastructure in underserved regions, supporting long-term teacher professional development, and mandating transparent reporting of AI tool evaluations, including limitations and adverse impacts.(UNESCO, 2023; UNESCO, 2019; DRCLAS ReVista, 2024)

Leaders should also engage stakeholders—students, parents, teachers, and communities—in deliberations about acceptable uses of AI in schools, from learning analytics to proctoring, recognizing that public trust is essential for sustainable innovation.

Section Summary

Translating the chapter's analyses into practice requires coordinated action by teachers, students, curriculum designers, and policymakers, all oriented toward a vision of AI-enhanced statistics education that foregrounds human reasoning, equity, and ethical responsibility.(UNESCO, 2019; Zhang, 2025)

12. DISCUSSION QUESTIONS AND REFLECTION PROMPTS

Reimagining learning goals: How would you revise the learning outcomes of an introductory statistics course at your institution to reflect the availability of AI tools? Which topics would you de-emphasize, and which would you elevate?

Designing AI-aware tasks: Choose a current assignment that primarily assesses computational skills. How could you redesign it so that students must use AI in a transparent, critical way while demonstrating their own reasoning?

Equity and access: In your context, which student groups are least likely to benefit from AI-enhanced statistics tools due to infrastructure, language, or prior preparation? What concrete steps could be taken over the next three years to mitigate these inequities?

Assessment integrity: Consider your course's major assessments. Where, if at all, should AI use be prohibited, and where could AI-assisted assessment better reflect authentic professional practice in statistics and data science?

Teacher learning: What forms of professional development (e.g., lesson study, peer observation, online communities of practice) would most effectively help you or your colleagues develop AASPK? How might you advocate for these supports in your department or system?

Policy priorities: If you could influence one institutional or national policy related to AI in statistics education, what would it be, and why? How would you justify its importance to stakeholders with differing priorities (e.g., efficiency, privacy, equity)?

Note: Any remaining numerical claims without explicit sourcing should be verified against up-to-date empirical studies or official statistics before publication.

REFERENCES

8allocate. (2025). *FERPA/GDPR for AI in education: A practical deployment checklist.* https://8allocate.com/blog/ferpa-gdpr-for-ai-in-education-a-practical-deployment-checklist/

AI4EDU. (2025). *Safeguarding student data in AI-driven education: EU AI Act and UNESCO's frameworks.* AI4EDU Consortium. https://ai4edu.eu/wp-content/uploads/2025/04/9a.-Safeguarding-student-data-in-AI-driven-education-EUAI-ACt-and-UNESCOs-Frameworks.pdf

Akintunde, O., Iyanda, R., & Osei, K. (2025). A data literacy competence model for higher education. *arXiv preprint arXiv:2504.15690.* https://arxiv.org/html/2504.15690v1

Athaluri, S. A., Manthena, S. V., Kesapragada, V. S. R. K. M., Yarlagadda, V., Dave, T., & Duddumpudi, R. T. S. (2024). Hallucinations in large language models for education: Challenges and mitigation. *International Journal of Technology in Learning and Education.* https://ijtle.com/issue-alldetail/hallucinations-in-large-language-models-for-education-challenges-and-mitigation

Baral, S., Sharma, K., & Singh, R. (n.d.). Student and instructor feedback on an AI-assisted grading tool. In *Proceedings of the ASEE Annual Conference.* American Society for Engineering Education. https://peer.asee.org/student-and-instructor-feedback-on-an-ai-assisted-grading-tool.pdf

Burgess, T. A. (2007). *Investigating the nature of teacher knowledge needed and used in teaching statistics* [Doctoral dissertation, Massey University]. IASE. https://www.stat.auckland.ac.nz/~iase/publications/dissertations/07.Burgess.Dissertation.pdf

Büscher, C. (2022). Design principles for developing statistical literacy. *Statistics Education Research Journal, 21*(1), 10. Advance online publication. DOI: 10.52041/serj.v21i1.80

Business Standard. (2025, January 1). 57% schools have functional computers, 53% have internet access. *Business Standard.* https://www.business-standard.com/india-news/57-schools-have-functional-computers-53-have-internet-access-govt-125010101044_1.html

BusinessWire. (2021, July 21). *Carnegie Learning announces new 3rd party study indicating that MATHia leads to better performance in Algebra.* https://www.businesswire.com/news/home/20210721005130/en/Carnegie-Learning-Announces-New-3rd-Party-Study-Indicating-That-MATHia-Leads-to-Better-Performance-in-Algebra

BusinessWire. (2023, March 30). *Study proves DreamBox Learning® significantly increases math achievement after only one hour of use per week.* https://www.businesswire.com/news/home/20230330005199/en/Study-Proves-DreamBox-Learning-Significantly-Increases-Math-Achievement-After-Only-One-Hour-of-Use-Per-Week

Carlson, J., & Johnston, L. (Eds.). (2015). *Data information literacy: Librarians, data, and the education of a new generation of researchers*. Purdue University Press. DOI: 10.26530/OAPEN_626975

Carnegie Learning. (n.d.). *Carnegie Learning publisher response to IMRA final report*. Texas Education Agency. https://im.tea.texas.gov/sites/default/files/evaluations/Carnegie%20Learning%20Publisher%20Response%20to%20IMRA%20Final%20Report.pdf

China, M. O. E. (2019). *UNESCO publishes Beijing Consensus on Artificial Intelligence and Education*. Chinese Ministry of Education. http://en.moe.gov.cn/news/press_releases/201909/t20190902_396913.html

CIDDL. (2024). *Summary of UNESCO AI competency framework for teachers.* https://ciddl.org/summary-of-unesco-ai-competency-framework-for-teachers/

D'Mello, S. K. (2017). Emotional learning analytics. In Lang, C., Siemens, G., Wise, A., & Gasevic, D. (Eds.), *Handbook of learning analytics* (pp. 115–127). Society for Learning Analytics Research., https://www.solaresearch.org/wp-content/uploads/2017/05/chapter10.pdf DOI: 10.18608/hla17.010

DRCLAS ReVista. (2024). Unequal beginnings: Artificial intelligence and Latin America's educational divide. *ReVista: Harvard Review of Latin America*. https://revista.drclas.harvard.edu/unequal-beginnings-artificial-intelligence-and-latin-americas-educational-divide/

EdTech Books. (n.d.). Constructivism. In *Student guide to learning theories*. https://edtechbooks.org/studentguide/constructivism

Educational Technology. (n.d.). *TPACK: Technological pedagogical content knowledge framework*. https://educationaltechnology.net/technological-pedagogical-content-knowledge-tpack-framework/

Eduten. (n.d.). *Teaching and AI: Eduten platform overview* [Presentation, GEP Forum]. Finnish National Agency for Education. https://www.oph.fi/sites/default/files/documents/Sirkus_Day%201_Slot%201_Eduten%20presentation_GEP%20Forum%20.pdf

Georgia Tech. (2024). *Georgia Tech's Jill Watson outperforms ChatGPT in real classrooms*. Georgia Institute of Technology. https://research.gatech.edu/georgia-techs-jill-watson-outperforms-chatgpt-real-classrooms

Giving Compass. (2023). Millions of students in the US lack access to high-speed internet. https://givingcompass.org/article/millions-of-students-in-the-us-lack-access-to-technology-and-high-speed-internet

Global Citizen. (2023). Millions of students in the US lack access to technology and high-speed internet. https://www.globalcitizen.org/en/content/verizon-innovative-learning-tech-program/

Google. (2024). *How we're improving AI literacy in young people*. https://blog.google/innovation-and-ai/technology/families/improving-ai-literacy-in-young-people/

GovInsider. (2023). *How Finland is using AI for predictive public services*. https://govinsider.asia/intl-en/article/how-finland-is-using-ai-for-predictive-public-services

Grassini, S., Laumann, K., & Skogstad, M. R. (2025). The impact of GenAI on learning outcomes: A systematic review and meta-analysis of experimental studies. *Learning, Media and Technology*. Advance online publication. DOI: 10.1016/j.learntechol.2025.00051

Herold, B. (2017, July). Personalized learning: Modest gains, big challenges, RAND study finds. *Education Week*. https://www.edweek.org/technology/personalized-learning-modest-gains-big-challenges-rand-study-finds/2017/07

Higher Ed Dive. (2023). *Beyond student progress: How Ivy Tech is approaching data analytics*. https://www.highereddive.com/news/beyond-student-progress-how-ivy-tech-is-approaching-data-analytics/405110/

Hundr, E. D. (n.d.). *Squirrel AI Learning*. https://hundred.org/en/innovations/squirrel-ai-learning

IJLTER. (2024). AI in the classroom: A systematic review of barriers to educator acceptance. *International Journal of Learning, Teaching and Educational Research, 23*(4). https://www.ijlter.org/index.php/ijlter/article/view/14081

India Today. (2025, January 3). Only 57% of schools have computers, 53% have internet. *India Today*. https://www.indiatoday.in/education-today/news/story/only-57-of-schools-have-computers-53-have-internet-udise-report-school-digital-infrastructure-2659262-2025-01-03

Jukes, M. C. H., Grijalva, L., & Zuilkowski, S. (2024). *Experimental evidence on the impact of an AI math tutor in Ghana* [arXiv preprint arXiv:2402.09809]. https://arxiv.org/pdf/2402.09809.pdf

Kearney, P. (n.d.). *Understanding the digital divide in education* [Video]. YouTube. https://www.youtube.com/watch?v=vgpHcEuo_90

Khan Academy. (2023). *University of Toronto randomized controlled trial of 11K students demonstrates a meaningful positive effect of Khan Academy on student learning*. https://blog.khanacademy.org/university-of-toronto-randomized-controlled-trial-of-11k-students-demonstrates-a-meaningful-positive-effect-of-khan-academy-on-student-learning/

Khan Academy. (2024). *Isolating the impact of EdTech in real-world classrooms: A Khan Academy study in a leading academic journal*. https://blog.khanacademy.org/isolating-the-impact-of-edtech-in-real-world-classrooms-a-khan-academy-study-in-a-leading-academic-journal/

Koehler, M. J., Mishra, P., & Cain, W. (2013). What is technological pedagogical content knowledge (TPACK)? *Journal of Education*, *193*(3), 13–19. https://www.bu.edu/journalofeducation/files/2014/02/BUJoE.193.3.Koehleretal.pdf. DOI: 10.1177/002205741319300303

Lukarov, V., Chatti, M. A., Thüs, H., Kia, F. S., Muslim, A., Greven, C., & Schroeder, U. (2018). Learning analytics case study in blended learning. In *Proceedings of the 10th International Conference on Computer-Supported Education* (Vol. 2, pp. 1–8). CEUR Workshop Proceedings., https://ceur-ws.org/Vol-2193/paper2.pdf

McLeod, S. (2024). Vygotsky's sociocultural theory of cognitive development. *Simply Psychology*. https://www.simplypsychology.org/vygotsky.html

Ministry of Education China. (2019). *UNESCO publishes Beijing Consensus on Artificial Intelligence and Education*. http://en.moe.gov.cn/news/press_releases/201909/t20190902_396913.html

Ministry of Education Singapore. (2023). *EdTech Masterplan 2030*. https://www.moe.gov.sg/education-in-sg/educational-technology-journey/edtech-masterplan

Ministry of Finance Finland. (n.d.). *National artificial intelligence programme AuroraAI*. https://vm.fi/en/national-artificial-intelligence-programme-auroraai

Mishra, P., & Koehler, M. J. (2006). Technological pedagogical content knowledge: A framework for teacher knowledge. *Teachers College Record*, *108*(6), 1017–1054. DOI: 10.1111/j.1467-9620.2006.00684.x

Nucamp. (2025). *The complete guide to using AI in the education industry in Finland in 2025*. https://www.nucamp.co/blog/coding-bootcamp-finland-fin-education-the-complete-guide-to-using-ai-in-the-education-industry-in-finland-in-2025

Pane, J. F., Steiner, E. D., Baird, M. D., & Hamilton, L. S. (2015). *Promising evidence on personalized learning* (Research Report RR-1140-BMGF). RAND Corporation. https://eric.ed.gov/?id=ED571009

Penn, G. S. E. (n.d.). *Learning analytics and artificial intelligence, M.S.Ed.* University of Pennsylvania Graduate School of Education. https://www.gse.upenn.edu/academics/learning-analytics-AI-online-msed

Pham, H. H., Dao, T. Q., Le, T. T. H., & Nguyen, D. D. (2022). The effects of ALEKS on mathematics learning in K–12 and higher education: A meta-analysis. *Investigations in Mathematics Learning*, *14*(1), 1–18. DOI: 10.1080/19477503.2021.1926194

Rao, V. N. V., Jeng, A., Drew, J., Kala, B., & Gongati, S. (2026). Students' Statistical Thinking When Using Generative AI: A Descriptive Case Study. *Journal of Statistics and Data Science Education : An Official Journal of the of the American Statistical Association*, *34*(1), 4–15. DOI: 10.1080/26939169.2025.2596684

Raspberry Pi Foundation. (2024). *Bringing AI education to 1.25 million students across Latin America*. https://www.raspberrypi.org/blog/bringing-ai-education-to-1-25-million-students-across-latin-america/

Ridsdale, C., Rothwell, J., Smit, M., Ali-Hassan, H., Bliemel, M., Irvine, D., Kelley, D., Matwin, S., & Wuetherick, B. (2015). *Strategies and best practices for data literacy education: Knowledge synthesis report*. Dalhousie University. https://www.semanticscholar.org/paper/Strategies-and-Best-Practices-for-Data-Literacy-Ridsdale-Rothwell/5a2f9bc40d78f58baf774d4e55f8377f796f105e

Schwartz, D. L., Chase, C. C., & Bransford, J. D. (2023). Resisting overzealous transfer: Coordinating previously successful routines with needs for new learning. *Educational Psychologist*, *48*(2), 89–106. https://pdfs.semanticscholar.org/5471/3b2d07caa89883822c9ad041dfeedf0efc24.pdf

Sharma, P. (2024). *The power of personalized learning: A meta-analysis* (Report No. ED646968). ERIC. https://files.eric.ed.gov/fulltext/ED646968.pdf

Sharma, S. (2017). Definitions and models of statistical literacy: A literature review. *Statistics Education Research Journal*, *16*(1), 149–163. DOI: 10.1080/23265507.2017.1354313

Tang, X., Zhu, J., & Chen, Y. (n.d.). *When adaptive learning is effective learning: Comparison of an adaptive learning system to teacher-led instruction* [Unpublished manuscript]. University of Hong Kong. https://www.studocu.com/hk/document/the-university-of-hong-kong/research-seminar-ii/when-adaptive-learning-is-effective-learning-comparison-of-an-adaptive-learning-system-to-teacher-led-instruction/108779520

Tech, C. E. N. T. U. R. Y. (2024). *CENTURY Tech report reveals significant positive impact of AI-powered learning on primary SATs outcomes.* https://www.century.tech/news/century-tech-report-reveals-significant-positive-impact-of-ai-powered-learning-on-primary-sats-outcomes

Tech, C. E. N. T. U. R. Y. (2025). *GCSE outcomes: An impact analysis of CENTURY.* https://www.century.tech/wp-content/uploads/2025/06/GCSE-Outcomes-Impact-Analysis-of-CENTURY.pdf

The Academic. (2025). AI-powered learning analytics for student success. *The Academic Journal, 3*(1). https://theacademic.in/wp-content/uploads/2025/08/47.pdf

UNESCO. (2019). *Beijing consensus on artificial intelligence and education: Outcome document of the International Conference on Artificial Intelligence and Education.* UNESCO. https://www.unesco.org/en/articles/first-ever-consensus-artificial-intelligence-and-education-published-unesco

UNESCO. (2023). *AI and education: Guidance for policy-makers.* UNESCO. https://www.unesco.org/en/articles/ai-and-education-guidance-policy-makers

UNESCO. (2024). *AI competency framework for students.* UNESCO. https://www.unesco.org/en/articles/ai-competency-framework-students

University of Miami. (n.d.). *AI-assisted grading with Gradescope.* Learning and Portfolio Technologies. https://lpt.it.miami.edu/resources/faculty-and-staff/leverage-ai-tools/ai-assisted-grading/index.html

Uwineza, I., Mugisha, J. F., & Nsengimana, V. (2025). The impact of artificial intelligence in secondary education: A case study of Wellspring Academy, Rwanda. *Journal of Research Innovation and Implications in Education, 9*(2), 111. https://www.jriiejournal.com/wp-content/uploads/2025/06/JRIIE-9-2-111-.pdf

Wild, C. J., & Pfannkuch, M. (1999). Statistical thinking in empirical enquiry. *International Statistical Review = Revue Internationale de Statistique, 67*(3), 223–265. DOI: 10.1111/j.1751-5823.1999.tb00442.x

WWC. (2013). *DreamBox Learning* [WWC Intervention Report]. Institute of Education Sciences, What Works Clearinghouse. https://ies.ed.gov/ncee/wwc/Docs/InterventionReports/wwc_dreambox_121013.pdf

Zhang, J. (2025). Meta-analysis of artificial intelligence in education. *Educational Technology Research and Development*. https://files.eric.ed.gov/fulltext/EJ1465704.pdf

Compilation of References

Abbasi, B. N., Wu, Y., & Luo, Z. (2025). Exploring the impact of artificial intelligence on curriculum development in global higher education institutions. *Education and Information Technologies*, *30*(1), 547–581.

Abe, E. C., & Birabil, S. T. (2022). Fostering creativity and critical thinking in 21st century classroom. *Innovare Journal of Education*, *10*(1), 8–16. DOI: 10.22159/ijoe.2022v10i3.44671

Abuhassna, H., Awae, F., Adnan, M. A., Daud, M., & Almheiri, A. S. (2024). The information age for education via artificial intelligence and machine learning: A bibliometric and systematic literature analysis. *International Journal of Information and Education Technology (IJIET)*, *14*(5), 700.

Adadi, A., & Berrada, M. (2018). Peeking inside the black-box: A survey on explainable artificial intelligence (XAI). *IEEE Access : Practical Innovations, Open Solutions*, *6*, 52138–52160. DOI: 10.1109/ACCESS.2018.2870052

Afan, H. A., Almawla, A. S., Al-Hadeethi, B., Khaleel, F., AbdUlameer, A. H., Khan, M. M. H., Ma'arof, M. I. N., & Kamel, A. H. (2024). LSTM model integrated remote sensing data for drought prediction: A study on climate change impacts on water availability in the arid region. *Water (Basel)*, *16*(19), 2799. DOI: 10.3390/w16192799

Afzaal, M., Shanshan, X., Yan, D., & Younas, M. (2024). Mapping artificial intelligence integration in education: A decade of innovation and impact (2013–2023): A bibliometric analysis. *IEEE Access*.

Afzaal, M., Nouri, J., Zia, A., Papapetrou, P., Norqvist, L., & Nilsson, M. (2021). Explainable AI for data-driven feedback and intelligent action recommendations to support students self-regulation. *Frontiers in Artificial Intelligence*, *4*, 715143. Advance online publication. DOI: 10.3389/frai.2021.723447 PMID: 34870183

AI4EDU. (2025). *Safeguarding student data in AI-driven education: EU AI Act and UNESCO's frameworks*. AI4EDU Consortium. https://ai4edu.eu/wp-content/uploads/2025/04/9a.-Safeguarding-student-data-in-AI-driven-education-EUAI-ACt-and-UNESCOs-Frameworks.pdf

Airaj, M. (2024). Ethical artificial intelligence for teaching-learning in higher education. *Education and Information Technologies*, *29*(13), 17145–17167.

Akhter, E. (2025). AI IN THE CLASSROOM: EVALUATING THE EFFECTIVENESS OF INTELLIGENT TUTORING SYSTEMS FOR MULTILINGUAL LEARNERS IN SECONDARY EDUCATION. ASRC Procedia. *Global Perspectives in Science and Scholarship*, *1*(01), 532–563. DOI: 10.63125/gcq1qr39

Akintunde, O., Iyanda, R., & Osei, K. (2025). A data literacy competence model for higher education. *arXiv preprint arXiv:2504.15690*. https://arxiv.org/html/2504.15690v1

Al Labadi, L., & Ly, A. (2025). Enhancing statistics education through Project-Based Learning (PBL) and the emergence of ChatGPT. *Teaching Statistics*, *47*(3), 200–218. DOI: 10.1111/test.12405

Alabi, R. O., Elmusrati, M., Leivo, I., Almangush, A., & Mäkitie, A. A. (2023). Machine learning explainability in nasopharyngeal cancer survival using LIME and SHAP. *Scientific Reports*, *13*(1), 8984. Advance online publication. DOI: 10.1038/s41598-023-35795-0 PMID: 37268685

Alam, A. (2023c). Intelligence unleashed: An argument for AI-enabled learning ecologies with real world examples of today and a peek into the future. In *AIP Conference Proceedings* (Vol. 2717, No. 1, Article 030001). AIP Publishing.

Alam, A., & Mohanty, A. (2022, December). Facial analytics or virtual avatars: Competencies and design considerations for student-teacher interaction in AI-powered online education for effective classroom engagement. In *Proceedings of the International Conference on Communication, Networks and Computing* (pp. 252–265). Springer Nature.

Alam, A., & Mohanty, A. (2023, January). Learning on the move: A pedagogical framework for state-of-the-art mobile learning. In *Proceedings of the International Conference on Data Management, Analytics and Innovation* (pp. 735–748). Springer Nature.

Alam, A. (2022). Impact of university's human resources practices on professors' occupational performance: Empirical evidence from India's higher education sector. In *Inclusive businesses in developing economies: Converging people, profit, and corporate citizenship* (pp. 107–131). Springer.

Alam, A. (2023a). Media multitasking with M-learning technology in real-time classroom learning: Analysing the dynamics in formal educational settings for the future of E-learning in India. In *Proceedings of the 2023 2nd International Conference on Smart Technologies and Systems for Next Generation Computing (ICSTSN)* (pp. 1–6). IEEE.

Alam, A. (2023b). The secret sauce of student success: Cracking the code by navigating the path to personalized learning with educational data mining. In *Proceedings of the 2023 2nd International Conference on Smart Technologies and Systems for Next Generation Computing (ICSTSN)* (pp. 1–8). IEEE.

Alam, A., Bhat, M. S., & Maheen, M. (2020). Using Landsat satellite data for assessing the land use and land cover change in Kashmir valley. *GeoJournal*, *85*(6), 1529–1543. DOI: 10.1007/s10708-019-10037-x

Alam, A., & Mohanty, A. (2024). Integrated constructive robotics in education (ICRE) model: A paradigmatic framework for transformative learning in educational ecosystem. *Cogent Education*, *11*(1), 2324487.

Albert, J., & Hu, J. (2019). *Probability and Bayesian modeling*. Chapman & Hall/CRC., DOI: 10.1201/9781351030144

AlDhaen, E., & Danish, F. (2024). Exploring the role of artificial intelligence in education: A survey-based study at University of Technology and Applied Science. In *Business Sustainability with AI* (Vol. 1, pp. 63–74). Springer., DOI: 10.1007/978-3-031-56345-4_7

Aldoseri, A., Al-Khalifa, K. N., & Hamouda, A. M. (2023). Re-thinking data strategy and integration for artificial intelligence: Concepts, opportunities, and challenges. *Applied Sciences (Basel, Switzerland)*, *13*(9), 8792. DOI: 10.3390/app13127082

Aljanabi, F., Dedeoğlu, M., & Şeker, C. (2024). Environmental monitoring of Land Use/Land Cover by integrating remote sensing and machine learning algorithms. *Journal of Engineering and Sustainable Development, 28*(4), 455-466. ttps://DOI: 10.31272/jeasd.28.4.4

Alkaissi, H., & McFarlane, S. I. (2023). Artificial hallucinations in ChatGPT: Implications in scientific writing. *Cureus*, *15*(2), e35179. DOI: 10.7759/cureus.35179 PMID: 36811129

Alkhater, N., & Danish, F. (2024). "The impact of artificial intelligence on students' learning experience." In Business Sustainability with Artificial Intelligence (AI). *Challenges and Opportunities, Springer*, *1*, 75–84. DOI: 10.1007/978-3-031-56345-4_8

Al-Labadi, L., Jazi, O. A., Ataei, M., Bao, K., & Yu, R. (2025). AI meets academia: Enhancing statistics education with ChatGPT in undergraduate courses. *TechTrends*, *69*(2), 143–154. DOI: 10.1007/s11528-025-01112-x

Allaire, J. J., Teague, C., Scheidegger, C., Xie, Y., & Dervieux, C. (2022). *Quarto* (Version 1.0) [Computer software]. DOI: 10.5281/zenodo.5960048

Allen, R. V. (1978). Automatic earthquake recognition and timing from single traces. *Bulletin of the Seismological Society of America*, *68*(5), 1521–1532. DOI: 10.1785/BSSA0680051521

Almasri, F. (2024). Exploring the impact of artificial intelligence in teaching and learning of science: A systematic review of empirical research. *Research in Science Education*, *54*(5), 977–997.

Alqahtani, N., & Wafula, Z. (2025). Artificial intelligence integration: Pedagogical strategies and policies at leading universities. *Innovative Higher Education*, *50*(2), 665–684.

Altınpulluk, H., & Alptekin, G. (2025). AI Literacy in Distance Learning: Analyzing Graduate Students' Competencies Across Key Variables. In *Proceedings of the World Conference on Education and Teaching* (Vol. 4, No. 1, pp. 48-60). DOI: 10.33422/etconf.v4i1.1058

Al-Zahrani, A. M., & Alasmari, T. M. (2024). Exploring the impact of artificial intelligence on higher education: The dynamics of ethical, social, and educational implications. *Humanities & Social Sciences Communications*, *11*(1), 1–12.

Amdan, M. A. B., Janius, N., & Kasdiah, M. A. H. B. (2024). Concept paper: Efficiency of artificial intelligence (AI) tools for STEM education in Malaysia. *International Journal of Science and Research Archive*, *12*(2), 553–559.

American Statistical Association. (2014). 2014 Curriculum Guidelines for Undergraduate Programs in Statistical Science, Alexandria, VA: Author. Available at https://www.amstat.org/education/curriculumguidelines.cfm

Amlasri, F. (2022). Simulations to teach science subjects: Connections among students; engagement, self-confidence, satisfaction, and learning styles. *Education and Information Technologies*, *27*(5), 7161–7181. DOI: 10.1007/s10639-022-10940-w PMID: 35153535

Ammann, P. J. L., Golde, J. M., & Akbik, A. (2025). "Question decomposition for retrieval-augmented generation." *Proceedings of the 63rd Annual Meeting of the Association for Computational Linguistics (ACL)*, 497–507. DOI: DOI: 10.18653/v1/2025.acl-srw.32

Ananny, M. (2022). Seeing like an Algorithmic Error: What Are Algorithmic Mistakes, Why Do They Matter, How Might They Be Public Problem? *Yale JL & Tech.*, *24*, 342.

Anderson, M. (2024). *Rekindle Your Professional Fire: Powerful Habits for Becoming a More Well-balanced Teacher*. ASCD.

Andersson, T. R., Markou, S., Requeima, J., Bruinsma, W. P., Vaughan, A., & Turner, R. E. (2023). Environmental sensor placement with convolutional Gaussian neural processes. *Environmental Data Science*, *2*(e32), 1–16. DOI: 10.1017/eds.2023.22

Andinasari, Z., Zulkardi, , Somakim, , & Wasiran, Y. (2019). Learning design of reciprocal proportionality using airplanes context. *Journal of Physics: Conference Series*, *1166*(1), 012018. DOI: 10.1088/1742-6596/1166/1/012018

Arrieta, A. B., Díaz-Rodríguez, N., Del Ser, J., Bennetot, A., Tabik, S., Barbado, A., & Herrera, F. (2020). Explainable artificial intelligence (XAI): Concepts, taxonomies, opportunities and challenges toward responsible AI. *Information Fusion*, *58*, 82–115. DOI: 10.1016/j.inffus.2019.12.012

Ashofteh, A., & Bravo, J. M. (2021). Data science training for official statistics: A new scientific paradigm of information and knowledge development in national statistical systems. *Statistical Journal of the IAOS*, *37*(3), 771–789. DOI: 10.3233/SJI-210841

Asif, M., Kuglitsch, M. M., Pelivan, I., & Albano, R. (2025). Review and intercomparison of machine learning applications for Short-term flood forecasting. *Water Resources Management*, *39*(5), 1971–1991. DOI: 10.1007/s11269-025-04093-x

Athaluri, S. A., Manthena, S. V., Kesapragada, V. S. R. K. M., Yarlagadda, V., Dave, T., & Duddumpudi, R. T. S. (2024). Hallucinations in large language models for education: Challenges and mitigation. *International Journal of Technology in Learning and Education*. https://ijtle.com/issue-alldetail/hallucinations-in-large-language-models-for-education-challenges-and-mitigation

Avalekar, U. A., Mehta, V., Mishra, B. R., Prasanna, L., Rajlakshmi, P. V., & Manjunath, T. C. (2025). The current advances in AI-driven education. In Babulak, E. (Ed.), *Educational AI humanoid computing devices for cyber nomads* (pp. 173–196). IGI Global Scientific Publishing., DOI: 10.4018/979-8-3693-8985-0.ch008

Babu, G. R., Maheswari, G., Parameshachari, B. D., & Ullo, S. L. (2020). PSO with LSTM deep learning model for land cover classification. *IEEE International Conference on Emerging Trends in Information Technology and Engineering*. https://arxiv.org/abs/2008.01635

Babu, K. S., Nagaraju, M. V., & Johnson, G. (2023). *Mathematics in everyday life: The hidden language of the world*. Shineeks Publishers.

Baker, T., Smith, L., & Anissa, N. (2019). Educ-AI-tion rebooted? Exploring the future of artificial intelligence in schools and colleges.

Baker, M. (2016). 1,500 scientists lift the lid on reproducibility. *Nature*, *533*(7604), 452–454. DOI: 10.1038/533452a PMID: 27225100

Ball, P. (2023). Is AI leading to a reproducibility crisis in science? *Nature*, *624*(7990), 22–25. DOI: 10.1038/d41586-023-03817-6

Banala, S., Panyaram, S., & Selvakumar, P. (2025). Artificial intelligence in software testing. In Chelliah, P., Venkatesh, R., Natraj, N., & Jeyaraj, R. (Eds.), *Artificial intelligence for cloud-native software engineering* (pp. 237–262). IGI Global Scientific Publishing., DOI: 10.4018/979-8-3693-9356-7.ch009

Banwo, B. O., Khalifa, M., & Seashore Louis, K. (2022). Exploring trust: Culturally responsive and positive school leadership. *Journal of Educational Administration*, *60*(3), 323–339. DOI: 10.1108/JEA-03-2021-0065

Baral, S., Sharma, K., & Singh, R. (n.d.). Student and instructor feedback on an AI-assisted grading tool. In *Proceedings of the ASEE Annual Conference*. American Society for Engineering Education. https://peer.asee.org/student-and-instructor-feedback-on-an-ai-assisted-grading-tool.pdf

Bargagliotti, A., & Franklin, C. (2015). The statistical education of teachers: Preparing teachers to teach statistics. *Chance*, *28*(3), 19–27. DOI: 10.1080/09332480.2015.1099362

Baumer, B. S., Kaplan, D. T., & Horton, N. J. (2014). R Markdown: Integrating a reproducible analysis tool into introductory statistics. *Technology Innovations in Statistics Education, 8*(1).

Bayaga, A. (2025). Leveraging AI-enhanced and emerging technologies for pedagogical innovations in higher education. *Education and Information Technologies*, *30*(1), 1045–1072. DOI: 10.1007/s10639-024-13122-y

Beckman, M. D., Çetinkaya-Rundel, M., Horton, N. J., Rundel, C. W., Sullivan, A. J., & Tackett, M. (2021). Implementing version control with Git and GitHub as a learning objective in statistics and data science courses. *Journal of Statistics and Data Science Education, 29*(sup1), S132–S144.

Bender, E. M., Gebru, T., McMillan-Major, A., & Shmitchell, S. (2021). On the dangers of stochastic parrots: Can language models be too big? *Proceedings of the 2021 ACM Conference on Fairness, Accountability, and Transparency (FAccT '21)*, 610–623. DOI: 10.1145/3442188.3445922

Bender, S. M. (2024). Awareness of artificial intelligence as an essential digital literacy: ChatGPT and Gen-AI in the classroom. *Changing English, 31*(2), 161–174.

Bennie, B., & Erickson, R. A. (2024). Obtaining and Applying Public Data for Training Students in Technical Statistical Writing: Case Studies with Data from U.S. Geological Survey and General Ecological Literature. *Journal of Statistics and Data Science Education : An Official Journal of the of the American Statistical Association, 32*(2), 217–226. DOI: 10.1080/26939169.2023.2195459

Ben-Zvi, D., & Makar, K. (2016). International perspectives on the teaching and learning of statistics. In Ben-Zvi, D., & Makar, K. (Eds.), *The teaching and learning of statistics* (pp. 1–10). Springer., DOI: 10.1007/978-3-319-23470-0_1

Bergen, K. J., Johnson, P. A., de Hoop, M. V., & Beroza, G. C. (2019). Machine learning for data-driven discovery in solid Earth geoscience. *Science, 363*(6433), eaau0323. Advance online publication. DOI: 10.1126/science.aau0323 PMID: 30898903

Berlin Declaration on Open Access to Knowledge in the Sciences and Humanities. (2003). *Max Planck Society*. https://openaccess.mpg.de/Berlin-Declaration

Bernardo, J. M., & Smith, A. F. M. (2009). *Bayesian Theory* (2nd ed.). John Wiley & Sons.

Bertolini, R., Finch, S. J., & Nehm, R. H. (2023). An application of Bayesian inference to examine student retention and attrition in the STEM classroom. *Frontiers in Education, 8*, 1073829. Advance online publication. DOI: 10.3389/feduc.2023.1073829

Biehler, R., Frischemeier, D., Gould, R., & Pfannkuch, M. (2024). Impacts of digitalization on content and goals of statistics education. In Pepin, B., Gueudet, G., & Choppin, J. (Eds.), *Handbook of digital resources in mathematics education* (pp. 547–583). Springer. DOI: 10.1007/978-3-031-45667-1_20

Blikstein, P., & Worsley, M. (2016). Multimodal learning analytics and education data mining: Using computational technologies to measure complex learning tasks. *Journal of Learning Analytics*, *3*(2), 220–238. DOI: 10.18608/jla.2016.32.11

Boels, L. (2023). Reflections on gaze data in statistics education. *Teaching Statistics*, *45*(S1), 40–51. DOI: 10.1111/test.12340

Boels, L., Lyford, A., Bakker, A., & Drijvers, P. (2023). Assessing students' interpretations of histograms before and after interpreting dotplots: A gaze-based machine learning analysis. *Frontline Learning Research*, *11*(2), 1–30. DOI: 10.14786/flr.v11i2.1139

Boettiger, C. (2015). An introduction to Docker for reproducible research. *Operating Systems Review*, *49*(1), 71–79. DOI: 10.1145/2723872.2723882

Bogner, K., Bui, T., Gupta, H., Sharma, A., Nguyen, H., Khandelwal, A., Addanki, R., Saha, A., & Nemani, R. (2021). A global, operational, real-time flood forecasting system using machine learning and remote sensing. *Nature*, *596*, 80–84. DOI: 10.1038/s41586-021-03600-2

Bonas, M., Datta, A., Wikle, C. K., Boone, E. L., Alamri, F. S., Hari, B. V., Kavila, I., Simmons, S. J., Jarvis, S. M., Burr, W. S., Pagendam, D. E., Chang, W., & Castruccio, S. (2024). Assessing predictability of environmental time series with statistical and machine learning models. *Environmetrics*, *36*(1), e2864. DOI: 10.1002/env.2864 PMID: 40017797

Boutilier, J. J., & Chan, T. C. Y. (2023). Introducing and integrating machine learning in an operations research curriculum: An application-driven course. *Transactions on Education*, *23*(2), 64–83. DOI: 10.1287/ited.2021.0256

Bozkurt, A., Karadeniz, A., Baneres, D., Guerrero-Roldán, A. E., & Rodríguez, M. E. (2021). Artificial intelligence and reflections from educational landscape: A review of AI studies in half a century. *Sustainability (Basel)*, *13*(2), 800. DOI: 10.3390/su13020800

Bray, A., Çetinkaya-Rundel, M., & Hardin, J. (2021). *infer: An R package for tidyverse-friendly statistical inference*. https://infer.netlify.app

Breiman, L. (2001). Statistical modeling: The two cultures (with comments and a rejoinder by the author). *Statistical Science*, *16*(3), 199–231. DOI: 10.1214/ss/1009213726

Bryan, J., & Hester, J. (2021). *What they forgot to teach you about R: The stuff you need to know about R beyond data analysis*. https://rstats.wtf

Bryan, J., Hester, J., & the The Stat 545 Tas. (2021). *Happy Git and GitHub for the useR*. https://happygitwithr.com

Brynjolfsson, E., & McAfee, A. (2017). *Machine, platform, crowd: Harnessing our digital future*. W. W. Norton & Company.

Bukar, U. A., Sayeed, M. S., Razak, S. F. A., Yogarayan, S., & Sneesl, R. (2024). Decision-making framework for the utilization of generative artificial intelligence in education: A case study of ChatGPT. *IEEE Access : Practical Innovations, Open Solutions*, *12*, 95368–95389.

Buolamwini, J., & Gebru, T. (2018, January). Gender shades: Intersectional accuracy disparities in commercial gender classification. In *Conference on fairness, accountability and transparency* (pp. 77-91). PMLR.

Burgess, T. A. (2007). *Investigating the nature of teacher knowledge needed and used in teaching statistics* [Doctoral dissertation, Massey University]. IASE. https://www.stat.auckland.ac.nz/~iase/publications/dissertations/07.Burgess.Dissertation.pdf

Burrill, G., & Pfannkuch, M. (2024). Emerging trends in statistics education. *ZDM Mathematics Education*, *56*(1), 19–29. DOI: 10.1007/s11858-023-01501-7

Büscher, C. (2022). Design principles for developing statistical literacy. *Statistics Education Research Journal*, *21*(1), 10. Advance online publication. DOI: 10.52041/serj.v21i1.80

Business Standard. (2025, January 1). 57% schools have functional computers, 53% have internet access. *Business Standard*. https://www.business-standard.com/india-news/57-schools-have-functional-computers-53-have-internet-access-govt-125010101044_1.html

BusinessWire. (2021, July 21). *Carnegie Learning announces new 3rd party study indicating that MATHia leads to better performance in Algebra*. https://www.businesswire.com/news/home/20210721005130/en/Carnegie-Learning-Announces-New-3rd-Party-Study-Indicating-That-MATHia-Leads-to-Better-Performance-in-Algebra

BusinessWire. (2023, March 30). *Study proves DreamBox Learning® significantly increases math achievement after only one hour of use per week*. https://www.businesswire.com/news/home/20230330005199/en/Study-Proves-DreamBox-Learning-Significantly-Increases-Math-Achievement-After-Only-One-Hour-of-Use-Per-Week

Cabrera, Á. A., Tulio Ribeiro, M., Lee, B., & Deline, R. (2023). What did my AI learn? How data scientists make sense of model behavior. *ACM Transactions on Interactive Intelligent Systems*, *13*(4), 44. DOI: 10.1145/3609565

Cadet, M. J. (2023). Application of game-based online learning platform: Kahoot a formative evaluation tool to assess learning. *Teaching and Learning in Nursing*, *18*(3), 419–422. DOI: 10.1016/j.teln.2023.03.009

Caliskan, A., Bryson, J. J., & Narayanan, A. (2017). Semantics derived automatically from language corpora contain human-like biases. *Science*, *356*(6334), 183–186. DOI: 10.1126/science.aal4230 PMID: 28408601

Callingham, R., & Watson, J. M. (2017). The development of statistical literacy at school. *Statistics Education Research Journal*, *16*(1), 181–201. DOI: 10.52041/serj.v16i1.223

Camerer, C. F., Dreber, A., Forsell, E., Ho, T.-H., Huber, J., Johannesson, M., & Hung, H. (2016). Evaluating replicability of laboratory experiments in economics. *Science*, *351*(6280), 1433–1436. DOI: 10.1126/science.aaf0918 PMID: 26940865

Cañas, J. J. (2022). AI and ethics when human beings collaborate with AI agents. *Frontiers in Psychology*, *13*, 836650. DOI: 10.3389/fpsyg.2022.836650 PMID: 35310226

Carlson, J., & Johnston, L. (Eds.). (2015). *Data information literacy: Librarians, data, and the education of a new generation of researchers*. Purdue University Press. DOI: 10.26530/OAPEN_626975

Carnegie Learning. (n.d.). *Carnegie Learning publisher response to IMRA final report*. Texas Education Agency. https://im.tea.texas.gov/sites/default/files/evaluations/Carnegie%20Learning%20Publisher%20Response%20to%20IMRA%20Final%20Report.pdf

Castro, I. K. G., Elquiero, N. M., & Fradejas, J. D. (2023). *Assessing machine learning methods in predicting dengue incidence using climatic factors in Region IV-A (CALABARZON), Philippines* (Bachelor's thesis). De La Salle University. Retrieved from https://animorepository.dlsu.edu.ph/etdb_bio/27

Ceballos, R. F., Gallano, R. C., & Visaya, L. D. (2024). Assessing the Relationship and Effect of Air Pollution [PM 2.5] on Child Respiratory Illness and Child Mortality in the Philippines. *Applied Environmental Research, 46*(3).

Çetinkaya-Rundel, M., & Rundel, C. (2018). Infrastructure and tools for teaching computing throughout the statistical curriculum. *The American Statistician*, *72*(1), 58–65. DOI: 10.1080/00031305.2017.1397549

Chambers, C. D. (2013). Registered reports: A new publishing initiative at *Cortex. Cortex; A Journal Devoted to the Study of the Nervous System and Behavior*, *49*(3), 609–610. DOI: 10.1016/j.cortex.2012.12.016 PMID: 23347556

Cheah, Y. H., Lu, J., & Kim, J. (2025). Integrating generative artificial intelligence in K–12 education: Examining teachers' preparedness, practices, and barriers. *Computers and Education: Artificial Intelligence*, *8*, 100363.

Chen, B. (2025). Beyond tools: Generative AI as epistemic infrastructure in education. *arXiv preprint arXiv:2504.06928.*

Chen, A. M., Palacci, A., Vélez, N., Hawkins, R. D., & Gershman, S. J. (2024). A hierarchical Bayesian model of adaptive teaching. *Cognitive Science*, *48*(7), e13477. DOI: 10.1111/cogs.13477 PMID: 38980989

Chen, L., Chen, P., & Lin, Z. (2020). Artificial intelligence in education: A review. *IEEE Access : Practical Innovations, Open Solutions*, *8*, 75264–75278. DOI: 10.1109/ACCESS.2020.2988510

China, M. O. E. (2019). *UNESCO publishes Beijing Consensus on Artificial Intelligence and Education*. Chinese Ministry of Education. http://en.moe.gov.cn/news/press_releases/201909/t20190902_396913.html

Chin, C., & Osborne, J. (2008). Students' questions: A potential resource for teaching and learning science. *Studies in Science Education*, *44*(1), 1–39. DOI: 10.1080/03057260701828101

Chowdhary, S., Selvakumar, P., Sangeetha, B., Sarvaani, V. V., Anute, N., & Sharma, M. (2025). The role of social capital in entrepreneurial development. In Martínez-Falcó, J., Sánchez-García, E., & Marco-Lajara, B. (Eds.), *Support networks for entrepreneurs: Social capital and strategic collaborations* (pp. 311–338). IGI Global Scientific Publishing., DOI: 10.4018/979-8-3693-9836-4.ch013

CIDDL. (2024). *Summary of UNESCO AI competency framework for teachers.* https://ciddl.org/summary-of-unesco-ai-competency-framework-for-teachers/

Clements, D. H., & McMillen, S. (1996). Rethinking "concrete" manipulatives. *Teaching Children Mathematics*, *2*(5), 270–279. DOI: 10.5951/TCM.2.5.0270

Clerc, O., Abdelghani, R., Desvaux, C., Poisson, E., Oudeyer, P. Y., & Sauzéon, H. (2026). *Teaching students to question the machine: An AI literacy intervention improves students' regulation of LLM use in a science task.* arXiv (Cornell University). https://doi.org/10.48550/arxiv.2604.01955

Coates, J. M., Santhanalakshmi, K., Dinesh, N., Gandhimathi, S., & Chandel, P. S. Mohit, (2025). "Assessment and evaluation in transnational staff development." In Morris G, Ye J (Eds.), Training and development in transnational higher education (pp. 387-406). IGI Global Scientific Publishing. DOI: DOI: 10.4018/979-8-3373-1897-4.ch019

Cohen, A. J., Brauer, M., Burnett, R., Anderson, H. R., Frostad, J., Estep, K., Balakrishnan, K., Brunekreef, B., Dandona, L., Dandona, R., Feigin, V., Freedman, G., Hubbell, B., Jobling, A., Kan, H., Knibbs, L., Liu, Y., Martin, R., Morawska, L., & Forouzanfar, M. H. (2017). Estimates and 25-year trends of the global burden of disease attributable to ambient air pollution: An analysis of data from the Global Burden of Diseases Study 2015. *Lancet*, *389*(10082), 1907–1918. DOI: 10.1016/S0140-6736(17)30505-6 PMID: 28408086

Cordovez, E. M. (2022). Teaching and Learning Music Technologically.

Cotton, D. R. E., Cotton, P. A., & Shipway, J. R. (2023). Chatting and cheating: Ensuring academic integrity in the era of ChatGPT. *Innovations in Education and Teaching International*, *61*(2), 228–239. DOI: 10.1080/14703297.2023.2190148

Crawford, K. (2021). *The atlas of AI: Power, politics, and the planetary costs of artificial intelligence*. Yale University Press.

Cukurova, M. (2025). The interplay of learning, analytics and artificial intelligence in education: A vision for hybrid intelligence. *British Journal of Educational Technology*, *56*(2), 469–488.

D'Mello, S. K. (2017). Emotional learning analytics. In Lang, C., Siemens, G., Wise, A., & Gasevic, D. (Eds.), *Handbook of learning analytics* (pp. 115–127). Society for Learning Analytics Research., https://www.solaresearch.org/wp-content/uploads/2017/05/chapter10.pdf DOI: 10.18608/hla17.010

Dai, K., & Liu, Q. (2024). Leveraging artificial intelligence (AI) in English as a foreign language (EFL) classes: Challenges and opportunities in the spotlight. *Computers in Human Behavior*, *159*, 108354.

Dano, J. B., Cruz, R., & Tiburan, C. (2023). Machine learning approaches for flood susceptibility mapping in the Philippines. *Natural Hazards*, *117*, 1885–1907.

Davies, N., & MacGillivray, H. (2024). Tribute to Peter Holmes and his statistical education achievements. *Teaching Statistics*, *46*(3), 122–126. DOI: 10.1111/test.12376

Davis, C., Bush, T., & Wood, S. (2024). Artificial intelligence in education: Enhancing learning experiences through personalized adaptation. *International Journal of Cyber and IT Service Management*, *4*(1), 26–32.

Dede, C., & Lidwell, W. (2023). Developing a Next-Generation Model for Massive Digital Learning. *Education Sciences*, *13*(8), 845. Advance online publication. DOI: 10.3390/educsci13080845

DeGroot, M. H. (2004). *Optimal statistical decisions*. John Wiley & Sons. DOI: 10.1002/0471729000

Deng, D., Wu, A., Qu, H., & Wu, Y. (2022). DashBot: Insight-driven dashboard generation based on deep reinforcement learning. *IEEE Transactions on Visualization and Computer Graphics*, *28*(1), 907–917. DOI: 10.1109/TVCG.2022.3209468 PMID: 36179003

Desir, S. W., Jr. (2024). High School Acceleration and First-Year College Student Success: Do Advanced Placement or Dual Enrollment Influence College Persistence Differently (Doctoral dissertation, University of South Florida).

Devi, V. A., & Naved, M. (2021). Dive in deep learning: computer vision, natural language processing, and signal processing. In Prakash, S., Parveen, R., & Ahmad, T. (Eds.), *Machine Learning in Signal Processing* (pp. 43–68). Taylor & Francis., DOI: 10.1201/9781003107026-5

Di Porto, F. (2023). Algorithmic disclosure rules. *Artificial Intelligence and Law*, *31*(1), 13–51. DOI: 10.1007/s10506-021-09302-7

Díaz Palencia, J. L. (2024). Applying the anthropological theory of didactics to enhance a multicultural approach to statistics education for engineering students. *Journal for Multicultural Education*, *18*(4), 435–446. DOI: 10.1108/JME-04-2024-0043

Diaz Pratiwi, M., Hernawan, A. H., & Fadillah, A. F. (2025). "Coding and Artificial Intelligence (AI) learning in teachers' perspective." Curricula: Journal of Curriculum Development, 4(1), 215–228. DOI: DOI: 10.31227/osf.io/8rj2m

Dieterle, E., Dede, C., & Walker, M. (2024). The cyclical ethical effects of using artificial intelligence in education. *AI & Society*, *39*(2), 633–643. PMID: 36185064

Dignum, V. (2019). *Responsible Artificial Intelligence: Developing and Using AI in a Responsible Way*. Springer. DOI: 10.1007/978-3-030-30371-6

Ding, A. C. E., Shi, L., Yang, H., & Choi, I. (2024). Enhancing teacher AI literacy and integration through different types of cases in teacher professional development. *Computers and Education Open*, *5*, 100178. Advance online publication. DOI: 10.1016/j.caeo.2024.100178

Ding, Z., Ji, Y., Gan, Y., Wang, Y., & Xia, Y. (2024). Current status and trends of technology, methods, and applications of human–computer intelligent interaction (HCII): A bibliometric research. *Multimedia Tools and Applications*, *83*(7), 12095–12114. DOI: 10.1007/s11042-023-18096-6

Dogucu, M., & Çetinkaya-Rundel, M. (2022). Tools and recommendations for reproducible teaching. *Journal of Statistics and Data Science Education : An Official Journal of the of the American Statistical Association*, *30*(3), 251–260. DOI: 10.1080/26939169.2022.2138645

Dong, L., Tang, X., & Wang, X. (2025). Examining the effect of artificial intelligence in relation to students' academic achievement in classroom: A meta-analysis. *Computers and Education: Artificial Intelligence*, *6*, 100185. DOI: 10.1016/j.caeai.2025.100185

Donoho, D. L. (2017). 50 years of data science. *Journal of Computational and Graphical Statistics*, *26*(4), 745–766. DOI: 10.1080/10618600.2017.1384734

Dorward, J., & Heal, R. (1999). National library of virtual manipulatives for elementary and middle level mathematics. In *WebNet World Conference on the WWW and Internet* (pp. 1510-1511). Association for the Advancement of Computing in Education (AACE).

Draidi Areed, W., Nguyen, T. T. T., Do, K. Q., Nguyen, T., Bui, V., Nelson, E., Warren, J. L., Doan, Q.-V., Sinh, N. V., Osborne, N. J., Richards, R., Tran, N. Q. L., Le, H., Pham, T., Hung, T. M., & Phung, D. (2025). A district-level ensemble model to enhance dengue prediction and control for the Mekong Delta Region of Vietnam. *PLoS Neglected Tropical Diseases*, *19*(9), e0013571. DOI: 10.1371/journal.pntd.0013571 PMID: 41022038

DRCLAS ReVista. (2024). Unequal beginnings: Artificial intelligence and Latin America's educational divide. *ReVista: Harvard Review of Latin America*. https://revista.drclas.harvard.edu/unequal-beginnings-artificial-intelligence-and-latin-americas-educational-divide/

Dudda, L., Kormann, E., Kozula, M., DeVito, N. J., Klebel, T., Dewi, A. P. M., Spijker, R., Stegeman, I., Van den Eynden, V., Ross-Hellauer, T., & Leeflang, M. M. G. (2025). Open science interventions to improve reproducibility and replicability of research: A scoping review. *Royal Society Open Science*, *12*(4), 242057. DOI: 10.1098/rsos.242057 PMID: 40206851

Dvir, M., & Ben-Zvi, D. (2023). Fostering students' informal quantitative estimations of uncertainty through statistical modeling. *Instructional Science*, *51*(3), 423–450. DOI: 10.1007/s11251-023-09622-y

Eaton, S. E. (2023). *Plagiarism in higher education: Tackling tough topics in academic integrity*. ABC-CLIO.

EdTech Books. (n.d.). Constructivism. In *Student guide to learning theories*. https://edtechbooks.org/studentguide/constructivism

Educational Technology. (n.d.). *TPACK: Technological pedagogical content knowledgeframework*. https://educationaltechnology.net/technological-pedagogical-content-knowledge-tpack-framework/

Eduten. (n.d.). *Teaching and AI: Eduten platform overview* [Presentation, GEP Forum]. Finnish National Agency for Education. https://www.oph.fi/sites/default/files/documents/Sirkus_Day%201_Slot%201_Eduten%20presentation_GEP%20Forum%20.pdf

Edwards-Fapohunda, M. O., & Adediji, M. A. (2024). Sustainable development of distance learning in continuing adult education: The impact of artificial intelligence. *Iconic Research and Engineering Journals*, *8*(1), 113–114.

Ekizer, F. N., & Yıldırım, S. S. (2023). 21st century skills and learning environments: ELT students' perceptions. *Educational Research Review*, *18*(6), 114–128. DOI: 10.5897/ERR2023.4332

Ellis, A. R., & Slade, E. (2023). A new era of learning: Considerations for ChatGPT as a tool to enhance statistics and data science education. *Journal of Statistics and Data Science Education : An Official Journal of the of the American Statistical Association*, *31*(2), 128–133. DOI: 10.1080/26939169.2023.2223609

Engel, J. (2017). Statistical literacy for active citizenship: A call for data science education. *Statistics Education Research Journal*, *16*(1), 44–49. DOI: 10.52041/serj.v16i1.213

Erduran Tekin, Ö. (2024). Academic self-discipline as a mediating variable in the relationship between social media addiction and academic achievement: Mixed methodology. *Humanities & Social Sciences Communications*, *11*(1), 1–9. DOI: 10.1057/s41599-024-03633-x

Errington, T. M., Mathur, M., Soderberg, C. K., Denis, A., Perfors, A., Ioannidis, J. P. A., & Nosek, B. A. (2021). Investigating the replicability of preclinical cancer biology. *eLife*, *10*, e71601. DOI: 10.7554/eLife.71601 PMID: 34874005

Ezeoguine, E. P., & Eteng-Uket, S. (2024). Artificial intelligence tools and higher education student's engagement. *Edukasiana: Jurnal Inovasi Pendidikan*, *3*(3), 300–312.

Farooqi, A., Das, D., Tripathi, M., Dutta, R., Goyal, N. K., & Sheikh, M. F. (2026). Navigating ethical frontiers in AI-driven geriatric care. In Stolakis, K., & Efthymiou, I. (Eds.), *AI for geriatric care in an aging society: Ethical, clinical, and policy challenges* (pp. 243–266). IGI Global Scientific Publishing., DOI: 10.4018/979-8-3373-5462-0.ch009

Farooqi, M. T. K., Amanat, I., & Awan, S. M. (2024). Ethical considerations and challenges in the integration of artificial intelligence in education: A systematic review. *Journal of Excellence in Management Sciences*, *3*(4), 35–50.

Feng, L., Ma, D., Xie, M., & Xi, M. (2025). Review on the Application of Remote Sensing Data and Machine Learning to the Estimation of Anthropogenic Heat Emissions. *Remote Sensing (Basel)*, *17*(2), 200. DOI: 10.3390/rs17020200

Ferrari, D. (2022). Teaching Bayesian Statistics. *PS, Political Science & Politics*, *55*(1), 230–235. DOI: 10.1017/S1049096521001244

Firat, M. (2023). How Chat GPT can transform autodidactic experiences and open education? *Theory and Practice in Language Studies*, *13*(3).

Fischhoff, B., & Davis, A. L. (2014). Communicating scientific uncertainty. *Proceedings of the National Academy of Sciences of the United States of America*, *117*(14), 7672–7675. DOI: 10.1073/pnas.131750411 PMID: 25225390

Fitrianto, I., Setyawan, C. E., & Saleh, M. (2024). Utilizing artificial intelligence for personalized Arabic language learning plans. *International Journal of Post Axial: Futuristic Teaching and Learning*, 30–40.

Fleischer, Y., Biehler, R., & Schulte, C. (2022). Teaching and learning data-driven machine learning with educationally designed Jupyter notebooks. *Statistics Education Research Journal*, *21*(2), 1–25. DOI: 10.52041/serj.v21i2.61

Fleischer, Y., Podworny, S., & Biehler, R. (2024). Teaching and learning to construct data-based decision trees using data cards as the first introduction to machine learning in middle school. *Statistics Education Research Journal*, *23*(1), 1–24. DOI: 10.52041/serj.v23i1.450

Floridi, L., & Chiriatti, M. (2020). GPT-3: Its nature, scope, limits, and consequences. *Minds and Machines*, *30*(4), 681–694. DOI: 10.1007/s11023-020-09548-1

Floridi, L., & Cowls, J. (2021). *The Ethics of Artificial Intelligence: Principles, Challenges, and Opportunities*. Oxford University Press.

Foltynek, T., Bjelobaba, S., Glendinning, I., Khan, Z. R., Santos, R., Pavletic, P., & Kravjar, J. (2023). ENAI Recommendations on the ethical use of Artificial Intelligence in Education. *International Journal for Educational Integrity, 19*(1), 12. Advance online publication. DOI: 10.1007/s40979-023-00133-4

Forero-Corba, W., & Bennasar, F. N. (2024). Techniques and applications of machine learning and artificial intelligence in education: A systematic review. *RIED-Revista Iberoamericana de Educación a Distancia, 27*(1).

Foster, E. D., & Deardorff, A. (2017). Open science framework (OSF). *Journal of the Medical Library Association: JMLA, 105*(2), 203. DOI: 10.5195/jmla.2017.88

Freire, P. (1970). Pedagogy of the oppressed (MB Ramos, Trans.). *New York: Continuum, 2007.*

Freire, P. (2025). *Pedagogy of freedom: Ethics, democracy, and civic courage.* Bloomsbury Publishing USA.

Frischemeier, D. (2020). Building statisticians at an early age: Statistical projects exploring meaningful data in primary school. *Statistics Education Research Journal, 19*(1), 39–56. DOI: 10.52041/serj.v19i1.118

Gacu, J. G., Monjardin, C. E. F., Mangulabnan, R. G. T., Pugat, G. C. E., & Solmerin, J. G. (2025). Artificial intelligence (AI) in surface water management: A comprehensive review of methods, applications, and challenges. *Water (Basel), 17*(11), 1707. DOI: 10.3390/w17111707

GAISE College Report ASA Revision Committee (2016). “Guidelines for Assessment and Instruction in Statistics Education College Report 2016,” [online]. Available at https://www.amstat.org/docs/default-source/amstat-documents/gaisecollege_full.pdf

Gal, Y., & Ghahramani, Z. (2016). Dropout as a Bayesian approximation: Representing model uncertainty in deep learning. *In Proceedings of the 33rd International Conference on Machine Learning* (Proceedings of Machine Learning Research, Vol. 48, pp. 1050–1059). https://proceedings.mlr.press/v48/gal16.html

Galan, J., & Kotze, D. J. (2024). Pedagogy of Planning Studios for Multidisciplinary, Research-Oriented, Personalized, and Intensive Learning. *Journal of Planning Education and Research, 44*(3), 1096–1108. DOI: 10.1177/0739456X221082502

Gal, I. (2002). Adults’ statistical literacy: Meanings, components, responsibilities. *International Statistical Review = Revue Internationale de Statistique, 70*(1), 1–25. DOI: 10.1111/j.1751-5823.2002.tb00336.x

Gal, I., & Ograjenšek, I. (2017). Official statistics and statistics education: Bridging the gap. *Journal of Official Statistics*, *33*(1), 79–100. DOI: 10.1515/jos-2017-0005

Gallant, T. B., & Rettinger, D. A. (2025). *The Opposite of Cheating: Teaching for Integrity in the Age of AI* (Vol. 4). University of Oklahoma Press.

Gamboa-Chacón, S., Meneses, E., & Chaves, E. J. (2025). Analysis of earthquake detection using deep learning: Evaluating reliability and uncertainty in prediction methods. *Computers & Geosciences*, *197*, 105877. Advance online publication. DOI: 10.1016/j.cageo.2025.105877

Gandomi, A. H., Chen, F., & Abualigah, L. (2023). Big data analytics using artificial intelligence. *Electronics (Basel)*, *12*(11), 2455. DOI: 10.3390/electronics12112455

García-Martínez, I., Fernández-Batanero, J. M., Fernández-Cerero, J., & León, S. P. (2023). Analysing the impact of artificial intelligence and computational sciences on student performance: Systematic review and meta-analysis. *Journal of New Approaches in Educational Research*, *12*(1), 1–17. DOI: 10.7821/naer.2023.1.1240

Garfield, J. B., Ben-Zvi, D., Chance, B., Medina, E., Roseth, C., & Zieffler, A. (2008). *Developing students' statistical reasoning: Connecting research and teaching practice*. Springer.

Garfield, J., & Ben-Zvi, D. (2008). *Developing Students' Statistical Reasoning: Connecting Research and Teaching Practice*. Springer Science & Business Media.

Gatete, D. O. (2025). Statistics: The Art and Science of Learning from Data. *International Journal of Research and Innovation in Social Science*, *9*(7), 285–301. DOI: 10.47772/IJRISS.2025.90700021

Gawlikowski, J., Tassi, C. R. N., Ali, M., Lee, J., Humt, M., Feng, J., Kruspe, A., Triebel, R., Jung, P., Roscher, R., Shahzad, M., Yang, W., Bamler, R., & Zhu, X. X. (2023). A survey of uncertainty in deep neural networks. *Artificial Intelligence Review*, *56*(S1, Suppl 1), 1513–1589. DOI: 10.1007/s10462-023-10562-9

Gebru, T., Morgenstern, J., Vecchione, B., Vaughan, J. W., Wallach, H., Daumé, H.III, & Crawford, K. (2021). Datasheets for datasets. *Communications of the ACM*, *64*(12), 86–92. DOI: 10.1145/3458723

Gelman, A., Carlin, J. B., Stern, H. S., Dunson, D. B., Vehtari, A., & Rubin, D. B. (2013). *Bayesian data analysis* (3rd ed.). CRC Press., DOI: 10.1201/b16018

Gentleman, R., & Temple Lang, D. (2007). Statistical analyses and reproducible research. *Journal of Computational and Graphical Statistics*, *16*(1), 1–23. DOI: 10.1198/106186007X178663

George, A. S. (2023). Preparing students for an AI-driven world: Rethinking curriculum and pedagogy in the age of artificial intelligence. *Partners Universal Innovative Research Publication*, *1*(2), 112–136.

George, A. S. (2024). Technology Tension in Schools: Addressing the Complex Impacts of Digital Advances on Teaching, Learning, and Wellbeing. [PUMRJ]. *Partners Universal Multidisciplinary Research Journal*, *1*(3), 49–65.

Georgia Tech. (2024). *Georgia Tech's Jill Watson outperforms ChatGPT in real classrooms*. Georgia Institute of Technology. https://research.gatech.edu/georgia-techs-jill-watson-outperforms-chatgpt-real-classrooms

Geron, A. (2021). *Hands-On Machine Learning with Scikit-Learn, Keras, and TensorFlow* (2nd ed.). O'Reilly Media.

Gholamzadeh Khoee, A., Yu, Y., & Feldt, R. (2024). Domain generalization through meta-learning: A survey. *Artificial Intelligence Review*. https://link.springer.com/article/10.1007/s10462-024-10922-z

Gibbons, S. J., & Ringdal, F. (2006). The detection of low magnitude seismic events using array-based waveform correlation. *Geophysical Journal International*, *165*(1), 149–166. DOI: 10.1111/j.1365-246X.2006.02865.x

Gigerenzer, G. (2004). Mindless statistics. *Journal of Socio-Economics*, *33*(5), 587–606. DOI: 10.1016/j.socec.2004.09.033

Gigerenzer, G. (2010). *Rationality for Mortals: How People Cope with Uncertainty*. Oxford University Press.

Gilster, P. (1997). *Digital literacy*. Wiley Computer Pub.

Giving Compass. (2023). Millions of students in the US lack access to high-speed internet. https://givingcompass.org/article/millions-of-students-in-the-us-lack-access-to-technology-and-high-speed-internet

Global Citizen. (2023). Millions of students in the US lack access to technology and high-speed internet. https://www.globalcitizen.org/en/content/verizon-innovative-learning-tech-program/

Gonda, D., Pavlovičová, G., Ďuriš, V., & Tirpáková, A. (2022). Implementation of pedagogical research into statistical courses to develop students' statistical literacy. *Mathematics*, *10*(11), 1793. DOI: 10.3390/math10111793

Goodfellow, I., Bengio, Y., & Courville, A. (2016). *Deep learning*. MIT Press.

Google. (2024). *How we're improving AI literacy in young people*. https://blog.google/innovation-and-ai/technology/families/improving-ai-literacy-in-young-people/

GovInsider. (2023). *How Finland is using AI for predictive public services*. https://govinsider.asia/intl-en/article/how-finland-is-using-ai-for-predictive-public-services

Goyal, N. K. (2025a). Security and privacy in IoT, fog, and blockchain networks. In Sathio, A., Rind, M., Awan, S., & Junejo, A. (Eds.), *Energy-efficient deep learning approaches in IoT, fog, and green blockchain revolution* (pp. 371–398). IGI Global Scientific Publishing., DOI: 10.4018/979-8-3373-0300-0.ch015

Goyal, N. K. (2025b). Weaponizing misinformation and cyberattacks on supply chains. In Bukhari, S., & Zafar, I. (Eds.), *Mass media and impact of fake news on supply chains* (pp. 177–210). IGI Global Scientific Publishing., DOI: 10.4018/979-8-3373-2175-2.ch007

Goyal, N. K., Dandotiya, M., Kumari, M., Kaloria, S., & Anushya, A. (2025c). AI-powered haptic devices for patient rehabilitation. In Mamodiya, U., Kalam, A., Bossoufi, B., Awad, M., & Somwanshi, D. (Eds.), *Integrating AI with haptic systems for smarter healthcare solutions* (pp. 143–170). IGI Global Scientific Publishing., DOI: 10.4018/979-8-3373-2307-7.ch007

Goyal, N. K., Dandotiya, M., Kumari, M., Sheikh, M. F., & Sharma, S. (2025d). Emerging job roles in the tourism sector leveraging artificial intelligence. In Silic, M., Luthia, M., Ahmad, F., & Chakraborty, P. (Eds.), *Empowering sustainable performance and competitive advantage in tourism* (pp. 89–126). IGI Global Scientific Publishing., DOI: 10.4018/979-8-3373-4546-8.ch004

Goyal, N. K., Dandotiya, M., Qurashi, J. A., Kumari, M., & Sharma, S. (2025e). AI-driven predictive analytics for disease management. In Ouaissa, M., Ouaissa, M., Imad, M., Qurashi, J., & Farooq, M. (Eds.), *Utilizing AI of medical things for healthcare security and sustainability* (pp. 231–276). IGI Global Scientific Publishing., DOI: 10.4018/979-8-3373-0690-2.ch008

Goyal, N. K., Kumari, M., Kushwah, V., Dandotiya, M., & Vijay, A. (2025f). Evaluating blockchain security: Trade-offs in consensus mechanisms. *IET Conference Proceedings,* 2024(38), 80–88. https://doi.org/DOI: 10.1049/icp.2025.0775

Grájeda, A., Burgos, J., Córdova, P., & Sanjinés, A. (2024). Assessing student-perceived impact of using artificial intelligence tools: Construction of a synthetic index of application in higher education. *Cogent Education, 11*(1), 2287917.

Grassini, S., Laumann, K., & Skogstad, M. R. (2025). The impact of GenAI on learning outcomes: A systematic review and meta-analysis of experimental studies. *Learning, Media and Technology*. Advance online publication. DOI: 10.1016/j.learntechol.2025.00051

Gruber, A., Gunzburger, M., Ju, L., Lan, R., & Wang, Z. (2023). Multifidelity Monte Carlo estimation for efficient uncertainty quantification in climate-related modeling. *Geoscientific Model Development*, *16*(4), 1213–1229. DOI: 10.5194/gmd-16-1213-2023

Guo, L. (2022). Using metacognitive prompts to enhance self-regulated learning and learning outcomes: A meta-analysis of experimental studies in computer-based learning environments. *Journal of Computer Assisted Learning*, *38*(3), 811–832. DOI: 10.1111/jcal.12650

Guo, S., Zheng, Y., & Zhai, X. (2024). Artificial intelligence in education research during 2013–2023: A review based on bibliometric analysis. *Education and Information Technologies*, *29*(13), 16387–16409.

Guttikunda, S. K.. (2021). Air pollution in South and Southeast Asia: Science-based solutions. *Atmospheric Environment*, *246*, 118093.

Haber, E., Jemielniak, D., & Kurasiński, A. (2025). Future trends and emerging tools. In Haber, E., Jemielniak, D., & Kurasiński, A. (Eds.), *AI in Writing and Research: A Roadmap for Higher Education* (pp. 187–202). Springer., DOI: 10.1007/978-3-031-91705-9_7

Haenlein, M., & Kaplan, A. (2019). A brief history of artificial intelligence: On the past, present, and future of artificial intelligence. *California Management Review*, *61*(4), 5–14. DOI: 10.1177/0008125619864925

Halaweh, M. (2023). ChatGPT in education: Strategies for responsible implementation. *Contemporary Educational Technology*, *15*(2), ep421. DOI: 10.30935/cedtech/13036

Hardin, J., Hoerl, R., Horton, N. J., Nolan, D., Baumer, B., Hall-Holt, O., Murrell, P., Peng, R., Roback, P., Temple Lang, D., & Ward, M. D. (2015). Data science in statistics curricula: Preparing students to "think with data.". *The American Statistician*, *69*(4), 343–353. DOI: 10.1080/00031305.2015.1077729

Hariyanti, F., Budayasa, I. K., & Setianingsih, R. (2025). The role of AI in enhancing statistical literacy: A systematic review in education. *Multidisciplinary Reviews*, *8*(1), 145–157. DOI: 10.31893/multirev.2025376

Hassan, N., & Woo, C. S. (2021, August). Machine learning application in water quality using satellite data. [). IOP Publishing.]. *IOP Conference Series. Earth and Environmental Science*, *842*(1), 012018. DOI: 10.1088/1755-1315/842/1/012018

Haugsbaken, H., & Hagelia, M. (2024). A New AI Literacy For The Algorithmic Age: Prompt Engineering Or Eductional Promptization? In *2024 4th International Conference on Applied Artificial Intelligence (ICAPAI)* (pp. 1-8). IEEE.

Hayes, K. R., Regan, H. M., & Burgman, M. A. (2021). Concepts and methods of uncertainty analysis in environmental risk assessment. In *Environmental Risk Assessment of Genetically Modified Organisms* (Vol. 3, pp. 189–206). CAB International., DOI: 10.1079/9781800621176.0028

Heath, M., Asim, S., Milman, N., & Henderson, J. (2022). Confronting tools of the oppressor: Framing just technology integration in educational technology and teacher education. *Contemporary Issues in Technology & Teacher Education*, *22*(4), 754–777.

Henrickson, L., & Meroño-Peñuela, A. (2025). Prompting meaning: A hermeneutic approach to optimising prompt engineering with ChatGPT. *AI & Society*, *40*(2), 903–918. DOI: 10.1007/s00146-023-01752-8

Herold, B. (2017, July). Personalized learning: Modest gains, big challenges, RAND study finds. *Education Week*. https://www.edweek.org/technology/personalized-learning-modest-gains-big-challenges-rand-study-finds/2017/07

Higher Ed Dive. (2023). *Beyond student progress: How Ivy Tech is approaching data analytics*. https://www.highereddive.com/news/beyond-student-progress-how-ivy-tech-is-approaching-data-analytics/405110/

Holmes, W., & Porayska-Pomsta, K. (2023). The ethics of artificial intelligence in education. *Lontoo: Routledge*, 621-653.

Holmes, W., Bialik, M., & Fadel, C. (2019). *Artificial intelligence in education: Promises and implications for teaching and learning*. Center for Curriculum Redesign.

Holstein, K., Wortman Vaughan, J., Daumé, H.III, Dudik, M., & Wallach, H. (2019, May). Improving fairness in machine learning systems: What do industry practitioners need? In *Proceedings of the 2019 CHI conference on human factors in computing systems* (pp. 1-16). DOI: 10.1145/3290605.3300830

Horton, N. J. (2023). Teaching reproducibility and responsibility workflows. *Journal of Statistics and Data Science Publication.* (Invited perspective / conference-linked publication). https://www.prodabi.de/wpcontent/uploads/Slides_Nick_Horton_Teaching_Reproducibility_and_responsible_Workflows.pdf

Hossain, M. E., & Islam, M. A. (2024). AI and the Future of Education: Philosophical Questions about the Role of Artificial Intelligence in the Classroom. *International Journal of Research and Innovation in Social Science*, *8*(IIIS, 3s), 5541–5547. DOI: 10.47772/IJRISS.2024.803419S

Hosseini, M., & Horbach, S. P. J. M. (2023). Fighting AI-facilitated research misconduct: The importance of involving multiple stakeholders. *Publications*, *11*(3), 43.

Hosseini, M., Horbach, S. P. J. M., Holmes, K. L., & Ross-Hellauer, T. (2024). Open science at the generative AI turn: An exploratory analysis of challenges and opportunities. *Quantitative Science Studies*. Advance online publication. DOI: 10.1162/qss_a_00337 PMID: 40124128

Huang, D. (2024). Innovative interactive instruction to enhance learning behaviors. *Journal of Innovation & Knowledge*, *10*(1), 100641. DOI: 10.1016/j.jik.2024.100641

Hüllermeier, E., & Waegeman, W. (2021). Aleatoric and epistemic uncertainty in machine learning: An introduction to concepts and methods. *Machine Learning*, *110*(2), 457–506. DOI: 10.1007/s10994-021-05946-3

Hundr, E. D. (n.d.). *Squirrel AI Learning*. https://hundred.org/en/innovations/squirrel-ai-learning

Hu, S., Guo, T., Alam, M. S., Koetaka, Y., Ghafoori, E., & Karavasilis, T. L. (2025). Machine learning in earthquake engineering: A review on recent progress and future trends in seismic performance evaluation and design. *Engineering Structures*, *340*, 120721. DOI: 10.1016/j.engstruct.2025.120721

Huser, R., Opitz, T., & Wadsworth, J. L. (2025). Modeling of spatial extremes in environmental data science: Time to move away from max-stable processes. *Environmental Data Science*, *4*, e3. DOI: 10.1017/eds.2024.54

IJLTER. (2024). AI in the classroom: A systematic review of barriers to educator acceptance. *International Journal of Learning, Teaching and Educational Research*, *23*(4). https://www.ijlter.org/index.php/ijlter/article/view/14081

India Today. (2025, January 3). Only 57% of schools have computers, 53% have internet. *India Today*. https://www.indiatoday.in/education-today/news/story/only-57-of-schools-have-computers-53-have-internet-udise-report-school-digital-infrastructure-2659262-2025-01-03

Iqbal, M., Khan, N. U., & Imran, M. (2024). The role of artificial intelligence (AI) in transforming educational practices: Opportunities, challenges, and implications. *Qlantic Journal of Social Sciences*, *5*(2), 348–359.

ISO/IEC. (2022). *ISO/IEC 22989:2022—Information technology—Artificial intelligence—Artificial intelligence concepts and terminology*. International Organization for Standardization.

Ispriyanti, D., Prahutama, A., & Taryono, A. P. (2018, May). Modelling space of spread Dengue Hemorrhagic Fever (DHF) in Central Java use spatial durbin model. [). IOP Publishing.]. *Journal of Physics: Conference Series*, *1025*(1), 012112. DOI: 10.1088/1742-6596/1025/1/012112

Jackson, M. C. (2021). Artificial intelligence & algorithmic bias: The issues with technology reflecting history & humans. j. Bus. &. *Tech. l.*, *16*, 299.

Jaiswal, R. K., Mukherjee, S., Raju, K. D., & Saxena, R. (2002). Forest fire risk zone mapping from satellite imagery and GIS. *International Journal of Applied Earth Observation and Geoinformation*, *4*(1), 1–10. DOI: 10.1016/S0303-2434(02)00006-5

Janssen, M., Hartog, M., Matheus, R., Yi Ding, A., & Kuk, G. (2022). Will algorithms blind people? The effect of explainable AI and decision-makers' experience on AI-supported decision-making in government. *Social Science Computer Review*, *40*(2), 478–493. DOI: 10.1177/0894439320980118

Jatileni, C. N., Sanusi, I. T., Olaleye, S. A., Ayanwale, M. A., Agbo, F. J., & Oyelere, P. B. (2024). Artificial intelligence in compulsory level of education: Perspectives from Namibian in-service teachers. *Education and Information Technologies*, *29*(10), 12569–12596.

Javed, T., & O'Brien, A. (2024). Teaching Together: A Cross-Cultural Analysis of Graduate Teaching Assistant Experiences and Pedagogy. Postgraduate Pedagogies, 4(1).

Jaya, I. G. N. M., Andriyana, Y., Tantular, B., Pangastuti, S. S., & Kristiani, F. (2025). Spatiotemporal Dengue Forecasting for Sustainable Public Health in Bandung, Indonesia: A Comparative Study of Classical, Machine Learning, and Bayesian Models. *Sustainability (Basel)*, *17*(15), 6777. DOI: 10.3390/su17156777

Jeon, I. S., Kang, S. J., & Kang, S. J. (2024). A staged framework for computer vision education: Integrating AI, data science, and computational thinking. *Applied Sciences (Basel, Switzerland)*, *14*(2), 235–250. DOI: 10.3390/app14219792

Jobin, A., Ienca, M., & Vayena, E. (2019). The global landscape of AI ethics guidelines. *Nature Machine Intelligence*, *1*(9), 389–399. DOI: 10.1038/s42256-019-0088-2

Joel Augustus, D., Asiegbu Victor, I., & Obinna, E. (2025). Leveraging artificial intelligence (AI) for educational development in Nigeria: Examining the challenges and opportunities. *Journal of Social Science*, 2(2).

Johnston, H., Wells, R. F., Shanks, E. M., Boey, T., & Parsons, B. N. (2024). Student perspectives on the use of generative artificial intelligence technologies in higher education. *International Journal for Educational Integrity, 20*(1), 2. Advance online publication. DOI: 10.1007/s40979-024-00149-4

Joque, J. (2022). *Revolutionary mathematics: Artificial intelligence, statistics and the logic of capitalism.* Verso Books.

Jordan, M. I., & Mitchell, T. M. (2015). Machine learning: Trends, perspectives, and prospects. *Science, 349*(6245), 255–260. DOI: 10.1126/science.aaa8415 PMID: 26185243

Jozinović, D., Lomax, A., Štajduhar, I., & Michelini, A. (2022). Transfer learning: Improving neural network-based prediction of earthquake ground shaking for an area with insufficient training data. *Geophysical Journal International, 229*(1), 704–721. https://academic.oup.com/gji/article/229/1/704/6447541. DOI: 10.1093/gji/ggab488

Jukes, M. C. H., Grijalva, L., & Zuilkowski, S. (2024). *Experimental evidence on the impact of an AI math tutor in Ghana* [arXiv preprint arXiv:2402.09809]. https://arxiv.org/pdf/2402.09809.pdf

Kaewpradit, K., Ngamchaliew, P., & Buathong, N. (2025). Digital screen time usage, prevalence of excessive digital screen time, and its association with mental health, sleep quality, and academic performance among Southern University students. *Frontiers in Psychiatry, 16*, 1535631. DOI: 10.3389/fpsyt.2025.1535631 PMID: 40195967

Kanamori, H., & Brodsky, E. E. (2004). The physics of earthquakes. *Reports on Progress in Physics, 67*(8), 1429–1496. DOI: 10.1088/0034-4885/67/8/R03

Karakose, T., & Tülübas, T. (2024). School leadership and management in the age of artificial intelligence (AI): Recent developments and future prospects. *Educational Process: International Journal, 13*(1), 7–14.

Karakozov, S. D., Natal'ya, I., Samylkina, N. N., & Samokhvalova, E. A. (2024). Variable teaching of artificial intelligence and data analysis basics in computer science general education course: Integrative approach and key components. *Siberian Pedagogical Journal, 6*(6), 9–23. DOI: 10.15293/1813-4718.2406.01

Karataş, F., Eriçok, B., & Tanrikulu, L. (2025). Reshaping curriculum adaptation in the age of artificial intelligence: Mapping teachers' AI-driven curriculum adaptation patterns. *British Educational Research Journal, 51*(1), 112–129. DOI: 10.1002/berj.4068

Karataş, F., Eriçok, B., & Tanrikulu, L. (2025). Reshaping curriculum adaptation in the age of artificial intelligence: Mapping teachers' AI-driven curriculum adaptation patterns. *British Educational Research Journal*, *51*(1), 154–180.

Kasneci, E., Seßler, K., Küchemann, S., Bannert, M., Dementieva, D., Fischer, F., Gasser, U., Groh, G., Günnemann, S., Hüllermeier, E., Krusche, S., Kutyniok, G., Michaeli, T., Nerdel, C., Pfeffer, J., Poquet, O., Sailer, M., Schmidt, A., Seidel, T., & Kasneci, G. (2023). ChatGPT for good? On opportunities and challenges of large language models for education. *Learning and Individual Differences*, *103*, 102274. DOI: 10.1016/j.lindif.2023.102274

Kearney, P. (n.d.). *Understanding the digital divide in education* [Video]. YouTube. https://www.youtube.com/watch?v=vgpHcEuo_90

Kelly, A. N. (2024). Whole Human Pedagogy: A Novel Framework for Education Abroad Praxis.

Kendall, A., & Gal, Y. (2017). What uncertainties do we need in Bayesian deep learning for computer vision? *Advances in Neural Information Processing Systems*, 30. https://papers.nips.cc/paper/7141-what-uncertainties-do-we-need

Khan Academy. (2023). *University of Toronto randomized controlled trial of 11K students demonstrates a meaningful positive effect of Khan Academy on student learning*. https://blog.khanacademy.org/university-of-toronto-randomized-controlled-trial-of-11k-students-demonstrates-a-meaningful-positive-effect-of-khan-academy-on-student-learning/

Khan Academy. (2024). *Isolating the impact of EdTech in real-world classrooms: A Khan Academy study in a leading academic journal*. https://blog.khanacademy.org/isolating-the-impact-of-edtech-in-real-world-classrooms-a-khan-academy-study-in-a-leading-academic-journal/

Kiker, G. A., Bridges, T. S., & Varghese, A. (2021). Modernizing multi-criteria decision analysis in environmental management using AI-based decision support. *Journal of Environmental Management*, *293*, 112836.

Kim, J. H., Kim, M., Kwak, D. W., & Lee, S. (2022). Home-tutoring services assisted with technology: Investigating the role of artificial intelligence using a randomized field experiment. *JMR, Journal of Marketing Research*, *59*(1), 79–96. DOI: 10.1177/00222437211050351

Kim, J., Lee, H., & Cho, Y. H. (2022). Learning design to support student-AI collaboration: Perspectives of leading teachers for AI in education. *Education and Information Technologies*, *27*(5), 6069–6104. DOI: 10.1007/s10639-021-10831-6

Kluyver, T., Ragan-Kelley, B., Pérez, F., Granger, B., Bussonnier, M., Frederic, J., & Willing, C. (2016). Jupyter Notebooks—A publishing format for reproducible computational workflows. In Loizides, F., & Schmidt, B. (Eds.), *Positioning and Power in Academic Publishing: Players, Agents and Agendas* (pp. 87–90). IOS Press. DOI: 10.3233/978-1-61499-649-1-87

Knuth, D. E. (1984). Literate programming. *The Computer Journal, 27*(2), 97–111. DOI: 10.1093/comjnl/27.2.97

Koehler, M. J., Mishra, P., & Cain, W. (2013). What is technological pedagogical content knowledge (TPACK)? *Journal of Education, 193*(3), 13–19. https://www.bu.edu/journalofeducation/files/2014/02/BUJoE.193.3.Koehleretal.pdf. DOI: 10.1177/002205741319300303

Koga, S. (2022). Characteristics of statistical literacy skills from the perspective of critical thinking. *Teaching Statistics, 44*(2), 59–67. DOI: 10.1111/test.12302

Koga, S. (2025). Lessons to demonstrate statistical literacy skills: A case study of Japanese high school students on reading statistical reports. *Journal of Statistics and Data Science Education : An Official Journal of the of the American Statistical Association, 33*(1), 77–89. DOI: 10.1080/26939169.2024.2334903

Krieglstein, F., Beege, M., Rey, G. D., Sanchez-Stockhammer, C., & Schneider, S. (2023). Development and Validation of a Theory-Based Questionnaire to Measure Different Types of Cognitive Load. *Educational Psychology Review, 35*(1), 9. Advance online publication. DOI: 10.1007/s10648-023-09738-0

Kruschke, J. K. (2015). *Doing Bayesian Data Analysis: A Tutorial with R, JAGS, and Stan* (2nd ed.). Academic Press.

Kruschke, J. K., & Liddell, T. M. (2017). The Bayesian New Statistics: Hypothesis testing, estimation, meta-analysis, and power analysis from a Bayesian perspective. *Psychonomic Bulletin & Review, 25*(1), 178–206. DOI: 10.3758/s13423-016-1221-4 PMID: 28176294

Kubo, H., Naoi, M., & Kano, M. (2024). Recent advances in earthquake seismology using machine learning. *Earth, Planets, and Space, 76*(1), 36. DOI: 10.1186/s40623-024-01982-0

Kuiper, S., & Sturdivant, R. X. (2015). Using online game-based simulations to strengthen students' understanding of practical statistical issues in real-world data analysis. *The American Statistician, 69*(4), 354–361. DOI: 10.1080/00031305.2015.1075421

Kumari, M., & Goyal, N. K. (2026). Artificial intelligence in the cryptocurrency ecosystem: Crime mechanisms, detection strategies, and legal perspectives. In Lin, L. (Ed.), *Innovations in cryptocrime and financial fraud* (pp. 245–282). IGI Global Scientific Publishing., DOI: 10.4018/979-8-3373-0675-9.ch007

Kumari, M., Kumawat, R., Tripathi, M., Suganthi, K., Goyal, N. K., & Sheikh, M. F. (2026). Blockchain for transparency and traceability in supply chains. In Khan, M., Mehmood, T., & Rao, M. (Eds.), *Maximizing operational efficiency at the intersection of supply chain management and marketing* (pp. 35–64). IGI Global Scientific Publishing., DOI: 10.4018/979-8-3373-3109-6.ch002

Kurniawan, D., Masitoh, S., & Bachri, B. S. (2025). Integrating AI in digital project-based blended learning to enhance critical thinking and problem-solving skills. *Multidisciplinary Reviews*, *8*(2), 334–348. DOI: 10.4081/mr.2025.312

Kurtz, G., Amzalag, M., Shaked, N., Zaguri, Y., Kohen-Vacs, D., Gal, E., Zailer, G., & Barak-Medina, E. (2024). Strategies for integrating generative AI into higher education: Navigating challenges and leveraging opportunities. *Education Sciences*, *14*(5), 503. DOI: 10.3390/educsci14050503

Lakens, D. (2021). The practical alternative to the p value is the correctly used p value. *Perspectives on Psychological Science : A Journal of the Association for Psychological Science*, *16*(3), 639–648. DOI: 10.1177/1745691620958012 PMID: 33560174

Lakshminarayanan, B., Pritzel, A., & Blundell, C. (2017). Simple and scalable predictive uncertainty estimation using deep ensembles. *In Proceedings of the 31st International Conference on Neural Information Processing Systems (NeurIPS 2017)* (pp. 6405–6416). Curran Associates, Inc.

Lau, A. C., Henderson, C., Stains, M., Dancy, M., Merino, C., Apkarian, N., Raker, J. R., & Johnson, E. (2024). Characteristics of departments with high-use of active learning in introductory STEM courses: Implications for departmental transformation. *International Journal of STEM Education*, *11*(1), 10. Advance online publication. DOI: 10.1186/s40594-024-00470-x

Lay, T., & Wallace, T. C. (1995). *Modern global seismology*. Academic Press.

Leal Filho, W., Kim, E., Borsatto, J. M. L. S., & Marcolin, C. B. (2025). Using artificial intelligence in sustainability teaching and learning. *Environmental Sciences Europe*, *37*(1), 124. DOI: 10.1186/s12302-025-01159-w

Leavy, A. M., Hourigan, M., & Fitzpatrick, M. (2024). Exploring the plight of the honeybee: Using data sensors and CODAP to support emerging bilingual learners in reasoning about big statistical ideas. *Statistics Education Research Journal, 23*(2), 1–24. DOI: 10.52041/serj.v22i2.706

Lee, A. V. Y. (2023). Supporting students' generation of feedback in large-scale online course with artificial intelligence-enabled evaluation. *Studies in Educational Evaluation, 77*, 101250. DOI: 10.1016/j.stueduc.2023.101250

Lee, D. (2020). Teaching statistics online to prepare educators for evidence-based practice. *Journal of Education for Teaching, 46*(3), 424–429. DOI: 10.1080/02607476.2020.1766303

Lee, Y. J., Davis, R. O., & Ryu, J. (2024). Korean in-service teachers' perceptions of implementing artificial intelligence (AI) education for teaching in schools and their AI teacher training programs. *International Journal of Information and Education Technology (IJIET), 14*(2), 214–219.

Legaki, Z., & Hamari, J. (2020). Gamification in statistics education: A literature review. In *Proceedings of the International GamiFIN Conference* (pp. 41–51). CEUR Workshop Proceedings.

Legaki, N. Z., Xi, N., Hamari, J., Karpouzis, K., & Assimakopoulos, V. (2020). The effect of challenge-based gamification on learning: An experiment in the context of statistics education. *International Journal of Human-Computer Studies, 144*, 102496. PMID: 32565668

Leong, W. Y., Leong, Y. Z., & San Leong, W. (2024, October). Artificial intelligence in education. In *Proceedings of the IET International Conference on Engineering Technologies and Applications (ICETA 2024)* (pp. 183–184). IET.

Lewicka, D. (2022). Building and rebuilding trust in higher education institutions (HEIs). Student's perspective. *Journal of Organizational Change Management, 35*(6), 887–915. DOI: 10.1108/JOCM-02-2022-0037

Li, K. W. (2022). An empirical study on integrating technology into statistics classroom practice. *Journal of Pedagogical Research, 6*(3), 112–136. DOI: 10.33902/JPR.202212339

Limbore, N. V., Anute, N., Ahluwalia, G. K., Chordiya, P. B., & Kalshetti, P. (2025). Ethical leadership and corporate responsibility. In Harriott, S. (Ed.), *Innovative approaches to managing conflict and change in diverse work environments* (pp. 193–218). IGI Global Scientific Publishing., DOI: 10.4018/979-8-3693-9556-1.ch009

Lim, E. M. (2024). Metaphor analysis on pre-service early childhood teachers' conception of AI (artificial intelligence) education for young children. *Thinking Skills and Creativity*, *51*, 101455.

Lim, T., Gottipati, S., & Cheong, M. (2025). What students really think: Unpacking AI ethics in educational assessments through a triadic framework. *International Journal of Educational Technology in Higher Education*, *22*(1), 56. DOI: 10.1186/s41239-025-00556-8

Lindley, D. V. (2000). The philosophy of statistics. *The Statistician*, *49*(3), 293–337. DOI: 10.1111/1467-9884.00238

Lin, T., Zhang, J., & Xiong, B. (2025). Effects of Technology Perceptions, Teacher Beliefs, and AI Literacy on AI Technology Adoption in Sustainable Mathematics Education. *Sustainability (Basel)*, *17*(8), 3698. DOI: 10.3390/su17083698

Lipič, N., & Ovsenik, M. (2020). The effect of statistical literacy on response to environmental change. *Organizacija*, *53*(2), 147–163. DOI: 10.2478/orga-2020-0010

Liu, R., Zenke, C., Liu, C., Holmes, A., Thornton, P., & Malan, D. J. (2024, March). Teaching CS50 with AI: Leveraging generative artificial intelligence in computer science education. In *Proceedings of the 55th ACM Technical Symposium on Computer Science Education,* Volume 1 (pp. 750–756). Association for Computing Machinery.

Liu, W., Dugar, S., McCallum, I., Thapa, G., See, L., Khadka, P., Budhathoki, N., Brown, S., Mechler, R., Fritz, S., & Shakya, P. (2018). Integrated participatory and collaborative risk mapping for enhancing disaster resilience. *ISPRS International Journal of Geo-Information*, *7*(2), 68. DOI: 10.3390/ijgi7020068

Li, X., & Mostafavi, A. (2025). Machine learning approach for disaster risk and resilience assessment in coupled human infrastructure systems performance. *npj. Npj Natural Hazards*, *2*(1), 56. DOI: 10.1038/s44304-025-00104-4

Lokhande, M., John Deva Prasanna, D. S., Ragupathi, T., Vaissnave, V., & Manjunath, T. C. (2025). "Novel ML algorithms for healthcare." In Ajibesin A, N G, Thangavel S (Eds.), Synergizing data envelopment analysis and machine learning for performance optimization in healthcare (pp. 113-134). IGI Global Scientific Publishing. DOI: DOI: 10.4018/979-8-3373-0081-8.ch005

Long, D., & Magerko, B. (2020). What is AI literacy? Competencies and design considerations. *Proceedings of the 2020 CHI Conference on Human Factors in Computing Systems (CHI '20)*, 1–16. DOI: 10.1145/3313831.3376727

Longo, A. (2024). The dystopian threat of AI in primary education. School Children and the Challenge of Managing AI Technologies, 47.

Luby, K. E. (2022). Strategies for Teachers that Reduce Anxiety and Promote Productive Struggle for Students in Secondary Mathematics Classes (Doctoral dissertation, Northeastern University).

Luckin, R. (2018). *Machine Learning and Human Intelligence. The future of education for the 21st century*. UCL institute of education press.

Luckin, R. (2025). Nurturing human intelligence in the age of AI: Rethinking education for the future. *Development and Learning in Organizations, 39*(4), 8–11. DOI: 10.1108/DLO-04-2024-0108

Luckin, R., Holmes, W., Griffiths, M., & Corcier, L. B. (2016). *Intelligence unleashed: An Argument for AI in Education*. Pearson.

Luckin, R., Holmes, W., Griffiths, M., & Forcier, L. B. (2016). *Intelligence Unleashed: An Argument for AI in Education*. Pearson Education.

Lukarov, V., Chatti, M. A., Thüs, H., Kia, F. S., Muslim, A., Greven, C., & Schroeder, U. (2018). Learning analytics case study in blended learning. In *Proceedings of the 10th International Conference on Computer-Supported Education* (Vol. 2, pp. 1–8). CEUR Workshop Proceedings., https://ceur-ws.org/Vol-2193/paper2.pdf

Lund, B. D., Wang, T., Mannuru, N. R., Nie, B., Shimray, S., & Wang, Z. (2023). ChatGPT and a new academic reality: Artificial intelligence-written research papers and the ethics of the large language model publishing landscape. *Journal of the Association for Information Science and Technology, 74*(5), 570–581. DOI: 10.1002/asi.24750

Lundberg, S. M., & Lee, S. I. (2017). A unified approach to interpreting model predictions. *Advances in Neural Information Processing Systems*, •••, 30.

Lundberg, S. M., & Lee, S.-I. (2017). A unified approach to interpreting model predictions. In *Advances in Neural Information Processing Systems 30 (NeurIPS 2017)* (pp. 4765–4774). Curran Associates, Inc.

Luptakova, I. D. (2023). Using a selected machine learning method in the R language in statistics learning. In *ICETA 2023 – 21st International Conference on Emerging eLearning Technologies and Applications* (pp. 348–352). IEEE. https://doi.org/DOI: 10.1109/ICETA61311.2023.10344171

Lye, C. Y., & Lim, L. (2024). Generative artificial intelligence in tertiary education: Assessment redesign principles and considerations. *Education Sciences, 14*(6), 569.

Mahmoud, C. F., & Sørensen, J. T. (2024). Artificial intelligence in personalized learning with a focus on current developments and future prospects. *Research and Advances in Education*, *3*(8), 25–31.

Majumder, R., & Reich, B. J. (2023). A deep learning synthetic likelihood approximation of a non-stationary spatial model for extreme streamflow forecasting. *Spatial Statistics*, *55*, 100755. DOI: 10.1016/j.spasta.2023.100755

Mann, H. (2024). *Artificial Integrity: The paths to leading AI toward a human-centered future*. John Wiley & Sons.

Marcus, G., & Davis, E. (2019). *Rebooting AI: Building artificial intelligence we can trust*. Vintage.

Markham, A. (2021). The limits of the imaginary: Challenges to intervening in future speculations of memory, data, and algorithms. *New Media & Society*, *23*(2), 382–405. DOI: 10.1177/1461444820929322

Marwick, B., Boettiger, C., & Mullen, L. (2018). Packaging data analytical work reproducibly using R (and friends). *The American Statistician*, *72*(1), 80–88. DOI: 10.1080/00031305.2017.1375986

Mata, L. (Ed.). (2022). *Ethical Use of Information Technology in Higher Education*. DOI: 10.1007/978-981-16-1951-9

Matos, T., Santos, W., Zdravevski, E., Coelho, P. J., & Pires, I. M. P. (2025). "A systematic review of artificial intelligence applications in education: Emerging trends and challenges." Decision Analytics Journal., 12. *Article*, *100441*, 1–20. DOI: 10.1016/j.dajour.2025.100441

Mavropoulos, T., Symeonidis, S., Tsanousa, A., & Zikos, G. (2021). Smart integration of sensors, computer vision and knowledge representation for intelligent monitoring and verbal human-computer interaction. *Journal of Intelligent & Robotic Systems*, *101*(2), 67–85. DOI: 10.1007/s10846-021-01377-z PMID: 34127879

Mayer, R. E. (2020). *Multimedia Learning* (3rd ed.). Cambridge University Press. DOI: 10.1017/9781316941355

McCaffery-Pomerleau, K. A. (2024). Unlocking the Power of Co-Collaboration: The Impact of Educator Involvement in Educational Technology Development (Doctoral dissertation, Northeastern University).

McCall, S. A. (2024). *A Troubling Inheritance: Reworking Problematic Curricula*. Rowman & Littlefield. DOI: 10.5040/9798216431817

McCarthy, J., Minsky, M. L., & ML, N. (1956). Rochester, and CE Shannon (1955). *Proposal for the 1956 Dartmouth Summer Research Project on Artificial Intelligence.*

McElreath, R. (2020). *Statistical rethinking: A Bayesian course with examples in R and Stan* (2nd ed.). Chapman & Hall/CRC., DOI: 10.1201/9780429029608

McFarland, D. A., Khanna, S., Domingue, B. W., & Pardos, Z. A. (2021). Education data science: Past, present, future. *AERA Open*, *7*(1), 23328584211052055. DOI: 10.1177/23328584211052055

McGovern, A., Ebert-Uphoff, I., Gagne, D. J., II, & Bostrom, A. (2021). The need for ethical, responsible, and trustworthy artificial intelligence for environmental sciences. *arXiv.* /arXiv.2112.08453DOI: 10.48550

McKinney, W. (2017). *Python for data analysis: Data wrangling with Pandas, NumPy, and IPython* (2nd ed.). O'Reilly Media.

McLeod, S. (2024). Vygotsky's sociocultural theory of cognitive development. *Simply Psychology*. https://www.simplypsychology.org/vygotsky.html

McNamara, D. S., Arner, T., Butterfuss, R., Basu Mallick, D., Lan, A., Roscoe, R., Roediger, H., & Baraniuk, R. (2022). Situating AI (and big data) in the learning sciences: Moving toward large-scale learning sciences. In Ouyang, F., Jiao, P., McLaren, B., & Alavi, A. (Eds.), *Artificial Intelligence in STEM Education: The Paradigmatic Shifts in* (pp. 427–449). Taylor & Francis., DOI: 10.1201/9781003181187-23

Mehra, J., Madaan, S., & Balu, N. Mohit, Manjunath T C, (2025). "The ubiquitous internet and smart computation available 24/7 for anyone and anywhere." In Babulak E (Ed.), Educational AI humanoid computing devices for cyber nomads (pp. 247-270). IGI Global Scientific Publishing. DOI: DOI: 10.4018/979-8-3693-8985-0.ch010

Meinlschmidt, G., Koc, S., Boerner, E., Tegethoff, M., Simacek, T., Schirmer, L., & Schneider, M. (2025). "Enhancing professional communication training in higher education through artificial intelligence (AI)-integrated exercises: Study protocol for a randomised controlled trial." BMC Medical Education, 25(1). *BMC Medical Education*, *307*(1), 1–9. DOI: 10.1186/s12909-025-07307-3 PMID: 40448046

Mendez-Carbajo, D., & Dellachiesa, A. (2023). Data citations and reproducibility in the undergraduate curriculum. *Harvard Data Science Review*, *5*(3). Advance online publication. DOI: 10.1162/99608f92.c2835391

Meresa, H., Murphy, C., Fealy, R., & Golian, S. (2021). Uncertainties and their interaction in flood hazard assessment with climate change. *Hydrology and Earth System Sciences*, *25*(9), 5237–5253. DOI: 10.5194/hess-25-5237-2021

Mike, K., & Hazzan, O. (2022). Machine learning for non-major data science students: A white box approach. *Statistics Education Research Journal*, *21*(2), 1–22. DOI: 10.52041/serj.v21i2.45

Milojevic-Dupont, N., & Creutzig, F. (2021). Machine learning for geographically differentiated climate change mitigation in urban areas. *Nature Communications*, *12*, 4025.

Ministry of Education China. (2019). *UNESCO publishes Beijing Consensus on Artificial Intelligence and Education.* http://en.moe.gov.cn/news/press_releases/201909/t20190902_396913.html

Ministry of Education Singapore. (2023). *EdTech Masterplan 2030.* https://www.moe.gov.sg/education-in-sg/educational-technology-journey/edtech-masterplan

Ministry of Finance Finland. (n.d.). *National artificial intelligence programme AuroraAI.* https://vm.fi/en/national-artificial-intelligence-programme-auroraai

Mishra, P., & Koehler, M. J. (2006). Technological pedagogical content knowledge: A framework for teacher knowledge. *Teachers College Record*, *108*(6), 1017–1054. DOI: 10.1111/j.1467-9620.2006.00684.x

Mitchell, M., Wu, S., Zaldivar, A., Barnes, P., Vasserman, L., Hutchinson, B., & Gebru, T. (2019). Model cards for model reporting. *Proceedings of the Conference on Fairness, Accountability, and Transparency (FAT* '19)*, 220–229. DOI: 10.1145/3287560.3287596

Mitchell, S., Potash, E., Barocas, S., D'Amour, A., & Lum, K. (2021). Algorithmic fairness: Choices, assumptions, and definitions. *Annual Review of Statistics and Its Application*, *8*(1), 141–163. DOI: 10.1146/annurev-statistics-042720-125902

Monett, D., & Paquet, G. (2025). Against the Commodification of Education—If harms then not AI. *Journal of Open, Distance, and Digital Education*, *2*(1).

Mousavi, S. M., & Beroza, G. C. (2022). Deep-learning seismology. *Science*, *377*(6607), eabm4470. Advance online publication. DOI: 10.1126/science.abm4470 PMID: 35951699

Mousavi, S. M., & Beroza, G. C. (2023). Machine learning in earthquake seismology. *Annual Review of Earth and Planetary Sciences*, *51*(1), 105–129. DOI: 10.1146/annurev-earth-071822-100323

Mousavi, S. M., Ellsworth, W. L., Zhu, W., Chuang, L. Y., & Beroza, G. C. (2019). CRED: A deep residual network of convolutional and recurrent units for earthquake signal detection. *Scientific Reports*, *9*(1), 10267. DOI: 10.1038/s41598-019-45748-1 PMID: 31311942

Mousavi, S. M., Sheng, Y., Zhu, W., & Beroza, G. C. (2020). Earthquake Transformer—An attentive deep-learning model for simultaneous earthquake detection and phase picking. *Nature Communications*, *11*(1), 3952. DOI: 10.1038/s41467-020-17591-w PMID: 32770023

Moyer, P. S., Bolyard, J. J., & Spikell, M. A. (2002). What are virtual manipulatives? *Teaching Children Mathematics*, *8*(6), 372–377. DOI: 10.5951/TCM.8.6.0372

Moyer-Packenham, P. S., & Westenskow, A. (2013). Effects of virtual manipulatives on student achievement and mathematics learning. [IJVPLE]. *International Journal of Virtual and Personal Learning Environments*, *4*(3), 35–50. DOI: 10.4018/jvple.2013070103

Muhammad, A. (2024). Combining symbolic AI and deep neural networks for robust real-time autonomous decision systems. *International Journal of Hybrid AI Systems*, *3*(2), 55–68. DOI: 10.13140/RG.2.2.23456.78901

Musa, N. S., Mirza, N. M., Rafique, S. H., Abdallah, A. M., & Murugan, T. (2024). Machine learning and deep learning techniques for distributed denial of service anomaly detection in software defined networks—Current research solutions. *IEEE Access : Practical Innovations, Open Solutions*, *12*, 60521–60537. DOI: 10.1109/ACCESS.2024.3360868

Natural Hazards. (2024). Early warning system for floods at estuarine areas: Combining artificial intelligence with process-based models. *Natural Hazards, 121*, 4615–4638. DOI: 10.1007/s11069-024-06957-8

Necula, S. C., Hauer, I., Fotache, D., & Hurbean, L. (2025). Advanced Hybrid Models for Air Pollution Forecasting: Combining SARIMA and BiLSTM Architectures. *Electronics (2079-9292), 14*(3). DOI: 10.3390/electronics14030549

Ng, D. T. K., Chan, E. K. C., & Lo, C. K. (2025). Opportunities, challenges and school strategies for integrating generative AI in education. *Computers and Education: Artificial Intelligence*, 100373.

Ng, D. T. K., Leung, J. K. L., Chu, K. W. S., & Qiao, M. S. (2021). AI literacy: Definition, teaching, evaluation and ethical issues. *Proceedings of the Association for Information Science and Technology*, *58*(1), 504–509. DOI: 10.1002/pra2.487

Nguyen, A., Kovyazin, V., & Pham, C. (2025). Application of Remote Sensing and GIS in Monitoring Forest Cover Changes in Vietnam Based on Natural Zoning. *Land (Basel), 14*(5), 1037. DOI: 10.3390/land14051037

Nguyen, A., Kremantzis, M., Essien, A., Petrounias, I., & Hosseini, S. (2024). Enhancing student engagement through artificial intelligence (AI): Understanding the basics, opportunities, and challenges. *Journal of University Teaching & Learning Practice*, *21*(6), 1–13.

Nickerson, R. S. (2000). Null hypothesis significance testing: A review of an old and continuing controversy. *Psychological Methods*, *5*(2), 241–301. DOI: 10.1037/1082-989X.5.2.241 PMID: 10937333

Nilsson, N. J. (2009). *The quest for artificial intelligence: A history of ideas and achievements*. Cambridge University Press. DOI: 10.1017/CBO9780511819346

Nisha Angeline, M., Gupta, M. K., Nazar, N., Elumalai, D., & Bhattacharya, S. (2025). Emerging materials for energy storage and environmental applications. In Muduli, K., Moharana, B., Ales, S., & Biswal, D. (Eds.), *Using computational intelligence for sustainable manufacturing of advanced materials* (pp. 53–72). IGI Global Scientific Publishing., DOI: 10.4018/979-8-3693-7974-5.ch003

Nosek, B. A., Alter, G., Banks, G. C., Borsboom, D., Bowman, S. D., Breckler, S. J., Buck, S., Chambers, C. D., Chin, G., Christensen, G., Contestabile, M., Dafoe, A., Eich, E., Freese, J., Glennerster, R., Goroff, D., Green, D. P., Hesse, B., Humphreys, M., & Yarkoni, T. (2015). Promoting an open research culture. *Science*, *348*(6242), 1422–1425. DOI: 10.1126/science.aab2374 PMID: 26113702

Nosek, B. A., Ebersole, C. R., DeHaven, A. C., & Mellor, D. T. (2021). The preregistration revolution. *Proceedings of the National Academy of Sciences of the United States of America*, *118*(15), e2101233118. DOI: 10.1073/pnas.2101233118 PMID: 29531091

Nucamp. (2025). *The complete guide to using AI in the education industry in Finland in 2025*. https://www.nucamp.co/blog/coding-bootcamp-finland-fin-education-the-complete-guide-to-using-ai-in-the-education-industry-in-finland-in-2025

Obidovna, D. Z. (2024). The pedagogical-psychological aspects of artificial intelligence technologies in integrative education. *International Journal of Literature and Languages*, *4*(3), 13–19.

Oddo, D.. (2025). Harnessing artificial intelligence to address climate-induced challenges in water resources management. *Frontiers in Water*, *7*, 1637341. Advance online publication. DOI: 10.3389/frwa.2025.1637341

OECD. (2023). *Recommendation of the Council on Artificial Intelligence* (OECD Legal Instrument OECD/LEGAL/0449). Organisation for Economic Co-operation and Development.

Olatunde-Aiyedun, T. G. (2024). Artificial intelligence (AI) in education: Integration of AI into science education curriculum in Nigerian universities. *International Journal of Artificial Intelligence for Digital Education*, *1*(1), 1–14. DOI: 10.2139/ssrn.4633644

Open Science Collaboration. (2015). Estimating the reproducibility of psychological science. *Science*, *349*(6251), aac4716. DOI: 10.1126/science.aac4716 PMID: 26315443

Ouyang, F., & Zhang, L. (2024). AI-driven learning analytics applications and tools in computer-supported collaborative learning: A systematic review. *Educational Research Review*, *41*, 100620. DOI: 10.1016/j.edurev.2024.100616

Owan, V. J., Abang, K. B., Idika, D. O., Etta, E. O., & Bassey, B. A. (2023). Exploring the potential of artificial intelligence tools in educational measurement and assessment. *Eurasia Journal of Mathematics, Science and Technology Education*, *19*(10), em2367. Advance online publication. DOI: 10.29333/ejmste/13428

Pande, C. B., Sidek, L. M., Varade, A. M., Elkhrachy, I., Radwan, N., Tolche, A. D., & Elbeltagi, A. (2024). Forecasting of meteorological drought using ensemble and machine learning models. *Environmental Sciences Europe*, *36*(1), 160. DOI: 10.1186/s12302-024-00975-w

Pandey, J. K., Rai, M., & Alam, E. (Eds.). (2025). *AI and ML in Early Warning Systems for Natural Disasters*. Bentham Science. DOI: 10.2174/97988988113891250101

Pane, J. F., Steiner, E. D., Baird, M. D., & Hamilton, L. S. (2015). *Promising evidence on personalized learning* (Research Report RR-1140-BMGF). RAND Corporation. https://eric.ed.gov/?id=ED571009

Pan, Y., & Gu, J. (2023). Empowering education: ChatGPT's role in teaching and learning statistics and data analytics. *International Journal of Technology in Teaching and Learning*, *19*(1), 34–51. DOI: 10.37120/ijttl.2023.19.1.02

Pathak, P., & Muralidharan, K. (2023). Bibliometric analysis and review of recent literature on flood susceptibility and trends in forecasting methods. *International Journal of Environmental Sciences & Natural Resources*, *32*(2). Advance online publication. DOI: 10.19080/IJESNR.2023.32.556337

Peach, R. L., Greenbury, S. F., Johnston, I. G., Yaliraki, S. N., Lefevre, D. J., & Barahona, M. (2021). Understanding learner behaviour in online courses with Bayesian modelling and time series characterization. *Scientific Reports*, *11*(1), 2823. DOI: 10.1038/s41598-021-81709-3 PMID: 33531544

Peng, R. D. (2011). Reproducible research in computational science. *Science*, *334*(6060), 1226–1227. DOI: 10.1126/science.1213847 PMID: 22144613

Peng, R. D. (2022). *Mastering software development in R*. Leanpub.

Peng, R. D., & Hicks, S. C. (2021). Reproducible research: A retrospective. *Annual Review of Public Health*, *42*(1), 79–93. DOI: 10.1146/annurev-publhealth-012420-105110 PMID: 33467923

Penn, G. S. E. (n.d.). *Learning analytics and artificial intelligence, M.S.Ed.* University of Pennsylvania Graduate School of Education. https://www.gse.upenn.edu/academics/learning-analytics-AI-online-msed

Perkins, M., Furze, L., Roe, J., & MacVaugh, J. (2024). The artificial intelligence assessment scale (AIAS): A framework for ethical integration of generative AI in educational assessment. *Journal of University Teaching & Learning Practice*, *21*(6), 49–66.

Perol, T., Gharbi, M., & Denolle, M. (2018). Convolutional neural network for earthquake detection and location. *Science Advances*, *4*(2), e1700578. DOI: 10.1126/sciadv.1700578 PMID: 29487899

Pétrin-Pomerleau, P., Vincent, C., Mairena, P. M. G., Yilmaz, E., Charbonneau, A. T., Husereau, T., & Jacob, G. (2023). The Bayesian approach is intuitive conditionally to prior exposition to these examples. *The Quantitative Methods for Psychology*, *19*(3), 244–253. DOI: 10.20982/tqmp.19.3.p244

Pham, B. T.. (2020). Flood susceptibility modelling using machine learning. *Water (Basel)*, *12*(4), 1138.

Pham, H. H., Dao, T. Q., Le, T. T. H., & Nguyen, D. D. (2022). The effects of ALEKS on mathematics learning in K–12 and higher education: A meta-analysis. *Investigations in Mathematics Learning*, *14*(1), 1–18. DOI: 10.1080/19477503.2021.1926194

Pitts, G., Rani, N., Mildort, W., & Cook, E. (2025). *Students' reliance on AI in Higher Education: Identifying contributing factors*. ArXiv.org. https://doi.org/10.48550/arxiv.2506.13845

Plesser, H. E. (2018). Reproducibility vs. replicability: A brief history of a confused terminology. *Frontiers in Neuroinformatics*, *11*, 76. DOI: 10.3389/fninf.2017.00076 PMID: 29403370

Poldrack, R. A., Baker, C. I., Durnez, J., Gorgolewski, K. J., Matthews, P. M., Munafò, M. R., Nichols, T. E., Poline, J.-B., Vul, E., & Yarkoni, T. (2017). Scanning the horizon: Towards transparent and reproducible neuroimaging research. *Nature Reviews. Neuroscience*, *18*(2), 115–126. DOI: 10.1038/nrn.2016.167 PMID: 28053326

Popper, K. R. (1959). *The logic of scientific discovery*. Hutchinson.

Posekany, A. (2025). Project-based learning connecting robotics and artificial intelligence. *Lecture Notes in Networks and Systems*, *1280*, 319–326. DOI: 10.1007/978-3-031-83523-0_30

Prahutama, A., Hakim, A. R., Ispriyanti, D., Yasin, H., & Warsito, B. (2021). Geographically weighted negative bivariate binomial regression for modelling the number of dengue diseases and their mortality in East Nusa Tenggara, Indonesia. *Journal of Mathematical and Computational Science*, *11*(6), 7971–7990.

Pruim, R., Kaplan, D. T., & Horton, N. J. (2017). The mosaic package: Helping students to 'think with data' using R. *The R Journal*, *9*(1), 77–102. DOI: 10.32614/RJ-2017-024

Purwitaningsih, L. M., & de Carvalho, A. C. (2022). Empowering local leaders in flood inundation mapping in Bagelen, Purworejo, Central Java. *Jàambá*, *14*(1), 1298. DOI: 10.4102/jamba.v14i1.1298 PMID: 36092748

Qayyum, F., Kim, D. H., Bong, S. J., Chi, S. Y., & Choi, Y. H. (2022). A survey of datasets, preprocessing, modeling mechanisms, and simulation tools based on AI for material analysis and discovery. *Materials (Basel)*, *15*(4), 1434. DOI: 10.3390/ma15041434 PMID: 35207974

Quiñones, D., Ruz, F., Díaz-Arancibia, J., Paz, F., Osega, J., & Rojas, L. F. (2024). Innovating Statistics Education: The Design of a Novel App Using Design Thinking. *Applied Sciences (Basel, Switzerland)*, *14*(18), 8515. Advance online publication. DOI: 10.3390/app14188515

R Core Team. (2024). *R: A language and environment for statistical computing*. R Foundation for Statistical Computing. https://www.R-project.org

Rabiatu, M. M., & Shehu, S. A. (2024). Adopting artificial intelligence (AI) in education: Challenges and possibilities. *Asian Journal of Advanced Research and Reports*, *18*(2), 106–111.

Rahmaty, M. (2023). Machine learning with big data to solve real-world problems. *Journal of Data Analytics*, *2*(1), 9–16. DOI: 10.59615/jda.2.1.9

Raiaan, M. A. K., Mukta, M. S. H., Fatema, K., Fahad, N. M., Sakib, S., Mim, M. M. J., Ahmad, J., Ali, M. E., & Azam, S. (2024). A Review on Large Language Models: Architectures, Applications, Taxonomies, Open Issues and Challenges. *IEEE Access : Practical Innovations, Open Solutions*, *12*, 26839–26874. DOI: 10.1109/ACCESS.2024.3365742

Ramachandran, K. K. (2024). Data science in the 21st century: Evolution, challenges, and future directions. *International Journal of Business and Data Analytics*, *7*(3), 201–219. DOI: 10.4018/IJBDA.20240703

Ramirez, E. A. B., & Esparrell, J. A. F. (2024). Artificial intelligence (AI) in education: Unlocking the perfect synergy for learning. *Educational Process: International Journal*, *13*(1), 35–51.

Rana, I. A., & Routray, J. K. (2023). Integrating AI tools into disaster risk reduction education. *International Journal of Disaster Risk Reduction*, *96*, 103878.

Rane, N. (2024). Enhancing the quality of teaching and learning through Gemini, ChatGPT, and similar generative artificial intelligence: Challenges, future prospects, and ethical considerations in education. *TESOL and Technology Studies*, *5*(1), 1–6.

Rao, V. N. V., Jeng, A., Drew, J., Kala, B., & Gongati, S. (2026). Students' Statistical Thinking When Using Generative AI: A Descriptive Case Study. *Journal of Statistics and Data Science Education : An Official Journal of the of the American Statistical Association*, *34*(1), 4–15. DOI: 10.1080/26939169.2025.2596684

Rasmussen, L. V., Whitley, E. W., & Welty, L. J. (2023). Pragmatic reproducible research: Improving the research process from raw data to results, bit by bit. *The Journal of Clinical Investigation*, *133*(16), e173741. DOI: 10.1172/JCI173741 PMID: 37581309

Raspberry Pi Foundation. (2024). *Bringing AI education to 1.25 million students across Latin America*. https://www.raspberrypi.org/blog/bringing-ai-education-to-1-25-million-students-across-latin-america/

Razzaq, S., Shah, B., Iqbal, F., Ilyas, M., Maqbool, F., & Rocha, A. (2023). DeepClassRooms: A deep learning based digital twin framework for on-campus class rooms. *Neural Computing & Applications*, *35*(11), 49815–49833. DOI: 10.1007/s00521-021-06754-5 PMID: 35017794

Reiss, M. J. (2021). The use of AI in education: Practicalities and ethical considerations. *London Review of Education, 19*(1). Advance online publication. DOI: 10.14324/LRE.19.1.05

Reynolds, L., & McDonell, K. (2021, May). Prompt programming for large language models: Beyond the few-shot paradigm. In *Extended abstracts of the 2021 CHI conference on human factors in computing systems* (pp. 1-7).

Ridgway, J. (2016). Implications of the data revolution for statistics education. *International Statistical Review = Revue Internationale de Statistique, 84*(3), 528–549. DOI: 10.1111/insr.12110

Ridsdale, C., Rothwell, J., Smit, M., Ali-Hassan, H., Bliemel, M., Irvine, D., Kelley, D., Matwin, S., & Wuetherick, B. (2015). *Strategies and best practices for data literacy education: Knowledge synthesis report.* Dalhousie University. https://www.semanticscholar.org/paper/Strategies-and-Best-Practices-for-Data-Literacy-Ridsdale-Rothwell/5a2f9bc40d78f58baf774d4e55f8377f796f105e

Robert, A., Potter, K., & Frank, L. (2024). The impact of artificial intelligence on students' learning experience. *Wiley Interdisciplinary Reviews: Computational Statistics, 2*(1), 75–84.

Robert, C. P. (2007). *The Bayesian Choice: From Decision Theoretic Foundations to Computational Implementation.* Springer.

Robin, J., Requena-Mesa, C., Benson, K., Alonso, L., Poehls, M., Carvalhais, N., & Reichstein, M. (2022). Space–time modeling of NDVI using ConvLSTM over sub-Saharan Africa. https://arxiv.org/abs/2210.13648

Rocha-Feregrino, G., & Sánchez, G. S. (2025). "Transforming the teaching of probability and statistics: The impact of AI-driven contextualization on architecture students' motivation." **Proceedings of the 2025 IEEE International Conference for the Future of Education*, 198–206. DOI: DOI: 10.1109/IFE63672.2025.11024621

Roderick, T. (2023). *Teach for climate justice: A vision for transforming education.* Harvard Education Press.

Romano, L. (2024). *The Transparency Problem in Higher Education Administration: Using a Grounded Theory to Create a Model for Rebuilding Trust.* St. John's University.

Romero-Rodríguez, M. E., Rodríguez-Donate, M. C., & Nieto-González, I. L. (2024). Improving active learning: Innovation in statistics education. In *Teaching innovations in economics: Towards a sustainable world* (pp. 371–384). Springer Nature.

Roscher, R., Bohn, B., Duarte, M. F., & Garcke, J. (2020). Explainable machine learning for scientific insights and discoveries. *IEEE Access : Practical Innovations, Open Solutions*, *8*, 42200–42216. DOI: 10.1109/ACCESS.2020.2976199

Ross, Z. E., Meier, M.-A., Hauksson, E., & Heaton, T. H. (2018). Generalized seismic phase detection with deep learning. *Bulletin of the Seismological Society of America*, *108*(5A), 2894–2901. DOI: 10.1785/0120180080

Russell, S., & Norvig, P. (2021). *Artificial intelligence: A modern approach* (4th ed.). Pearson.

Sajadi, A. (2024). Optimizing Data Input Interfaces Through User Error Analysis: A Statistical and HCI-Driven Approach. *International Journal of Advanced Human Computer Interaction*, *2*(2), 67–77.

Saldanha, L., & Thompson, P. (2002). Conceptions of sample and their relationship to statistical inference. *Educational Studies in Mathematics*, *51*(3), 257–270. DOI: 10.1023/A:1023692604014

Sana, E., Fitriani, A., Soetarno, D., & Yusuf, M. (2024). Analysis of user perceptions on interactive learning platforms based on artificial intelligence. *Journal of Computer Science and Technology Application*, *1*(1), 26–32.

Šarić-Grgić, I., Grubišić, A., & Gašpar, A. (2024). Twenty-Five Years of Bayesian knowledge tracing: A systematic review. *User Modeling and User-Adapted Interaction*, *34*(4), 1127–1173. DOI: 10.1007/s11257-023-09389-4

Sari, W., Astrada, A., Septiana, V., & Pamungkas, R. A. (2025). Screen Time and Emotional Development Among Indonesian Preschoolers: A Comparative Study Across Socioeconomic Contexts in Jakarta. *Media Publikasi Promosi Kesehatan Indonesia*, *8*(9), 1001–1012. DOI: 10.56338/mppki.v8i9.7879

Sarkar, A. (2025). Bridging the Divide: A Systems Thinking Approach to Inclusivity in AI Development and Education. Available at *SSRN* 5097669. DOI: 10.2139/ssrn.5097669

Sarwar, M. A., & Ms Saima, A. G. (2024). The role of artificial intelligence in shaping the future of education at higher secondary level. *Journal of Education and Social Studies*, *5*(1), 34–45.

Schenk, M., Drechsel-Grau, C., & Stefanek, M. (2024). Uncertainty, risk, and decision-making in science education. *Science & Education.* Advance online publication. DOI: 10.1007/s11191-024-00544-w

Schwab-McCoy, A. (2019). The state of statistics education research in client disciplines: Themes and trends across the university. *Journal of Statistics Education : An International Journal on the Teaching and Learning of Statistics*, *27*(3), 253–264.

Schwartz, D. L., Chase, C. C., & Bransford, J. D. (2023). Resisting overzealous transfer: Coordinating previously successful routines with needs for new learning. *Educational Psychologist*, *48*(2), 89–106. https://pdfs.semanticscholar.org/5471/3b2d07caa89883822c9ad041dfeedf0efc24.pdf

Schwarz, J. (2025). The use of generative AI in statistical data analysis and its impact on teaching statistics at universities of applied sciences. *Teaching Statistics*, *47*(2), 118–128. DOI: 10.1111/test.12398

Seabold, S., & Perktold, J. (2010). Statsmodels: Econometric and statistical modeling with Python. *Proceedings of the 9th Python in Science Conference*, 57–61. DOI: 10.25080/Majora-92bf1922-011

Sekti, B. A. (2025a). AI Technology Management Concepts and Strategies. In *AI Technology Management and Value Creation* (pp. 1–32). DOI: 10.4018/979-8-3373-2497-5.ch001

Sekti, B. A. (2025b). IT Service Information Security Management. In *Cases on Information Systems Service Management* (pp. 61–93). DOI: 10.4018/979-8-3373-2352-7.ch003

Sekti, B. A. (2025c). Machine learning and artificial intelligence (AI) in manufacturing. In *Integrating Digital Innovation and Integrated Frameworks in Manufacturing* (pp. 255–292). DOI: 10.4018/979-8-3373-1082-4.ch011

Sekti, B. A. (2025d). Machine Learning vs. AI: Key Concepts. In *Implementing Enterprise Cybersecurity With AI* (pp. 1–27). DOI: 10.4018/979-8-3373-2252-0.ch001

Selvaraju, R. R., Cogswell, M., Das, A., Vedantam, R., Parikh, D., & Batra, D. (2017). Grad-CAM: Visual explanations from deep networks via gradient-based localization. *Proceedings of the IEEE International Conference on Computer Vision*, 618–626. https://doi.org/DOI: 10.1109/ICCV.2017.74

Selwyn, N. (2019). *Should Robots Replace Teachers? AI and the Future of Education*. John Wiley & Sons.

Shah, P. (2023). *AI and the Future of Education: Teaching in the Age of Artificial Intelligence*. John Wiley & Sons.

Sharma, P. (2024). *The power of personalized learning: A meta-analysis* (Report No. ED646968). ERIC. https://files.eric.ed.gov/fulltext/ED646968.pdf

Sharma, P., Kumawat, R., Jain, G., Keswani, G., Goyal, N. K., & Sheikh, M. F. (2026). Machine learning-based intrusion detection systems for healthcare Internet of Things (HIoT). In Shieh, C., Goel, P., Horng, M., & Pandey, H. (Eds.), *Resilient healthcare Internet of Things systems: Architectures, security, and trust* (pp. 185–214). IGI Global Scientific Publishing., DOI: 10.4018/979-8-3373-7610-3.ch007

Sharma, S. (2017). Definitions and models of statistical literacy: A literature review. *Statistics Education Research Journal, 16*(1), 149–163. DOI: 10.1080/23265507.2017.1354313

Shi, X., & Wang, B. (2025). "Exploration of interdisciplinary project-based teaching driven by generative AI." *Proceedings of the 4th International Conference on Educational Innovation and Multimedia Technology*, 454–465. DOI: DOI: 10.2991/978-94-6463-750-2_45

Shoufan, A., & Esmaeil, A. (2026). *AI Hallucination from Students' Perspective: A Thematic Analysis*. arXiv (Cornell University). https://doi.org/10.48550/arxiv.2602.17671

Shoukat, W., Rizwan, N., & Khan, M. T. (2025). The role of artificial intelligence (AI) tutors in personalized learning: Benefits and challenges. *Journal of Social Signs Review, 3*(4), 1–13.

Siddiqui, M. T., Mansoori, M. V., & Yadav, A.Mohammad Talha Siddiqui. (2025). AI-enabled pedagogy: Advancing education through innovative teaching tools and the AI-TEACH model. *Journal of Informatics Education and Research, 5*(1), 1–20. DOI: 10.52783/jier.v5i1.2261

Sindakis, S. (2023). "Promoting creativity and critical thinking: Fostering 21st-century skills in education." Academia World News, 1–6. DOI: DOI: 10.13140/RG.2.2.34567.89123

Sperling, K., Stenberg, C. J., McGrath, C., Åkerfeldt, A., Heintz, F., & Stenliden, L. (2024). In search of artificial intelligence (AI) literacy in teacher education: A scoping review. *Computers and Education Open, 6*, 100169.

Spiegelhalter, D. J., Abrams, K. R., & Myles, J. P. (2004). *Bayesian Approaches to Clinical Trials and Health-Care Evaluation*. Wiley.

Srivathsa, B. S., Pandey, H., & Naganandini, G. (2025). Future trends in education: The impact of AI, data science, and immersive technologies. In Naganandini, G. (Ed.), *Future Prospects of AI and Data Science* (pp. 115–132). IGI Global., DOI: 10.4018/979-8-3693-8292-9.ch007

Steib, N., Büchter, T., Eichler, A., Binder, K., Krauss, S., Böcherer-Linder, K., Vogel, M., & Hilbert, S. (2024). How to teach Bayesian reasoning: An empirical study comparing four different probability training courses. *Learning and Instruction*, *95*, 102032. DOI: 10.1016/j.learninstruc.2024.102032

Stodden, V., Leisch, F., & Peng, R. D. (Eds.). (2014). *Implementing reproducible research*. CRC Press. DOI: 10.1201/b16868

Stodden, V., McNutt, M., Bailey, D. H., Deelman, E., Gil, Y., Hanson, B., Heroux, M. A., Ioannidis, J. P. A., & Taufer, M. (2016). Enhancing reproducibility for computational methods. *Science*, *354*(6317), 1240–1241. DOI: 10.1126/science.aah6168 PMID: 27940837

Stodden, V., & Miguez, S. (2014). Best practices for computational science: Software infrastructure and environments for reproducible and extensible research. *Journal of Open Research Software*, *2*(1), e21. DOI: 10.5334/jors.ay

Suharyo, S., Nugroho, A., & Wibowo, H. (2024). Artificial intelligence in the context of curriculum design for primary and secondary education. *Humanika*, *30*(2), 208–217. DOI: 10.14710/humanika.v30i2.60563

Suzuki, W. (2021). *Good Anxiety: Harnessing the Power of the Most Misunderstood Emotion*. Simon and Schuster.

Sweller, J. (2023). The Development of Cognitive Load Theory: Replication Crises and Incorporation of Other Theories Can Lead to Theory Expansion. *Educational Psychology Review*, *35*(4), 95. Advance online publication. DOI: 10.1007/s10648-023-09817-2

Taddeo, M., & Floridi, L. (2020). How AI can be a force for good. *Science*, *361*(6404), 751–752. DOI: 10.1126/science.aat5991 PMID: 30139858

Tahir, M., Hassan, F. D., & Shagoo, M. R. (2024). Role of artificial intelligence in education: A conceptual review. *World Journal of Advanced Research and Reviews*, *22*(1), 1469–1475.

Tang, X., Zhu, J., & Chen, Y. (n.d.). *When adaptive learning is effective learning: Comparison of an adaptive learning system to teacher-led instruction* [Unpublished manuscript]. University of Hong Kong. https://www.studocu.com/hk/document/the-university-of-hong-kong/research-seminar-ii/when-adaptive-learning-is-effective-learning-comparison-of-an-adaptive-learning-system-to-teacher-led-instruction/108779520

Tang, K. H. D. (2024). Implications of artificial intelligence for teaching and learning. *Acta Pedagogia Asiana*, *3*(2), 65–79.

Tech, C. E. N. T. U. R. Y. (2024). *CENTURY Tech report reveals significant positive impact of AI-powered learning on primary SATs outcomes*. https://www.century.tech/news/century-tech-report-reveals-significant-positive-impact-of-ai-powered-learning-on-primary-sats-outcomes

Tech, C. E. N. T. U. R. Y. (2025). *GCSE outcomes: An impact analysis of CENTURY*. https://www.century.tech/wp-content/uploads/2025/06/GCSE-Outcomes-Impact-Analysis-of-CENTURY.pdf

Teegavarapu, R. S. (2024). *Imputation Methods for Missing Hydrometeorological Data Estimation*. Springer International Publishing AG. DOI: 10.1007/978-3-031-60946-6

Tengö, M., Hill, R., Malmer, P., Raymond, C. M., Spierenburg, M., Danielsen, F., & Folke, C. (2021). Weaving knowledge systems in IPBES, CBD and beyond—Lessons learned for sustainability. *Current Opinion in Environmental Sustainability*, *53*, 101016.

The Academic. (2025). AI-powered learning analytics for student success. *The Academic Journal, 3*(1). https://theacademic.in/wp-content/uploads/2025/08/47.pdf

Thekdi, S., Tatar, U., Santos, J., & Chatterjee, S. (2023). Disaster Risk and Artificial Intelligence: A Framework to Characterize Conceptual Synergies and Future Opportunities. *Risk Analysis : An Official Publication of the Society for Risk Analysis*, *43*(8), 1641–1656. DOI: 10.1111/risa.14038 PMID: 36316234

Theobald, E. J., Hill, M. J., Tran, E., Agrawal, S., Arroyo, E. N., Behling, S., Chambwe, N., Cintrón, D. L., Cooper, J. D., Dunster, G., Grummer, J. A., Hennessey, K., Hsiao, J., Iranon, N., Jones, L.II, Jordt, H., Keller, M., Lacey, M. E., Littlefield, C. E., & Freeman, S. (2020). Active learning narrows achievement gaps for underrepresented students in undergraduate science, technology, engineering, and math. *Proceedings of the National Academy of Sciences of the United States of America*, *117*(12), 6476–6483. DOI: 10.1073/pnas.1916903117 PMID: 32152114

Tian, N., Zheng, J.-X., Li, L.-H., Xue, J.-B., Xia, S., Lv, S., & Zhou, X.-N. (2024). Precision Prediction for Dengue Fever in Singapore: A Machine Learning Approach Incorporating Meteorological Data. *Tropical Medicine and Infectious Disease*, *9*(4), 72. DOI: 10.3390/tropicalmed9040072 PMID: 38668533

Tintle, N., Chance, B., Cobb, G., Rossman, A., Roy, S., Swanson, T., & VanderStoep, J. (2015). *Introduction to statistical investigations: High school binding*. John Wiley.

Topaz, M., Peltonen, L. M., Michalowski, M., Stiglic, G., Ronquillo, C., Pruinelli, L., & Fukahori, H. (2025). The ChatGPT effect: Nursing education and generative artificial intelligence. *The Journal of Nursing Education*, *64*(6), e40–e43. PMID: 38302101

Trabelsi, Z., Alnajjar, F., Parambil, M. M. A., Gochoo, M., & Ali, L. (2023). Real-Time Attention Monitoring System for Classroom: A Deep Learning Approach for Student's Behavior Recognition. *Big Data and Cognitive Computing*, *7*(1), 48. Advance online publication. DOI: 10.3390/bdcc7010048

Trnkoczy, A. (2009). Understanding and parameter setting of STA/LTA trigger algorithm. *In New manual of seismological observatory practice (NMSOP)*. GFZ German Research Centre for Geosciences. https://api.semanticscholar.org/CorpusID: 145040868

Tu, Y., Chen, J., & Huang, C. (2025). Empowering personalized learning with generative artificial intelligence: Mechanisms, challenges and pathways. *Frontiers of Digital Education*, *2*(19), 1–18. DOI: 10.1007/s44366-025-0056-9

Tyralis, H., & Papacharalampous, G. (2024). A review of predictive uncertainty estimation with machine learning. *Artificial Intelligence Review*, *57*(4), 94. DOI: 10.1007/s10462-023-10698-8

UNDRR. (2022). *Global Assessment Report on Disaster Risk Reduction 2022: Our World at Risk.*

UNESCO. (2019). *Beijing consensus on artificial intelligence and education: Outcome document of the International Conference on Artificial Intelligence and Education*. UNESCO. https://www.unesco.org/en/articles/first-ever-consensus-artificial-intelligence-and-education-published-unesco

UNESCO. (2023). *AI and education: Guidance for policy-makers*. UNESCO. https://www.unesco.org/en/articles/ai-and-education-guidance-policy-makers

UNESCO. (2023). *Guidance for generative AI in education and research*. UNESCO.

UNESCO. (2024). *AI competency framework for students*. UNESCO. https://www.unesco.org/en/articles/ai-competency-framework-students

University of Miami. (n.d.). *AI-assisted grading with Gradescope*. Learning and Portfolio Technologies. https://lpt.it.miami.edu/resources/faculty-and-staff/leverage-ai-tools/ai-assisted-grading/index.html

Upadhyaya, A. N., Debnath, P., Rani, P., Selvakumar, P., Manjunath, T. C., & Bhattacharya, S. (2025). AI-based disaster prediction and early warning systems. In Mobo, F. (Ed.), *AI and emerging technologies for emergency response and smart cities* (pp. 55–74). IGI Global Scientific Publishing., DOI: 10.4018/979-8-3693-9770-1.ch003

Ushey, K. (2023). *renv: Project environments for R* (Version 1.0.3) [R package]. https://rstudio.github.io/renv

Uwineza, I., Mugisha, J. F., & Nsengimana, V. (2025). The impact of artificial intelligence in secondary education: A case study of Wellspring Academy, Rwanda. *Journal of Research Innovation and Implications in Education*, *9*(2), 111. https://www.jriiejournal.com/wp-content/uploads/2025/06/JRIIE-9-2-111-.pdf

Vallat, R. (2018). Pingouin: Statistics in Python. *Journal of Open Source Software*, *3*(31), 1026. DOI: 10.21105/joss.01026

van Dis, E. A., Bollen, J., Zuidema, W., van Rooji, R., & Bockting, C. L. (2023). ChatGPT: Five priorities for research. *Nature*, *614*(7947), 224–226. DOI: 10.1038/d41586-023-00288-7 PMID: 36737653

Van Wart, M., McIntyre, M., Zhang, J., Medina, P., Ni, A., & Njualem, L. (2025). The perceived importance of active learning techniques in online STEM courses. *Computers and Education Open*, *9*, 100309. DOI: 10.1016/j.caeo.2025.100309

VanderPlas, J. (2016). *Python data science handbook: Essential tools for working with data*. O'Reilly Media.

Vashishth, T. K., Sharma, V., Sharma, K. K., Kumar, B., Panwar, R., & Chaudhary, S. (2024). AI-driven learning analytics for personalized feedback and assessment in higher education. In *Using traditional design methods to enhance AI-driven decision making* (pp. 206–230). IGI Global Scientific Publishing. DOI: 10.4018/979-8-3693-0639-0.ch009

Vaswani, A., Shazeer, N., Parmar, N., Uszkoreit, J., Jones, L., Gomez, A. N., Kaiser, Ł., & Polosukhin, I. (2017). Attention is all you need. *In Proceedings of the 31st International Conference on Neural Information Processing Systems (NeurIPS 2017)* (pp. 6000–6010). Curran Associates, Inc.

Vicente-Saez, R., & Martinez-Fuentes, C. (2018). Open science now: A systematic literature review for an integrated definition. *Journal of Business Research*, *88*, 428–436. DOI: 10.1016/j.jbusres.2017.12.043

Wagenmakers, E.-J., Wetzels, R., Borsboom, D., van der Maas, H. L. J., & Kievit, R. A. (2012). An agenda for purely confirmatory research. *Perspectives on Psychological Science : A Journal of the Association for Psychological Science*, *7*(6), 632–638. DOI: 10.1177/1745691612463078 PMID: 26168122

Wagenmakers, E., Marsman, M., Jamil, T., Ly, A., Verhagen, J., Love, J., Selker, R., Gronau, Q. F., Šmíra, M., Epskamp, S., Matzke, D., Rouder, J. N., & Morey, R. D. (2018). Bayesian inference for psychology. Part I: Theoretical advantages and practical ramifications. *Psychonomic Bulletin & Review*, *25*(1), 35–57. DOI: 10.3758/s13423-017-1343-3 PMID: 28779455

Wahba, F., Ajlouni, A. O., & Abumosa, M. A. (2024). The impact of ChatGPT-based learning statistics on undergraduates' statistical reasoning and attitudes toward statistics. *Eurasia Journal of Mathematics, Science and Technology Education*, *20*(7), 1–14. DOI: 10.29333/ejmste/14726

Wang, H., Tlili, A., Huang, R., Cai, Z., Li, M., Cheng, Z., Yang, D., Li, M., Zhu, X., & Fei, C. (2023). Examining the applications of intelligent tutoring systems in real educational contexts: A systematic literature review from the social experiment perspective. *Education and Information Technologies*, *28*(7), 9113–9148. DOI: 10.1007/s10639-022-11555-x PMID: 36643383

Wang, J., & Li, J. (2024). Artificial intelligence empowering public health education: Prospects and challenges. *Frontiers in Public Health*, *12*, 1389026. PMID: 39022411

Wang, K., Ling, C., Chen, Y., & Zhang, Z. (2023). Spatio-temporal joint modelling on moderate and extreme air pollution in Spain. *Environmental and Ecological Statistics*, *30*(4), 601–624. DOI: 10.1007/s10651-023-00575-6

Wang, X., Zhang, Y., & Zhu, R. (2022). A brief review on algorithmic fairness. *Management System Engineering*, *1*(1), 7. DOI: 10.1007/s44176-022-00006-z

Wang, Y., & Jin, J. (2024). Research on Bayesian Statistics Teaching with R. *International Journal of Education and Humanities*, *12*(1), 39–40. DOI: 10.54097/5zh7f436

Wardani, I. S., & Fiorintina, E. (2023). Building critical thinking skills of 21st century students through problem based learning model. [Jurnal Pendidikan Indonesia]. *JPI*, *12*(1), 45–54. DOI: 10.23887/jpiundiksha.v12i3.58789

Warner, B. (2025). *Edtech for Multilingual Learners: 48 Fun and Flexible Activities for Every Classroom*. ASCD.

Watson, J., & Smith, C. (2022). Statistics education at a time of global disruption and crises: A growing challenge for the curriculum, classroom and beyond. *Curriculum Perspectives*, *42*(2), 171–179.

Weber, F., Ickstadt, K., & Glass, Ä. (2022). shinybrms: Fitting Bayesian regression models using a graphical user interface for the R package brms. *The R Journal, 14*(2), 96–120. https://rjournal.github.io/. DOI: 10.32614/RJ-2022-027

Wickham, H., Averick, M., Bryan, J., Chang, W., McGowan, L., François, R., Grolemund, G., Hayes, A., Henry, L., Hester, J., Kuhn, M., Pedersen, T., Miller, E., Bache, S., Müller, K., Ooms, J., Robinson, D., Seidel, D., Spinu, V., & Yutani, H. (2021). Welcome to the Tidyverse. *Journal of Open Source Software, 4*(43), 1686. DOI: 10.21105/joss.01686

Wild, C. J., & Pfannkuch, M. (1999). Statistical thinking in empirical enquiry. *International Statistical Review = Revue Internationale de Statistique, 67*(3), 223–248. DOI: 10.1111/j.1751-5823.1999.tb00442.x

Wilkinson, M. D., Dumontier, M., Aalbersberg, I. J., Appleton, G., Axton, M., Baak, A., Blomberg, N., Boiten, J.-W., da Silva Santos, L. B., Bourne, P. E., Bouwman, J., Brookes, A. J., Clark, T., Crosas, M., Dillo, I., Dumon, O., Edmunds, S., Evelo, C. T., Finkers, R., & Mons, B. (2016). The FAIR Guiding Principles for scientific data management and stewardship. *Scientific Data, 3*(1), 160018. DOI: 10.1038/sdata.2016.18 PMID: 26978244

Williamson, B., & Eynon, R. (2020). Historical threads, missing links, and future directions in AI in education. *Learning, Media and Technology, 45*(3), 223–235. DOI: 10.1080/17439884.2020.1798995

Willis, A. S. (2023). Teachers' cultural, social and emotional capabilities: How teacher compassion and humility is an antecedent to student confidence. *Pedagogy, Culture & Society, 31*(1), 91–108. DOI: 10.1080/14681366.2021.1884122

Wilson, G., Bryan, J., Cranston, K., Kitzes, J., Nederbragt, L., & Teal, T. K. (2017). Good enough practices in scientific computing. *PLoS Computational Biology, 13*(6), e1005510. DOI: 10.1371/journal.pcbi.1005510 PMID: 28640806

Winner, L. (2017). Do artifacts have politics? In *Computer ethics* (pp. 177–192). Routledge. DOI: 10.4324/9781315259697-21

Withers, M. M., Aster, R. C., Young, C. J., & Chael, E. P. (1996). High-frequency analysis of seismic background noise as a function of wind speed and shallow depth. *Bulletin of the Seismological Society of America, 86*(5), 1507–1515. DOI: 10.1785/BSSA0860051507

Wongvorachan, T., He, S., & Bulut, O. (2023). A Comparison of Undersampling, Oversampling, and SMOTE Methods for Dealing with Imbalanced Classification in Educational Data Mining. *Information (Basel)*, *14*(1), 54. Advance online publication. DOI: 10.3390/info14010054

WWC. (2013). *DreamBox Learning* [WWC Intervention Report]. Institute of Education Sciences, What Works Clearinghouse. https://ies.ed.gov/ncee/wwc/Docs/InterventionReports/wwc_dreambox_121013.pdf

Xia, Q., Weng, X., Ouyang, F., Lin, T. J., & Chiu, T. K. (2024). A scoping review on how generative artificial intelligence transforms assessment in higher education. *International Journal of Educational Technology in Higher Education*, *21*(1), 40.

Xie, Y., Allaire, J. J., & Grolemund, G. (2020). *R Markdown: The definitive guide*. CRC Press. https://bookdown.org/yihui/rmarkdown

Xie, X. (2023). Influence of AI-driven inquiry teaching on learning outcomes. *International Journal of Emerging Technologies in Learning*, *18*(21), 23–38. DOI: 10.3991/ijet.v18i23.45473

Xing, Y. (2024). Exploring the use of ChatGPT in learning and instructing statistics and data analytics. *Teaching Statistics*, *46*(2), 95–104. DOI: 10.1111/test.12367

Yang, C., Chiang, F. K., Cheng, Q., & Ji, J. (2021). Machine learning-based student modeling methodology for intelligent tutoring systems. *Journal of Educational Computing Research*, *59*(6), 1015–1035. DOI: 10.1177/0735633120986256

Yang, J., Gong, P., Fu, R., Zhang, M., Chen, J., Liang, S., Xu, B., Shi, J., & Dickinson, R. (2013). The role of satellite remote sensing in climate change studies. *Nature Climate Change*, *3*(10), 875–883. DOI: 10.1038/nclimate1908

Yang, S., Zhao, H., Xu, Y., Brennan, K., & Schneider, B. (2024, August). Debugging with an AI tutor: Investigating novice help-seeking behaviors and perceived learning. In *Proceedings of the 2024 ACM Conference on International Computing Education Research-Volume 1* (pp. 84-94). DOI: 10.1145/3632620.3671092

Yang, W., Wei, Y., Wei, H., Chen, Y., Huang, G., Li, X., Yao, N., Wang, X., Gu, X., Amin, M. B., & Kang, B. (2023). Survey on explainable AI: From approaches, limitations and applications aspects. *Human-Centric Intelligent Systems*, *3*(3), 161–188. DOI: 10.1007/s44230-023-00038-y

Yang, Y., Zhuang, Y., & Pan, Y. (2021). Multiple knowledge representation for big data artificial intelligence: Framework, applications, and case studies. *Frontiers of Information Technology & Electronic Engineering*, *22*(12), 1551–1558. DOI: 10.1631/FITEE.2100463

Yim, I. H. Y., & Su, J. (2025). Artificial intelligence (AI) learning tools in K–12 education: A scoping review. *Journal of Computers in Education, 12*(1), 93–131.

Yixuan, Z., & Xiaohua, Z. (2025). "Research and design of an AI-integrated online learning system." **Proceedings of the 2025 7th International Symposium on Educational Technology*, 211–220. DOI: DOI: 10.1109/ISCBI64586.2025.11015364

Yodplob, T., & Ketsuwan, C. (2025). Modified Seoul National University Renal Stone Complexity Scoring System for Predicting Stone-Free Status After Extracorporeal Shock Wave Lithotripsy. *Research and Reports in Urology, 17*, 279–286. DOI: 10.2147/RRU.S534829 PMID: 40800736

Yoon, C. E., O'Reilly, O., Bergen, K. J., & Beroza, G. C. (2015). Earthquake detection through computationally efficient similarity search. *Science Advances, 1*(11), e1501057. DOI: 10.1126/sciadv.1501057 PMID: 26665176

Yue, M., Jong, M. S. Y., & Ng, D. T. K. (2024). Understanding K–12 teachers' technological pedagogical content knowledge readiness and attitudes toward artificial intelligence education. *Education and Information Technologies, 29*(15), 19505–19536.

Zawacki-Richter, O., Marín, V. I., Bond, M., & Gouverneur, F. (2019). Systematic review of research on artificial intelligence applications in higher education—Where are the educators? *International Journal of Educational Technology in Higher Education, 16*(1), 39. DOI: 10.1186/s41239-019-0171-0

Zhang, J. (2025). Meta-analysis of artificial intelligence in education. *Educational Technology Research and Development*. https://files.eric.ed.gov/fulltext/EJ1465704.pdf

Zhang, X., Chen, G., Cai, L., Jiao, H., Hua, J., Luo, X., & Wei, X. (2021). Impact assessments of Typhoon Lekima on forest damages in subtropical China using machine learning methods and Landsat 8 OLI imagery. *Sustainability (Basel), 13*(9), 4893. DOI: 10.3390/su13094893

Zhang, Y.-L., Yu, Z.-C., & He, C. (2025). Uncertainty-aware neural networks with manual quality control for hydraulic fracturing downhole microseismic monitoring: From automated phase detection to robust source location. *Petroleum Science, 22*(11), 4520–4537. DOI: 10.1016/j.petsci.2025.07.017

Zhou, X., Zhang, J., & Chan, C. (2024). Unveiling students' experiences and perceptions of artificial intelligence usage in higher education. *Journal of University Teaching & Learning Practice, 21*(6), 126–145.

Zhu, J., Li, S., Wei, Y., & Song, J. (2023). On-site instrumental seismic intensity prediction for China via recurrent neural network and transfer learning. *Journal of Asian Earth Sciences*. https://www.sciencedirect.com/science/article/abs/pii/S1367912023000718

Zhu, W., & Beroza, G. C. (2019). PhaseNet: A deep-neural-network-based seismic arrival time picking method. *Geophysical Journal International*, *216*(1), 261–273. DOI: 10.1093/gji/ggy423

Zieffler, A., Garfield, J., Delmas, R., & Reading, C. (2008). A framework to support research on informal inferential reasoning. *Statistics Education Research Journal*, *7*(2), 40–58. DOI: 10.52041/serj.v7i2.469

Zou, T., Shi, J., Wang, M., & Lin, C. (2025). Inverse Design of Structured Electrodes in Lithium Metal Batteries: Integrated High-Throughput Phase-Field Modeling and Machine Learning. *Advanced Functional Materials*, , 12788.

About the Contributors

Roel Ceballos earned his Doctor of Philosophy in Statistics from the University of the Philippines Los Baños under the DOST-ASTHRDP scholarship. He currently serves as a faculty member and research mentor at the University of Southeastern Philippines. Dr. Ceballos has over a decade of experience in statistical consulting, data science, and quantitative research, with contributions spanning public health, environmental risk analysis, educational reform, and disaster preparedness. He has co-authored peer-reviewed journal articles, technical reports, and institutional studies, including work on child mortality, dengue surveillance, air pollution, disaster resilience metrics, and educational leadership. A dedicated statistics educator, Dr. Ceballos has led the development of innovative teaching strategies and elective courses in environmental statistics and data literacy. His research is driven by a commitment to ethical, inclusive, and context-sensitive applications of statistics, especially in developing country settings. He actively advocates for statistical literacy, equity in education, and the responsible integration of AI in pedagogy.

***

Ashraf Alam is currently serving as an Assistant Professor in the Department of Education at the National Institute of Technology Calicut, Kozhikode, India. Dr. Ashraf has been recognised among the World's Top 2% Scientists by Stanford University and Elsevier, reflecting his scholarly engagement with critical questions at the intersection of pedagogy, sustainability, technology, ethics, innovation, and social change. His academic contributions include more than seventy-five Scopus-indexed publications and over one hundred presentations delivered at national and international academic forums. His work has appeared through reputed academic platforms including Elsevier, Springer, Taylor & Francis, Wiley, Routledge, Sage, Emerald, and IEEE. He holds a Ph.D. in Education from the Indian Institute of

Technology Kharagpur, where his research engaged with foundational concerns in educational philosophy, innovation, and pedagogical transformation.

John Riz Bagnol is a researcher and PhD student at the Université de Technologie de Compiègne (UTC) within the Compiègne Applied Mathematics Laboratory (LMAC). His research centers on Random Forests and machine learning applications for hazard risk assessment and disaster reduction. With a background in university instruction and a passion for applied mathematics, he focuses on enhancing predictive capabilities for environmental safety.

Anagha Bhope is an accomplished academician and management educator serving as an Associate Professor at the Balaji Institute of Modern Management (BIMM), Sri Balaji University, Pune. With extensive experience in higher education, she has made significant contributions to teaching, research, and academic development in the field of management studies. Known for her student-centric teaching approach, Dr. Bhope integrates theoretical concepts with practical industry perspectives, enabling learners to develop analytical thinking, leadership skills, and professional competence. Her academic interests include organizational behaviour, human resource management, business strategy, and contemporary management practices. She actively participates in research activities and contributes scholarly work through publications, conferences, and academic collaborations that address emerging challenges in business and management. In addition to her teaching responsibilities, she is actively involved in curriculum development, mentoring students, and supporting institutional initiatives aimed at enhancing academic quality and industry engagement. Through her dedication to education, innovation, and knowledge dissemination, Dr. Anagha Bhope continues to play a vital role in shaping future management professionals and strengthening the academic excellence of Sri Balaji University, Pune.

Anthony Capili is an Associate Professor and former Program Head of the BS Statistics program at the University of Southeastern Philippines. He holds a PhD in Statistics with a cognate in Mathematics from the University of the Philippines Los Baños. He earned both his BS in Statistics (cum laude) and MS in Applied Mathematics from the University of Southeastern Philippines. Dr. Capili was a DOST scholar during his undergraduate studies and a DOST ASTHRDP scholar while completing his doctoral degree. His areas of specialization and research interest include time series analysis, experimental design, response surface methodology, and regression analysis.

Shiney Chib is presently working as Professor, Dean Academics, and Research Head at Datta Meghe Institute of Management Studies, Nagpur, and previously served as the Director of the institute from 2015 to 2023. She is also appointed as Adjunct Faculty at SEGI University, Malaysia. With proven expertise in academic leadership and team building, she has successfully organized numerous national and international conferences, Management Development Programs (MDPs), Faculty Development Programs (FDPs), and various intra- and inter-college academic events. Her academic credentials are extensive, including qualifications such as B.Tech, multiple MBA degrees, M.Com, LL.B, PhD, MPhil, and postgraduate qualifications across management, psychology, public administration, and related disciplines, and she is currently pursuing a second PhD in Psychology. Her contributions to education have been recognized with prestigious awards including the Distinguished Educator Award, Rajiv Gandhi Excellence Award, Mahila Ratan Gold Medal for Academic Excellence, and Eminent Educationist Award. She has significant international exposure, having represented India at international conventions in Germany, chaired and participated in global conferences in Japan and Hong Kong, and served as a paper reviewer for international academic forums in Taiwan and Korea.

Ahmad Darmawan is a researcher in the fields of information technology and education at Esa Unggul University, Jakarta, Indonesia. His research interests focus on the integration of information technology in education, digital learning systems, educational data analytics, and the development of technology-enhanced learning environments. He has been actively involved in academic research and applied projects aimed at improving the quality of education through innovative digital solutions and data-driven approaches. His work reflects strong analytical thinking, interdisciplinary collaboration, and a commitment to advancing modern educational practices. Ahmad actively contributes to collaborative research initiatives and scientific publications that support the development of effective and sustainable digital education systems.

Victor Paul dela Cruz works at the University of Southeastern Philippines as faculty of Mathematics and Statistics, College of Arts and Sciences, handling both foundation and core courses in Statistics. He graduated Bachelor of Science in Statistics and Master of Science in Applied Mathematics from the University of Southeastern Philippines. He also earned Data Science Track short course and secondary education units. He is interested in the statistical analyses and modeling, data visualization, and Machine Learning in the fields of Education, Economics, Social Sciences, and Public Health. He is Licensed Professional Teacher and Career Service Professional eligible. He presented the various conferences related to statistics and education.

Oya Ekici is an Associate Professor in the Department of Business Administration (Quantitative Methods) at the Faculty of Political Sciences, Istanbul University, where she has been a faculty member since 2013 and has served as Vice Chair since 2023. She holds a B.A. in Economics (English-taught program), and M.A. and Ph.D. degrees in Econometrics from Istanbul University, and conducted her postdoctoral research at the Department of Statistics, Duke University. Her teaching covers undergraduate and graduate courses in statistics, Bayesian data analysis, decision theory, data analytics, and operations management. Her research interests include Bayesian statistics, time series analysis, MCMC methods, decision-making processes, and macroeconomic applications, with a strong emphasis on interdisciplinary quantitative modeling.

David Gray is a statistician and Assistant Professor in the Department of Mathematics and Statistics at the University of Liberia. He obtained his doctorate in Statistics from the University of the Philippines Los Baños. Dr. Gray specializes in Bayesian statistics, financial risk modeling, multivariate statistics, survival analysis, and quantitative research applications. His research interests are centered on applying statistical methods to solve problems related to development, health, education, and finance in Liberia. In addition to his involvement in curriculum development and higher education training, Dr. Gray has prepared and delivered lectures on mathematical statistics, applications of probability models, multivariate statistical techniques, business research methodology, and other quantitative subjects. He firmly believes that statistics teaching should not only be clear but should also focus on methodology and its application in solving social issues. A committed scholar and nation-builder, Dr. David Clarence Gray continuously contributes to the development of statistics and research in Liberia and other countries.

Mustafa Kayyali is an ardent advocate for excellence in higher education, driven by a relentless pursuit of quality, recognition, and innovation. Their journey in academia started with a Master's in Quality Management and Evaluation in Higher Education from Universitat Oberta de Catalunya, followed by a Ph.D. in Quality Management from Azteca University. These academic pursuits have laid a strong foundation for their expertise in Accreditation, Quality Assurance, and Higher Education Rankings. As an entrepreneur, researcher, translator, and publisher, they are deeply involved in various facets of the academic world. Their diverse interests encompass Management, Translation, Interpretation, and Academic consulting, contributing to a well-rounded understanding of the industry. Throughout their career, they have made significant contributions to academic literature, with more than 40 published papers and 30 book chapters to my name. Additionally, they take pride in having translated 6 books, bridging language gaps, and promoting knowledge exchange on a global scale. They are committed to fostering positive change in higher education and contributing to its continuous improvement.

Sumit Kushwaha is an Associate Professor in the Department of the Directorate of Research, Innovation, and Consultancy (DRIC) at Chandigarh University Uttar Pradesh, Unnao. He is actively engaged in academic research, innovation, and consultancy activities, contributing to the university's research ecosystem. With a strong commitment to advancing knowledge, Dr. Kushwaha focuses on interdisciplinary research and promotes collaboration between academia and industry. He plays a vital role in guiding students and researchers, fostering innovation-driven projects, and supporting consultancy initiatives. His contributions reflect a dedication to academic excellence, research development, and the practical application of knowledge in real-world contexts.

Mohammad Norman Gaza Laksono is a quantum physics researcher with a strong background in condensed matter physics and computational quantum mechanics. He earned his physics degree from Universitas Indonesia and master study at Uppsala University, Sweden. He has conducted extensive research on nodal-line semimetals at the Quantum Lab of Universitas Indonesia and has served as a research assistant at the National Research and Innovation Agency (BRIN). His work focuses on quantum computing, semimetals, and nuclear and particle physics, contributing to advancements in theoretical and applied quantum research. With experience in both experimental and computational approaches, he continues to explore quantum materials and their potential applications in next-generation technologies.

TC Manjunath was born on 6th February 1967. He did his B.E. from RV College of Engg. in 1989 (B'lore Univ), M.E. in Robotics & Automation from Govt.'s LD College of Engg., (Gujarat Univ., Ahmedabad) in 1992 with FCD-First Rank & PhD in Systems & Control Engg. from IIT Bombay in the year 2007, got best research scholar award for the entire IITB. He is currently working as the Dean Research (R & D) and as Professor in Dept. of Computer Science & Engg. with specialization in IoT, Cyber Security, Blockchain Technology in Rajarajeswari College of Engineering, Bengaluru, Karnataka. He has got a teaching (academic), research & administrative experience of more than 35+ years (10 years as Principal & 8 years as HoD, 1 year as Dean Research & rest as faculty) and has published more than 1500+ research papers in various national & international journals & conferences, with 175+ patents, 100+ book-chapters, 25 awards, 100s of Keynote talks and also published 25 text books in various field of science, engineering & technology, completed projects worth Rs. 9 Crores till date & guided 10 PhD scholars in VTU. He is a member of 30 Professional Society Chapters and is a fellow of IE, IETE, AMIEE, Sr. Member of IEEE and a chartered engineer.

Arvinder Kour Mehta is a distinguished academician, researcher and professional with over 15 years of corporate experience and 9 years of teaching experience. She holds 4 post graduation and PhD reflecting her commitment to continuous learning and excellence. She contributes significantly to the corporate landscape as a corporate trainer and presently working as Assistant professor at Yeshwantrao Chavan college of Engineering.

Mamta Mishra is a distinguished academician and administrator, currently serving as Professor and Head of the Department of Management Studies at Sinhgad College of Engineering, Pune. With extensive experience in management education, she has been instrumental in advancing academic excellence, curriculum development, and research initiatives within the department. Dr. Mishra is known for her commitment to quality teaching, mentorship, and institutional development, and she actively contributes to the professional growth of students and faculty through leadership, scholarly activities, and industry–academia engagement.

Nehru P is an esteemed Assistant Professor at B.S Abdur Rahman Crescent Institute of Science and Technology. With a strong academic background and a passion for education, Nehru has been inspiring and guiding students in the field of Generative AI and Blockchain. His research interests include Plant disease prevention and he has published several papers in renowned journals and conferences. Nehru's dedication to teaching and research has made a significant impact on the academic community, and he continues to be a valuable asset to the institution.

Selvakumar P is currently an Associate Professor in the Department of Science and Humanities at Nehru Institute of Technology, Coimbatore, Tamil Nadu, India. Prior to joining Nehru Institute of Technology, he held positions as an Assistant Professor in the Department of Science and Humanities various engineering colleges in Coimbatore, Tamil Nadu, India, spanning from 2011 to 2023. Dr.P. Selvakumar's academic and research interests lie primarily in the field of phytochemistry. He has made significant contributions to his field, with an impressive record that includes 30 journal publications, 12 patents, and 20 conference papers. Additionally, he has organized 5 seminars and conferences, further demonstrating his commitment to academic and scientific exchange. Throughout his career, Dr. P.Selvakumar has been recognized for his dedication and excellence in teaching, having been honored with several awards, including the Best Teacher Awards. He holds a prominent position in the academic community, contributing actively to research.

Saravanan R, serve as an Assistant Professor at Vinayaka Mission's Law School (VMLS), Vinayaka Mission's Research Foundation (Deemed to be University), Chennai campus. I hold an LL.M in Maritime Law (with distinction) from Gujarat Maritime University. My academic and research experience includes contributing to the GMU–ISWAN Joint Research on Seafarers' Recruitment and Placement and assisting the National Human Rights Commission (NHRC) in developing the Handbook on the Rights of Seafarers.At VMLS, I teach Maritime Law, Labour Law, and Constitutional Law, integrating policy and practical perspectives into legal education. My research interests extend to, Admiralty Law, Maritime labour regulations, IPR and human rights in emerging global contexts.I am deeply committed to advancing interdisciplinary legal research and guiding students toward exploring contemporary issues in law, technology, and innovation with a focus on justice, ethics, and social impact.

Pallapati Ravi Kumar is currently serving as an Assistant Professor in the Department of Computer Science and Engineering at Koneru Lakshmaiah Education Foundation (K L University), located in Vaddeswaram, Guntur, Andhra Pradesh, Bharat. He is dedicated to academic excellence and research in the fields of Deep Learning and Data Science. With a strong commitment to fostering innovation and analytical thinking among students, he actively contributes to both teaching and research activities within the department. His academic and research pursuits focus on developing intelligent systems and data-driven solutions that address real-world challenges through advanced computational techniques.

Resa mae Sangco is a Filipino statistician and researcher who earned her Doctor of Philosophy in Statistics from the Institute of Statistics, University of the Philippines Los Baños (UPLB). Her doctoral work, "Development of a Health Coverage Index at the National and Sub-National Levels in the Philippines," offers a pioneering framework for measuring disparities in health service access, delivery, and financial protection across the country. Dr. Sangco's research spans health economics, universal health coverage, time series analysis, spatial analytics, econometric modeling, big data applications, and public sector program evaluation. She has conducted and co-authored various studies involving ARDL modeling, probabilistic forecasting, health expenditure analysis, and insurance industry analytics, and demonstrating a strong command of both theoretical and applied statistics. Beyond her academic achievements, Dr. Sangco is engaged in professional statistical and research communities, advocating for evidence-based policymaking and capacity-building among young statisticians.

Binastya Anggara Sekti has been a lecturer at the Faculty of Computer Science, Esa Unggul University, Jakarta, since 2016. He is actively involved in the Artificial Intelligence and Information Security Study Group. He holds a Bachelor's degree in Informatics Engineering from the Bandung Institute of Technology and a Master's degree in Information Systems Management from Trisakti University, Jakarta. Prior to entering academia, he accumulated over 25 years of professional experience as an IT practitioner in various companies across Jakarta. His work focused on developing data centers for internet service providers and delivering IT solutions for the manufacturing and oil & gas sectors. His research interests include artificial intelligence, cybersecurity, and the development of IT infrastructure.

Fe Monique Tagaytay is a faculty member at the University of Southeastern Philippines and a multidisciplinary researcher working at the intersections of communication, media, education, and society. Her work spans communication studies, media and information literacy, discourse, and education, examining communication practices and interactions and how these shape society and educational landscapes. She has published on topics including new media use, representation, and educational contexts, and has contributed to collaborative and interdisciplinary research across the humanities and social sciences. She also serves as a Department Editor of the Southern Philippines Journal of Research and Development and previously served as Director of the university's Gender and Development Office. Musni-Tagaytay holds a Master of Arts in Education and is currently pursuing a Doctor of Education.

Index

A

B

C

D

E

F

G

H

I

L

M

O

P

R

S

T

U

V

www.ingramcontent.com/pod-product-compliance
Lightning Source LLC
LaVergne TN
LVHW080912300926
849162LV00003B/651